INSIDE ? 7

BY

Gary David Bouton

Barbara Mancuso Bouton

Mara Zebest Nathanson

Daniel Will-Harris

J. Scott Hamlin

Robert Stanley

New Riders

201 West 103rd Street, Indianapolis, Indiana 46290

Inside Photoshop 7

Copyright © 2003 by New Riders Publishing

International Standard Book Number: 0-7357-1241-7

Library of Congress Catalog Card Number: 2001096940

Printed in the United States of America

First Printing: July 2002

06 05 04 03 02   7 6 5 4 3 2 1

Interpretation of the printing code: The rightmost double-digit number is the year of the book's printing; the rightmost single-digit number is the number of the book's printing. For example, the printing code 02-1 shows that the first printing of the book occurred in 2002.

Trademarks

Warning and Disclaimer

Publisher
David Dwyer

Associate Publisher
Stephanie Wall

Production Manager
Gina Kanouse

Managing Editor
Sarah Kearns

Acquisitions Editor
Jody Kennen

Development Editor
Jake McFarland

Copy Editor
Kathy Murray

Product Marketing Manager
Kathy Malmloff

Publicity Manager
Susan Nixon

Manufacturing Coordinator
Jim Conway

Cover Designer
Gary David Bouton

Compositor
Gloria Schurick

Proofreader
Julia Prosser

Indexer
Joy Dean Lee

Media Developer
Jay Payne

Technical Reviewers
Mara Zebest Nathanson
Dave Huss

Contents at a Glance

Table of Contents

Part IV   Photoshop for Photographers

About the Authors

Gary David Bouton and Barbara Mancuso Bouton. Gary is an author and illustrator who turned to computer art after 20 years as a traditional artist. *Inside Photoshop 7* is Mr. Bouton's 13th book on the World's Most Popular Image Editing program. His other titles include books on CorelDRAW, the Internet, 3D modeling, and multimedia. Gary and his wife Barbara have attended conferences as lecturers, written columns for trade papers, and written chapters for school books (themselves being adolescents at heart). Gary fools with a vintage Rickenbacker in his spare time, and he can get that killer chord from the beginning of the Beatles' "A Hard Day's Night" out of it. Barbara performs local consulting work, and Gary is desperately trying to learn new applications, such as Poser 4 and Alias|Wavefront's Maya. In their spare time, Gary and Barbara host a three-satellite web endeavor, where they post new info on books, sell art t-shirts (Gary's art, naturally), and offer free illustrated tutorials on just about everything for download. Gary holds six international awards in DTP and graphic design, and is also a modeling freak.

You can reach Gary by driving down Woods Path to Elmcrest and turning right on Pawnee Drive, or you can email him at Gary@GaryDavidBouton.com.

J. Scott Hamlin is the director of Eyeland Studio (www.eyeland.com). Eyeland Studio is a web content design studio specializing in Flash game production and original content design. Eyeland Studio produces several products sold over the web and on CD-ROM. Eyewire.com, one of the world's largest stock imagery companies, carries Eyeland Studio's products. Eyeland Studio's past client list includes Nokia, Procter & Gamble, Sun Microsystems, MTV Europe, Nabisco, and Extensis Corporation. Scott also writes for *Computer Arts Special* magazine and *AV Video and Multimedia Producer* magazine. Eyeland Studio also is the creator of SwiftLab (www.swiftlab.com).

Mara Zebest Nathanson is a graphic artist who uses her knowledge and skills in both volunteer work and commercially. Mara donates much of her time to a local school corporation, providing technical support to teachers and administrators in designing brochures, letterhead, logos, and even t-shirts. Commercially, she designs newspaper and magazine ads, as well as a variety of other graphics. This is Mara's second time as a contributing author and technical editor for the *Inside Photoshop* series.

Robert Stanley is a freelance artist living with his family in Southern California. His clients have included 20th Century Fox, MTV, *Cigar Aficionado*, and Grammercy Pictures. Robert can rip through a phone book with his bare hands and has created cold fusion in his bathtub. He was the real inventor behind Velveeta™ cheese and wrote several songs for Lennon-McCartney while in kindergarten. That same year, Robert told Thomas Knoll to call it the *toolbox* instead of the *sandbox* when he played with Thomas and the Photoshop interface at recess.

Daniel Will-Harris is a writer and designer whose clients include Addison-Wesley, Bitstream, Corel, Microsoft, NetObjects, Peachpit Press, Prentice Hall, Simon & Schuster, the State of California, WordPerfect, ViaFone, and Xerox.

His own site, www.will-harris.com, was one of the first 5,000 sites on the web, and it showcases a wide variety of work, including web and logo design, computer clock screensavers at www.ElementOfTime.com, and useful desktop yoga exercises at www.MyDailyYoga.com.

www.will-harris.com also features unique designer fonts and his own EsperFonto™ System (in use by Bitstream, Hewlett Packard, and Corel), the web's first interactive typeface selection system.

Daniel's opt-in email www.SchmoozeLetter.com combines autobiography, fiction, and web tips into an entertaining mix that critics have called, "The only email newsletter anyone would ever really want." Daniel created and edited www.eFuse.com, the friendly place to learn how to build a better web site.

Daniel has written, designed, and produced seven books (including one of the first about DTP on the PC), designed dozens more, and has edited and written for countless magazines around the world.

A book version of his SchmoozeLetters will soon be in print, as well as a new book called "Wallet Reading, your personality in your pocket," and a novel called "Frickingenius.com."

About the Technical Editor

 **Dave Huss** is an avid digital photographer, technical writer, and graphics and desktop publishing consultant. Dave has authored over 13 books on photo editing and has taught at conferences around the world. He was part of the Photoshop World Dream Team, and his photomontages have won several international awards.

Dedication

Usually, you find, "For my wife, my cat, my family, my gardener, and my friends" in a book dedication. But, you know, after writing more than a dozen books on Photoshop for New Riders, I found out that I can pretty much say whatever I want in a dedication.

So here goes:

How would you like to feel, in a way, that you were partially responsible for a cure for cancer? For AIDS? For Parkinson's, MS, or Lou Gehrig's Disease? I think I'd feel positively wonderful, because it always seems like it's "the good ones" who go first, and some of my friends are currently suffering from one or more of these diseases.

Want to help? You can by joining Folding@Home. Folding@Home studies protein folding, protein misfolding, aggregation, and related diseases. Folding@Home uses client software downloaded to volunteers' computers to achieve extraordinary computing power. This distributed computing model, coupled with novel computational methods, allows Folding@Home to simulate timescales thousands to millions of times longer than previously achieved. This has allowed researchers to simulate folding for the first time and to direct their approach toward examining folding-related diseases.

Join the *Inside Photoshop 7* Folding@Home team by entering our team number, 2842, in the team number field in the Folding@Home software Configuration dialog box. Let's show the world one way that artsy-fartsy folk can make significant scientific contributions.

Who can fold at home:

Macintosh, Windows, and Linux users with any kind of Internet connection, even behind a firewall. You need an established Internet connection only when sending in completed work and getting new work, depending on how fast your machine is and how long the Folding program runs. This typically works out to anywhere from once a day to once every 3 days.

Results will be published in scientific journals, and then the raw data will be posted online for anybody and everybody to use at no cost.

At present 80,000 computers around the world are running Folding@Home.

The following are quotes from the site:

"One of our project goals is to simulate protein folding in order to understand how proteins fold so quickly and reliably, and to learn how to make synthetic polymers with these properties. What happens if proteins don't fold correctly? Diseases such as Alzheimer's disease, cystic fibrosis, an inherited form of emphysema, and even many cancers are believed to result from protein misfolding."

"In addition to biomedical applications, learning about how proteins fold will also teach us how to design our own protein-sized 'nanomachines' to do similar tasks. Of course, before nanomachines can carry out any activity, they must also be assembled."

"We never have enough money for research and we never have enough money to spare. THIS time, you can do a world of good simply by leaving your machine on at night and donating the processor cycles to medical research."

Please, *please* go download the latest version of the screensaver with easy instructions from:

http://folding.stanford.edu

http://folding.stanford.edu/faq.html

Acknowledgments

I don't know how Adobe does it. With each new version, the engineers and other folk pack more power, features, enhancements, and just plain "good stuff" into Photoshop. Photoshop has gotten way too big for a single writer to show you what all this power is good for. So I asked some of the best people in the business to help me. J. Scott Hamlin and his partner Scott Balay, Mara Nathanson, Robert Stanley, Daniel Will-Harris, and Dave Huss have all contributed to this book.

You can check out their bios in the "About the Authors" section, but I can tell you that they were being modest when they wrote their bios. All of these folks are experts in the areas I asked them to write about, and I wouldn't be surprised if you own a few of the books they've written. I am so grateful and proud to have them grace the pages of this book.

Getting this book into your hands took not only the talents of what we privately called the "Ocean's 11" writing consortium, but also the skills and patience of the publishing professionals at New Riders Publishing and the support of many throughout the graphics industry.

I want to thank all of them from the bottom of my heart:

- First, I want to thank Jody Kennen for moral support (directed toward a guy who *has* no morals, mind you <g>), a string of critical back-and-forths almost every other day over the phone and email—which kept this book organized along the road from idea to printed page, and mostly for allowing us to show each other that we're human: we catch colds, we get tired sometimes, we fall off the roof hanging Christmas ornaments. Jody, thanks. I mean it.

- Thanks to Associate Publisher Stephanie Wall. She's on the top of this list, and also toward the top of my list of professional workmates during the course of writing this humble tome. She did everything in her power to help organize a big-time effort here; and most of all, she made it abundantly clear to me that she believes in me as a talent. Thank you, Stephanie—that's as eloquent as I get...

- Thanks to Jake McFarland, Developmental Editor for, once again, letting me tell the story my way. The *Inside Photoshop* series is FAR from being a "formula" book, and it's always eggshells you walk on when you break conventions and rules. Thanks for being a "good egg" (OUCH!), Jake.

- A big thank you to my Publisher, David Dwyer. David and I have had the pleasure to work together for six years now (during which time, his title always seems to progress up the totem pole, while I'm still an author. Hmmmm <g>); and during the course of our relationship, David has seen me as more than a writer—he's allowed me to contribute to the book's overall feel—I get to design the color signature and even draw the book cover art. Don't I sound like Martha Stewart?

Seriously, these things mean a lot to me, David, because to call myself an author means I'm defining myself, and self-definition leads to self-limitation. Thank you for letting me be myself in New Riders' books, David.

- Thanks to my wife, my friend, and my Talent Liaison (or more appropriately, "Talent Wrangler"—which means she handled the mail and the calls so I could write). Barbara, we have a long history with New Riders, and I know we have a longer one with each other. Thank you, mate.

- Many thanks to Richard Cordero, who played an extremely heavy hand in the correctness and ease of reading "Color Calibration" in the IP6 book, along with Barbara Bouton. Richard was kind enough to help with this book's version of the chapter (Chapter 7), so you're getting the straight story on a very important set of imaging issues. Thank you once again, Richard.

- Thanks to Ed Guarente, our Photographer of the Airwaves. When Mara and I did not have the setup or the equipment to photograph something we needed for a tutorial, we called Ed. Ed would download a rough sketch from us, get his digital camera, get the scene set up, and email us about three different exposures of the image we needed—to size and everything. This shows two things:

    1.) Ed is leveraging technology about as well in his craft as is technologically possible at this point.

    2.) It doesn't hurt that all of us use Road Runner.

Can you imagine doing this kind of stuff within ½ hour, going from coast to coast? FedEx has gotta be quaking in their running shoes! Thanks, Ed. I owe you more than a dedication in this book for your spirit of giving.

- Thanks again to Ron Pfister (http://www.imaginationmagic.com) for his beautiful Hawaii photography he is sharing with me…and you all. Thanks, Ron.

- Thanks to Stu Winders for designing a model of a castle for me for the Gary Cauldron section. I had not the time nor talent to build elegant castles the way Stu did (in less than 24 hours, mind you!). And Stu, if I'm ever in New Zealand, I'll buy you a pint.

- Thanks to Marc Pawliger and Chris Cox at Adobe Systems for answering all my questions, and then some, during the beta cycle. Also thanks to Chris Conner, and especially for letting us participate in the creation of this product through suggestions and the beta-cycle channels. Special thanks to Anjali Ariathurai, Adobe Systems Beta Coordinator, and Karen Gauthier from Adobe, for accommodating our special needs during the writing of this book. You folks were incredibly responsive and helpful. We needed that to write this book.

- Many, Many thanks to Mark Goodall of XARA, Ltd. Mark made it possible at the last moment for Windows users to get a trial edition of XARA X on the Companion CD (no slight here; it's a Windows-only program). See the ad in the back of the book for an incredibly low-priced offer on a program I have been using for five years to get stuff like book covers, annotations, charts, and technical drawings done. And I've done fun stuff, too, that you can find on the gallery at www.xara.com. Mark, thank you for listening to me, and I realize that you've probably lost huge clumps of hair as a result of reading emails from me that started out with the sentence, "Mark, wouldn't it be neat of Xara did …". You and Kate Moir have been the most responsive business contacts I've ever had the privilege to know. Thank you both.

- Thanks to J.B. Popplewell and Amedeo Rosa at Alien Skin for extending the money-saving offer on their fantastic Photoshop plug-ins. We sort of have a running gag between us, so look for aliens—some of them wearing t-shirts—in various places in this book.

- A hearty thanks to Cliff Weems, Founder and CEO of Auto FX, and also to Debra Boring for offering our readers a special discount in this book on DreamSuite gel series, and DreamSuite series 1. They are knockout filters.

- Thanks to Richard Harris (the Creative Director at Wacom, not the guy who played Dumbledore in Harry Potter), for an excellent amount of savings, right here in this book, on Wacom's superb tablets.

- Thanks to Kathy Murray and Gina Kanouse for making certain the book is a "good read." Sentences have a way of getting jumbled from the mind to the keyboard sometimes! Thank you, sincerely.

- Thanks go to Jay Payne for mastering a CD that is accurate, despite how complex we made it for you!

Now, it's only fair that the hard-working co-conspirators to this book should be able to thank a friend or two, too. So here goes:

Mara Zebest Nathanson would like to thank her friends and family members for their support and encouragement. A special thanks to my husband, Richard, and my kids,

David and Leah, who constantly keep it real (for me) with their never-ending supply of laundry. And a big *thank you* to Robert Stanley, an infinitely wonderful and extraordinary friend.

Robert Stanley would like to thank his wife and children for putting up with everything that goes on during the writing process. Robert would also like to thank Bill and Kayre Morrison for their friendship (and the use of the character Roswell) and Mara Nathanson for all of her hard work and dedication in the cause of "getting it right."

Dear reader, these ladies and gentlemen have, pardon the phrase, *really busted* to bring information to the world, because they love the arts or communication and content creation, and they also love to share. If you care at all about the downward trend in media content, visit these sites, make a contribution, or start out on your own creating *true content*—the stuff we all *really* like to read.

A Message from New Riders

As the reader of this book, you are our most important critic and commentator. We value your opinion and want to know what we're doing right, what we could do better, in which areas you'd like to see us publish, and any other words of wisdom you're willing to pass our way.

As the Associate Publisher for New Riders, I welcome your comments. You can fax, email, or write me directly to let me know what you did or didn't like about this book—as well as what we can do to make our books better. When you write, please be sure to include this book's title, ISBN, and author, as well as your name and phone or fax number. I will carefully review your comments and share them with the authors and editors who worked on the book.

Please note that I cannot help you with technical problems related to the topic of this book, and that due to the high volume of email I receive, I might not be able to reply to every message. Thanks.

Fax:	317-581-4663
Email:	stephanie.wall@newriders.com
Mail:	Stephanie Wall
	Associate Publisher
	New Riders Publishing
	201 West 103rd Street
	Indianapolis, IN 46290 USA

Visit Our Web Site: www.newriders.com

On our web site, you'll find information about our other books, the authors we partner with, book updates and file downloads, promotions, discussion boards for online interaction with other users and with technology experts, and a calendar of trade shows and other professional events with which we'll be involved. We hope to see you around.

Email Us from Our Web Site

Go to www.newriders.com and click on the Contact Us link if you

- Have comments or questions about this book.
- Want to report errors that you have found in this book.
- Have a book proposal or are interested in writing for New Riders.
- Would like us to send you one of our author kits.

- Are an expert in a computer topic or technology and are interested in being a reviewer or technical editor.

- Want to find a distributor for our titles in your area.

- Are an educator/instructor who wants to preview New Riders books for classroom use. In the body/comments area, include your name, school, department, address, phone number, office days/hours, text currently in use, and enrollment in your department, along with your request for either desk/examination copies or additional information.

Introduction

A New Version, a New Crew, and a New Format for the Book

To borrow from umpteen million advertisements, "You won't find a fresher (book on Photoshop) than ours." Why? Because we used the freshest ingredients—we are a new, expanded authoring staff with wildly divergent opinions on Photoshop 7, but we are all in agreement that this is an important version release.

Before explaining the new format of the book, I'd like to doff my cap and introduce you to the talent that is driving this book:

- Gary David Bouton is the same affable guru who has helmed this book since its first version in 1994. Many gray hairs later, Gary still has that passion for both exploring a new program and writing about it in the same way you'd write a letter to a friend.

- Mara Zebest Nathanson is back again, to our delight. She tackled not only a wonderfully intricate and beautiful chapter, but she also tech edited the majority of the book.

- If you know anything about fonts, you know the name Daniel Will-Harris. I begged and kicked and screamed until he said yes to writing a typography chapter. And after five minutes of independent exploration of Photoshop 7, you'll understand *why* you need to dig heavily into Daniel's chapter and the art of type.

- J. Scott Hamlin and his partner Scott Balay are pretty darned dominant on the web with their unique style of web page presentation. Scott will show you some innovative web graphics and animation design in this book, and Scott (the *other* Scott!) covers a powerful new tool in Photoshop—scripting—and Photoshop Actions.

- Dave Huss has been Mr. Corel Photo-Paint for years. He's the Answer Man when it comes to bitmap graphics, and we're proud he's aboard this version to cover selections, image retouching, and a whole lot of necessary stuff in Photoshop in a dry, humorous style that Bouton has yet to learn!

- Mr. Robert Stanley's energies in recent years have gone into his work on "The Simpsons," and other graphically demanding projects in Hollywood. I'm extremely pleased he put down his brush (yes, he's a traditional artist who took up computer graphics—so there's decades of experience in his noggin) to show us how to perform magic and create photoreality using Photoshop. Robert also has written two versions of *The Complete Idiot's Guide to Photoshop* for Que Publishing. You'll find he's more typecast in *this* book than the others <g>.

How could you ask for a more pleasing mix, a better group of professionals, all with the same goal:

We're going to save you precious time learning and conquering Photoshop.

What's This "New Format" Stuff?

It's really quite simple. For ages, we've made *Inside Photoshop* a logical progression—you enter the first chapters as a novice and exit the book as a qualified user. So why mess with a good thing? One clear answer: To make it *better*.

Inside Photoshop 7 was designed around a "hub system." Now, it's not a real hub, or the book would be round instead of rectangular; but we're talking a core of reference chapters surrounded by parts in the book which appeal to different audiences. You'll probably even find that you're the audience for all the parts of the book. The point was to make the book quickly accessible to readers who have a specific need. If you're a novice, spend some time in the core section of the book. Don't worry; we don't do reference sections like you might believe—there are actually fun, learning-based tutorials mixed in between lists and valuable shortcuts.

On the other hand, if you want specific photo-retouching advice, you'd go straight to the part of the book called "Photoshop for Photographers".

We think this simplifies the structure of the book and makes it even easier for you to learn on the fly and become a Photoshoppist (who earns money from their new-found skills) quicker than ever.

Okay, I'm Hooked. What's Behind the Content of the Book?

Inside Photoshop 7 is a fully guided tour of the behind-the-scenes magic this program can produce. The authors take you through comprehensive steps in each chapter to show you how to produce award-winning work—photorealistic or otherwise. Our approach is a straightforward and simple one: it is our belief that every attention-getting image has to begin with a *concept*. You then choose the tools to complete the goal, and, by working through a set of procedures, finish the work. It is our intention to show you a task, to examine what needs to be done, and then to provide the steps you need to bring the piece to completion. By structuring the book in this way, we make it possible for you to be able to apply the "methodology" shown in this book to a *multitude* of personal and professional assignments.

An Omnibus Approach Provides Help for All Classes of Designers

Photoshop 7 has a streamlined interface, which is much more logically laid out than previous versions; but at the same time, pros are going to need to check out where stuff has been relocated, such as the Paint Bucket tool. (Hint: It's on the Gradient tool flyout.)

The program also features commands and palettes you'll find in other Adobe products. For example, a seasoned PageMaker or Illustrator user can get down to work in Photoshop 7 more quickly.

The authors have therefore chosen to presume practically *nothing* in teaching you this new program. Naturally, you need to feel comfortable with your computer's operating system; you need to know how to save, copy, and move a file; and proficiency with a mouse or a digitizing tablet will get you where you're going in Photoshop 7 more quickly than if you just unpacked a computer from a box moments ago! The authors have chosen to take a "step back" attitude from Photoshop 7 to better include users who might be unfamiliar with such things as anti-aliasing, interpolation, alpha channels, and other computer graphics terms. Again, if it's fundamental features you need to know, start at the core section.

As the theme of the book goes, *everyone* is new to Photoshop 7; it's an adventure for the pro and the beginner alike, and we didn't want to leave out anything in the steps, the notes, the text, or the discovery process. Do not take the attitude of, "Yeah, yeah, I know about the Lasso tool, so I'll skip this section." There are new features on the Lasso tool flyout on the toolbox, and you'll be missing out on valuable information if you "gloss" a chapter. The authors didn't presume anything, so as a reader, you shouldn't either!

Taking the Road to Adventure

Let us make learning Photoshop 7 an excursion, an adventure. As most adventures go, you must pack a few things first—intangible things like a positive attitude, a concept, a proficiency with your computer, and an eagerness to learn. And last but not least, you should have a map, so you can instantly find your way from Point X to Point Y, while ignoring entirely Point A. The authors have *provided* the map (it's called "this book"!), and the following sections describe this map by way of explaining some of the conventions of *Inside Photoshop 7*.

Figure I.1

Push Down and Twist: Directions for Accessing This Book

Most of the examples described in the book are documented in a step-by-step format. If you follow along, your screen should look like this book's figures, except that your screen will be in color. Each chapter leads you through at least one set of numbered steps, with frequent asides explaining why we asked you to do something. The figures show the results of an action, and we explain what the effect should look like.

Most of Photoshop 7's tools have different, enhanced functions when you hold down the Shift, Alt, or Ctrl keys (Shift, Opt, ⌘ Command keys, for Macintosh users) while you click a mouse button or press other keyboard keys. These *modifier keys* are shown in the steps as Ctrl(⌘)+click, Alt(Opt)+click, Ctrl(⌘)+D, and so on. *Inside Photoshop 7* is a multiplatform documentation of the application; Windows key commands are shown first in the steps, followed by the Macintosh key equivalent (enclosed in parentheses). The primary difference in Photoshop 7 across platforms is the "look" each operating system lends to interface elements.

As you can see in Figure 1.2, we believe that most Windows users can readily get down to work in Photoshop under Mac OS X.

Meanwhile, in Figure 1.3, the "Chrome" skin (many Windows skins are available for XP) surrounds exactly the same contents as those shown in Figure 1.2. We see minute functional differences between platforms, which means that you'll see very few differences in the way this book explains Photoshop for the two platforms.

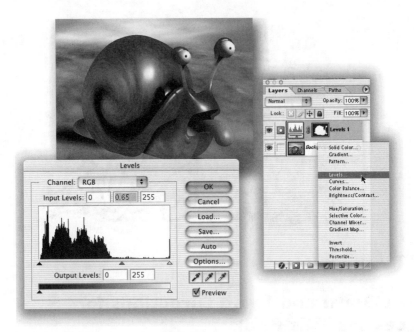

Figure I.2   The Macintosh interface is clean and attractive, and all the controls in Photoshop are easy to locate.

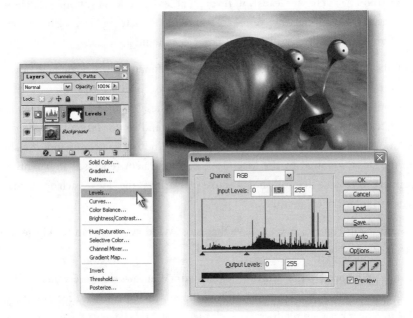

Figure I.3   Windows, Macintosh—it's all the same Photoshop when you remove the "padding" that the platform adds.

Note

Windows Versus Macintosh   Okay, here's a list of the *real* differences in features between the Windows and the Macintosh versions of Photoshop 7:

- In Windows, when you are in full-screen mode without the menu or title bar on an image, you can still access the menu because a flyout button appears on the top of the toolbox.

- On the Macintosh, you can roll up the toolbox at any time by double-clicking the palette tab at the very top of the toolbox. A second double-click rolls the toolbox down.

- The Document Sizes field and the Zoom Percentage field on the Macintosh version of Photoshop are located on the bottom of the current image window. In Windows, the Document Sizes and Zoom Percentage field are on the Status Line at the bottom of the screen, where you also can see options displayed for the currently selected tool.

- As of this writing, the Adobe Gamma control panel automatically loads upon installing Photoshop 7 on the Macintosh. You can find this utility under the Apple menu, Control Panels. The Adobe Gamma Control Panel might or might not automatically load during installation while running Windows ME, NT/2000, or Windows XP. Be sure to check out the (Photoshop 5) Goodies, Calibration folder if Adobe Gamma didn't load into the system Control Panel. There will be instructions in the Calibration folder on how to manually install Adobe Gamma. (Hint: do it—it's the best global gamma adjustment utility you can find for your computer, and it's free.)

To show you how easy it is to follow along in this book, here's how we tell you to access the Feather command:

1. Press Ctrl(⌘)+Alt(Opt)+D (Select, Feather), and then type **5** in the Pixels field. Click OK to apply the feathering.

The translation? You hold down the first key while you press the second and third keys (then release all three keys to produce the intended result), or you can access the command the "hard way" through the menu commands enclosed in parentheses. The authors are trying to get you comfortable with modifier keys rather than menu commands because this constant reinforcement (highlighted throughout the book) will eventually enable you to work more efficiently in Photoshop 7. Function keys appear in this book as F1, F2, F3, and so on.

If the steps in an exercise are available in both Windows and Macintosh formats but they are significantly different, we fully explain the steps you need to complete the task on both platforms.

The figures in this book were taken in Windows NT/2000 and XP; there simply isn't room in this book to show all the versions of Windows, UNIX, and Macintosh interfaces! Again, where there is a significant difference in the way something is accomplished on a specific platform, this book details specific steps to be used.

Terms Used in This Book

The term *drag* in this book means to hold down the primary mouse button and move the onscreen cursor. This action is used in Photoshop to create a marquee selection and to access tools on the toolbox flyout. On the Macintosh, dragging also is used to access *pull-down menus*; Windows users do not need to hold the primary mouse button to access flyout menus and main menu commands.

Hover means to move your cursor onscreen without holding a mouse button. Hovering is most commonly used in Photoshop with the Magnetic Pen and Magnetic Lasso tools, and it is also used with the Eyedropper tool when you are seeking a relative position in an image and want to know the color value beneath the tool. (Hint: Display the Info palette, F8, to determine the values the Eyedropper reads.)

Click means to press and release the primary mouse button once.

Double-click means to press twice, quickly, the primary mouse button. Usually you double-click to perform a function without the need to click an OK button in a directory window or dialog box. Additionally, when you double-click a tool in Photoshop's toolbox, the Options palette appears.

Shift+Click means that you should hold down the Shift key while you click the primary mouse button.

Special (Not Ordinary) Things We Used in This Book

Throughout this book, several conventions are used to clarify certain keyboard techniques and to help you distinguish certain types of text (new terms and text that you type, for example). These conventions include the following:

Special Text

Information you type is in **boldface**. This rule applies to individual letters, numbers, and text strings, but not to special keys, such as Enter (Return), Tab, Esc, or Ctrl(⌘).

New terms appear in *italic*. Italic text is used also for emphasis, as in "*Don't* unplug your computer at this point."

We Use Nicknames for Well-Known Products

Inside Photoshop 7 would be an even larger book than it already is if every reference to a specific graphics product or manufacturer included the full brand manufacturer, product name, and version number. For this reason, you'll frequently see Adobe Photoshop 7 referred to as simply "Photoshop" in the text of this book. Similarly, Adobe Illustrator is referred to as "Illustrator," and other products are mentioned by their "street names."

New Riders Publishing and the authors acknowledge that the names mentioned in this book are trademarked or copyrighted by their respective manufacturers; our use of nicknames for various products is in no way meant to infringe on the trademark names for these products. When we refer to an application, it is usually the most current version of the application, unless otherwise noted.

Contents at a Glance

The authors recommend that you use *Inside Photoshop 7* as a reference guide, but it was also written as a string of hands-on tutorials. And this means that you might benefit most from the information in the book by reading a little at a time. We are aware, however, that this is not the way everyone finds information—particularly in an integrating graphics environment such as Photoshop's, where one piece of information often leads to a seemingly unconnected slice of wisdom. For this reason, most chapters offer complete, self-contained steps for a specific topic or technique, with frequent cross-references to related material in other chapters. If you begin reading Chapter 4, for example, you will learn a complete area of image editing, but you can build on what you've learned if you thoroughly investigate Chapter 16 as well.

Inside Photoshop 7 is divided into nine parts, with the Appendix and special instructions for installing components of the Companion CD in Part IX, "The Back O' the Book." Here's a breakdown of what's in store:

Part I: Getting Your Feet Wet

Let's face it; we all like to play with non-toxic stuff before reading the instructions. So it is with Photoshop. Indulge! We put you through your paces only *later* in the book!

Chapter 1: Getting Creative When You Have No Idea What You're Doing

In this one-chapter part of the book, Gary Bouton lets you play with some really cool imagery—and guess what? There are no grades! Just moosh stuff, and twist and rotate things to your heart's content. The chapter's contents are merely suggestions on the best way to moosh and rotate—and it helps you get your hands dirty and have fun with Photoshop in a few opening exercises.

Part II: Photoshop Core Concepts

This part of the book is the "hub" from which all creative things flow. This is a reference part, but it also is a hands-on, "let's memorize this stuff" chapter. You become a more powerful Photoshoppist after you've pored through the chapters in this part so that you can better travel off and become the creative individual that *you* have in mind.

Chapter 2: Optimizing and Customizing Photoshop Preferences

Gary Bouton helps you make sure that Photoshop works for you, and not the other way around. Chapter 2 shows you all the little neat things spinning around the interface—and beneath and behind it—and we offer suggestions on the smartest, most time-efficient and friendly way to "mold" your own interface. Photoshop will work faster, and you'll be happier with the results after reading this chapter.

Chapter 3: Harnessing the Power of Selections

Dave Huss takes you around the virtual block with a potpourri of selection techniques, because one selection method does not fit all. Find out which method to use on which type of image or painting to accurately and invisibly separate areas with which you want to work.

Chapter 4: Enough Selections! The Layers and Shapes Chapter

In this chapter, Gary shows you just how valuable layers can be when you want to create a really sophisticated and elegant presentation. Layers also are an alternative for selection definition over channels—you can learn it all right here. Also get complete control over the vector shapes, the palette, and the Options bar options, and gain experience as you would in Illustrator or other vector programs. Vectors are a scalable, smooth, and welcome addition to Photoshop's bevy of tools.

Chapter 5: Working with Channels and Paths

Gary Bouton takes you on an exploration of channels—why you need them and the creative ways in which to manipulate them. Then, we hunker down and pull apart (carefully) the Pen tools, and see how vectors are manually created in Photoshop. Because you can stroke paths and make selections based upon their geometry, they are positively career-savers.

Chapter 6: Using the Clone Stamp, Healing Brush, and Patch Tools

New to this version of Photoshop are the Healing Brush and the Patch tools. In Chapter 6, Gary Bouton shows you exactly how the Clone Stamp tool works (through example, natch'), which is about 25% of the total power of Photoshop. Then you get some fun and educational assignments to help you become familiar with the other new cloning tools. (I *really* like the Patch tool and used it frequently to put this book's graphics together.)

Part III: The Important and Headache-Causing Stuff: Calibration, Input, and Output

Part III of this book lassos the fly in the ointment, helping you anticipate and work around irritation and inconsistencies you might experience as you are displaying, printing, or exporting your Photoshop creations.

Chapter 7: Understanding Photoshop's Color Management System

Chapter 7 was originally written by Richard Cordero and Barbara Bouton in the version 6 book and was updated by Gary Bouton for this book. If you are after color-critical work, this chapter is a must, and you should probably read it before any of the other chapters. Why? Because your system's calibration will affect your work in all the examples and tutorials in this book.

Chapter 8: Input, Output, and Resolution

In Chapter 8, Dave Huss discusses, in *human* terms, the best way to acquire an image, what your alternatives are, how many samples you need to take of an image (or physical art to make it print correctly), and a formula or two that you should tuck in your back pocket before you go off photographing or scanning things.

Part IV: Photoshop for Photographers

Here is another, time-tested, popular "spoke" in the hub system of this book. Yes, finally, we are devoting an entire section to photographers and their special needs. No typography, no illustrations—just the artist's eye, the lens, and Photoshop.

Chapter 9: Basic Picture Editing

Chapter 9 was written by Dave Huss for everyone who wants to use Photoshop, but needs a little help with the terms and procedures professional photographers use to get the raw material they mold and shape in Photoshop. Photography is not the same game it used to be—today you have digital cameras, the web as a showplace, and look, ma...very few minutes to wait and very few chemicals. Let Dave help you prepare for the road to today's photography and tomorrow's photographer.

Chapter 10: Color and Tone Correction

In Chapter 10, Gary Bouton covers everything you need to know about correcting a photo for color and tone: from basic Brightness/Contrast, through Levels and Curves, all the way to working with Variations and selectively restoring a photo.

Chapter 11: Restoring an Heirloom Photograph

Chapter 11 is one of two parts. Originally written by Gary Bouton and updated by Dave Huss, this chapter is a must-read if you have a shoebox full of precious but deteriorating images. Who doesn't? Learn the secrets to coping with water damage, artificial tints applied to black-and-white pictures that simply don't cut it, and other surface defects on heirloom images.

Chapter 12: Retouching an Heirloom Photograph

Chapter 12 is meant to help you go beyond restoration and to create an image "as you remember it." Gary Bouton (with updates by Dave Huss) takes you a step beyond the reality of a repaired photo that becomes a treasure once again. Call it photo-idealism.

Part V: Photoshop for Artists

Photographers are not allowed to look at this part of the book. I'm kidding, I'm kidding! This part of the book's hub is devoted to creating airbrush-type cartooning, doing some advanced photorealistic painting, and filling in those paths you learned about earlier.

Chapter 13: Using Paths

Now that you've been through Bouton's chapters on paths, you're all set to put them to artistic purposes. What??? Help!!!

Not to worry—Mara Nathanson's chapter will put you on the right, um—*path*, and you'll create a stunning piece of "orange crate art" in the process.

Chapter 14: Bringing Out the Artist in You

Robert Stanley positively wails in Chapter 14. It's more than a bunch of helpful tips; read this chapter, and you're well on your way to Wish Fulfillment. Ya' just have to read it.

Chapter 15: Out of This World A.R.T. (Advanced Rendering Techniques)

Robert's got an interesting acronym going on in the title of this chapter. Robert's a pro; learn from a pro; become a pro. It's that hard and that simple.

Part VI: Typography and Special Effects

What is type? Who started type, and why is it so small on medicine bottles? We can't provide all the answers, but dig this: Photoshop 7 had type handling controls that match Illustrator feature-for-feature, and almost rival PageMaker and InDesign. They're *that* good, and you deserve to get a background on typography—its preferred use and tricks and tips—before you set that next paragraph.

Chapter 16: Typography

Daniel Will-Harris shows you, (typo)graphically, the do's and don'ts of typesetting and choosing the best font for expressing a thought. The leading authority on fonts, Mr. Will-Harris is a widely known columnist; and to get him to write for this book, Bouton promised to hand-kern his entire type collection. (That was a joke.)

Chapter 17: Special Effects with Type

Gary Bouton shows you four situations in which you need a little something above and beyond what Photoshop automatically provides. Do you need wrap-around text? How about a "Hawaiian postcard" look for a client? Dig in right here, and you'll see how type meets graphics in Photoshop.

Part VII: Photoshop for the Web

You didn't think we'd leave out the fastest form of graphics communications from this toe-buster of a book, did you? And who is the best person to teach this stuff? J. Scott Hamlin; you've seen his work just about everywhere on the web, and I had to pry him away from his *own* best-selling books with a tire iron to get him to write for this book.

Chapter 18: Creating Interface Elements

Scott Hamlin designed a fun trip for those of you who need guidelines for successful web communication. Less is more; move the design over by one pixel—advice you can count on, and then go off and make your own cyber-masterpiece!

Chapter 19: Rollovers, Slicing, and Optimization

Scott Hamlin leads you through—with great results—the adage, "make every pixel count on the web." Scott's whipped up a healthy serving of tips, innovative approaches, and just plain talk from a genius who knows about these sorts of things. Your web buttons will animate, your images will be small but beautiful, and you'll have learned yet another aspect of successful electronic communications.

Chapter 20: Animation

Scott Hamlin shows you other ways to get your point across using animation. Heard of Flash and Adobe LiveMotion? These vector forms of animation are fun to create and leave your audience gasping at your graphics prowess. Get the inside scoop; chances are 10 out of 10 that Adobe or Macromedia has already snuck the components for watching these animations into your browser!

Chapter 21: Scripting and Actions

Scott Balay, Scott Hamlin's professional partner, tackles scripting and actions in this chapter. You might be familiar with Actions since version 4 of Photoshop, but Scott Balay puts a new spin on everything, including Photoshop's new scripting language. And check out the CD—Scott said he'd put some interesting sample scripts on it!

Part VIII: Photoshop Tricks and Closing Thoughts

This part rounds out the book with a healthy dose of practical insight and experiential mastery techniques (in other words, *tips* and *tricks*). You'll learn how to do a number of specialized, attention-getting and time-saving techniques before we finish up and set you free to create your own exciting Photoshop masterpieces.

Chapter 22: Gary Cauldron and Photoshop Tips

J. Rowling's book and the obvious play on Gary's name made it inevitable that the theme was going to be Photoshop magic to close out the tutorials in the book. But wait until you see this chapter on Photoshop Magic—it required 70 manuscript pages and three typewriter ribbons (which is hard to do because I use a laser printer). This book has been a labor of love for me to create, and I just wanted to share it *all* on the occasion of our 10th anniversary writing graphics books for New Riders. This bag of tricks contains a great collection of neatly sliced, advanced tricks that you follow step-by-step.

Probably, the best "trick" that you'll learn in this chapter is that there's no such thing as magic, but only a mystery you've yet to ingeniously solve. That sounds like I'm pushing the creative ball back into your court without so much as a shred of advice about where to go from here—what's next for you when the book's done? Well, there's Chapter 22½.

Chapter 22½: Where Do We Go from Here?

It's not about Photoshop. It's about *you*. How do you feel about a career in graphics once your head has stopped spinning from this book? How do people get into the business? Can you make a good living? What should you expect, and what's the most important thing to hold in your mind as you walk out into the sunshine and start looking at the real world and all the commercial trappings that go with it?

Amazingly, it's all in about five pages. It's the least we could do for our readers.

Part IX: The Back O' the Book

Don't you hate reaching the end of a good book, only to find that the authors skimped on the research they put into it?! Everyone who works with a computer has a natural curiosity about where to learn more, where to find the best sources for more tools, and what stuff means when they read it out of context.

Appendix A: The *Inside Photoshop 7* CD-ROM

This tells precisely what the *Inside Photoshop 7 Companion CD* is all about. On the CD, you will find a number of important resources for your continuing adventures in Photoshop, long after you've poured through the pages in this book:

- **Resource files for the chapter examples.** We recommend that you work through the steps shown in this book, using files (carefully prepared by the authors) that demonstrate specific procedures and effects. The files, located in the Examples folder on the Companion CD, are platform-independent and can be used on any Macintosh or Windows system with Photoshop 7 installed. Sorry, Photoshop 7 itself is *not* included on the Companion CD! You need to bring *some* ingredients in the recipe for imaging fame and fortune to the party yourself!

- *The Inside Photoshop eGlossary.* This Acrobat PDF file contains color examples, shortcuts, definitions, and other material pertaining to this book, to Photoshop, and to computer graphics in general. We recommend that you install the OnLine Glossary on your system, and then launch Adobe Acrobat Reader when you need a quick explanation of something. Acrobat Reader comes on the Adobe Photoshop CD.

Note

Author's Note   The Glossary, even though it's almost 300 pages, does not include Photoshop 7-specific information. To be honest, we're offering the version 6 eGlossary, which contains more than 90% of what you might need to look up in version 7. Hey, we were kinda' busy when it came time to update this valuable guide.

- **Fonts, textures, and scenes in Windows and Macintosh formats.** The authors have produced a fairly extensive collection (in our opinion) of frequently needed items for web pages, traditional publication, and other types of media construction. Check out the Boutons folder on the Companion CD; these are completely unique, one-of-a-kind, Photoshop-oriented files and programs.

- **Extras.** Shareware, demo versions of working programs, and utilities provided on the Companion CD are hand-picked items we have used and recommend. There are certain restrictions on some of the ShareWare, and please don't confuse "ShareWare" with "FreeWare." If you find something on the Companion CD that is useful in your professional work, please read the Read Me file in the folder where you found the utility or file, and register (pay a small fee) to the creator of the program.

Appendix B: Keyboard Shortcuts and Power User Tips

Mara Nathanson and Dave Huss have compiled a beautiful resource—*computer tidbits.* All too often we forget that these beige boxes don't learn for themselves, they don't wash your car…in fact, there's a lot of reasons for having a child over having a computer. Discover some basic facts, some not-so-basic tricks of the pros, and get to the root of why your computer is sticking its virtual tongue out at you with a "Type 10 error," or "Windows has closed this program because it was irritating."

The Index

The mark of a well-written book is only as good as its index. New Riders has the best indexers in town, and if you can't wait to thumb through the pages for something, check the Back O' the Book.

Ads and Goodies

Last, but certainly not least, don't overlook the special discount offers you'll find at the back of the book. These offers can save you hundreds of dollars!

Hey. It's So Complex, It's Simple

Electronic imaging is such a wonderful, magical thing that it's impossible to keep the child in us quiet. For that reason, many of the examples in this book are a little whimsical—they stretch reality a tad, in the same way you'll learn to stretch a pixel or two using Photoshop. We want to show you some of the fun we've had with a very serious product, and hope that perhaps we will kindle or fan the flame of the creative spark in you, as well.

Part I

Getting Your
Feet Wet

Chapter 1

Getting Creative When You Have No Idea What You're Doing

When you are given the choice between gooshing your fingers in Play-doh for a few hours or helping to design the integration controls for an automated forklift...quick, which one would you choose?

There isn't a right or wrong answer here, but we were kinda hoping that you're the "gooshing" type. Why? Because this is a book on art and not forklifts. But more importantly, you can actually learn a lot from topographically rearranging child's modeling clay. Some things you just pick up by experimenting. And if you're new to Photoshop, the program may seem as complicated as the innards of a forklift, but we are going to make this complex image editing program (Photoshop) fun—yes, *fun* for you to goof around with. In this chapter, we have a handsome, goofy picture on several layers just waiting for you to alter, and you will assuredly learn some Photoshop truths through your (guided) tour.

So come along, it's only the beginning of the book, and you can honestly tell your boss you're researching the program while you're having a ball!

Meet Bouton's Idea of a Picnic

If you open picnic.psd from the Examples/Chap01 folder of the Companion CD, you will see a sight, *fer shur*. We have an alien sporting a shameless plug for a software company on its T-shirt, a duck swimming in a watch, a rock pile with a face looking on, some fruit, a gnome with a mushroom (at least he's bringing something to the picnic), and naturally, a pest—in the form of a hovering insect. Every picnic *has* to have insects.

The first thing we ought to do, therefore, is not to *kill* the insect, but instead to stash its component parts away in a layer aet.

What's a layer set? Read on!

Introducing Layers and Layer Sets

To understand layer sets, you first need to understand Photoshop layers. Photoshop layers can store non-transparent design or photographic elements. Those elements are held in place by transparency all around, which means that you can see the non-transparent contents of a layer underneath. For example, if you open picnic.psd from the Examples/Chap01 folder on the Companion CD (you're going to have to eventually), and then press F7 to display the Layers palette, you will see that there are about a quatrillion layers in the image. Why, oh why did author Bouton do this? Simple: So you can experiment with one item in the image without disturbing the others.

Now, the process does become a little confusing when you have odd ends and pieces of objects all on separate layers, so the most prudent thing to do when working on any multi-layered image is to keep components of one element in one place. A layer set helps you solve that problem by keeping all the crumbs on one cookie.

In the steps that follow, you will put the bumblebee, along with its left and right wing, in a layer set you create…

Creating and Using a Layer Set

1. With the picnic.psd file open in Photoshop, scroll up the Layers list until you can see Right wing, Bumble, and Left wing titles.

2. On the Layers palette, click the flyout menu button (circled in Figure 1.1) and then choose New Layer Set from the menu. A dialog box appears—type **Bumble** for the name and then click OK.

Figure 1.1   Create a new layer set for keeping elements together on the Layers palette.

3. A tiny folder icon appears on the Layers palette list with the title Bumble. Drag the titles for Bumble, Left wing, and Right wing from the palette to the folder icon. Although the bumblebee is still visible in the image window, you can now delete it, move it up or down in layer order, or make all three layers invisible with a single click. (Depending on the order in which you placed the three layers in the layer set, the wings may now appear behind the bee. But don't worry about that.) Pretty powerful stuff. Keep Photoshop and this image open; we've yet to begin messing it up.

Admittedly, organizing insect parts is not an auspicious opening to a playful chapter. We'll correct this in the following section where you get a true feel for the power of layers.

Changing Layers and Moving Objects

Before continuing, choose the Move tool (on the upper right of the toolbox; shaped like an arrow with a street intersection symbol) and make certain that the Auto Select Layer checkbox on the Options bar (upper left of your screen) is unchecked. You can check it later, after you've read about preferences in Chapter 2, "Optimizing and Customizing Photoshop Preferences." Now, as you can see, there are a lot of things wrong with this picture: the fruit has no color, the gnome looks happy even though he's a gnome—and *the tree has a faucet tap on it*! The gnome might benefit from some professional help, but you can move the tap to its rightful place on the keg (we aren't sure what's in the keg; we assume it's apple cider) in about two editing moves.

Here's how:

Tapping a Keg

1. Right-click (Macintosh: hold Ctrl and click) over the tap on the tree. The context menu pops up and tells you that there are three layers directly under your cursor. Choose the tap choice, and the Layers palette will highlight the tap title on the list to indicate that this is the layer you are editing (see Figure 1.2).

Note

For those of you who feel a tad rebellious and want to maneuver to different layers *without* selecting the Move tool and turning on the Auto Select Layer option as we suggested, try this: Ctrl(⌘)+click on the tap layer to jump instantly to that layer. Additionally, a Ctrl(⌘)+click (with the Move tool active) temporarily toggles the Auto Select feature on.

2. With one deft move of the cursor, drag the tap layer to the keg layer. One problem here: the duck is going to get its watch wet now that the tap is positioned correctly. This is no problem if you understand how to link layers and move them together. And besides, who invited the duck, anyhow?

3. Click on the QT shadow layer, and then click in the column to the left of the QuackTime layer title, as shown in Figure 1.3. You've connected the layers now; not in the same way that you collected the insect parts, but linking is good for moving things in tandem.

Right-click (Ctrl+click) to change the current editing layer to those layers on the context menu (directly under the cursor). Choose the layer named tap.

Figure 1.2   Right-clicking (Macintosh: hold Ctrl and click) over a point on a multi-layer image (when Auto Select Layer is turned off) takes your cursor to the layer that you choose on the context menu.

Link layers to move them in unison

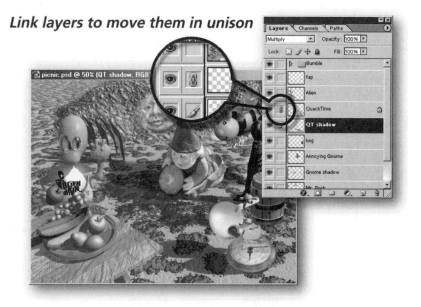

Figure 1.3   Linking layers is easy. Choose a "base" layer and then click the link icon on layers above or below the base layer.

4. Drag the duck-in-the-watch and its shadow to the left, out of wetness' way and into safety. Keep Photoshop open and save this image to your hard disk to speed up the action.

The next weird item on our "let's muck it up" list is the face in the stone pile. Why isn't he smiling? Wanna make him smile?

Using the Liquify Command

If you skipped past version 6 to arrive directly at Photoshop 7, or if you're new to the program, the Liquify command (which has moved from the Image menu to the Filter menu) is very much like KPT Goo (part of Corel KPT6) and the VALIS Group's Flo', except for two things.

First, Liquify produces more refined results than the other two products—with a lot of practice, you can actually make Aunt Tilly look slimmer or do a proboscis reduction on your friend, thus saving your relatives and friends thousands of dollars in plastic surgery. Liquify turns the target image into soft, pliable pixels—this author's favorite. Of course, the most predictable use for the command is to do unflattering things to pictures of late-paying clients.

Second, and this is unfortunate, Liquify cannot produce a movie of distortions like Goo and Flo' do. But hey, we're talking Photoshop and not Adobe Premiere, which is the program in the movie game. In the following exercise, you'll do something almost that amazing by transforming a grumpy rock into a smiling one for the occasion of the picnic.

Using the Liquify Command

1. Right-click (Macintosh: hold Ctrl and click) over the rock face to display the context menu, and then choose the entry "Mr. Rock." (Warning: The author does all sorts of cloying, Mr. Rogersish naming conventions in this chapter.) The layer with the rock face is the current editing layer.

2. Choose Liquify from the Filter main menu. As you can see in Figure 1.4, only the rock is subject to editing in the Liquify box. This figure shows some important numbers we'll reference in the following steps, so mark this place so that you can return to it easily.

3. Click the Zoom tool in the left tools column of the interface. Zoom into the rock face until it's approximately the size shown in Figure 1.4. On the right side of the interface, choose a 30-pixel brush tip (circled in Figure 1.4), and change Reconstruction to Smooth. This choice is more processor-intensive than the others; but hey, we all have P4s and G4s these days so brute force comes easy in Photoshop, right?

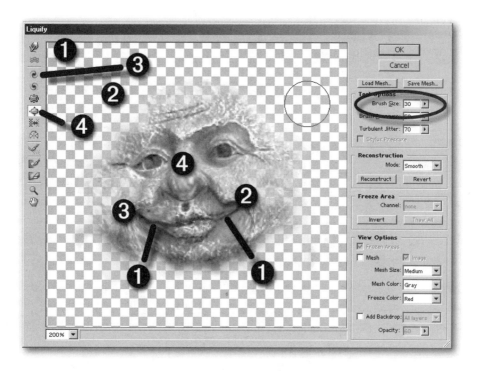

Figure 1.4   There are tons of editing controls in the Liquify dialog box. This section runs
through the most striking and popular commands.

4. Click the top icon in the left column in the box. This is the Warp tool; and if
   you're new to the Liquify command, you might want to turn on tool tips from
   the Preferences menus after you close this dialog box so that you can work more
   and hunt less.

5. Pull on the rock's lips: first pull the left side farther to the left, and then pull the
   right side farther to the right (see item 1 in Figure 1.4).

6. Now, a smile, especially on a rock, should be a subtle thing—the corners of the
   lips turn up, like what Clint Eastwood does instead of actually smiling. Choose
   the Twirl counterclockwise tool (item 2), and then rub the tool over the right
   corner of Mr. Rock's lips. He smirks now—but you still need to even out the
   smile.

7. Click the Twirl clockwise tool and repeat Step 6, this time on the left edge of Mr.
   Rock's lips (item 3). Oh, boy, he's happy now!

8. Finally (optional): Click the Bloat tool (item 4) and click Mr. Rock's nose a few
   times. No, this doesn't directly contribute to the tutorial—it just looks funny.
   Click OK to apply the changes to Mr. Rock, close the Liquify command, and get
   back to the picnic.

Tip

If you want to see quickly how far you've come using the Liquify tool, you can press Ctrl+Z a few times to undo your changes.

9. Keep Photoshop open. We have to pretend now that the section coming up is a reference section.

In the world of Photoshop, there's something called *modes*. It will not make a lot of sense right now if you're just beginning, but Photoshop can eventually (and potentially) blend the visual information (the image area) on one layer with the underlying layer(s). The way in which the data (image area) is blended is called a *mode*. There are 22 layer modes (modes into which you subject an entire layer's contents) and 23 painting modes (all the layer modes plus the Behind mode, which enables you to (apparently) paint on the back of a layer, thus preserving the image data on the front of the layer.

The following section introduces you to the different modes so that you can make intelligent choices about which mode to use in your own work. You'll also understand, after reading the next section, why we ask you to choose certain modes for stuff in the picnic image.

Photoshop Modes: A Dry Definition of Each Blending Mode

Well, I'm lying—the explanations here will be terse but not dry. I don't write "dry." Learning about modes now is important because they control the way the painting and drawing tools in Photoshop affect the image you're working on. As you go through the exercises in the book, you'll be glad you had this primer up-front (really, you will). The following list gives you a quick introduction to the modes you'll use most often:

- **Normal mode.** Normal mode is the default mode for painting and compositing and is the standard mode for a layer. When a color or selected image area is composited into the background, Normal mode replaces the underlying pixels with the pixels you added to the image. It's a straightforward replacement of background pixels. You can change the opacity of the paint or selection before finalizing an edit by clicking and dragging the Opacity slider, which is found both on the Layers palette for compositing and merging layers and on the Options bar when you're painting.

- **Dissolve mode.** Dissolve mode corrupts a selection or paint stroke by randomly distributing foreground pixels throughout the selected area. Dissolve mode is useful for painting; it can create an instant "texture" to which you can apply other effects and create complex designs. Dissolve mode also can produce some fairly unaesthetic blends of a selection into a background image. Blending layers together in Dissolve mode can be equally unphotogenic.

- **Behind and Clear modes.** These modes can be used only on layers, and these are painting modes, not layer modes; background images can't be painted clear or behind. Behind mode treats opaque pixels as masked, and only the transparent pixels on a layer can receive color. This creates a simulation of painting on the back side of a sheet of acetate, where a design has already been painted on the front. Clear mode changes opaque pixels to transparent and can be used with the Paint bucket tool, the Paintbrush tool, the Pencil tool, the Fill command, and the Stroke command. You must be in a layer with Lock Transparency deselected to use this mode. Additionally, you can use the Edit menu's Fill and Stroke commands to apply Clear to the edges or interior of a selection.

Tip

When you click and drag the Eraser tool through opaque pixels on a layer, it creates the same effect as Clear mode. You may find that erasing is a more straightforward way of removing a pixel's opacity than using Clear mode.

- **Multiply and Screen modes.** These are perhaps two of the most useful modes for painting and compositing that you, as a designer, could want. Multiply mode has the opposite function of Screen mode. When you paint in Multiply mode, the foreground color (indicated on the toolbox) combines with an image's colors to decrease brightness on the area you're painting. Painting in Multiply mode always produces a darker color, and the effect can look like soft charcoals or designer markers that have saturated the paper. When you use it as a mode for compositing floating selections, Multiply mode emphasizes the darker values of the selection as it's blended into the background image. Lighter colors in the selection disappear when you deselect (thus blend) the selection. Multiply is great for creating shadows, which you'll see in the examples shown in other chapters.

  Screening "bleaches" a lighter foreground color out of an image when you are painting, and Screen mode always produces a lighter color. Stay tuned for an example of using Screen mode in an exercise to follow.

- **Color Burn mode.** This mode looks at the color information in each channel and darkens colors on the bottom layer by increasing the contrast. If the Color Burn mode is used on a layer of white, there is no change in the appearance of the overall image.

- **Linear Burn mode.** This mode examines the channel colors in the target layer (the layer causing the change in Linear Burn mode) and darkens the color in the bottom layer to blend color by decreasing the apparent brightness. There is no change in the appearance of the overall image if the target layer is white.

- **Overlay mode.** This mode intensifies the highlight and shadow areas of the image you paint over; it also adds intense highlight and shadow areas to the background image when you assign Overlay mode to a floating selection. The *midtones* of an image—the areas that have neither highlights nor shadows—are tinted with the current foreground color when you use Overlay mode for painting, and floating selections assigned Overlay mode blends most of the color values into the background image. Overlay is a great mode for creating ghost-like objects in an image and for superimposing titles.

- **Soft and Hard Light modes.** These are combination effect modes; both Soft and Hard Light modes react to the base color (the color found in the background image you paint or composite a selection into). If a background area has a brightness of greater than 50%, Soft Light mode lightens the paint or composite selection, and Hard Light screens the paint or composite selection. If the underlying background has pixels that fall below a 50% brightness value, Soft Light darkens the area, and Hard Light multiplies the color values. This means that you can achieve a selective Screen and Multiply effect at once when you choose Hard Light as the painting or compositing mode. Use these modes with partial Opacity settings to achieve different effects.

- **Vivid Light.** This message burns in or dodges out the colors by changing the contrast, depending on the color(s) on the layer you're messing with. If the blend color is lighter than 50% black, the image is lightened by decreasing the contrast. If the blend color is darker than 50% black, the image is darkened by increasing the contrast. We'll be using this mode to help the alien in this picnic image color its fruit. Where's the Lucky Charms leprechaun when you need him?

- **Linear Light.** This mode works very much like the Vivid Light mode except that brightness is the governing force, not contrast. If the blend color(s) is lighter than 50% black, the image is lightened by increasing the brightness. If the blend color(s) is darker than 50% black, the overall image is darkened by decreasing the brightness.

- **Pin Light.** Similar to the two previous commands, Pin Light replaces colors with a break point at 50% black—no contrast or lightness is involved in the process. If the blend color(s) is lighter than 50% black, pixels darker than the layer upon which you are working are replaced, and pixels lighter than the blend color (the color on the active layer) do not change. If the blend color is darker than 50% black, pixels lighter than the blend color are replaced, and pixels darker than the blend color do not change. A warning, however: This author has played with this mode for over three months and has yet to figure out how to make a beautiful area in an image using it.

- **Darken and Lighten modes.** Darken mode affects only the pixels in the image that are lighter than the foreground color. Equal or darker pixels are not affected. Conversely, Lighten affects only the pixels in the image darker than the foreground color you selected. Darken and Lighten modes produce painting and compositing effects that are much more subtle than Screen and Multiply modes, but they are closely related. You may decide to use Lighten or Darken modes for painting when Screen or Multiply produces results that are too intense.

- **Difference mode.** This mode evaluates the color of both the image area you paint and the current foreground color. If the foreground color is brighter, the background color is changed to the color opposite its original value. Painting over an image with white produces the most dramatic results; therefore, few background images contain a value brighter than absolute white!

- **Exclusion.** This mode creates an effect lower in contrast than Difference mode. Painting with white on an Exclusion mode layer inverts the bottom layer color values. Painting with black produces bupkis, nada, nothing.

- **Hue mode.** Hue mode paints with the foreground shade only. The Luminosity and Saturation of the image area you paint is unaffected. This mode is terrific when you want to tint areas.

- **Saturation mode.** If your foreground color is black, Saturation mode converts color areas to grayscale. If your foreground color is a color value, this mode, along with each brush stroke, amplifies the underlying pixels' basic color value by reducing the gray component. The non-black foreground color you selected doesn't affect what happens. You have to play with Saturation mode to understand its possibilities in your own work.

- **Color mode.** This mode changes both the Hue and Saturation of a selected image without altering the background image's tonal composition—the quality that comprises visual detail in most photographic images.

- **Luminosity.** This increases the lightness qualities in the image. This powerful mode doesn't change color values. Use it sparingly when lightening, say, an oversaturated color area in an image. When using Luminosity mode with a brush, set the Opacity on the Brushes palette down to about 30%.

There. Whew! I think that's all of them!

Take a look at Figure 1.5, and here's a Quick Teaser quiz: If the alien's fruit is all grayscale, what painting mode would be the best to make it look really juicy—even if it's fake fruit?

Well, Color mode would help the fruit, but it wouldn't give it the intensity of the Vivid Light mixing mode.

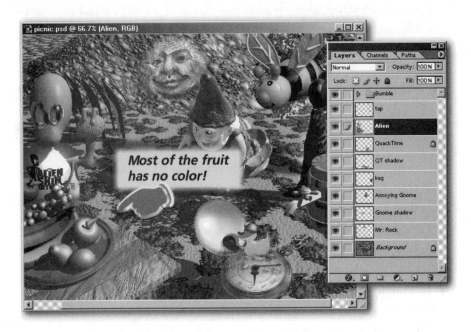

Figure 1.5   The guests really don't care which blending mode you use on the fruit—but you do. This section has given you a handy reference of all the blending modes to help you decide which one you need.

Painting Grayscale Fruit with a Photoshop Mode

Okay, I pre-empted myself in the last paragraph, but what you are about to do is both amazing and rote. You're painting, which means you have to stay within the lines. You choose a mode for the layer on top of the target layer when you perform modifications on new layers. You cannot change the layer you want to work on without changing the overall look.

By the way, that's a lime in the fruit bowl. The alien's got the lemon, and it's already colored, anyway...

Adding Color to Grayscale Fruit

1. On the Layers palette, click the Alien layer title. The alien shares this layer with the fruit. (Don't read anything into this.)

2. Click the Create a new layer icon (the turned page icon on the bottom of the Layers palette). Heads up—this is both a truism and a shortcut in Photoshop: New layers are always created one layer on top of the current layer, and the new layer becomes the current editing layer. That's why you needed to click the Alien layer. Now, double-click the layer title (currently titled Layer 1) and type **Fruit Color** in the text field. You gotta keep track of layers and the only way to do this is by using understandable names and layer sets. Before continuing, be sure to Lock Transparent Pixels on the Fruit Color layer by clicking the tool in the Lock bar on the Layers palette.

3. On the top of the Layers palette, choose Vivid Light from the modes drop-down box.

4. Click on what is called the Foreground Color Selection box. Adobe calls it this, and so shall we, to keep their documentation and ours in synch. In the color picker (the result of clicking on the color selection box), choose a red color (R:175, G:62, B:62) to define a juicy red apple. Click OK. Press B to switch to the Brush tool.

5. Choose the 19-pixel hard tip brush, as shown in Figure 1.6. You can right-click (Macintosh: hold Ctrl and click) when the Paintbrush tool is chosen to put the Brush Preset picker palette right at the point of your cursor. This makes selecting a brush easy. Press Enter (Return) to exit the palette once you've chosen your brush. Then start painting away on the apple. Cool, eh?

6. Change the foreground color for the lime, and again, you want a green (R:56, G:154, B:10), but a dull green for the pear (R:90, G:145, B:70). As a matter of fact, you might want to put a hit or two of brown (R:145, G:100, B:70) on the pear (try this with a soft round 21-pixel brush and lower the Flow on the Options bar to 20%). In Photoshop, you can apply paint using strokes, but the cursor can also remain stationary, and successive clicks simulate airbrush "hits" on the canvas, each hit making the applied color a little more pronounced.

7. Okay, the banananananas. Get out a deep green from the color picker (R:60, G:120, B:30). Click the Airbrush option on the Options bar, and set the Flow of the Airbrush down to about 38%, as shown in Figure 1.7. Figure 1.7 is not shown in color, but if you just touch-up the tips of the bananas with the Airbrush-type tip, the bananas will look more realistic.

8. The bunch of grapes should be a walk in the park for an experienced fruit colorist by now. Make the foreground color selection box a ripe purple (R:70, G:17, B:116). You might want to choose a slightly smaller brush tip, take the Airbrush option off, and raise the Flow back to 100%. Then daub away until the bunch is purple. If you want to be super-finickey, you can (finally!) choose a pale brown and color the grape bunch stem. Me? I let this one ride. Gray is so close to the real color of grape bunch stems, I called it quits right here.

Create a new layer icon

Figure 1.6   Choose a color, a mode, and a brush tip to bring this fruit to life.

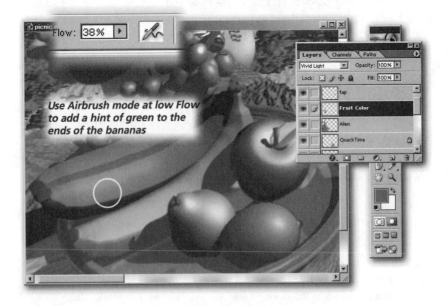

Use Airbrush mode at low Flow
to add a hint of green to the
ends of the bananas

Figure 1.7   Make two-toned bananas by detailing the ends with green. They will also stay
fresher this way.

9. Keep Photoshop open; there's more fun—oops, *research*, coming up.

Making Your Own Brush Tip and Quick Masking with It

This section opens up two more features of Photoshop for you to use—the Brush Tip Shape menu within the Brushes menu, and the Layer Mask mode. You are to grasp quickly how to use the custom brush tip, but a Layer Mask might sound as oblique as a "rotary simulatory activator."

The Layer Mask mode in Photoshop is, quite simply, a "gimme back" facility. You appear to be erasing when painting in Layer Mask mode, but here's the safety chute—no erasure or edit is permanent until you peel the Layer Mask off the image. Photoshop then asks you whether you want to apply the erasures, or discard the mask…which will return everything on that layer to a state before you did any editing. I wish I had this feature back in (physical) still-life drawing with a (physical) pencil at my (physical) university!

No sense in hangin' around now. Here's the plot: the duck on the pocket watch is lying pretty flat on the ground, and we think it should have a blade or three of grass growing up around the watch. By erasing part of the duck's watch on the bottom, it will appear that grass is growing around the watch. And to paint (erase) shapes that look like grass, you need to make a brush that looks like a blade of grass.

Here goes!

Growing Grass in the Picnic Image

1. Choose the Brush tool from the toolbox, and then click the menu icon (to view the Brushes palette options) on the top right of the Options bar. (You can browse ahead to Figure 1.8 if you want to see what the icon looks like.)

2. Click on the Brush Tip Shape title on the Brushes menu (at the top left), and then click on the 13-pixel hard round diameter tip. Now, you're going to distort this brush tip, but not to worry. No changes are permanent unless you specify it—the next time you call up brush tip 13, it will be round and happy again. And there's not time in the book to teach you about permanent changes…you'll learn that later.

3. With your cursor, squash the roundness of the tip by dragging the dots on the sides of the tip toward the center (see the point to which the finger is pointing in Figure 1.8). Then drag the arrow so that it is almost upright. As you can see in the preview window at the bottom of the menu, the stroke sort of looks like a blade of grass. This is good. (If your preview window doesn't update automatically, don't worry about it.) Click Enter (Return) to close the menu, and it's time to move on to the Layers palette.

You also can adjust the brush inside this menu dialog box by entering the numbers shown in Figure 1.8 for Angle, Roundness, Spacing, and so on.

4. Click the QuackTime layer to make it the active layer. Click the Add layer mask icon (pointed out in Figure 1.8) to create a layer mask on the selected layer title. Now, you are ready to do some sophisticated editing. The colors should default to black and white (with Black as the foreground color) when in Layer Mask mode.

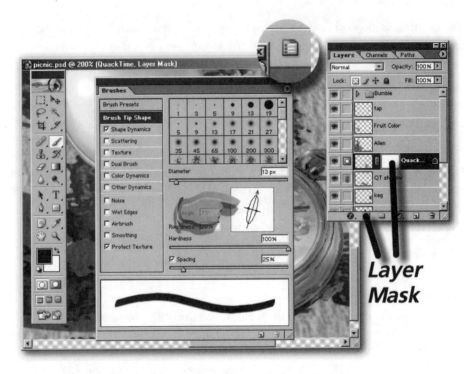

Figure 1.8   Create a unique brush tip for a special assignment, and then enter Layer Mask mode by adding a layer mask to the layer you intend to edit.

5. Zoom into the bottom of the pocket watch. Trick: Press Ctrl(⌘)+the plus key on the keypad until the image is at 200% viewing resolution—you don't always need to slow down your work to shift views by choosing the Zoom tool. Hold the spacebar (to toggle to the Hand tool) and drag within the image window until the pocket watch is in plain view.

6. Make some strokes with the custom tip, going upward from outside the bottom of the watch to inside the watch. As you can see in Figure 1.9, it really does look as though grass is infringing on the watch.

7. In Figure 1.10, I've decreased the opacity of the shadow layer underneath the duck so you can better see the grass illusion. Uh-oh. My boss doesn't think "QuackTime" is funny and wants a different duck in the image. I have to agree—I'd prefer a duck that brings its own food and drinks to the party. But

you need to see what happens when you delete a layer mask before we delete the duck. Click the thumbnail (the layer mask thumbnail) to the right of the image thumbnail on the layer title, and drag it into the trash icon on the bottom of the Layers palette. A question box similar to the one shown in Figure 1.10 pops up. Choose Apply to make your erasures permanent, and the pocket watch appears with permanent deep gouges on the bottom of it, masquerading as blades of grass.

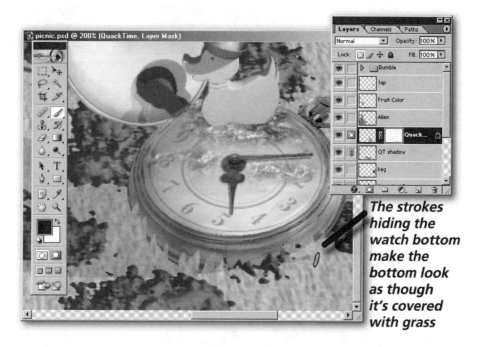

Figure 1.9   Remove parts of the bottom of the watch with your custom strokes, and you create a convincing illusion grass is growing over it. How long did this guy wait for the picnic to begin?

8. Now, drag the QT shadow layer into the trash icon, because you will be deleting the object of the shadow (the duck swimming in the watch) shortly (see Figure 1.11). Adobe gives you no warning that you deleted a layer—and never will. As we agreed (or at least as *I* agreed), the duck in the watch has gotta go. But before you drag its title into the trash on the Layers palette, why not move it to the left so the tap on the keg doesn't spill any precious liquid onto the watch face? Do this by pressing V to switch to the Move tool (or hold down the Ctrl(⌘) key to temporarily select the Move tool). Choose the QuackTime layer and scoot the little soon-to-be-doomed fellow over approximately 2 screen inches. You can now drag the QuackTime layer onto the trash icon.

Figure 1.10   Click Apply when you drag a layer mask thumbnail into the trash—and the areas you've erased are gone from the picture for good.

Figure 1.11   Delete layers by dragging their titles to the trash icon; and when the Move tool is chosen, you can either drag the contents of a layer or use the keyboard arrow keys to move a layer's contents.

Tip

When you choose the Move tool and tap the keyboard arrow keys to move the contents of the current editing layer, the layer contents move by one pixel per stroke. If you want to "super nudge" the contents to move them 10 pixels at a time, hold Shift while you press the arrow keys.

9. Now that the duck is gone, we can openly make rude remarks about him. We also need to create a shadow for the keg. The duck was hiding this area. Creating a shadow for the keg is easy. First, click the Annoying Gnome layer title, and then click the Create a new layer icon on the Layers palette. Now the target layer for the shadow is beneath the Keg layer (see Figure 1.12).

Figure 1.12   To enhance the reality of the scene (?), you need to put a shadow on its own layer directly above the Annoying Gnome layer.

10. Rustle up the Elliptical Marquee tool on the toolbox, and drag an ellipse at the bottom left of the key, touching its base (see Figure 1.13). Black should be the current foreground color. If it's not, click the Default Color icon in the toolbox. Now press Alt(Opt)+Delete (Backspace) to fill the marquee selection with black.

Figure 1.13   Fill the marquee selection with foreground color.

> **Tip**
>
> We haven't gotten into the nature and physics of marquee selection yet (gimme a break—it's only Chapter 1); but FYI, if your ellipse doesn't look situated as we have it in Figure 1.13, drag (from the inside of the selection) with the Elliptical Marquee tool *before* filling it, and you will have moved only the selection and not the contents of the selection marquee.

11. The shadow is too opaque and dense when compared to the other shadows in the image. Deselect the marquee selection (pressing Ctrl(⌘)+D is the pro's way of doing this), and then crank the Fill control down to about 50%, as shown in Figure 1.14. Now you've got your perfect keg shadow. Name the new layer by double-clicking on the layer title and typing something modest but tasteful, like **Keg Shadow**.

12. It's time to bring in the new duck, so save your changes to the picnic.psd file, and keep Photoshop open while we set up the next set of steps.

Figure 1.14   Reduce the Fill amount on the Keg Shadow layer, and the shadow looks
more realistic.

Note

What's the diff' between Fill and Opacity? Opacity applies to both a layer's contents and
any effects associated with that layer, such as embossing or a drop shadow. When you
change a layer's opacity, you change the percentage to which it blocks the view of the
next layer. A layer at 100% opacity totally obscures the lower layer. A layer at a lower
capacity allows some of the lower layer to show through. Fill (which is really named Fill
Opacity) affects only the painted or drawn shapes or pixels on a layer and doesn't
change any layer effects that have been applied. This means that if you have applied a
Drop Shadow effect to a layer and change the Opacity setting, the entire layer becomes
increasingly transparent as you reduce the Opacity value. If you reduce the Fill Opacity
value on that same layer, only the pixels on that layer—and not the Drop Shadow
effect—are changed.

The following steps are pretty simple. By the way, if you've been following along on your
own monitor, you are learning a lot of key concepts. We *told* you this would be fun—and
educational!

Meet the New Duck

Now you need to add a new duck—with his own beverage—to the scene (no getting into the keg for this boy). To make it easy on you, the duck has been pre-sized and even has a shadow of the correct opacity attached to his tail feathers. This means that moving the duck into the picnic picture is the bulk of the task ahead.

Ready? Duck!

Copying and Moving a Picture Element into Position

1. Open the Duck with soda.psd file from the Examples/Chap01 folder on the Companion CD. Notice that the duck is surrounded by transparency, which means you can simply copy the whole layer to the picnic scene.

2. With a clear view of both the image window and the Layers palette, and with the Duck with soda image in the foreground, click the layer title on the Layers palette, and then drag the title into the picnic image, as shown in Figure 1.15. You might never go back to copying and pasting in Photoshop after learning to do it this way.

Figure 1.15   Dragging a Layers palette title into an image window is equivalent to copying and pasting the image.

3. Close the Duck with soda.psd file at any time. With only picnic.psd open, use the Move tool to drag the duck into a position similar to that shown in Figure 1.16, and rename the new layer on the Layers palette. Let's reposition a few layers. Drag the tap layer so that it's above the keg layer. The Duck with beverage layer should now be positioned on top of the tap layer. If necessary, drag the title upward or downward, and drop it on top of the tap layer title.

Figure 1.16 If this were a freezing spring day, would this be a cold duck on tap?

4. Save the image; keep Photoshop open and the screen door closed. Next we're going to edit the insect hanging out in the Layer Set folder.

Creating Your Own Special Effects Without a Clue as to What You're Doing

The bumblebee, for your amusement, is a photo of a child's toy we picked up at Pier 1 Imports. Most of the images in the picnic image, however, are rendered models (the keg is one such example). Bouton worked very hard to match angle and lighting effects for the photos versus the models. One thing we didn't particularly care for was that the bumbler came with wheels but no wings. Bouton modeled the wings in a powerful 3D program called trueSpace, complete with some alpha channel transparency, and the two wings and the bumblebee seem to work, artistically.

What doesn't work, however, is that if the picnic is supposed to be a photo (*in my dreams*), the wings would not be clearly defined as they flutter. And yet the bumblebee seems happily suspended in space without exerting energy.

We're going to change all that here and now.

Unpacking the Insect and Adding Wings

Yes, you read this section heading correctly. You are going to add wings of different opacity and angle to the bumblebee. This will create at least a cartoon representation, if not a somewhat real vision, of the bee fluttering its wings. And then perhaps we'll wipe that grin off its face.

Let's start with the introduction of another advanced Photoshop interface move and hide all the layers from view except the layer set.

Let It Bee

1. Drag the top edge of the palette to extend the Layers palette, if necessary, so the scroll bar disappears, and then in one lightning, expert stroke, drag your cursor down the visibility column, starting below the Bumble layer set. Isn't this wild? You can blank out the whole image except for the layer you want by simply stroking downward in the visibility column. I'm *impressed*.

2. Double-click the Zoom tool to zoom into 100% viewing resolution. You might need to pan with the Hand tool, open the window a little to get a good view of the bumblebee, and provide some space beneath it to create a new wing.

3. Click the right-facing triangle to the left of the Bumble layer set. The triangle then points down, and the contents of the layer set can now be addressed on the level of individual layers.

4. Ctrl(⌘)+click on the Right wing layer title. This action puts a marquee selection around the non-transparent areas of the layer. The wing is perfectly selected.

5. Hold Ctrl(⌘)+Alt(Opt) and then drag the wing to below the bee, as shown in Figure 1.17. This set of steps is sort of the "hard way" to add more wings to the bumbler, but know that this technique will come in handy in your own work for the future. The wing is now what we call a *floating selection* until you press Ctrl(⌘)+D to deselect it and let it fall on the same layer as the original Right wing (but don't press Ctrl(⌘)+D just yet).

6. Press Ctrl(⌘)+T. Introducing…the Free Transform feature. Did you know that you can rotate, distort, and otherwise mangle a selection area in an image to your heart's content, and then apply the transformations all at once, in one operation? This is terrific because the more you stretch and mutate areas in a bitmap image, the more the pixels can begin to lose their position. The result is poor image quality and focus. But Free Transform lets you play until either the cows come home or you press Enter (Return) to apply the changes to the image.

Figure 1.17   Copy the wing onto the same layer. Use the Move tool in combination with the Alt(Opt) key to duplicate the wing.

7. Drag the center circle of the Transform box to the lower-left corner of the box because you are going to make the right wing flap, and all the right wings (there will be three) need to have the same origin point. Otherwise, this bumbler will look stupid.

This center circle is called the *reference point*. By default, the reference point is in the center of an object. Certain adjustments, such as rotate, revolve around this reference point. This means that if the reference point is located in the center of an object, the object will rotate…um…around its center point. By moving the reference point to the lower-left corner, rotations will respond to this new location instead.

8. Right-click (Macintosh: hold Ctrl and click); and from the context menu, choose Rotate. Putting the Transform box in Rotate mode is not hard if you've been doing it for a while (you hover the cursor over a corner of the box), but let's make the steps foolproof for those of you who've never done this before. Put your cursor in the upper right of the Transform box, and pull clockwise. By how much? Check out Figure 1.18 for the answer. (Hint: See the Options bar for a clue.)

Figure 1.18   Pull the wing copy clockwise so that its beginning will hook up with the original wing's beginning.

9. Press Enter (Return) to finalize the rotation. Now, right-click (Macintosh: hold Ctrl and click). The wing should still be selected (if it's not, lasso select it). Press Ctrl(⌘)+Shift+J (a shortcut for the Layer via Cut operation).

The wing is now on a layer called Layer 1, but we're not going to rename these wings you are creating. There is a next-to-zero chance you will confuse the wings as we build this flying bee.

10. On the Layers palette, drag the Opacity down to 67% or so, choose the Move tool, and deselect the duplicate wing if needed (this is an automatic process when you choose Layer via Copy or Cut). Then move the wing up to where it should join the bee (see Figure 1.19). Do you see where this is going?

11. Make a copy of this layer by dragging Layer 1 to the Create a new layer icon at the bottom of the Layers palette. Press Ctrl(⌘)+T to put the wing in Free Transform, move the rotation center point, and then rotate the wing. Figure 1.20 shows you this.

Figure 1.19   To suggest motion (especially motion like you see in those stroboscopic images), reduce the opacity of the duplicate wing and put it in its place.

Figure 1.20   Make a third wing for the right side of the bumble bee. You can rotate this copy of a copy up or down—the important part is where you place it in the composition.

12. Repeat Steps 6–11 with the Left wing layer, making certain that as you create new layers for the left wing, the new layers are *behind* the bee body (in other words, below the Bumble layer on the Layers palette list).

13. Seal up the Bumble layer set folder by clicking the triangle to the left of the Bumble title. Now return the rest of the scene to visibility by dragging up the visibility column on the Layers palette, starting at the Background layer—this is the reverse of what you did to hide all the layers in one fell swoop (see Figure 1.21). The wings look good, but even with all that work on the bee, it's still smiling. Darn…

Figure 1.21   A group of wings at different opacities and angles definitely suggests motion.

14. Press Ctrl(⌘)+S; keep the file open.

For the sole reason that man has historically found it easier to destroy than to build, I'm proposing that after all your hard work on the insect, you hide it, and we put a sun in the picture. This will not be just any sun; it should to be a comical sun about 200% larger than we need it to be for the picture. Oh, what to do? (Clever segue, huh?)

Copying and Resizing the Sun (Handling "Big Data")

I remember it as though it were yesterday…an Adobe exec was telling me that Photoshop 4 now handles "big data." If my phone had had a camera attached, the Adobe

Systems person would have seen my dumb stare. Big data. Okay, what on Earth is big data?

Well, part of big data is Photoshop's capability to import an image to a layer that is *larger* than the image window. You can move the image around in the window *ad infinitum*, and as long as you do not crop the image or otherwise edit it.

Why is this important? Because shortly you are going to drag the sun title into the picnic scene, and even though it is larger than the image window, you will be able to use the Free Transform's Scale mode to shrink the sun and drag it to where it belongs in the composition.

This is neater than you might believe. You won't appreciate this feature until you need to use it—unless, of course, you remember Photoshop 3.

Copying and Scaling "Big Data"

1. On the Layers palette, click the eye icon to toggle the visibility off for the Bumble layer set. Open the Sun.psd image from the Examples/Chap01 folder on the Companion CD. Using the Ctrl($\mathcal{H}$)+the minus key method of zooming out, zoom out on both images in the workspace. At 50% viewing resolution, you can see that the sun ain't going to make it into the picnic picture. Or will it?

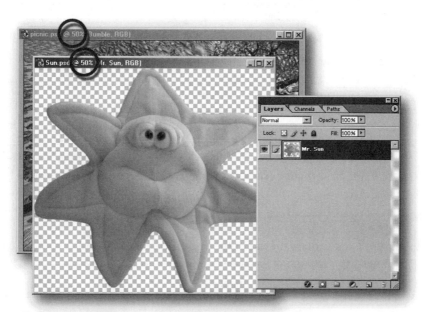

THE SUN IS **HUGE** WHEN COMPARED TO THE PICNIC SCENE! GET SUNGLASSES!!

Figure 1.22   Hey, some sun is nice and everything, but this guy looks as though he's a replacement bulb for the *actual* sun when it burns out or breaks.

2. Click on the title bar of Sun.psd to keep it in the foreground, drag the Mr. Sun title from the Layers palette, and drop it on the picnic image. Drag Mr. Sun to the top layer, if it did not land there, as shown in blistering detail in Figure 1.23. You can close the Sun.psd file.

Figure 1.23   Yo, Bouton. We got a size problem here.

3. Drag the corner of the picnic window to maximize the picnic window size so that you can see some of the image window's neutral-colored background. Now press Ctrl(⌘)+T. Surprise! Free Transform works even outside the image window! Hold Shift to maintain the proportions of the selected sun and then drag inward (on a corner of the bounding box), toward the center of the sun. Take a break from the shrinking action to drag in the center of the transformation box to relocate the sun. If you do not do this, the sun will both shrink and try to reposition itself outside of the image window. See Figure 1.24 for the action in progress.

4. When the sun is about the size of the duck, press Enter (Return) or do it like the pros—double-click inside the Transform box to finalize your editing work.

5. Press Ctrl(⌘)+S; keep the file open.

Free Transform works even when an element falls outside the image window

Figure 1.24   Even though the sun falls outside of the image window, the Free Transform feature works on the entire image.

Are you getting the sinking feeling that the author listed all those wild modes earlier in the chapter, and that's that—end of story? Far from it. In the upcoming section, you are introduced to the Paths palette and use a very special blending mode to make the sun *really* shine—none of this limbs-hanging-off-an-orb stuff, as we have at present.

Stroking a Path and Blending Modes

If you've picked up a trade magazine or seen just about anyone's web site these days, you know that Photoshop's capability to blur is being put to good use. Specifically, the Gaussian Blur filter has been making the rounds for around seven years, popular because it produces a bell-shaped distribution curve which, not surprisingly, imitates real-world phenomena, such as drop shadows and glows.

Well, one way to make the sun look as though it's hotter than it really is, is to stroke a path that is the outline of the sun, keep this stroked path on top of the sun, blur the layer, and then put the layer into a special blend mode.

Huh?

Don't worry. Follow the steps.

Introducing Paths and Creating a Sun Stroke

1. Now that the sun is in its proper place, Ctrl(⌘)+click on its layer title on the Layers palette. (Notice that named layers keep their names even when they are transported to different image windows.) Click on the title itself to make sure this is the target layer, and then Alt(Opt)+click on the Create a new layer icon. The Alt(Opt) twist here presents you with a dialog box in which you name the layer, which saves renaming it later. Type **Sunshine** in the Name field and then press Enter (Return).

2. Now, to select the sun's silhouette, which will be used as the path, Ctrl(⌘)+click the Mr. Sun layer title. See Figure 1.25 for a visual example of what's going on right now.

Figure 1.25   Load the sun's silhouette as a selection marquee. Shortly, you'll turn its shape into a path.

3. On the Layers palette, click the Paths tab to view the Paths palette. The Paths palette is ordinarily used in combination with the Pen tools, but for this assignment, all you need to do is convert the shape of the marquee to a path. Click the Make work path from selection icon, as shown in Figure 1.26, and Photoshop auto-traces the selection with a vector, non-printing path.

Figure 1.26   You can stroke a work path with as large, as small, or as weird a Paintbrush
tip as you can find.

> **Note**
>
> Please do not freak out about paths at this point. If you've used a vector program, such
> as XARA, Adobe Illustrator, or CorelDRAW, you know that paths are simply vector
> directions on a page. They cannot mess up your work in Photoshop because, intrinsically,
> they have no physical form in this bitmap editing program until you fill or stroke the
> path.
>
> You'll find a lot more information on paths and the Pen tools in Chapter 13, "Using
> Paths." Everything is sailing smoothly here, and remember—this is only the first chapter,
> but you're learning some advanced techniques.

4. Now that you have a work path (which you can leave as an unsaved path; you
   will not need it after you stroke the path), set up the tool with which you'll stroke
   the path. Set the foreground color to a golden color. (Actually, you can use the
   Eyedropper tool to sample a foreground color from the sun itself.)

5. Choose the Paintbrush tool. (This is very important. If you don't choose the
   brush before you stroke, the Paths palette defaults to the Pencil tool and the
   stroking looks crummy.) Choose the 100-pixel diameter, soft tip brush from the
   Brushes palette, and then click on the Stroke path with the brush icon, as shown
   in Figure 1.27. Wow! Intense, huh? Too intense, and that's why we have more
   steps to do. Right now, this figure makes the sun look like he's in the bottom of a
   laundry basket!

Figure 1.27   Have Photoshop stroke the path with a fairly large brush tip and you're well on the way to creating a very special effect.

6. Drag the work path on the Paths palette into the trash icon. Click the Layers tab to return to the Layers palette, choose the Hard Light mode from the modes drop-down list. You'll see the sun in all its glory onscreen, and of course we have the grayscale version, Figure 1.28, right here.

Note

The section, "Photoshop Modes: A Dry Definition of Each Blending Mode," earlier in this chapter, is what the author used to discern which mode to use. It's a handy reference and deserves one of those fluorescent sticky notes placed on that page!

7. Press Ctrl(⌘)+S; keep the file open.

It's only fair to end this chapter with a grand finale—besides, you've had almost enough of beginner's tricks, and I need to take a nap. In the following section, you use a secret trick in Photoshop to align perfectly an imported layer, and then get your hands on what is extensively used in the photography section of this book, the Levels command.

Figure 1.28   Hard Light appears to be the logical choice of blending modes for the stroked path. It creates a glow, but also allows the sun's face to poke through the stroke.

Working a Stein into the Picture

The author rendered a model of a glass stein, complete with partial transparency, using Caligari trueSpace. This modeling program happens to have two features (besides the rendering quality) that make it an assignment-saver for Photoshop work. First, trueSpace enables me to render the stein to any reasonable dimension, which means that I could render the somewhat diminutive stein practically swallowed by a large background—specifically for the same dimensions as the picnic picture.

The other feature? trueSpace renders *alpha channels*. You'll learn more about the virtues (and indispensable qualities) of alpha channels later in this book, but all you need to know about them for now is that an alpha channel can describe the shape and opacity of any object in the scene—and Photoshop can load channels as selections.

So let's go for it. Let's see how to add a stein to the table in the scene and then learn how to tonally balance the stein.

Using the Shift Modifier when Copying Layers

1. Open the stein.tif image from the Examples/Chap01 folder on the Companion CD.

2. Choose the Move tool. Click the Channels tab to view the Channels palette and then Ctrl(⌘)+click the Alpha channel on the Channels palette that describes the form of the stein. Switch back to the Layers palette, and sure enough, the outline of the stein has a selection marquee going around it (see Figure 1.29).

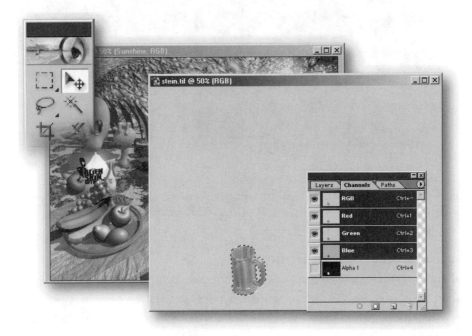

Figure 1.29   Load the selection of the stein in the Channels palette, and a selection marquee will appear around the object in the Layers palette view.

3. While holding Shift, drag the stein using the Move tool into the picnic.psd image. Surprise again! The stein landed perfectly on the table the alien is hogging. Why? Because the Shift key sends Photoshop a message to copy the stein to the relative center of the other image. In other words, I knew in advance where the stein should go, so I rendered it so both images were the same size. (I'm sure this is a better trick than it sounds!) If you understand this centering thing, you can copy and paste internally (from within Photoshop; from window to window) with perfect accuracy. In your Photoshop work, you might need to duplicate layers to different image windows, and the Move tool and the Shift key combination are your...well, your *key* (see Figure 1.30).

4. Press Ctrl(⌘)+S; keep the file open.

Figure 1.30 The stein is copied to its relative position in the picnic image. Holding Shift is the trick.

Got a minute to balance the tones in the stein? It looks washed out in the picture. And perhaps you want to give the stein a shadow that falls on the table.

The Levels Command and More Shadow Work

At this point, all you need to know is that the Levels command is sort of like the Brightness/Contrast control on your TV—only better. You can tune the highlights, the shadows, and the midtones, which is very useful for bringing out image detail. (Did you know most visual content in an image is in the midtones?). You're going to use the Levels command with confidence and gusto because we have steps for you to follow. Further, we think you can "wing" a shadow on the table from the stein. You've learned a headful in this chapter, and we need to cram in two more things, okay?

Finessing the Stein

1. With the Stein as the current editing layer on the Layers palette, press Ctrl(⌘)+L. This takes you to the Levels command…and it's a terrific keyboard shortcut for a much-used feature.

2. Drag the far left, black triangle under Input Levels to about 61. This makes the stein take on some blacks, where it used to be washed out. Now, we need some light areas.

3. Drag the white slider on the far right to the left until the Input field for this slider reads 216, as shown in Figure 1.31. As you can see, this is a visually interesting stein now—good contrast and motion of tones across its face.

Figure 1.31   Use the Levels command to sort out tonal "blahs" in an image area.

4. Press Enter (Return) to make the Levels changes and return to the picnic.

5. Click the Sunshine layer title on the Layers palette, and then click the Create a new layer icon. The new layer is beneath the stein.

6. Zoom in on the stein, and with the Lasso tool, try really hard to draw the simple shape you see in Figure 1.32. This is an experimental chapter; give it another try if the shadow looks wrong on your first try.

7. Click the Eyedropper tool and click to sample a shadow color from one of the darker hues in the wooden table. This sets the foreground color in Photoshop.

8. Press Alt(Opt)+Delete (Backspace) to fill the selection. On the Layers palette, drag the Fill down to about 62%, and change the mode to Multiply. You can press Ctrl(⌘)+D at any time.

9. Press Ctrl(⌘)+S; keep the file open.

Figure 1.32   Create a shadow for the stein. You can do it with only a tug or two on the Lasso tool.

Note

Um…we almost made it out of this beginning chapter without discussing how Photoshop's sliders work. It might be in Adobe Systems documentation, but we don't want to take any chances.

Slider boxes are actually a two-in-one affair. For example, you can specify Opacity on the Layers palette two different ways: You can type a value in the Opacity field by typing the value and pressing Enter (Return), or you can reveal a hidden slider by clicking and holding the triangle to the right of the field.

I take responsibility for this oversight for which I will surely be punished.

There's one more command we can teach you that will conclude our "gooshing" of Photoshop and its features like so much clay. Check out Figure 1.33—you don't have to do anything but look at the bumbler. You now know how it was resized (using the Free Transform Scale mode command), but why is it now looking to the left?

By the way, the way the bumblebee is pointing now is wrong, because the light is striking its left side, instead of following the scene's emanation of light from the right. But, right or wrong, it was fun to do the following:

1. Click the Bumble layer set folder.

2. Press Ctrl(⌘)+T to put the folder in Free Transform.

3. Right-click (Macintosh: hold Ctrl and click) and then choose Flip Horizontal from the context menu.

Figure 1.33   You can put a layer set into Free Transform and come up with time-saving steps for editing.

Now you're not a beginner anymore, and it's going to be harder and harder to amaze you with the stuff to come!

We're up to the challenge, though.

Summary

This chapter was a light-hearted romp through some of Photoshop's really cool features, but ask yourself: how much did I learn and how can I apply it to an idea of my own? That's the *true* key to learning Photoshop—you can learn commands at your own speed, but you can't put a time value on the experience of discovering what the tools are good for and how creative you can be with them. As your experience grows, you form a sort of yin-yang relationship with Photoshop; that is, you bring a working knowledge of tools and a concept to Photoshop, and Photoshop helps you create it. Conversely, you can explore and discover what features can do, and this might influence the direction you take with a photo or a piece of art. And as far as exploring and uncovering, this chapter has barely exposed the surface to the standard for image editing. You saw some neat stuff, but turn the pages. Turn the pages! There's a *lot* of neat stuff about Photoshop in this book.

Next up: Preferences, options, and how to customize Photoshop so that sitting down with it each time is like sitting down to talk to an old friend. Master the controls, and you'll quickly master principles that bring your work to life.

Part II

Photoshop Core Concepts

Chapter 2

Optimizing and Customizing Photoshop Preferences

Okay, so you needed a new set of wheels, and you picked this century's hottest car, the Daimler-Chrysler P.T. Cruiser. This popular auto mixes a little bit of the past and a little of today's car style and engineering.

But wait, as long as you're spending half your trust fund, you might as well go for the two-tone cream and maroon model. And you might as well add a pair of fake fur cheetah fuzzy dice to the mirror. And your mp3 file collection on CDs deserves a Blaupunkt stereo system with JBL speakers.

Then you wake up. "What have I done?" you ask. The answer lies in this chapter's title (clever segue, huh?). You've just customized and specified preferences to an awesome piece of machinery. Guess what? Photoshop 7 has so many preferences from which to choose, you might want to set aside a whole afternoon with PS 7 and this chapter. We're going to show you how to work more quickly—and with better results—than if you simply drove Photoshop 7 right off the lot.

Glomming Over Photoshop's Preferences

The good news is that there's an entire tabbed menu of preferences in Photoshop; all you need to do to display it is press Ctrl(⌘)+K. The not-so-good news, however, is that there's also some useful stuff on the tabbed pages that are "logically opaque" (in other words, unfathomable) to beginners and even some intermediate users. So our best advice is to follow our lead about which preferences to select. We'll show you examples and perhaps a mini-tutorial or two, and then you can decide for yourself what you're going to hold and what you're going to fold.

In Photoshop, press Ctrl(⌘)+K now so that you can get started on the following section.

General Preferences

The first tab you come to in Photoshop Preferences relates to the broadest changes you can make: how Photoshop displays, hides, or reveals things in the interface. Let's take the tour.

Color Picker

The color picker appears when you click on the foreground/background selection boxes on the toolbox. The Preferences dialog box enables you to choose from among three options. We recommend selecting Adobe's color picker, shown as item 1 in Figure 2.1.

Put your thumb or a paper clip on this page so that you can refer to it as we proceed ahead and illustrate some of the General Preferences.

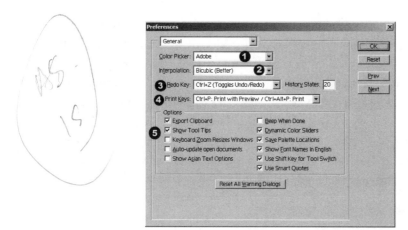

Figure 2.1   The first preference you get to select within Photoshop is the type of color picker used.

Why do we recommend Adobe's color picker? Because it can be configured in many different ways, and at least one is sure to fit your work style. In Figure 2.2, you can see the default Windows color picker and the Macintosh color picker. The Macintosh version has a more robust selection of color modes for color choosing, but there is a flaw in its design; it specifies color components between 0 and 100% in RGB color mode, and Photoshop, most other programs, and Windows use the 0 to 255 increment. This means that you need to translate the values (and that means—ugh—*math*) to communicate color specifications to Photoshop users who use Adobe's color picker.

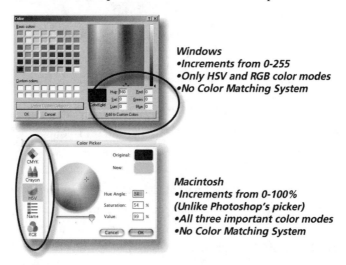

Windows
•Increments from 0-255
•Only HSV and RGB color modes
•No Color Matching System

Macintosh
•Increments from 0-100%
(Unlike Photoshop's picker)
•All three important color modes
•No Color Matching System

Figure 2.2   Windows and the Macintosh color picking choices are limited and are best used by applications whose programmers didn't feel like making a program color picker.

In contrast, Photoshop's color picker—as shown in Figure 2.3—supports the mapping of its color field by each component of four color models (RGB, LAB, CMYK, and HSB). For example, you can click the S in the HSB area, and the color field changes its configuration. The Macintosh color picker also supports over a dozen color-matching specifications, including the legendary PANTONE. So when a client says, "Hobkins, I want the label on the can to be PANTONE 1485c," you can access the PANTONE collection of swatches by clicking on Custom in the Adobe color picker, typing the PANTONE number until it appears, and clicking OK to use this color in an image window…and, while you're at it, tell the guy your name is not Hobkins.

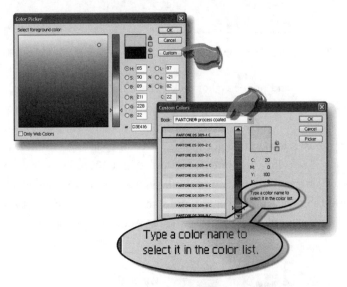

Figure 2.3   Many of your would-be clients will insist on exact color matching. And no program does it better than Photoshop.

Okay; let's leaf back to Figure 2.1 and the General Preferences menu. Or better yet, why not sit in front of your computer, open Photoshop, and read along?

Interpolation

An easy way to remember what the Interpolation setting is all about is to remember the word *interpretation*. (Interpolation is marked as item 2 in Figure 2.1.) When you command Photoshop to stretch or shrink an image, it has to calculate (take a guess at—interpret) additional pixels to fit into the image, or it must decide which pixels to remove to make a smaller image.

Whether you are shrinking or stretching an image, it will have some detail loss because Photoshop has to make an estimate of the number of pixels to add or remove.

Fortunately, Photoshop (and very few other applications) uses Bicubic "guesstimating" when removing or adding pixels. This is the most accurate math method for evaluating which pixels go where. Bicubic sampling searches across, up, down, and diagonally to the target pixel that's getting added or deleted. The process then uses a weighted average of pixel colors to color in the new region if you're shrinking a file, or it creates new pixels using a weighted average if pixels need to be added to the new image. This means that if, say, the region of an image is primarily green, you can expect Bicubic sampling to make the region mostly green, with a very minor color influence from only one or two pixels that are not green.

Your other choices are Bilinear (Photoshop only looks in two directions for neighboring pixel colors) and Nearest Neighbor, which is not an interpolation method at all. Nearest Neighbor simply puts the neighboring color next to a pixel when an image is enlarged. Nearest Neighbor is a phenomenally inaccurate choice for interpolation. However, if you need to increase the size of, for example, a screen capture of a palette (as we do in this book), Nearest Neighbor is terrific. The process simply makes the horizontal and vertical dimensions twice as large resulting in an image area that's four times larger than the original—with no smoothing or averaging or fuzzy text.

To make this fairly lofty concept more "creative-person friendly," check out Figure 2.4. There's a dot that's been resized using the three different methods.

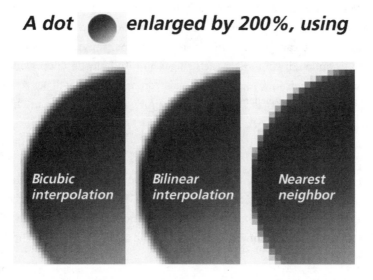

Figure 2.4 Stick with Bicubic Interpolation. Your new 1.4GHz muscle machine with 256MB RAM can handle the calculations in a flash.

Redo Key

You have your choice of using Y or Z with the Ctrl(⌘) modifier key to redo and undo editing moves (item 3 in Figure 2.1). We recommend Ctrl(⌘)+Z because many of our readers are experienced with other applications that also use Ctrl(⌘)+Z to undo a move. By the way, you will find it extremely frustrating if you want to go back several steps and use this command—repeating Ctrl(⌘)+Z for multiple undos does not work. The command for progressively removing edits in an image is Alt+Ctrl+Z (Macintosh: Opt+⌘+Z).

The History States control, off to the right of the Redo Key selection, specifies how many steps back in a file (how many undo times) you can tap into. Each History State requires a hunk of RAM to store the undo data; so the number of states you enable is a balancing act between how big a safety net you want and the amount of RAM you have installed on your computer. The default number of History States is 20. This means that you can undo the previous 20 commands or tool strokes you made. After you make your 21st command or stroke, the undo state for the first command or stroke is deleted to allow room to undo the most current command or tool stroke.

So even though you'd probably like to set this option to a thousand—*don't*. If you have 96MB of RAM installed on your computer (the minimum amount of RAM that Photoshop requires to run), 10 is probably a reasonable setting for History States. If you have 128MB of RAM (the amount you *really* need to run Photoshop so you don't feel as though you're working underwater), 20 History States is a good figure. If you have lots and *lots* of RAM, you can probably bump up the number some. But whatever number you set for this option, if your system acts sluggish or if Photoshop pops you a warning that available memory is low, you probably have too many History States set. Besides, if you plan on making more than 20 mistakes at a time, you don't belong in Photoshop— you belong in government work.

Print Keys

You're undoubtedly going to want to see printouts of your creations as you work on your compositions. Wouldn't it be nice to bypass the File, Print menu selection by using a shortcut key? You can set up Print Keys in the Preferences dialog box by using the—you guessed it—Print Keys selection (see item 4 in Figure 2.1). The default method sets up the keys as follows:

- Press Ctrl(⌘)+P to print
- Press Ctrl(⌘)+Alt(Opt)+P to Print Preview

If you prefer, you can reverse these settings so that you can press Ctrl(⌘)+Alt(Opt)+P to print and Ctrl(⌘)+P to preview your work. To make the change, just click the Print Keys down-arrow and select the alternate option.

Options

Ah, now we come to item 5 on the General Preferences dialog box (refer to Figure 2.1). Some of these options are useful features; others matter not a whit. Adobe has not cleaned this palette up, but instead has added to it. Some commands are vestigial organs from a time when a Macintosh Classic or an i386sx was considered a fast machine.

Please take a look now at the preferences on your monitor; we are going to have you change some of the defaults.

- **Export Clipboard.** Yes, by all means. Now this means that you must also "flush" the clipboard after you've pasted a Photoshop piece into a different application, because holding anything on the clipboard takes up system resources. To perform clipboard flushing, choose Edit, Purge, Clipboard from the main menu.

- **Show Tool Tips.** Um, these balloons that pop up when your cursor lingers over a toolbox icon aren't exactly tips. In other words, the pop-ups won't tell you nearly as much about a chosen tool as the status bar will (we recommend that you always have Window, Status Bar checked). What tool tips *will* do is name the tools on the toolbox for you, provide the shortcut key, and occasionally tell you what a button is supposed to do on the Options bar. We recommend leaving Tool Tips on for your first few months with PS7, and as you memorize and familiarize, you may find the tips to be a distraction, and you can turn them off by unchecking the box.

Tip

Undo That Again, Will You?   By the way, the Ctrl(⌘)+Z Undo/Redo toggle has nothing to do with Step Forward and Step Backward, a multiple undo/redo that is available both as part of the History palette and two commands under Edit in Photoshop. You might want to memorize Alt(Opt)+Ctrl(⌘)+Z to undo actions you've made more than one step ago.

- **Keyboard Zoom Resizes Window.** This sounds like a bizarre tabloid headline, doesn't it? Actually, there are a number of ways to zoom in and out of an image window. One of the first ways that experienced, ancient Photoshoppists like me used to shortcut the zooming process (without using the toolbox tool) was to press Ctrl(⌘) and then press the plus and minus keys on the numerical keypad.

We recommend that you keep this checkbox checked because it doesn't make much sense to zoom into an image and then have to resize the window. This option is your one-stop shop for image navigation.

- **Auto-Update Open Documents.** If you are in a studio, or even working remotely over the Internet on a collaborative piece, you want to check this option. Why? Because PS7's new Workgroup feature enables several people to work with the same image. This is a boon to desktop publishing professionals because Larry in Seattle can be composing the page while Phil in Delphia can be color correcting the image. If you don't auto-update the file, you will not keep current with the revisions going on within your workgroup. Leave this one checked unless you run a standalone computer.

- **Show Asian Text Options.** There's really no reason for showing Asian text options unless you are Chinese, Japanese, or Korean. When this option is enabled, these options appear on the Paragraph and Character palettes—Asian characters use a double-byte character system, whereas English and West European characters are single-byte in complexity.

- **Beep When Done.** This option causes you to run around the office making beeping sounds when you've finished an assignment. *Onnnnnnly* kidding. Actually, this is another vestigial organ in Photoshop. There was a time when you'd apply a Gaussian Blur to a 3MB image—and you had time to go out for lunch, a haircut, and have your taxes done. And Photoshop's beep after a tediously long operation was welcome because it woke you up so that you could proceed editing. But today's G4s and Intel Pentium 4s (at this writing, P4s are up to 2gHz in speed, compared to the "super-fast" 50mHz of 486 machines in 1995) are number-chewing monsters, and I personally have not heard Photoshop beep ever since processor speed got to be around 500mHz or so. Leave this option off, and if you're a fan of beeping, drop your money on the ground at a drive-through that has a lot of folks behind you who are in a hurry. In addition to beeping, you'll learn some new words, too.

- **Dynamic Color Sliders.** Check this option. There's no way to get an accurate idea of the result of mixing colors on the Color palette without seeing how one component of a color affects the color range of a different component. This option doesn't slow you down at all, and it's kinda fun watching the sliders change color.

- **Save Palette Locations.** Check this option unless several other people use your computer at work. It is a pain in the neck arranging palettes so that you can work on large images (or even small ones), and it is twice the pain to have to reset the location of the palettes after you return to your work.

- **Show Font Names in English.** Again, Chinese, Japanese, and Korean fonts are unlike your garden variety Georgia TrueType or Type 1 Garamond. If you want to use double-byte fonts such as these, and you were brought up with the alphanumeric system of Europe and the U.S., check this option. It'll make finding the font you need on your machine a lot easier.

- **Use Shift Key for Tool Switch.** This is a safety feature. If you do not check it, you can make mistakes in choosing tools if you're a keyboard kinda guy or gal. Unchecked, for example, pressing G will toggle the Bucket tool with the Gradient tool. Do you want this to happen? If not, check this option. Then, tools assigned to that button alternate only when you hold Shift and press G.

  Better still? Invest a moment to choose the tool from the toolbox. This author is not sold on memorizing toolbox keyboard shortcuts (there are *plenty* of other, more productive shortcuts in this program to memorize, believe me!), and this option will *not* activate a tool with no shortcut letter next to it in a group. For example, the only way to get to the Convert Point tool is to hold the Pen tool until the flyout does its thing, and then you choose the Convert Point tool.

- **Use Smart Quotes.** This means that you can use *smart* quotes from people like Ben Franklin, Samuel Clemens, and John Cleese. Dumb quotes abound in our times…okay, I'm pulling your leg here. "Smart quotes" is a PlainTalk phrase for "typographer's quotes" or "Curly Quotes." If you check this option, the text you create in Photoshop will look more professional, and you will not have to look up the scan code (for example, a left typographer's quote in Windows requires that you remember, and type, 0147 while holding the Alt key.) Wotta trial! Thank you, Adobe, and leave this option checked. (The only exception to this is the case in which you want to express something in inches. If that's the case, you need to turn off Smart Quotes and type the symbol ").

- **Reset All Warning Dialogs.** This option is pretty self-explanatory. Photoshop has some warning dialog boxes, most of which have to do with color management profiles that can be prevented from displaying ever again by checking an option on the face of the dialog box. But if the dialog box never again shows its face, how are you going to get the chance to uncheck the option if you change your mind and want to be warned?

  Simple: Press Ctrl(⌘)+K and click the Reset All Warning Dialogs button at the bottom of the General Preferences dialog box.

Which brings us to page 2 of the Preferences. Not to worry; General Preferences was the longest of the tabbed pages to explore.

File Handling

You get to the next page of the Preferences dialog box by clicking the Next button. This page is all about File Handling, as you see in Figure 2.5. This handles how thumbnails of images are created, how TIFF and PSD files are saved (this is a critical choice now in version 7), and how you want your workgroup to work. Let's begin.

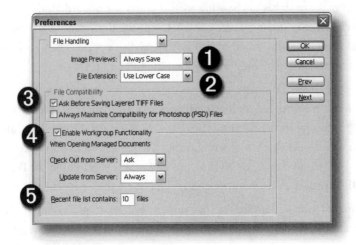

Figure 2.5   The File Handling Preferences dialog box.

Image Previews

Image previews is one area in Photoshop where operating system differences between Windows and Macintosh are evident. The biggest difference is that the Mac OS supports more image previews and that it does not, by default, use file extensions to indicate the kind of file or program that can be used to open the file. Image previews are miniature pictures of the actual image contained in a file. These miniature versions of the file are also sometimes called *thumbnails*.

The default setting for the Image Previews drop-down list, Always Save, is the setting we recommend you use (item 1 in Figure 2.5). Your other choices are Never Save and Ask When Saving. These settings do exactly what they say. Saving an Image Preview is particularly useful for files saved in Photoshop's PSD file format. Photoshop PSD files, when saved with a preview image, show up as little thumbnails of the file on your desktop and in folders (when Large Icons is the viewing mode). In Photoshop's Open dialog box, if you choose Thumbnails from the View menu, PSD, TIF, GIF, PNG, and JPG files will display as miniature pictures, which makes it very easy to spot the file you want to open.

But the Open dialog box isn't the only place you'll see thumbnails. Now that Photoshop 7 also has a File Browser, you'll be able to see image previews in the browser window as well (see Figure 2.6). All of this makes it that much more important that you save a thumbnail with your image. It adds only about 2K to the total saved file size, which is a flyspeck in a time when an 80GB hard disk is about $250.

Figure 2.6   Photoshop 7's new File Browser.

Note

Not All It's Cracked Up to Be   The File Browser is a new feature that will certainly be welcome to users who don't have cataloguing software. But what kind of graphics person, in 2002, doesn't already have cataloguing software? Admittedly, Adobe's implementation is comprehensive, but so are other standalone applications, such as Ulead's Album 7. At the time of this writing, Adobe's File Browser, accessed from within Photoshop, brought this author's system to a…I guess the polite phrase would be "a lull." Is it a good idea to add a file browser to an already immense application, using valuable resources for something not related to image editing? The jury's still out.

File Extension

The next option in the second page of the Preferences dialog box, File Extension, allows you to choose the letter case of file extensions (see item 2 in Figure 2.5). Use Lower Case is the default. Unless you have an in-house rule that says that all filenames have to be uppercase, leave Use Lower Case selected. Who on earth wants a file extension shouting at them from a long list of files?

L Case

File Compatibility

In the File Compatibility area of the Preferences dialog box, Ask Before Saving Layered TIFF Files should be checked (item 3 in Figure 2.5). Adobe is sort of hamstrung between still image artists who want the TIFF format to remain the same as it's always been so that Photoshop users on both platforms can access an image in this format. Also, those who do not own Photoshop usually can view a TIFF. But the digital video industry has been pleading for a TIFF version that can contain layers since…well, since digital video editing has been around.

For the user, you need to pay attention and not accidentally save a layered image to the TIFF format.

> **Tip**
>
> **Special Considerations for Client Files**   The problem caused by layers in a TIFF file you send to your client isn't the only headache you can cause with image files that can contain special features. Get rid of those paths in your image before you send it to press or for placement in a DTP document. The authors had an experience where an accidentally included path acted like a clipping path when the TIFF was sent to a printer!
>
> Learn from our mistakes, eh?

Ah, another interesting option: Always Maximize Compatibility for Photoshop (PSD) Files. Each new version of Photoshop comes with tons of new features. The downside to all the new features is that older versions of Photoshop, as well as other programs that can import Photoshop files, don't *know* about the features. At best, these programs will ignore stuff in the file that they don't understand (type layers, effect layers, and so on), and, at worst, these programs may not be able to open the newer version Photoshop files at all. Backward compatibility issues have always focused on Photoshop's native file format, PSD files. But now, because Adobe has enhanced the capability of the TIFF and PDF file formats, you need to watch out for backward compatibility problems with files saved in these formats as well.

For these reasons, the default setting for the Maximize Backwards Compatibility option is enabled. When this option is checked, extra information is saved along with TIF, PDF, and PSD images, creating flattened versions of the files. Doing so allows the programs that don't know about the latest version of Photoshop to open those files. Be aware, however; saving this extra version of the file within the saved file increases the file's size noticeably.

It's really your call. Our recommendation is that if you are working in an enterprise where there are many licenses for Photoshop, all different versions, you bite the bullet and use backward compatibility. But for small groups of users who all have version 7—why needlessly plump up the saved file size? Use the extra disk space for MP3 files!

Enable Workgroup Functionality When Opening Managed Documents

OFF Enabling workgroup functionality sounds like a swell idea, huh? It *is*—you can work with others on an assignment across the room, on an intranet, or the Internet (see item 4 in Figure 2.5). But there are some considerations about this setting you need to know. Under When Opening Managed Documents, you have two options:

- **Check Out from Server.** Your choices are to Ask whether you want Workgroup functionality on, to Always have it on, and to Never have it on. Again, this is a pretty simple decision—the choice depends on your work environment. Obviously, Never is an option for those who do not need workgroup functionality.

- **Update from Server.** If more than one person is working on a document, you should select Always from the drop-down list. Who wants to update a file only to have someone else working on it un-update it? Keep Groupware files current is the rule here.

Recent File List Contains

The setting Recent file list contains (item 5 in Figure 2.5) is a boon to all Photoshop users, Macintosh and Windows alike. Most Windows applications have included this feature in the past, but now not only do both platforms have this option under File, but you *OK* can set the number of files you want to retrieve. Many of this author's programs limit him to the last four used files, but Photoshop 7 will let you crank it up to the *last 30* used files!

You'll never lose your file on your hard disk again, even if you use only the default of 10 of your most recent files. This feature requires *no* additional memory usage.

The Macintosh File Handling Preferences Box

You have slightly different choices on the File Handling page of the Preferences dialog box on the Macintosh, shown in Figure 2.7, so here's the scoop on the different options.

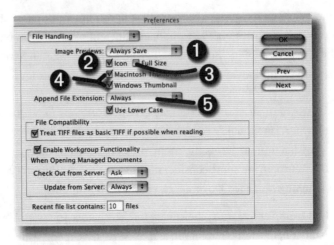

Figure 2.7   The Macintosh dialog box for File Handling Preferences has options that are different from those in Windows.

Image Previews

As with the preferences in Windows, Image Previews gives you the choice of Always Save, Never Save, and Ask When Saving (item 1 in Figure 2.7), but there's also a sub-choice here. Do you want to save to Icon, Macintosh Thumbnail, Windows Thumbnail, and/ or Full Size?

- **Icon.** (See item 2 in Figure 2.7.) Displays the picture at 32 × 32 pixels on the desktop and in folder windows. This is a very sensible option to check and adds practically nothing to the saved file size.

- **Full Size.** (See item 3 in Figure 2.7.) Whoa! Isn't a full-size image preview redundant? No—what is meant here is that some applications, such as Quark, can place and link at full-page preview at a resolution of 72 pixels per inch. The actual picture might be the same size in inches, but its resolution could be something such as 266 pixels per inch. Yes, this option does, indeed, significantly increase the size of your saved file, but you will work more quickly in Quark when the on-page image links out to the 72 pixel per inch preview for display.

- **Macintosh or Windows Thumbnail.** (See item 4 in Figure 2.7.) This is the image you see in preview boxes. The image is larger than an icon thumbnail and smaller than a Winnebago. Check this option if you want the saved file size to be a little larger than the icon option but want to have an easier time previewing files before you load them. Your choice of Windows and/or (you can choose both) Macintosh thumbnail has to do with the final destination of the file. Are you a Macintosh user who sends work to a Windows service bureau? Then make your preview choice here.

Append File Extension

In the options for Append File Extension (item 5 in Figure 2.7), you have Never, Ask, and Always as choices in the Append File Extension option. If you design for the web, browsers insist on file extensions. Many, many web servers use UNIX as the operating system, and GIF, JPEG, and HTML files *must always* have the file extensions (*.gif, *.jpg, and *.html, respectively) appended to a document name for the server to successfully pass the correct image type to the visitor's browser. And even if there weren't a web, there are multiplatform companies out there, which make it that much more difficult to share your work with Windows users if neither of you know the file format.

The rest of the preferences are the same as in Windows, so we're essentially done with the Macintosh Preferences dialog box. It's time to move on to the Display & Cursors page of the Preferences dialog box.

Display & Cursors

Back on the Windows side now, the Display & Cursors page of the Preference dialog box enables you to choose how cursors, image channels, and the images themselves are presented onscreen. Take a look at Figure 2.8, and get a load of those callouts!

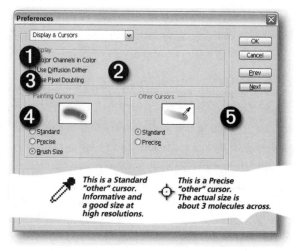

Figure 2.8   The Display & Cursors page of the Preferences dialog box.

Display

In the Display area, there are three options you get to set:

- **Color Channels in Color.** (See item 1 in Figure 2.8.) We've been puzzling about this one for a long time and have concluded that to show, for example, a blue channel in shades of black and blue would simply be a visual reminder that you are working in the blue channel. We recommend that you turn this novelty *off* and work with color component channels in *grayscale* because this is the way color information is stored—as varying amounts of tones (grayscale): the whitest being full contribution of the component color to the color composite (RGB) image, while 100% black indicates no contribution. Additionally, you can easily lighten or darken the channel with a number of toolbox tools and commands to refine a component of an image.

- **Use Diffusion Dither.** (See item 2 in Figure 2.8.) This option applies only to users whose video card has something like 20KB of video memory—as well as to many laptop users. Seriously, you will almost never work on a system today that doesn't support 24-bit color, so you can leave this box unchecked. This option will dither images that are beyond the video capacity of your system settings for video.

- **Use Pixel Doubling.** (See item 3 in Figure 2.8.) Enable this? Not really, unless you want to view your movements on an image at half the image area's resolution. It's disconcerting to see an image area move at low resolution and then to normal resolution after it's been moved. Today's processors usually remove any need for this fancy screen mapping while you edit.

Painting Cursors

In the Painting Cursors area (item 4 in Figure 2.8), you have three choices for the display of a painting cursor: Standard, Precise, and Brush Size. These cursors include the Paintbrush cursor and the Clone Stamp tool—in other words, tools that apply paint, as opposed to editing, selection, annotation, and other cursors. For this selection, we recommend the Brush Size option. This option shows you the outline of the tip of your current painting tool, which is darned handy when you have, say, a 300-pixel diameter brush defined—you can see exactly what you're going to hit and what you'll miss while editing an image.

Other Cursors

When you get around to choosing Other Cursors (item 5 in Figure 2.8), we recommend the Standard cursors as the choice, for two reasons. First, a Standard cursor is

Standard

going to show you onscreen exactly which tool you are using; and with as many new tools as Photoshop has, this is a blessing. Figure 2.8 shows a magnified view of the Precise cursor. Our biggest complaint is that it is *small*, especially on 1024-by-768 and higher screen resolutions. However, if you need pin-point accuracy, to change a single pixel onscreen, you'd want the Precise (crosshair) cursor. And you know what? You do not have to come to this Preferences box to access a Precise cursor, for *any* tool. Simply press CapsLock, and poof!—you've toggled to a Precise cursor.

Let's tackle the invisible now—Transparency and Gamut preferences. Click Next. Onscreen, of course—not in this book.

Understanding How to Choose Transparency & Gamut Settings

It's funny, but the correct choice on the Transparency & Gamut page of the Preferences dialog box depends entirely upon the color content of the image at hand. Keep an eye on Figure 2.9— we will be referring back to it.

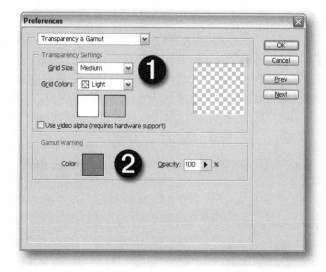

Figure 2.9   The Transparency & Gamut page of the Preferences dialog box.

First of all, what if there is an odd chance that what you are editing has a light checker pattern to it? The default Transparency grid color is light checkered (item 1 in Figure 2.9), and as you can see in Figure 2.10, the transparency default is about as worthwhile as going to sea in a tea strainer.

HOW ON **EARTH** DO YOU USE THE DEFAULT TRANSPARENCY CHECKERS ON AN **IMAGE** WITH CHECKERS?

HEY, A QUICK MASK ISN'T VERY USEFUL IF THE COLOR AND AMOUNT OF OPACITY BLEND INTO THE PICTURE, EH?

Figure 2.10 You must choose—and rechoose—colors for CMYK gamut saturation and for transparency design, depending upon the specific image you are editing.

As far as the Gamut Warning color goes (item 2 in Figure 2.9), if you want Photoshop to display a tinted overlay in areas in your image that cannot be faithfully reproduced in CMYK colors, you'd usually press Ctrl(⌘)+Shift+Y (or choose View, Gamut Warning). The default for this is gray at 100% opacity. So here's the obvious question now: How can you tell something's out of gamut if the original picture contains a lot of grays, as shown in Figure 2.10?

In the following set of steps, we'll demonstrate a problem and then show you how to fix it using four keystrokes.

Changing Transparency Display

1. Open the visible.psd image from the Examples/Chap02 folder on the Companion CD. You will want to zoom to the word "visible" in the image to do the editing.

2. Display the Layers palette by pressing F7 if necessary, and click the Add Layer Mask button (the icon is a circle within a rectangle, to the right of the "f" button) on the bottom of the Layers palette.

3. Choose the Paintbrush tool, choose the 19-pixel tip from the Options bar, and press D (default colors). If it is necessary, Press X to make black the foreground color. Make sure Opacity is set to 100% and then start hiding the image background by painting over it. Carefully work your way to the edge of the "v" in "visible." Stop when you think you've trimmed around the outside edge of the "v". See Figure 2.11 to see what you are supposed to be masking.

Figure 2.11   Add a layer mask, and then start painting around the "v" to remove the background.

It's very hard to tell where the transparent background ends and the graphic begins, isn't it?

4. Press Ctrl(⌘)+K, click the top drop-down list in the Preferences dialog box, and choose Transparency & Gamut.

Don't even *try* to remember the shortcut key because it is displayed next to the name of the Preference page. There are much more useful shortcut keys to remember—such as Ctrl(⌘)+K.

5. Click the foreground color swatch, choose green from the color picker, click OK, then click the other swatch for the grid and make it the same color of green, as shown in Figure 2.12. Click OK to apply the changes.

6. Maximize your view by clicking the Maximize/Restore window button (Macintosh: drag the window edges away from the image), hold the spacebar and drag in the window until you see the area you were editing.

Wow! There were areas you didn't even *see* that are unedited, aren't there? See Figure 2.13. Now that you've defined a different color transparency grid, you can accurately trim around the lettering. The Polygon Lasso tool helps when you're working around the straight edges.

The point's been made here, so it's really not necessary to edit completely around the lettering. But if you want the experience of working with the Paintbrush tool, choose a tip that is two sizes smaller for going around the lettering. When the white background is completely gone, drag the Layer Mask thumbnail onto the trash icon on the Layers palette, and choose Apply in the attention box that appears.

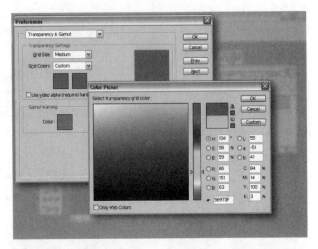

Figure 2.12   If you want a good view of the edges to mask in this image, choose a color not found in the image—a strong green.

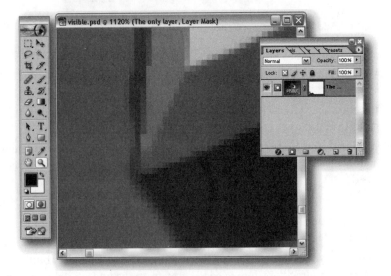

Figure 2.13   Well, oops. Your view of both the transparent regions and the foreground design are important to perform accurate masking.

7. You can save visible.psd to your hard disk, or simply close it without saving. Keep Photoshop open.

Determining Which Units and Rulers to Use

You can specify units for rulers two different ways in Photoshop. Whenever you press Ctrl(⌘)+R, rulers pop up to the left and top of the document window. Besides being able to measure things, the rulers are the only interface elements that enable you to drag guides from them (which means that if you need to place a guide, you need the rulers visible).

Tip

Displaying Units & Rulers Preferences   To go directly to the Units & Rulers Preferences page, press Ctrl(⌘)+R to display the rulers, and then double-click a ruler.

In the Rulers drop-down list, we suggest that you specify pixels (unless you work somewhere that uses centimeters or picas) and choose points for Type (and every once in a while picas), as shown in Figure 2.14. As you can see, you also can set the rulers to inches by pressing F8 to beckon the Info palette.

Why pixels and not inches for the rulers? Pixels are an absolute measurement, while inches depend on the resolution of the image file. Hey, if you do a little planning to work smarter and faster, you get more time for lunch.

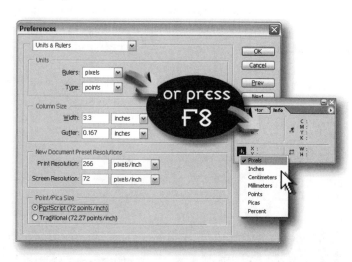

Figure 2.14   Make choices that make sense to your working methodology in the Units & Rulers Preferences dialog box.

As for the Column and Gutter choices, you may well wonder what they are! This setting is for desktop publishing: You might change it, for example, when your client has a need for a photo that runs across the gutter or simply fits in one column. The Gutter is set to inch values here although Photoshop ships with the default measurement of picas. We put these values in because they are the column and gutter width settings for a default PageMaker page. Hey, why not? For best results, get the specs from your client before goofing with the column and gutter distances.

Photoshop gives you the option of saving print and display settings you want to apply to all the images you create. You make these choices in the New Document Preset Resolutions area. Here you can choose the print and screen resolution at which the image is printing and displayed.

- **Print Resolution.** The default for printing, 300ppi (pixels per inch, not dots per inch), is fanciful. Later in this book, we'll cover commercial printing and the math behind it. A coffee table book, a luxurious item, is printed at about 2,540 dots per inch. This translates to 266 pixels per inch for a 1-to-1 printing. 300 pixels per inch is too large a capture for most Photoshop user's needs.

- **Screen Resolution.** Although some Windows products and Windows itself set screen resolution at 96 pixels per inch, this is not the commonly adopted standard. It's 72 pixels per inch (which, comfortably, is the same measurement as a typeface point—72 per inch). Leave this setting at 72.

- **Point/Pica Size.** This option should be left at 72 points per inch. We are creating electronic documents and using PostScript technology in Photoshop, so the traditional standard is not of use to us.

Figure 2.15 shows an example of changing units of measurement to pixels. Every command that uses units of measurement, such as the Canvas Size command shown here, is displaying image attributes in pixels.

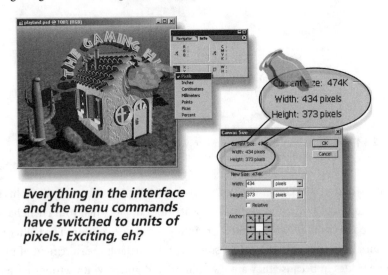

Everything in the interface and the menu commands have switched to units of pixels. Exciting, eh?

Figure 2.15   Your clients may give you "exotic" units of measurement. Trust us—you're equipped to handle that with the Units & Rulers Preferences dialog box.

What do you say we check out the Guides, Grid & Slices Preferences next?

Checking Out the Guides, Grid & Slices Preferences

The next Preferences menu controls how guides, a grid, and HTML slice guidelines appear on an image in Photoshop (see Figure 2.16).

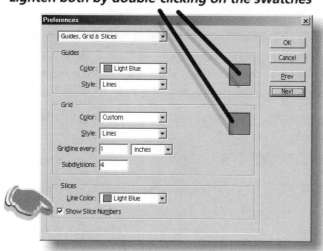

Figure 2.16 The Guides, Grid & Slices Preferences dialog box.

- **Guides.** Guides were introduced in Photoshop 4 and are a big hit, and a big help, for users. The only possible gripe is that the default color of medium blue for guides is probably too dark for richly colored images. We suggest, at your discretion, that you click the color swatch on this menu, take a ride to the color picker, and choose a lighter color.

  For those of you who are new to Photoshop, *guides* are non-printing screen elements that you pull out of rulers (press Ctrl(⌘)+R) to help you align vertical and horizontal elements. You can hide guides, but it's a better idea to put them back into the rulers—to avoid embarrassing presentations. Any tool can be used to pull guides out of the ruler, however; only the Move tool can be used to put 'em back.

- **Grid.** Again, the Photoshop Grid is another non-printing element that assists in accuracy and alignment of areas on layers and so on. It is in this section box that you can set the increments and subdivisions of the Grid. Grid increments are set independently of the Units & Rulers specifications.

Can you imagine Units & Rulers getting into a fight with Guides, Grid & Slices? We see nothing wrong with the conventional ruler layout for the Grid—a tick every inch with four subdivisions. It's all dependent on the way you work. If you work on the web, for example, you might want to set the Grid to 10 pixels a tick with, say, 5 subdivisions every tick to ensure precise web media placement (the web is one place where *every pixel* counts in design work).

- **Slices.** Slices are actual pieces of an image file that you create using the Slice tool. (You learn about slices and web page creation in Part VII of this book). Essentially, this setting gives you the option of showing the slice numbers. The numbers become part of the filenames of the slices, so it's probably a good idea to leave this option checked. Who knows; later you might decide to edit a slice of an image without the hassle of locating it or creating the sliced image a second time.

  You can choose the color of the indicator (again, non-printing and invisible on the web) of the slice boundary. This author finds that electric orange works nicely with almost any image.

Getting Some Control Over Screen Appearances of Elements!

Okay, in terms of non-printing screen elements, we've covered the guides, the grid, and the slices. Coming up soon will be selection edges (affectionately known as "marching ants"), Target Paths (which involve using the Pen tools, discussed in Chapter 5), two gandarks, a swozzle, and a pnuph. Okay, I was exaggerating toward the end there; however, it's not funny when you've ganged up a bunch of screen aids and want to hide them from view in one fell swoop.

Choose View, Show, Show Extras Options to display the dialog box you need. Adobe calls these screen elements "extras." Figure 2.17 shows the dialog box with the different screen elements that you can hide if you choose.

If you uncheck an item, you cannot use the Ctrl(⌘)+H shortcut to Hide and Show Extras. So we recommend that you leave checked every screen element you regularly use. Then, a simple Ctrl(⌘)+H toggles the visibility and invisibility of the screen elements. Remember that you are *not* deleting anything; you're *hiding it from view*.

Let's hop over to plug-ins and scratch disks next.

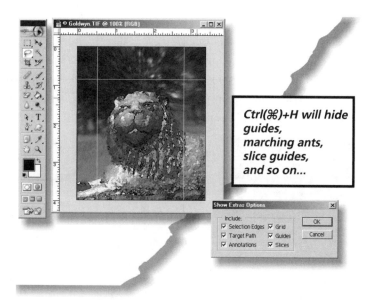

Figure 2.17   You can unclutter the screen by hiding screen elements that are not part of your image.

Plug-Ins, Scratch Disks, Memory and Image Cache

Photoshop handles memory very elegantly, but it doesn't know the memory and hard disk specs of your system. Therefore, the final two Preferences boxes are where you find the *real* control—how to fine-tune Photoshop's performance.

Ranking the Importance of Scratch Disks

The scratch disk is probably as important a preference in Photoshop as color settings are for the workspace. Photoshop needs hard-disk space in which it saves history pieces, clipboard pieces, multiple copies of an active file for undo purposes, and more. If you do not give it enough hard-disk space, your work could come to a grinding halt even with gigabytes of RAM on your system.

Let's get the trivial preference here out of the way so that we can talk memory management with you.

Specifying the Directory for Plug-Ins

Plug-ins, those third-party enhancers from Alien Skin, Andromeda software, and others, can be installed to Photoshop's Plug-Ins directory (item 1 in Figure 2.18). Now, here's the catch: what if you also own, say, Painter and you want to use the same plug-ins in Painter? No problem. You create a folder on one of your drives, plunk your third-party plug-ins in the folder, and then point Photoshop toward this folder as an additional place to look for plug-ins. By the way, you need to check the Additional Plug-Ins Directory option so that Photoshop will go looking the next time you start it. Changes to the plug-ins folder location(s) don't take place until you restart Photoshop.

Figure 2.18   You can specify up to four temporary locations on your system's hard disk(s) where Photoshop can store parts of files, multiple undo images, and other things.

Legacy Photoshop Serial Number

Some plug-ins will not work without a legitimate Photoshop serial number (item 2 in Figure 2.18). Well, the sequencing of the registration number has changed with version 7, and this might keep third-party plug-ins from working. So put in your registration number from a previous version of Photoshop if your plug-ins aren't plugging in.

Okay, on to memory management…

Doling Out System Resources to Photoshop

It might come as a surprise to new users that Photoshop doesn't use that nice hunk of temporary space you set away for applications to use. Nope, Photoshop wants its *own* space that no other application is going to touch while it is running—and it wants it to be as large as possible. Adobe, like virtually no other company, knows how to handle memory. This means where other applications might gag and crash handling a 40MB image file, Photoshop can do it—*if* you set up memory and scratch disk allocation the way it wants.

As a rule of thumb, Photoshop wants to work with three to five times the size of a saved image file. That means that if you are working on a 5MB file, you need to have 15 to

25MB free of both scratch disk space and physical RAM. If you have less scratch disk space than RAM, Photoshop will not use any more RAM than it has scratch disk space. Therefore, if you have 1GB of RAM and have assigned Photoshop 200MB of scratch disk space, Photoshop will use only 200MB of that huge RAM amount you have installed.

In the Scratch Disks area (item 3 of Figure 2.18), you can see that the author has specified two drives for scratch disk space. The first one, drive J, was exclusively created when the hard disks were partitioned to be used only by Photoshop. Hard disks are cheap— image work is much larger than it used to be—and this author felt that 3GB was plenty of room in which Photoshop could play. The secondary drive specified is a drive that simply has a lot of room on it. As you can see, you can specify up to four scratch disks. Big recommendation here: Windows ME and later versions defragment drives while you're not watching so that the drives are always optimized. This is not true on the Macintosh. Macintosh users should defragment and optimize their scratch disks regularly using a utility, such as those made by Symantec.

Finally in this version of Photoshop, both Windows and Mac OS handle memory in similar ways. This means that the memory handling techniques you'll read about in the following section applies equally to Macintosh and Windows users.

Scratch Disk Assignment and RAM Requirements

Windows and the Mac dynamically resize the memory pool to allow applications to extend their use of RAM while you work. But it's still a good idea to devote hard-disk space to as many drives as you can afford in the Plug-Ins & Scratch Disks page of the Preferences dialog box. Good candidates to which you can assign a scratch disk location are these:

- **A drive that has a lot of free space.** I've gone overboard with my own system, but even 1GB is not unreasonable, and naturally, you get this space back after you close Photoshop.

- **A drive that does not use a compression scheme.** Microsoft DriveSpace is *not* cool on the drive to which you assign the primary scratch disk. Compressed drives shouldn't even exist in 2002. Get a big hard disk instead of compressing.

- **A drive that has been defragmented.** As mentioned before, use the Disk Defragmenter utility to optimize any drive to which you assign scratch disk status if your OS doesn't have native clean-up features.

Your first choice should be the drive that happens to have the most free, uncompressed space. If you have any other drives that have a lot of free space, you can assign them as second, third, and fourth drives. Photoshop *honestly needs* this kind of hard-drive space to enable you to work quickly and flawlessly in it. You might even want to re-think running other applications while Photoshop is loaded to give maximum memory support to Photoshop.

> **Warning**
>
> **Don't Put a Scratch Disk on Your C Drive**   It is not a good idea to put a scratch disk on your C drive. Not only is this usually the drive where your operating system is located, but it's also where temp folders for other applications are placed. If you attempt to dynamically resize a space on a drive on Windows that's been assigned as a scratch disk, you *will* have system problems.

When you allocate a scratch disk space on a Macintosh system, the procedure is similar to the one for Windows. Pick a large drive with nothing on it, use a utility such as Norton Utilities to defrag the drive, and use no drive compression on the target drive. Pick as many as four locations for scratch disk space.

The first thing you ought to do to optimize RAM use is check your system to see how much RAM is available. A lot of the older G3s, the colorful (no flat screen) iMacs, and some of the G4s shipped with 64MB of physical RAM, and you need 128MB to work comfortably in Photoshop. So call and order some more RAM.

Even with 128MB of RAM, applications other than Photoshop are memory hogs (*all* of today's programs are), and if you absolutely need to run an application along with Photoshop, here's what you need to do:

Allocating RAM to Photoshop on a Macintosh

1. Start your machine and do *not* run any applications.

Running an application or logging on to check your email will potentially fragment your system's memory and give you an inaccurate reading in Step 3.

2. Start any other application you think you will want to use while Photoshop is running. Ideally, you should have no other program running, but doing this is a productivity dampener.

3. Go to Finder, and choose About This Computer from the Apple menu. This box will tell you what the largest unused block of RAM available is. Let's suppose the number is 120MB.

4. In Finder, choose the Adobe Photoshop program icon and choose File, Get Info.

5. Regardless of what values are in the box, in the Info window, set the Preferred Size to no more than 90% of the Largest Unused Block value you saw earlier, such as 90% of 120MB.

6. Close out of the Info box and launch Photoshop.

Return to the Preferences dialog box by pressing Ctrl(⌘)+K; then choose Memory & Image Cache from the drop-down list to queue up for the next section.

Memory & Image Cache

Cache setting for images help speed up their display in the same way that caching on your system helps speed up display of frequently used screen areas. The default level is 4, and we see no need to change this, because it is a good trade-off between snappy display and overall system performance.

The Use Cache for Image Histograms is not really a preference you want. We recommend that you leave this unchecked. Even if you have the system resources to dedicate to caching histogram information, caching is performed on a *sampling* of pixels in the image, instead of *all* the pixels in the image.

The Available RAM you dedicate to Photoshop depends on how much total RAM your machine has. As you can see in Figure 2.19 for Windows and Figure 2.20 for the Macintosh, the Mac has the most RAM, with a total of 384MB. Adobe suggests at least 128MB of RAM for Photoshop, so math tells us that about 50% of available RAM can be used by Photoshop, with a matching amount of scratch disk space.

Figure 2.19   Set the Maximum memory used by Photoshop to at least 96MB. 128 is better, and 256MB is better still.

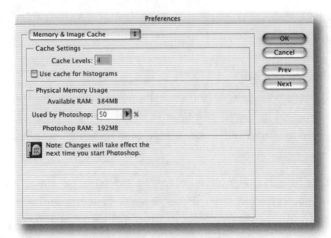

Figure 2.20   The Macintosh handles memory differently, and much better for Photoshop users, with the introduction of OS X.

Tip

Getting More RAM Space   If, by chance, your editing work exceeds the RAM and scratch disk space, Photoshop will begin to swap in and out elements it needs to complete your work and this really drags your system down.

Also, you can set Maximum memory usage to 100%, but doing this is sort of a fairy tale. You aren't actually committing 100% of your system's resources to Photoshop—the Windows OS will not allow this. The OS needs resources of its own and will hang onto whatever it needs.

Strong hint: Buy RAM, and keep a large space on one or more of your hard disks free.

You actually decrease efficiency of Photoshop as the RAM dedicated approaches 100%. This happens because the Windows system itself can use software caching, and Photoshop and Windows will fight over how much RAM is actually available.

Note

Keeping an Eye on Your Resources   If you click the triangle on the status bar (Macintosh: on the bottom scroll bar) and choose Efficiency from the pop-up, you will be in constant touch with how much RAM Photoshop is actually using (the indicator will read 100%). You will also be able to see whether Photoshop is swapping out to hard disk. If the Efficiency drops to 58%, for example, you should (1)Save and close the file, and/or simplify it by merging unused layers, and (2)buy more RAM!

Whew! Do you feel like you've been locked in a (Preferences) box for about a week? Okay, come out in the sunshine now—you've optimized all the base-level stuff in Photoshop, and now it's time to make your preferences in the *working space*. Make Photoshop's workspace truly your own.

Doing Some Photoshop House Cleaning

Photoshop 7 is *just about* everything to everyone. This means that whatever type of graphics you are interested in creating, Photoshop's got your number, so to speak. However (and this is a BIG "however"), Photoshop sort of keeps things you might or might not need hanging out there in the interface. Additionally, there's some quasi-hidden stuff with which you should acquaint yourself.

Let's start with the master control panel for Photoshop's collections of neat stuff. Technically, it's called the Preset Manager.

More Choices and More Control with the Preset Manager

The Photoshop CD is crammed to the gills with options for fills, brush tips—you name it. And how do you get to this cornucopia?

The Preset Manager (Edit, Preset Manager) is your "one stop shop" for accessing exactly what you need when you pick up a tool (see Figure 2.21). After you have displayed the Preset Manager, click the drop-down list (item 1) for Preset Type, and then choose from categories by clicking that tiny button (circled in Figure 2.21). As you can see, you also can choose how the members of a category are presented on palettes (we recommend, for example, Small Thumbnail for the Brushes collection, at least for the default brushes).

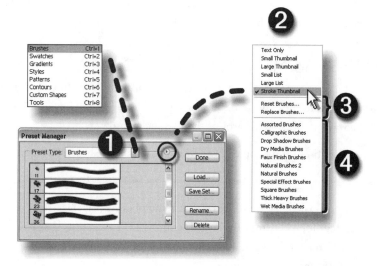

Figure 2.21   The Preset Manager gives you complete control over eight creative
elements found within Photoshop.

To briefly explain a fairly intuitive selection process, follow the bouncing balls in Figure 2.21:

- Clicking the down button on the Preset Type field (item 1) displays the eight types of palettes from which you can customize the appearance and choose from Photoshop's collection. Brushes have been chosen here.

- Clicking the encircled icon in Figure 2.21 opens the menu for the Preset Manager (item 2). For the default brushes, you can get away with a small thumbnail display on the Brushes palette, but for exotic stuff such as the Wet Media brushes, you will probably want a Stroke Thumbnail display.

- Now, item 3 brackets Reset Brushes and Replace Brushes. What's the diff'? Resetting the Brushes returns the Brushes palette to the "normal," round hard and soft-tipped brushes—ideal for image editing. Replace Brushes leads you to a directory box, where you must scout (needlessly) for a brushes palette file.

- Item 4 in Figure 2.21 is the reason why you really don't need to use Replace Brushes, shown in item 3. All of Photoshop's brushes collections can be found here. Now, if you or someone else has created a Brushes palette, then you'd either want to put the file in with the other Brushes files (in the Photoshop7/Presets/Brushes folder) or go through the hassle of tracking down the file every time you want to use it. The choice is obvious, eh?

You can perform the same customizing with Styles, Patterns, and so on—and it's all done the way we've shown you with the Brushes palette.

Who Wants So Many Palettes in a Group?

As you've surely noticed, extra palettes in this version have been bunched up in a way that practically suffocates the poor Layers palette. You do not have to keep palettes grouped the way Adobe Systems groups them, doncha know.

Our recommendation for a happier, less cluttered desktop is shown in Figure 2.22.

Allow us to explain the construction work going on in Figure 2.22.

- The History palette is useful, but if you remember Alt(Opt)+Ctrl(⌘)+Z , this is the shortcut for a "History Backward" command. This means that you don't really need the History palette in the Layers group—you can call it when you need it from the Window menu.

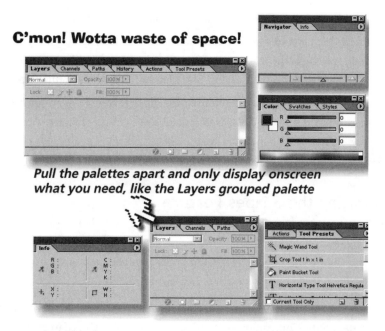

Figure 2.22   For 99% of your daily palette needs, simply remember F6, F7, and F8.

You click and hold the title of a palette, and then drag to pull it free from a palette group. Conversely, you drop a palette on top of a group title bar to add it to the group.

- Actions and Tool Presets seem to work well together, and you do not need them onscreen all the time, so why not group them together and close the palette? Besides, you can access the tool presets from the Options bar (more on them later in this chapter—it's a wonnnnnnn-derful feature).

- The Navigator palette has got to be about the least useful innovation as of Photoshop 4, but it's still around. Harsh criticism? No. You can use the Hand tool to bop around an image without the need for a palette, regardless of the image size. And you also can Zoom in and out to replace what the Navigator palette does. Still, if you're attached to it, leave the Navigator palette together with the Info palette. This author has the Info palette on his machine set up as a stand-alone group of one palette.

- Similarly, the Color, Swatches, and Styles fit together nicely; this is the default configuration—we suggest you leave it this way.

Terrific! Now, no grouped palette has more than three members, and they are configured logically. Here are the magic keys to make your workspace even more user-friendly:

- F6 toggles the Styles, Color, and Swatches palette on and off.

- F7 toggles the Layers, Channels, and Paths palette on and off. You will probably want this palette in the workspace all the time, however. The Options bar and the Layers/Channels/Paths palette account for around 85% of this author's design work.

- F8 toggles the Info palette on and off. This shortcut key is a very quick way to change unit of measurements, as described earlier in this chapter.

Wait. We're not done yet. More customizing ahead!

Customizing the Shapes Feature

In Photoshop 6, shapes were introduced. Shapes are vector designs on a palette, and typically, you create a vector mask layer when you create a shape in an image window, as is being done in Figure 2.23. Do not worry too much about Shapes right now; they are covered in Chapter 4. What we're doing here is showing you how to access different shapes.

Replace Shapes is selected in Figure 2.23. The reason? We've put some really inventive Shapes palettes on the Companion CD, and to access them, you need to choose either the Load Shapes or Replace Shapes command. Then again, as you can see in the figure, Photoshop ships with a bunch of different shape themes, shown at the bottom of the palette menu.

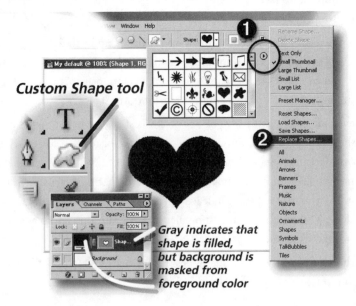

Figure 2.23   Choose the Custom Shape tool, and then on the Shapes palette, choose Replace Shapes.

To try your hand using different shapes, do this: Click the down arrow next to the Shapes icon on the Options bar. Then click the menu flyout button, and choose Replace Shapes. Navigate to the Examples/Chap02 folder on the Companion CD. Click icons.csh, and then click Load.

Click the Shape layers icon on the Options bar. Open a new image window, and go to town clicking on shapes. Then marquee drag a shape (hold Shift to constrain proportions of the shape). Fun, eh? And best of all, shortly you'll learn how to make a shapes palette of your own.

As you can see in Figure 2.24, you can choose different options for the shapes you create. If you click the down arrow to the right of the Shapes icon, the Custom Shape Options appears. (This feature is explained more fully in Chapter 4.) If you toggle off the link icon (item 2) in Figure 2.24, whatever the shape allows to peek through under the layer will *not* move in synch if you choose to move the shape on the layer.

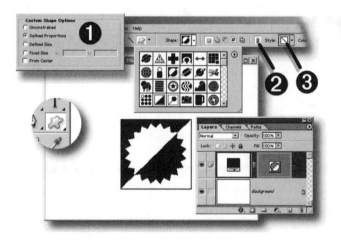

Figure 2.24   Use your own Shapes with Photoshop's Shapes feature.

Finally, item 3 shows that no style has been chosen for the shape. A style is a combination of different effects that produce gem-like or stone-like qualities (again, more in Chapter 4). With no style, what shows through the shape is the underlying foreground color. Double-click the left thumbnail on the Layers palette, and you will see that you can change layer colors by making the change in the color picker.

Styles and Their Components

Figure 2.25 shows that a shape has been given a style, specifically one of the Glass Button collection styles. All you do to add a style to a shape is click the style icon by selecting it from the drop-down palette on the Options bar or from the Styles palette (F6).

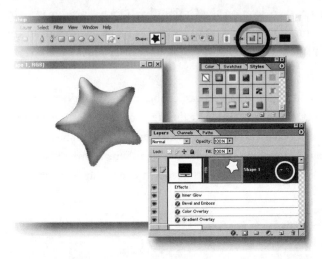

Figure 2.25   You can drag a style icon and drop it on top of a shape, or you can simply click the styles icon.

Why don't you create a shape now in a new window? That way, you'll see what goes into a style.

Figure 2.25 shows that there is a down arrow to the right of the Shape thumbnail on the Layers palette. Click the triangle, and all the effects that go into making the current style are revealed to you. You can change any aspect of the style that has been applied by double-clicking on a style effect, and then changing the default settings. Changing a component of a style applies only to what you added it to in the image window; a style on a palette cannot be changed unless you explicitly delete or otherwise modify the style.

Adding Your Own Shape to Photoshop

So far, we've touted the Shapes tools as the best thing since those wash-off tattoos—however, we didn't tell you that you, too, can make a collection of shapes and use them. Now, we assume that you have not read Chapter 5 yet, and therefore, you are not familiar with the Pen tool. This is okay—this chapter is on customizing. The working knowledge of tools comes later.

Start by clicking the Pen tool. Draw anything you like—a doodle is fine—and close the path by clicking on its origin point, the first point you started with. If you're not familiar with the Pen tool, attempt a simple shape for now, such as a rectangle, by clicking at the points that make up the corners.

You can now add the shape to the current shapes palette in two easy steps:

1. Choose Edit, Define Custom Shape.
2. In the Shape Name dialog box, type the name of the shape, as shown in Figure 2.26. Done!

Figure 2.26   Creating a new shape on a Shapes palette is as easy as 1-2-3, without the 3.

You might want to use the Blank.csh file in the Examples/Chap02 folder to populate a palette with your own designs. This palette has only one shape that you can delete after adding at least one of your own creations (palettes have to have at least one object).

If you're wishing now that you had the same control over defining brush tips as you do now with vector shapes—well, you *do*!

Come on—let's take a trip to the brush tip controls. They blast version 6's options away.

Exploring Near-Infinite Brush Variations

If the heading to this section were true, you'd have to plod through a near-infinite chapter! Fortunately, we've collected for your enjoyment the really interesting variations on brush tips and presented them in this section. We've also provided you with only necessary explanations of the less-than-spectacular controls—for those, you can go off and experiment on your own.

Levels of Brush-Building Complexity: Part I

There are two areas you can dig into with the Brushes controls; we need to be careful not to mistake the Brush Preset picker from the Brushes palette. The Brush Preset picker is where the saved brush tips are offered up for you to use. But when you want to truly customize a brush or to build your own, the Brushes palette is "Shape Central." Without further diversion, let's take a look at how you can build one of your own brushes with the Brush Tip Shape controls—the less elaborate and confusing of the controls.

Here are the steps you need to create a unique tip for the Brush tool:

Creating a Custom Brush

1. Click the menu icon on the Options bar (item 1 in Figure 2.27). A menu drops down into the workspace with way too much information for mere mortals to understand. Click the Brush Tip Shape button to simplify things and avail yourself of only the tools you immediately need.

2. Round brushes are the staple of Photoshop—you can't retouch images without them. However, each round brush is based on an existing one, so click the 19-pixel hard brush on the Brushes palette within this menu box. Then, click the arrow inside a circle at the top right of the menu (item 2 in Figure 2.27), and choose New Brush from the flyout menu. When the Brush Name dialog box appears, name the new brush **23 elliptical, hard** and press Enter (Return).

   If this arrow is not visible, click the Brushes tab (at the top of the palette) and drag it well away from the Options bar. You then will have access to the arrow (item 2 in Figure 2.27).

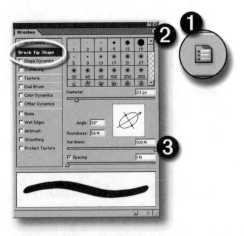

Figure 2.27   The Brush Tip Shape controls enable you to create a rudimentary custom brush that could be ideal for photo-retouching.

3. Drag the diameter slider over to the right so that it reads 23px (or type this number into the Diameter field and then press Enter (Return).

4. Drag one of the dots in the brush tip proxy box (near item 3 in the Figure) closer to the center of the brush—the brush shape becomes elliptical. Do not worry about the Angle and Roundness fields; we're experimenting here and if you want to get precise, you can always come back to these controls.

5. Drag the arrow in any direction you choose. As you can see in the preview window, a stroke will now become thicker and thinner, depending on the direction in which you stroke.

6. We'll get to the Hardness slider in a moment. For now, leave it and the Spacing slider alone. You now have a new brush with the name you have given it at the end of the currently loaded Brushes palette. Keep Photoshop open; there's more in store.

It is important to understand—and I guess right now is a good time—that Photoshop has brush tips that fall into two different classes: those that are based on math (and can be squished and have hardness altered) and those that are built from a captured bitmap design. We've not touched the bitmap sort yet, but we will soon. With both math-based and bitmap brush tips, you have the option of increasing Spacing. Spacing is the distance between one paint daub and the next. When you drag the Paintbrush tool, you are actually making oodles of individual daubs that are spaced so closely together that it appears to be—and for all purposes, *is*—a continuous line.

You do not need a tutorial to walk you through Spacing, but you can take a moment and experiment on your own. Choose a small soft round tip, and increase the spacing for it on the menu (see Figure 2.28). You'll see the continuous stroke break up into individual dots, and if you paint with the setting you've chosen, you can make a path of dots. Spacing is much more useful when the individual paint daubs represent something, such as stars or other mini-designs on the Brushes palette. Painting with dots wears thin in the amusement department fairly quickly.

The next set of steps are going to be the world's shortest tutorial, because you will play with only one control—an important one—Hardness.

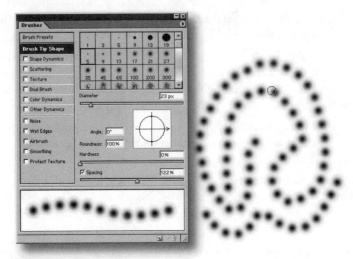

Figure 2.28   Spacing is the control that can break up a continuous stroke a brush makes into its components.

Using the Hardness Control

1. Click the 19-pixel hard tip brush on the palette, and choose New Brush from the palette flyout. Name the brush **23 pixel soft tip, round**. Do not goof with the Angle and Roundness controls this time.

2. Drag the Hardness slider all the way to the left.

3. Check out the preview window at the bottom of the menu (see Figure 2.29).

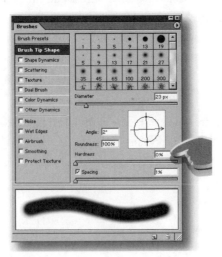

Figure 2.29   Create a soft brush of the diameter you like for special occasions, such as image retouching.

4. You now have a small brush that is ideal for retouching, using the Brush or other painting tool (such as the Clone Stamp tool). And let's face it—professional retouching requires a lot of subtlety, and a totally soft round brush is very hard to detect in a finished piece of retouching—it's a bit harder than the airbrush option, but softer than using the Pencil tool.

Tip

Changing Brush Tip Size   At any time, you can change the size of your brush tip without leaving the scene of your retouching or designing efforts. Right-click (Macintosh: hold Ctrl and click) when a painting tool is chosen, and up pops the Brush Preset picker with a Master Diameter control at the top. A changed brush is not a saved brush, but you can save a setting very quickly by adding the configuration—even the present foreground color—to the Brush Preset picker, the top left icon on the Options bar (which looks like a page icon).

So you say you want more control over brush tips? We hear you, and the following sections are going to take you on a (pleasant) roller coaster ride of options you can put at your mouse tip.

Tip

In Favor of Tablets   A digitizing tablet is really an enhancer to these new brushes in Photoshop. They give you more control than using a point-and-click device, and Photoshop is able to recognize the pressure-sensitive input—which means you'll get more work that appears genuinely hand-drawn. Hint: Wacom's Graphire 2 tablet and stylus comes with Painter Classic—a wonderful graphics arsenal addition and frequently a helpful mate to Photoshop.

Using Brush Presets: A First Look

We're not going to dig too deeply in this section because *every* option on the Brush Presets section of the Brushes menu has at least three sub-options. If you need a simple solution for the "round-tip, soft" blahs, however, this section will show you how just a few clicks can take you to an arresting new look for painting.

Let's do it in tutorial format, just because my publisher told me to:

Oh, Those Brush Presets

1. Click the Brush Presets tab on the Brushes menu. Now, before we go changing stuff (not to worry; changes here are not permanent, although we'll discuss how to make permanent changes shortly), why don't you click some of the weird new brush tips on the Brushes palette and see which properties suddenly have a check mark next to them?

2. Okay. Let's stop clowning around while we're learning. Click the 19-pixel hard brush tip, and then draw a stroke on an empty canvas. Hmm, round on both ends of the stroke and fairly unremarkable. Click the Scattering checkbox, marked as item 1 in Figure 2.30. Now drag the brush. Wowee! The page looks like a marbles championship! Keep Figure 2.30 handy because we'll be referring to this figure for a few more steps.

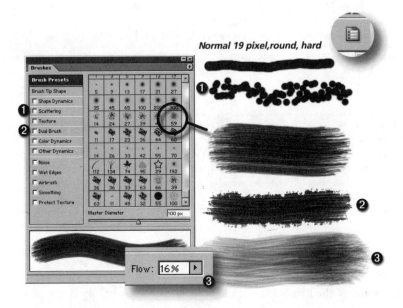

Figure 2.30   There are permutations piled upon permutations in the Brush Presets area. Chances are that you can design a brush tip no one has even thought of yet.

3. Choose the 59-pixel brush tip (circled in the figure) that looks like a splatter. Stroke it across the canvas. Pretty neat, huh? It looks like an actual, physical brush stroke. How can we improve its realism? Click the Dual Brush checkbox and make a stroke (item 2 in the figure). Okay, perhaps this is not what you had in mind, but an explanation might help things here. Dual Brush means that all four sides of a brush stroke display the ends of the stroke—the unevenness, or whatever the effect of a particular brush tip may be. Not all brushes will make such a pronounced effect—in fact, round tip brushes are a total dud when used in combination with Dual Brush. Uncheck Dual Brush.

4. There's a brush tip enhancer that isn't even in the Brushes menu; it's called Flow, and it's on the Options bar. Crank Flow down to about 16%, as shown in item 3 of Figure 2.30, and make a stroke with this 59-pixel splatter tip. Now, you can see the hairs on the brush and the stroke looks a lot more realistic.

Keep Photoshop open because we're really going to turn this customized brushes stuff on its ear in the following section.

Noise, Wet Edges, and Color Dynamics

In the steps that follow, you experiment with far more interesting effects (although I'm sure you feel that the ones you've been using are thrilling!). So, to pile superlative upon superlative before getting to the point, let's do some knock-out stuff that was only a dream in Photoshop 6:

More (and More Complex) Brush Presets

1. Get out a new, blank, white image window or erase what you've been using. Choose the 100-pixel, soft-edged tip from the palette, as you see in item 1 in Figure 2.31.

2. Click the Noise checkbox and make a brush stroke. Wild, eh? It looks like a horizontal cat's tail in a marsh, or something. This stroke is neither soft nor hard—think about stroking a path using a brush this size or smaller.

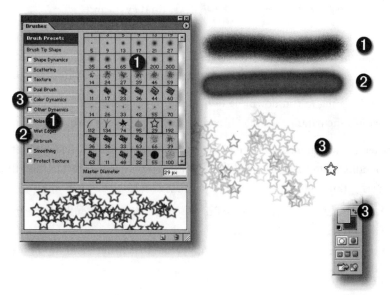

Figure 2.31 These are the Noise, Wet Edges, and Color Dynamics modifiers for brush tips.

Again, not all brush tips will work as well as the one we recommend here for the Noise filter. Soft edges produce the most attention-getting effect. If you still have Fill set to 16% on the Options bar (from the last exercise), try a few brush strokes with it turned back up to 100%.

3. Click the Wet Edges checkbox. Make a stroke; it looks like finger painting, right? A visual example is marked as item 2 in Figure 2.31.

4. Color Dynamics is one of my favorite parameters. Choose the hollow star or the leaves tip from the Brushes palette, and then click Color Dynamics to select it. Set the color selection boxes on the toolbox to diametrically opposing colors. Green and blue will do. Now stroke away. You can't see the color changes in Figure 2.31 (item 3), but the individual components of the stroke cycle colors from green in the spectrum to blue. A little note here: if your toolbox's color selection boxes are black and white, no color cycling will take place as you stroke.

Let's now take a look at how the rest of the modifiers change brush shapes. And we'll even show you how to build a really interesting new brush shape of your own.

Brush Dynamics, Textures, and Making Your Own Sophisticated Tip

Guess what? There's a "trap door" in the Brushes menu that we haven't opened yet. Right now, check the Shape Dynamics checkbox, and then click its title. Wow! A whole new world of strange new options has taken the place of the Brushes palette. Things like Control and Jitter and Angle are listed. Whatever do they mean?

Well, first, unless you have a pressure-sensitive digitizing palette, you aren't going to get much out of the Control drop-downs. This is not to say you cannot experiment, but the Fade option seems to cause the most apparent change in the behavior of the brush tip.

Second, we're going to run down the terms found in this "Fine-Tuning Center" so that you can adjust the parameters quickly and confidently on your own.

- **Jitter.** Means randomness, straying from the default. Therefore, if you set Roundness Jitter up high, you'd get a brush tip that produces thick and thin strokes (thin where the random Roundness decides to be un-round (elliptical).

- **Shape Dynamics.** Should be the first place you stop when designing a custom brush tip (see Figure 2.32). This area on the menu has controls for size (and variation in size as you paint), Angle (with variations…Jitter), and Roundness (also with variations).

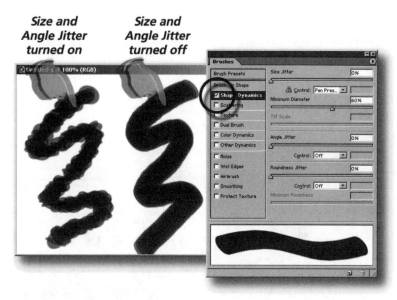

Figure 2.32   When you select Shape Dynamics in the Brushes menu, the controls for other parameters such as size, Angle, and Roundness appear.

- **Texture.** This area gives you a big chance to mess with the look of the brush stroke. Shortly, when we run through a mini-tutorial, you add a predefined texture to the brush stroke. When a brush tip already looks as though it's a captured bitmap and has texture, adding texture makes the tip look more complicated. And because nature is a very complex place, the more complex a brush tip, the more natural it looks.

- **Other Dynamics.** These other dynamics are Opacity and Flow controls, and you can access more of them from the Options bar. However, when Flow is used at a low setting (in other words, your digital pen is slightly clogged) you can simulate paint build-up by stroking over areas a different number of times.

The Noise, Wet Edges, and other options at the bottom of the palette have no secret door to variations, and their purpose is self-explanatory. However, the Protect Texture checkbox is of great interest to us brush-builders. When you have the ultimate texture to tip into the brush recipe and then decide to change parameters, you might wind up with a different texture in the Texture dialog box. Click this option to retain the texture (under Texture) while you design your brush tip.

Ready to test drive the Brushes controls with a little back seat driving? Of course you are!

Making a Sophisticated Brush Tip

1. Get out a clean sheet of image window (item 1 in Figure 2.33). Choose white as the color with a size as small as 1" square, 72ppi, and Grayscale.

Figure 2.33   Create a noisy image, and then enlarge a section to become your brush tip (at least the *beginning* of it).

2. Choose Filter, Noise, Add Noise. Crank up the Amount all the way to 400%. Choose Gaussian Distribution. Here the Monochromatic option is irrelevant because this is a grayscale image (item 2). Press Enter (Return).

3. With the Rectangle Marquee tool, drag a small rectangle (a quarter inch is fine), and then press Ctrl(⌘)+T to put the rectangle and its contents in Free Transform mode (item 3). Drag a corner away from the center of the selection until you can clearly see the dots of the noise.

4. Press Enter (Return) or click the checkmark on the Options bar to execute the enlargement of the selected section. Now, press Ctrl(⌘)+Shift+J to cut the selection to its own layer.

5. Drag the Background layer to the trash icon so that you can see more clearly what you have to work with on Layer 1.

6. Using the Eraser tool set to about 35 pixels and in Airbrush mode (which you select on the Options bar), soften the edges of the dotted rectangle on the layer. (Hint: See Figure 2.34, item 1.) Choose Edit, Define Brush, and then name it in the dialog box something you'll remember, such as **My first brush tip**. Then, make a stroke or two on a new canvas, first with the Flow turned up to 100%, and then with Flow at 20%. What a difference Flow makes!

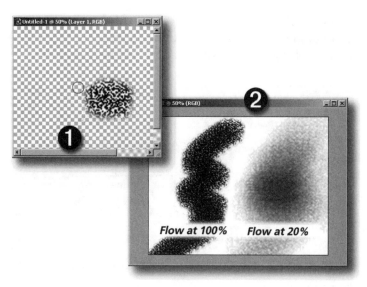

Figure 2.34   The Flow control allows more detail to be visible and also enables you to build up a texture using multiple strokes.

7. Okay, now you're ready for the big time. Click the Brushes menu on the Options bar, and to be cool, use only the Shape Dynamics. You can see the settings and an example of the stroke in Figure 2.35.

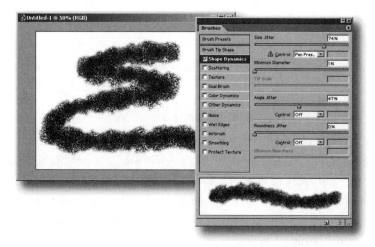

Figure 2.35   Using only the Shape Dynamics controls, you've turned an interesting brush art tip into a *very* interesting one!

8. Okay, it's boogie time—click Texture, then specify 100% Depth (see Figure 2.36), and choose one of the preset textures from the drop-down box. Use Hard

Mix and then drag the brush around the canvas. It's a pretty interesting, organic-looking brush stroke, eh? Ooops—make sure Flow is still at 20% on the Options bar or your strokes will look too heavy and be lacking in character.

Figure 2.36   Wow! Did *you* create that? You bet, with a little prodding and Photoshop's new Brushes controls.

9. You might want to save this brush now in a more accessible place. Click the Brush on the far left of the Options palette, and add it—with your own inspired name—to Tool Presets. You can close the working canvas now at any time. Keep Photoshop open.

So now you have total control over how brushes and shapes appear within the work-space. Next let's see how to make a palette obey your beck and call.

Layers, Layers—Oh How Do You Control Layers?

The technique for leveraging layers in your work is a topic covered in future chapters. For now, we're just going to show you how to *manage* them because, after all, this is the *reference* section of this book.

Copying and Naming Layers

Photoshop is most decidedly "layer-centric"—if you're working efficiently (in other words, if you've read this book!). You will find layers indispensable, and almost every editing move (or perhaps every other editing move) somehow involves using layers.

Take out the Icons.psd image from the Examples/Chap02 folder on the Companion CD. You're going to learn some tricks here and now...

Naming and Propagating Layer Content

1. With the Icons.psd image open, press F7 if the Layers palette isn't open on your desktop. If it is, let it sit there for a moment.

2. As you can see, the top layer containing the icon is labeled "Gluntwerp," a dumb and useless name for the purposes of this assignment. Double-click the name and—surprise, fellow Photoshop users. Photoshop finally lets you rename a layer in place. Type **Icon** in the space, and press Enter (Return) to apply the new name (see Figure 2.37).

Figure 2.37   You can rename a layer (or channel, or path) simply by double-clicking the current name and entering the new name in the text field.

3. Click and hold the layer name on the Layers palette. Drag the layer title onto the Create a new layer icon at the bottom of the Layers palette. Repeat this four times, as you see in Figure 2.38. What is the lesson here? Well, there are two: First, a copy of a layer is always placed precisely over the original; so in this case, you cannot see that there are four images of that icon. Second, because you duplicated the layers in this way, they are conveniently numbered for you on the Layers palette.

4. Choose the Move tool and right-click (Macintosh: hold Ctrl and click) on the image window. Actually, you can use any tool you please, but you're going to be using the Move tool in a step or two. As you can see in Figure 2.39, any layer that has content (non-transparent pixels) is listed on the context menu. Note that this works only if you click directly on the desired image element. Now, because we have all these icons stacked up, let's separate them a little. Choose icon copy from the context menu, and this layer lights up on the Layers palette, indicating that this is the new editing layer.

By the way, if you've chosen Auto Select Layer on the Options bar, you've ruined Step 4! Uncheck this option—if you're just starting out with Photoshop, this feature can get you into tons of editing trouble. And then, of course, you'll be late delivering your assignments, and you will most likely starve.

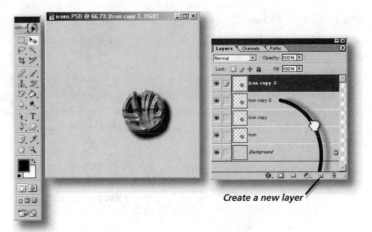

Figure 2.38   Duplicate layers are numbered automatically if you drop the desired layer onto the Create a new layer icon.

Figure 2.39   Right-click (Macintosh: hold Ctrl and click) to bring up the context menu. You can then choose to activate any layer with content that is beneath your cursor.

5. Aw, why not choose icon copy from the context menu? Now, with the Move tool (and only the Move tool), you can scoot the Icon copy visual contents up and to the left of the stack of icons. If you have been fooling around with other features for a while and need a quick reminder of which icon you just moved, right-click (Macintosh: hold Ctrl and click), as shown in Figure 2.40, and click the only logical choice (the choices are icon copy and Background).

6. Move a few more icons out of the way of the original one. Oh, okay—we'd be remiss if we didn't show you the option to Auto Select Layer. Click the checkbox on the Options bar, and then click an icon. The Auto Select Layer option causes the Layers palette to jump to the layer containing the top item you click. You will see the Layers palette change the highlight for the current editing layer, as shown in Figure 2.41. You can close the file without saving changes.

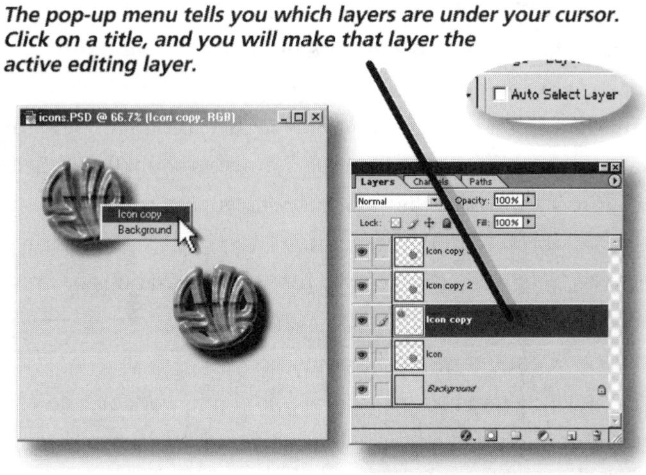

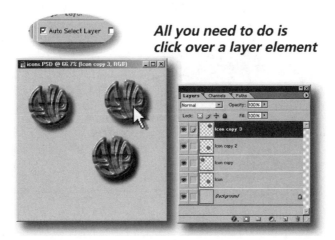

The pop-up menu tells you which layers are under your cursor.
Click on a title, and you will make that layer the
active editing layer.

Figure 2.40   This context menu is very handy, when used in combination with the
Move tool, to quickly identify areas on the image.

Remember that Auto Select Layer is an option, but again, this option of auto-selecting
can work against you because it's so easy to accidentally click a different image area after
you've auto-chosen the layer you need. It's best to leave this option turned off. If you
have the Move tool active, it is more efficient to select this feature on demand by simply
Ctrl(⌘)+clicking on an object to jump quickly to the layer that contains that object.

All you need to do is
click over a layer element

Figure 2.41   The Auto Select Layer feature puts layer choosing—and inadvertent
mistakes—at your fingertips.

Let's drift back to those custom brushes to show off a new feature we've only hinted at
so far: the Tool Preset feature.

Introducing the Tool Preset Palette

Of the scores of innovations Adobe Systems has brought to Photoshop 7, the one this author is most impressed with is the Tool Preset palette. The Preset palette is always up there on the Options bar, and it's a good, *quick* way to save a configuration for any tool. And to add the icing on the cake, you can sort saved presets so that the palette presents only the tool you want to use and the permutations you've created and saved. This means, for example, that if you want the orange-tipped square 43-pixel brush tip, you do not have to wallow through presets that refer to Lasso customizations or Eraser tools.

A Real-World Tool Preset Palette Simulation

In the steps to come, you'll create a brush, specify a color for it, work on a design, and then pretend you take four months off to go to Barbados (*in your* dreams!), only to come back to a layout that needs the exact same brush, color and all. Oh, what to do? What to *do*???

You do the following steps…

Working with the Tool Preset Palette

1. Create a brush tip you can call your own (or pick a different name than "your own"), and pick a color, any color, from the color selection boxes on the toolbox. See Figure 2.42—you remember this stuff from the previous section.

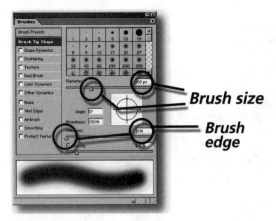

Figure 2.42   Create a brush tip that you're certain you will totally forget about after some rest and recreation.

2. Click the Tool Presets picker (it's the first icon on the left in the Options bar). When the Tool Presets picker opens, click the Create new tool preset icon near

the upper-right of the palette (it's the icon that looks like a page of paper that's partly turned over). In the resulting New Tool Preset dialog box, type a name for the brush (such as **Sunny soft brush**), check the Include Color checkbox, and then press Enter (Return) to close the dialog box.

3. Open the icons.psd image from the Examples/Chap02 folder on the Companion CD. Double-click the Gluntwert title and rename this layer **Icon** once more. Then make a pathetic design, such as the one the author created, using the brush, as shown in Figure 2.43.

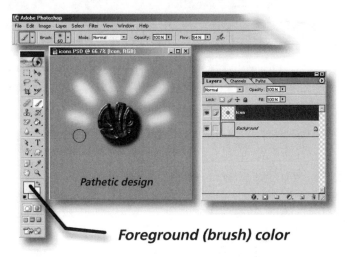

Foreground (brush) color

Figure 2.43   This is more than just a custom brush you are using—it also is a saved brush, for use a little later or after your vacation in Barbados.

4. Dash off on vacation, leaving no one responsible for watering your office flowers, and then come back to the office, totally relaxed, blood pressure on the floor someplace, barely a pulse, and then discover that the sunny icon design you made needs revision. Blood pressure rises.

5. Open the Tiffletrom.psd image from the Examples/Chap02 folder on the Companion CD. Mr. Tiffletrom now owns the company, and instead of a round logo, he wants a square one with the sunny paint strokes. Oh, wow…big changes, huh?

6. Click the Brush tool, click the Tool Presets icon (you remember where it is after vacation?), check the Current Tool Only checkbox, and choose Sunny soft brush, as illustrated in Figure 2.44.

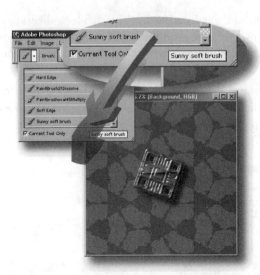

Figure 2.44   Photoshop has an excellent memory. So do elephants, but elephants
don't come with a Tool Presets palette.

7. Complete the design, as shown in Figure 2.45. Mr. Tiffletrom is so impressed with
your stamina, sheer raw talent, and vigor that he gives you a promotion and
makes you the head of the Barbados office.

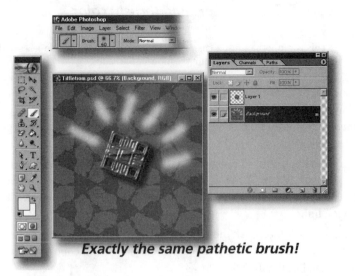

Figure 2.45   The completed design, which radiates creativity, is your ticket to
Happily Ever After.

End of fairy tale.

Let's move on to the Actions palette. We've got some good news for users who need the Brightness/Contrast menu but are sick and tired of going to the main menu and then doing the sub-menu shuffle to reach this command.

Using Actions to Add Keyboard Shortcuts

After some tough Photoshop artistic challenges, you might already know how valuable keyboard shortcuts are—especially ones such as F7, which is used to hide and display the Layers palette.

Well, Contrast/Brightness was demoted a few versions ago, and this author uses it a lot for special effects (such as those found in some of these screen figures). The drawback is that I could have a birthday while wading through Image, Adjustments, Brightness/Contrast…accessing it from the main menu just takes me too far away from my work.

So let's invent a Photoshop Action that assigns Brightness/Contrast to F11, a key few people use in Photoshop.

Actions for Keyboard Shortcuts

1. Open the Actions palette from the Window menu. Click the menu flyout button (circled in Figure 2.46), and then choose New Action. In the New Action dialog box, type **Brightness/Contrast** in the Name field, leave Set at its default, assign the action a function key (F11), and then click Record.

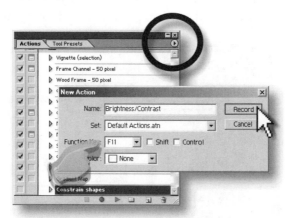

Figure 2.46   Record an action that is activated with a function key.

2. Click the menu flyout button again on the Actions palette, and then choose Insert Menu Item, as shown in Figure 2.47. The dialog box stays onscreen.

Figure 2.47   Later you'll learn to create really fancy Actions, but for now, we want Brightness/Contrast to pop up at a keystroke!

3. Follow the numbered items in Figure 2.48. The first step is to reconfirm the Insert Menu item. As you can see in this figure, you need to mouse your way to the desired command. Choose Image, Adjustments (item 2).

4. Click Brightness/Contrast (item 3), and then click OK in the Insert Menu dialog box (item 4).

5. Finally, click the STOP button on the bottom of the Actions palette (item 5). You're done. In fact, you can close the Actions palette now, and the command will work!

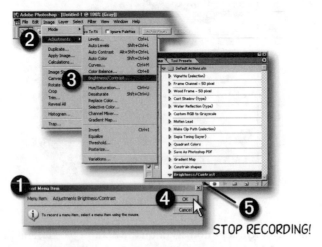

Figure 2.48   A few simple steps make the Brightness/Contrast command pop up when you press F11.

Coming up: Selections versus masks. Don't put your money on a winner yet...

What's the Difference Between Selections and Masks?

Adobe Systems sometimes leaves this author speechless because of the way in which things are named. For example, a Quick Mask, which is an overlay you paint on image areas to declare "I want this area selected," can mark either a selected area or a masked area.

It really doesn't matter that Photoshop has tacked the word *mask* onto at least 15 things that can produce selections in addition to masking. Quick Mask can both protect from editing the area you mask over (in which case, it's truly a Quick Mask) and make areas you tint on top of the image *available* for editing (in which case, you are defining a selection and not a mask).

You will thank me for this later if you are just coming to Photoshop. Let's perform a short series of steps to make sure that when you want a selection, you get a selection, and when you want a mask, you get a mask.

Quick Masking…and Quick Selecting

1. Open the Daisy.tif image in the Examples/Chap02 folder on the Companion CD. Make certain that on the toolbox, the foreground color selection box is black (press D for the default colors, and if necessary, press X to switch black to the foreground).

2. Figure 2.49 shows a magnified view of the Quick Mask icon. To its left is the Standard Editing mode button, the button that will most frequently be selected as you work. Double-click the Quick Mask button. The Quick Mask Options dialog box appears.

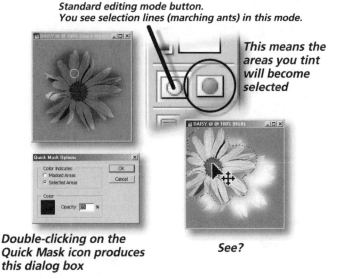

Figure 2.49   With the Quick Mask tool configured this way, it's actually a "Quick Selection" tool.

3. Click the Selected Areas button in the dialog box, and then press Enter (Return). Now, only places where you apply tint over the image will be selected when you return the image to Standard editing mode (the act of double-clicking the Quick Mask icon automatically puts the image into Quick Mask mode after the dialog box is closed).

4. Get out a small round, soft tip to tint the daisy (precision is not an issue here—we're not master maskers yet). Paint over the daisy, and then click the Edit in Standard Mode button on the toolbox (or press Q to toggle Quick Mask on and off). A marquee appears around the daisy. Click the Move tool on the toolbox, and then you can move the daisy around. Stop when the novelty fades.

5. Okay. Go to the File menu and choose Revert (and let's start fresh again). Alt(Opt)+click the Quick Mask icon. As you can see in Figure 2.50, the icon reverses coloration, so the *outside* of the circle has tone (we've changed the preference to "Masked Areas"). In Selected Areas mode, the circle had a tone on the icon.

Figure 2.50   In "true" Quick Mask mode, everywhere you tint is protected from editing.

6. Paint again, this time filling the daisy with tint. When you've finished, click the Edit in Standard Mode icon. You will see the daisy outlined with "marching ants," but the edge of the image has ants, too. This means the background is selected, and the daisy truly is masked.

Wanna prove it to yourself?

7. Choose the Gradient tool, then choose a nice, complex, Chrome preset gradient, and then drag the tool in the image window. Surprised? Hope not. The background accepts the gradient while the daisy is still all nice and neat because it was *not* selected.

Pin the daisy on your lapel or on a bucket hat, and keep Photoshop open.

There's one last stop we need to make to consider through our examination of things that can be changed to suit your tastes. Guess what? Photoshop has a spell checker now.

Spell Checking and Photoshop

Photoshop's spell checker is sort of like a tasting spoon at Baskin-Robbins. The checker is serviceable, but for heavy-duty text formatting, spell checking, and other word processing tasks—you should use a word processor.

Still, it's nice to be able to do spot checks in Photoshop, and the following steps will show you how to check the spelling in your creations.

Performing Spell Checking and Increasing the Number of Words

1. Open the GrandFunc.tif image from the Examples/Chap02 folder of the Companion CD.

2. Deliberately mistype **Grand Func Railway** (two lines of text and a 48 point ornamental font will do fine).

3. Highlight **Func** and then choose Edit, Check Spelling. A box pops up that suggests word alternatives. You pick the correct spelling from the Check Spelling dialog box, and then click Change, as shown in Figure 2.51.

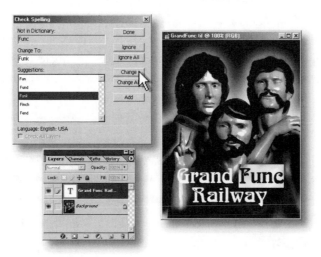

Figure 2.51   Photoshop's spell checker can prevent large mishaps unless the Oxford English Dictionary is your "light reading" at bedtime.

4. You receive a call. The band has changed its name to The Brawloney Brothers. Fair enough. You type this name in the image window, and as part of a well-oiled routine, you summon the spell checker. Guess what? Brawloney is not in the spell checker, mostly because it's not a word. But you're going to be doing business with the band for a while, so you need to add Brawloney to the spell checker for future checking (see Figure 2.52).

Figure 2.52   It's easy to customize Photoshop's spell checker.

Keep Photoshop open and go see the Brawloney Bros.—or whatever they're calling themselves this week. I hear they're opening for McCartney in Chicago in a few months...

The Well

If you're one of those users who is comfortable with 800×600 video resolution, you may never see Photoshop's palette well. It's on the far upper right of the screen at 1024×768 and higher, and it's a place where you can drop palettes.

Palettes stay neatly arranged and you can display a palette from the well by clicking on its title (see Figure 2.53).

Figure 2.53   The Well is available only at 1024 × 768 video resolutions and higher.

Well. I believe we've come to the end of the preferences, options, and customization of Photoshop. Admittedly, it was a quick look <g>, but you have your hands on important stuff you need to complete a lot of the tutorials in this book. What you learned here will also help you work quicker, smarter, and with a greater sense of self-satisfaction.

Summary

Like the fire extinguisher on a public building wall reads—in case of emergency, break open this chapter. We created this chapter for you so that Photoshop tasks would go more smoothly. Yes we are opinionated, but a strong point of view is always beneath reproach <g>. The number of sections we covered are too numerous to recap here, but if you take away a sense of confidence after reading this (or even referring to it as you plunge into the later parts of the book), then it's been as worthwhile to you as it's been writing it.

Next stop is selections. At last count, there are 14 ways to select something in Photoshop, which means parts of the tutorial images we toss at you *have* to have one means or another for being selected! Selecting image areas is at least 50% of the power of Photoshop, so let's move right ahead and get your hands on a tremendous piece of learning power.

Chapter 3

Harnessing the
Power of Selections

All photo-editing work can be lumped into

two general categories: You are working on

the entire image (removing a color cast,

cropping, rotating, and so on) or you are

working on a portion of an image, perhaps removing backgrounds from people or objects, creating special effects like a soft focus background, or doing any of a host of other common tasks. Photoshop provides an assortment of tools for selecting the portion of the image with which you want to work.

Basic Selections 101 with Lab

The selection tools in Photoshop have the unique purpose of defining the part of the image you want to use. The area you define is called a *selection,* and all the tools you use to make the selections are known as *selection tools.* Simple enough, eh? The number of selection tools may not seem so simple at first, however; in fact, if you are new to Photoshop, the choices may seem overwhelming. This chapter will help you get a handle on which tool to use in different circumstances and show you basically how the tools work.

The concept of selection is something we work with all the time—perhaps without knowing it. If you have ever used a stencil in Photoshop, you have used a selection. The stencil allows you to apply paint to one part of the material while protecting the rest. Another example of a selection that is closer to home (literally) is using masking tape to mask off the parts of a room where you don't want to paint (which for me would be the whole room). Selections in Photoshop act just like a stencil or masking tape when it comes to applying an effect to a selected part of an image. Now that you've got the concept, let's look at the most basic of the selection tools—the Marquee tools.

Introducing the Marquee Tools

The Marquee tools, shown in Figure 3.1, are used to create selections in the shapes of rectangles, ellipses, rows, and columns that are 1-pixel wide.

The best way to see how these tools work is to use them to create some neat stuff. So, let's jump right in and make a poster for the National Wildflower Center in Austin, Texas. Our theme for this program is the World of Texas Bluebonnets, and to make such a world, we'll use the Elliptical Marquee tool.

Figure 3.1   The Marquee tools provide the basic building blocks for many selections.

Creating a World of Flowers

1. Open BluebonnetField.tif from the Examples/Chap03 folder on the Companion CD.

2. Select the Elliptical Marquee tool from the toolbox by placing the cursor over the Marquee tools icon and clicking the small black triangle in the lower-right corner of the button. This opens the tool selection.

For this next step, make sure that the Info palette is visible. If it's not, go to the Window menu and choose Info. This enables you to use the Width and Height numbers in the lower-right corner as a guide while you carry out the next step. Your circle doesn't have to be the exact same size, but the circle I created was about 286 (pixels). If your measurements currently aren't in pixels, you can click the plus symbol (+) in the lower-left corner of the Info palette and choose Pixels from the drop-down list.

3. Place the cursor near the center of the photograph. Click and hold the mouse button, and press Alt(Opt)+Shift; then drag the mouse outward to form a circle roughly in the position shown in Figure 3.2. When the circle looks about the right size, release the mouse button and the keys. The edge of the selection is marked by a flashing black-and-white marquee that has come to be called "marching ants."

Note

Adding to the Marquee Tools   Holding down the Alt(Opt) key while making a selection with the Marquee tools starts the selection in the center and moves outward from there. Adding the Shift key constrains the Marquee tool to a perfect circle (or a perfect square, in the case of the Rectangular Marquee tool). Also, if you would like to move the selection to a better position, just click and drag it to relocate the selection (or use the arrow keys to move it). This only works as long as the Marquee tool is active.

Figure 3.2 Hold down Alt(Opt)+Shift, and drag out a circle. The figure has the selection
highlighted to make it easier to see, but your own selection will not have
this highlight.

4. Press Ctrl(⌘)+C to copy the selection. Only the contents of the selection will be copied to the clipboard.

5. Press Ctrl(⌘)+V to paste the selection onto a new layer (the selection marquee disappears). If it is not already showing, open the Layers palette (F7) to see the new layer. Because you are going to need the selection again (it was lost when you used the Paste command), go to the Select menu, choose Reselect, and the marquee returns. You need this selection before applying the next filter; otherwise, the shape of the sphere will distort.

6. Now go to the Filter menu, choose Distort, Spherize, and use the default setting of 100%. The bluebonnets have been distorted as though they were in a glass ball (as shown in Figure 3.3).

Figure 3.3   The selection allows the Spherize filter to be applied to the top layer without distorting the shape.

7. Press Ctrl(⌘)+H to temporarily hide (or turn off) the visibility of the selection marquee to make this next step a little easier.

Tip

Hiding and Displaying Marching Ants   When you press Ctrl(⌘)+H to hide a selection, the selection is still active. If you need to see the selection again (to reassure yourself that it is still there), just press Ctrl(⌘)+H again to toggle the visibility back on.

8. Select the Dodge tool from the toolbox. Right-click (Macintosh: hold Ctrl and click), and then choose the soft 100-pixel brush, set the Range to Midtones, and Exposure to 50%. To make this look like a glass sphere, you need to lighten the edges. The trick to this effect is to apply just the edge of the brush inside of the selection edge. We expect to see a little more light reflected near the top upper-left part of the sphere, so apply additional strokes of the Dodge tool here (see Figure 3.4).

Figure 3.4 Applying the Dodge tool along the edges defines the edge of the selection.

9. Press Ctrl(⌘)+D to deselect the image. (Even though the selection is hidden, it is still active, which means that you need to deselect it when you are finished with the selection.) On the Layers palette, click the Background layer to make it the active layer. Go to the Filter menu and choose Blur, Guassian Blur with a Radius of 2.0. Click OK. Click Layer 1 to make this the active layer. Press V to switch to the Move tool and drag the wildflower sphere to the right of the image, as shown in Figure 3.5.

10. On the Layers palette, click the Background layer once more. Click the Create new fill or adjustment layer icon at the bottom of the Layers palette and choose Hue/Saturation. In the Hue/Saturation dialog box, check Colorize and change the settings to Hue 36, Saturation 25, and Lightness 0 (see Figure 3.6). Click OK. Now you should have a brightly colored sphere of bluebonnets on top of what appears to be a sepia tone photograph. If you would like to add just a slight amount of color to the Background layer, lower the Opacity for the Hue/Saturation adjustment layer to 60%.

Figure 3.5   You can use the Move tool to position the finished "wildflower world" anywhere in the image.

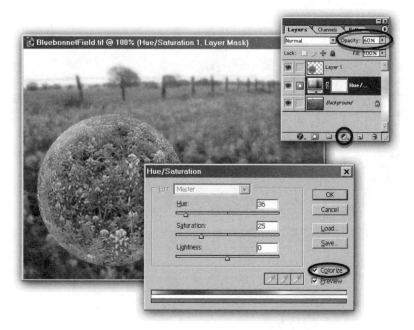

Figure 3.6   The Hue/Saturation command makes the background look like a sepia print.

Now you'll place a title on this poster.

11. Press D for default colors. Press X to switch white to the foreground. Choose the Horizontal Type tool from the toolbox. On the Options bar, choose Impact as the font at 48 points, and select Right align text. Click in the document and type **A World of TEXAS Bluebonnets** (pressing Enter once after typing the word *of* and again after the word *TEXAS*). Hold the Ctrl(⌘) key to toggle to the Move tool and reposition the text if needed (see Figure 3.7). When the text is the way you want it, press Ctrl(⌘)+Enter (Return) to commit the text to a layer. Click the triangle in the upper-right corner of the Layers palette and choose Flatten Image.

12. Go to the Filter menu and choose Render, Lens Flare. In the Lens Flare dialog box, choose the default settings of 100% for Brightness and 50-300mm Zoom for Lens Type. In the Flare Center preview box, drag the marker to position it, as shown in Figure 3.8.

Figure 3.7 Add text and then flatten the image to prepare for the next step.

Figure 3.8 This wildflower poster looks a lot better in color.

Tips and Tricks Using Marquee Tools

So what did you do in the preceding exercise? You used several key combinations to extend the use of the Marquee tools. These combinations are referred to as *modifier keys.* This is what they do:

- **Shift key.** When you press Shift *after* you press the mouse button, it constrains the Ellipse tool to a circle and the Rectangle marquee to a square. If you don't use Shift, getting a selection that is a perfect square or circle is nearly impossible.

- **Alt(Opt) key.** Pressing Alt *after* you press the mouse button makes the marquee expand outward from the center. If you don't use this option, the marquee is created diagonally from the upper-left to the lower-right. Centering the selection without Alt can take forever.

Tip

Position a Selection While Making a Selection At any point while creating a selection (without lifting your finger off the mouse), you can press the spacebar to reposition the selection marquee by dragging it with the mouse. Release the spacebar, and continue to create the marquee selection.

The Marquee tool modifier keys are unique in that the action they perform is relative depending on whether they are pressed before or after the mouse button is pressed. If the modifier key is pressed *before* the mouse button, the action changes.

The Marquee Tool Options Bar

If this is the first time you have worked with Photoshop, you may think the Marquee tools are quite limited. After all, how often will you need to select a square, rectangle, ellipse, or circle? The truth is that you can create just about any shape imaginable using these tools if you learn how to use some of the features found on the Options bar (see Figure 3.9).

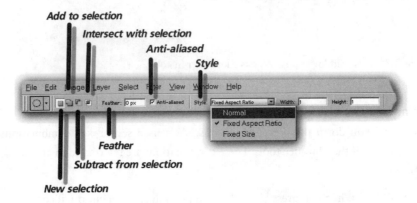

Figure 3.9   The Options bar adds more capability to the Marquee tools.

Here is a brief breakdown of what the items on the Options bar will do. You can refer to Figure 3.9 as the items are explained:

- **New Selection.** When you select this option, a new selection is created. If there is an existing selection, selecting this option cancels out the existing selection and replaces it with the new one you create. There are modifier keys that will override this (which are covered later in this section).

- **Add to Selection.** This option adds to an existing selection. If you have made a selection and would like to add to the selection without using the icons on the Options bar, you can press Shift to get the same result.

- **Subtract from Selection.** If you have an active selection and would like to subtract from that selection, you can select this option (or use the modifier Alt(Opt) key).

- **Intersect with Selection.** If you choose this option when a selection is active, the result will be the intersecting areas of two selections. The key combination that can produce the same results is Alt(Opt)+Shift.

Note

Boolean Operations   These modifications to existing selections are sometimes called *Boolean* operations, named after George Boole (1815-1864), a British mathematician who invented a simple way to describe algebraic operations using the terms *and*, *but not*, and others. Unfortunately, a digital device was needed to carry out the Boolean operations, and that was not to happen for more than 100 years! Nonetheless, Boole was named a fellow of the Royal Society in 1857.

- **Feather.** This option allows you to give the selections a soft edge by blurring and building a transition boundary between the selection and surrounding pixels. This also gives the selection corners a rounded appearance because the greater the number, the more you blur (or soften) the hard-edge results of the selection.

- **Anti-aliased.** This options smoothes the jagged edges of a selection by creating transition pixels between the edge and background.

- **Style.** There are three styles, as you see here:

  - **Normal.** This option enables you to determine the size of your selection as you drag.

  - **Fixed Aspect Ratio.** This option enables you to fix a ratio for your selection. For example, if you want the selection to be twice as high as it is wide, you would enter 2 in the Height and 1 in Width.

  - **Fixed Size.** This option enables you to enter values for Height and Width to create a precise selection (when the dimensions are known).

The Marquee tools interact with existing selections in four different ways. The default setting for the Marquee tools is *New Selection*. The ones you will use most often to interact with existing selections are the *Add to* and *Subtract from* settings. By using the Marquee tools in combination with these settings, you can make almost any irregular shape imaginable. The last setting, *Intersect with selection*, is a little unusual in that when you drag it over an existing selection, only the part of the selection that the two selections have in common will remain. Don't worry about this one for now; there won't be too many situations in which you'll need it—but that doesn't mean you shouldn't experiment. Once you understand what it can do, you might discover a time when this option fits perfectly with what you want to accomplish. That one time will make you glad you gave it a chance.

Feathering the Selections

Until now, we have been considering selections that have a hard, defined edge. The circle mask used in the previous exercise had an anti-aliased option. Anti-aliasing gives an edge a smooth look as opposed to a jagged bitmapped look. But don't get the smooth look of anti-aliasing confused with feathering. *Feathering* builds a transition along the edges, in effect blurring the edges.

You will want to give a selection a soft edge in many different circumstances. One reason might be that you are removing a person or a thing from a photograph and placing it into another photograph. Using a feathered selection enables you to blend the subject into the picture more smoothly. You need to be careful with the amount of feathering you apply to the mask, however. Usually, just a few pixels are sufficient. If you put in a large amount of feathering, the object looks like it is glowing or has fur.

Figure 3.10 was created using Photoshop's selection tools. After I made the selection, I applied three different settings of feathering and copied the image to the clipboard each time. Of the three copies of Michelle, the one on the left was made using a selection that was not feathered; the middle one used a 3-pixel feather, and the one on the right had a feathering value of 9 pixels. Although the higher feathering setting in the image on the right loses tiny detail in her hair, it gives it a desirable softening effect; but remember that this smoothing effect on hair (as in this example) isn't always the effect you might be after.

Note

Feathering Is Relative   The feather effect produced by any particular setting is controlled by the size of the image. For example, I took the original photograph of Michelle on my digital camera at a high-resolution setting, and as a result the image is pretty large. On an image with a greater resolution, a 3-pixel feather would have less of an effect. Conversely, a small resolution file might find the 3-pixel feather setting to be too much.

Although you can do many things with the Marquee selection tools, they serve a pretty basic function. When you need to create an irregularly shaped selection, it is time to take on the Lasso tools.

Figure 3.10   Use of feathering produces much softer edges when a subject is copied out
of a photograph.

Rounding Up the Lasso Tools

Located under the Marquee tools in the toolbox, the Lasso tools are a collection of three
different tools you can use to draw both straight and freehand edges when making an
irregularly shaped selection. The three tools are as follows:

- Lasso tool
- Polygonal Lasso tool
- Magnetic Lasso tool

Unlike the Marquee tools, which produce closed shapes, the Lasso tools let you draw
a meandering path around a subject and return to the beginning point to finish the
selection. If you release the mouse button or double-click it (depending on which tool
you are using), Photoshop will make a straight line back to the starting point to complete
the selection. So unless this result is your intention, make sure that you return to the
starting point when using the Lasso tools.

These tools all act similarly. In the grand scheme of things, the Lasso tool is designed to
draw freehand selections, and the Polygonal Lasso tool creates a selection made up of a
series of straight lines. If you want to create a selection that combines both straight and
rounded edges, you can toggle between these two tools by pressing the Alt(Opt) key
while keeping your mouse button pressed. You might want to practice switching between

these two tools because mastering this trick can come in pretty handy. If you start out making a freehand selection with the Lasso tool, keep the mouse button clicked as you drag. When you want to switch to making straight edges in the middle of the selection process, stop dragging (but keep the mouse button pressed), and press the Alt(Opt) key. As long as you keep holding the Alt(Opt) key, you are free to release the mouse button and click only on corners that make up the straight line. If you want to return to the Freehand Lasso tool, stop and press the mouse button; then release the Alt(Opt) key and continue dragging. Whew! Trust me—it's a lot easier to perform than it is to describe!

Note

Polygon Definition   According to the dictionary, the noun *polygon* is defined as any multi-sided figure. Polygon is *not* a dead parrot ("Polly gone"—ya gotta *work* with me here). Therefore, the Polygonal Lasso tool is appropriately named.

The Magnetic Lasso tool will automatically detect the edge of an object for you, on one condition: There must be a high contrast between the color of the object you are selecting and the background color surrounding the object. When the colors are similar, this tool might not work as anticipated; otherwise, it can save you a lot of work. If this condition applies to a part of the object but not the entire object, you can press and hold the Alt(Opt) key to toggle between the Magnetic Lasso tool and the Lasso tool, which allows you to finish the selection freehand.

Don't be intimidated by complicated selections. You might think, "Man, I couldn't sign my name with a mouse to save my life." You're not alone. Very few of us can. That's why Photoshop has made so many ways available to create a selection. In addition, all the methods available can be combined to make selecting something as easy as possible. So switch selection tools, switch selection *methods*—whatever works. And there are many ways to make it work.

Now, if it is still important to you to sign your name digitally, you might want to consider using a graphic tablet instead of a mouse. If you want to look into these handy devices as an alternative, the industry standard for graphic tablets is Wacom Technology (www.wacom.com). Does this mean you absolutely need a graphics tablet to make a Lasso selection? Of course not! It is completely possible to make irregular selections with a mouse. Not only is it possible, at least three of this book's authors do it all the time.

Getting the Best Selections (in the Least Amount of Time)

Whether I'm doing art layout for work or for community projects (read: free), I have spent the past 10 years making selections. In that time, I have come up with a short list of dos and don'ts that might save you some time and trouble. Ready? Read on.

Do Make a First Rough Cut Selection

If the object you want to select is large and has a lot of meandering edges, make a ballpark selection first. You can take two routes with this possible solution:

- You can make a general selection just *outside* the object (precision is not necessary at this point). Then put the selection on a separate layer and use a layer mask to paint away what you don't need. Layer masks are very forgiving. What I mean by this is that when you are working in Layer Mask mode, mistakes are easily fixed. You paint with black to remove unwanted parts of the selection, and if you make a mistake, paint with white to correct it.

- The other choice is to make a general selection just *inside* the object (again precision is not crucial), and then go into Quick Mask mode. Pressing Q toggles you in and out of Quick Mask mode. You create a selection by painting. You will see a tinted color (the default is red) appear where ever your selection is being made. Don't worry, you are not really painting tint on your object; the tint appears to let you see where your selection will be. Similar to the Layer Mask, you paint with black to apply the tinted color, and paint with white to correct mistakes. Your goal is to add the tinted paint to finish the selection you started. This is a good place to try combining selection tools. When you press Q again to toggle out of Quick Mask mode, you will see your tinted paint change to a selection (or marching ants).

Zoom and Move

Set the Zoom to Actual Pixels to get an up-close-and-personal look at your image and do the fine-point editing you need to do. Use either Ctrl(⌘)+Alt(Opt)+0 (zero) or double-click the Zoom tool in the toolbox. Yeah, I know, if the image is large; it no longer fits on the screen, but that doesn't matter. There are several ways to move around when this close, but probably the best way I know is to press the spacebar, and the currently selected tool toggles to the Hand tool (as long as you keep the spacebar pressed). This is really a lifesaver.

You've magnified your view of an area to see it better. You are drawing a selection and you find that you have come to an edge of the document window. You need to move past the edge of the document window, but don't want to lose the selection you've started (you're still in the middle of making this selection). When that happens, press the space-bar, drag the image to expose more of the subject on the screen and let go of the space-bar to pop back to your selection tool. Then simply finish where you left off.

Adding Some and Taking Some

Using the Add to selection and Subtract from selection modes, you can begin to shape the selection to fit the subject you are trying to isolate. Here is a trick that will save you time when you are doing this part. First, instead of clicking the buttons on the Options bar, use the key modifiers to change between modes. Pressing Shift changes to the Add to selection mode and pressing Alt(Opt) changes to the Subtract from selection mode.

Just remember that these modifier keys must be pressed *before* you click the mouse. If you use these modifier keys often, you will find that using them becomes second nature. You'll be surprised by how quickly you will be able to work with one hand on the keyboard and the other on the mouse. You'll soon know instinctively which key to press without even looking—kind of like touch-typing.

Also, if you know you'll be using the Add to selection and Subtract from selections frequently, you can choose one of these options on the Options bar. This way you need to use only the modifier key for the mode that you didn't pick to switch to the other mode.

Get in Close

On some areas, you may need to zoom in at levels even greater than 100%. Photoshop enables you to zoom up to 1600%, which must be for selecting microbes and stray elec-trons. Try to remember two more shortcuts: Ctrl(⌘)+plus and Ctrl(⌘)+minus. These shortcuts allow you to zoom in and out of the document quickly. The only problem is that these shortcuts have become so instinctive for me—I've become *so* used to using them—that it never fails to disappoint and frustrate me when I press Ctrl(⌘)+plus while in Microsoft Word, and it *doesn't* zoom in on the document.

Now and again return to Fit to Screen just to keep a perspective on the whole image. Speaking of keeping a perspective—when taking the time to refine your selection, keep in mind some questions to ask yourself to gauge how much time to invest in this selection. Here are some examples of real situations that should help you gauge the degree of exactness you want in making your selection:

- Are the edge colors of the object you are selecting almost identical to the background colors? If they are roughly the same color, investing a lot of time producing a detailed selection doesn't make much sense because a feathered edge will work just fine.

- Will you be resizing the final image? If you are going to be making the current image larger, every detail will stick out like the proverbial sore thumb. This means that any extra time you spend to make the selection as exact as possible will pay big benefits. If you are going to reduce the size of the subject, a lot of tiny detail will be lost when it is resized so you don't need to invest a lot of time in the selection.

- Is this a paid job or a freebee? Creating a complex selection is a time-consuming process. I once spent nearly half a day on a single selection. You may not want to let the payment issue be the sole determining factor, but keep in mind that free, complicated jobs and paying, complicated jobs both can take the same amount of invested time.

Let's Lasso Somebody

Okay, enough theory. Take a soda break if you need one, and when you return refreshed, we'll put some of this theory into practice and make some selections. The next exercise involves a groomsman named Jon in a cluttered church office wearing a ridiculously overpriced rental tuxedo. If his mother is going to frame this photograph, the background must be replaced with something a little less cluttered.

Combining Selection Methods

1. Open the TuxedoJon.psd file from the Examples/Chap03 folder on the
   Companion CD.

Note

Controlling the Magnetic Lasso The Magnetic Lasso tool can be a great timesaver
when it comes to making selections. Essentially you move the tool along the edge of the
area you want to select. A high-contrast, well-defined edge works best. On edges that
are poorly defined—when the colors inside and outside the edge are close to the same
color—the tool needs a little help from you.

Using the tool is quite simple. Click once at the point where you want to begin the
selection. This point is called a *fastening point*. Now move the tool (slowly and without
holding down the mouse button) along the edge. Fastening points will appear along the
edge of the selection as the computer tries to determine where the edge is. At some
point, the computer will guess wrong. When it does make a wrong guess, stop and
press Backspace. Each time you press the key, Photoshop removes the last point on
the selection. Continue to do this until you get to a point on the selection back on the
actual edge. You can try adding fastening points again, but usually when the Magnetic tool
guesses wrong, there is either a low-contrast edge or there is something nearby (not on
the edge) that is pulling the tool away from the edge.

At this point, you have several choices. You can change the settings in the Options
bar and attempt to click your way through it—but this is not the best alternative.
Instead, try clicking to create fastening points where you would like them to go, or
press the Alt(Opt) key to switch temporarily to the Lasso tool; and while pressing the
mouse button, drag the mouse along the edge. If the edge confusing the Magnetic Lasso
is composed basically of straight lines, you can switch to the Polygonal tool by holding
down the Ctrl(⌘) key and then click from point to point.

2. Choose the Magnetic Lasso tool and pick an area of high contrast between Jon
   and the background. Click at the edge of Jon and the background (his tuxedo
   is a good starting place). After you click, release the mouse button and simply
   drag a line around him. When you reach Jon's hair, or another area of low
   contrast, you may find it easier to define this area if you hold down Alt(Opt)
   to toggle to the Lasso tool and click and drag to make a selection near this area.
   Release Alt(Opt) when you're back to high contrast areas. Don't worry if your
   selection has mistakes (see Figure 3.11). You will fix those later.

If you would like to do this exercise without all the work of making a selection, you can
use a ready-made selection. Step 3 explains how to make use of this selection. Otherwise,
skip Step 3, and continue on to Step 4 to refine the selection.

Figure 3.11   Using the Magnetic Lasso tool, you can quickly make an initial selection of Jon from the background.

3. *Optional:* Click the Channels tab to view the Channels palette and Ctrl(⌘)+click the Tight Jon Outline channel. A selection of Jon will load. If the marching ant selection appears around the edges of the document, press Ctrl(⌘)+Shift+I to invert the selection. Click the Layers tab to move back to the Layers palette. Skip to Step 6.

4. Press D (default colors). Click the Quick Mask mode icon on the bottom of the toolbox. If the red tint color is not on Jon (but on the background instead), Alt(Opt)+click the Edit in Quick Mask Mode icon below the color boxes on the toolbox to switch the tint to Jon.

5. Press B to switch to the Brush tool. On the Options bar, choose a soft round 5-pixel brush. Mode should be set at Normal, and Opacity and Flow should be at 100%. Press Ctrl(⌘)+plus sign to zoom in so that you can get a good look at the edges where Jon meets the background. Press the spacebar to toggle to the Hand tool when you need to maneuver around the image as you work. With black as the foreground color, paint in areas of Jon that might have been missed. Press X to switch to white as the foreground color and paint over mistakes or areas of the background that were included in the selection process. The goals are to have Jon covered in red tint and to exclude the background (see Figure 3.12). Press X to switch back to black if needed. When you are satisfied with the selection (or the red tint area), press Q to exit Quick Mask mode and turn the red tint area back into a selection.

Figure 3.12   Use the Quick Mask mode to refine your selection.

One of the ways to emphasize the subject is to blur the background using Gaussian Blur. The problem with this approach is the background. It is so cluttered that by the time that you get it blurred enough to do the job, it looks sort of surreal. On top of that, Jon and the couch on his right are the same distance from the camera, so the perspective doesn't look right. For the best results, let's replace the background with a different one.

6. Press Ctrl(⌘)+J to move Jon to his own layer. Click the Background layer to make this the active layer. Open the Background.tif image from the Examples/Chap03 folder on the Companion CD. Position both documents so that you can see both (zoom out if necessary). Click the title bar of the Background.tif image to make it the active document. Hold down the Shift key and drag the Background layer into the TuxedoJon.psd document window (see Figure 3.13). Holding down the Shift key will position the new background so that it is centered in the document window. Close the Background.tif image without saving any changes.

Figure 3.13   Shift+drag the new background image into the TuxedoJon document.

7. Wow, the photograph has now replaced the previous cluttered one. Actually, the old background is still there, simply hidden by the new background. To prove the original photo is still there, click the eye icon on Layer 2 to toggle the layer's visibility to off and the old background becomes visible. Click the Layer 2 eye icon again and the new background returns. Wait, it gets even better: select the Move tool in the toolbox and with the top layer selected, you can move the background image around to position it.

8. *Optional:* If you see on Jon areas of the old background that need to be removed, click Layer 1 (Jon's layer) to make it the active layer. Click the Add layer mask icon at the bottom of the Layers palette. The default colors (black and white) should still be your foreground and background colors. Press B for the Brush tool and use black to paint away unwanted areas. Press X to switch and use white to paint back any mistakes you might make. When Jon appears perfect, right-click (Macintosh: hold Ctrl and click) on the layer mask thumbnail and choose Apply Layer Mask to apply your changes (see Figure 3.14). Press Ctrl(⌘)+Shift+S if you would like to save this image to your hard disk.

Using a selection allows you to replace a background without losing the original background.

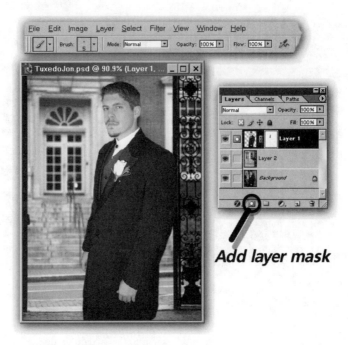

Figure 3.14 Use a layer mask if necessary to touch up any missed areas of old
background on Jon.

Saving and Loading Selections

In the previous exercise, you had the opportunity to load a selection that I had made
instead of creating it yourself. After making that particular selection (which took only
about five minutes), I saved it as part of the Photoshop file. If a selection is not saved as
a selection, it is lost as soon as the file is closed—even if the file is saved as a Photoshop
PSD file.

The Alpha Channel

So, how do you save a selection? If you invest a lot of time making a selection, you should
be able to save it. The process is simple—you use the Alpha channel. Sounds like a
science fiction channel on your local cable TV, doesn't it? The Alpha channel actually is

not a channel at all, but rather the name assigned for additional channels (in the Channels palette) used as general-purpose storage space in a graphics file. You can rename these channels, of course, but Photoshop will generate the Alpha channels in numerical order. The new channel is still technically referred to as an Alpha channel (or simply a channel) to differentiate it from the image mode channels (such as the Red, Green, and Blue channels found in an RGB document). How many Alpha channels can fit into a Photoshop file? Good question. How big a file can you live with? Adobe allows an image to have up to 24 channels (which includes color and Alpha channels), but be warned that the more channels saved in a file, the higher the overall file size of the document.

Saving a Selection

So let's get back to the original question of saving a selection. You can get the same result a couple of different ways.

One method is to go to the Select menu and choose Save Selection. This opens the Save Selection dialog box, shown as item 1 in Figure 3.15. If the image already has an existing channel, you can add your new selection to the existing one or you can save the selection to a new channel. Choose New and give the channel a descriptive name (as was done for the TuxedoJon image in the previous steps).

The second method is to view the Channels palette and click the Save selection as channel icon at the bottom of the Channels palette (or Alt(Opt)+click to view a dialog box that will allow you to name the channel). An Alpha channel with the selection information is generated (item 2 in the figure). Another way to rename an Alpha channel is to double-click the channel title to select the channel name; then type the new name (similar to renaming layers on the Layers palette).

You must save the image as a Photoshop (.psd) or a TIFF (.tif) file to save the channel information. If you don't save in one of these formats, Photoshop will do you the courtesy of giving you a single obscure warning message that there are some features that will not be saved in the format that you have chosen before you save in that format and lose the channel forever.

Figure 3.15   The Save Selection dialog box (item 1) or the Channels palette (item 2) will give you access to saving your selection as a channel.

Loading a Selection

When you open the file and want to access the saved selection from the channel, display the Channels palette and Ctrl(⌘)+click the channel with your selection, or open the Select menu and choose Load Selection. Open and pick the name of the Alpha channel that you or someone else tucked away into the image. This may surprise you, but many stock photography companies offer selections in their photos. Two of these companies are Photospin (www.photospin.com), a great online photo subscription service, and Heremera (www.hermera.com), which offers large collections of photo objects on CDs (lots and lots of CDs).

Magic Wand Tool Magic

The Magic Wand tool is a great selection tool for selecting areas that contain similar colors. You need to know a few things about this tool to produce the best results. This section helps you figure out how the tool works and then do some cool stuff with it.

The first fact about the Magic Wand tool is that it's not magic (surprised?). Until now, all the selection tools have involved either closed shapes or lassos that surround the area to be selected. The Magic Wand tool acts more like dropping a stone in a calm pool of water. The selection ripples outward from the starting point and continues radiating outward, selecting similar (and adjacent) colored pixels until it reaches pixels whose color or shade is noticeably different from the starting point. These pixels are not included in the selection. The next exercise helps you understand how the Magic Wand tool works.

In this exercise, you use the Magic Wand tool and a few other Photoshop features to create a photo composite from two photographs. In this case, I have an excellent exterior photo taken on a bright summer day in a rural Texas town, but I cannot see inside the building. I also have a great photo taken of a stairway in Ybor City, Florida. Our job will be to combine the two into a photo that can be used in a brochure for the purpose of increasing awareness of the problem of urban decay in the inner city.

Tip

Using the Magic Wand   One of the first problems you may discover with the Magic Wand tool is that clicking in an area doesn't always produce a uniform selection. Instead, you may get many little selection "islands" that pop up randomly within the initial selection. This happens because of a difference in color value from the starting point pixels and the pixels that make up these "islands."

You can resolve this issue several ways. You could Shift+click all of the individual "islands" with the Magic Wand tool until they are all included in the selection, but this is not the most efficient way to resolve the problem (although I'm embarrassed to admit that I am guilty of using this practice on occasion myself). Instead, try choosing Select, Similar; or try increasing the Tolerance setting, and reselect the same area again. The Contiguous option on the Options bar also acts in the same manner as Select, Similar when Contiguous is checked. The selection will stop when it bumps up against pixels of different colors. When Contiguous is unchecked, the selection will include *all* similar colors within the image or within the layer (which brings us to another option to consider). When the Use All Layers option is checked, the selection is based on the entire image. When Use All Layers is unchecked, the selection is based on the image information of the active layer only.

Keep in mind that sometimes the selection "islands" are a result of areas that are vastly different in color. In this case, (if you still want these "islands" to be included in the selection), choose a Marquee or Lasso tool, and hold down the Shift key (Add to selection) while making a selection shape over the "islands." That should resolve the issue.

Something else worth mentioning: when you use Select, Similar to add to a selection, another problem could arise. If the selection goes too far into the part of the image that you *don't* want selected (especially at the edge of an object), there is another trick to consider. Did you know that when you use the Similar command, Photoshop uses the current Tolerance setting to determine which pixels can be included in the selection? This means that after you do an initial selection with the Magic Wand tool (at a Tolerance level of 32, for example), you can set the Tolerance option to a lower value (perhaps somewhere between 4–8) before going to the Select, Similar menu option. Then colors that are much closer to the original starting point will be the only ones added to the original selection.

An Exercise in Pane (*Window*pane, That Is)

1. Open the OldWindows.tif file from the Examples/Chap03 folder on the Companion CD. From the toolbox, choose the Magic Wand tool.

2. On the Options bar, check the Contiguous option and set Tolerance to 30. Click in the center of a windowpane as shown in Figure 3.16. The selection instantly expands to select all of the black pixels in the pane. Because the Contiguous checkbox was checked, the selection stopped at the edge of the windowpane.

Figure 3.16   The Magic Wand tool quickly selects all the black pixels in the windowpane.

3. To select the rest of the windowpanes, go to the Select menu and choose Similar. Now Photoshop selects all the pixels in the image that are within the Tolerance setting. Because there are no other black pixels in the image, all of the pixels in the windowpanes are selected (see Figure 3.17).

4. Open the OldStairs.tif image from the Examples/Chap03 folder on the Companion CD. Press Ctrl(⌘)+A to select the entire image. Press Ctrl(⌘)+C to copy the image to the clipboard. Close the file without saving any changes.

5. With the OldWindows.tif image as the active document, choose Edit, Paste Into (or press Ctrl(⌘)+Shift+V). The photograph of the stairs now appears to be the view through the windowpanes, as shown in Figure 3.18. The Paste Into command created a new layer containing the new background image of the stairs, along with a layer mask that reveals only the areas that initially were selected. With the Move tool, you can move the stairs photograph around (this is slightly different from the method used to move a new background into the TuxedoJon exercise, earlier in this chapter). Now let's get even more creative.

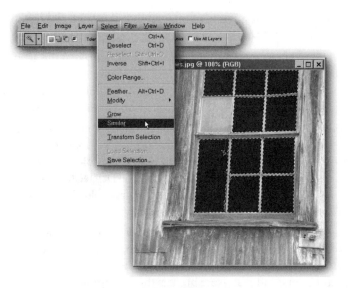

Figure 3.17 Use the Select, Similar command to add the remaining black windowpanes to the selection.

Figure 3.18 Using the Paste Into command, you are able to put stairs into the windows.

You have one pane of glass left, and, even though it is dirty, it should be at least a little transparent. To accomplish this, you need to create another selection.

6. On the Layers palette, click the Background layer to make it the active layer. If the Magic Wand tool is not active, press W to make it active. Change the Tolerance setting to 15 so that the selection will be limited to the pixels only in the dirty window pane. Click in the center of the dirty window pane.

7. To make the glass transparent, you'll modify the layer mask (on Layer 1). On the Layers palette, click the thumbnail of the layer mask on Layer 1. Click the foreground color of the toolbox, and change the color to a medium gray (R:129, G:129, B:129). Click OK. Press Alt(Opt)+Delete(Backspace) to fill the selection on the layer mask with this medium gray color. You learn more about layer masks after the exercise.

8. Dirty windows are never uniformly dirty, so for a touch of realism, press B to switch to the Brush tool. On the Options bar, choose an irregularly shaped brush, such as the Spatter 46-pixel brush. Set the Opacity to 35%. Press D for the default colors, and make sure black is the foreground color (if not, press X to switch black to the foreground). Click once or twice in the window pane to make it appear as though there are smudged areas that are dirtier than other areas (thus less transparent). Or maybe you would like to drag across the window pane with the brush. Experiment and use the History palette to undo any brush strokes you don't like. When you are satisfied with your results, press Ctrl(⌘)+D to deselect. The resulting image is shown in Figure 3.19.

9. As a finishing touch, you should make some tonal adjustments so both photographs look like they belong together. On the Layers palette, click the Background layer to make it the active layer. Click the Create new fill or adjustment layer icon at the bottom of the Layers palette and choose Levels. In the Levels dialog box, change the middle Input level from 1.00 to 0.45 (as shown in Figure 3.20) and click OK. If you would like, you can save this file to your hard drive as a .psd file to maintain the layers or flatten and save in a file format of your choice.

Figure 3.19   The dirty—but still transparent—window adds a realistic touch.

Figure 3.20   Use a Levels Adjustment layer to make a tonal adjustment to the background image. When you use an adjustment layer, you have the flexibility of changing or tweaking the settings for the Levels command at any time.

The Layer Mask

We have used a layer mask in two examples in this chapter, so we should talk a little about this marvelous feature. What *is* a layer mask? The layer mask shares a layer controlling the image on the layer it occupies, determining what is visible and what is not. Areas on the mask that are white are 100% opaque or visible, while areas of the mask that are black are completely transparent. So it figures that if we were to paint a brushstroke on the layer mask that was 50% gray, the contents of the layer under the brushstroke would be 50% transparent. In the last exercise, we made the glass semi-transparent by using a gray tone and painting part of the layer mask under the glass with brush tools set at an opacity of 35%. That resulted in the layer containing the glass to become 65% transparent (100% − 35% = 65%). Don't worry about the math. It isn't like I calculated the amount, I just tried several different settings (God bless Undo) until I found one I liked.

In the previous examples, we created a layer mask by either clicking the Add layer mask icon at the bottom of the Layers palette or by converting an existing selection into a layer mask with the Paste Into command.

Replacing an Overcast Sky

Taking photographs on an overcast day is always a mixed blessing. Because of the clouds, the illumination is diffused—and that's good. But these kinds of clouds also make the horizon of a landscape photograph uninteresting—which isn't so good. The Magic Wand tool can be used in this type of situation to make an easy selection of the overcast sky. After you have selected the sky, you can replace it with an artificial one created in Photoshop or with another photograph of a sky with clouds that appear more interesting. Let's move on and see how this is done.

Adding a Cloudy Sky

1. Open the dscn0349.tif image from the Examples/Chap03 folder on the Companion CD. Press W to switch to the Magic Wand tool. On the Options bar, set the Tolerance to 70 (this high setting ensures that all of the areas around the branches will be tightly selected). Click in the upper-right area of the sky. The selection marquee shown in Figure 3.21 shows the edges of the initial selection.

2. Choose Select, Similar. Wow! Now you have more selected than you wanted. That's easy to fix.

3. Choose the Rectangle Marquee tool from the toolbox. On the Options bar, click the Subtract from selection icon. Click and drag a marquee over all of the area in the lower part of the photograph, where there's no sky, as shown in Figure 3.22.

Figure 3.21 The Magic Wand tool is essential for replacing an overcast sky.

Figure 3.22 Use the Rectangle Marquee tool and the Subtract from selection option to correct the unwanted areas of the selection.

It may help to drag the corner of your document window to give yourself some working room when making this rectangular selection. Start the drag on the left edge (around the tops of the monuments). Don't forget to include the highest monuments near the trees in the marquee selection. If you need to reposition the selection as you create it, hold the spacebar while you continue to keep the mouse button pressed. This allows you to drag and reposition the marquee selection while you are creating it. When you have the marquee in the desired location (a tight fit above the monuments at the top edge), release the spacebar and continue dragging down to the lower-right corner of the document.

4. Change the foreground color to a believable sky blue color (R:104, G:148, B:238), and leave the background color white.

5. From the Filter menu, choose Render, Clouds. The result of the Clouds filter is generated randomly. In other words, the result differs each time it is used. Therefore, if you don't like the results on the first try, press Ctrl(⌘)+F to repeat the last filter used until you are pleased with the results. Another little-known trick is to hold down the Alt(Opt) key when you choose Filter, Render, Clouds— the result is a sharper, more severe rendering. When you have a result that pleases you, press Ctrl(⌘)+Shift+F to open the Fade dialog box (or go to the Edit menu and choose Fade Clouds). In the Fade dialog box, change the Opacity to 50%, set the Mode to Hard Light (you can also try the Pin Light mode as an interesting alternative—see Figure 3.23). The replacement sky looks realistic enough to pass as the real thing. Press Ctrl(⌘)+D to deselect. Press Ctrl(⌘)+Shift+S to save the file on your hard disk as WildFlowers.tif. Keep the file open for the next exercise.

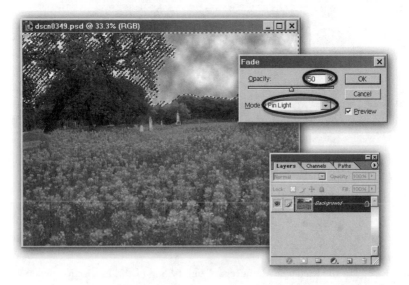

Figure 3.23   This may be an artificial sky, but it looks better than the original slate gray one it replaced.

Making a Quick Panorama Using Selections

Selections also can be used to move parts of images around quickly without using the clipboard. In this exercise, you are going to use the WildFlowers.tif image from the previous example and make a panorama image.

Creating a Panoramic View

1. If the WildFlowers.tif image from the previous exercise is not already open, open this file now.

2. Your first goal is to make the image a little wider. The background color should still be white. If it's not, press D for default colors (and press X if necessary to make white the background color). Right-click (Macintosh: hold Ctrl and click) the title bar of the image and choose Canvas Size. In the Canvas Size dialog box, check the Relative checkbox, change the Width to 665 (pixels), and change the Anchor point to the button on the middle-left (see Figure 3.24). Click OK and the photo now has a white rectangle on the right side.

> **Note**
>
> **Coloring Your New Canvas Size**   When the Canvas Size dialog box is used to enlarge the document dimensions, Photoshop will automatically use the background color to fill in the added space. This might be a helpful fact to keep in mind if you have a situation in which you intentionally want a specific color for the additional space added to the canvas size. The exception to this rule is that if there is no Background layer, the resulting expansion will then be transparent.

3. Choose the Rectangle Marquee tool from the toolbox. The Feather setting on the Options bar should be set to 0 pixels. Drag a selection beginning at the top of the original photograph to the right side of the farthest white monument and move down to the bottom right edge where the image ends and the new canvas begins (see Figure 3.25). Don't forget that you can hold down the spacebar as you make the selection to reposition the marquee selection close to the monument (then release the spacebar and continue to drag to complete the selection). Now the fun begins.

Figure 3.24 Use the Canvas Size dialog box to expand the Width of your document by adding three more inches to the right side.

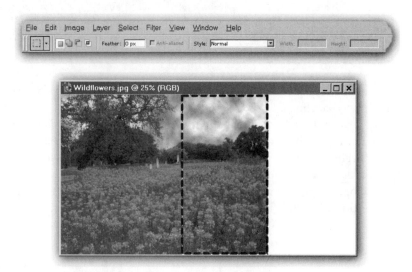

Figure 3.25 Make a selection with the Rectangular Marquee tool, similar to the one shown here.

4. Hold down the Ctrl(⌘)+Alt(Opt) keys and the cursor changes to a double arrow. Still holding these keys, click inside the selection and drag it until it fills the new area you created. If you have the dexterity, press the Shift key as you drag to restrain the movement horizontally; otherwise, you can adjust the position using the up and down arrow keys. The selection should look like Figure 3.26.

Figure 3.26   Works great, but the seam prevents it from looking real at this point.

5. Press Ctrl(⌘)+D to deselect. On the Options bar, change the Feather setting to 3 pixels. The goal here is to patch the seam area and to break up the repeating patterns. The most obvious repeated pattern is where the two selections overlapped. Drag a selection from the line of trees to the left of the break, as item 1 points out in Figure 3.27. Using the same technique you used in Step 3, Ctrl(⌘)+Alt(Opt)+click inside the selection and drag it over the break (as item 2 shows). When you're satisfied, press Ctrl(⌘)+D to deselect.

Don't forget to set the Feather option back to the default of 0 for the next time you use the Rectangular Marquee tool.

6. Look at the image and you will see more patterns that literally scream repair. To finish the job, choose the Clone Stamp tool from the toolbox. On the Options bar, choose the soft round 100-pixel brush (the remaining settings should be the defaults shown in Figure 3.28). Carefully pick areas that you want to use to patch the trouble areas, then press Alt(Opt), and click a sample area. Click in the trouble spots to repair the seams or any repetitious patterns you want to minimize. Press Alt(Opt) to sample new areas frequently; and if you don't like a particular brush stroke, don't forget that you can use the History palette (or Ctrl(⌘)+Alt(Opt)+Z to undo as many steps as the History palette allows). Figure 3.28 shows the final results.

Figure 3.27   Use another selection (item 1) and move it over the seam (item 2) to help break up the repeating pattern near the seam. The goal is to make it look like a single photograph.

Figure 3.28   A finished panorama in less than five minutes.

Summary

If you take away only one lesson from this chapter, I hope it's an understanding of how important selections are to working magic with your images. Photoshop isn't a mind reader; if you want to separate an object from a background, you have to select the object. Likewise, if you want to apply a filter to only a small section of an image, you must select the small section of the image to let Photoshop know what you want to change.

The second important concept I hope you grasped is the way you can combine all forms of selection tools to make a single selection. You are not limited to one tool for each job. Continue to think in terms of the best tool—or *combination* of tools—to make the job at hand as easy as possible. And don't forget to use Boolean functions when applicable (such as the Add to selection or Subtract from selection modes). The fact that Photoshop offers such a large variety of ways to create a selection makes it an extremely flexible and powerful program in which to work.

Chapter 4

Enough Selections!
The Layers and
Shapes Chapter

Although, apparently, Photoshop layers
and the Shapes tools have nothing in common, when you get to real-world assignments, you'll find yourself continually
using first one feature and then the other.

Why? Adobe has made creating shapes very simple, somewhat like opening a template of a design. To make image creation even easier, Adobe invented something called vector masks. *Vector masks* are pre-designed shapes—they act as tiny portals to layers underneath the layer upon which a vector mask resides, or they can appear as shapes against the background. You can change their color and add all sorts of wonderful effects to them. But…vector masks—shapes—work only on *layers*, and that's why these two features are grouped into a single chapter.

Examining the Flexibility of Layers

Layers have been a Photoshop feature since version 3.0 (shortly after electricity was discovered). In passing years, Adobe has made the layers feature so powerful that today it almost overshadows Photoshop's most-used feature: the shipload of different ways you can select image areas.

In the sections that follow, you become familiar with Layer modes, layer locking, layer linking, clipping groups, clipping paths, layer sets, layer ordering, layer deleting, and Layer effects. Is learning *all* this stuff necessary? Yes, most certainly so; once you make layers a part of your Photoshop knowledge, you will work at least twice as fast as the next (uneducated) guy or gal.

First, we felt you'd benefit most from a potpourri-style tutorial, where you learn exactly what you need to know about a *number* of different layer tools and features. You'll see how efficiently you can work to perform complicated image editing.

Introducing the "Pocket Contents" Image

If someone were to ask you to empty the contents of your pockets on a table:

- You're probably being booked for a crime, and
- You'll notice that from an artistic standpoint, the composition formed by dumping your pockets is dimensional. Everything is not neatly ordered and distributed. This could be considered to constitute *layers* of things. Your keys might be above some folded money, and the folded money partially hides some pocket change.

The point here is that realistic image composition inherently has a depth of field; things go in front of and behind other elements. This is where Photoshop layers come in handy. They can help imitate real-world compositions.

Now, imagine you're Jim Carrey—the only comedian whose adopted planet is Earth—and you're asked to dump out your pockets on a table. The contents would probably be like the contents of the Pocket.psd image you'll work with in a moment.

The image looks like any other table top scene, except this scene was rendered in a modeling program, and everything is on different layers. FYI, shadows are attached to everything using the glow and shadow technique you will become familiar with in Chapter 5, "Working with Channels and Paths." Let's start off slow and easy as you learn how to manipulate the ordering of layers.

Investigating Layer Order

1. Open the Pocket.psd image from the Examples/Chap04 folder on the Companion CD, and save it to your hard disk using the same name and file type. This image is 600 by 800 pixels, with a resolution of 72 pixels per inch; zoom in or out if necessary to see all the contents of the image window.

2. Press F7 to display the Layers/Channels/Paths/And So On grouped palette. Press V to switch tools to the Move tool.

   And remember this shortcut: When the toolbox is partially hidden or closed, pressing V selects the Move tool directly, saving you the trouble of looking through the toolbox for the tool you need.

3. Right-click (Macintosh: hold Ctrl and click) over the 15ball in the image. As you can see in Figure 4.1, the context menu offers two layers presently underneath your cursor, called the 15ball and the Background. Click the 15ball choice, and you will see that the 15ball layer on the Layers palette is highlighted. You've made the 15ball layer the current editing layer.

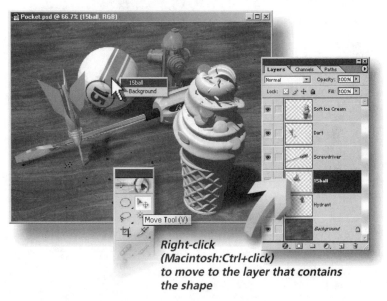

Figure 4.1   Move directly to a layer you want to edit by right-clicking (Macintosh: hold Ctrl and click) the area you want to edit.

Warning

Avoid Auto Select Accidents   When the Move tool is selected, the Options bar offers a checkbox for Auto Select Layer. We don't recommend using this option if you're a novice to Photoshop—or even an intermediate user. When the option is checked, if you click anywhere in the image with the Move tool, you immediately move to the layer that was underneath your cursor. Can you see how this option can be both confusing and hazardous to your work?

You can take a safer route to select a layer quickly when the Move tool is active, however. Simply Ctrl(⌘)+click to move to a specific object on that layer. This enables you to change layers when it's convenient and avoids the accidental layer jumping you might do if Auto Select were enabled.

4. Drag the 15ball downward so that it is between the dart and the ice cream. Let's say we want the 15ball to play a more predominant role in the composition. No problem. On the Layers palette, drag the layer title for the 15ball up *between* the Soft Ice Cream layer and the Dart layer, as shown in Figure 4.2. This puts the 15ball layer between the dart and ice cream layers. And like me, you might not hit the "sweet spot" on the palette on your first try. If you release the layer title *on top of* a layer, it then resides *directly beneath the layer* upon which you dropped it. This technique might be worth a few practice stokes on your own.

Figure 4.2   Move the order in which layers are organized to place an object in front of another.

> **Note**
>
> **Moving Through Layers, the Fast Way**   We acknowledge that we are cramming your head with stuff here. If you feel you have the memory (the carbon-based, organic kind), you can learn a keyboard method to change a selected layer's position in the stack of layers. Press Ctrl(⌘)+] (right bracket) to move the chosen layer up by one layer. As you might expect, to demote a layer, press Ctrl(⌘)+[(left bracket), one stroke per layer downward in the stack.
>
> Photoshop uses the same ordering commands for layers as Illustrator and PageMaker do for objects.

5. Play around with the position of the 15ball as much as you like. There's no exam at the end of this chapter. It's sort of fun to see how the shadow and pool ball cover different layer items. Keep the image and Photoshop open.

A Photoshop layer has more than one property. A layer is not only a container in a stack of other layers—it also can be changed with respect to opacity and how the layer's contents blend with layers underneath it. Come explore layer properties in the following section.

Changing the Appearance of a Layer

If you change a property of a layer in Photoshop, you also are likely to change the same property of whatever is on that layer. There are eight things that you can do to a layer, *without* mixing a layer with an additional, modifying layer (covered later in this chapter). The sections that follow introduce you to these different properties.

Opacity

When you're using a selection tool or the Move tool, you can change the opacity of a layer and its contents by doing the following:

- Planting your cursor in the Opacity field and typing. If you type a single digit, this represents 10 times the opacity applied. In other words, type 5, and 50% will appear in the number field. A zero (0) represents 100% opacity. Typing two numbers, one right after the other—no pausing—will enter these two numbers in the number entry field. Typing 5 and then 7, for example, will make the opacity 57%.

- Typing a number value when your cursor is *anywhere* in the interface. This, too, affects the opacity of the current layer. This may not be your preferred method because it might be unsettling to type a number while working in a channel and inadvertently change the opacity of a layer.

- Click the Soft Ice Cream layer title, click and hold on the palette's opacity flyout button, and then drag the opacity down to 57%, as shown in Figure 4.3. This is the direct, hands-on opacity determining method.

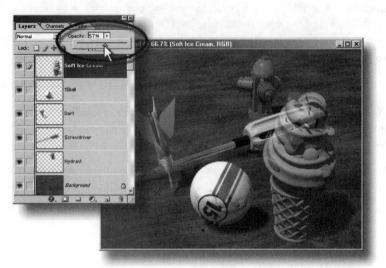

HEY, IT'S SUMMER. ICE CREAM DISAPPEARS **FAST!**

Figure 4.3   Create semi-transparent objects on a layer. Assign the layer partial opacity.

The Modes Drop-Down List

In Photoshop, you can paint using a certain mode you choose from the Options bar, and you also can put an entire layer's contents into most of the same modes. Photoshop has 22 modes, which means that you have 22 different ways to blend a layer into the under-lying layers.

After using layer modes in several versions of Photoshop, I have discovered that there are four modes you'll use regularly: Normal, Multiply, Screen, and Overlay. You also will experiment on your own and find the perfect blending mode for your own images, but let's cover the "basic four" here and now:

- **Normal.** Normal is the default mode, and the blend between the target layer and the layer(s) underneath is simple math. For example, if a layer is 50% opaque and the image underneath is 100% opaque, the resulting image at any point will be a color combination of 50% layer and 50% background image. Try making a bright blue background and a bright red layer, and then tuning the layer down to 50% opacity. The resulting color, in Normal mode, is a deep purple.

- **Multiply.** This is a terrific blending mode for working shadows into images. Multiply mode replaces colors with a combination of layer colors that is subtractive in regions that are less than 50% in brightness. Huh? Okay, think of staining something light in color with a blue marker pen. Only the target area gets darker. Now, imagine a white marker. Writing across the surface of something with the white marker causes no difference in the surface's color—due to the fact that no subtractive color process is going on with a light color and a light target in Multiply mode.

- **Screen.** If Multiply mode is like staining something, Screen mode is like bleaching something; it's the exact opposite effect. In Screen mode, lighter colors become more intense, while deeper colors do not change (and again, 50% brightness is the break point for what Photoshop considers light and dark). Try out Screen mode in the Pocket image, on the partially visible Ice Cream Cone layer. As you can see in Figure 4.4 (and *much* better on your own monitor), Screen mode really brings out the whites of the vanilla ice cream, and the deeper shadow areas on the cone seem to vanish.

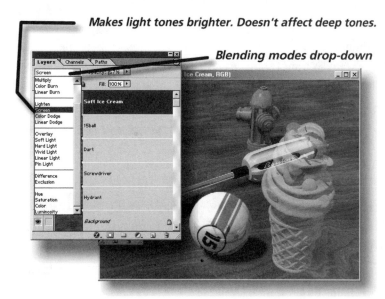

Figure 4.4   Screen mode is useful if you have a layer with light colors that you want to separate off a dimly lit background.

- **Overlay.** This mode produces an effect somewhat similar to placing a colored gel over an image. Overlay mode blends the image color with the Overlay color. Highlights and shadows do not change in brightness, but colors with a brightness between shadows and highlights are screened if they are over 50% in brightness. Additionally, colors are multiplied if the image's original color is less than 50% bright. You'll see a good example of this color mode in Chapter 5 with the ball and the pattern on the ball.

There are two more ways in which you can change the appearance of a layer, and both controls are located to the left of a layer title on the Layers palette.

Fill

The Fill slider on the Layers palette enables you to achieve two different kinds of opacity on a single layer. The Opacity setting controls the transparency of the layer; a setting of 100% means that the layer beneath the current layer cannot be seen through the objects on the selected later. A setting of 50%, however, fades the layer to allow 50% transparency so that objects on other layers will be visible through the current one. Fill (which is short for Fill Opacity) actually enables you to fade out the pixels or shapes you draw on the selected layer. It is used primarily when you have applied a layer effect, such as Emboss or Drop Shadow. When you reduce the Fill value, the pixels on the layer become increasingly transparent, but the layer effect remains.

Give the Fill control by trying this: Using the Pocket image (we're going to trash this image through the course of the chapter, so don't worry about messing it up), click the Soft Ice Cream layer, and with Opacity at 100%, drag the Fill slider down to about 50%. Ooooh, ghostly ice cream!

Now let's restore the Fill setting to 100% for this layer. We have more to do with this image, and you can always mess with the Fill feature (it's new to Photoshop 7, by the way) on other layered images later.

Visibility and Edibility Icons

The Layers palette shows two columns to the left of any layer. These columns contain icons that let you know which layers are visible and available for editing. The leftmost one concerns us here. Be patient—we'll get to the second one soon.

- The visibility icon, in the leftmost column, is pretty self-explanatory. If there's an eye in the box, this means you can see the contents of the layer. If you click the eye, it disappears, and so does the visibility (and editing) of the layer's content.

Tip

Hide It and You Won't (Accidentally) Edit It   Photoshop users have been leveraging the power of the visibility icon for years by turning the visibility of a layer off so that no accidental editing can happen to the layer.

Also, the Lock feature (new to version 7) has an option for painting. If you click the brush icon, you'll get one of those international "do not" symbols if you try to paint this layer.

- The column to the left of the visibility column is called the Layer Link Mode column, and the appearance (or absence) of a link icon tells you whether a layer is linked. But you may actually see a few different icons in this column, depending on which state the layer is in. There are four possible states into which you can toss a layer: the target layer state, the Layer Mask state, the Layer Link mode, and the lock list. In the target layer state, the icon resembles a paintbrush; in layer mask, it looks like a gray rectangle with a white circle; and in layer link mode, the icon appears to be a chain. When you choose one of the lock list items, a small padlock appears to right of the layer name.

Target Layer State

You can paint on only one layer at a time in Photoshop, and you choose that layer by either keyboarding your way to a layer or by clicking its title on the Layers palette. When the layer is highlighted, it is called the target layer. A paintbrush icon in this column's box indicates that this layer is the target (current editing) layer. The title bar on the image also lists the current layer.

Layer Mask State

Later in this chapter, you edit the Pocket composition, using the layer mask. The quickest way to put a layer into the Layer Mask state is to choose the layer, and then click the icon that is second from the left on the bottom of the Layers palette. When a layer is in Layer Mask mode, you see the same icon in the box in the second column next to the Layer title.

What's this state *do*? Layer masks enable you to control the parts of the image you want to be able to edit, hide, or reveal. But not to worry! We're getting ahead of ourselves here, and you *will* play with the Layer Mask state later in this chapter!

Layer Link Mode

You'll be doing a step-by-step procedure with the Layer Link state later in this chapter, too. If you click in the second column box when the Paintbrush icon (target layer) isn't there, this layer turns into a *linked* layer, and a tiny chain appears in the column box. This layer is linked to the target layer, and if you use the Move tool to move the target layer's contents, the linked layer's contents moves correspondingly. This is a terrific feature when you have two objects aligned on different layers and you want to move them both, but you do not want to merge the layers. A click in a box that contains the link icon unlinks the layers.

We've saved the least critical three controls for layers for last. Don't worry if you find you are not using them daily in your work.

The Lock List

You've had a taste of this list with the Lock Image Pixels (that teeny brush icon). This horizontal list above the top layer title is probably used most often by intermediate to advanced users, primarily because these users are the ones who create intermediate to advanced *problems* in an image, and locking features are art-savers.

We have no tutorial to show you how the Lock choices work, so you might want to open a new image, and add a layer to it now. To do this, click the folded page icon directly to the left of the trash icon on the bottom of the Layers palette. Then use the Paintbrush tool to paint something, any color, on the layer.

The default setting for the layer Lock feature is Lock nothing. This means that *no* part of the layer is protected against accidental editing. You can paint over the first strokes you've made in the image window, and you also can paint over empty areas of the layer.

When you're ready to try out one of the Lock options, you can choose from Lock transparent pixels, Lock image pixels, Lock position, or Lock all. The paragraphs that follow explain each of these choices a bit more.

Set the Lock feature by clicking Lock transparent pixels, the first icon next to the word "Lock" (see item 1 in Figure 4.5). Enabling this feature locks the current opacity of the layer, no matter what the current setting might be. Any areas on that layer that have even 1% opacity (and it's doubtful any of us can see a 1% opaque area) cannot become more opaque, regardless of what tool you use to paint.

The next icon, Lock image pixels, shown as item 2 in Figure 4.5, keeps you from painting on the layer. Item 3, Lock position, stands for "no moving stuff, bud." With this icon selected, you cannot use the Move tool to accidentally or intentionally move any non-transparent areas on a target layer. Finally, item 4, Lock all, stands for "you cannot do anything to this layer; it is locked against *everything*."

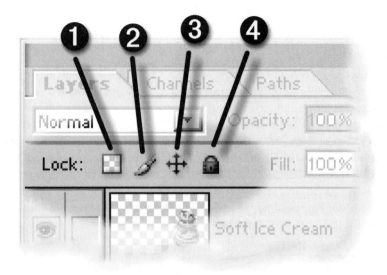

Figure 4.5   The Lock feature can disable painting over areas, prevent moving areas on a layer, and completely prevent editing on the target layer.

You'll definitely use more options in your first months with Photoshop, but it's nice to see some of the most common ones and know what they do. Let's get back to our Pocket masterpiece, and explore more layer features.

New! Layer Sets

New to Photoshop is the layer set feature. Layer sets enable you to pack away multiple layers so that they can't be seen cluttering up your Layers palette. You can organize all layers related to a specific item, for example, in one layer set. When you're working on the layer set, all layers are available to you. When you're finished with that set, you can hide the layers by closing the layer set. To get a feel for this, let's continue messing up the Pocket.psd image.

Packing Away Layers You Don't Need

We'll let you in on the ending of the Pocket.psd story here: eventually, you will be editing only the dart and the 15ball against the background. This means that the tiny hydrant, the screwdriver, and the ice cream cone serve no purpose other than to distract us.

Here's how to pack the three layers away in a layer set. You no longer need to worry about deleting superfluous layers, only to find out later that they weren't superfluous!

Using the Layer Set Feature

1. On the Layers palette, click the menu flyout triangle near the top right of the palette.

2. Choose New Layer Set from the menu, item 1 in Figure 4.6. A dialog box pops up, item 2 in Figure 4.6. Type **Unused Pocket Items** in the Name field, and because this is our first time using this feature, make the color of the layer set violet. Pass Through is a mode assigned only to layer sets. This means that any of the contents of the layer set that are activated (to activate, you open the layer set folder and click the eye icon) will appear in Normal mode. You also can do some weird stuff like assigning Color mode to the layer set, which causes every acti-vated layer in the layer set to take on the "parent" Blending mode. Leave the mode at Pass Through and then click OK. Onscreen, the closed set entry on the Layers list will be violet…very easy to locate.

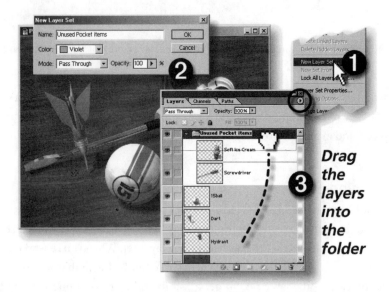

Figure 4.6   Create a new layer set—a container for layers—as easily as you create new layers.

3. Drag the Hydrant, the Screwdriver, and the Soft Ice Cream layers into the Unused Pocket Items title on the Layers palette, item 3 in Figure 4.6. The layers will disappear from the Layers palette, but you'll clearly see these layers again if you click the right-facing triangle next to the layer set name (the triangle toggles the layer set folder open and closed—for viewing or hiding the layers within the palette).

4. Close the layer set title by clicking the down triangle to the left of its name, and the triangle then faces right. Hide the images in the layer set by clicking the eye icon to deselect it.

5. Press Ctrl(⌘)+S to save the file. Keep the image and Photoshop open.

> **Tip**
>
> **Seeing What's in a Layer Set**   You can see the contents of a hidden layer set in the image window by clicking the layer set title's eye icon. If you click the layer set title's triangle so that it faces down and the title expands to show thumbnails of the contents of the layer set folder, you can edit layers in the Layer Set exactly as you would do with layers outside the set. You must, of course, have the eye icon and the brush icon enabled for the selected layer title before you can do any work with that layer's contents.

Let's do something that's impossible in the real world. In the following section, you'll work with the layer mask feature to make it look as though the dart is harpooning the 15ball. And you'll do it without the need for woodshop tools.

Using the Layer Mask Feature

A layer mask does something a little more substantial and dramatic than the name suggests. When you put a layer into Layer Mask mode, you can erase and restore image areas using selection or painting tools, but none of the changes are permanent. You can take a few minutes to refine the edge of an object on a layer, save the file, and open it up in a week, and still the changes you've made are *proposed* ones—nothing you see is permanent until you remove (apply) the layer mask. Let's get to the example of the layer mask, the dart, and the 15ball in the Pocket image.

Creating a Unique Composition Through Layers

You need to do two things to get the dart looking as though it was thrown at the 15ball by a small explosion. First, the dart needs to be on the top layer. Next, you need to remove part of the dart's tip and part of its shadow, combine the two dart pieces, and position them over the 15ball.

That's the plot. Let's get hatching…

Pinning Down a 15ball

1. Drag the Dart layer title on the Layers palette to the top of the individual layers, as shown in item 1 of Figure 4.7. Or, if you remember the key commands for this, press Ctrl(⌘)+] (right bracket) until you can see the Dart title above the 15ball title.

2. Move the dart closer to the 15ball by using the Move tool to drag the Dart layer, as shown in item 2 of Figure 4.7.

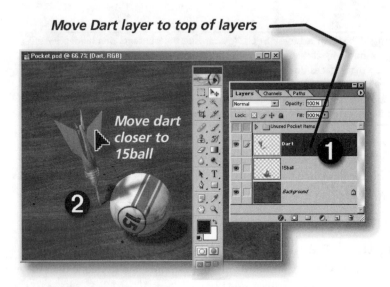

Figure 4.7   The dart should be in front of the 15ball, and the two objects should be
close to one another.

3. Zoom in (Ctrl(⌘)+plus sign) so that you have a good view of the tip of the dart,
and place that dart tip on the upper left of the pool ball. As you can see in Figure
4.8 a 100% viewing resolution does the trick. Now, click the Layer Mask icon
with the Dart layer as the active layer. Weird stuff is going to happen when you
go to apply the Paintbrush tool and the foreground color!

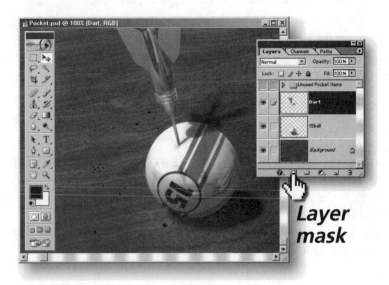

Figure 4.8   When a layer's layer mask is in place, you are editing the visibility of areas;
you are not moving or painting them.

4. Click the Swap foreground/background colors icon if necessary to make black the current editing color. The Swap icon looks like a bent, two-headed arrow; you'll find it to the upper right of the color selection boxes on the toolbox. Choose the Paintbrush tool, and then right-click (Macintosh: hold Ctrl and click) to produce the Brushes palette over your work. Click the 19-pixel tip (this is the *default* palette of tips from which you're working), and press Enter to make your choice—and make the floating palette disappear. Drag the Paintbrush cursor over the tip of the dart, shortening the tip by about 50%. Do the same to the tip on the shadow of the dart.

Black hides objects on a layer, and applying white restores the hidden areas. So if you goof, press X to swap foreground and background default colors, and restore what you wiped out.

5. When your editing is finished (it should look pretty much like item 1 in Figure 4.9), drag the *right* thumbnail on the Dart layer title into the trash icon. Make sure it's the *right* side one you're trashing—this is the layer mask thumbnail (see item 2 in Figure 4.9). If you drag the left thumbnail into the trash, you delete *the entire layer.*

Figure 4.9   Dragging the layer mask thumbnail into the trash means that you're serious about what you've painted to hide, and you want to permanently delete the hidden areas from the file.

6. Next, the "last chance" attention box pops up (see Figure 4.10). When you trash a layer mask, Photoshop asks you whether you want to Apply the mask (permanently deleting hidden image areas), Cancel (think twice about trashing the hidden areas), or Discard (throw away your masking work and return everything to the way it was).

Go for it. Click Apply with a swift, definitive keystroke.

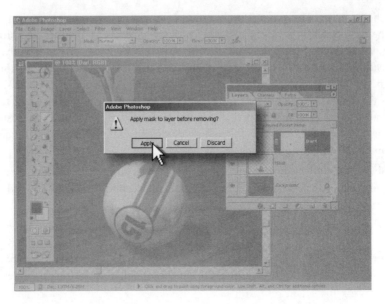

Figure 4.10   What a polite program!

7. As you've probably noticed, there's a gap now between where the shadow of the dart ends and where the dart tip begins. This is a tad unrealistic, no? Press Ctrl(⌘)+S at this point, keep the image and Photoshop open, and we'll show you a trick in the following section for the precise union of dart and shadow.

There was a term a long time ago for what Adobe used to call an image area that was floating on top of the current editing layer. The name was *floating selection*. Adobe has dropped the term in recent versions and doesn't even tell you what's going on when you float an image area; however, that's okay. In the next section, we are going to show you how to create a floating selection and make it work for you.

Floating and Aligning the Dart with Its Shadow

As of version 4 of Photoshop, selection tools were redesigned to create selections, but they could not move the *contents* of the selection. Now the Move tool takes care of such feats as moving image areas on layers.

But by using a shortcut key and the arrow keys on your keyboard, you define a pretty broad selection around the dart and still place it precisely where you want it in the image.

Let's try out a new technique:

Finishing the Weird Composition

1. With Dart as the target layer (I think there is an unintentional pun in there someplace), choose the plain Lasso tool, and drag a selection marquee around the dart, as shown in Figure 4.11. Be careful not to select any of the dart shadow.

Figure 4.11   The selection might seem broad, but in reality, you are only selecting the non-transparent pixels on the layer—the dart.

2. With the Lasso tool still chosen (and Feathering made 0px on the Options bar), place it inside the selection marquee and then hold Ctrl(⌘). The cursor turns into a tiny Move tool with a pair of scissors hanging off of it. This means that if you move the marquee right now, the action will cut the selected area's contents from the layer. Nothing but transparency surrounds the dart, so this action is not destructive—*and* the dart selection is now hovering above the Dart layer.

3. While holding the Ctrl(⌘) key, press the down- and right-arrow keys until the dart meets the tip of its shadow, as shown in Figure 4.12. You'll notice also that as soon as the marquee selection is moved, the marquee changes shape to conform to the non-transparent areas within the selection. This is a nice visual confirmation that you are moving the right thing on a layer.

Figure 4.12   Hold Ctrl(⌘) and then use the keyboard arrow keys to nudge the selection toward the tip of the shadow.

Tip

Add Power to Your Keypress   Just in case "power-nudging" sounds like fun to you, let us tell you what it is. You can hold Shift while you press the arrow keys to nudge a selection by 10 pixels instead of by one. This makes your fingers all twisted, but it can save time when you need coarse movement editing, followed by precise movements.

4. Press Ctrl(⌘)+D to deselect the marquee, use the Move tool to reposition the dart so that it looks like it's piercing the 15ball, and you're done! In Figure 4.13, you can see the finished piece. I'm going to frame my copy and put it in the game room (right next to the conservatory...*in my dreams*).

    Keep Photoshop open, save the Pocket image, and keep it open, too.

Figure 4.13   Reality is what you make it in Photoshop.

For the super fussy-at-heart, there is a mistake in the finished dart and pool ball image—in the shadow of the dart. Right now, the shadow extends in a linear fashion away from the dart tip, when, in reality, if a dart happened to get stuck in a pool ball, the shadow on the pool ball would be curved, and then it would be linear as soon as the shadow hits the table top.

You know what? Who's going to notice? I am *exceptionally* nit-picky on aspects of photorealism in Photoshop pieces, but this is one inaccuracy that you can afford to let go. Why? Because the shadow of the dart is at such a steep angle that it is severely distorted, and the average viewer will not notice that the shaded part of the pool ball doesn't shade it with an arc.

The sub-lesson here is that if you create an image that is dramatic and striking and appealing and all that, most viewers will skip over the small flaws.

Coming attractions: You're going to use an Adjustment Layer to enhance the tones in the Pocket image.

Imagine Color Correction by Painting It On

I hope the title is a catchy one here. For the most part, you change the color and tones of object areas in Photoshop by selecting them, apply feathering so the transition between edited and original areas is not severe (or noticeable), and then get out that Curves or Levels command.

You don't actually need to create a selection to perform color and tone corrections. Adjustment Layer fills enable you to paint on a layer that is above your target layer, and instead of applying paint, you're applying tone, color, or other corrections.

Photoshop's Department of Corrections

Adjustment Layers were a hands-down boon to photographers using Photoshop because they provided the photographer with a preview of one or more different tone or color corrections. And this could be done without touching the digitized image.

Photoshop's Adjustment Layers include the useful correction commands found on the Image, Adjust drop-down menu. Also (although we don't have an assignment that shows this off) *everyone*…even non-photographers…can play through "what-if" scenarios without damaging the goods, because in addition to Adjustment Layers, non-photographers can experiment with the Fill Layer feature. (To use the Fill Layer feature, choose Layer, New Fill Layer; then select the type of Fill Layer you want to create (Solid Color, Gradient, or Pattern). A dialog box appears, asking you to name the Fill Layer and choose the Color, Mode, and Opacity settings. After you enter a name, make your choices, and click OK, you are presented with the current set of fill choices that apply to the type you selected. Choose the one you want from the pop-up dialog box and click OK to make the change.

> **Note**
>
> **Modifying Palettes**   As you may remember from Chapter 2, "Optimizing and Customizing Photoshop Preferences," you always can change the offerings of a palette by using the Presets Manager.

And like the layer mask, the tone of the color you apply to the Adjustment Layer determines how predominant the effect is. White shows off the effect at 100%, black doesn't show the effect at all, and 254 other levels of gray can be used to bring out a little or a lot of Adjustment Layer effect. Moreover, Adjustment Layers change the appearance of every layer underneath them, not only the closest layer underneath.

In the following example, you are going to decrease the brightness of the pool ball and dart while holding the brightness of the table top. With layers, this task is a lot easier than it sounds.

Applying a Dynamic Fill Layer

1. Create a link between the Dart and the 15ball layer, as shown in Figure 4.14, and then use the Move tool to move the pair up so that the two objects are vertically centered in the image. (This has nothing to do with Adjustment Layers. This step simply didn't fit into the preceding set of steps).

Figure 4.14   The Layer Link feature is on the Layers palette. Click in the empty box in the right column next to the layer thumbnail to link a layer to the current editing layer.

2. Click the Create new fill or adjustment layer icon (the half moon icon next to the New Layer icon), as shown in Figure 4.15, and then choose Brightness/Contrast from the list. Note that we've moved the list over in this figure so that you can see both the Create new fill or adjustment layer icon and the pop-up menu.

Figure 4.15   Choose Brightness/Contrast from the many Adjustment Layer selections.

3. In the Brightness/Contrast box that pops up, drag the Brightness slider to –20, as shown in Figure 4.16. Click OK. All layers in the Pocket image lose brightness, and a new title on the Layers palette appears: Brightness/Contrast.

Figure 4.16   With the Adjustment Layer's Brightness/Contrast, you begin tuning the brightness of the picture with a –20 setting (the final brightness you want for unedited areas of the image), and add color (using a brush or a fill) to bring parts or all of the image back to the original brightness.

4. Let's simply play here for a moment. Take the Paintbrush tool, choose a medium-sized tip (Right-click (Macintosh: hold Ctrl and click), click the tip

from the palette, and then press Enter to close the palette). Black should be the fore-ground color. Make a few strokes on the wood area of the image. As you can see on your screen, and in Figure 4.17, when you apply black to the Adjustment Layer (the chosen layer on the Layers palette), you are negating the brightness change you specified; and wherever you stroke, the wood becomes its original color.

Foreground black color restores original wood brightness.
So does a good furniture polish.

Figure 4.17   Look at the Adjustment Layer fill (mask) thumbnail on the Layers palette. Wherever you apply black in the image, the image takes on original brightness, and the thumbnail shows where you applied color.

5. Okay, let's do what we came here for. Hold Ctrl(⌘) and click the Dart layer title on the layers palette, and then hold Shift+Ctrl(⌘) to add the 15ball layer to the selection by clicking its Layers palette title (see Figure 4.18).

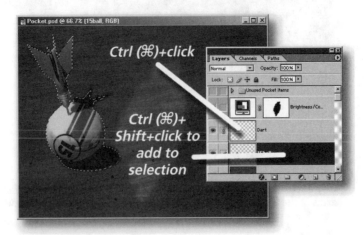

Figure 4.18   Create a selection marquee in the image by adding one shape's outline to another on a different layer.

6. Press Shift+F7 (or Ctrl(⌘)+Shift+I; they both produce the same result) to invert the selection marquee in the image so that everything except the dart and the ball are selected.

7. Make certain that when you created the selections you did not change target layers! The Adjustment Layer should be the present editing layer. Press Alt(Opt)+Delete (Backspace), and then press Ctrl(⌘)+D to deselect the marquee. You've filled the Dynamic layer with black—except where the objects are— and the wood table top in the image takes on its original brightness. Now let's lighten the objects by half the brightness by which they were decreased.

8. Repeat Step 5, but do not invert the selection. The ball and dart are now selected. Be sure one or the other of the layers is chosen, and apply 50% black to brighten these objects by half. Inside the selection marquee, with a selection tool chosen, right-click(Macintosh: hold Ctrl and click), and then choose Fill from the context menu.

9. The Fill dialog box pops up. Choose Foreground color from the Use drop-down list, and then type **50** in the Opacity box, as shown in Figure 4.19. Click OK. Press Ctrl(⌘)+D to deselect.

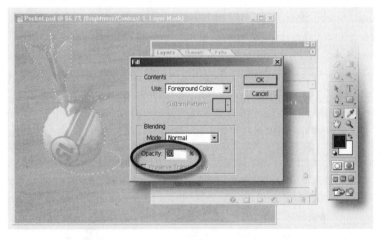

Figure 4.19   To make the selected area halfway between its current and its original brightness, fill the selection with 50% black.

If you look carefully at the Adjustment Layer thumbnail icon, or press Alt(Opt) while clicking the thumbnail to make the masking of the Adjustment Layer fill appear in the image window, you'll see that the entire layer is black (no effect) and the shapes are 50% black (50% of the effect). You can accomplish this "half bright" editing move by choosing a 50% black foreground color and then stroking in the selection, but filling it was quicker, right? You now know two ways to change an Adjustment Layer's effect. To go back to image view in the image window, Alt(Opt)+click again to toggle the display back to the image with the Dynamic Fill layer affecting it.

10. Let's pretend you are servicing a client in these steps. The client looks at the tone changes you made and decides that he likes it better the way the image was originally. Clients, right? You drag the Adjustment Layer title into the trash icon. If your client is less of a pain and likes your tone adjusting work, you can keep the image with an Adjustment Layer on it or flatten the image to make your editing changes permanent. Flatten image is located on the Layers palette menu flyout.

11. You can close the image at any time after saving it. Keep Photoshop open. We've finally exhausted layer tricks, and we'll now move on to shapes.

Step 11 isn't 100% accurate. Shapes have a lot to do with layers, so don't say sayonara to them yet. It's on to the easiest methods for creating complex designs in Photoshop—with shapes—vector masks.

Shapes and Clipping Paths

Although Chapter 3, "Harnessing the Power of Selections," covers the use of path-making tools, Adobe Systems wants *every* user to get with the program and start using the power of vector paths in Photoshop, right from Day One. Okay, suppose it's Day Two or Three with you and Photoshop; we are still going to show you the easiest way to start using vector paths. Paths travel under the guise of something called *shapes* in version 7—these are pre-made paths that you can fill, stroke, base a selection upon, and so forth. And shapes give you a way to get started understanding the relationship between vectors and designs that are filled with pixels. Shapes are a sort of vector container for the bitmap rendering you do in Photoshop.

So without further ado, let's play with some pre-made shapes we've created for you on the CD (they're really cool), and discover the different relationships vector graphics have with Photoshop 7 features.

Building Upon a Simple (But Cool) Shape

Okay, here's a perfect chance to show you a relationship between a vector design and layers in Photoshop. In the steps that follow, you will copy a path from a collection of shapes on the Companion CD, fill it to turn it into the base layer of a clipping group, load the selection, and then pile on some layer effects to create stunning artwork in less than five minutes.

By the way, the shapes you'll see in this section were all taken from the Haxton Logos typefaces on the Companion CD. So if you decide you like creating art using the steps to follow, there's plenty more shapes where these came from.

Here's how to create a shape on a layer from a path shape:

Copying and Using Paths

1. Open the Shapes.tif image from the Examples/Chap04 folder on the Companion CD.

   Although this does not affect the way you use this file, I've filled the vector shapes; so when they are hidden, you can still see the designs I put in this document.

2. Click the Paths tab of the Layers/Channels/Paths/Tra La La palette, and then click the Shapes by Bouton title. All the paths will appear in the image window.

3. Choose the Path Selection tool, and then marquee drag on the train stencil in the Shapes.tif image window, as shown in Figure 4.20.

Marquee select this guy

Path Selection tool (new name since version 6)

Figure 4.20   Technically, all the designs are one big, composite path, because they are stored under one title. The Path Selection tool enables you to select only the train paths from all the rest in the image window.

4. Press Ctrl(⌘)+C to copy the path to the clipboard.

   You can use the Path Selection tool to drag a copy of a path to a different image window, but we don't have a new window yet. Just a tip here.

5. Create a new image window. Make it 3 inches by 3 inches at 72 pixels/inch, RGB Color mode, and Contents: White. This is a tad larger image window than the train, but you'll be adding special effects to the train, so we'll leave a little elbow room in the new document.

6. Press Ctrl(⌘)+V, and then name the Work Path **Train**. Double-click the path title to get the Save Path name box. Center the train path in the image window by marquee selecting the train path with the Path Selection tool, and then dragging it.

7. On the Layers palette, create a new layer, leave it as the current editing layer, and press D (default colors); then on the Paths palette, click the Fill path with fore-ground color icon, as shown in Figure 4.21. Finally, click an empty area of the Paths palette's list area to hide the path. Congratulations! You've just created a shape on a layer that can now be used for a number of things, not the least of which is the base layer for a clipping path.

   Save the design as Train.psd in Photoshop's native format, and keep Photoshop open.

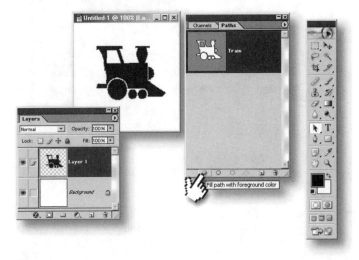

Figure 4.21   Use the Fill path with foreground color icon to give the shape some substance.

Here come the fireworks. Now that you've created a "stencil" of the train on a layer, you can fill this stencil, move it around, and add layer effects to it.

Introducing Clipping Groups

I think within the context that Adobe uses "clipping" in Photoshop, we can consider it the opposite of masking. Instead of everything outside of a selection being opaque, the *inside* of a shape is a container for whatever you choose.

Clipping groups can be very useful when you have dozens of different patterns, for example, and want to see what they look like on a shirt pattern. You make the shirt pattern the base of a clipping group, and then anything you toss on top of this layer—on different layers—becomes the fill. And you can move the container around and the pattern will travel, too.

Let's walk through the following steps to demonstrate the power of clipping groups.

Creating a Clipping Group

1. Click the Create new layer button on the Layers palette (it's the folded page icon next to the trash icon). By default, this is named Layer 2.
2. Choose the Gradient tool from the toolbox. On the Options bar, choose the linear style of filling, and then from the drop-down list of preset gradients, choose the yellow/violet, orange, blue preset. Press Enter (Return) after you click the icon to let Photoshop know you are sincere in your selection.
3. Drag the Gradient tool from the top to the bottom of the image window. The gradient now covers the train shape.
4. Hold Alt(Opt) and then click between the two layer titles on the Layers palette. As you can see in Figure 4.22, your cursor turns into a novel design; and after clicking, the top layer is clipped to fill only the train shape. We call the top layer the *clipping layer* and the train shape the *base layer*. Heads up for the Note that follows.

   If there were any transparency on the gradient layer, you could add another layer, and it, too, could be viewed only through the portal that the train design has become.

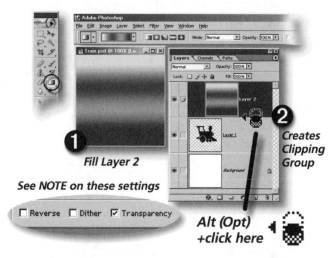

Figure 4.22   The thumbnail of Layer 2 on the Layers palette has shifted to the right, telling you that you've successfully made the base layer a host for the visual contents of Layer 2.

Note

Fun with Gradients   There are three options on the Options bar when the Gradient tool is active, and they're kinda obscure. First, the Reverse checkbox enables you to quickly reverse the order of colors in the current gradient. Dither should be unchecked if you're composing artwork for the web. If you are designing for color printing, you probably should check dither because dithering is noise; and if you add noise to a gradient destined for print, the noise will disguise the *banding* that inevitably occurs when you move an RGB image to the smaller color space of CMYK printing. Transparency is an option relating to any transparency that might be in a gradient you use or create. Keep this option checked unless you want your gradient to fill 100% of a layer, with no transparent areas.

5. For fun, click the Layer 1 title (it's underlined now because it is a base layer for a clipping group); and then with the Move tool, move the train around. You will see different areas of the partially concealed gradient layer. Now, click the box in the second column to the left of the thumbnail on the gradient layer (where a paintbrush icon would be if this were the current layer). A chain link appears. and now the base layer and the gradient layer are linked. Try dragging the train around. You'll notice that the contents remain static within the stencil of the train. This happens because the base layer is now linked to the gradient.

6. For even *more* fun, let's try something else. First, move the Train.psd image to the top left of the screen so that you can preview the effects as you modify them. Then, choose Layer 1 (the base clipping group layer), and click the "f" icon on the bottom of the Layers palette; then click Bevel and Emboss. Doing this brings up a huge options palette called Layer Style. Drag the Depth slider to about 500% for a default emboss that's really noticeable and deep in shading. Now, click the Drop Shadow title, check the Drop Shadow box, and play with the sliders, as shown in Figure 4.23, until you get a soft but noticeable shadow. Click OK.

   You can add as many effects as you like in this dialog box by clicking the effect title. Only until you click OK are the effects displayed in your image. And even then, you can change your mind and delete them by dragging an effects title into the Layers palette's trash icon.

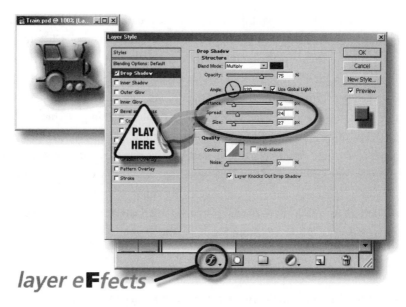

Figure 4.23   You can "mix & match" effects to be applied to the target layer using the Layer Styles command.

7. As you can see in Figure 4.24, you've created something of a mini-masterpiece without even calling on your drawing prowess. Why not save this file to your hard disk, come back to it some other time, and paint the train different colors? You can close the image at any time, but keep Photoshop open.

Figure 4.24   You do not have to be a born artist to create striking visuals for a web site, a greeting card from an inkjet printer, or whatever. Simply use Adobe's (or Bouton's) preset shapes, and add a few layer effects.

Let me point out here that Adobe ships with 12 (at this writing) Shapes palettes that you access from the Options bar when you choose the Custom Shape tool. Click the down-arrow to the right of the shape icon on the Options palette. Then, click the triangle in a circle in the upper right of the palette, and choose Replace Shapes, a misnomer—the current Shapes palette is simply hidden back in the Presets files folder of your hard disk. To add shapes to an image window, you choose one by double-clicking it (which also closes the palette), and then hold Shift (to constrain proportions) and drag diagonally in the image window. This creates, by Photoshop default, a Vector Mask, similar to a path you create using the Pen tools (covered in Chapter 5, "Working with Channels and Paths"). Although you have to admit that preset shapes are quick to implement, we'll tell you right now that vector masks have special properties we'll cover; and later in the chapter, we'll show you how to create a Custom Shape palette of your own.

Now it's time to take a look at the most simple of paths to create—vector masks. What are they good for? How do you convert them to other types of image objects? You're going to find the following section to be a very integrating experience.

Working with a Vector Mask Layer (Shapes)

A vector mask layer has some nice options for enhancing your work, but at the same time, you'll discover that there are many things you've learned about Photoshop features that are not available to a Shapes layer. For example, changing the color to a gradient within the "container" shapes you create is not possible.

The best way to get a feel for Shapes is to experiment for yourself. The following steps take you on a fairly thorough investigation of these vector masks.

Note

A Shape by Any Other Name...   Before we get too far into the game, we need to clear up an ambiguity of terms Adobe has bestowed on the Shapes tool. Technically, only the Shapes Layer tool creates a shape because, hey, that's what it's called, and it produces distinctly different results in an image window than the Paths and the Fill Pixels modes on the Options bar.

All three modes on the toolbar use the Shapes tools, however. I think we can all keep a little more of our hair where it belongs if we accept the term *shapes* to mean a design that's a result of using any of the Shapes tools, regardless of whether the Shapes tool produces a vector mask, a simple path, or foreground colors in the shape of a checkmark, a speech balloon, or whatever.

Creating a Shapes Layer

1. Open a new image, choose Photoshop Default Size from the Preset Sizes drop-down in the New dialog box, choose RGB color mode, and choose White as the contents. Press Enter.

2. Click the foreground color selection box (marked as item 1 in Figure 4.25), and choose a light purple as the color you paint with and the color that will be peeking through the shapes on the Vector Path layer.

3. Drag the face of the Shape tool on the toolbox, and then choose the Polygon tool (item 2 in Figure 4.25). Immediately, the Options bar sprouts new choices for you to make, and (as of this writing) the far left tool (item 3) is the active shapes mode—called, fairly enough, Shape Layers. Check the following Note for other choices you can make whenever you choose the Shape tool.

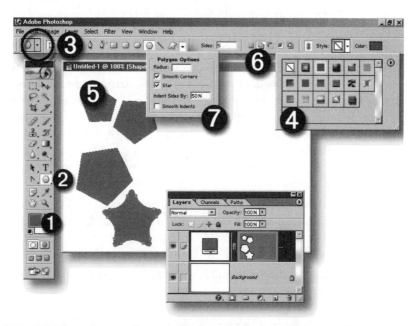

Figure 4.25 When you choose a Shape tool, many options are available to you for creating a shape, its contents, and what is shown in non-path areas.

Note

Paths and Fills for Shapes The other modes for Shape creation are Path creation and Fill Pixels fill modes. If you click the Fill Pixels mode icon, the shapes you drag are plain pixels against the current layer or the background. These modes pop up on the Options bar the moment you choose a Shapes tool. For comparison here (this is a new topic) the Shape Layers tool produces a shape on a new layer when you drag with the tool, and you can turn off the vector outline if you like by clicking the right thumbnail on the new layer.

continues ▶

If you choose the Path icon, every shape you draw will be a vector shape, but it will not clip the layer underneath it, nor will it have a fill.

Once you've thoroughly pored through this chapter and Chapter 5, you might find that the Path mode in combination with Shapes tools is the way to work. For now, we'll keep digging through stuff for you <g>.

Now, after you've created your first shape, the Boolean buttons on the Options bar (subtract from, add to, and so on) will become active. Because we want to draw oodles of shapes, click the Add to shape area icon (item 6 in Figure 4.25). Now, every shape will be on the same layer and will *not* create a new layer (try managing 47 layers!) when you create your second shape.

4. Click the Layer Style drop-down list button (item 4 in Figure 4.25), and then click the No Style, international symbol. Now every time you create a polygon, the polygon will simply be foreground purple with no layered effects on it. You can add effects later; you'll see how momentarily.

5. Start click+dragging in the image window (item 5 in Figure 4.25). You will create polygons of different sizes. If you want to create variations on the polygon, click the Options down button to the right of the Shapes button on the Options bar. Every preset shape (such as the Polygon, the Rounded Corner Rectangle, and so on) has different parameters you can change at any time. For the Polygon, you can turn it into a star, with any degree of sharpness between points. Check it out—item 7 in Figure 4.25 marks the Polygon Options used to create the unusual star in the display.

6. Stop when you've created about four or five polygons. You will see an unusual thumbnail for this layer on the Layers palette. Paths are shown in miniature in the thumbnail, and the thumbnail looks quite a lot like a layer mask thumbnail (giving you a clue as to what to expect we can do with this layer soon).

7. Keep the image window open and keep Photoshop open.

Tip

Create It Once, Use It Many Times with Presets   See the circle around the shape icon in the very upper-left corner in Figure 4.25? That's the Presets button. If you go through the trouble of designing a really neat polygon (such as a purple rounded-edge star) and think you want to use it months from now, save yourself the steps of replicating the effect by clicking the down arrow to expose the Tool Presets palette, clicking the triangle in the circle in the top right, and choosing New Tool Preset. Give the preset an interesting name in the dialog box, and you can recall the tool and its customized options from the palette at any time in the future.

Earlier, we mentioned restrictions on editing a Shapes layer. Let's be a little more positive and explore next what you *can* do with Shapes layers.

Editing Clipping Path Layer Components

Although you cannot fill a Shape layer with a photograph, pattern, or unique gradient fill, you can edit the container shape using the Direct Selection tool, you can move shapes using the Path Selection tool, and you can add styles. But most importantly, you can *change your mind* about any of the edits mentioned earlier. Nothing is carved in stone on a Shapes layer until you choose Layer, Rasterize (change to pixels from a vector), and then click Shape.

So let's play a little with some properties of the Shape layer. Um, your image might not look like mine (because we are not the same person), but you will get the general idea of the flexibility of Shapes layers.

Manipulating a Shapes Layer

1. Make sure that a Shapes tool is chosen (or you won't see a Styles box on the Options bar) and then click the down arrow to the right of the international "no" symbol. This extends the Style palette, which you can see marked as item 1 in Figure 4.26. The palette might seem hidden, but if you click the down arrow to reveal it, and then click the encircled triangle (upper right), you have several more palettes from which to choose. (To replace the current collection, click one, and then click OK.) Glass Buttons produces a neat effect. But *don't* do that yet. Click Sunset Sky (item 2), and immediately every polygon on that layer turns to multicolor glory…as not seen in Figure 4.26 because this darned book is in black and white.

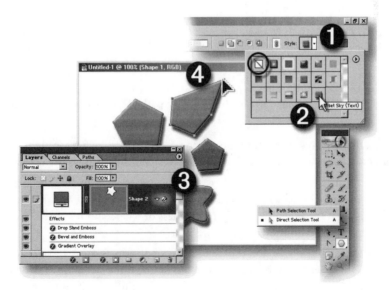

Figure 4.26   You apply a style to the entire layer. Anything within a path takes on the layer's style.

2. Click the down triangle to the right of the Shape thumbnail on the Layers palette to display the layer set (item 3 in Figure 4.26).

Warning

A Slight Workaround   We used the Dodge tool to make this triangle apparent in this figure, because at the time of this writing, the triangle and the Effect symbol are black against Windows Millennium, Windows 2000, and Windows XP Windows Classic interface dark blue. To fix this, you need to right-click the desktop, choose the Appearance tab and in the Scheme drop-down, pick Spruce or Rose.

Note

Routes to the Styles Palette   The Options bar is not the only place from which you can access the Styles palette. This palette is grouped with the Colors and Swatches palettes and can be called by choosing Window, Styles. We simply think you don't need this palette out all the time and accessing it from the Options bar is, um, *tidier*.

Suppose you want to change the style of this layer. You can do so by clicking a new style on the Styles palette. Suppose, on the other hand, that you want to change a component of the Style; this is why we have a drop-down box beneath every Layer title that is a Shapes layer. You double-click, and you're off to change the component upon which you clicked. You also can add a component by clicking the Effects button (the round one with the "f" inside of it) on the bottom of the Layers palette and then choosing a component. And, natch, you can get rid of a style component by dragging its title into the Trash icon at the bottom right of the Layers palette.

Note

Don't Go Changin'   By the way, you are affecting only the art in the image window by doing any/all of the above. You are not changing a Style on the Styles palette at all.

In addition to coloring the shape, you also can distort it and move it. In the following steps, you'll see how to rearrange stylized vector paths. That sounds almost scientific, doesn't it?

3. Click the Direct Selection tool on the toolbox. It might be hidden right now, so hold the Path Selection tool if this is the case, and then choose the direct Selection tool from the tool flyout.

4. Click any polygon to select it, and then click an anchor point and drag it, as item 4 in Figure 4.26 shows. Notice that regardless of where you relocate a point, the fill extends to accommodate the new shape.

5. Switch to the Path Selection tool and move a polygon. Surprise! Even though these paths have the same fill were created on the same layer, the Path Selection tool enables you to individually sort these shapes out! And if you want all the shapes to move as one, notice the Combine button on the Options bar. (This change isn't shown in the figure.)

6. Okay, let's say we're getting bored using the Sunset Sky style for all our polygons. Double-click the solid color thumbnail on the left of the layer title on the Layers palette. When the Color Picker appears, choose a light purple color, and then press Enter (Return) to define this new color. Now, click the international "no" swatch on the Styles palette. Woweeee! Everything inside the shapes is the color of purple you specified.

7. Now let's say you've grown weary of looking at all the straight edges. Choose the Convert point tool from the Pen tools flyout on the toolbox, and then click+drag on an anchor on one of the polygons. As you can see in Figure 4.27, clipping path layer elements obey the same rules as a regular path. You can move path elements, reposition their anchor points, bend path segments, and even use the Add Point and Delete Point on the clipping paths.

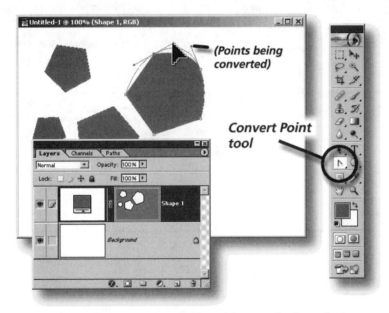

Figure 4.27   The subpaths in a vector mask (Shapes) layer can be changed using the Pen tools and selection tools.

8. Click the "f" icon in the bottom left of the Layers palette. Choose Bevel and Emboss from the pop-up list, and then click OK in the Layer Style dialog box to accept the default properties for the embossing. In your own work, you should spend time in this dialog box to fine-tune the effect you want to apply. Feedback for your tuning is immediately shown onscreen; but if you are running less than 800×600 video resolution, the art probably is obscured by the Styles dialog box. The effect also can be seen in a square in the lower right of the dialog box.

9. Click the "f" icon, and then choose Drop Shadow. Again, click OK in the dialog box to accept the defaults, and you are returned to the image.

10. This image is pretty dull without a background. Open Ppaper.tif from the Examples/Chap04 folder on the Companion CD.

11. With the Move tool, drag the title on the Layers palette into the image window with the shapes. Then, drag the title for the background all the way down so that it is beneath the clipping paths layer. Finally, drag the background, if necessary, so that it fills the whole background of the image window (see item 1 in Figure 4.28).

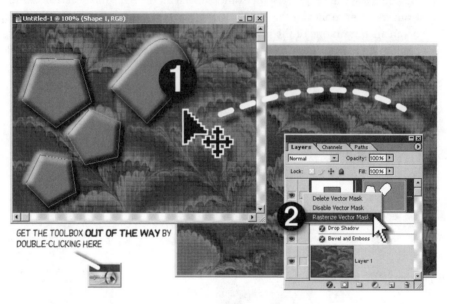

Figure 4.28   Copy a background to the target image window, move it to the bottom layer, and then convert the vector mask layer to a layer mask.

You also can drag an image in an image window into another image window to copy it, but dragging the title on the Layers palette is sometimes easier—an image window can cover another window, but it will not cover a Photoshop palette.

Tip

Copying on Center   If you want the contents you are copying from one window to land in the center of a different image window, hold Shift while you drag. This is a particularly nice feature if you want to duplicate the contents of a layer and you want the contents positioned exactly as they are in the original image.

12. Right-click (Macintosh: hold Ctrl and click) over the path thumbnail on the Layers palette, and then choose Rasterize Vector Mask, as item 2 shows in Figure 4.28. The effect you've created is that the paths no longer exist on the clipping path layer, and it's not a clipping path layer anymore. Now, it's a *layer mask*.

13. Choose Layer, Rasterize, and then choose Fill Content. The shapes are no longer linked to the layer fill (the left thumbnail on the Shape title on the Layers palette).

14. Click the right (the right, the *right*, not the left!) thumbnail on the title, and then drag it into the trash icon. A dialog box pops up asking whether you want to Apply the mask before removing. Click Apply. You now have your embossed, drop-shadow images on a transparent layer on top of the tapestry background layer.

15. You can save this image to your hard drive, if you'd like. You can close the Ppaper.tif image at any time, but keep Photoshop open.

Pretty neat, huh? Do you realize that you've created a wonderful design without once picking up the Paintbrush tool? You've been taking full advantage of Photoshop's features, both old and new.

You've turned vector paths filled with styles into an ordinary opaque area on a layer; now it's time to take a shape and turn it into a clipping path.

Using a Shape Layer as a Clipping Path

Read this carefully: there is practically *no* difference between a shape layer and a clipping path. The only difference is that you assign an image a Clipping Path status through the context menu, and then life is good. The vector mask (found on the left of the three tools when you choose a Shapes button) can be filled with almost anything except photos and can be moved about on its own special layer. Unlike version 6, you will not see the effect of a clipping mask if you try to apply it to an image using the previous version's commands.

With a shape—created by you or anyone else—you can set up a document so that the entire image is one color and a small design area allows the viewer to peek through to the layer underneath. Have you seen travel agency posters of say, the Bahamas, and the word *Bahamas* has a beach scene peeking through? Same thing—and that's what we came here for.

Here's how to do the trick of "peek through" masking so you can use it in Photoshop or any other program that reads clipping paths.

Inverting and Refining a Shape Layer

1. Open the Chick.tif image from the Examples/Chap04 folder on the Companion CD. If you click the Paths tab, you will see (as Figure 4.29 shows) that there is already a plain (non-Shapes) outline path around the chick (we saved you the effort, but you should practice using paths, since you learn about them in Chapter 5).

Figure 4.29 A chick outline path has already been provided for you on the Paths palette.

2. Click the Chick Path title on the Paths palette, and then click the Load path as a
selection icon in the bottom of the Paths palette to select the path. Make the Path
Selection tool the active tool. Right-click (Macintosh: hold Ctrl and click)
anywhere in the document window, and choose Clipping Path from the context
menu (see Figure 4.30). Click OK.

Figure 4.30 Turn an ordinary path into a clipping path, using the Clipping Path command.

3. Save the image in TIFF format to your hard disk as Chick.tif.

4. Open a desktop publishing program or Illustrator, and choose to place the Chick.tif image into a document. In Figure 4.31, we've set up a document that needs a chick hanging out in front of the 3D text. Perfect! The clipping mask hides all the other mess around the chick in the original picture.

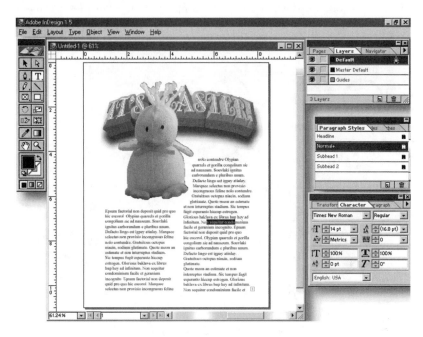

Figure 4.31   Import an image with clipping layer attributes, and you can position the cropped image anywhere.

5. You can close the host program now without saving (the point's been made in this section), but keep Photoshop open.

Here's a quick tutorial to show you the versatility of paths as they can exist as clipping paths, vector masks, or just plain paths. Suppose that you drew an ordinary path, and you now want the path to be part of a Shapes layer. Additionally, you want an inverted mask—the whole page is colored, and the shape is knocked out of the design. Hard?

Not if you follow these steps:

Designing an Inverted Vector Mask Layer

1. Open Ocean.tif from the Examples/Chap04 folder on the Companion CD.

2. Choose the Shapes tool from the toolbox, and then drag the image borders away from the image so that you can "lasso" the entire image with a vector mask.

3. Choose the Shape Layers tool (item 1 in Figure 4.32). Click the Rectangle Shape tool (item 2), and then choose a deep marine blue by clicking the Color swatch on the Options bar and accessing the color picker.

4. Drag from upper left to lower right in the image (item 3 in Figure 4.32). Now, and this is an important one, click the Booleans Subtract From tool (item 4). This creates conditions where any path dropped on the Shapes layer will remove a shape through the marine color and expose the underlying ocean.

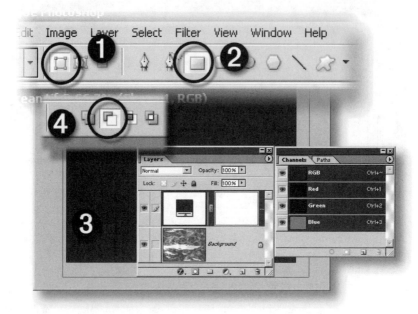

Figure 4.32   Photoshop should look like this at this point.

5. Open the Shapes.tif image, click the Path tab to view the Path palette, and click the Shapes by Bouton title to view the paths. With the Path Selection tool, marquee select the ship's wheel, as shown in Figure 4.33. Press Ctrl(⌘)+C to copy this symbol to the clipboard, and then close Shapes.tif.

Figure 4.33   Copy the wheel shape to the clipboard.

6. Press Ctrl(⌘)+V to paste the wheel into the image. Surprise! Because you chose Subtract From from the Options bar, Photoshop is showing only the subtracted area where the background and the path meet—the wheel drills out a shape from the blue background. You can see ocean within the wheel, as shown in Figure 4.34. But the wheel looks like it was designed for a 4 year old. It needs to be bigger in the design. Oh, what to do? Ya proceed to Step 7!

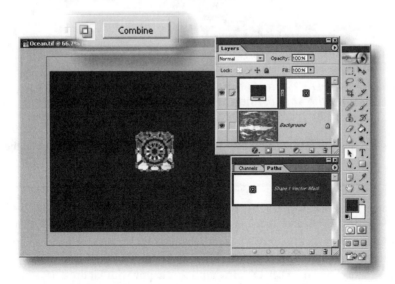

Figure 4.34   The Subtract command is terrific for removing shapes from a plain Shapes background and showing the layer underneath.

Note

Putting It All Together with Combine   The Combine button on the Options bar is shown in Figure 4.34 for good reason. If you want to reposition a path that has a bunch of subpaths, like the wheel does, clicking Combine enables you to move the design around the canvas using the Path Selection tool. But you must click the Combine button while all the anchor points in the design are highlighted.

If you deselect the shape and decide to move it later, you must use the Direct Selection tool to marquee select all the anchor points in the design and then drag the design around.

7. Press Ctrl(⌘)+T to put the Free Transform box around the shape, and then hold Shift and drag away from the wheel's center using a corner handle (see Figure 4.35).

Press Ctrl (⌘)+T to put the Free Transform box around the shape, and then hold Shift and drag away from the wheel's center using a corner handle.

Figure 4.35   Press Ctrl(⌘)+T to put the Free Transform box around the shape, and then hold Shift and drag away from the wheel's center using a corner handle.

8. Press Enter to finalize the operation when the wheel is the size you want. Hmm, an emboss effect would really help define the wheel. Click the Effects button on the bottom of the Layers palette, and then choose Bevel and Emboss. Play with the controls, and then take a look at the image by holding the Styles dialog box title bar and moving it out of the way for a moment. When you're happy with the transformation, click OK. The author is happy with Figure 4.36, so he clicked OK, too.

Figure 4.36 Add any effect you like to the wheel to make it look more pronounced in the composition.

9. You can save (or not) the Ocean composition. What you've learned about the flexibility and possibilities of vector masks is the real lesson here.

Note

Shortcut Those Anchors (or, Anchors Away!)   If the anchors on a path are highlighted, this means that the path—and not other image areas on a layer—is selected. So you can get away with a Ctrl(⌘)+A ploy instead of fussing with selecting all the anchors and copying.

Now that I've described how to access the Adobe shapes, let's see how you can create your own collection of preset shapes. Adobe doesn't know what your company wants you to design over and over again, right? And neither do I!

Creating, Saving, and Reusing Shapes

I think you'll design better paths by hand if you read Chapter 5 right now, but the wonderful thing about books is that they are not linear. You can indeed skip over this section, read up on how the Pen tool works, and then come right back here. If you want to use one of Bouton's shapes, that's fine for this section, too. We're not stressing how to design a path here—we're focusing on how to make an existing path easy to reach and modify from within Photoshop.

So get out a path or get out Logo.tif, and we'll begin.

Storing Shapes in Photoshop

1. Copy Blank.csh from the Examples/Chap04 to your hard disk—then make it the default palette. Do this by choosing the Custom Shape tool and clicking the down arrow to the right of the Shape title on the Options palette. This action extends the palette so that you can click the flyout menu button (top right on the palette) and choose Replace Shapes. Navigate to Blank.csh and select it.

   Note that the author could not create an entirely blank palette, so there is a star on the palette that you can delete after you've added at least one new shape to the palette.

2. Open either an image with a saved path you created, or open Patio.tif from the Examples/Chap04 folder on the Companion CD. If you're working with the CD design, copy the file to your hard disk and then open it in Photoshop. For those of you who have read Chapter 5 first and are now path gurus, create your design (it can be anything), and then save the file as Patio.tif, the same file stored in the Chap04 folder.

3. Click the Paths tab to view the Paths palette. You see that two paths have been created; you want Path 1 for this example. Click Path 1 to select it.

4. Now, as you see in Figure 4.37, choose Edit, Define Custom Shape. Doing this displays the Shape Name dialog box, and you should now name the shape. You're naming the shape because you can customize a shapes collection to be presented to you only by name on a palette.

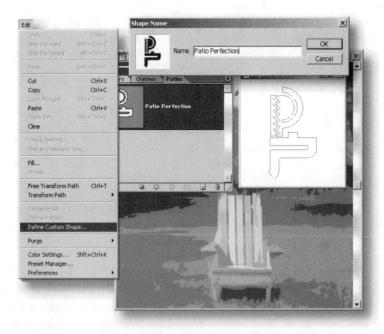

Figure 4.37   Create your logo using path tools so that you can make the logo easy to access from a Shapes palette in the future.

5. Click the Shapes arrow on the Options bar, as shown in Figure 4.38. Wow! Your Patio Perfection logo is right next to the star, and you can click it and use it ad infinitum or ad nauseum!

Figure 4.38 This is how you grow a palette of your own. By the way, you might want to rename the palette from a folder window when Photoshop is closed to help you remember its contents later.

Note

Adding More Shape(s) to Your Life   Now that you know how to add shapes to the Custom Shapes palette, you may want to load even more. You can add some other shapes I've created by clicking the Shapes down-arrow, clicking the flyout button, and choosing Load Shapes. When the dialog box opens, click Logos.csh and click OK. The additional logos are added to your current Shapes palette, and you're good to go.

6. On the Options bar, the Shape Layer option should still be selected. Hold Shift, and then drag the cursor from the upper left downward in the patio image. Stop before you've reached the chair in the image (see Figure 4.39).

7. Click the Style button, click the flyout button, choose Glass Buttons from the list and click OK in the confirmation box. Click the shape thumbnail on the Layers palette, and then give the yellow icon a click and amazingly, as shown in Figure 4.39, you now have quite an impressive picture, with special effects and everything!

Figure 4.39   Create a vector path logo layer using a shape you specified yourself.

8. Just because we haven't used it in this chapter, click the Type Tool. Choose lemon yellow as the foreground color, choose any "serious" font you like from the Options bar, and complete the logo's "P"s by adding "atio" and "erfection." With the Type Tool active, click near the top "P" and type "atio." Highlight the text and increase or decrease the point size (on the Options bar) until it's sized something like the text you see in Figure 4.40. Change tools to the Move tool (the text is a permanent entry on its own layer and the current layer is the type layer), and move the type until it appears to be centered in the composition. Repeat this process to type "erfection" near the lower "P" (of the logo).

And yes, this figure is tricked up to show Type tool options instead of showing the Move tool. You've *seen* the Move tool before!

Figure 4.40   Hey, you can create slides for presentations easily when you understand what tools are, where they are, and what they can do.

9. This is a good-looking presentation piece. Save it to your hard disk in Photoshop's PSD format, and you can close it at any time. Keep Photoshop Open.

I would say, "Not bad!" for nine steps. In fact, I *will*. You did *terrific*, starting with nothing; and nine steps later, using a little stock art, you've created an attention-getting slide or logo for a company.

By the way, if you want to store a copy of the logo vector path as a regular, normal path that's hard to accidentally delete, (with the Shape layer as the active layer on the Layers palette) double-click the clipping path's title on the Paths list. Name the path, and it's now a saved path in addition to a vector mask.

Wow! How many different ways have we explored paths and shapes? To create a clipping group, to add styles to a path, to fill a path, to turn a Shape into a clipping path…okay, I'm exhausted already.

But not too tired to show you one more way to put a twist into the flexible, indispensable path in Photoshop. Let's see how to create a path based on pixel color or a selection marquee.

Creating a Path from Different Image Properties

This is the "I got to creating images from paths. Now where's the way back?" section of this chapter. There are good tools for auto-creating paths, and there are excellent ways to do it. And we're going to show you both the tools and the methods you need.

First comes the book's shortest set of steps, which you use to add text to an image. Then you click a button to perform tracing.

Here goes:

Making a Work Path from a Selection

1. Create a new image; size is unimportant. Simply make sure the image is large enough to see, without magnification, in the workspace.

2. Click the Type tool, and type any character from any font. Because a point is about equal to a pixel, you'd best make this single character 100 points or more (a little more than an inch) so that Photoshop is tracing a shape and not a fly speck.

3. On the Layers palette, Ctrl(⌘)+click the type layer to create a marquee selection of the outline of the character.

4. On the Paths palette, click the Make Work Path from selection icon, as shown in Figure 4.41, and then press Ctrl(⌘)+D to deselect the selection. Yup. It's that simple to auto-create a path from a selection. End of tutorial, but keep the image open for a moment.

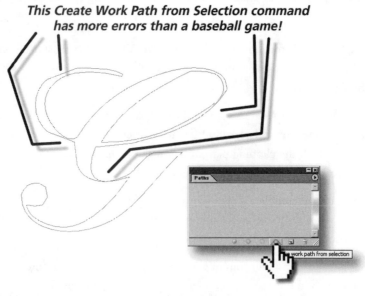

Figure 4.41   There's an icon you click in Photoshop to make any selection into a path (or collection of subpaths). The resulting path is of questionable benefit, though.

To be fair in our analysis of Photoshop's auto-trace feature, you can specify the degree of error (the Tolerance) with which a selection is traced. To access the Tolerance feature, Alt(Opt)+click when you click the Make work path from selection icon.

However, making the Tolerance a smaller value (the default is only two pixels…you don't get much smaller than that) will not necessarily increase the fidelity of the newly created path, which was shown in Figure 4.41. Do you really want to go with using this path? I'd say not without exporting it to Illustrator and making significant changes. Let's face it—this path is a dud.

Okay, you know by now that we are not going to leave you hanging. There's a new feature in Photoshop that enables you to create a precise path based on text. And the reason why it is so precise is that the method doesn't read what's onscreen. Instead, this method you're going to learn searches the typeface's outline file and creates a path based on sound, solid numbers and geometry.

The following exercise shows how to take any typeface character and turn it into an accurate path outline. (Hint: Symbol fonts will probably be of the most use. Save them to a Shapes palette as you did earlier.)

Using the Create Path Feature

1. Click the character you created in the last exercise by using the Move tool to select it.
2. Choose Layer, Type, Create Work Path, or Convert to Shape

   That's it! Click the Paths palette tab and save the work Path as a named path, and then save it to your collection of preset shape paths.

After you've saved a path based on the character, you can do all the things you've learned in the rest of this chapter to turn the character path into High Art. Check out the precision with which Photoshop created a path from the type in Figure 4.42.

BROAD CREATIVE HINT: USE THE LAYER,
TYPE, CREATE SHAPE (OR PATH)
FOR TRACES AS ACCURATE AS THIS ONE

Figure 4.42   It takes only two steps to accurately create a path (or group of subpaths) from a typed character.

Is this the end of the *paths saga*? Hardly; Chapter 5 gets you intimately involved in the *creation* of paths (we've been providing you with premade examples, and it *would* be nice if you worked out with the Pen tools!), so you have the option in Photoshop of using the paths of others or your own. If you take away one thing from this section, hopefully it's that paths are a welcome feature in Photoshop, and Adobe keeps making the capability of paths stronger and stronger with every release.

Summary

This chapter summary was originally going to be (ecch!) a bulleted list. But if you read the Table of Contents, you'll see that we indeed covered a lot of ground in Photoshop 7, dealing with only two features. If you can take to heart (IOW, *remember* <g>) a handful of techniques here, you've already become more dynamic and powerful in expressing yourself with pixels.

Earlier in this book, I mentioned that selection-making is the most refined and sought-after feature in Photoshop. As a means to this selecting-stuff goal, we have covered three main features in Photoshop: layers, paths, and channels. Chapter 5 gets you into the creation of paths and also explores about a billion ways (okay, *ten*) to manipulate image channels to create more compelling, more evocative artwork.

Chapter 5

Working with Channels and Paths

Photoshop layers have stolen a lot of the

glitz and glamour from other features that

can be used to edit images. To become a

Photoshop pro, however, you need to

understand *all* the big-time features in Photoshop, whether they seem sexy on the surface or not.

Image channels and paths have been features of Photoshop before there were layers (back in version 2.5), and today, you still can do some pretty amazing stuff with channels and paths that cannot be easily performed using layers. So call this a trip down Memory Lane, or call it a passage to a more thorough understanding of the entirety of Photoshop: You're going to see some fascinating *and* relevant stuff in the sections to follow.

Channels: A Definition and the Keys to Mastering Them

Let's pretend we can revisit grade school and are listening in on a lecture concerning how light is broken down into components. The professor whips out a prism, places it near sunlight (which is very close to absolute white), and ker-blooey…the white light is broken down into its components.

Although this is all very illuminating, it does not describe the *principle* of additive primary colors: the colors your computer monitor uses to make up all the colors you can imagine. What we need to do in our imaginary trip back to 4th grade is to come up with an equally imaginary device—a perverse prism—that will allow us to do the exact opposite of what a prism does. In Figure 5.1, you can see my own personal perverse prism. It's being fed red, green, and blue components on the left, and white light comes out the right side. What does this tell us? That three components—*channels* we'll call them—are the primary additive components that together at full intensity create white.

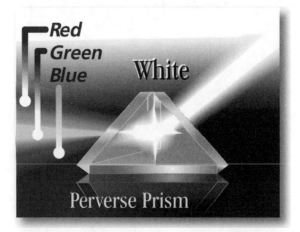

Figure 5.1   If a prism gathered components of white light and blended them, the action would essentially be what your monitor and video card does to create *additive color*.

Searching for More Colors

A good question right now is, "Hey, how do you get colors *other than white* using additive colors?" The equally good answer is in this bulleted list:

- You combine less than all three primary color channels at maximum brightness. For example, if you do not use green or red at all, the resulting color is blue. And if you mix green and blue together and ignore red, you arrive at the color cyan.

- You do not use the full brightness of a primary color in the mixture of additive colors. Orange, for example, is the result of mixing the red channel at full intensity, and the green channel at 50% intensity.

Figure 5.2 shows what happens when the first part of my answer is demonstrated using stage lights. Yes, I know the book is in black and white, but if you own stage lights (or even three flashlights with primary-color cellophane over them—*hint, hint*), you will see the secondary additive colors where two colors converge. Cyan, magenta, and yellow are called *complementary colors* in the additive color system, because they are a result of two neighboring colors in the color spectrum.

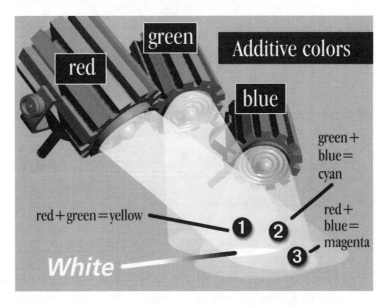

Figure 5.2 Additive colors have secondary, or complementary, colors. Add two primary colors to get a secondary color.

We're not done yet, and we cannot get to the fun assignments that follow unless we digress briefly into subtractive colors. You'll thank us someday for it; this discussion ties a lot of cosmic color theory stuff together.

Understanding Subtractive Colors

Most of us didn't get the straight story from our grade school teacher concerning primary colors. In fact, there might be some readers out there who will argue with me that red, blue, and yellow are the primary colors, because Mrs. Griswell said so before you were old enough to reach a steering wheel.

Well, it is true that red, blue, and yellow are primary colors, but *not in the additive color model*. You probably didn't get to fool around with primary colored lights in grade school, and chances are that the instructor used to pass out crayons as art materials. Pigments, such as crayons, house paint, artist's oil paints, and clothing textile paints, are all part of the *subtractive color system*. Instead of getting white when you mix all pigments together, you get black. Be sure to take a look at Figure 5.3; Gary worked hard to illustrate this point.

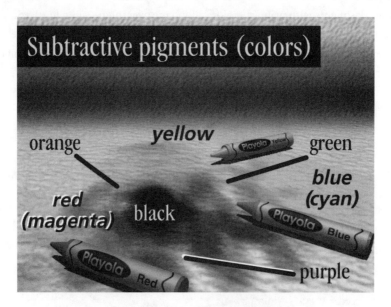

Figure 5.3   If you mix two subtractive colors together, you get a complementary color. All three colors added together at full intensity equals black.

Here's the interesting part: Commercial printing presses use subtractive colors, and the colors used to make up a composite (full-color original) picture are cyan, magenta, and yellow. Cyan is mighty close to blue, and magenta is close to red, so you can see now how your grade-school crayons were fairly close to what is used commercially to produce *process color*. We call this *CMYK color*.

The "K" is sort of unexpected in the abbreviation for cyan, magenta, and yellow. The "K" stands for **key**, or black. A key plate is used in printing to complete the visible range of whatever you are printing. Let's make life easy and simply call it the *black plate*. A black plate is added to the cyan, magenta, and yellow printing plates because pigments are not totally pure; some light is absorbed into the art material instead of being bounced back at you. So the average of all three intensities of colors on the color plates is used to generate this black plate, and color printing is not only possible, but also pleasing to look at. Without that fourth printing plate, you'd wind up with sludge-like browns in areas that should be black.

In the section to follow, you will get hands-on work with channels to visually demonstrate the additive light system, but also to have a little fun in Photoshop. Some erudite (fancy-talking) individuals in the computer graphics field will call the following section *ChOps*—short for "channel operations." I will simply call it "learning and having a ball by goofing around with some features in Photoshop."

Working with Color Channels

With the exception of the Macintosh color picker and a few applications, the intensity in each (primary) color channel that makes up an image goes from 0 (black) to 255 (white). This makes good sense when you consider that what we often say that a 24-bit/pixel image (also called a *TrueColor image*, when referring to it as displayed on a monitor) has three channels—red, green, and blue. Therefore, each channel gets 8 bits of color expression to the channel: 8 times 3 equals 24.

Eight bits of color intensity (or *tone*, or *brightness*) in a channel means that there are 2 to the eighth power of different brightness possibilities in each channel... or (we did the math for you; it only took an hour) 256 unique tones. And it's no coincidence that 256 (one channel's color capability) brought to the third power (there's three channels), equals 16.7 million possible total colors (or 2 to the 24th power).

In the example to follow (whew...thank goodness Bouton is going to shut up with this theory stuff for a while!), you are going to take a scene and add a green pear to it—*not* by painting it into the composite color channel, but instead by first masking all three channels (producing a black pear in the scene—no color channel is making a brightness contribution), and then adding a white pear shape to the green channel. The result is going to be a green pear. Why? Because the green channel will be the only channel that contributes brightness to the overall scene (also known as the *color composite*, or *RGB color channel*—this channel is shown at the top of the Channels palette).

Plop that Companion CD into your system's CD player, locate Examples/Chap05 folder, and let's get sailing...

Painting a Picture Using Channels

1. Open both the Basic.tif image and the Pear.psd image in Photoshop, found in the Examples/Chap05 folder on the Companion CD. Arrange both image windows so that you have a clear view of both images.

2. Press F7 if the Layers/Channels/Etc./Etc. palette isn't currently onscreen. Click the Channels tab.

   Now, if this is one of your first times out with Photoshop, you might want to click the flyout menu on the Channels palette, choose Options, and then click the largest icon on the Options palette; then close the options box. This ensures that even if you're running at a high screen resolution, you will be able to see the magic that is about to take place.

   Notice that in Figure 5.4, there are callouts that show which color channels contain brightness, and therefore contribute to the overall color scene, and which areas in which channels do not. For example, in the Blue channel, the entire top of the channel thumbnail is white. Do you know why? It's because the color composite of this image has a pure blue sky—100% brightness (white) is needed to create pure blue in the color composite. Take a moment to review this figure.

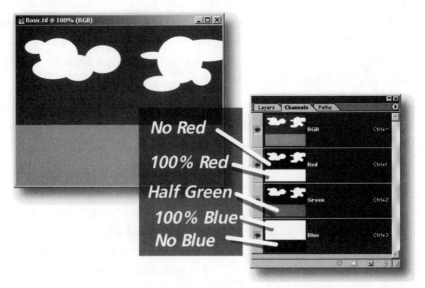

Figure 5.4 All color scenes are made up of color components—channels. And within the channel are tones that tell Photoshop how much of a particular primary color contributes to an overall scene.

3. With the Move tool chosen, drag the black pear into the RGB view of the Basic.tif image, as shown in Figure 5.5. Then, press Ctrl(⌘)+E to merge the layer that contains the black pear with the background design. This is not a mandatory editing move—it simply makes this assignment easier to follow if we aren't messing around with layers.

Note

Changing Channels   If you're uncertain of how to see the color composite image in an image window, press Ctrl(⌘)+tilde (~). Most intermediate users switch channels by clicking the channel thumbnail on the Channels palette. The channels are clearly labeled.

The way the author switches channels is with a remote control.

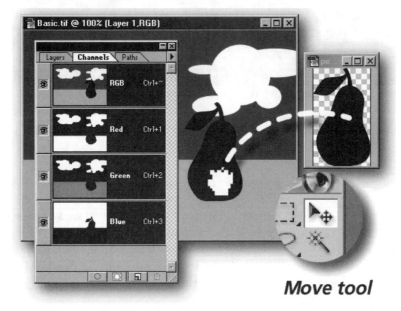

Move tool

Figure 5.5   Drag the black pear into the RGB channel of the Basic.tif image. Leave it to the right of the composition.

You will notice that every component channel turned black (0 color contribution) when you dragged the pear into Basic.tif.

4. Guess what comes next? Yup—you need to turn the black pear shape into a white pear shape, so it can contribute 100% brightness (full-color channel intensity) to the Green channel. Click the title bar to the Pear.psd image to make it the current image window in the workspace. Now press Ctrl(⌘)+I. This is the keyboard shortcut for inverting colors in an image. Ya got a white pear now.

5. Click the Green channel thumbnail with the Basic.tif image in the foreground of the workspace. Click the pear image to make it the current editing image. It does not matter what your channel, view of the pear shape is—all channels, including the RGB composite channel contain a white pear. Press Ctrl(⌘)+A to select all of the pear shape, and then use the Move tool to drag the pear shape into the Green channel view in the Basic.tif image window, as shown in Figure 5.6. With the Move tool, align the pear shape with the black pear outline that's in the green layer. Surprise! You will see a green pear emerge in the RGB color thumbnail of the image on the Channels palette!

*Move an inversed copy of the pear shape into the silhouette of
the first pear using the Green channel*

Figure 5.6   Adding 100% brightness to the green layer will result in a green object within
the RGB color composite view (the view we normally use) of the image.

6. Click the RGB channel thumbnail on the Channels palette to see a full-size version of your new composition in the image window. Okay, pears don't get this
green except in wax fruit stores, but you've just learned an invaluable lesson for
future channel editing in Photoshop. Class dismissed. You can close the Pear and
the Basic images at any time without saving.

A principle was shown in the preceding assignment. It was not meant to teach you how
to paint or edit, for there are quicker ways to put a green pear into a scene. Now that
you're getting a feel for this "goofing with channels"—or *gotcha*, as the non-erudite
author calls this stuff—let's progress to editing an image that would be somewhat hard
to color correct without digging into a channel.

Nice Picture, Rotten Weather

If you live in an area of the U.S. like the author's, you get an average of about five sunny
days a month. It's a photographer's nightmare—all the skies in the images look like the
color of lint. Not to worry; overcast skies are simply a combination of red, green, and
blue colors mixed in equal amounts. A neutral shade of black is the result of red, green,
and blue being applied in equal amounts, at less than full strength.

Let's get inventive here. *Hmmm*…if skies are supposed to be shades of blue, why not
accentuate the Blue channel in a picture and play down the Green and Red channels? We
frequently "goose" a screen capture here and there to bring out a property we want you
to see; to exaggerate a result. But we were shocked when we saw how much detail in the

sky was hidden there when the green and red were reduced in the image you will use in a moment.

Using a nice picture of an art deco building with little or no sky detail, here's how to add visual interest to the image by re-working the colors in the channels:

Revealing Scene Objects by Manipulating Channels

1. Open the Mohawk.tif image from the Examples/Chap05 folder on the Companion CD. (The image is the Niagara-Mohawk power company building here in town; that explains the file name.)

2. Click the Magic Wand and then click on the Channels palette, the Red channel layer. Okay, you should notice a mild amount of tonal variation in the Red channel, but it's all basically off-white. Set the Tolerance on the Options bar to 32 (a number the author came to through trial and error; 32 out of a possible 256 tones is a moderately narrow tolerance for selecting pixels).

3. Click the Anti-Aliased checkbox on the palette to make a smooth selection edge, and finally, click the Contiguous checkbox. If you don't do this, *every* instance of the color the Magic Wand selects will be chosen in the picture—including the interior of the building!

4. Click the Magic Wand tool as shown in Figure 5.7. As you can see, the sky is selected, and the building has no selection marquees inside its silhouette.

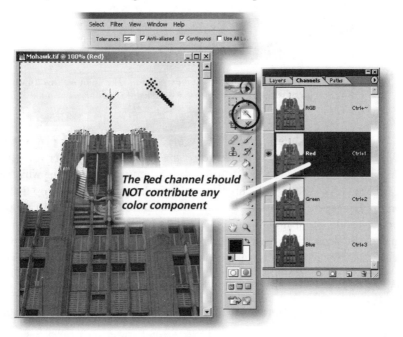

Figure 5.7   Select the part of the channel that is making more of an overall color contribution than it should.

5. Press Ctrl(⌘)+L to display the Levels command. This feature can re-tune the brightness values in an image according to three zones: highlights, midtones, and shadows. In the Input area, drag the black point and the midtone sliders to the right, as shown in Figure 5.8. What you're doing here is telling Photoshop that the channel's black point exists at much more than 0 on a scale of 0–255. The black point, which is the slider control farthest to the left, is currently set at 51, and the midtone slider is set to .16, as you can see in the Input Levels fields in the figure. You can use these settings if you like or come up with something that suits you better.

Figure 5.8   Except for sunsets, there usually isn't any red in the sky. Remove this unwanted primary color. Use the Levels command on part of the channel to make it darker (reduce its overall contribution to the RGB image).

The effect? The channel's visual contents become darker. You can play around with these input settings if you like to get the effect you want. After you get the input levels the way you want them, on the Output scale, reduce the white point to about 203, as shown in Figure 5.9. Again, you are telling Photoshop that white in this image actually starts at 203 on a scale of 0–255. Click OK. So, although you've lied to Photoshop in only one step, you will notice that the color thumbnail of the sky is taking on a cyan color. This happens because although you've eliminated the red, there is still a dollop of green in the total area of the sky in the image.

Warning

Be Careful with the Midtone Slider   Don't go too far to the right with the midtone slider, or you won't see white clouds in the picture. Instead, you'll see only shades of blue when you've finished this assignment.

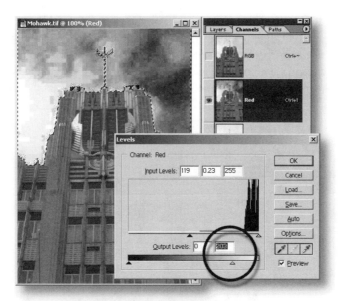

Figure 5.9   Negate any pure (255 brightness scale) contributions to the Red channel by
lowering the white point Output level.

6. Perform Step 5 on the Green channel, as shown in Figure 5.10. As you can see, it
only takes a slide to the right with the midtones control to really make the sky
come alive in the image thumbnail and in the image. Click OK to apply the
changes and return to the workspace.

Make the Green channel dense by increasing the midpoint

Figure 5.10   By darkening the Red and Green channels, the image is left with brightnesses
in the blue range, and this produces a mottled, realistic sky in the picture.

7. Click the RGB color channel thumbnail on the Channels palette. You will see a sky with different tones (but no white clouds because white requires red, green, and blue at full intensity). Figure 5.11 *suggests* the results—hey, it's a black and white book, and we even exaggerated the tones in this figure to give you a better idea of the picture after experimenting with channels.

Figure 5.11   Emphasizing a channel while playing down the others is a good method for bringing out the detail of the image as your human eye envisions it. Forget about what photography taught you—it's the aesthetics of the image that count!

8. You can choose to save the image at this point (TIFF is a good format), or close it without saving. Now that you realize the point of the assignment, there's no real need to keep the product. Changing the tone in one channel of an image is only one way to bring out qualities that the original picture did not show. Let's get creative in the next section and *add* to the image detail that was never there.

Filtering a Channel

By this late date (IOW, five minutes after you've installed Photoshop!), you must surely have experimented with the filters and your favorite (or least favorite) photo. Photoshop is well-known for its special effects prowess; over 100 filters ship with the program.

Let's choose a particular filter, and instead of applying it to the photo, we'll apply it to a single channel and see how artistically we can mess up an image. Hey, *New Media* runs stuff like this all the time:

Applying a Filter to a Color Channel

1. Open the Big_Dip.tif image from the Examples/Chap05 folder on the Companion CD. Double-click the Zoom tool to move your viewing resolution of the image to 100%, and then drag the window borders away from the image, if necessary, to see the whole image onscreen.

2. Click the Channels tab of the Layers/Channels/Blah/Blah palette, and then click the Green channel title to make this channel appear in the image window. Why are we doing this? Because we want to mess up the image a little, not a lot. And as you can see in Figure 5.12, the Green channel contributes some but not all of the component colors.

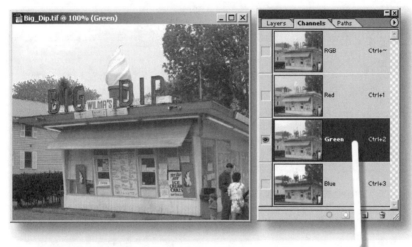

Green channel is fairly dim. This means it makes a so-so color contribution to the overall image.

Figure 5.12   If you want to make minor color changes to an image, find a channel that has very little visual information. The more dense the tones, the less contribution to the overall image this channel makes.

3. Choose Filter/Artistic/Colored Pencil. In Figure 5.13, you can see that the Colored Pencil filter *really* messes around with original tones! The Green channel's filtered tones will create a very different type of image. Click OK to apply the filter and return to the workspace. Click the RGB channel to view the full results.

4. In Figure 5.14, you can see a grayscale version of the finished image. You can choose to save the file to the TIFF format, or simply close it without saving—that's what *I* do to keep my hard drives clear of experiments that aren't of the artistic quality of the Mona Lisa. Keep Photoshop open. There's more fun with channels ahead.

Figure 5.13   By changing tones in the channel, you're actually mixing new amounts of red, green, and blue in the image to make a dramatic effect.

Figure 5.14   Sorry that this figure is in black and white! If you perform the steps, on your screen, you'll see an image that appears to have been taken under fluorescent lighting about 50 years ago, at sunset, with mild solarization (similar to inverting tones in an image). And all you did was filter a single channel!

We tend to take it for granted that the component colors onscreen (and in slides) are aligned. In other words, we hardly think (or worry) that, for example, the Red channel will be misaligned with the two other channels. In fact, a lot of monitors have a convergence feature that keeps the cathode guns in the back of the monitor aligned to hit exactly the same area of phosphors on the screen.

Hey, part of art is whimsy and going against convention. Let's see in the following section how art is achieved by deliberately misaligning the visual information in channels.

Using Offset Channels to Create an Effect

You can use any image you like for the following steps, but we've provided you with a perfectly good one: a hand-drawn cartoon in color. The trick I'm going to show you generally works best with cartoon figures, pictures of people you don't like, and simple, colorful objects such as billiard or croquet balls and informal dinnerware (Pier 1 stuff).

The Sunday color funnies in the newspaper have gained over the years a rightfully sorry reputation of printing inks that are out of register. I've seen colors fall at least 1/4" out of their target on a bad day. However, this mis-registration effect has become somewhat of an artistic icon. And here's how to reproduce it digitally:

Creating Misaligned Channels

1. Open the Geek.tif image from the Examples/Chap05 folder on the Companion CD. Or use a picture of your boss.
2. Open the Channels palette (press F7), and then choose the Move tool. The Move tool needs to be chosen because you cannot use the keyboard arrow keys when any other tool is chosen. And you will be nudging. Figure 5.15 shows the players in this assignment.

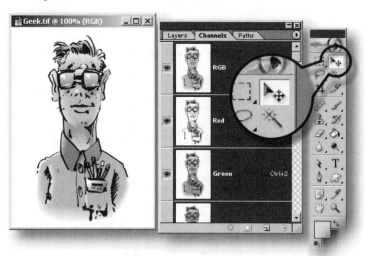

Figure 5.15   An image, the Channels palette, and the Move tool are all you need to create a comic book effect in Photoshop.

3. Click the Green channel title on the Channels palette. Nudge the Green channel up by 2 pixels by tapping twice on the up arrow, and then nudge the channel to the left by two pixels by tapping the left arrow by 2 pixels (see Figure 5.16).

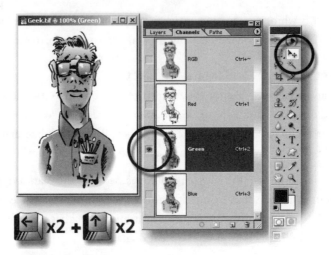

Figure 5.16   You're knocking the alignment of the Green channel's contents away from the other channels by tapping the arrow keys when the Move tool is chosen.

4. Click the Red channel to make it the current editing channel. Nudge the channel down by two pixels and to the right by two pixels.

5. Click the RGB title on the Channels palette's list. Yeah, yeah, Figure 5.17 is in black and white, but it should give you a fair idea of the wonderful effect caused when the three component channels in an image don't line up. For larger images, nudge the channels away from the center by more than 2 pixels; use your own artistic taste.

Figure 5.17   A comic book look can be achieved simply by throwing the color channels in an image off-center.

6. If you used your own image in these steps, you might want to save the image to your hard drive in the TIFF file format. Similarly, if you really like this weird version of one of the author's cartoons, save it. If you see the potential of this trick in your work and have no need for a test image, close it without saving.

Coming up next is a technique for adding text to an image *without* disturbing the graphic arrangement of the image. You'll *create* a channel, add some text, and …we don't want to spoil this now—read on!

Alpha Channels: Storage Space for Special Information

So far, we've played with what an image can provide—a number of color channels that together make up a color image. But don't think for a moment that an image can have only three channels: CMYK images have four channels, and Duotone images have two color channels. CMYK is a necessary color space because printing inks cannot capture RGB colors completely with fidelity. So Cyan, Magenta, Yellow, and Black simulate computer art colors. Soft-proofing (looking at your image with CMYK "spectacles") is covered in Chapter 7, "Understanding Photoshop's Color Management System." And Duotone is a color mode that uses a color plate in addition to a grayscale plate to make the gray tones look richer…truth be known, black ink doesn't provide total coverage on paper of the design you create.

In addition to the channel information that makes up an image, you can *add* a channel of grayscale visual information to an image for purposes we'll discuss in a moment. Targa format can hold one extra channel, as can Macintosh PICT files. TIFF images can hold several extra alpha (information) channels, and Photoshop's native PSD file format can hold up to 32 channels (a ridiculously luxurious amount). Before Photoshop refined the Layers feature, alpha channels were a must because this is where you could store and retrieve selection areas you created with the Lasso tool or the Quick Mask tool. Suppose you were in the middle of some really intricate selection work, and Mom called you for dinner. No problem—you saved your work to an *alpha channel.*

Using an Alpha Channel to Store Typography

As you will see in this chapter, alpha channels can be used to store selection information such as an area or the outline of text, and also to save texture images to be used with the Lighting Effects filter. Alpha channels are handy enough that we should take some steps toward mastering them. And those steps are as follows…

Creating a Type Effect Using an Alpha Channel

1. Open the Flowers.tif image from the Examples/Chap05 folder on the Companion CD.

2. This is a step that should be a Note or mentioned in *every* assignment. Move the Flowers image to the upper left of the screen. Then, click the Type tool. By moving the image window, you are assured that you can see the text as it is rendered to the image while the Type toolbox is open. You cannot move image windows once a dialog box, filter, or other menu item or palette has been called. But you can always move the dialog box.

3. Now that the Type tool is chosen, you can access the Character and Paragraph palettes by clicking the menu icon on the right of the Options bar (marked as item 1 in Figure 5.18). Choose a pretty font from the Character palette (item 2), and you can either experiment with the right font size for this image or take our word for it that 110 points will be a good size. Type **Flowers** on the image. Highlight the text, click the Color swatch on the Options bar, and then choose white from the color picker if the foreground color (and the text) is not already white. Then use the Move tool to position the text on the image (item 3) to give you a good idea that the point size will accommodate the whole word. Check out Figure 5.18 to see what I'm describing here.

Figure 5.18   Create text that has ornamental features and scale it in the Type tool dialog box so that it will fit nicely on the background.

4. Click OK to get out of the color picker. If text is still highlighted, click in the text to view the text. Press Ctrl(⌘)+Enter (Return) to apply a layer of editable text to the Flowers image. If necessary, hold down the Ctrl(⌘) key to toggle to the

Move tool and center the text. So what did this have to do with channels? Wait a
sec and you'll see. On the Layers palette, Ctrl(⌘)+click the text layer title—this
creates a marquee selection around the lettering.

5. On the Channels palette, Alt(Opt)+click the Save selection as channel icon at the
bottom of the Channels palette. By using the Alt(Opt) modifier key, an options
box pops up before saving the selection of the text to a new alpha channel. Here's
where you can make life easy on yourself. Although native color component channels all work on the "black contributes no color; white contributes a lot of color"
principle, alpha channels can skip this rule because alpha channels are not pictor-
ial information channels. In Figure 5.19, you can see the Alt(Opt)+click (item 1)
that brings up the Options box (item 2), and you should check Color Indicates
Selected Areas. Do you know why? Because it's far more intuitive to write with
black on white than it is to perform a "blackboard" thing where you have to draw
using white on a black alpha channel to define selections.

Click OK to add the lettering outline to the new alpha channel, and press
Ctrl(⌘)+D to deselect the selection marquee.

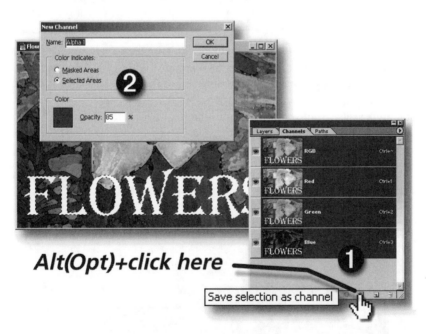

Figure 5.19   Alt(Opt)+click the Save selection as channel icon, and then choose whether you
want to work black on white or white on black in the new alpha channel.

6. Okay, the lettering has been saved as black on white in the alpha channel. How
do you get it to work as a selection marquee? Glad you asked: Either hold
Ctrl(⌘) and click the image thumbnail on the Channels palette list (the tiny
picture of the alpha channel), or (more conventionally) click the Channel title
and then click the Load channel as selection icon (see Figure 5.20).

Figure 5.20   Load the visual information stored in the alpha channel as a selection marquee.

7. Here's the really fun part: Click the RGB channel title on the Channels palette list, and then click the Background layer to make it the current editing layer. Next, poke the Text layer's eyeball in the eye to hide it. Then press Ctrl(⌘)+L to display the Levels dialog box.

8. Again, carefully arrange the image window so that when the Levels dialog box pops up, it doesn't cover the picture. As shown in Figure 5.21, drag the white point and the midpoint slider close to the left of the Input levels scale. This lightens the area inside the selection marquee, but the visual content—the flowers—is still quite visible. Can you think of, oh, about a million situations where you need to add a title without disturbing the image? Here's the ticket (okay, here's one of many tickets). Click OK. Press Ctrl(⌘)+D to deselect the text.

Figure 5.21   By moving the midpoint and white point sliders to the left, you are assigning pixels lighter colors than they originally had. The effect is an eye-pleasing one, and one you can use on many occasions.

9. There's no big need to hang on to this assignment, so close the image without saving. Keep Photoshop open.

So far, we've covered color channels, saving to alpha channels, and loading selections from channels. Channels and selections seem to be irrevocably intertwined as Photoshop features go. Let's pay another visit to selecting and saving to a channel, but this time there's a twist. You'll be using the Quick Mask feature for selecting and applying an effect to the image.

Setting Up and Using the Quick Mask Feature

The Quick Mask is an excellent feature that professionals use all the time when they want to select by painting over something instead of creating an outline around the part of the design (as selection tools do). The only problem with the Quick Mask feature, and it's not a big one, is that when you switch from Quick Mask to Standard Editing mode, you *must* then save that marquee selection to a channel—or your selecting work has gone into the dumpster.

You have a challenge here, but pssssst, *we don't grade papers*, so don't get all nervous. Let's see how you can select using the Quick Mask feature. And then save to a channel.

Isolating an Image Element and Saving It

1. Open the Ducks.tif image from the Examples/Chap05 folder on the Companion CD. Double-click the Zoom tool, and then drag the window edges away from the image so that you can see the whole image.

2. Press D (default colors), and then, if your Quick Mask icon on the bottom of the toolbox looks like the top icon in Figure 5.22, don't do anything…you're cool. But if the icon looks like a clear circle with shading *outside* of the circle (shown in the bottom right of the figure), then uh-oh; your paint strokes will represent masked areas when you switch back to Standard Editing mode. This is easy enough to correct: Hold Alt(Opt)+click the Quick Mask icon and it inverts the selection and masked areas.

3. Select the Brush tool and click the Brush down-arrow in the Options bar. When the Brushes palette appears, drag the Master Diameter slider to turn the selected brush into a 35-pixel hard edge tip. Then, carefully paint around the edge of the tulip, gradually working inward until the whole tulip is painted over.

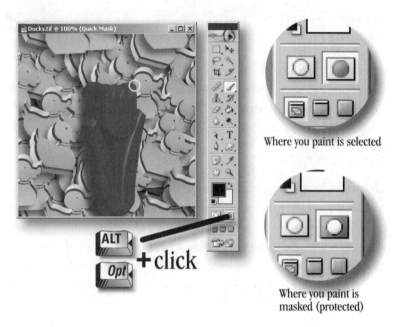

Where you paint is selected

Where you paint is
masked (protected)

Figure 5.22   Apply Quick Mask tint to the tulip to select it from the background.

Tip

Undo Painting Messes   As you'll remember from the chapters on selections, if you make a mistake, press X to make white the current foreground color, and then drag through the mistake to erase it (which in effect paints the pixels white). Then, press X again to change the color back to your previous selection and continue painting.

4. Click the Standard Editing icon to the left of the Quick Mask mode icon; the tint areas you painted become the "inside" of a selection marquee at the edges of the Quick Mask. The background is not selected.

5. Click the Channels tab of the grouped palette, and then click the Saves selection as channel icon, as shown in Figure 5.23. By default, the channel is named "Alpha 1." If you want to get fancy and make up your own alpha channel name, hold Alt(Opt) as you click the icon on the bottom of the Channels palette. Doing this saves the selection, but first prompts you with an options box in which you can enter a name for the alpha channel, such as "Tulip," or "liposuction," or "bowling league night."

Tip

Taking the Direct Route   You also can type directly into a name field on a title on the palettes. This is new to PS 7. Double-click a name, and then type the name you want.

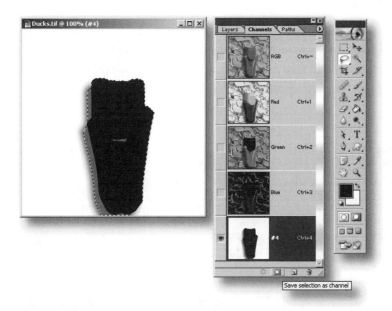

Figure 5.23   Save a selection based on your painting work with the Quick Mask option.

At any time in the future, you can load the saved selection in Alpha 1 by Ctrl(⌘)+clicking its title on the Channels palette. From there, you can copy or cut the selection to a new layer to eventually make a whole bunch of tulips in the image or copy the tulip to the clipboard and then to a new image window.

6. You can close the image at any time without saving it. Or you might want to experiment with it later. In either event, close the image and keep Photoshop open.

An alpha channel, as you know, does not have to hold photographic content. An alpha channel doesn't need to carry selection information, either, to be useful. In the section that follows, you will see how an alpha channel can hold a texture rendering—specifically a scan of crumpled paper—that can be used to add dimension and texture to any image.

Using a Texture and the Lighting Effects Filter

If you're into independent experimenting with Photoshop (as opposed to experimenting under the guidance of this book), you may have hit upon the Filter/Render/Lighting Effects filter. You might have had the impression that you can change the lighting in an image with this filter. Nooooope—you can only treat an image as though it's hanging on the wall, and you're directing lighting at the picture.

But there's a secondary use for the Lighting Effects filter that is very cool, and it might remind you of Corel Painter's Apply Surface Texture command. In Photoshop, you can fill a channel with a pattern and then use the Texture Channel feature to emboss the RGB color channel with a texture image of your choice.

In the steps that follow, you use an image of crumpled paper (which also happens to be a seamless tiling image) to fill an alpha channel. You then apply this Texture Channel feature to only the background of the image, giving the image a crumpled appearance and making it a real attention-getter (the good kind, we hope).

Creating a Canvas with Character

1. Open the Crumple.tif image from the Examples/Chap05 folder on the Companion CD. While you're at it, open egg.tif from the same folder. You'll need it later in this exercise.

2. Choose Edit, Define Pattern, as shown in Figure 5.24. Photoshop 7 saves patterns by using a dialog box, so those of us who've used previous versions of Photoshop will get a little surprise here. You do *not* need to have the pattern selected if it takes up the whole image window, by the way.

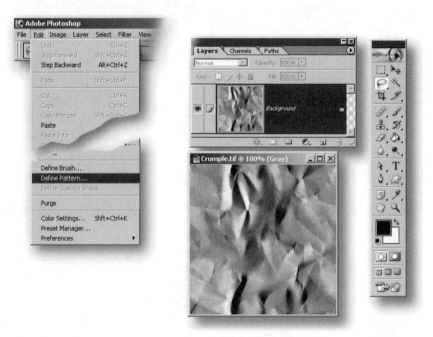

Figure 5.24   Choose Edit, Define Pattern to display the dialog box for saving patterns to a collection you can then apply to image areas later.

3. In the Pattern Name dialog box, type **Crumple**, as shown in Figure 5.25, and then click OK. The pattern is now saved to Photoshop, and even if you close and then re-open Photoshop, the program remembers that you've saved a texture named "Crumple." Close the **Crumple.tif** image without saving changes (it is no longer needed at this point).

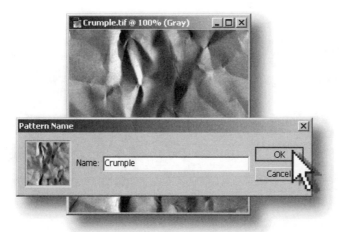

Figure 5.25   Name the pattern you want to save. Later in your adventures, you can have the Patterns palette display only the name of the fill, a thumbnail (the default presentation), or a list of all the patterns you've saved.

4. Select the egg.tif image you opened earlier. You now need to create an alpha channel into which you can tile the sampled pattern. And like paths, it's probably a good idea to name the channel as you create it. First, Alt(Opt)+click the Create New Channel icon on the bottom of the Channels palette. Then, when the New Channel dialog box appears, type the name for the channel. **Crumple** is swell, as shown in Figure 5.26. Click the Color Indicates: Selected Areas option—this means light areas of the pattern will remain light instead of inverted with the denser areas—and then click OK. We need to do this to select the background and not the foreground.

5. Choose Edit, Fill. Choose Pattern from the Use drop-down list. A palette within a dialog box pops up, and you can choose the crumpled paper pattern by clicking it (see Figure 5.27) and then pressing Enter.

Note

Using the Paint Bucket Tool   You also can fill a channel or selection by using the Paint Bucket tool, which is kinda hidden in this version of Photoshop. You click and hold the Gradient tool in the toolbox until the tool flies out to display the Paint Bucket tool. Like all the tools, options for the Paint Bucket are displayed on the Options bar.

Tip

Displaying Patterns the Way You Want 'Em   When the dialog box for Fill is displayed, it's your chance to turn the Pattern palette into a list or name-only presentation. Click the flyout button (the right-facing triangle on the top, right of the palette) and choose the type of display of patterns you want. Also, to change the name of a pattern, right click (Macintosh: hold Ctrl and click) the swatch and choose Rename Pattern.

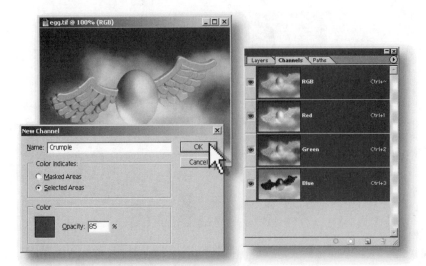

Figure 5.26   It's important to name the channels you create, but your Color Indicates choice is even more important.

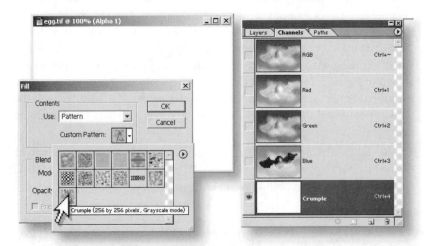

Figure 5.27   You can see the list of patterns you've saved and also customize the view of the collection while the Fill dialog box's patterns list is displayed.

6. Press Enter (Return) after making your pattern selection, and you will see that the Alpha channel 1 is filled from edge to edge with the crumpled paper pattern. Again, the sample crumpled paper was carefully designed not to show tiling marks.

7. Press Ctrl(⌘)+tilde (~) to return your view of the image window to RGB composite (normal) view. Choose Filter, Render, and then choose Lighting Effects. Hint: Run 800 by 600 or better to use this filter. The dialog box is huge.

8. Choose Directional as the Light Type from the drop-down list. This light type is like very distant illumination—you can avoid putting overexposed spots (hot spots) on the canvas by using this light type.

   Your other choices here are Spotlight and Omni. The Omni light is not that easy to control—you might have problems keeping a hot spot off the target image. The Spotlight option puts a "scoop" in the picture where the edges of the spotlight are cut off by the sudden drop-off of light, characteristic of a real-world spotlight. Experiment with these other types on your own—you might find a legit use for them in the future.

9. Drag the light source dot (on the line in the proxy window—sneak a peek at Figure 5.28) toward or away from the image to set the amount of overall light in the image. In practice, the lighting should match the original brightness of the image. A good way to check this is by moving the Lighting Effects box and comparing the proxy window's illumination to the original image. Practice this three times, tops, and you'll be a pro at the technique.

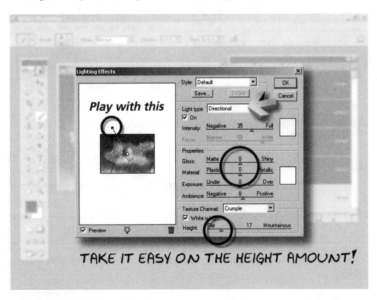

Figure 5.28 Besides imitating light being cast at an image, the Lighting Effects filter can be used to add texture—dimension—to your favorite image. Or mine.

10. Make sure that the Gloss and Material sliders are at zero (0). You do not want to add any other effects besides texturing to the image. Naturally, these controls can be of use in your own assignments when you want to make a selection area really slick-looking.

11. In the Texture Channel drop-down list, choose Crumple, and choose White is high by clicking in the checkbox. White is high means that white areas in the texture channel will appear to rise, and black or in-between shades will appear to recede, exactly as the crumpled paper image appears.

12. Before clicking OK, drag the Height slider to the left, until a 17 appears, as shown in Figure 5.28. The crumpled paper channel has a lot of contrast, so to use it as a texture map (an image that simulates elevations), you do not need a lot of its effect.

13. Click OK, and voila, you should have a crumpled egg picture, as shown in Figure 5.29. Chances are that you own a better picture to do this texturing stuff with, so after this assignment, you might as well check around your hard disks for a good target image *that you made a copy of* and a good seamless pattern (strong hint: the Boutons folder on the Companion CD has a bunch of them), and then texturize it.

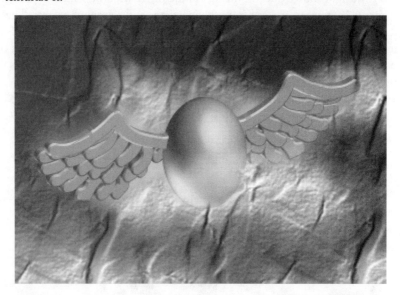

Figure 5.29   Using a Texture channel on an image is a particularly good way to set up a photograph to look antique when printed on an inkjet printer.

14. You can close the image at any time without saving it. Keep Photoshop open.

Tip

For More Information   Check out Part V, "Photoshop for Artists," and you'll see how to paint textures into alpha channels to really make the RGB composite image look like a painting.

This concludes our section on Photoshop channels. You now have enough information to get really creative and seize a lot of the power of "channel operations."

In the section to follow, you'll become acquainted (intimately) with the vector part of Photoshop: paths.

Paths, as in Those Things in Illustrator and CorelDRAW

It's pretty neat that Adobe Systems has beefed up the vector tool part of Photoshop, because vector graphics and pixel-based images are two entirely different types of computer graphics. You will almost never confuse vector artwork with bitmaps, but through Photoshop, you can take the best properties of both kinds of graphics and meld them into *very* special bitmap images.

An Introduction to Vector Tools Before You Use Them

I found that with my own tutelage, it was better to know what a tool did by (gasp!) reading the manual instead of getting down to work and drowning in sludge—a result of driving before you take the car out of park, as it were. Adobe documents the tools very well in the Photoshop owner's manual, but what we're going to do here is show you the relationship among the tools, show how certain tools are superfluous most of the time, and explain how to best use the tools (including the shortcuts and the motions you'll use to design stuff). Illustrator users have an advantage here, due to the fact that Photoshop's Pen tool group is almost exactly like Illustrator's Pen set.

Not to worry. We're gonna knock on every door in the neighborhood, as follows.

In Figure 5.30, you can see what happens when you click and hold on the top-facing tool, on a flyout palette, on the toolbox. From here, you can select any of the path drawing tools and one modifying tool—the Convert Point tool. Most of the tools here are self-explanatory, except for the Convert Point and Freeform Pen tools.

- The Freeform Pen tool is used by simply dragging it around an image. When you stop dragging, path segments and anchor points appear (a path can be open or closed). Anchor points are the square dots between path segments that can be manipulated using other tools to change directly neighboring path segments. Additionally, you can make the Freeform Pen tool magnetic (check this option on the Options palette), so that all you have to do is click an edge where one color meets a different one in an image and then hover the cursor along the color edge, and the Freeform Pen does the rest by tracing the edge. If this is what you want from the tool, we recommend clicking at regular intervals with the tool to lay down anchor points. Why? Because the more anchor points you create, the more accurate the finished path will be.

- The Convert Point tool is used for changing the property of an anchor point. When a path passes through an anchor point, it does not have to do so smoothly. By dragging on an anchor point with this tool, if the path passing through the point is sharp, the tool will make the anchor point smooth. And if you tug on a direction point (covered shortly) that belongs to an anchor point, you'll make a smooth transition through the point a sharp transition. Finally, if you just click on an anchor point with this tool without dragging, you'll straighten out the path segments that meet at the anchor point.

As you can see in Figure 5.30, the Auto Add/Delete checkbox appears on the Options bar whenever you use the Pen tool. This diminishes the need for the Add Anchor Point tool and Delete Anchor point tool. With this checkbox checked:

- Whenever you click an anchor using the Pen tool, the anchor is deleted (and the path changes shape).

- Whenever you click a path segment, an anchor is created. And you can use the Convert Point tool to change the properties of the new anchor.

So there are two tools on the Pen tool flyout you really never need to access.

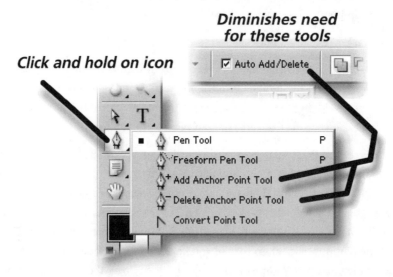

Figure 5.30   The flyout on the toolbox that offers all the vector drawing tools in Photoshop.

Note

Bookmark It!   You'd do well to bookmark this section for future reference as you work on assignments of your own.

Perhaps Adobe felt the Pen tool flyout was long enough and wanted to start yet another flyout for path-handling tools. In Figure 5.31, you can see the flyout for the path selection tools: the Path Selection tool and the Direct Selection tool. We're going to run through what the Path Selection tool does first, because you may not need to use it very often (so we're getting the function of it out of the way to better concentrate on the more productive vector tools).

Figure 5.31   The Path Selection tool flyout.

Let's test drive the Path Selection tool to provide good examples for the occasions that call for it.

Using the Path Component Selection Tool Two Ways

1. Open the Doodle.tif image from the Companion CD. You won't see any paths in the image window right now because they are not selected.

2. Press F7 to display the Layers/Channels/Paths/YaDaDa grouped palette, click the Paths tab, and then click the title on the Paths list called "Doodles" (it's the only path group in the image). Magically, the paths appear in the image window.

Note

> **Work Paths**   Work paths do not belong to a specific layer. Paths created using the Shape Layer tool (covered in Chapter 4, "Enough Selections! The Layers and Shapes Chapter,") are always confined to a specific layer, however.
>
> You can modify, stroke, and fill work paths (and named/saved paths) to apply color to any layer you choose. The paths in Doodles were preserved in this CD image file because it is a *saved* work path; you save a path by double-clicking the work path's title on the Paths palette and then naming it. Then, from session to session, the path will remain intact in the image.

3. Choose the Path Selection tool from the flyout on the toolbox. Now, click the spiral doodle in the Doodles.tif image. All the anchor points will become filled, indicating that the entire shape has been chosen and can now be modified independently of the dot-shaped path.

   Note that Show Bounding Box is now an option on the Options bar. This is a good choice to click if you immediately want to rotate, distort, skew, or apply other Free Transform distortions to the selected path. But we're here to find stuff in the interface, and this is only one of two ways to send the selected path spinning.

4. Right-click (Macintosh: hold Ctrl and click), and then choose Free Transform Path from the Context menu. Immediately, control boxes for transformations appear on the Options bar, and you can type a specific amount to change the orientation or shape of the shape…but this is more boring than applying a transformation manually (and helps the author show off another point with the tool).

5. Hover your cursor at a corner of the transform box, and then drag up and to the left. As you can see in Figure 5.32, I've rotated the spiral shape by -10 degrees (positive rotation is clockwise in Photoshop). Why don't you do this now, too? (If you're interested in a shortcut, simply enter **-10** in the Transform field in the Options bar.)

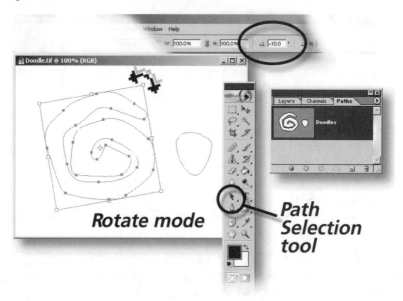

Figure 5.32   The Path Selection tool is really neat. (Do I have to have *all* good figure captions in this book?)

6. Heads up! To finalize the transformation, press Enter (Return). If you've goofed up the shape somehow and want another crack at rotating it, press Esc(ape). This negates any proposed transformations you've made. You also can use the History palette to back your way out of an error (Window, Show History).

Okey-dokey; you've seen one use for the Path Selection tool. Here's the other one:

7. With the Path Selection tool, marquee select both shapes (in other words, start dragging in the upper left of the image window and drag diagonally to the bottom right).

8. Now the Options bar looks entirely different, as shown in Figure 5.33. You have the option of aligning the two paths vertically and horizontally.

> **Tip**
>
> **Distributing Paths**   When you have more than two paths selected, you also have the choice of distributing the paths by position, which is a good way to evenly space the elements of a pattern.

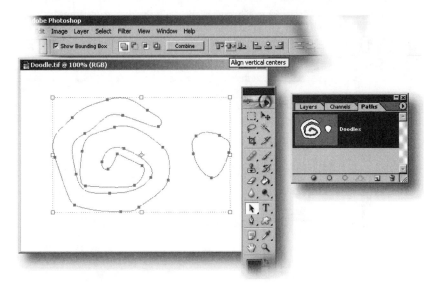

Figure 5.33   If you select two paths, your options for editing your work with the Path Selection tool are to align the paths vertically and/or horizontally.

9. That's it. That's "The Show" with the Path Selection tool. You can close Doodles.tif at any time and keep Photoshop open.

As I mentioned earlier, this chapter explores the manual use of path creation and editing tools. Photoshop shapes are also paths, but creating them is an automated routine, and instructions on working with shapes is in Chapter 4.

The next section provides more than you'd ever want to know about Photoshop paths. This is a "memorize everything you can" kind of section, but if you come away with only three things about Photoshop path tools, you'll be working like a pro later in this chapter.

The Anatomy of a Path

Before we do anything, click the Pen tool on the toolbox. As you can see in Figure 5.34, the Options bar displays three different icons that will have an impact on the design you create. *Do not* click the left icon; this icon will create a new (Shapes) layer and many of the rules you will learn about hand-drawn paths will not apply (clipping paths are covered in Chapter 4, however).

Instead, click the center icon, as shown in Figure 5.34. This is the normal work and saved path mode for path creation.

Tip

What About the Right Icon?   By the way, the right icon enables you to draw shapes that are immediately converted to pixels—no vector path or otherwise is involved. You might want to use this mode in combination with the Shapes tool (which calls up the Shapes palette on the Options bar) to make quick signs or flyers, when your graphics needs are undemanding.

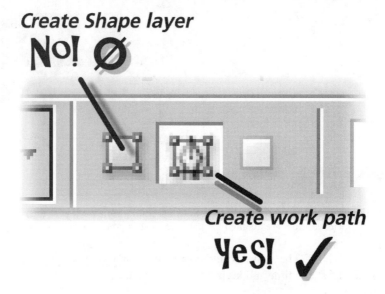

Figure 5.34   Create work paths using the Pen tool and other tools by first choosing the Path mode on the Options bar.

Anchors and Segments

Let's take a look at how the Pen tool is used to draw. A *path* in Photoshop consists of several components:

- First, there is the *segment*—a path segment always has an anchor point at the beginning and end of it.

- These *anchor points* determine the course of a path as it passes through the point. When you click with the Pen tool, successive clicks create anchor points with straight path segments in-between anchors.

- If you *drag* while you click, you create a *curved* path segment between where you are dragging and your previous click or drag. Also, when you drag while you're holding the primary mouse button, your finishing point is not an anchor point but a different component of paths: the direction point.

- A *direction point* is at both ends of a curved segment, sprouting off the very last anchor point you make. Direction points are connected to an anchor by direction handles, which determine the severity and direction of a curved path segment by the location at which you position the direction point.

Now you know how to make a straight path segment and how to bend it as you progressively create a path. But how do you change the property of an anchor point, and how do you reposition it? Aha! Read on!

The Direct Selection Tool

You can access the Direct Selection tool by clicking it on the toolbox, but why change tools in the middle of an artistic effort? The smarter, easier way to access this important tool is to hold Ctrl(⌘) while the Pen tool is selected. You can then use the Direct Selection tool to bend a path segment (you click an anchor to reveal the direction points used to steer the curve). The Direct Selection tool also can be used to click an anchor and move it. This reshapes a segment of the path.

Figure 5.35 provides a review of anchor and segment techniques using the Pen and Direct Selection tools.

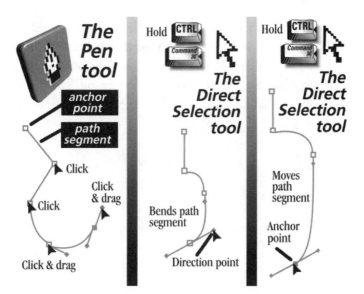

Figure 5.35   By using modifier keys, you can create paths and anchors and also change the curve of a path and reposition anchor points.

The more you work with Pen tools, the easier it becomes to make outlines of complex shapes in an image. The path can then be turned into the cleanest selection marquee you've ever seen by clicking the Loads path as selection icon on the bottom of the Paths palette.

Note

Staying Out of the Toolbox   It is entirely possible—because the author does it all the time—to use only the Pen tool and not to go fishing in the toolbox for other path tools. In the next section, you'll learn about the Convert Point tool. If you can access the Pen tool, the Direct Selection tool, and the Convert Point tool through modifier keys, why waste a visit to the toolbox and be taken away from your image work?

Half the trick to Photoshop is to learn ways (shortcuts) to keep your cursor close to your work. Who wants to run out to the paint store for varnish when they've spent hours sanding a chair? You want to continue and not interrupt the creative process.

The Convert Point, Add Anchor, and Delete Anchor Tools

Like the Direct Selection tool, the Convert Point tool can be accessed without leaving the Pen tool. Hold Alt(Opt) and you toggle from the Pen tool to the Convert Point tool. As described earlier in this chapter, the Convert Point tool determines whether a path segment is straight or curved (by clicking an anchor point) and can change the direction of the path as it travels through an anchor point (by click+dragging with the tool to expose the direction points and then dragging on a selection point).

Also, probably the least-used Pen tools you'll encounter are the Add Anchor and Delete Anchor tools, all shown in Figure 5.36. Why don't you need the "plus and minus" anchor tools? Because when you click the Pen tool, the Options bar provides a checkbox called Auto Add/Delete. Check this box, and then click a path segment: a new anchor appears. Conversely, clicking over an anchor with this option checked will delete the anchor point (and reshape the path).

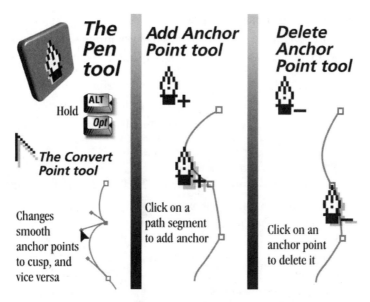

Figure 5.36   You can access the Convert Point tool by holding Alt(Opt) with the Pen tool chosen. And the plus and minus anchor tools are not used often.

Hopefully, you've seen here that six tools can be whittled down to two (the Path Selection tool and the Pen tool), if you know what the modifier keys are and understand the options. I hate to say this, but the very *best* way to become proficient with the vector tools in Photoshop is to set aside 15 minutes a day with the tools and an image. Follow the contours in the image where colors meet, and refine the paths you draw. Within a week, you'll never understand why you'd use any other tool for selecting stuff!

Okay, we've stressed paths enough without telling you what they are good for! In the next section, you'll deal with a real-world situation that calls for the use of the Pen tools. At least, the assignment is real in *my* world.

The Pen Tool and Special Effects

In the history of Photoshop, part of the "signature" of the program has been really life-like shadow and glow creation. There are a number of ways to create shadows and the inverse, glows, but the way you'll learn in the sections to follow involves using the path tools to accurately define the area that is to glow.

Easy Selections: Using Straight Paths

If you look ahead to Figure 5.37, you'll see that the dice in the image are composed of nothing but straight lines—*path segments,* in the parlance of Photoshop's Pen tool.

To place a glow around either of the dice, you first must define its outline. This is where you'll use the Pen tool. Now, the outline of a die is a closed one, so to learn something new in the steps to follow, you'll create a closed path. All set?

Creating a Closed Path

1. Open the bones.tif image from the Examples/Chap05 folder on the Companion CD.
2. Choose the Pen tool from the toolbox, as shown in Figure 5.37. Make sure that you choose the Work Path icon on the Options bar.

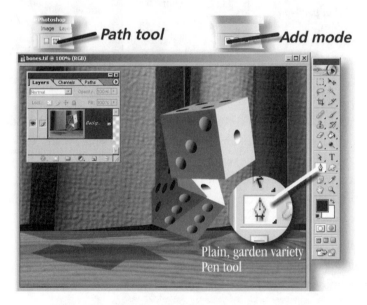

Figure 5.37 Choose the Pen tool, and use clicks—not clicks and drags—to create an outline around straight-edged shapes.

3. Hold Ctrl(⌘) plus the spacebar to toggle to the Zoom In tool, and then click over the top die until you are at 100% viewing resolution. If you are running a high resolution, such as 1024 by 768 pixels on a large monitor, you can either ignore this step or zoom in closer because the image will probably load at 100% to begin with.
4. Follow the instructions on Figure 5.38. Click at the vertices of the die. If you cannot see all of the die's vertices from your view through the image window, hold the spacebar and drag in the opposite direction you want to view. This is

the shortcut to the Hand tool. Whenever you want to view the left of an image, for example, you drag to the right.

When you reach the beginning anchor point, click it to close the path. You can tell that your cursor is positioned correctly when the cursor changes to a tiny pen point with a circle in the bottom right.

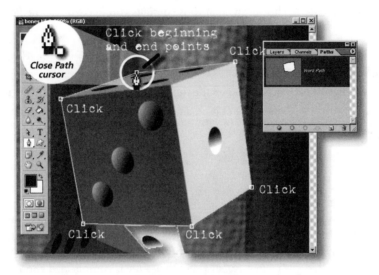

Figure 5.38   Click any place along the outline where there is a sharp turn in direction, and then click once over the beginning point to close the path.

Whenever you create a path, it is called a *work path* on the Paths palette. What does this mean? Only one thing: a work path is overwritten as soon as you start creating a new path. And we don't *ever* want this to happen accidentally in your work, so you need to know how to turn a work path into a saved path that will remain indefinitely within the Psd, Tif, and Tga file formats:

5. Click the Paths tab on the grouped palette, and double-click the work path title on the palette's list. A dialog box will appear.

6. Type **Bone** in the Name field, and then press Enter (Return) to turn the work path into a saved path. Keep your work and Photoshop open.

Paths are wonderful, because

- They add virtually nothing to the saved file size. Alpha channels, in comparison, increase a file's saved size by about 25 to 33%.

- You can add to a saved path as long as it is visible on-screen, and new paths you create can be considered all part of one saved path, even if the shapes don't touch one another (this is called a *discontinuous* path, in AdobeSpeak).

- Paths are invisible when you print an image, and they do not belong to any layer, which means that you can use the same path a number of times on a number of layers, as you will soon see.

I should point out that although paths do not print, things such as clipping paths have a visual effect on a layout. This means that those designs you make using the Pen tool do not print.

Using a Path to Create a Selection

Now that you have created a path, here's the fun part: putting the path to some *use*! First, we need to copy the die shape and put it on a new layer. By doing this, we can put a glow *behind* the shape so it *looks* like a glow.

C'mon. *Let's (rock) and roll them bones*:

Making a Selection Based on a Path

1. On the Paths palette, Ctrl(⌘)+click the Bone title. This modifier key command loads the path as a selection and then hides the path from view so that it cannot accidentally be deleted. You can use both the Backspace key and the Delete key to delete a selected path. Now, forget I said that—life is complicated enough—and check out Figure 5.39.

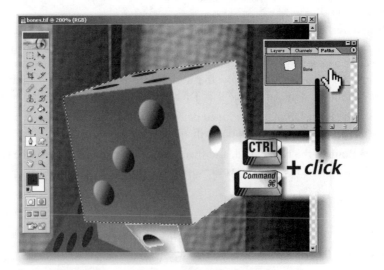

Figure 5.39   Ctrl(⌘)+click the path title to both make a selection based upon the path's outline and to hide the path from accidental editing.

2. Choose a selection tool (the Rectangular Marquee tool is fine). Doing this changes the commands on the context menu so that they offer the choice you want at this point. Right-click (Macintosh: hold Ctrl and click), and then choose Layer via Copy from the Context menu, as shown in Figure 5.40. If you're in a shortcut kind of mood, you can press Ctrl(⌘)+J to do the same thing.

Figure 5.40   Copy the selection of the die to a new layer.

By taking this shortcut instead of going to the main menu to create a layer and copy something to it, you have to pay the price of accepting the default name for the new layer—in this case, Layer 1. You can change the name of the layer at any time by double-clicking the title and then typing whatever you please, but in this simple, two-layer composition, it's really not necessary to label absolutely everything.

3. Click the Background layer title on the Layers palette so that you will be working on the Background from this point on. Keep Photoshop and the image open.

Next, you will apply a glow to the die, using the Background layer as the target layer for the applied glow.

Using a Soft-Edge Brush Tip for Creating the Glow

As mentioned earlier, there's more than one way to create a glow or shadow in Photoshop. Many people design a shape that is larger than the object and then apply the Gaussian blur filter. However, we don't need to do this when we have a perfectly good path that can be stroked with a soft brush tip. Paths can be copied, stroked, used as the basis of a selection, filled—you name it.

Note

Copying Paths   To copy a path, hold Alt(Opt) while clicking a path using the Direct Selection tool. Then drag the duplicate away from the original path. The duplicate and the original path are part of the same composite path because they belong to the same title on the Paths palette.

To copy a path to its own space in Photoshop, select the path, press Ctrl(⌘)+X, unselect the current path by clicking a blank area on the Paths palette's list, and then press Ctrl(⌘)+V.

Here's how to finish the piece:

Stroking a Path

1. Choose the Paintbrush tool from the toolbox, right-click (Macintosh: hold Ctrl and click) to access the Brushes palette, select the 100 (pixels) soft tip, and then press Enter (Return) to make the palette go away. You should be working on the Background layer now.

2. Your new foreground color should contrast with the rest of a dim scene, and if these are to be lucky dice, choose a strong orange-yellow from the color picker as the color that will be stroked across the path.

3. On the Paths palette, click the Bone title to view the path. Click the Stroke path with brush icon on the bottom of the Paths palette, as shown in Figure 5.41.

Figure 5.41   Unless you specifically choose the Paintbrush tool for stroking the path, Photoshop will use the Pencil tool at its current size setting.

4. If you want to remove the path from the creation (you no longer need it), drag the path title to the trash icon on the Paths palette.

5. To make this image one that can be saved to all different kinds of file types—including the proprietary Windows BMP and Macintosh PICT formats—the image must be flattened now. On the Layers palette, click on Layer 1 to make this the active layer. Press Ctrl(⌘)+E. This command is the shortcut for Merge Down and does the trick here.

6. Choose File, Save As, and then save the file to a format that doesn't have to discard visual information. TIFF is my personal favorite, but there are enhanced TIFFs and plain TIFFs; you need to uncheck the Layers checkbox in the Save As dialog box to make a "normal" TIFF image that everyone with an image viewer can see. Later, you might want to send your work to a friend by making an email attachment. In this case, you'd want to open the TIFF image in ImageReady and visually tune the piece so that image details that are lost through compression don't really show. You can close the image at any time. Keep Photoshop open.

Okay, enough of the simple stuff. If you're really willing to grow as an artist, we must place an annoying challenge before you. We're kidding about the annoying part; in the next section, you'll design a flower shape using paths, duplicate and twist the paths, and then fill them using a special fill mode to transform a blue ball into a *decorated* blue ball.

Taking Paths to the Max

Hey, you've glommed onto all these fun facts about paths and Pen tools, and so far, you've only used one of the tools. You start simple—you get simple results. What say you design a flower shape using two of the Pen tools, with curves and everything we discussed? After this following lesson, you can consider yourself Master (or Mistress, or Mattress) of Photoshop Paths.

To Make a Flower, Start with a Single Petal

In Figure 5.42, you can see the image stickem.tif. It's darker here in the figure than it is on the Companion CD—we want you to see clearly what it is you're going to create. No doubts about it—the outline is a complex path, but with instructions, you'll do it with plenty of time left over to watch *The Sopranos*.

stickem.tif @ 100% (RGB)

Silhouette of those stupid vinyl stickers
people put in the tub to hide cracks in tile work

Figure 5.42   The assignment? Trace around the outline of the flower in this file using
the Pen tools.

Let's get down to business. Now, for once, we figured that the first seven steps in this
assignment could also be called out in a screen figure. So if you get lost, look to Figure
5.43. *I myself* got lost twice doing this, and this figure saved my neck. Open the
Stickem.tif image from the Examples/Chap05 folder and zoom into a petal to about
300% viewing resolution. You need this close-up view to see exactly where the anchors
should be placed.

Creating a Flower Petal by Tracing

1. With the Pen tool, click a point at the vertex that comes before the beginning of
   a petal (see Figure 5.43, item 1).

Tip

"Stretching" Your Abilities   Whether you use paths every day or you are just beginning to learn how to use them, you may find that the Pen tool's "rubber band" option
makes your life easier. To turn on this feature, select the Pen tool and click the Pen
Options down-arrow (to the right of the Custom Shape tool on the Options bar). When
the Pen Options box appears, click the Rubber Band checkbox. Click outside the box to
close it.

2. Click at the beginning of the petal. We're working clockwise in this example.
3. Click, hold, and drag at the next location, shown as item 3. As mentioned earlier,
   when you do this maneuver, you wind up with a curve, and your cursor is hanging onto a direction point and not the anchor it created. Weave the cursor a little
   until you see the curve conform to the template of the petal.

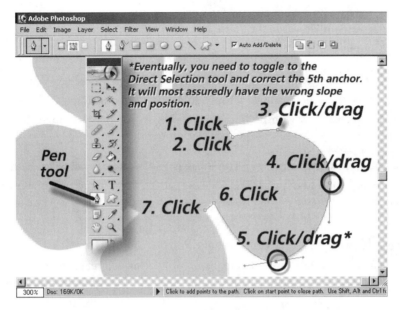

Figure 5.43   You can't go wrong if you stick to this road map.

4. Click and drag at about the center of the petal, as shown in item 4. Generally, when you are creating a path, you need an anchor approximately every 90 degrees. The example shows that the middle of the petal is about 90 degrees away from the third anchor point. When you do it this way, editing an anchor point is easy, you can control the curve precisely, and the direction handles aren't so long you have to go scrolling all over the screen to edit a curve.

5. Click and drag on the point shown as item 5. We have a slight problem to fix due to the fact that you've been drawing curves, and you're going into an anchor point that sharply bends the path as the path travels through it. Don't try to make this path segment conform precisely to the outline of the petal. Instead, make the curve fit the petal in this area as closely as possible, and you'll edit the anchor point later.

6. Click but don't drag a sixth anchor at item 6.

7. Click again as shown at item 7 in the figure.

8. Hold Ctrl(⌘) to toggle to the Direct Selection tool, and then click the fifth anchor. Drag the anchor or the direction points that are now visible (because you clicked the anchor). Make the curve conform to the outline you are tracing.

9. Repeat Steps 3–8 to close the path and complete the flower design. You can pick up where you left off by toggling back to the Pen tool and clicking the last anchor. Now click and drag a starting curve once more. When you come back to the first anchor, hover the cursor over the anchor until you see a tiny circle in the bottom right of your Pen tool cursor. This is the indication that your cursor is in the correct position to close the path.

10. Save the path by double-clicking the work path title on the Paths palette, and name the path **Flower** in the dialog box that pops up. Click OK, and keep this piece and Photoshop open.

In case this set of steps is too lengthy for you, and you want to proceed, you can open the stickem.psd file from the Examples/Chap05 folder on the Companion CD. There you'll find the completed path with nothing surrounding it, so you can copy it to the ball image.

Uh-oh. The clock says it's time for a Fun Break now. This means you will copy the path to an image of a ball and duplicate and scale the pattern to make multiple flower designs on the ball.

Creating Many Flowers from a Single Path

Copying and making the flowers different sizes on the ball will make the ball look more lifelike. So let's get to it, using the Path Selection tool and the Free Transform mode.

Mapping Out a Decoration for the Ball

1. Make sure that the flower pattern in stickem.tif is visible. Then press Ctrl(⌘)+C. You don't have to select a path before copying it; however, you do have to make sure no marquee selection exists, or Photoshop will copy the image area instead of the path.

    Um, you also can toss the Path title into a different image window to copy it there.

2. Close the stickem.tif image. (You can choose whether to save it. It's sort of served its purpose.) Open the Ball.tif image from the Examples/Chap05 folder on the Companion CD. Zoom in or out until you can see the whole image in the workspace.

3. Press Ctrl(⌘)+V to paste the path into the picture. Now, in case you accidentally deselect the path, choose the Path Selection tool from the toolbox, as shown in item 1 of Figure 5.44.

4. Click the path, and press Ctrl(⌘)+T to enter the Transform tool. Right-click (Macintosh: hold Ctrl and click) and choose Scale from the context menu, as shown in item 2 Figure 5.44.

5. The flower path looks nice, but it's too large if you want several designs on the ball. Click and hold a corner of the Scale bounding box, and then hold Shift and drag toward the center of the selection, as shown in Figure 5.45. Stop when the flower pattern is about two-thirds of its original size.

    The Shift modifier key keeps the path in proportion as you scale it. You also can press the link button on the Options bar in the Scale section (it's the only link icon on the Options bar), and then you do not have to hold the Shift key while you proportionately scale.

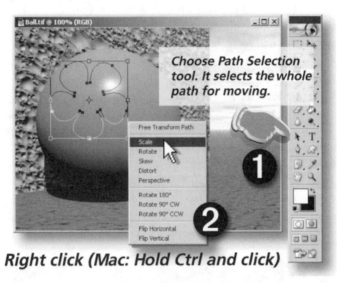

Figure 5.44   Choose the Scale command to make it possible for the path to be scaled up or down.

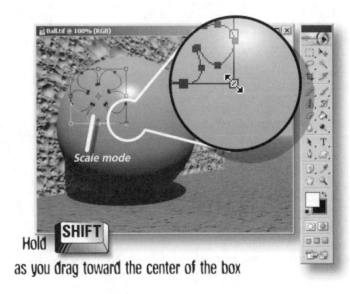

Figure 5.45   Drag toward the center to make a smaller flower; drag away from the path center to make a larger flower design.

6. Now's your chance to reposition the flower. Click inside the bounding box and drag the flower. To finalize your Transform edits, press Enter (Return).

7. Let's try a different tool to make a bunch of flowers of different sizes. Choose the Direct Selection tool. While you click the flower path, hold Alt(Opt), and then drag away from the flower. Yay! You've cloned the pattern!

   Now, if you want to, say, rotate the duplicate path, release Alt(Opt), right-click (Macintosh: hold Ctrl and click), chooseh, and press Ctrl(⌘)+T to enter the Transform tool Free Transform Path, and then hover your cursor slightly away from a corner of the bounding box until it turns into a bent arrow. Drag up or down and the duplicate pattern will rotate. You also should make the duplicate a different size (you already know how to do this) and move it to a new location on the ball.

8. Create about five flowers. It doesn't matter whether a flower path goes outside of the ball. You'll be painting and then cleaning up your painting work soon, so it's only natural—as with an actual ball—that parts of the pattern are obscured from your viewpoint. Figure 5.46 shows the work you've done in Steps 7 and 8.

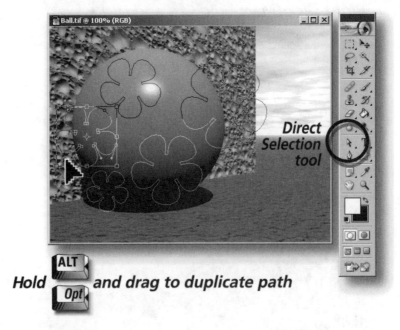

Figure 5.46   Use the Direct Selection tool to duplicate paths and drag on a path segment while the whole path is selected to move the path.

9. Save your work to the hard disk. Keep the design and Photoshop open.

It's time now to apply foreground color to the path areas and put the painted flowers in a special mixing mode for combining with the ball image. We'll also do a little Layer Mask editing to perfect the design (you can review this technique Chapter 4). Here's how to finalize the piece:

Overlaying a Flower Pattern

1. With the Direct Selection tool, click an empty area of the design so that no path has its anchors highlighted (indicating that it's selected). When no path is selected, but all are visible, you can apply color using all the paths that are present without selecting every one of them.

2. Click the Loads path as a selection icon on the bottom of the Paths palette. This is a different way to load a selection and hide the paths, as explained earlier in this chapter. You can do almost anything two or more different ways in Photoshop.

3. Click the Layers tab on the palette, and then click the Create new layer icon on the bottom of the palette. Choose a bright orange color from the color picker by clicking the foreground color selection box on the toolbox. Click OK to exit the color picker after selecting your color.

4. Press Alt(Opt)+Delete (Backspace), and then press Ctrl(⌘)+D to deselect all the selection marquees. Now, you've got your bunch of flowers; however, something smells fake here.

   When you cover an area with solid paint on a layer to work on top of the background layer, valuable image info is hidden, such as shading and highlights. To make the flowers look like they were painted on plastic, you need to choose a different mixing mode than Normal, the default. We cover mixing modes on the Quick Reference sheet for more info. But for now...

5. Choose Overlay mode from the modes drop-down list on the Layers palette. Overlay is a mixing mode where highlights and shadows show through from layers underneath, and the objects on the layer mix with the underlying color so that the two colors combine and the brightness of the color on the Background layer is preserved. So you've got sort of a dirty orange pattern of flowers on the ball—I'm not knocking it; the image looks nice! Besides, this is the same effect as when a ball manufacturer silk-screens a bright pattern on a cool, neutral-colored plastic toy. See Figure 5.47 to see where we are now in the steps.

6. If you did as recommended earlier, one or two of the flowers go outside of the silhouette of the ball. No problem. Here you'll find that the Layer Mask technique we worked with in Chapter 4 comes in handy once again. Click the Layer Mask mode tool at the bottom of the Layers palette and make sure that black is the current foreground color (press D).

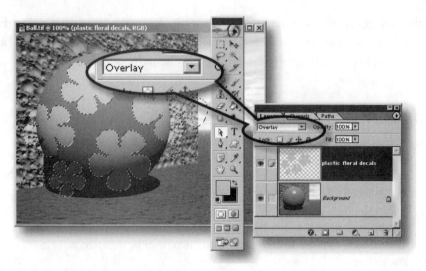

Figure 5.47   Use Overlay mode to better blend the flower patterns "into" the ball shape.

7. Zoom into about 300% viewing resolution, and then hold the spacebar to scroll your view in the window so you can see one of the offending, overlapping flower designs. Choose the Paintbrush tool, right-click (Macintosh: hold Ctrl and click), and choose the 13-pixel diameter tip.

8. Stroke over the outside edge of the ball until all the paint outside the ball has been removed (see Figure 5.48). Then do the same thing to any other overlapping flower shapes.

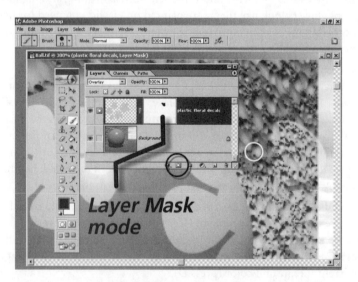

Figure 5.48   Use the Layer Mask feature to hide areas you don't want visible in the finished design, and then trash the mask and the unwanted pixels to finish the image.

9. When you've got the flowers looking right, click the mask thumbnail on the Layers palette (be sure to select the mask thumbnail, to the right of the thumbnails—*not* the image thumbnail), and drag it into the trash icon. Click Apply in the dialog box that pops up. (Like you don't know what you're doing! *Duh!*) Those pixels that were outside the ball are now gone forever.

10. If you'd like to change the color of the flowers, or further experiment with the image, save it now in Photoshop's native file format—PSD. This is the only file format that retains Photoshop layers. If you think you're done and want to pack away your masterpiece as a single-layer work, choose Flatten Image (from the Layer menu), and then press Ctrl(⌘)+S to save it as the TIF it began its life as.

11. Take a well-deserved break. I think there's a Diet Pepsi toward the back of the fridge, behind the Chinese take-out.

In Figure 5.49, you can see the finished piece in black and white (trust me, it's a mind-blower in color). There's nothing in the image to suggest that this is a retouched image because you chose the right blending mode for the flower designs and trimmed away the excess that was outside the ball's silhouette.

Figure 5.49   One of the outstanding characteristics of Photoshop is that with the right information, you can turn a nice picture into a *better* picture.

You've done it. You've worked your way through perhaps one of the hardest chapters in this book. Is there more to the tale of paths? Yes, but we'll cover this in a more relaxed atmosphere throughout the book…

Well, I'm going to draw a path around *myself* right now, convert it to a selection, and then cut out of here. Or move to a different layer. Or something. What's important is the Summary, as follows…

Summary

You could spend a year learning all the undocumented or vaguely documented features in Photoshop, and I'm glad my publisher gave me the space to concentrate on stuff that's really important to your growth as an artist. Channels and paths might not be on everyone's lips when you create a slick piece of art, but if you follow my examples in this chapter, you'll be doing stuff that other Photoshoppists cannot do, because they understand the "Oh, wow!" Lens Flare filter and the Emboss filter, but don't know how to create the kind of eye-catching edits *you* can perform now.

Channels and paths are core components of Photoshop; they are much overlooked in light of all the web stuff packed into the program now. By understanding the core elements, you bring yourself one step closer to a professional artist wielding a *verrry* powerful tool.

In Chapter 6, "Using the Clone Stamp Tool, the Healing Brush, and Patch Tools," we heal, we patch, and we clone. No, it's not plastic surgery—it's an exploration of new tools for photo retouching in Photoshop, and a brush-up course on the Clone Stamp (formerly the Rubber Stamp) tool. When a photo is in trouble, these can be the most valuable tools to use for invisible mending. C'mon, let's take a look at what you're armed with when a photo comes across your desk in tatters.

Chapter 6

Using the Clone Stamp, Healing Brush, and Patch Tools

Photoshop's toolbox has a logical layout. On top are the selection tools, in the middle are editing tools (mostly painting tools), and on the bottom are productivity tools, such as the Measure, Eyedropper, and Note tools. You use some of these tools with Photoshop rulers and guides. (The commands for displaying rulers and guides are found in the View menu).

The Clone Stamp tool, however, is neither beast nor fowl—you use it for editing, but it doesn't use paint. And now, to add to these "I don't know what to call them" breed of tools are the Healing Brush and the Patch tools. I guess it's not really important in which category these tools belong, as long as you know that you really need them to create Photoshop magic. Rarely does a day go by when I don't use the Clone Stamp tool. And it's time to run through these tools so that you know the right occasion to depend upon them.

Copying Pixels Is the Name of the Game

As opposed to replacing colors with other colors, the Clone Stamp tool and its two brothers in this chapter use borrowed, existing areas in the image to fix a blemish, an unwanted spot, or a sofa (as you will soon see). This is great news for photographers because the days of using an airbrush, physical or digital, are over!

Taking Out the Virtual Trash

I took the first picture here on trash day—evidentally my neighbors wanted their old sofa out of the neighborhood, but they'd put it out so many days in advance of the haulers that it sort of became an icon—kids were playing on it and it gave me a visual clue when to turn right to get to our house!

We can't do anything about the hauling date, but we can certainly move the sofa out of the picture using the Clone Stamp tool.

Now, there's one *very* important thing about the Clone Stamp tool that you should know. The Clone Stamp tool needs you to set a source point for sampling (in this case, the lawn to cover the sofa) and a point for painting. These two points always remain the same distance from one another, which creates a problem if you are not careful. If you allow the sampling point to wander into the area where you first started cloning, the image over which you've cloned will begin to reappear. This is *not* what you want. So you need to keep a watchful eye on where the sampling point is moving and do not stray into your work with the cloning tip—you sample and resample frequently from different areas.

Ready to get rid of this sofa?

Making a Sofa Disappear

1. Get the Sofa.tif image from the Examples/Chap06 folder on the Companion CD. It's very attractive, as you can see in Figure 6.1.

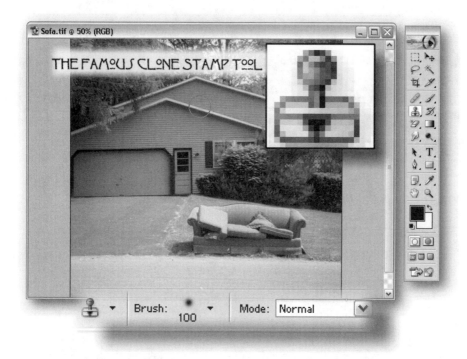

Figure 6.1   I have this belief that ridiculous pictures don't just happen. They *wait* for you to run and get your camera.

2. Choose the Clone Stamp tool, and choose a soft round 100-pixel brush from the Brush Preset picker. Alt(Opt)+click some grass to the right of the sofa, release the Alt(Opt) key and then start painting at the right side of the sofa. Do not get overzealous, or what we warned about will happen, as you can see in Figure 6.2 where I deliberately let my Clone Stamp tool extend farther than the distance between the tool tip and the original sampling point. And what do you get? You get a sofa arm pushed over by two feet with the dust ruffle still hanging out toward the right edge of the image.

3. Sample the grass frequently and use short strokes into the sofa. Resample, and with every row of pixels that you manage to cover, the sofa is going bye-bye (see Figure 6.3).

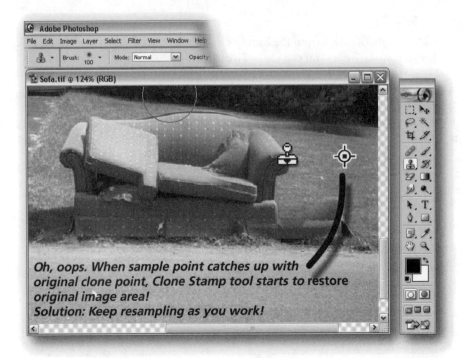

Figure 6.2   Don't let this happen to you. Resample frequently to prevent the sampling point from traveling into unwanted territory.

Figure 6.3   Use short strokes to cover the offensive image area, but don't let the source point stray and foul up the action.

4. You need to trim the area where the grass meets the road. So Alt(Opt)+click the edge of the road/lawn on the right, and then clone over where the sofa is out in the street, as shown in Figure 6.4.

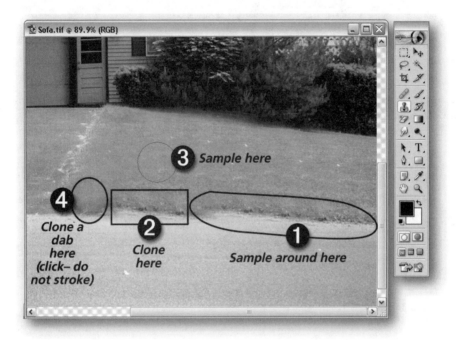

Figure 6.4   You need to completely erase this sofa, and that means cloning over the street, too.

5. There's one last area that needs a "hit" of the Clone Stamp tool, and that's where the driveway, the road, and the lawn meet. Alt(Opt)+click to sample the area where the lawn edge meets the driveway or road areas and clone in any trouble spots where the sofa remains. Perfect! If you want to add a few extra touches, you might try sampling some areas of grass and clone away any evidence of repeated patterns from the grass (such as a pesky white spec in the grass that has a tendency to repeat).

6. The lawn looks a little bare, and this is optional, but because our neighbors were so delightfully diligent about putting out big-time trash, I think we should park a rusted tractor in its place. Open Cruiser.psd from the Examples/Chap06 folder on the Companion CD. With the Move tool, drag the tractor into the Sofa.tif document, as shown in Figure 6.5. Kinda homesy and provincial, isn't it? <g>

Figure 6.5   You can fix anything with the Clone Stamp tool. What you do after that is your own business!

Right beneath the Clone Stamp tool on the toolbox is the Pattern Stamp tool. Let's investigate.

Working with the Pattern Stamp Tool

Unlike the Clone Stamp tool, the Pattern Stamp tool gives you no visible source point from which to sample the pixels the cursor lays down as you drag. Nope. In this case, you load a pattern for the tool, and the tool just keeps painting away, which strongly suggests that your target pattern is a repeating tile.

Luckily, we have just such a repeating tile for you and a host image right around the corner. Here they come!

Using the Pattern Stamp Tool

1. Open the plum.ai image from the Examples/Chap06 folder on the Companion CD. When the Rasterize dialog box pops up, tell it you want the plum to be 66 pixels in Width, and RGB color mode. Click OK to create the raster image from the plum's vector information.

2. Right-click (Macintosh: hold Ctrl and click) the title bar of plum.ai, and choose Canvas Size. Give yourself a little elbowroom and make the canvas 200 by 200 pixels.

3. Open the Pattern.psd image from the Examples/Chap06 folder on the Companion CD. In the plum.ai image, use the Rectangular Marquee tool to make a fairly tight selection (the tighter the selection, the more plums per inch in the pattern, so leave a little room, see Figure 6.6).

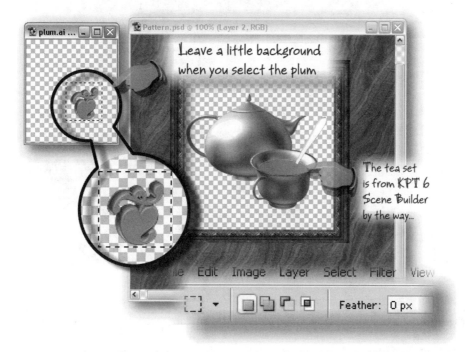

Figure 6.6   Make a selection marquee that will represent one whole tile for the Pattern Stamp tool to use.

4. Choose the Brush tool and set the painting mode to Behind on the Options bar (a 45-pixel brush will cover the area fairly well). Hold down the Alt(Opt) key to toggle to the Eyedropper tool and sample a green color from the plum. Paint the inside of the selection marquee. Do not deselect the marquee. Choose Edit, Define Pattern, and why not save the default name of **Plum**? Click OK.

Don't forget to turn the painting mode for the Brush tool back to Normal for the next time you need to use this tool.

5. Click and hold the Clone Stamp tool on the toolbox until the flyout appears. Choose the Pattern Stamp tool. On the Options bar, choose a brush tip (a 65-pixel brush might work well for this image). Click the title bar of the Pattern.psd file

to make this the active document. Click the Create a new layer icon at the bottom of the Layers palette. Drag this new layer (Layer 3) below the bottom layer (Layer 1). Make sure that the pattern you just saved is showing in the Pattern drop-down list on the Options bar, and then start painting away, as shown in Figure 6.7. Remarkable, eh?

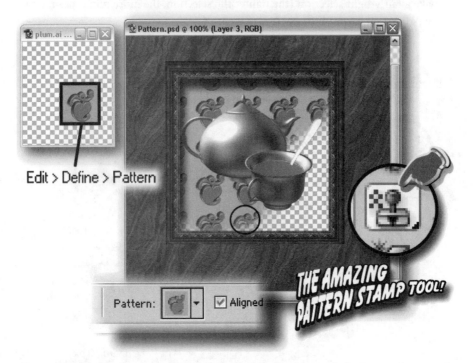

Figure 6.7   Apply the tile again and again merely by stroking with the Pattern Stamp tool.

6. I'd say, "Quit when you're done, and then frame the piece," but the piece is already framed, no?

Note

3rd Party Plug-in for the Frame   The frame in the Pattern image was created 1-2-3 by Alien Skin's Splat! Group of filters. Check out the ad in the back of this book for a special offer from the aliens.

This covers the Stamp tools. Now let's get into a totally new feature or two to make your editing life easier.

Introducing the Healing Brush Tool

Adobe has created a way to retouch images, Clone Stamp style, but much better in many respects. The Healing Brush tool not only clones away unwanted areas, but it also takes into account lighting and texture, which means that your work is truly invisible. One thing I found about the tool: you do not want to use the Healing Brush tool on image areas the size of a car. Dents, marks, small nicks, and other surface blemishes suit the Healing Brush just fine.

We were visiting Lysander in upstate New York last year, which is the pollination capital of the world. These folks turn out a lot of honey and even have a bee statue erected in a park. Well, wouldn't you know that some kid spray painted "M.E. + M.E." in a heart on the base of the statue (see Figure 6.8). Either there are two kids in Lysander who are in love or one kid who is narcissistic.

Figure 6.8   Imagine this! Defacing a community monument!

Fixing this is no problem when you have the Healing Brush tool. Let's visit Lysander and clean up this graffiti.

Using the Healing Brush Tool

1. Open the Lysander.tif image from the Examples/Chap06 folder on the Companion CD.

2. Choose the Healing Brush tool from the toolbox. For an image this size, you will need a 44-pixel soft-tip brush. Right-click (Macintosh: hold Ctrl and click) and then from the Brush picker, pick a brush and use the Diameter slider to make the tip 44 pixels in diameter (Hardness should be 0%).

3. On the Options bar, choose Replace as the mode. Replace is a stronger mode than Normal—it preserves noise, film grain, and texture at the edges of the brush stroke.

4. Zoom into about 1:1 viewing resolution and then Alt(Opt)+click a vacant concrete area next to the lovers' heart to sample the concrete.

5. Brush over the heart. Resample and do this again. The amazing thing here is that Photoshop is calculating light and texture; the Clone Stamp tool cannot do this (see Figure 6.9).

Figure 6.9   The Healing Brush really goes a long way toward "healing" a broken photograph!

6. Continue resampling and stroking into the heart until it's completely gone. Look at that concrete! There's not a *trace* of tampering! Check out Figure 6.10. You *have* to try this one out yourself!

Figure 6.10   The Healing Brush should be called the Magic Brush! Look at how thoroughly and perfectly you can get rid of a stain!

The Healing Brush tool can really come in handy for images where you might want to give yourself (or others) a little digital cosmetic work. This tool shines on images where you might want to remove the wrinkles or "bags" from under your eyes (or maybe blemishes from your skin). If you have such an image lying around, give this tool a test drive by sampling a smooth area near your eye; then make one smooth brush sweep under the eye and watch your wrinkles disappear. What would you pay to have a *real life* brush that could do this?

There's one more tool you need to familiarize yourself with, and this one is a mindblower. It's the Patch tool.

The Patch Tool at Work

I have seen many "patching" tools in other programs in the past. Boy, am I glad Adobe got it right the first time out. It was worth the wait! This Patch tool examines the problem area, allows you to define an area from which to take a patch, and as you drag the patch over the problem area, Photoshop calculates lighting and other parameters, and you *cannot see* where the patch has been performed!

Let's walk through something simple, like taking a grocery sticker off a Granny Smith apple:

Using the Patch Tool

1. Open the Breakfast.tif image from the Examples/Chap06 folder on the Companion CD.

2. Choose the Patch tool from the toolbox. Click the Source button on the Options bar. Now use the Patch tool to drag a tight circle around the sticker on the apple. The sticker is the "source" (see Figure 6.11).

Figure 6.11   The word "source" with respect to the Patch tool means, "the area that needs fixing."

3. Now, drag the selection marquee down to an area of the apple below the sticker (the goal is to drag to a good sample area for the Patch tool to make calculations.) As you can see in Figure 6.12, the patch changes color slightly and accommodates you by covering that sticker in a way that would take 10 minutes using only the Clone Stamp tool.

Note

Source Versus Destination   The Patch tool performs its repair calculations based on one of two methods. You can either choose Source or Destination on the Options bar.

If **Source** is the chosen option from the Options bar, you need to drag in the image to select the area you want to repair. Then drag the selection border to the area from which you want to sample. When you release the mouse button, the originally selected area is patched with the sampled pixels.

If **Destination** is chosen as the option on the Options bar, you drag in the image to select the area from which you want to sample. Then drag the selection border to the area you want to patch. When you release the mouse button, the newly selected area is patched with the sample pixels.

In other words, you have the choice of selecting the damaged area first (the source) and moving it to a good sample area, or selecting the good sample area first (the destination) and moving it to the damaged area. Either method works. You also can choose a pattern on the Options bar to be used as the sample pixels for repair work.

Notice that the selection process for the Patch tool is similar to other selection tools. In fact, you can make a selection with Photoshop's selection tools before choosing the Patch tool. If you are using the Patch tool to make your selection, you can use Shift to *add to your selection*, Alt(Opt) to *subtract from your selection*, or Alt(Opt)+Shift to use *the intersection area of two selections*.

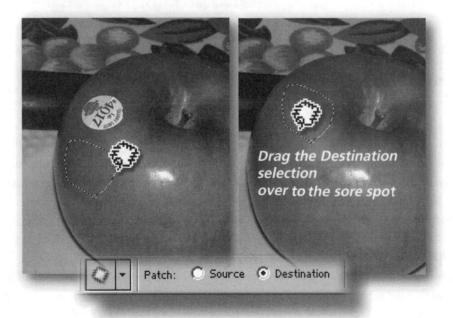

Figure 6.12   The "patch" neatly covers *and* conforms to the texture surrounding it.

4. That's about it for a Patch tool tutorial. Take a look at Figure 6.13. Can you see any trace of a sticker?

Figure 6.13   The Patch tool flawlessly repairs the sticker area without a lot of cloning work.

Don't put this picture away yet!

This chapter has been light on demanding techniques because its only purpose is to acquaint you with a very important tool—the Clone Stamp tool—and its relatives. You will get plenty of opportunities in the rest of this book to exercise your knowledge of the tool(s) at various points through these pages. The tools I use the most frequently are the Clone Stamp tool, the Free Transform tool, and the Pen tools. (I started my graphics exploration with a tiny computer and CorelDRAW, so I like vectors!).

Optional Independent Study

If you look at the Breakfast picture once more, you'll realize that the Granny Smith sticker on the apple is the least of the problems. To wit:

- There are some lovely coffee stains on the outside of the mug in the back of the picture. Solution? The Healing Brush tool.

- The red plastic spoon in the cereal doesn't really cut it. You can remove the spoon just like you did with the sofa, using the Clone Stamp tool.

- Now, here's the stumper. The bowl is chipped in the front (see Figure 6.14).

Figure 6.14   Ooops! Well, there goes the set.

The real trick here is to know when *not* to use the Clone Stamp tool. You cannot repair a missing arc in the bowl with areas around it that clearly arc in different directions.

The secret? Copy an area of the bowl lip next to the missing piece. It also helps to put the healthy bowl lip selection on its own layer by pressing Ctrl(⌘)+J. Then put the copy in Free Transform mode and swing it around so that it covers the lip chip.

By the way, you can at any time hide both a selection and the Free Transform bounding box by pressing Ctrl(⌘)+H. This enables you to precisely place the replacement without being distracted by selection marquees or the bounding box of the Transform tool (see Figure 6.15).

Figure 6.15   You can't use the Clone Stamp tool for everything! Sometimes, you have to use your noodle—and a different Photoshop feature. Make a selection of a healthy lip area for the bowl to use as a replacement for the chipped area.

Figure 6.16 shows the selected area being moved and rotated into position.

Figure 6.16   Press Ctrl(⌘)+T and use the Transform tool to rotate the selection and reposition it in the damaged area.

The rest of the bowl is easily repaired with, yes, the Clone Stamp tool.

Hey, how many chapters tell you what to do, but also what *not* to do? <g>

Summary

You have three very powerful photo-retouching tools at your disposal in Photoshop. You can paint using parts of an image instead of mere colors. Practice with these tools—the more they become a part of you, the more readily and easily you can employ them. And know when to use other tools! Good judgment is worth its weight in hours saved from futile work any day.

Part III

The Important and Headache-Causing Stuff: Calibration, Input, and Output

Chapter 7

Understanding Photoshop's Color Management System

We all like surprises, like being treated to breakfast in bed on an ordinary day, or finding that we've won the 12 million dollar state lottery. But there are some surprises that no one wants to receive, like having uninvited relatives permanently bond themselves to your sofa at the exact same moment that your special someone is about to arrive for a romantic evening, or chomping into a wax pear thinking it's the real thing.

The unpleasant surprise that haunts the dreams of graphic artists and photographers usually involves color. Specifically, the problem is "color-gone-wrong." No one wants to spend hours staring at the monitor getting the delicate blush on a model's face just right, or tweaking the color of this month's Sweater of the Month Club sweater only to have the model's blush look like a rash and the sweater take on a royal blue hue instead of regal purple when printed. But just about the only way to avoid the unpleasant and often expensive problem of color-gone-wrong requires the help of a workable color management system—CMS.

The purpose of a color management system is to supply users with tools they can use to control the colors in images so that they remain as true as possible all through the process—from acquisition to final output. Ideally, such a system should work effortlessly and flawlessly and should be constrained from producing color perfect output only by the laws of physics itself.

Ideally, the photo of a pear you scanned should be the same color when displayed and when printed; and in a perfect world, the scanner's output should look like the physical pear.

Guess what? The world is not perfect, and neither is any color management that was or is available. But it *did* get a whole lot better and even worth using on an everyday basis when Adobe introduced a new, comprehensive color management system in Photoshop 6. The Adobe CMS works pretty much the same in professional Adobe products, such as Photoshop, Illustrator, and InDesign. And because the Adobe system is based on the use of an international standard for creating ICM (color) profiles (descriptions of how a device handles color), color managed files from Photoshop work as expected with other manufacturers' software and hardware.

So why are we rehashing a Photoshop 6 feature in a book on Photoshop 7? Simple— because color management is very important and because it is not the most intuitive or easy thing for most people to understand and embrace. Many Photoshop users just skipped over the feature as best they could and continue to work in a graphics world where color is more likely to go wrong than right. Also, it's possible you upgraded straight from version 5 to 7, and never read this chapter in our version 6 book.

If you were one of the brave and became a whiz at managing color consistency using Adobe CMS in Photoshop 6, you probably have more time to spend doing the things that you love to do. Learning how to use Photoshop's color management tools is not only for folks whose day gig is in a studio, either. If you have a digital camera and you like to retouch family photos or create and print your own holiday cards, you've already found out how much time and how many pieces of expensive inkjet photo paper it takes to produce *one copy* that has colors you anticipated.

What you are going to learn in this chapter is the most important thing you can learn about Photoshop—how to get predictable, consistent output and how to get your scanner, monitor, and printer to display approximately the same thing. This is the graphic artist's dream, but it doesn't come without a price, and that price is this—a very serious, very technical chapter.

Our advice up front is that you take two or three days to digest what we teach in this chapter. We also realize that the other chapters in this book are light and occasionally humorous when compared to this chapter. So, keeping in mind that you're human and need a break when involved in anything serious, we present to you Figure 7.0. Now, this is a funny picture. Anytime you find your attention drifting from this chapter, turn back to this page.

Aren't you glad the authors have a sense of perspective?

Figure 7.0   Return to this page and this image anytime you're reading this chapter and find that you're in over your head.

Understanding Photoshop's Color Management System (CMS)

Up 'til now, establishing a color-managed workflow was something attempted only by large organizations with big, fat budgets for equipment and dedicated color management technicians. And it didn't always work, even for them. Photoshop 5 introduced a color management process for the individual desktop, and Photoshop 5.5 improved upon that beginning. But those efforts fell short of being impressive; and most users, including us, continued to run, screaming, for the exits. Even talking about color management was too horrible to contemplate.

Well, times have changed. Adobe's new color management system (also referred to as CMS) is probably the single most important feature in Photoshop 7, in Illustrator 10, and in every other new Adobe product coming down the pipeline. Adobe deserves a lot of credit, but so do Apple and Microsoft and a whole bunch of other companies that make up the International Color Consortium (ICC). All these companies have made a serious commitment toward making color management work. It is now possible for mere mortals to understand and use color management. This is great news!

Having a usable system for managing color is a big deal. It is headline news. It is worth writing home about. Why? Because when you have set up your system to use color management and you've learned how to use these new color management tools, you'll never again have to play the "What color is it, really?" game. The colors you see on your monitor will be surprisingly close to what will come streaming out of a high-speed printing press or tumbling out of your desktop inkjet printer.

Adobe has made a splendid CMS that works the same in all of its products. Apple and Microsoft have done their part by providing operating system–level support for color management, so that every program, even non-Adobe programs, can use color management. Equipment manufacturers have made descriptions of the color capabilities of their products available so that the information can be "plugged into" the CMS. Now you can master the concepts of color management and take up the new tools that have been placed at your disposal.

Coming to Terms with Color Management

To be frank, color management is still not an easy topic to understand and it can't be mastered by reading a few paragraphs. But we promise you that it is possible to learn, that it is worth the effort, and that if you take your time going through this chapter, you will be able to use Adobe's CMS and still have enough brain cells left to do creative, artistic work.

In this section, we take a look at some of the key terms used in talking about color management. Along the way, you'll catch a little of the history of the way this newest CMS evolved.

Color Spaces and Color Gamut

Throughout this chapter, you frequently are going to see the terms color spaces and color gamut. *Color space* is a model for representing color in terms of values that can be measured, such as the amount of red, green, and blue in an image. CMS works with standard color spaces, including RGB (Red, Green, Blue), Lab (L for relative lightness, a for colors from red to green, and b for colors from blue to yellow), and CMYK (Cyan, Magenta, Yellow, Black). *Color gamut* refers to a contiguous range of colors describing the limitations of a device or image. Color gamut might be called *color capability* when referring to a specific color space. "How many colors can this model accurately represent?" is the question put forth by color gamut.

Life would be very boring and one dimensional if the universe and every man-made device had only one color space. That's not the case, however, and so the issue of color gamut is a big concern for anyone involved in color-critical work. Here's a quick summary explaining why:

- Every device—monitor, printer, printing press, camera, film, ink, and media combination—can produce only a limited number of colors.
- No two devices or processes have the exact same color gamut.
- Even two printers or monitors of the same make and model vary from each other, although new generations of desktop printers with built-in densitometer (color measuring device) and automatic self-calibration tend to be reliable from printer to printer.
- A device changes in its color-rendering capability because of age, lighting, or other operating conditions.

Ugh. These varying factors drive digital artists and production people up a virtual wall!

Color Calibration

Before you explore the Adobe CMS further, you need to calibrate your devices. What do we mean by the term *calibrate*? *Calibration* is the process of bringing a device, such as a printer or monitor, to an absolute standard to ensure consistency over time and across devices of the same make and model. That is, you are attempting to make the color gamut and characteristics of a physical device adhere to some empirical, mathematically perfect standard.

Calibration is critical when you want accurate color output on a monitor. A good place to start is to match the white point and gamma from monitor to monitor, using monitor calibration software, such as Adobe Gamma, or third-party software and hardware when vailable.

Working Space

Time for a new term: *working space*, which includes RGB and CMYK color spaces. A *working space* is the pool of possible colors available when you edit a file. In the early days of color management, the monitor's color capability (color gamut) was the same as the space in which you worked with your image (the working space). If there were only one monitor in the world, and it never changed, you could consider the color gamut and the working space to be the same. But such is not the case, and a CMS shouldn't assume it is.

A much better idea is to assign actual numbers to specific color values (sometimes referred to as *data*) and then reference and manipulate the data within the context of an ideal, standard working color space, rather than use the settings of a fallible and limited physical device. How is such an ideal, a standard, established when the world is full of so many different types of monitors, printers, scanners, and other devices? Read on!

Commission Internationale de l'Eclairage (CIE)

CMS creators needed a uniform way to describe the color space of devices and standard color spaces. They also needed to define a standard set of rules that govern the way information about color values is exchanged between color spaces that do not overlap.

In the 1930s, the Commission Internationale de l'Eclairage (CIE), based in France, began the task of establishing color standards by assigning numbers to every color visible to the human eye. The color spaces the CIE defined, such as CIELAB, form the foundation of device-independent color for color management. The group's work was only a beginning; however, it did not resolve the color management issues encountered in electronic publishing. Who had PageMaker in 1930?

International Color Consortium (ICC)

In 1993, the International Color Consortium (ICC)—a group of companies recognized as leaders in the fields of electronic publishing, software development, and digital prepress—formed a committee to establish standards for *electronic* color publishing. The ICC based its standardized color information on the CIELAB color space and developed device profiles that would easily transfer color information from one device to another and from one computing platform to another.

Here is the problem the ICC tackled: Each printing device, scanner, digital camera, and monitor has its own way of *rendering* a color (that is, assigning a meaning to a color). This meaning is called the device's *color space*.

Monitors, for example, specify colors as values of red, green, and blue (RGB). The values R:100, G:20, B:30 specify a certain shade of red on a particular monitor. These values are said to be *device-dependent*; if these values are sent to a second monitor with different colored phosphors, a different color red will be displayed. If they are sent to a printer that describes colors as percentages of cyan, magenta, yellow, and black (CMYK), yet another different red will be printed.

Which is the correct color? The color seen on the first monitor? The color seen on the second monitor? Or the color printed on the printer?

Photoshop 7 Color Working Spaces

Fast forward to today. To enable Photoshop to provide uniform ways of describing color space, Adobe needed to offer several different standard color working spaces. Thanks to the foundation laid by the CIE and the ICC, Adobe was able to do so. For RGB images Photoshop offers sRGB, Adobe RGB 1998, Apple RGB, and Colormatch RGB working spaces. For CMYK working spaces, Photoshop offers US Web Coated SWOP, US Web Uncoated, US Sheetfed Coated, US Sheetfed Uncoated, Japan Standard, Euroscale Uncoated, and Euroscale Coated.

Establishing these color working spaces wasn't enough. How could that information be exchanged between devices?

Enter ICC profiles.

ICC Profiles

ICC profiles are an essential element of the color management equation. Because no device can be brought into perfect calibration, and because no two devices—monitors, printers, or scanners—perform identically even if they are the same make and model, profiles are created to *document* the ways a specific device strays from the standard. What kind of documentation is this? Well…

The Adobe CMS uses ICC standard device profiles to ensure that colors are accurately converted across devices. *Profiles* are data files that record all the relevant information for a particular device, including its color space, capabilities, and limitations. Each profile relates a device's color space to the CIE-referenced color space. By doing so, a profile assigns an absolute meaning to each color that a device can produce.

When you transfer an image between two devices that have ICC profiles, a *Color Management Module* (CMM) compares the ICC profile of the source device (such as the monitor) with the ICC profile of the destination device (such as the printer) to create consistent color results. With the information contained in the ICC profile, the CMM transforms colors in image files to produce consistent color simulation on the monitor and the proofing device. For every RGB value in the monitor color space, for example, the color transformation produces a similar CMYK value in the printer's color space. If a color space specified on one device falls *outside* the color gamut of another device, the CMS may automatically reassign the actual values put out from the devices to preserve the *relationship* of colors from one device to another. The CMS in effect *remaps* colors that fall outside of the other device's gamut, *but* …it does so in a way the human eye accepts.

Note

In Windows It's ICM   Because the Windows operating system had already assigned the ICC suffix to another system component, Windows refers to ICC profiles as ICM. The suffixes ICC and ICM are interchangeable in the language of CMS.

How do you *get* ICC profiles? Adobe and your operating system offer generic profiles for popular brands of monitors. In Photoshop, Adobe also offers Adobe Gamma, which creates a custom ICC profile the Adobe CMS can use to understand how your monitor handles color. (Hang on. We cover Adobe Gamma next.)

Even if one of the generic profiles fits your monitor, we recommend that you create a custom ICC profile. It is *not* recommended (at least, not by the authors) to use preset monitor profiles. They are of little value, due to aging and varied viewing conditions of the devices that the profiles describe. Custom profiles are always better. After all, would you rather have a picture of an ideal family or a picture of *your* family?

Note

Profiling   When you create an ICC profile for your monitor, you are making a *system-level* adjustment. This means that *any* program that is color management–capable uses the ICC profile you've created for your monitor.

You can (and should) have multiple ICC profiles for printing devices—one profile for one specific working condition. *But use only one profile at a time.* Also, be careful to use the correct profile for the current condition. For example, you may have one profile for your inkjet printer that you use with the manufacturer's standard glossy paper and another that you use with a third party's glossy paper.

In addition to performing regular calibration (hey, stuff ages) and profiling the monitor, an artist should try to maintain consistent lighting conditions. The monitor needs to be calibrated and profiled at least once a month. Of all the devices that require ICC profiles, the monitor loses its calibration the quickest.

Translation, Please

The Color Management Module (CMM), mentioned earlier, is a color transformation engine that translates data from one device's color to another via an independent color space. The CMM receives the necessary information from the profiles so that it can accurately transform a color from one device to another. The CMM interprets the data and, in essence, says to the monitor, "The file data says to display a blue that has the RGB values of 66, 66, 150; but I've looked at your profile, and you always make things too red. You will display RGB value 60, 66, 150 so that it *looks like* the ideal 66, 66, 150. *Photoshop doesn't have to know about our arrangement.* When it does something to the color 66, 66, 150, use the color in the file data."

When Photoshop performs an operation that requires it to calculate a new color value, that color must be contained in the current working space. The working space's color mode and the position and size of the color gamut of the working space are determined by the ICC profile. Successfully moving color values from one color space to another is a difficult problem because color spaces do not generally share the same color gamut. How is this conversion done?

To bring all the possible color spaces into a common space where accurate color translation becomes possible, a very large device-independent color space is needed. For example, to translate monitor colors to printer colors, a space must exist that is large enough to encompass all *device-dependent spaces* (spaces that are unique to a specific device) as well as standard color spaces. At the heart of Adobe's Color engine is a Profile Connection Space (PCS) that is device-independent and has a large enough color gamut to hold both the source and the target color spaces. That PCS is based on the CIELAB color space.

Figure 7.1 shows a representation of Lab color space. It is tongue-shaped because visible light is broken down into uneven amounts, with green being predominant. Our eyes are more sensitive to greens than to blues or reds; hence, the distortion in the shape of a color space. In the color section in this book, there is an image (a color image, natch) of the CIELAB color model in two dimensions and three dimensions. It also shows how Adobe RGB (1998)—our recommendation for working spaces—neatly fits inside of the gamut of the Lab space.

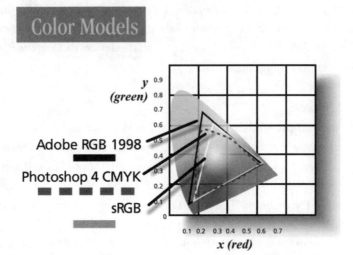

Figure 7.1   Different color spaces often fit inside one another and often overlap.

In the illustration, the working space is Adobe RGB 1998. This color space, larger than anything your monitor can show you, fits within the translation color space, making it possible for every point in the space to be mapped—without color loss—to the translation space (Lab). The colors in printer space, whether it's a commercial press or an inkjet, are CMYK. They represent a smaller space than RGB color and have a few areas that RGB cannot reproduce. Fortunately, the translation layer *can* reproduce those colors. That is why, in the illustration, the printer space eclipses the monitor space slightly, but overall, fits within the working space.

Adobe Gamma

At the time of this writing, Adobe Gamma is available in Photoshop 7 only for Windows. Macintosh users might want to skip this section, but *do* refer to the ColorSync information that came with your OS.

The term *gamma* is the error measured between a straight, linear mapping of voltage applied to your monitor's circuitry and brightness you see on your monitor. Huh? Okay, example time:

Suppose that you were holding a lever that applied voltage to your monitor's blue phosphors. In theory, the screen would be black at zero voltage, medium blue (half blue) at half power, and as bright a blue as possible at full voltage. This is a linear plotting of voltage versus brightness, and it *does not exist*. There is a *sag* in the midrange of the voltage versus brightness graph, which is why we perform gamma correction.

Note

> **Gamma Settings Debate Rages On**   You may have heard that Windows gamma is
> 2.2, and it's 1.8 for the Macintosh. Do not be confused by the Control Panel's default
> settings for gamma; don't argue with them. Monitor gamma is different than the gamma
> of working spaces. Some CMS experts tend to favor 2.2 for both platforms. You very
> well could have a profile for your monitor that is 2.2, but find that Photoshop's working
> space displays images with deeper midtones than you'd expect.

When you installed Photoshop, the setup program installed a feature called Adobe
Gamma in your Control Panel(s) folder. In Windows, the Control Panel is under Start,
Settings, Control Panel. You can use this Adobe Gamma Control Panel and your eye to
calibrate your monitor or adjust its gamma.

The Adobe Gamma Control Panel actually does more than just adjust your monitor's
gamma. It also builds an ICC profile of your monitor that your operating system CMS
can use instead of the default one that was installed when you installed your monitor or
operating system. In fact, the Adobe Gamma Control Panel provides a much better profile, one that is tailored to the way your monitor actually operates and not just what the
engineering specification for the monitor said should be happening.

Note

> **Use Third-Party Software If Your Work Is Color Critical**   If your work is color
> critical, you may want to use a more precise, less subjective method to calibrate and
> profile your monitor. Third-party folks like Monaco, X-Rite, and Gretag Macbeth all offer
> special color measurement hardware and software that produces a more precise result,
> but a result that can cost anywhere from $300 to tens of thousands of dollars. For most
> people, however, the Adobe Gamma software does good enough profiling for the
> monitor, and the price certainly can't be argued.

For most computers, Adobe Gamma's control of the monitor's white point and gamma
affects your view of everything and every program displayed onscreen, whether it uses
color management or not. (The *white point*, or *highlight*, is the lightest part of the picture; it is the point along the range of tones in an image after which light tones appear
white.)

There are some situations in which Adobe Gamma doesn't have full control: Windows
NT 4 and some Windows 95 machines with video cards do not allow software to manipulate display hardware on a global basis. If you use Windows NT 4 or Windows 95 and
have one of the stubborn video cards, you're not totally out of luck—Windows allows
programs, such as Photoshop and PageMaker that "understand" color management, to
alter the display and use the information Adobe Gamma provides (along with the info

in the ICC profile) to adjust the information sent to the display, even if every program and the system itself do not permit that alteration and adjustment. On the Windows NT 4 operating system, the ICM must reside in the Color folder within the System32 folder to be available to graphic applications that support system-level profiles.

The good news is that Adobe Gamma works under Windows 98, Windows ME, Windows 2000, and Windows XP.

Warning

Watch Out for Double Color Management   If you use Adobe Gamma to calibrate and set the gamma of your monitor, don't use another program's software to do the same thing. Pick one system and use it.

Color Clipping

You now know that, for physical reasons, every device—monitor, printer, camera—is limited in the number of colors it can access. The group of colors available to a device— its *color space*—differs from that of other kinds of devices (monitors and printers, let's say). When one color space can express 10 shades of green, for example, you will see nice transition or good detail in parts of the image that use green. But what happens when you ask a different device to display the same image, and that device has a smaller color space or one with less variety in the number of greens available to it? What if it can express only two shades of green? All 10 of the greens will have to be expressed as one or the other of the two available greens in the new color space. The result will be a poster effect—areas of flat, saturated color where lots of different colors (green, in this example) used to be. This posterization of color is called *color clipping*. The way a color that is clipped is mapped into the new gamut is called *rendering intent*. We talk more about rendering intent later.

Color clipping can happen when you move an image between standard color spaces, such as RGB and CMYK, and when you move between subsets of each color space (Adobe RGB to sRGB, for example) or between the color gamuts that different inks or dyes can produce. It is the color management engine that uses the ICC profiles for the different devices and its color gamut to determine the best way to resolve the differences in color capability.

If you're striving for a lighter color or a more saturated one and nothing seems to work, you've reached the greatest possible parameters for such a color when it is output using the media and methods you've chosen. To get the color you want, you'd have to step outside the image's color gamut. In the CMYK print world, that usually means adding an extra ink, called a *spot color*. A *spot color* is a custom ink that is prepared to represent a color that's unavailable in the CMYK color space. It is applied as a separate color plate, in addition to the cyan, magenta, yellow, and black printing plates.

Preparing to Create a Custom Profile

Before we start building custom profiles and plugging them into the system, let's look at other issues that impact color management. Getting these issues squared away will make your custom profile more accurate.

Check Out Yourself, Your Environment, and Your Equipment

All the color profiling and monitor calibration on earth won't help you achieve color consistency across devices if you don't get your physical working conditions in order. Here are a few questions you should ask yourself:

- Have you been to the eye doctor lately?

- Are you taking cold medication? If so, it will really affect your color perception.

- Have you cleaned the smudges off your eyeglasses? Your glasses aren't tinted, are they? Did you remember to park your sunglasses at the door?

- Have you wiped the monitor screen clean lately? You aren't using a glare filter or one of those polarizing privacy screens, are you?

- Is the monitor warmed up? Has it been on for at least 30 minutes before you use it for color work or before you create a new profile?

- Do you work in a windowless room or one with heavily draped windows? You should, because the constantly changing qualities of natural light make it impossible to achieve accurate consistent color.

- Is your artificial lighting even? No bare bulbs peeking out from under their shades? No hot spots reflected in the monitor or shadows cast across it?

- Is your lighting a neutral, subdued white? Or is the light in your workspace too blue (or green) because it is lit with fluorescent tubes, or too yellow because incandescent lamps provide your lighting. See whether you can get your boss to install professionally color-balanced lighting, or at least try to get the fluorescent tubes that profess to have fuller frequency ranges to mimic daylight. If you are using fluorescent bulbs, the next time they need replacing, change them to 5000K bulbs, available at most home improvement stores. You may have to experiment a bit to get the right lighting for your particular workspace. In the meantime, just being aware of the effect of the lighting in your environment is important.

- Are your walls, furniture, curtains, posters, paintings, and plants all a nice neutral, medium gray? Probably not. Be aware that light reflecting off everything in the room can change the color of the light in the room and alter your perception of the colors on your screen and the output from your printer.

- Did you know that even the color of your clothing can make a difference? If your work is color critical, put on a light gray lab coat or artist's smock when you sit down to work. Who knows; your customers might be so impressed with your "technical" uniform that you could charge more. Or more likely, if you pay attention to everything on this list and in this chapter—your color work will be so dead on, your customers will *beg* to pay you more. Wouldn't that be nice? (This is a rhetorical question.)

- Have you extended the neutral gray color scheme to your desktop wallpaper, Windows title bars, and other screen elements? Let the color live in your work and not in your immediate surroundings.

Tip

Desktop Color   Ideally, a 50% gray desktop would help you evaluate colors without influence. However, cursors tend to disappear at R:128, G:128, B:128.

So go a little lighter or darker with your desktop so that it is color-neutral, but you can still make out your cursors.

We know you're anxious to get to the fun stuff, creating something in Photoshop or ImageReady, and that you'd like to finish all this hardware, techie stuff ASAP. But just as you have to do your exercises if you want to keep fit and trim, you have to put in some time now to get your *system* in shape so that you can enjoy the good life of a successful Photoshop user.

Read Your Monitor Manual

Before you start to calibrate and create a profile for your monitor using Adobe Gamma or any other calibration device, you need to find out on which color temperature your monitor bases its display. A monitor's temperature, also called its *white point*, is a value measured in degrees Kelvin that describes the point at which white light is produced from equal amounts of red, green, and blue light. Monitors are designed to operate at a white point that matches one of the standard illuminant temperatures defined by the CIE standards body. Some monitors offer a selection of operating temperatures from which the user can pick, while others offer only one fixed setting.

As you can see in Table 3.1, the default white point setting for Windows monitors is 6500 degrees Kelvin. This may be referred to as 6500K, D65, or daylight. The Macintosh OS default color temperature is 9300K (D93, or Cool White). The color temperature most often used in the publishing (to paper) community is 5000K (D50 or Warm White, Page White, or Paper White), because it produces a view that more closely resembles material printed on white paper. Other common white point settings are 5500K and 7500K. One of the latest trends among the CMS gurus is using 6500K for both platforms.

Table 3.1   Default White Point Settings

Environment	Default White Point	Standard Abbreviation	Commonly Referred To As
Windows	6500K	D65	Daylight
Macintosh	9300K	D93	Cool White
Publishing Paper	5000K	D50	Warm White, Page to White, or Paper White

Check your monitor's manual, its onscreen help, or the manufacturer's web site to see whether your monitor offers a user-definable color temperature and find out how to make that selection. If your monitor does offer a choice of color temperature or white point, you should choose based on the work you do most often. If your work centers around print, use the monitor's controls to set the white point at 5000K. If you design mostly for web or onscreen presentation, you could set your white point to the default temperature of the operating system used by most people who view your work. Or you could split the difference and set your hardware temperature to 7500K, if your monitor offers that choice (the author's monitor doesn't). Or you could set it to match the default setting for your operating system.

Older and some inexpensive monitors may not offer user-definable color temperature, but you should still see what the fixed temperature of the monitor is. Whatever type of monitor you have, find out what the current white point setting is, change it if you can and want to, and then write it down. You will need this value handy when you use Adobe Gamma to calibrate and make an ICC profile for your monitor.

If you are unable to find any of this information, don't panic. Adobe Gamma has a measurement feature that will provide an approximate value for your monitor's white point.

Setting the color temperature and gamma when calibrating and profiling the monitor can be referred to as "setting the *target*." In work environments with more than one monitor, it is important always to use the same target when you're trying to achieve consistent color from one workstation to another.

Install the Latest Drivers for Your Equipment

Before you begin to set up your system and Photoshop to use color management, make sure that you have installed all the latest drivers for your equipment. Monitor, video card, scanner, and printer manufacturers often update their drivers to fix bugs and to add or update the ICC profiles they have created for their products. These default manufacturer profiles are what you'll use if you don't create custom-made profiles for your equipment. In addition, the manufacturer profiles are often used by products that profile things, including Adobe Gamma, as a basis for the custom profile.

If you don't know which video card is installed in your computer, you can find out in Windows by right-clicking on the Desktop, selecting Properties, and choosing the Settings tab. In the Display area, the monitor name and display adapter name will be displayed. If you're a Mac user, even though Adobe Gamma is used with Macs, you can ensure that the video card software is current by using the Apple Profiler in OS 8.x or later. If you're working with OS X, just select Auto Updater after launching System Preferences.

Another great source for video card updates is your computer's manufacturer. They, of course, have an investment in your system working optimally. For example, I own several Dell computers. When I go to Dell's support site online, I click the link to my specific computer. After telling the site which operating system I am using, it displays the newest video drivers available for my computer/video card. This brings up an important point.

Warning

Download the Right Drivers   Regardless of where you get your updated video drivers, be careful that you download only the driver for the operating system you are using. As a general rule, it is best to avoid beta software drivers. Although most of the time they represent the latest and greatest, if this is your first color profile, it doesn't make sense to add the potential confusion of beta software drivers to the mix.

So, fire up your Internet browser or give customer service at each place a call, and get the newest drivers the equipments manufacturers have to offer. Follow their instructions for installing the drivers on your computer.

Creating an ICC Profile for a Monitor

Okay—gamma, brightness/contrast, and other parameters lie ahead of us. Follow these steps to create an ICC profile for your monitor, under Windows, using Adobe Gamma:

Profiling Your Monitor

1. If you haven't done so already, go to your monitor manufacturer's web site and download the most recent driver, and then follow their instructions to install it for your monitor.

2. With Photoshop and other applications closed, open the Control Panel(s) (folder), and double-click the Adobe Gamma icon.

   The Adobe Gamma control panel opens. You can choose to work with a single dialog box that has a number of different tasks, or use a step-by-step method that involves a Windows Wizard.

3. Click to set the Control Panel option, and then click Next. We'll show you how the single dialog version of this application works (shown in Figure 7.2), but you're free to switch to the step-by-step method at any time by clicking the Wizard button.

   In the Description field, you should see one or more profiles listed for your monitor. These profiles are already installed on your system and assigned to your monitor. If there are two, one was probably installed when you installed your operating system and the other is the one you just downloaded and installed from the monitor manufacturer. Unless you told the install program differently, the last installed profile is the one currently in use.

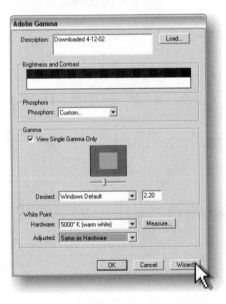

Figure 7.2   If you want to walk through the process of using the Adobe Gamma Control Panel screen by screen, click the Wizard button.

4. Highlight the profile you just installed in Step 1, and type a meaningful name, like **Downloaded 4-12-02**, to indicate that you downloaded the profile on April 12, 2002. This will make it easier to pick the profile from a list if you choose to use this profile at a later date.

Adobe Gamma will base the new profile being created on the highlighted profile in the Description field.

5. Click the Load button if you want to base the new profile on a profile other than the one currently in the field.

6. Using the controls on your monitor, increase the Contrast to 100%, or set it as high as the control will go. With your eye on the Brightness and Contrast section of the Adobe Gamma Panel, use the monitor's brightness control to adjust brightness up or down until the gray squares in the gray-and-black checkerboard strip are almost black (see Figure 7.3). The goal is to end up with an almost black-and-black checkerboard strip above a crisp, bright white strip. If the white gets dirty, be sure to increase the brightness.

Figure 7.3   Use your monitor's brightness and contrast knobs or onscreen controls to make the gray squares in the Adobe Gamma Control Panel almost black.

Warning

Changes to Contrast and Brightness Will Affect Profiles   If you change the monitor's contrast and brightness settings later in the profile-making process, or at any time in the future, the profile will no longer be accurate and you will have to create a new profile. If your monitor has external knobs that adjust brightness and contrast, you should use duct tape—or something stronger—to tape them down so that they can't be changed by accident.

7. Change the Phosphors setting only if you are *absolutely certain* that what is shown is wrong. If you are *certain* it is wrong, but you don't know what the right setting is, the best guess would be Trinitron.

Adobe Gamma sets the Phosphors properties based on information from the manufacturer's profile. If you installed the latest driver and profile from your monitor's manufacturer, you probably won't have to make any changes with the Phosphors drop-down list. For many users, the setting will be Custom; you should leave it alone and move on to the fun control: Gamma.

8. Make sure that the View Single Gamma Only option is checked. Then, lean back and squint, and drag the slider to the left or to the right until the solid tone in the center has the same apparent tone as the stripes outside the box.

You just defined gamma by using a composite control that applied the same gamma setting to each of the three RGB channels. This "one-gamma-setting-fits-all-channels" method works just fine for most people. If you want greater control or if you think that your monitor's RGB channels are a little out of synch with each other, however, clear the View Single Gamma Only option and, one by one, drag the slider under each box until the center box fades into the striped frame around it. Then move on to the next step.

If you are using Windows NT 4 or Windows 95 with certain video cards, you will not have the option of choosing a setting from the Desired drop-down list, as shown in the next step. This is a limitation imposed by the operating system and not by Adobe Gamma. Some Windows 95 users, and all Windows 98, ME, 2000, and XP users will have the option available to them and should follow the advice in the next step.

9. Choose Windows Default, Macintosh Default, or Custom from the Desired drop-down list—these are the options as of this writing; however, as we mentioned earlier, Adobe has no plans to implement Adobe Gamma on the Macintosh platform. I chose Windows Default (see Figure 7.4) because I'm working on a Windows computer. If you choose Custom, you will need to enter a value in the field next to the drop-down. We don't recommend choosing a custom setting unless you are experienced in color management and have a very compelling reason to do so.

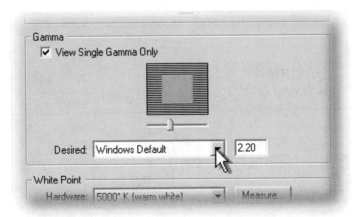

Figure 7.4 Choose from the (Gamma) Desired drop-down. Your choice should match your operating system.

In the White Point area of the Adobe Gamma Control dialog box are two drop-down lists. The first refers to the actual hardware setting of your monitor.

10. Click the Hardware drop-down list and choose the color temperature your monitor actually uses. Earlier in the chapter, this is the value you set or determined in the "Read Your Monitor Manual" section.

11. If you were unable to determine the hardware setting, or if your monitor is old and you think it might not be operating as well as it used to, click the Measure button next to the Hardware drop-down list. Follow the onscreen instructions carefully. Removing all ambient light means the room should be dark. You may even want to wait until night to do this if your workspace has windows. Click the center square when you are done. The entry in the Hardware drop-down list will now read Custom.

The Adjusted drop-down box offers the same color temperature choices as the Hardware drop-down list did. Adobe Gamma can override the hardware settings and force the monitor to display other standard white points.

The lighting conditions present when you're calibrating and profiling the monitor should be maintained when you use that profile. If you use other lighting conditions, you should recalibrate and reprofile. In other words, don't calibrate your new computer in the store and expect the profiles to hold true when you get the machine home.

12. If you ever need to use a nonstandard white point, choose Custom from the list, and enter the values that describe the custom white point.

If your monitor can display the color temperature you want to use, choose Same as Hardware from the Adjusted drop-down list. If your monitor has a fixed color point of 9600K, for example, and you want to use a 5000K white point to more closely mimic paper, then choose 5000K from the Adjusted drop-down list, as shown in Figure 7.5.

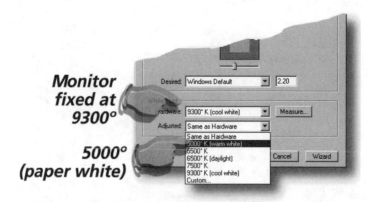

Figure 7.5   Choose a color temperature in keeping with the way you view your final output in Photoshop.

13. Click OK, and then in the Save As dialog box, give a descriptive name to your monitor's custom profile. On the Macintosh, the file extension would be .PF; in Windows, it's *.ICM.

For example, I'm calling the settings for one of my machines *Win XP machine 4-18-02.icm*. In this way, I can tell how recently I profiled the monitor.

14. Click Save, and then click OK in the Gamma Control Panel to finish calibrating and profiling your monitor.

It probably took longer to read how to calibrate and profile your monitor than it took to actually *do* it! This is a good thing, because if you want to keep your colors consistent, you really should recalibrate and reprofile your monitor at least once a month, even if nothing noticeable has changed in the environment. Recalibrate and reprofile right away if something *does* change in the environment. Changing a light bulb or repainting the room both qualify as events that should cause you to open up Adobe Gamma and run through it one more time.

Now that every color management–aware piece of software on your system has a target profile for your monitor, it will be easier to establish color consistency when you print or do web work in Photoshop. The next thing to do is to set up a working color space for Photoshop.

Photoshop and the CMS look in specific folders for profiles. The location of the folder that stores profiles depends on the operating system you use. Table 7.2 shows where you should save profiles you've created or obtained if you want to make them available for use.

Table 7.2   Required Locations for ICC Profiles

Operating System	Installed Location of ICC Profiles
Windows NT version 4	WinNT\system32\Color
Windows 2000	WinNT\system32\spool\drivers\color
Windows XP	WinXP\system32\spool\drivers\color
Macintosh OS using ColorSync, earlier than version 2.5	System Folder, Preferences, ColorSync Profiles
Macintosh OS using ColorSync version 2.5 or later	System Folder, ColorSync Profiles

To recap: You've profiled your monitor, and the operating system has assigned that profile to your monitor. Now it is time to open Photoshop and start setting up the rules for the way it should do its part in the color-management process.

Setting Photoshop's Color Management Defaults

Setting Photoshop Color Setting defaults doesn't take much time, but it does require a little thought to make them work best with the kind of work you do most. These settings can be changed at any time. They are defaults, which means they are the rules Photoshop will use unless you tell Photoshop to do something else. You always can override default settings on a per-file basis; when you find that you frequently are overriding the default settings, just press Ctrl(⌘)+Shift+K and set new defaults.

To make matters even simpler, Adobe has come up with different collections of settings that suit common needs of different types of work: printing to U.S., European, or Japanese printing presses; creating graphics for the Internet; working in the color spaces of Photoshop 4; or turning off color management. If one of the default settings is good for your kind of work, your stay in this dialog box will be brief. But if the defaults don't cut it for you, or you just want greater control over things, there are lots of choices you can make. In the next sections you'll discover what all the choices are, and I'll offer some recommendations for what you should choose.

Most of the recommendations are based on the premise that you are looking for a good, general-purpose workspace profile: one that enables the monitor's color capability to show through, one that embraces most other color output spaces, and one that gives a reasonably accurate view of images that come from different color spaces. Some images might be RGB, some might be Lab color, while others might have been saved in CMYK mode. It all depends on where you work!

A Word on Your "Out of the Box" Experience

You haven't ruined anything if you ran Photoshop for the first time and answered no to Photoshop's offer to help you determine Custom color settings. It only means that you need to press Ctrl(⌘)+Shift+K and change one or two things in the Color Settings box to get a better color space than the default going in Photoshop. More importantly, the authors have selected Adobe RGB 1998 color space when saving all the images on the Companion CD. You will get annoying, confusing dialog boxes when you open every image on the CD if you do not go with our recommendations concerning color space.

In a nutshell, as of this writing, Adobe has chosen sRGB as the default color space in Photoshop, and the authors disagree. We feel you should be working most of the time in Adobe RGB 1998 color space. Read on!

The Color Settings Dialog Box, or Laying Down the Rules

This section takes you to color management central, the Color Settings dialog box. We won't cover this as an exercise with lots of numbered steps because we don't know what the best choices for you will be. That's up to you to decide. What we do want to do is explain what all the choices mean and translate the parlance of color management into more understandable and accessible terms.

Here's what we'd like you to do to make following along easier: Open Photoshop (you do not need an image to be open), and then choose Edit, Color Settings, or press Ctrl(⌘)+Shift+K. The Color Settings dialog box pops up onscreen, where you can refer to it as you proceed through the following sections.

The Color Settings dialog box on your screen (and in Figure 7.6) has two major functions. It is used to define the default working color space that will be used when you create an image and to "tag" the image with the ICC profile of the workspace. The workspace tag is kind of like a short biography that tells what color space the file was born in and where it currently lives. The tag also is used to set the rules or color management policies for what happens when you work with files that don't have workspace tags or have tags that don't match the default space you've set. Your work is not harnessed to the profile, however. When you choose File, Save As, you can uncheck the ICC profile box, and Photoshop will protest a little in the form of a warning, but this is cool.

Now, for most folks, the choices shown in Figure 7.6 should be perfect for getting right down to work in Photoshop. If your screen doesn't look like this figure, manually select the options so that your screen will match what you're reading here. As mentioned earlier, the authors cannot adopt Adobe's decision to make the default space the teensy, web-friendly sRGB color space—we need more room if we're going to create something good.

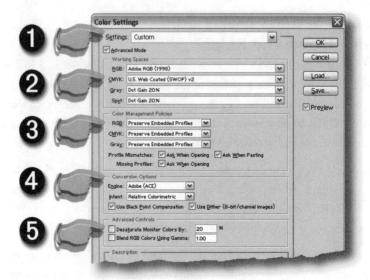

Figure 7.6 There are five areas you need to set in the Color Settings dialog box to make the workspace foolproof and easy to work in.

The Settings Drop-Down List

You use the Settings drop-down list to choose either a preset collection of settings or to select independently the various settings in the dialog box. Adobe has provided some very useful presets, and you, of course, can also create your own presets and choose them from this drop-down list. When you choose one of the presets in this drop-down list, the preset specifies and sets all the other fields and options in the dialog box for you. If none of the shipping color setting files meet your needs, for example, go through the dialog box, make your choices, and then save all the changes you've made to a new color setting file. From then on, you can access your custom settings with the convenience and precision of the shipping presets. You can even share these settings with other people by giving them the file that was created.

If you click the arrow for the Settings drop-down list you'll see that Adobe has provided the following presets:

- **Color Management Off.** As good as it is under most circumstances to use color management, there are times when you definitely want to turn it off. The most common reason for turning off color management is to create graphics that in their finished version will be viewed only onscreen, by users with different monitors and operating systems, or for video work. Examples of such material would be onscreen help files, reference material, and multimedia presentations.

- **Emulate Photoshop 4.** Photoshop 4 was the last version of Photoshop that did not have any color management features. Internally, both Macintosh and Windows versions of Photoshop 4 (and earlier versions) used a working space based on the characteristics of a Macintosh monitor. Choose this preset if you are working with files created in early versions of Photoshop, files you used successfully in projects of that era, which you might need to reproduce. Choose them also when you are working with older graphics and DTP software that does not have color-management features.

- **Europe Prepress Defaults, Japan Prepress Defaults, and U.S. Prepress Defaults.** Each of these three separate presets defines conditions suitable for common commercial press conditions of the specific region. These are generic conditions and are good as a starting point for creating a custom definition for the area of the world and the kind of press/ink sets and paper conditions you typically use.

- **Photoshop 5 Default Spaces.** This preset lands your Photoshop working space back in the sRGB mode, which we tell you is only good for screen presentations and web work. Make this your preset only if you did oodles of work in Photoshop 5 and if you have no business that requires photographic realism when going to print.

- **Web Graphics Default.** The settings specified by this preset are optimal for creating graphics that will be viewed on the web or on an intranet through ICC-aware web browsers.

- **ColorSync Workflow (Macintosh OS only).** Choose this setting if you are using ColorSync version 3.0 or higher and if you are using the ColorSync Control Panel to choose profiles.

Working Spaces

The settings in the Working Spaces section of the Color Settings dialog box, shown as item 2 in Figure 7.6, determine which of the many ICC profiles is the default working space profile assigned to newly created files. It's critical to understand here that when you convert from, say, RGB to CMYK, the resulting color space to which the CMYK image is saved is not necessarily the CMYK space you want. The image will default to the current CMYK working space in the Color Settings dialog box. Unless you only have one output device, and you've chosen the profile for that device in the Color Settings box, you will get more accurate results by changing color mode using Image, Mode, Convert to Profile, instead of depending on the Image, Mode colors listed in the main menu.

The Working Spaces section of the Color Settings dialog box contains four drop-down lists labeled RGB, CMYK, Gray, and Spot, respectively. The working space for each color mode is defined by the ICC profile you want to attach automatically to new documents that use the same color space: RGB, CMYK, Grayscale, or Multichannel.

When the Advanced Mode option is checked, the ICC profiles available at the system level are displayed. Those are the ones in the ColorSync folder (Macintosh) or Color folder (Windows). If you have loaded profiles in these locations and you need to access them, you should activate the Advanced Mode.

Choosing from the RGB Working Spaces Drop-Down List

When you click the down arrow to expose the choices offered by the RGB drop-down list, you may find a *huge* list of profiles from which to choose. The number of profiles in the RGB drop-down list depends on the number of RGB profiles loaded at the system level, and whether the Advanced Mode is activated. If Advanced Mode is not activated, the list is rather short. The profiles are grouped into the following categories:

- **Custom.** (Available in Advanced Mode only.) At the top of the list is Custom RGB. If you choose this option, you can define your own custom RGB space. Unless you are an expert in color management trying to solve a particular problem, we strongly recommend that you avoid the potential masochism in creating your own RGB workspace. That said, the only reason ordinary Photoshop users might use this feature would be to create a profile for BruceRGB. (For information on BruceRGB, see the Note at the end of this section.)

- **Load RGB and Save RGB.** (Available in Advanced Mode only.) These two commands are found in the second section of the drop-down list. Load RGB enables you to cruise your hard disks for an ICC profile that's not in the system level Color folder—oddly, this is not an option when Advanced Mode is not checked. Photoshop can convert the monitor setup file (*.AMS) into an ICC profile if you save it by using the Save RGB command after you've loaded it with the Load RGB command. Save RGB will save any currently chosen RGB workspace profile to any location on your hard disk, which is handy when you need to share a custom profile with another Photoshop user.

- **Other.** This section contains any profile you've created with the Custom command but have not yet saved with the Save RGB command.

- **Monitor RGB.** This is a straightforward choice to use Adobe's sRGB space. Although the colors on your screen will look lush on your monitor and on others who are, for example, visiting your site—it's a limited color space and not good for much other than web graphics.

- **Standard Working Spaces.** This part of the list contains the profiles that are the best as default working spaces. Unless you are working under unusual conditions, you should choose one of the profiles in this section. The profiles are Adobe RGB (1998), Apple RGB, ColorMatch RGB, and sRGB IEC61966-2.1 (commonly referred to as sRGB). The profiles are described in more detail here:
  - **Adobe RGB (1998).** A good all-around RGB working space with a color gamut large enough to produce decent RGB or CMYK printed output. This is our recommendation as a default working space.
  - **Apple RGB.** A good working space if your finished work will be seen only on Macintosh OS monitors, or if you are using older software that is not capable of color management. This is the working space used by the Emulate Photoshop 4 preset. This author uses Apple RGB space on a Windows XP machine occasionally to work between Apple and Windows systems, for comparison's sake.
  - **ColorMatch RGB.** Corresponds to the color space of the Pressview monitor. A small color space, it is sometimes used for images that will be output to a CMYK commercial printing press. Many prepress experts prefer to use a larger space than this for print work.
  - **sRGB IEC61966-2.1.** The working color space of choice for the creation of web graphics. If you think you will use an image on the web and also in print, choose Adobe RGB (1998) as your work space instead. sRGB is too narrow for print work, even on RGB inkjet printers.

  On the Macintosh, ColorSync RGB is also available as a standard working space. The actual working space used when Macintosh ColorSync is chosen depends on what you've chosen in the Apple ColorSync control panel (or in System Preferences when using OS X).

- **More RGB Profiles.** (Available in Advanced Mode only.) The last section of the list contains all other RGB profiles available in your computer's System level Color folders. You'll see all kinds of default device profiles for monitors, printers, scanners, and cameras, as well as profiles installed by RGB equipment you own. A few standard working spaces are listed here also: they include NTSC (1953) and PAL/SECAM,SMPTE-C, which refer to TV and video color spaces and CIE RGB and Wide Gamut RGB, which are both very wide, large color spaces that are *not* recommended unless you are working with files that are 16 bits per channel.

Adobe RGB (1998) is the best overall choice for working with or creating images that will output in a variety of ways. Logos, for example, typically are used in print, on the web, in videos, and on product packaging. If you want to be able to set and forget your workspace profile, Adobe RGB (1998) is the one to choose because it is the most flexible workspace. If you want to tweak images from the moment the first pixel is laid down, you should choose one of the special-use profiles that will work best for your intended output.

Note

Meet BruceRGB   One other standard RGB space, BruceRGB, is worth mentioning. Bruce Fraser, a prepress guru and writer, felt that Adobe RGB was too large a color space and that ColorMatch was too small for most prepress work. BruceRGB has become one of the accepted standard workspaces in the pre-press world. Unfortunately, Adobe doesn't install BruceRGB profile along with the other standard RGB working spaces. You can use the Custom RGB feature described earlier, however, to create this profile. To obtain the values you must enter in the Custom RGB dialog box to create the profile; and for other information about the color space, visit Mr. Fraser's web site. You'll find the address in the "Resources" section at the end of this chapter.

Choosing from the CMYK Workspaces Drop-Down List

The profile you choose in the CMYK drop-down list is the profile that will be applied to new CMYK images you create. You should be aware that what you specify as your default working CMYK space also is the default space when you use the View menu's proofing feature. Unless a custom proofing space is specified, the default CMYK working space is used for the soft-proof view, even when the image being proofed is an RGB image or has a different CMYK working space. The structure of the drop-down list parallels that of the RGB list, as you see here:

- **Custom.** When you click the CMYK Custom option, you'll see a dialog box that will be familiar if you ever looked at or changed the CMYK settings in Photoshop 5.5. If you need to tweak the settings of an existing profile or create one of your own, this is the place to do it. But if you are trying to re-create a custom setting you created and saved in an earlier version of Photoshop, it's easier to use the Load CMYK and Save CMYK options instead.

- **Load CMYK and Save CMYK.** Use these two commands to load new ICC profiles you may have obtained or to load CMYK Setup files (*.API) or Separation Setup files (*.ASP) you may have created in previous versions of Photoshop. Use Save CMYK to save a loaded ICC profile to disk or to convert and save a CMYK Setup file or Separation Setup file you've loaded to the now-standard ICC profile that Photoshop 7 uses.

- **Other.** This section contains any profile you've created with the Custom command and have not yet saved with the Save CMYK command.

- **Standard CMYK Workspaces.** This section contains the profiles you'll use most often. These standard profiles were designed to describe the colors that can be printed using various kinds of presses and papers under print conditions typical in the U.S., Europe, and Japan. You should choose for your default the profile that matches the CMYK press conditions you most often use. If you are working with files from Photoshop 4 or earlier or files that will be used in older publishing programs that are not capable of color management, you may prefer to choose a standard profile—the Photoshop 4 Default CMYK or Photoshop 5 Default CMYK profile—from the next section on the list instead. On the Macintosh, ColorSync CMYK is also available as a standard working space. The actual working space used when Macintosh ColorSync is chosen depends on what you've chosen in the Apple ColorSync Control Panel, which is accessed in System Preferences under OS X.

  Generally, the CMYK ICC profile you use for soft-proofing would be the same one you use for conversion from RGB or Lab to CMYK.

Choosing from the Gray Workspace's Drop-Down List

By now you've surely (and correctly) guessed that the Gray drop-down is used to specify which profile is used by default with grayscale images. This one has a twist—it has two custom commands:

- **Custom Dot Gain.** (Available in Advanced Mode only.) Choose this command to display the Custom Dot Gain dialog box, where you can enter values or click points and drag on the curve to create a profile that matches the way dot gain occurs at different halftone percentage points when printed. *Dot gain* is the amount by which a printed halftone dot increases or decreases in size when the ink, dye, toner, or other pigment is applied to the printed surface. To determine how to construct the curve, you should use a densitometer to take readings from a gradient bar that actually used the same inks, media, and output device you will ultimately use. For example, if the densitometer produces a reading of 16% when it reads the 10% portion of the gradient tint bar, you would type **16** in the 10% field of the Custom Dot Gain dialog box. If you do not have access to test prints, ask the folks who run the press which values you should use.

- **Custom Gamma.** (Available in Advanced Mode only.) With this command, you can create a profile for grayscale images that mimics their display on a monitor that has a custom gamma setting. Gamma determines the contrast of the midtones in an image. If you want to use a profile that reflects the gamma settings for Macintosh and Windows monitors, use either the Gray Gamma 1.8 or 2.2 settings at the bottom of the list.

- **Load Gray and Save Gray.** (Available in Advanced Mode only.) Use these commands either to load custom gray ICC profiles you may have obtained but that are not installed or to save a custom setting you've created.

- **Other.** This section contains any profile you've created with the Custom command but have not yet saved with the Save Gray command.

- **Standard Gray working spaces.** The balance of the list contains standard profiles that reflect dot gains of 10, 15, 20, 25, and 30 percent. Typically, you get this sort of information is by asking the pressman who is familiar with the (device-dependent) physical printing press. This dialog section also contains standard profiles called Gray Gamma 1.8 and Gray Gamma 2.2. Gray Gamma 1.8 mimics the default gamma of a Macintosh OS monitor and also corresponds to the default grayscale setting used in Photoshop 4 and earlier versions. Gray Gamma 2.2 corresponds to the default gamma of a Windows OS monitor. Choose the default setting that most closely matches the behavior of your most common grayscale output.

Choosing from the Spot Working Spaces Drop-Down List

The default choice you make in the Spot working spaces drop-down list differs from the others in that it governs the way spot color channels and duotones display. These profiles are the only ones that are not attached to files themselves, as you would embed other types of profiles in saved files. The choices here are identical to those offered in the Gray working spaces drop-down, except that Custom Gamma and the two Gray Gamma choices are not available here. You create custom dot gain profiles and choose between standard default profiles based on the same information and concerns you would use for dot gain in the Gray working spaces. If the system level Color folder holds custom Grayscale ICC profiles, another section (the custom Grayscale set) will appear after the Standard set.

Color Management Policies

The default working spaces profiles you just went through apply primarily to newly created files. But what happens when you open a file that doesn't have a color management profile attached to it, or that has a different working space profile attached to it than the default profile you've selected? Similarly, what happens when you cut from and paste into images that have different working spaces? The Color Management Policies section in the dialog box (see item 3 in Figure 7.6) takes care of situations in which profiles are mismatched. Adobe calls the actions taken by Photoshop to reconcile color mismatches and missing profiles the *Color Management Policies*.

Each of the three drop-down lists—RGB, CMYK, and Gray—offers the same three Color Management Policy options:

- **Off.** This setting doesn't exactly mean no color management at all. It means that an ICC workspace will *not* be assigned to newly created files. This is not to say that the working spaces you have designated are not affecting the soft-proofing capabilities while you are working on a newly created file in Photoshop. Very large gamut RGB working spaces usually create printed output that is prone to excessive clipping, so a choice here other than off might be the solution when you aren't happy with the output.

    Off also means that profiles attached to documents that are opened will be ignored, and they will be discarded if they do not match default working space. On the other hand, if the profile of the opened document matches the current default profile, the profile will be preserved.

    And Off means that when part or all of an image is pasted into another image, the colors will be added based on their absolute numeric value.

Note

Perception Versus Numerical Value in Color Conversion   When the numerical value of a color takes precedence in determining how colors are translated from one color space to another, the perceived color often changes, and many observers would not think it a faithful translation. The reason is that the perceived color of inks and dyes is greatly affected by the surface to which they are applied. For example, when a numerically specified color (RGB 97, 176, 224) is applied to newsprint it appears darker and duller than the same color printed on glossy, coated cover stock.

When the perceived appearance takes precedence over the numerical value of a color, the goal is to create a color that appears to be the same on newsprint as on cover stock, even though the actual ink or combination of inks used is wildly different. Maintaining perceptual color fidelity is very important when you are working with corporate colors or most photographic material.

- **Preserve Embedded Profiles.** This color management policy means that profiles attached to open documents are used and preserved. When material from one file is copied into another and the working space profiles of the two do not match, this policy attempts to maintain perceptual color values when the receiving image is an RGB or grayscale image and will use absolute numeric color values when the receiving image is a CMYK image.

- **Convert to Working.** When this policy is in effect, the default behavior is to convert all opened images to the current working color space regardless of whether they have a profile attached. Additionally, when image data is copied from one file into another, the appearance of the color always takes precedence, regardless of the color mode of either image.

We recommend that you use the Preserve Embedded Profiles Color Management Policy for all three color modes. You always can change the profile that is attached to an image, but we believe that is a decision you should make consciously and not have happen on a default basis.

Second Guessing Default Color Management Policies

The default policies are useful but they are not always what you really want to have happen. For this reason, Adobe has provided you with the option of asking Photoshop to notify you whenever there is a mismatch between image profiles when documents are opened or created, and when you open an image that doesn't have a profile. We recommend that you always keep the Profile Mismatches and Missing Profiles options checked so that you get to make these critical color decisions.

Having Photoshop notify you of mismatches or missing profiles when you open a document is a good idea if your workflow has only a few workstations and the artist is trained to make such choices. In a high-volume workflow with many workstations, however, such on-the-spot decision making can really slow things down.

Advanced Color Settings Options

We've now covered all the Color Setting options that Adobe thinks most people need to make. But other options are available in this dialog box. If the Advanced Mode option in the upper-left corner of the dialog box is checked, the dialog box expands to reveal additional important color management settings. Even if you don't want to change these default settings, you should read on because the choices offered in the section on Conversion Intents are those you are asked to make when you convert an image's profile, when you choose a custom soft-proofing profile, and when you assign a print profile.

Check the Advanced Mode option in the Color Settings dialog box if it is not already checked, and let's move on to the next section.

Conversion Options: Which Engine to Use

Now we'll take a look at the Conversion Options section of the Color Settings dialog box (item 4 in Figure 7.6). The default color management engine used in new Adobe products is ACE (Adobe Color Engine). Windows 2000 and XP users can choose to use Microsoft ICM engine instead of Adobe's engine, and Macintosh users can use the ColorSync engine instead, if they prefer. All three engines are similar because all three are based on Linotype AG's LinoColor Color Management System.

At first glance, the Adobe engine provided in all new Adobe products seems like a great choice because having the same engine available on both Macintosh and Windows makes trading files between the two operating systems entirely compatible. But because the Adobe ACE engine can be accessed only by Adobe products, you might not want to use Adobe's color management engine. Color management engines really should belong to the operating system so that they are available to all programs that use color management.

In the ideal world, we'd all be 125 pounds, blonde, rich, never flame a jerk in a newsgroup…and only one color management engine would be used, and it would work exactly the same on any operating system. But we haven't reached—and are not likely ever to find ourselves in—such a world. Unless you count Hollywood as a "world."

So what engine should you use? Use the one that is used by the most people who will handle the file. If you, your colleagues, clients, service bureaus, and printers use only Windows ME or higher, choose the Microsoft ICM system; if everyone in the chain uses Macintosh OS systems, choose the ColorSync engine. If your files move across platforms now, or may in the future, your best bet probably is to choose the Adobe ACE engine, because Adobe graphics products are the leading products on both platforms, and the ACE engine works identically on both platforms. What you want to strive for is *consistency*. For the purposes of this book, we will assume that you are using the Adobe ACE engine.

Conversion Intents

Intent, in the context of color management, is not exactly what it sounds like. It does *not* mean what your plans are; instead, it asks, "What overall rules do you want to use when you're moving an image from one color gamut to another?" Whenever you change the profile an image uses, the color management engine must somehow decide how the numbers that define the colors are changed or how the interpretation of those numbers changes to fit within the confines of the new profile. Exactly how this conversion takes place is governed by the source and destination profiles. When the source and destination profiles are created, they usually are assigned a default rendering intent. This default intent can be overridden by applications capable of designating rendering intent, like Photoshop.

Four intents have been defined by the ICC: *Perceptual* (sometimes called Image), *Saturation* (sometimes called Graphic), *Absolute Colorimetric*, and *Relative Colorimetric*. These four intents are used by all color management engines. Only one of the four intents can be applied during a conversion, but any one of the four could be specified. Which rendering intent you choose as the default intent depends on which qualities of your original image you want to preserve during a color transformation from one gamut to another. As mentioned earlier, it is important to understand what these intents do because you are asked to choose an intent whenever you convert an image's color space, when you choose a custom soft-proofing profile, and when you assign a print profile. A brief description of each of the four intents follows.

Perceptual Intent

Perceptual intent usually is the best choice for working with photographic images. When you choose Perceptual, the white points of the source and the destination color spaces are matched to each other. Then all the colors in the source space are shifted to new color values that maintain the original relative difference between colors. This means that the actual color values (the numbers) are changed in a way that preserves the overall look of the image rather than preserving the actual colors.

Because photographic and photorealistic images most often are moved from a large RGB editing working space to a smaller RGB or CMYK printing space, source colors either have to be clipped or the gamut of colors needs to be compressed. The Perceptual intent avoids having to clip colors, which would result in loss of image detail, by desaturating the colors in common between both spaces. Desaturating the common colors produces the room needed to assign color slots to colors that would otherwise be clipped. Consequently, using Perceptual rendering sacrifices absolute color fidelity to preserve detail and the overall look of the image. Perceptual's strategy of using desaturation works particularly well for photographic images that are making the large-to-small color space transition, because the human eye doesn't notice the desaturation of colors as much as it notices color clipping or posterization.

When images are being converted the other way around, from a small color gamut to a destination with a larger color gamut, the Perceptual intent would not be the best choice for a photograph or photorealistic image. Because almost all the colors will fit within the new, larger space, desaturation of common colors is no longer necessary to avoid excessive loss of detail due to clipping. Consequently, conversions of photographic and continuous tone images from smaller to larger color spaces usually turn out better if the Relative Colorimetric is chosen for the conversion intent.

It is also important to note that because Perceptual intent maintains the relationships between colors by remapping most, if not all, colors in an image by compressing them to fit into the new gamut, Perceptual would not be the correct choice when the destination gamut is very small—a flexographic newsprint press, for example. In that instance, it would be better to take the clipping hit and try to remap manually the colors that have turned to mud.

Saturation Intent

Saturation is a good intent to choose for images in which the actual color (hue) is not as important as the purity or distinctiveness of the color. The Saturation intent is most often used for business graphics, such as bar graphs, pie charts, and presentation graphics. These kinds of graphics typically don't require precise color matching; rather, they need non-subtle, easily distinguishable color that makes reading data easy or that doesn't wash out when projected. The rules inherent in the Saturation intent essentially tell the conversion process to focus on producing distinctive colors rather than maintaining an exact color specification. The Saturation intent is also good for re-creating psychedelic posters of the 1960s and for producing cartoons.

Absolute Colorimetric Intent

Absolute Colorimetric is the conversion intent most often used when the most important goal is to ensure that as many colors as possible in the source image are matched exactly in the destination image. Colors that cannot be matched exactly in the destination space will be clipped. White points in the source and the destination color gamuts are not matched. *Color clipping* (total saturation of an area in an attempt to render a specific color) will occur during a move from a profile with a large color gamut to a profile with a smaller color gamut, but the colors that do fall within output gamut are faithfully preserved. When a color(s) is clipped, it is generally moved to the edge of the new gamut, which generally translates as "muddy." Clipping also can take several dissimilar colors and assign them to the same color in the new gamut. With the power of preview soft-proofing, the artist has the opportunity to remap manually those colors that will be clipped before the change occurs. This intent is the best one to use when you are working with corporate logos, spot colors, or other specific colors that must be used in an image.

Relative Colorimetric Intent

Relative Colorimetric intent is our pick for best overall choice, and we're sorry if we made you muddle through the other options—but to be a Photoshop guru, ya gotta know this stuff. Relative Colorimetric intent maps the white point (the hottest point in an image—absolute white) of the source profile to that of the destination profile, and then shifts all the colors so that they maintain the same relative position to the white point. Source colors that fall out of gamut in the destination profile's color space are clipped (changed to the nearest color in gamut).

Resorting to clipping colors (reducing the number of unique colors) instead of preserving the absolute number of different colors by desaturating some of them is what makes Relative Colorimetric intent different from Perceptual intent. It is a good choice if the destination space is capable of producing almost all the colors, or if you have done a lot of tweaking to bring colors into the destination's gamut. Examples of this would be if you turned on gamut warning and then used color correction techniques to bring the color used in the image into the CMYK gamut, or if you used only web-safe colors when creating the image. You should base your default rendering intent on the nature of the images you work with and the kind of output to which these images typically are sent.

The Conversion Options section contains two other options, which we'll look at next.

Black Point Compensation

The tonal range of an image is determined by the number of intermediate grays the image contains between pure white (the white point) and pure black (the black point). ICC profiles have rules that govern how and when white points are matched to each other when conversions take place, but surprisingly, they don't have rules about how black points should be matched. When black points are not considered when an image's color space is converted, the translation between color spaces does *not* always look as good as it should or would if the black points had been evaluated. Adobe has developed a fudge factor, called *black point compensation*, that evaluates source and destination black points and then makes corrections to help ensure that the blacks in the converted file aren't blocked in or washed out. But like most workarounds, it doesn't suit all situations. The rule of thumb commonly used is that the Use Black Point Compensation option should be enabled when you're converting an image from RGB to CMYK or from one CMYK profile to another, and that it should not be enabled when you're converting from one RGB space to another.

Note

Controlling Contrast   The human eye is more sensitive to tonal changes in the low end of the spectrum than it is to changes approaching the white point. This is another reason why it's important to control the contrast of darker tones.

Black Point Compensation should also be avoided when the conversion from RGB has a destination gamut in which the paper and inks used have a low black density, such as CMYK newsprint, which has a washed-out black.

Use Dither (8-Bit per Channel Images)

Dither refers to a process (dithering) that uses different colored dots, shapes placed close to each other, or patterns made up of different colors—to fool the viewer's eye into seeing a color that is not actually there. When small specks of colors are intermingled, the brain blends the viewed colors together, and interprets them as the color that would be produced if the colors were actually mixed together. This phenomenon of human vision is what makes both the painting style of Pointillism and CMYK halftone printing work. Activating the Use Dither (8-bit per channel) option enables profile-conversion processes to use dithering to reduce the perceived amount of banding that is caused by color clipping. This is a good option to use, but it will increase file size and make file compression techniques less effective.

Advanced Controls

The last set of options in the Color Settings dialog box is Advanced Controls, consisting of Desaturate Monitor Colors By and Blend RGB Colors Using Gamma (item 5 in Figure 7.6). Adobe recommends that only advanced users use this option, but we're not sure that its useful even for advanced users. Desaturating the monitor colors by a user-definable percentage could, if you have a really good imagination, give you a general idea of what colors that cannot be displayed on the monitor might look like when output. The second option, Blend RGB Colors Using Gamma, is more useful than desaturating your monitor, but only if a specific image will be created and output from Photoshop. The default gamma setting of 1.0 for this option produces slightly better color choices on the edges of sharp color transition in RGB images. You probably shouldn't bother to enable either of these options.

Wow—we've looked at *all* the options in this dialog box. You might want to recalibrate your *eyeballs* now! The only other thing to do is to click the Save button to save a color settings file if you've made changes that aren't the preset color settings files. And that, fellow Photoshoppist, brings us back to where we were before we started looking at the settings in this dialog box.

Choosing Between Assigning and Converting to Profile

The default color settings you have specified and the color management policies you've set in the Color Settings dialog box are not the only place where profiles can be assigned to images. The Image, Mode menu is another. It has two very important entries, Assign Profile and Convert to Profile, that perform very different functions. And it is *quite* important that you understand the difference.

When we look at an image we've created and saved, it is irresistible not to imagine that an *actual* image of some sort exists inside the file image; a cyber version of a photographic print. In actuality, the image is just a bunch of numbers that represent the individual flecks (pixels) of color. Photoshop reads these numbers, figures out what to do with them in terms of color, and then puts them onscreen. Our eyes and our brain then take in all the bits of color and decide what they represent, what they look like. Is it a representation of a loved one or just a splash of color?

Some of the rules Photoshop uses to figure out what to do with the numbers it finds in image files are found within Photoshop's own program code. This part of the process of making an image out of numbers is out of Photoshop users' hands. It reflects the logic, decisions, and preferences of the programmers who wrote the Photoshop code. If a CMS is used, Photoshop's actions are guided and modified by an additional set of rules: the rules laid out in ICC profiles that are used in concert with the image. You decide which profile rules are associated with an image file.

Assigned Profile

Photoshop uses ICC profiles in two ways. It looks to an *assigned profile* for instructions on how to interpret or change the numbers in the file. Assigning a profile to an image tells Photoshop how to interpret the numbers in an image file. When you use the Image, Mode, Assign Profile command to assign to an image a profile other than the default one you designated in the Color Settings dialog box, you are telling Photoshop to look at the numbers as though they had been changed to fit the requirements of some other color space. But the numbers, the data in the file, have not really changed.

An assigned profile instructs Photoshop how to interpret the numbers. The assigned profile is similar to a statement that might be associated with or assigned to this paragraph—a statement that says, "The groups of letters that form this paragraph are to be thought of as being English words that are arranged in a way that makes sense to English language readers. Additionally, if any modification (editing) takes place, interpret that in the same way you interpret the original paragraph."

But a new profile could be assigned to take the place of the first one; the new one could say to interpret the groups of letters in the paragraph according to the rules and grammar of the German language. This new interpretation might not be very pleasing or be the best way to interpret the current order and grouping of the letters, but it would let you know how much or little of the intended communication would be understood if "output" to a German language speaker. In both cases, the only things that change are the *interpretation* instructions (assigned profile) and not the actual letters, their grouping, or their sequence.

Changing an assigned profile is a game of "what if…." What would this data, these colors, look like if they were transferred to another color space? The color space could be anything that you have an ICC profile of—another monitor, a television, an Epson inkjet print, an HP inkjet print, a press using newspaper, or a Matchprint.

This is the important thing to remember: Assigned profiles tell Photoshop and other color management–aware programs how to *interpret* the data.

But sometimes you want to *change* the data, not just its interpretation. To use the English-German analogy, sometimes we want to change the letters and their order, translate the data to make it is useful in another context, so that the paragraph makes sense to a German reader. In color management terms, that means that the data within the file, the numbers themselves, must be changed. The way that is done is covered in the next section.

Note

Changing Your View   Dr. Alvy Smith, who founded PIXAR and is partially responsible for inventing the HSB color model, has a profundity that would seem to fit right in here:

Change your *view* of the data before you change the data.

In other words, when you change your view, and you've been shown plenty of examples of how to change image view, you are not disrupting original data. Nor are you making the potentially false presumption that your monitor is calibrated perfectly, and the person who did the artwork's system was off.

When you make *physical* changes to image data, you can almost never get back to the original's content. It's kinda like a turnstile in a subway station—try exiting from one of the ones that are for entrance. Manipulating the colors in an image, similarly, is a one-way trip. Choose to change your view as a first, second, and third measure for viewing a file accurately.

Using Profiles to Change the Color Mode of an Image

As stated before, profiles are sets of rules, definitions of color spaces, which programs use to interpret color data. But profiles also are used to provide some of the rules on how to actually change the data in the file to make all the colors fit within a particular color space.

The intent—Perceptual, Saturation, Absolute Colorimetric, or Relative Colorimetric—chosen for the conversion also provides rules to guide the conversion process.

To continue with the English-German language analogy, a bilingual person who acts as the translator (the CMS) would look at the letters (the numerical color data), consult the rules of the German language (the destination profile) and the German language dialect that is desired (the intent), and then change the letters (the data) so that the data would actually be transformed from something that could be translated into German—to something already written in German.

If you want to permanently change the data in an image file, use the Convert to Profile command on the Image, Mode menu. Read the previous sentence out loud once or twice; it is an important concept.

This is not the only way to change the data in an image file. Photoshop users have been changing file data for years whenever they changed an image's color mode, from RGB to CMYK, for example. You still can go the traditional route, using the Color commands at the top of the Image, Mode menu, but you will give up the ability to fine-tune the process. When you use the Convert to Profile command you choose which ICC RGB profile or which ICC CMYK profile you want to use. The traditional color mode commands use the default ICC profile settings you set in the Color Settings dialog box.

Note

Precise Conversion   Internally, Photoshop uses the Lab color model as the heart of the conversion engine when going from one Image, Mode to another. So, the conversions are still fairly good, but not as precise as choosing Convert to Profile.

Putting Theory into Practice

If your head hurts from trying to assimilate all this data, you're in good company (see Figure 7.0 again). Color management is *not* a topic to digest the first or even the second time around. But when the light bulb goes on in your head and you shout, "Eureka! I really understand how this works!" you will have moved a long way from hoping your print jobs go OK, to *knowing* what they will look like before you see the finished results. So let's put into action the concepts of color management we've discussed. We'll start by creating a custom Color Settings preset file and then practice assigning and converting profiles.

Creating a Custom Color Settings File

1. Launch Photoshop, if it is not already open.

2. Press Ctrl(⌘)+Shift+K to display the Color Settings dialog box. Make sure that the Advanced Mode and Preview options are checked. Make the changes specified in the following four steps, if the options are not already set that way.

3. Set the RGB working space to Adobe RGB (1998); the CMYK working space to U.S. Web Coated (SWOP); the Gray and Spot working spaces to Dot Gain 20%.

4. Set all three Color Management Policies to Preserve Embedded Profiles. Check both Ask When Opening options and the Ask When Pasting options.

5. In the Conversion Options section, set the Engine to Adobe (ACE). Set the Intent to Relative Colorimetric. Check both the Use Black Point Compensation and the Use Dither options.

6. Make certain that the options in the Advanced Options section are not checked.

7. Click the Save button. In the Save dialog box that appears, use the Save In drop-down and other controls to navigate your way to the folder in which the other color setting files are saved, if you are not already there. Then type *IP7* in the File name field, and click Save.

8. In the Color Settings Comment dialog box that appears, type something that describes these settings, such as **Set used for exercise in Inside Adobe Photoshop 7 book, that definitive guide**—Um, you get the picture. Click OK.

   IP7 now appears as the selected setting in the Settings drop-down list.

9. Click OK to put these settings into use.

You now can choose the IP7 set of custom settings just as you would the ones that Adobe provided.

Now that you have the IP7 defaults set, you will be sure to get the same results as we do in the exercises that follow. As promised, the next set of steps gives you hands-on experience with assigned profiles.

Color Management Policies in Action

1. Choose File, Open, and open Vision.tif from the Examples/Chap07 folder on the Companion CD. This file has no profile attached, so a warning box should appear.

2. In the Missing Profile dialog box that appears (see Figure 7.7) choose the Assign Working RGB: Adobe RGB (1998) option. Click OK. Vision.tif opens.

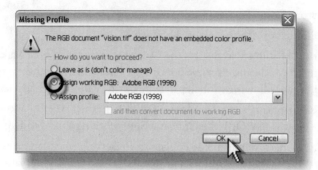

Figure 7.7   The Missing Profile dialog box appears when you open files to which a color management profile is not attached. Use its options to assign a profile.

You could choose any working space by selecting one from the drop-down, but because you don't know which working space this file was created in, and you haven't decided on a use for this file, the best choice is to assign Adobe RGB (1998). If you knew this file would be used for web use only, choosing sRGB also would be okay. Remember—at this point you are only deciding how Photoshop should interpret and show the file to you; you have not changed any of the numerical data in the file.

If you had chosen the third option, Assign Profile, and picked from the pop-up list the same profile as the default working profile, and checked the "and then convert the document to working RGB" option you would have done two things at once. You would have set the interpretation of the data to Adobe RGB (1998) and changed the data (the word *convert* is the clue) to data that fits in Adobe RGB (1998) space. If you chose to assign some other profile, you would have made your view of the file that of the assigned profile; but with the option checked, the data would have been converted to the working space profile Adobe RGB (1998). It is usually not a good idea to create a mismatch when you open a file; doing so distorts your view and can lead to unexpected color shifts when the assigned profile is eventually matched to the data profile.

3. Press Shift+Ctrl(⌘)+S to open the Save As dialog box. Note that toward the bottom of the dialog box, in the section labeled Color, the option ICC Profile: Adobe RGB (1998) is checked (see Figure 7.8).

Figure 7.8   The Color section of the Save As dialog box has options for embedding profiles in images.

If you leave this option checked, the profile you assigned and noted here will be embedded in the file. This will become the profile that always governs your view of the file until you either assign a new profile or convert to another profile. If you remove the check from the profile, the file will not be color managed. Until you close the file, however, your view of the file will be from the perspective of the Adobe RGB (1998) profile.

4.   Find a place on your hard disk to save the file, and then click Save. In the TIFF Options dialog box, leave LZW Compression unchecked, and choose the Byte order of your choice. Do not check the Image Pyramid box, and then click OK. Leave the image open.

Note

Image Pyramids   An Image Pyramid is an extra added attraction to Adobe's extension of the TIFF file format's capabilities, similar to saved layers. Image Pyramid is a multi-resolution file format that can be used in programs such as InDesign. Interestingly, Image Pyramid is not supported by Photoshop itself. So choose this, and you just locked the door without your keys!

To recap, you've opened an image that did not have a color management profile attached to it and assigned a working profile to the file. You then embedded the profile in the file by saving the file to disk with the profile option checked. But how do you change the assigned profile for a file that already *has* a profile? In the next section, you'll seek out the rather obviously named Assign Profile command.

Changing the Assigned Profile

1. With Vision.tif open in Photoshop's work space, choose Image, Mode from the menu. Note that at the top of the Image menu, RGB is checked. From this section of the menu, you could change the file to an entirely different color mode, like Grayscale or CMYK, but you can't change to a different RGB color space.

2. Choose Assign Profile from the Image, Mode menu. In the Assign Profile dialog box that appears (see Figure 7.9), be sure the Preview option is checked. As you can see, this dialog box offers three choices: Don't Color Manage This Document, Working RGB: Adobe RGB (1998), and a Profile drop-down list that contains the standard RGB working spaces as well as every other RGB profile that has been made available to the CMS.

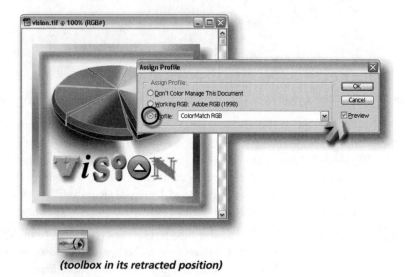

(toolbox in its retracted position)

Figure 7.9   With the Preview option checked, you can see how different assigned profiles would look.

3. Now choose US Web Coated (SWOP) v2 from the Profile drop-down list. Notice that the colors in Vision.tif become duller—you've gone from a wide color gamut to a fairly narrow one, and the nuances of the Vision picture are getting discarded. This is what the file would look like in the editing window if you were to click OK now. But remember, you are changing only the interpretation, your *view* of the data, and not the data itself. (But this is what the data would look like if you *did* convert it.) Choose other profiles to see how they affect the view of Vision.tif. Then click Cancel to close the dialog box without changing the Assigned profile. Leave Vision.tif open in the work space.

Okay, let's say a client calls to say they've decided they really want to use the Vision.tif file on the web, but that they have decided not to use it for their print campaign. So you figure that now's the time to get this image prepped, and one of the first steps toward doing that is to move the file to the preferred color space of the web, sRGB IEC61966-2.1. To move the file to that color space, you need to do more than simply change the assigned profile; you need to change the data in the file to ensure that all the colors in the image are within the smaller color space the web uses. To change the data, you must convert the profile, and you'll see how to do that in the next set of steps.

Converting a Profile Means Changing the Data

1. Press Shift+Ctrl(⌘)+S to open the Save As dialog box. Choose the As a Copy option, and then click Save. Because converting profiles involves changing the data, this is the right time to make a backup copy of Vision.tif. You or the client may change your mind at some point about the way you want to use this file.

2. With Vision.tif open in Photoshop's workspace, choose Image, Mode, Convert to Profile from the menu. The Convert to Profile dialog box opens (see Figure 7.10). Position the dialog box so that you can still see most, if not all, of Vision.tif, and make sure the Preview option is checked.

The Convert to Profile dialog box is divided into three sections. The first lists the profile of the Source Space. This corresponds to the working color space profile. The middle section, Destination Space, is where you choose a profile that defines which color space and color mode the CMS will change the data to fit inside. The last section, Conversion Options, should look familiar; it involves options, such as Intent and color management engines, that you learned about earlier in the chapter.

3. Click the arrow next to the Profile drop-down list. Notice that in addition to the standard RGB color spaces you saw in the Assign Profile dialog box, this list includes profiles not only for RGB but also for other color modes.

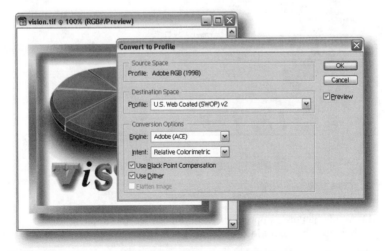

Figure 7.10   Use the Convert to Profile dialog box to convert from one color profile to another in the same color mode or in an entirely different color mode. This is the preferred way to change from RGB to CMYK.

4. Choose sRGB IEC61966-2.1 from the Profile drop-down list. Notice that the image got brighter, not duller as it did in the previous exercise, because the dialog box opens with a CMYK profile chosen, instead of the current working profile. And CMYK is always duller than RGB, even sRGB.

5. While watching to see how the image changes or doesn't change, try each of the four rendering intents. You'll notice that for this image, there is little if any change in the image preview when you change the rendering intent. For some images there would be noticeable changes.

   Based on the earlier discussion of Intents, Relative Colorimetric is probably the best choice. This is not a photograph; and with the white-to-gray squares and the full spectrum gradient at the bottom, maintaining the white point, and then using absolute values where possible, this will most likely produce the best conversion of values.

6. Choose Relative Colorimetric from the Intent drop-down list. To see what will happen if you choose Relative Colorimetric, you can look at the preview if you have that option selected (see Figure 7.11). Leave the Engine option set at Adobe (ACE), leave Use Dither checked, and uncheck Use Black Point Compensation. As mentioned earlier in the section, "The Color Settings Dialog Box, or Laying Down the Rules," the rule of thumb is to turn off Black Point Compensation when you're converting from one RGB profile to another.

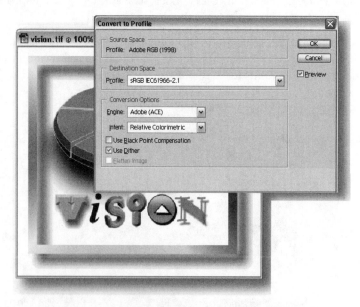

Figure 7.11   With the Preview option checked, you can see how different Intent choices change the look of the image.

7. Click OK. Press Alt+Ctrl (Macintosh: Opt+⌘)+Z three times, pausing between clicks to see what effect the Convert to Profile had on the image colors. The shift in

color is particularly noticeable in the greens. This is not surprising because Adobe RGB (1998) has a lot more green in its color space than does sRGB IEC61966-2.1. By the third Step Backward, the image should be back in Adobe RGB (1998) mode; leave it there and leave the image open in Photoshop's work space.

Tip

Look in File, Save As for the Current ICC Profile   If you ever get confused as to which profile is currently the assigned profile, choose File, Save As, and look at the Color section of the dialog box. The profile listed next to ICC Profile is the current assigned profile. You then can cancel out of the save by pressing Esc or clicking Cancel.

Seeing how the image changes depending on which profile you assign or convert might have given you the idea that whenever you want to see how a particular image will look when it's output to the web or to print you could or should change the image profile. *Don't!* There is a much easier, safer, and more elegant way to do it. It's called *soft-proofing* an image. Read on, and you'll find that Adobe has tucked this time-, money-, and fingernail-saving feature in the View menu.

Soft-Proofing, or Seeing Onscreen What an Image Will Look Like When It's Printed

Because Adobe's soft-proofing feature is driven by ICC profiles, it is a very good idea to collect ICC profiles for every device you use in your work and for every output device your work will be sent to. Getting your local commercial printers to give you an ICC profile for their press, let alone for their press using the exact paper and ink you want to use, is next to impossible. What *is* possible is to get ICC profiles for traditional hard-proofing materials, such as Matchprints. Most printers will set up their presses to produce results that match the color of an agreed upon hard-proof. What also is possible is to obtain the ICC profiles of the wonderful new inkjet printers that many folks are using for short-run printing.

Additionally, you already may have noticed that Adobe and your operating system have gifted you with generic ICC profiles for many proofing devices and conditions, as well as default ICC profiles for standard press conditions. Generic ICC profiles are never as precise as custom-made ICC profiles, which is why we showed you how to create a custom ICC profile for your monitor instead of using the default one. But using generic profiles with a CMS is better than not using any CMS at all. So hop on the WWW, go to the manufacturers of the equipment you and your customers use, and download the profiles for the devices. It is worth your while to collect ICC profiles for some of the more popular inkjet printers made by Epson, HP, and others. If you don't own one of these printers now, you really should put it on your wish list. Install the profiles, and then move on to the next example.

> **Note**
>
> **Printer Profiles and Paper Color**   Most ICC printer profiles are based on a specific paper color, generally a neutral bright white.

Soft-Proofing and Color-Correcting an Image

1. Vision.tif, the file we've been using, should still be open in Photoshop's workspace. In the last example, we converted the profile associated with the image from Adobe RGB (1998) to sRGB IEC61966-2.1, and then used the Undo command to cancel the conversion of the data and the assignment of a new working profile.

2. Choose View, New View. A new window opens; it contains an additional view of the original image, not a new copy of the image. Arrange the two image windows so you can see each image.

3. Choose View, Proof Setup, Custom. In the Profile drop-down list, choose the profile for the inkjet printer you have installed. In the Intent drop-down list, leave the entry as Perceptual, check Use Black Point Compensation, and check Simulate: Paper White, as shown in Figure 7.12. Click OK.

   If you don't have any inkjet or other desktop color printer profiles installed, use the Euroscale Coated profile.

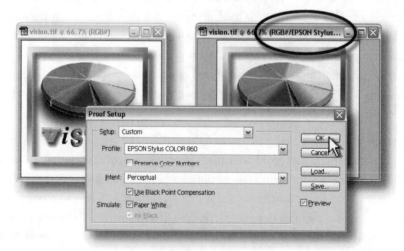

Figure 7.12   In the Proof Setup dialog box, choose the output device to which you want to print, and Photoshop will display the document more or less as it will print.

4. Notice that the title bar of the inactive window remains the same but that the active image title bar now reads RGB/Epson Stylus Color 860 (your title bar will read whatever you've loaded as a profile). The Epson Stylus Color 860 part corresponds to the Epson printer picked in Step 3 and is your soft-proof view. Notice that the colors in the RGB/ Epson Stylus Color 860 window are duller than in the original RGB window. The data hasn't changed; only your view has. Think of it as looking at the RGB/ Epson Stylus Color 860 image with Epson glasses on.

Chances are 100% that the image in the soft-proof window is not everything you hoped it would be. The solution? Edit the image. Because these two windows are different views of the same image, any edits you make will be reflected in both windows. It doesn't matter which window is the active window when you make the edits. To improve this image for printing to the inkjet printer, move on to the next step.

5. Click the Create new fill or adjustment layer icon at the bottom of the Layers palette (fourth icon from the left). Choose Color Balance from the menu (Ctrl(⌘)+B). The Color Balance dialog box appears. Drag it off to one side so that you can see the images. Make sure that the Preview option is checked.

The neutral background and the white-to-black boxes across the top of the image in the soft-proof window show an unwanted color cast. Because you've most likely chosen a different printer to soft-proof to than we have, you may not have a color cast, or it may be different from ours. Make your adjustments to suit your image. For the purposes of this example, we'll report what works according to our setup and what looks good to us.

Although you have set up and are using the CMS in Photoshop, you should not abandon the use of the Info palette for color feedback (correcting by the numbers). Your experience with your intended target device, combined with the Photoshop CMS, will yield better results than simply using either CMS or experience/Info palette alone.

6. Keep your eyes on the soft-proof window—that is the window you want to look good. The problem appears to be mostly in the midtones. Preserve Luminosity should be checked. Drag the Cyan slider toward Red (right) to a value of +7; drag the Magenta slider toward Green (right) to a value of +14; drag the Yellow slider toward Yellow (left) to a value of −3, as shown in Figure 7.13. Click OK.

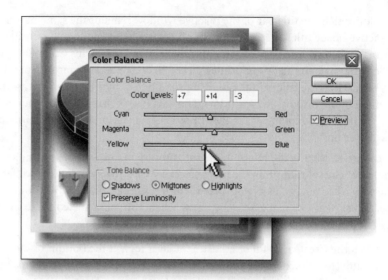

Figure 7.13   Use a Color Balance adjustment layer to remove an unwanted color cast that will develop when the image is printed to the inkjet.

Now the soft-proof window doesn't have a color cast, but the original window does. That is okay. An image often looks terrible on-screen but prints beautifully. That happens because the monitor and the printer have different color spaces. If you want good printed output, don't get hung up on how it looks on-screen in the working space. Pay attention to the soft-proof view.

7. Click the Create new fill or adjustment layer icon on the Layers palette. Choose Levels Layer on the menu. The image lacks punch because it doesn't really have a good white or black point. Drag the White point slider to around 226. Drag the Black point slider to around 13, and drag the Midpoint slider left to about 1.14, as shown in Figure 7.14. Click OK.

8. Take a good look at the preview window. If you like what you see, flatten the image by choosing Flatten Image from the Layers palette menu.

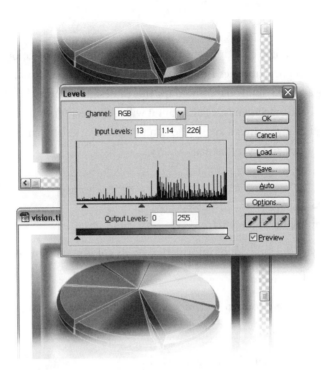

Figure 7.14   Use a Levels adjustment layer to create a better tonal range.

9. Choose File, Save As. In the File name field, enter *Vision for Inkjet.* Notice that the image still has the original profile listed in the Color section, and not the inkjet profile you proofed to. That is because the proof view was a *view* and not a *conversion* of the data to a new color space. You did change data when you edited, but it was changed in the context of the working space, not the proofing space of the inkjet. Click Save.

When it comes time to print the image to the inkjet printer and get the results you saw in the proof, you will want to change the data. You can do that by using the Convert to Profile command you experimented with in a previous example, or you can choose to do it as part of the print process.

Bear in mind that although it takes fewer steps to specify the conversion from the print dialog boxes, you don't get a chance to preview the different Intent options. Consequently, we recommend that you use the Convert to Profile command to change the data in the image and assign the same profile you used for soft-proofing.

Summary

That's it! If you've followed along, you've just joined the ranks of color management specialists. And you probably need to focus on postcards of Hawaii to rest your eyes for a week or so. We realize that you may hold the title of designer a little closer to your heart than that of color management specialist, but it will look great on your résumé. That line will signal to all that you are an artist who can produce work that can be counted on to look fabulous in any and every media.

Resources

http://www.apple.com/colorsync/

Apple's ColorSync site has a lot of information on its color management engine.

http://www.pixelboyz.com

Bruce Fraser's site, where you can find out more about the BruceRGB color working space.

http://www.cie.co.at/cie/

Commission Internationale de L'Eclairage (CIE)

http://www.linocolor.com

Heidelberg CPS GmbH has some good beginner information on color management. They also have information on very expensive software to create ICC profiles.

http://www.inkjetmall.com/store/

Inkjetmall.com, a division of the famous Cone Editions Press, is a great place to buy ICC profiles for Epson printers. These profiles not only profile the printer but also specific paper and ink combinations. The site even offers a few free profiles.

http://www.color.org

International Color Consortium(ICC)

http://search.microsoft.com/

Microsoft has lots of information available on color management, but it is not neatly organized in one place. Your best bet is to do a search on its site, using the keywords "color management" or "ICC profiles."

http://www.praxisoft.com

Good information on color management is available on the Praxisoft site. They also sell a reasonably priced (under $100) program called WiziWYG that can create good custom ICC profiles for your scanner and for printers.

http://www.xrite.com/

X-Rite, Inc., makes all kinds of hardware tools for measuring color and calibrating devices. Most of their solutions are rather high-end, very precise, and geared in price toward large, big-budget operations.

Chapter 8

Input, Output, and Resolution

Before you can use Photoshop to enhance

or combine images, you first must get the

images into the computer. The most obvi-

ous way to do this is to open an existing

file. Another option is to purchase artwork

or photographs from a stock agency, another artist, or a photographer. But what if the source materials you want to work with are right under your nose?

You may be able to use the old photos you have lying around, or perhaps you have the perfect idea for an image that involves using an everyday object you already have in your possession. There's one problem, however; how do you convert those images in your photo album or objects in your supply closet into digital files that you can use in Photoshop?

With the advent of inexpensive scanners, relatively inexpensive digital cameras, and the Internet, you now have the ability to digitize your existing treasured photographs and get access to hundreds, if not thousands, of digital pictures. This chapter is all about getting and preparing those items and objects for use in Photoshop. The next section introduces you to a few fundamental concepts you need to understand before you start working with the different aspects of image editing.

Bringing Images into Your Computer

Although it would be nice to be able to stick your favorite photograph into a slot on your computer and have it appear on the computer screen, the process isn't that simple. You must first convert a photograph to a digital file before it can be opened in Photoshop. Some images, like photographs taken using digital cameras, are already in a file format that can be opened by Photoshop; photographs taken with traditional film cameras, however must be converted into graphic files using a scanner. There are several options available to get images into your computer—or more importantly, Photoshop:

- If you have a creative side, you could use Photoshop or other tools to create your own images—Painter, Poser, and Bryce come to mind. The disadvantage to this option is that it may require a great deal of time and skill. The advantages might be that this form of digital imagery could be the exact look you're after— a look that could range from illustrated to photorealistic.

- You can use a digital camera to acquire an image. Digital-camera technology has made great progress, and although early cameras produced rather poor-quality images, today's cameras can produce excellent pictures.

- You can use a common flatbed scanner to digitize artwork, photographs, and yes, some of those small objects you have lying around the house.

- You can use a transparency scanner to digitize a slide or negative of a photograph. Depending on the scanner you're using, this method for making a digital file of a photograph can give you better quality than a flatbed scanner.

- You can send your images on a roll to many, many digital imaging services (Wal-Mart offers the service; it's nearly *ubiquitous*) and have your images scanned on expensive machines and written to PhotoCD. The disadvantage of this technology (and yes, we *have* touted the PhotoCD in past versions of this book) is that PhotoCDs are expensive when compared to buying a decent $700 to $900 camera and never paying for the service again. Also, PhotoCD technicians are not responsible for cleaning the film before scanning, and the wait time is mega-cyber-years when compared to putting an image into your computer yourself.

Getting Images from the Creative Side

If creating your own artwork from scratch isn't something you feel entirely confident about, you can purchase illustrations and stock photography from third-party companies, many of which can easily be found on the Internet. The cost can vary. Typically you might find a fee-per-image basis, or you might get the option of purchasing a CD containing a small collection of similar images. Other sites offer access to their entire collection for an annual subscription fee. One of my personal favorite sites that offers an extremely interesting range of work, not to mention high-quality images, is www. creatas.com.

Getting Pictures from Digital Cameras

In the span of a few short years, digital cameras have changed the way we approach photography. Early digital cameras were expensive and produced relatively poor-quality photographs. Today's entry-level digital cameras produce excellent results, cost much less, and give you the ability to take thousands of photos at little or no cost. The principal advantage of digital cameras over their film counterparts is that although the initial investment in the camera is much greater, the images captured by digital cameras can be instantly reviewed and used. This means that as soon as you take the pictures, they are ready in digital format—in other words, no scanning. You also have no film to buy or develop.

> **Note**
>
> **Digital Camera Advantages**   One of the greatest advantages to taking pictures with a digital camera is the immediate feedback. If you did something wrong—maybe you didn't center the subject matter or the lighting was wrong—you can get immediate feedback on these issues. But even *more* important, you can try again to perfect the image you were trying to capture—immediately, right at that moment—well, you get the point.

Connecting a Digital Camera to Your Computer

Whichever type of digital camera you use, after you take the picture, you need a way to get the pictures off the camera's media and into the computer. To do this, you need a physical connection between the camera and the computer. This can be done several ways (listed here from slowest to fastest):

- **Serial connections.** The original digital cameras used only serial connections. This type of connection was complicated to set up and very, very slow. If your camera's only connection is a serial connection, you should definitely consider the purchase of a digital camera media reader—called a *card reader*—which reads the images off the camera's memory card and enables you to copy them to your computer.

- **Dedicated card readers.** Card readers come in different sizes, shapes, and interfaces. For desktop computers, the most popular dedicated readers are those with a USB (Universal Serial Bus) interface. Dedicated USB readers move pictures from the media to the computer at high speed and are *hot swappable* (which means they can be plugged into the computer or removed without restarting the computer), which is not the case with all interfaces. PC Card (PCMCIA) readers are also quite popular with both Mac and PC laptops due to their small size and low cost. Regardless of the type of reader that is used, when it is connected to the computer, the camera's media appears on the computer desktop as a disk drive.

- **USB connections to the camera.** Most of the newer digital cameras connect directly to the computer with a USB cable. This is the best way to get pictures from a digital camera to a computer. Install the camera's control software that comes with the camera and, similar to a card reader, the camera's control software will launch when the camera is connected to a computer. You also have the option of importing the images into Photoshop the way you would import a scanned image, but I don't recommend this because using the camera's import and cataloging software is generally the best way to go. For best results, if you want to go the Photoshop route, remember to connect your camera to the computer before launching Photoshop.

Using Digital Camera Software

Generally, digital cameras come with either a Windows Imaging Acquisition (WIA) interface or TWAIN interface. By the way, TWAIN has evolved from using SCSI to the new popular Firewire, a USB, and USB 2 technology. The WIA is the primary software you need to install. It's the bridge to help your camera communicate with your computer and allow you to transfer images to the computer quickly.

After the camera's control software is installed, Photoshop only needs your camera plugged into the computer in order to recognize it. You can access your camera's software from within Photoshop by following these steps:

Plugging into Photoshop

1. Make sure that the camera is attached to the computer and is turned on.
2. Launch Photoshop.
3. Go to the File menu and choose Import, WIA Support…, as shown in Figure 8.1.

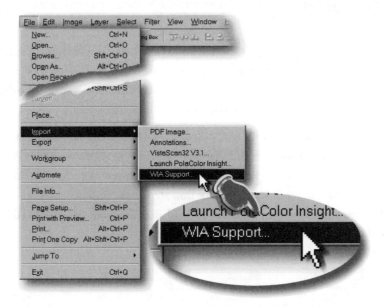

Figure 8.1   Clicking the WIA Support option launches the interface for the digital camera.

4. The software interface launches and allows you to choose which images to load into Photoshop. As you can see in Figure 8.2, you can choose to select one, a few, or all images. The option to delete the images from the camera also is available on this interface.

Figure 8.2   Select the images you want, and (with this particular camera and software) click the Get Pictures button to load the images into Photoshop.

Don't forget to delete the images off the memory card after you've transferred them to the computer. You'll want to free up the space on the memory card for your next photo shoot. You often can do this directly by using the controls on the camera or with the software that came with the camera. For either method, it's usually a simple process.

When I plug my camera into the computer, the WIA software automatically launches whether I'm using Photoshop or not. If I were to use the WIA interface outside Photoshop, it provides a series of screens to walk me through the process of downloading images from the camera. As you can see in Figure 8.3, the final step on the Scanner and Camera Wizard offers the option to delete the images on the card after the images download (this option is checked in the figure).

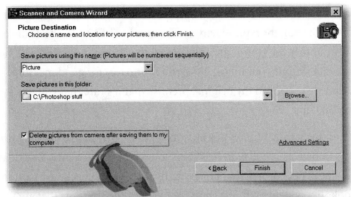

Figure 8.3   With many digital-camera setups, you can download all the images into the specified folder and then delete the images from the card in a single step.

Scanning Pictures

Scanners, like digital cameras, have enjoyed a dramatic price drop over the past few years, and as a result, they have become a normal part of many home and small office systems. The scanner is a marvelous tool that can turn almost any photograph, printed image, or even 3D object into a graphic image file that can be brought into Photoshop for enhancement, correction, or restoration. You probably need a scanner—even if you own a digital camera—to handle those old photos and negatives you need to scan and save as digital images for their preservation.

Flatbed Scanners

When buying a scanner, you always see the advertised specs boasting some high scanning-resolution capability. Although some of these specs might be important to the quality of the image the scanner is capable of producing, you will rarely find the need to scan at the highest setting when using a flatbed scanner. I personally almost never need to scan above 300 dpi. How do you know what you need? Simple. Consider what you plan to do with the image.

For example, if you just want a quick copy of an image to send in an email message to your aunt, you want to scan at a low resolution (around 72 dpi) to keep the file small. If you are scanning an image that will be sent to a professional printer or you want to edit the image after you scan it, scan at the higher resolution of 300 dpi.

When you are dealing with a professional service, ask how many lines per inch (lpi) they need to output. They might typically give you a number of 133. A good rule of thumb is to double this number for your scanning (input) dpi. In this case, 266 will yield a sufficient resolution to output your image. So if you round up (for good measure) to 300 dpi, you can see that we're back to my original premise that it's rare that you will need to scan images above 300 dpi.

By the way, it is this setting of lines per inch (or line screens) in professional printing that causes what is known as *moiré pattern*. When you scan a printed image, such as a picture from a magazine article or newspaper, it usually develops a checkered pattern or something that looks like a plaid on it. When the patterns of the tiny dots that are used to print the picture (called *screens*) are scanned, it develops its own pattern. You can reduce (not eliminate) these patterns in two different ways:

- Your scanning software may have the ability to minimize the moiré effect with the Descreen option. Some scanning software has a preset for this. For example, your software might have a setting for *newspaper and magazines,* which means the descreening is accomplished automatically for those items.

- The second possible way around this pattern is accomplished by using Photoshop filters. Go to the Filter menu and choose Noise, Despeckle.

Note

A Word on Descreening   Be aware that regardless of how an image is descreened, the result is a softer picture—meaning it loses some of its sharpness. This may be a small price to pay for the reduction of those annoying moiré patterns. Using the Unsharp Mask filter can help alleviate this problem.

Here are some scanning tips and tricks to help you get the most out of your scanning ventures.

Avoid Scanning Nightmares by Ordering the Right Prints

Now promise not to make fun of me if I confess something to you. Many years ago (before I owned my first computer and scanner), I used to take my film into one of those one-hour places and hand it over to the clerk. Every time the clerk would ask, "Would you like those in Matte-Finish or Glossy?" Personally, I didn't think twice about my answer. For some unknown reason, I liked the Matte-Finish better.

Well, I've since grown to hate that choice of my past. It makes for a flatbed-scanning nightmare. That bumpy surface shows up in your scans as noise and grain. If you open the ScanFlatbed.tif image from the Examples/Chap08 folder on the Companion CD, you will see an example of this problem first-hand.

Although all scanned images contain *some* noise and grain, you can help minimize this problem by choosing a smoother surface for your prints.

Note

Faux Matte Finish   Not all, but many photo-finishers don't even create honest Matte-Finish images. It's easier for them to process all the day's images as glossy and then hit your order of pictures with dulling spray. Now, guess what that does to the graphical information in your pictures? Okay, I'll answer: It *hides* it!

Keeping Your Scanning Surface Clean

I know this sounds really simple, but most users don't do it. Keep a small bottle of glass cleaner and a lint-free paper wipe right by the scanner; otherwise, you may not remember to clean the glass.

Take reasonable care of your scanner, and protect the glass and scanner with an acetate sheet when you're scanning something messy, dusty, or potentially harmful to the glass. If you always remember to use the acetate, your scanner will thank you and you'll be able to look forward to many years of creating fun and innovative designs using direct-scanned images.

Tip

Foggy Glass   When you are checking your glass for cleanliness, you may notice a faint fogging on the bottom side of the copy glass. This occurs sometimes and as a rule, has little to no effect on the scanned image. Do not attempt to remove the glass unless the manufacturer has provided instructions on how to do so safely.

Making the Scan

The following sections apply to most scanners and offer thoughts and recommendations that are the result of many years of scanning everything from photographs to cookies (no kidding). They are grouped into two general categories: scan preparation and scanner operation.

You can do a few simple things to ensure that you get the best possible scan each time. First, you should clean the scanner glass, as mentioned previously. Next, align the picture on the scanner glass. Photoshop has an excellent Image, Rotate Canvas command that can be used to correct any misalignment of an image on the scanner, but for best results, spend the extra time making sure that the image is correctly aligned from the start.

> **Note**
>
> **Why Not Rotate?**   Whenever you rotate an image in Photoshop, the image suffers from mild deterioration, which reduces the overall sharpness of the image. The exception to this rule is when images are rotated in increments of 90°; those rotations do not produce any loss of sharpness. Again, you can see why aligning the image properly in the scanner is the best way to go.

After the glass is clean and the image is aligned, you're ready to scan. The actual mechanics of making the scan vary depending on your scanner and software. Throughout the rest of this chapter, we've focused on specific scanning situations to show you the best ways to get the highest-quality possible images from your scans.

> **Note**
>
> **Scanning and Copyrights**   A word to the wise: Just because you *can* scan it, doesn't mean you *should* scan it. Sounds sort of Zen, doesn't it? I am sure most of you are aware that nearly everything in print is copyrighted in one form or another. Most of these are obvious. For example, you wouldn't think of scanning a photograph from an issue of National Geographic and selling it as wallpaper for your desktop. (You wouldn't, right?) Although that would be an obvious copyright infringement, others are more subtle. As strange as it sounds, it is not legal to make copies of any photograph that was made by a professional photographer or studio. Examples of this are school photos and wedding pictures taken by the pro—not the cheesy ones taken with the disposable camera during the reception. It is a fact of law that even though you may have paid this person or organization to take the picture of you or your loved ones and paid for the materials, the image still belongs to them and it is a violation of U.S. Copyright law to duplicate them. So be careful what you scan.

Transparency Scanners

The film scanner, which once was popular only with professionals, is now finding its way to a larger consumer base. One of the reasons for its growing popularity is the fact that, like most items, film scanners have come down in price over the years. The film scanner also produces excellent results compared to its flatbed counterpart. Figure 8.4 compares an image scanned with a flatbed scanner (shown on the left) with the same image scanned with a film scanner (shown in the right). If you go to the Examples/Chap08 folder on the Companion CD and open the ScanFlatbed.tif and the ScanNegative.tif, you can view these two images up close. Besides the obvious clarity in the ScanNegative.tif, you can see more detail and richness in color that is lacking in the flatbed version.

Figure 8.4   The image on the left was scanned using a flatbed scanner from a print that had a matte finish. This caused additional problems with the scan because it produced an excessive amount of noise or grain in the image. The image on the right was scanned from the negative. The result is a clearer, more detailed, and brighter image.

Here are some tips to keep in mind that will help you get the best possible scans from your film scanner:

- **Handle with care.** Make sure that your negatives are dust, hair, and fingerprint free—this is extremely important. If there is any foreign substance on either side of the negative, the scanner will see it and add it to your image. And although some film scanners have a built-in technology to account and adjust for dust, dirt, and scratches, you want to make sure you keep possible distortions to a minimum. Cleanliness goes a long way in acquiring a great image when you are using a film scanner.

- **Invest in some film-handling equipment.** For best results, use a pair of cloth film-handling gloves before you even think about taking your negatives out of their sleeves. Also, resist the urge to blow the dust off a negative. Do you really want that stubborn shred of celery projected at your film? Instead, dust both sides of the film with a compressed-gas duster such as Dust-Off by Falcon. The gloves and the compressed gas can be found in most photo stores and online.

- **Keep the negatives safe when you are finished with them.** Put the negatives back in their original carriers or plastic sleeves. Negatives scratch easily, so handle with care.

- **Film grain.** Although someone who works with film on a regular basis might intuitively know this one (and think to themselves, "Yeah—*duh!*"), it might not be as obvious to the rest of us. The film speed of your negatives affects the clarity of the scan. A high ASA (now called *ISO*) film will produce an extremely grainy scan.

Working with Kodak PhotoCDs

One of the easiest ways to get a digitized version of an image these days is to take your film or negatives to a photo-finisher and ask that the media be transferred to a Kodak PhotoCD. The processing lab then uses Eastman Kodak's proprietary PhotoCD (PCD) writer to scan your negatives and write the images to a CD-ROM that can be read by your computer's CD-ROM drive. This means that with only a camera, a CD-ROM drive, and a willingness to write a check for PhotoCD processing, you can get good-quality digital image files of your photographs. In 2002, you'll be hard pressed to find a photo-finisher who *doesn't* offer PhotoCD writing as a service.

Note

PCD Writers   PCD writers are a combination film scanner and file writer. After each negative is scanned, the PCD writer (a very expensive piece of hardware) writes a single PhotoCD file for that image. The PhotoCD file format is a proprietary compressed format that Photoshop and many other graphic applications can read.

A photo-finisher might or might not actually have a PCD writer on its premises. As mentioned earlier, the PCD hardware is extremely expensive, so don't expect a "mom and pop" photo-finisher or even a big retailer, such as Target or Wal-Mart to have this machine at its store. Usually, when a local photo-finisher offers PhotoCD service, the film you give them is shipped to a large custom-processing plant that has a PCD writer. Because the processing probably won't be done locally, you might have to wait at least two days to get your finished PhotoCD back from your local photo-finisher.

On your end, ordering a PhotoCD is simple. You bring either undeveloped film or negatives to the photo-finisher (slides will cost more because of the extra time required to handle each slide) and tell the clerk that you want a Kodak PhotoCD made of the images. You have the option to have your images written to the PhotoCD in a specific sequence, either on a frame-by-frame basis or roll by roll. You will be charged an additional fee for PhotoCD developing.

A single PhotoCD can contain about 120 images. It's a good idea to bring several rolls of film or several strips of negatives to the photo-finisher because doing this conserves space on the PhotoCD. You also can have images added to a partially filled PhotoCD, but this decreases the overall space on the PhotoCD.

When you get the PhotoCD from the photo-finisher, all you need to do is plop the CD into your CD-ROM drive and launch Photoshop. There is nothing special about a PhotoCD; physically, it is the same as any other CD you might load. PhotoCD image files can be copied from the PhotoCD and stored on hard disk, stored on removable media like Zip or Jaz cartridges, or even written to another CD-ROM. What makes a PhotoCD special is the file format in which the images are stored, and the compression format, which is part of the file format.

Understanding the Kodak PhotoCD Format

Each image on a Kodak PhotoCD is stored in a single file called an *image pac*. The following five sizes (resolutions) of the image can be opened from a single image pac:

- 72KB (128 by 192 pixels)
- 288KB (256 by 384 pixels)
- 1.13MB (512 by 768 pixels)
- 4.5MB (1024 by 1536 pixels)
- 18MB (2048 by 3072 pixels)

The image pac file itself actually contains the file at 4.5MB only. An application's PhotoCD import filter uses a proprietary method of interpolation (resizing), along with special hinting information found in the image pac, to produce the other sizes from the 4.5MB file. *Interpolation*, or resampling, is the method of resizing images by adding pixels to make an image larger or subtracting pixels to make it smaller.

Because the five different sizes of the image are not actually stored in a PCD file, a combination of compression/decompression and interpolation must take place when you choose to open the image in Photoshop at the 72KB, 2.88KB, 1.13MB, or 18MB size. I recommend that you choose to work with the 4.5MB size image whenever it is practical because it will have the sharpest focus. The reason? Even the best interpolation reduces the focus of an image as pixels are added or removed to create a new image size.

The PCD writer prints an index print to go along with every PhotoCD. The *index print* (tiny, numbered thumbnails of all the images stored on the PhotoCD) is something you *don't* want to lose because, from the outside, every PhotoCD looks identical. The numbers next to the thumbnails on the index print correspond to each image file on the PhotoCD—the first image on a PhotoCD is Img0001.pcd, the second is Img0002.pcd, and so on. Because the thumbnails are so tiny (and as added insurance in case you lose the index print), you might want to take advantage of Photoshop's Contact Sheet feature to create your own, more legible digital contact sheet. You can find the Contact Sheet feature by opening the File menu and choosing Automate, Contact Sheet II.

Note

Keep Your Index Print(s)   When you are sending in the CD for more transfers, hang on to your previous index prints. The lab doesn't need the prints, and they are trashed after the new index print is printed to update the contents of the CD. This gives you a backup of the CD contents before the latest transfer.

So, the inevitable question looms, "How does this compare to other image acquisition methods?" Today, I must say that a digital camera produces the best images you can work with in Photoshop, and PhotoCDs prove to be approximately the same or a little less quality than image-negative scanner images. Why? Because you treat your own images with kid gloves, while a PhotoCD plant handles your images like a business.

Output Essentials

What's written here is a lecture cleverly disguised as a reference guide, which is cleverly disguised as a chapter section. Specifically, it is a section on output—we tend to use the term *output* these days because hard copy isn't necessarily rendered to paper. You can print to film, to glossy paper, to t-shirt—there are oodles of ways you can get an image off your monitor and onto something in the physical world.

Throughout this section, I'm going to hand you tools in the guise of math formulas and nuggets of information that will do the following things:

- Give you the confidence that your printing skills are top-notch.
- Give you the straight story on many of the parameters surrounding the action of output, not the myths floating around that cause you headaches and make your work look crummy.

Let's begin with a simple term that you will hear more and more often as you gain experience with both personal and commercial printing. The word is *interpolation*.

Interpolation Means "Interpretation"

Interpolation is a neat-sounding word, isn't it? Many of us have a vague notion (within context) of what interpolation means, but you need to understand *precisely* what it means when you're using it on your work.

Interpolation in computer graphics is an application's *interpretation* of what something should look like, especially when it does not have sufficient data to carry out your request. Interpolation is always an *averaging* process of some kind. For example, suppose that you have a color image that is 4 pixels wide and 4 pixels high. You want the image to be twice the size: 8 pixels by 8 pixels.

There isn't a program on earth that will create the new image using sensitivity and artistic talent. The reason why is obvious: Computers have neither talent nor intuition—these are human qualities. This is why *you* run the computer, and not the other way around!

When you resize an image up or down, Photoshop searches for data to help support the application's decision on how the resizing of the image will look. You are the one who determines how extensively Photoshop uses interpretation—how much Photoshop searches to come up with new data for the image.

Bicubic Interpolation

Bicubic interpolation is the most sophisticated and elegant of Photoshop's resizing methods. This method also requires the most processing power, although in 2002, you will probably not notice even the slightest lag while Photoshop interpolates because our computers are so powerful. Figure 8.5 shows an image that is 4 pixels high and 4 pixels wide (outstanding art it's not), with 2 horizontal and 2 vertical pixels containing a color. I've drawn imaginary grids on the images on the right to help you visualize what's going on here.

The bottom of Figure 8.5 shows what you can expect from Photoshop when you command it to use bicubic interpolation (the default interpolation method) to make this artwork 8 pixels wide by 8 pixels high.

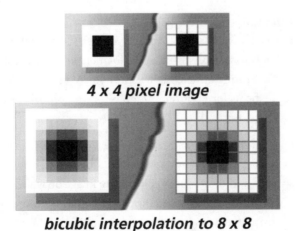

4 x 4 pixel image

bicubic interpolation to 8 x 8

Figure 8.5   By default, Photoshop uses bicubic interpolation to resize an image or an image area.

You can conclude the following from bicubic interpolation:

- The resizing of the art makes the component pixels in the new image appear a tad fuzzy.

- Photoshop makes a smooth transition between background color and foreground color. This effect is particularly important when you work with images whose *pixel count* (the number of pixels in the image) is far greater than the pathetic 16 pixels total you are looking at here.

Okay, so how did Photoshop come up with the intermediate pixels and pixel colors to "fill in" the gap caused by resizing the neighboring pixels? The term *bicubic* here means that Photoshop "looked" in the horizontal, the vertical, and the diagonal directions, beginning with each pixel and then scouting outward. The new pixels are an *average* of the original pixel color and the original pixel's *neighboring* pixel color. Photoshop performs a weighted average of the pixel and its neighbors along three directions and fits the new pixel between the original pixel and its neighbor.

Artistically speaking, you probably want to use bicubic interpolation all the time, whether increasing or decreasing an entire image or a selection. When an image is resized to be smaller, perhaps for display on a web page, bicubic interpolation makes the new image somewhat fuzzy, too. This happens because you're commanding Photoshop to toss away pixels from the original artwork, and Photoshop must reassign the remaining pixels an average of the original colors at any given point. And this ain't easy, because, again, machines and applications are very poor at guessing. They do the next best thing, which is called *averaging*!

Bilinear Interpolation

When you're making an image larger or smaller, you can also use bilinear interpolation. Bilinear interpolation is less processor-intensive than bicubic because it does less examining of pixels before creating or deleting pixels. If you're using a processor that meets the minimum requirements for Photoshop 7, however, you probably won't notice a difference in speed.

The result of bilinear averaging (as shown in Figure 8.6—go peek ahead) might not be obvious with very small images, as my now-famous 8-by-8 pixel artwork demonstrates. However, the new pixels and/or new pixel colors in an image on which you've used bilinear interpolation will not be as faithful to the original image because you commanded Photoshop to perform a decent, but not thorough, investigation to come up with data to be averaged.

> **Note**
>
> **Where There Is Blurring, Use Sharpening to Correct Fuzziness**   Okay, so this "wisdom" is not all that profound, but you should make it standard operating procedure that whenever you make a dramatic change in the number of pixels in an image, a trip to Photoshop's Sharpen filters is the smartest course of action. Not only is it easier to use the Sharpen command to fake restoring the focus of a large image made smaller, you also can use it to repair the focus of a small image made much larger through interpolation.
>
> I recommend the Unsharp Mask filter at all times, except when you're creating a button or an icon for a web page—when a 400-by-400 pixel image, for example, is reduced to 32 by 32 pixels. In this case, the Filter, Sharpen, Sharpen command produces an image that's a little exaggerated around the edges, but effectively communicates your artwork at a very small size.

From a math standpoint, the difference between bilinear and bicubic interpolation is that bilinear interpolation does not weight the average of samples it invents from existing image data, and it only searches in two directions—vertical and horizontal—to come up with new colors and/or new pixels. Qualitatively, you have no reason to change this interpolation preference in the General Preferences dialog box. Many applications out there do not even offer the option of bicubic interpolation.

Nearest Neighbor Interpolation

Nearest Neighbor interpolation is the crudest, quickest way to shrink or enlarge an image. It is also so wildly inaccurate in the visual results when you apply this method to an image, it rightfully earns the name "*no* interpolation"! Nearest Neighbor interpolation might only be of some use if you are increasing the size of an image by an exact, whole amount, such as four times or 16 times an original's size. Using Nearest Neighbor is safer in this situation because pixels are square, and when you increase the height of an image by two, you are also increasing the width by two. Therefore, twice the resolution of an image file means four times its original size.

Can you see now that the Nearest Neighbor method performs no calculations or averaging, but merely repeats the pixel color at the edge of the original? This can lead to really ugly and inaccurate work, especially if you are increasing the size of an image by a fractional amount or an amount that lies between two whole integers. In Figure 8.6, I increased the size of my famous 16-pixel artwork from 4 by 4 pixels to 6 by 6. As you can see, the deck was stacked: There is a 100% chance that Nearest Neighbor resampling will return an image area that is incorrect in size, when a number such as 150% the original size is applied to the image. The "magic numbers" to use with Nearest Neighbor resampling are 4×, 16×, and multiples thereof.

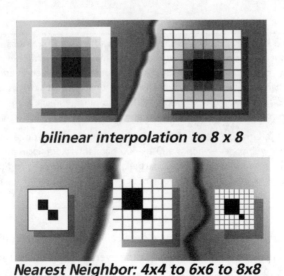

bilinear interpolation to 8 x 8

Nearest Neighbor: 4x4 to 6x6 to 8x8

Figure 8.6   Nearest Neighbor evaluation of an image to be shrunk or enlarged will usually create uneven, inaccurate image areas.

I've spent a good deal of time running down the types of interpolation Photoshop offers, not because I want you to change your preferences, but because I want you to understand the visual results of interpolation. Photoshop is not the only thing on earth that uses interpolation—image-setting devices (printers) and film recorders use averaging processes, too, and your hard copy of an image can be nicely or ineptly rendered. Now that you understand the difference between methods, you have an important question to ask a service bureau (or tech support) that you did *not* have when you began this chapter.

Going from Continuous Tones to Halftones

Contrary to what the name might suggest, a halftone is *not* 50% of a tone! Halftones are the lifeblood of commercial printers and the only way you can get a continuous tone representation on paper. Continuous tones versus halftones merit a brief explanation, and then this section will get into the types of halftones that are at the designer's disposal.

What's the Difference Between Continuous and Halftones?

When you look at the world, and there's a sunset with a rock in the vicinity, you'll see a subtle, *continuous*, falloff of light on the rock. There's no sudden, abrupt area of tone missing, as the light gradually changes on the rock's surface. This is a continuous tone image, because nature has every color with which to display images as the sun emits a spectrum, and your eyes are equipped to receive the parts of the spectrum that depict the rock's tones.

On the other hand, a halftone consists of precisely *two* colors—not exactly our sunset scene! A halftone consists of an arrangement of dots (the foreground color, usually made up of black toner) against the paper (background) color. So how do you capture photographic qualities when your output is to a laser printer? You *simulate* continuous tones, and this is done by the software instructing the printer to place dots of toner at different spatial intervals on the paper.

I've created an exaggerated example in Figure 8.7 of what a halftone sample looks like when compared to a continuous tone that transverses the page from black to white.

Warning

Before You Write In   *Please* don't bust my chops over the reality that this book is printed using dots on paper, and therefore could not possibly truly represent a continuous tone. This book is printed at 2,540 dots per inch, you can't even see the dots without a magnifying glass, and there's really no better workaround for showing you the principles of halftoning.

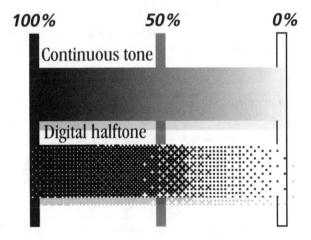

Figure 8.7   A continuous tone image makes seamless transitions between light and dark. Halftone images must rely on the density of toner dots at any given area to simulate a continuous tone.

The pattern you see in the halftone in Figure 8.7 is an exaggeration of what anyone would expect from a laser printer. I think the resolution of the halftone is something like 15 lines per inch, which is so coarse a resolution you could drive your new car through there and not touch the paint.

We'll get into the mystical term *resolution* shortly and demystify it. Next, let's take a look at how digital halftone cells help the accuracy with which a halftone image represents reality.

The Digital Halftone Cell

When you learn about halftoning, it is helpful to imagine a grid placed above your original, continuous tone work. This imaginary grid helps define every inch on the image in terms of density. Suppose, for example, that you have a photo of an ice cream cone against a white background. Slip a screen from a window or a door on top of the photo, and you will see something interesting happen. Pick a cell in the screen; pick it anywhere. Then, take a look at the tone of the photo that is framed by the cell in the screen window.

If the tone is 50% black, what Photoshop and your printer would do is fill half an invisible, corresponding, digital screen on top of the printed page with a halftone cell that occupies 50% of the cell.

Now here's where it gets weird for a moment. In traditional printing, commercial printers have historically put a physical film screen over a photograph to make a halftoned copy. And the halftones are round (usually), and each halftone dot is confined to a predetermined cell in a line of halftone dots. In Figure 8.8, you can see a digital halftone cell compared to a traditional halftone. Digital halftone cells contain square (or rectangular) dots of toner ink, but you can see in this figure how digital halftone cells closely mimic traditional coverage on a piece of paper or film. On the bottom of this figure, you can see the specific coverage amounts.

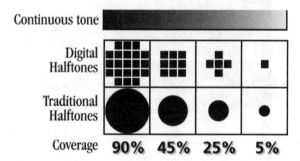

Figure 8.8   Digital halftone cells are filled with a given number of dots that when viewed together (from a distance!) represent a specific tone.

The following section gets into PostScript technology and how it affects printing. The reason for this excursion into the PostScript world is that, among other things:

- PostScript technology was the first and has traditionally been the real method of organizing toner dots (or emulsion on film) so that they truly mimic traditional, physical halftone screens. Hewlett-Packard and software companies offer PostScript emulation (supposed to be as good as the "real thing"), but PostScript is a patented Adobe technology and many print and service bureaus today approach emulation with reluctance for image setting.

- Because PostScript technology extends beyond merely organizing dots into pre-press, there are math formulas you really should know (I'll do the pencil work for you in this chapter) and refer to if you ever want to make your own camera-ready art from a personal printer for commercial, ink-on-paper printing.

PostScript and Image Resolution

It's almost impossible to talk about PostScript rendering of images without talking about image resolution. Many readers have written to me in past years asking me what the input should be for a particular image, and I always have to respond with a question: What is your intended *output* for the file? It makes very little sense to choose an input resolution without first knowing whether the image is going to press, going up on the fridge, or going across the World Wide Web. Let's take a brief look at PostScript technology, and then get involved with *resolution*—both its meaning and how to calculate it.

PostScript as a Halftone Dot Shaper

Using PostScript to render a continuous tone image, you can expect the most faithful of halftone renderings possible today. Other printing technologies put different-sized dots on a page, but they are not organized in screen lines that pressmen use. In Figure 8.9, on the left is a (nearly <g>) continuous tone image of a duck. On the right is a PostScript halftone rendering of the same image. I've used only 30 dots per inch (dpi) on the PostScript duck, which is a foolishly low resolution, but it helps display the individual dots better. Can you see how every tone on the left duck has a corresponding-sized dot that, together, represent the continuous tones?

Continuous tone duck

PostScript™ halftoned duck

Figure 8.9 A continuous tone image compared to a PostScript rendition of the same image.

Not long after the invention of the traditional, physical halftone screen, the publishing world yearned for a little more flexibility in *how* a halftone is rendered. Must a single halftone always be circular? When a screen is applied to a continuous-tone image at an angle other than right angles, what do you wind up with?

To answer these questions, take a look at Figure 8.10. Elliptical dots are being used to fill the digital halftone cells, and the screen created by Photoshop is placed at a 45° angle.

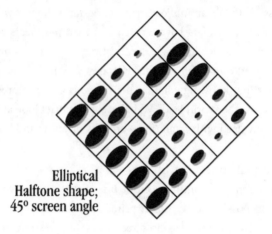

Figure 8.10   Photoshop offers six different shaped halftone dots, one of which is elliptical, plus a custom function, and any angle for the screen you choose.

You might want to squint at Figure 8.10 to get a better idea of how stylized a halftone print can be when you use halftone dots that are not circular. We'll be getting into Photoshop's print options later in this chapter. Many interrelated factors determine the best halftone print of your work. I'll try to cover them all in the least confusing way.

The first factor in image rendering is called *resolution*. Resolution determines how your print looks and also can tell you how many samples per inch you should set your scanner to take.

Image Resolution Is a Fraction

Several accurate analogies could help you better understand the term *resolution* as it applies to computer graphics. I'm going to choose speed—specifically, the speed of a car—to help illustrate this concept.

When you measure the speed of a car, it is conveyed in one set of units over a different set of units, such as 55 miles (a unit of distance) per hour (a unit of time). Image resolution is expressed similarly: Resolution can be defined as units of data over units of distance. When someone tells you that an image is 2" by 2" at 150 pixels/inch, they are expressing the number of pixels in an inch; this is the resolution of the image.

On the other hand, and unfortunately this happens all too frequently, if someone tells you that an image is 200 pixels by 200 pixels, they have not told you the resolution of the image at all! How many pixels per inch is this 200 pixel by 200 pixel artwork? A pixel (short for *pic*ture *el*ement) is merely a placeholder, an entity of no fixed size that holds a color value. For example, Red:128, Green:214, and Blue:78 is the best description of a pixel that anyone could come up with. But *resolution* is the expression of how *many* pixels you want per inch.

If someone tells you that an image is supposed to be 2" by 2", you need to ask them what the resolution is before you can create such an image. Conversely, if you are told that the resolution of an image is 300 ppi, you'd better ask this person what are the physical dimensions of the image, as expressed in inches, picas, cm, or so on.

Note

Image Dimensions Are Inversely Proportional to Image Resolution   Because a pixel is the unit of measurement for the numerator of the resolution fraction (for example, 65 pixels/inch) and because a pixel is only a placeholder, you have the flexibility of changing the size of an image by changing the resolution. And the visual information in the image will not change at all. For example, a 10" by 10" image at 100 pixels/inch can also be displayed as a 5" by 5" image at 200 pixels per inch.

You can tell that no image detail has changed when you change resolution because the size of the image file remains the same. Keep this Profound Wisdom handy when you lay out print work, and you will accomplish the assignment 100% correctly all the time.

Let's take a stroll through the interface of a scanner and put all these nuggets of advice I'm writing into order!

Scanning to the Right Size

I have a fictitious assignment here that involves scanning a piece of wood to 8 ½" by 11" with ¼" trim around each side (so I need about 9" by 11 ½" scanned). As I mentioned in the previous section, a pixel is a placeholder that only takes up space once you have entered it as the numerator of the resolution fraction. Now here's a key that will unlock many graphics doors for you:

Note

An Image Expressed Only in the Number of Pixels It Contains Is an Absolute Amount   You learned in the previous note that resolution is somewhat flexible; you can decrease dimensions and increase resolution, and the number of pixels will remain the same. A good way to measure images destined for the web or other screen presentations is by the number of pixels in the image. For example, a 640×480 screen capture will always contain 307,200 pixels, regardless of the monitor on which it is displayed.

Figure 8.11 shows a number of callouts that I'll explain shortly. What you're looking at is the TWAIN interface (a "corridor" between the scanning hardware and Photoshop, the imaging software). The piece of wood shown in the figure is a preview of the object I'm going to scan.

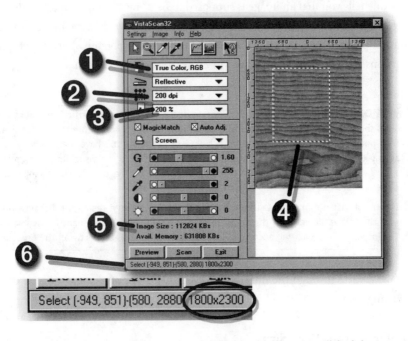

Figure 8.11   Your scanner's interface might not look like this, but you will find the same options on most models.

Let's begin examining this scanner interface based on my need for a 9" by 11 ½" scan of some wood. First question, right? "At what resolution do you need the scan?"

I need the scan to be 200 pixels per inch because my inkjet printer's resolution is 600 dots of ink per inch, and the guy at Epson told me that I should scan at ⅓ the final output resolution. This is not a number that is carved in stone, but typically, for non-PostScript inkjet printers that use error diffusion as a rendering technique (which is impossible to quantify because the dots of ink are not arranged in rows), ⅓ the output should be your scanning input.

Let's begin with explanations of the callouts:

1. **Color mode.** This should seem familiar; you see a Mode drop-down list every time you press Ctrl(⌘)+N in Photoshop. I've chosen RGB color here; however, there will be times when you want to scan in Grayscale, and most scanners offer this option.

Note

Grayscale Images Are ⅓ the Size of RGB Images   The reason for this is that RGB images have three channels of image information, while grayscale images have only one channel (brightness).

2. **Resolution.** I want to get into a quarrel with scanner manufacturers because they label the resolution in *dpi* (dots per inch), and scanners are actually scanning *samples* per inch (or *pixels* per inch). A dot is *not* a pixel. I've set the resolution to 200 here because my final output to my ancient inkjet printer is 600 dpi.

Note

Resolution and Inkjets   Because inkjets do not use PostScript technology, it is very difficult to estimate which sampling resolution of an image will adequately fill the bill when printing to one of these guys.

Here's the straight story: You sample at ⅓ the *true* resolution of the inkjet printer. I stress "true" here due to the fact that a lot of inkjet manufacturers have artificially increased resolution through interpolation. For example, an inkjet that touts 1,440 dpi, but actually renders at 600 dpi (interpolated up to 1,440 dpi) by 1,440 dpi requires ⅓ the sampling resolution of the *lower* number, which means that you sample at 200 pixels per inch for that *true* 600 dpi output.

3. **Scale.** Most scanners allow you to zoom in on whatever is on the scanner's platen. Because I've got a large sample of wood here, I want the scan to be 1 to 1 (100%). But if you, for example, wanted to scan a postage stamp and print it at 8 ½" by 11", you'd use the scale option to really zoom into the stamp. Scaling does affect resolution. If you Scale a scan at 200%, for example, you are scanning four times the information that you'd be scanning at 100% (twice the width, twice the height).

4. **Cropping area.** Scanners enable you to pick only the portion of the sampled object you want. My scanner (this is *not* shown in the figure) will tell me in pixels or in inches how large my crop box is. Generally, you choose the interface's cropping tool and then drag to select the part of the image you want scanned. Most scanners also come with rulers in the preview window, so guesswork is not required.

5. **Image size.** This feature tells you how much RAM is needed to hold and acquire the image and is also a good indicator of what the saved file size is. You'll note in this figure that the image size is about 11MB. This means that to scan from within Photoshop, I have to have at least this amount (ideally about three times the amount) of RAM and scratch disk space available. With today's systems, this is not an issue like it used to be a few years ago.

6. **Absolute measurement.** As described earlier, the height and width of an image as measured in pixels is an incomplete description. I've got 1,800 pixels in width by 2,300 pixels in height marqueed in the preview window. What makes these numbers meaningful is that I'm scanning at 200 samples/inch. This means that 1,800/200=9 (inches) and 2,300/200=11.5 (inches).

End of story! You click the Scan button, and in moments you can save the image, which is perfectly proportioned to hard disk, and print it later.

I've overlooked a few scanning issues in this section, such as interface options for contrast gamma control, saturation, and so on. My belief is to always "get it right in the camera" so your Photoshop correction work is not so prolonged, but I've honestly never seen a scanner preview that was good enough to evaluate corrections you might make using the interface controls. If an image looks halfway decent in preview, I scan it, and then use Photoshop's features to make the image perfect.

We need to put the world of resolution and the world of PostScript together now so that you have some sort of guide to follow when your scanner isn't my scanner, and your output device is not mine, either!

The Input/Output Chart

In Figure 8.12, I've put together a short list of scanning resolutions, the resolution of the printed work, and the expected file size of an acquired image. All of these values presume that you are using PostScript technology—non-PostScript rendering technology is very difficult to measure because non-PostScript printing does not follow any of the rules of traditional screening.

Various Output and Input Resolutions

For a 4" by 6" image at 1:1 sampling versus printing resolution

Resolution of Printed Work	Lines per Inch Output Device Uses	Recommended Scanning Resolution	File Size
300 dpi	45 lpi	90 to100 samples/inch	570 KB
600 dpi	85 lpi	170 samples/inch	1.99 MB
1200 dpi	125 lpi	225 samples/inch	3.48 MB
2450 dpi	133 lpi	266 samples/inch	4.86 MB

Figure 8.12   Choose the printer resolution that most closely matches your printer, and you can see how large you should scan and what the line-screen frequency should be.

When rules in science are followed, the results are totally predictable. The same is true of PostScript technology—there are rules that govern its operation, and the next section presents you with the math you need to create the best camera-ready prints.

A Whole Bunch of Printing Math

Before you even consider making your own camera-ready prints, you should pay a call on the fellows who are going to make the printing plates, and ask the following questions:

- What is the line-screen frequency and angle?
- What are the topmost and bottommost tones your presses can hold?

In Figure 8.13, you can see the "times 2" rule. Commercial press houses do not measure the resolution of a halftoned image in dots. Images are measured in *lines* of dots, and the expression *lpi* (lines per inch) is relevant to your work.

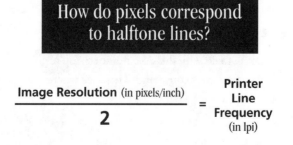

$$\frac{\text{Image Resolution (in pixels/inch)}}{2} = \text{Printer Line Frequency (in lpi)}$$

Figure 8.13   Your image's resolution has to be twice the print house's line-screen frequency.

If a press house tells you that their line-screen frequency is 100 lpi, then according to the formula in Figure 8.13, you need to scan an image (or modify the resolution using Photoshop's Image, Image Size command) at 200 samples (pixels) per inch. If you do this, your halftoned image will be optimal.

Now, toner dots from a laser printer are fused to the paper; the page is instantly dry. Such is not the case with offset printing, where *ink* is rolled onto paper. Ink bleeds, and there are very few press houses that can hold a screen that contains 100% black. The area on the printed page would be a puddle of ink. On the bright side, there is a screen limit to the lowest density of the screen (the white point). 100% white has to meet the next darker value, and the closer you keep the white point to your second brightest tone, the more even the print will look. And that point leads us to Figure 8.14.

How do you calculate lightest and darkest halftone areas?

256 - [Halftone Density (in percent) x 2.56] =

Brightness value

Figure 8.14   Print presses are wet, and laser prints are dry. Somehow, you need to change the tonal scheme of a print so that the print house's presses don't leave a puddle of ink on your work.

When you've got your image balanced to your liking, make a copy of it, and perform some tone reduction so that the press house can make plates from your work. Let's say that the pressman tells you that the presses can hold 10% (90% black) and 97% (3% white) on the top end of the tonal range.

Let's plug these values into the equation shown in Figure 8.14.

$$256 - [90 \times 2.56] = 230.4 = \textbf{25.6}$$

Great. What are you going to do with this 25.6 number? You're going to press Ctrl(⌘)+L in Photoshop to display the Levels command. Then, see where the Output Levels area is at the bottom? You type **25.6** in the left field.

Similarly,

$$256 - [3 \times 2.56] = 7.68 = \textbf{248.32}$$

This is the number you type in the right Output Levels field. Click OK, save the image, print a copy, and cart it off to the print house.

Now, there is a trade-off between the number of shades of gray that a laser printer can simulate and the line frequency of the print. This might not be of value in your work with a commercial printer, but it does serve as an intro here for personal printing—how to optimize the image that you're going to send to your folks.

Lines/Inch Versus Shades of Gray

This section header sounds like a weird football game, doesn't it? Actually, you can do some fun stuff and actually bring certain images up to print house specs if you understand the relationship between line-screen frequency and the number of tones a printer can simulate using digital halftone cells.

In Figure 8.15, you can see the equation. We'll plug some numbers into the equation shortly.

How many shades of gray can your printer simulate?

$$\frac{\text{Printer Resolution (in dpi)}}{\text{Printer Line Frequency (in lpi)}} = n^2 = \text{shades of gray}$$

Figure 8.15   You can change the number of grayscale values if you are willing to sacrifice image resolution.

Sometimes, you might want a "special effect" to enhance the visual content of a print. If you reduce the lines per inch the printer produces, you can get this effect and also increase the number of shades the printer is capable of producing. You're not changing the resolution of the printer; you're simply playing with the input.

Let's say your printer is capable of 600 dpi; a PostScript printer will output about 85 lines per inch. So let's plug these numbers into the equation:

600 (dpi)/85 (lpi) = 7.06 (squared) = **49** unique shades

Forty-nine unique shades of black will probably not get you where you're going. Most grayscale images have almost 200 unique tones. Let's try lowering the line screen to 45 lpi (a fairly low, but acceptable, resolution).

600 (dpi)/45 (lpi) = 13.33 (squared)=**196**

Whoa! Not bad! This means that there will be practically no banding when you are representing a continuous tone image at 45 lines per inch.

Hey, how else can you make personal, tack-em-on the-corkboard prints look super-special with limited resolution and money?

PCL Printing and Error Diffusion

Although the demands of PostScript printing are higher than non-PostScript printing, we would be nuts to ignore the alternatives to PostScript printing.

Hewlett-Packard has a very decent Resolution Enhancement Technology that belongs to the PCL (Printer Command Language) family of rendering technologies. Every printer manufacturer has a different technology, but HP seems to hold the lead on high-fidelity, non-PostScript rendering.

On the left in Figure 8.16 is the duck created using HP printing technology at 30 dpi. The results of the technology are not as elegant as PostScript printing, but the duck definitely has halftone shades across its body. The halftones are not really good enough to make a press screen, but again, these prints are for you and your family and not the world.

On the right in Figure 8.16, you see a duck rendered using error-diffusion printing. Error-diffusion printing can be done from several applications other than Photoshop, or you can actually turn an image into an error-diffusion print by using Photoshop's Image, Mode, Bitmap command—and by then printing it as a normal image. Error-diffusion printing makes a soft, pleasing image using non-PostScript technology, but you absolutely *cannot* take one of these prints to a press house without getting laughed out the door! Error-diffusion prints are not rendered in lines, and they have no regard for digital halftone cells.

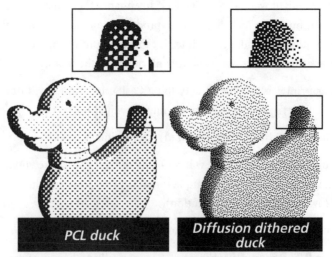

PCL duck

Diffusion dithered duck

Figure 8.16   Printer Command Language and error-diffusion printing are only two of the non-PostScript methods for making an interesting personal print.

Mezzotints

A line of digital halftone cells is not the only way to represent continuous tones. Mezzotinting is not as refined a printing process as PostScript, and a mezzotint image is usually highly stylized—your attention can be torn between the visual content of the image and the way that the print is executed, using lines, dots, and "worms" (more on this in a moment).

There's one newspaper in America that refuses to use halftoned photographs of any-one—pictures of financial moguls are done using a mezzotint screen. Figure 8.17 is a cold-hearted parody of the newspaper, using a line-type mezzotint. As you can see, the screening process is quite visible, but you can make out the face of the gentleman, and the combination of the two properties is aesthetically pleasing.

Figure 8.17   Inflation actually has a positive effect on most pool toys.

Stochastic screening produces tiny shapes that look like worms, and the patterns actually are measured in worms per inch. Figure 8.18 shows a stochastic print. Stochastic print-ing is all computer-generated—print houses cannot duplicate a pattern that shifts according to the input brightness of an image at any given point. To the right of the sto-chastic duck is a line-screen mezzotint that shows highlights going at one cut angle and the deeper shades moving in a different line direction.

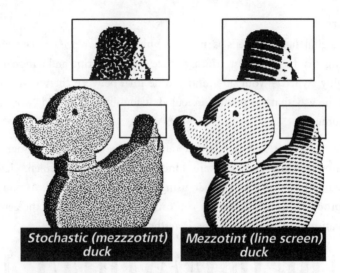

Figure 8.18   If you do not mind a pattern competing for the visual content of an image, mezzotinting could be your ticket.

After this glowing review of other screening types, particularly mezzotints, I've got some good news and some bad news. The bad news is that Photoshop has a Mezzotint filter under Filter, Pixelate that isn't within miles of the quality effects and options Adobe's products are known for. You could not create the mezzotint effects I've shown you in the past two illustrations using Photoshop's Mezzotint filter.

The good news is that Andromeda Software offers a comprehensive assortment of different mezzotint screens that give you complete control over line frequency, angle, and so on. The Screens filters are available in demo format at http://www.andromeda.com—all you need is a credit card and a fast Internet connection.

So far, we've spent a good amount of time on the fine points of printing, but not much explanation on how you print from Photoshop. Allow me to correct this oversight…

Printing Options in Photoshop

Now I'd like to cover two categories of output that are under Photoshop's roof. First, printing from Photoshop is not as effortless as, say, printing from Microsoft Word. But then again, you're printing *art* from Photoshop, while you're printing formatted text from Word—and there's a chasm of sophistication you'd need to ford to bring the two application printing engines even remotely closer together.

Let's first look at how Photoshop lets you know when the resolution of a file you want to print needs tuning.

The Image Size Command: A Career-Saver

Remember the "image dimensions decrease as resolution increases" line a few pages back? Well, Photoshop is a very strict enforcer of correct image dimensions, because it's a waste of paper to allow an image to be printed with clipping, all because the dimensions were not set up correctly.

Figure 8.19 shows an image I want to print. Before printing, however, I clicked the Document Sizes area in the workspace, and a frame popped up that tells me that this image is going to print right off the edges of my paper.

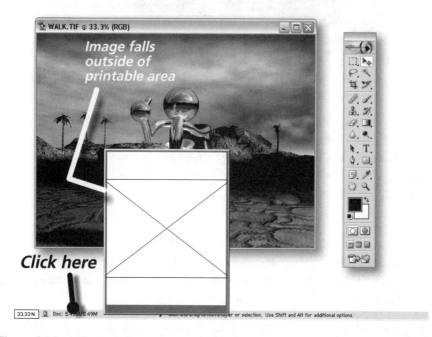

Figure 8.19   Before printing, make it a practice to check the image frame. The "x" shows the extent of the image when printed at the current dimensions and resolution.

Figure 8.20 shows that when I pressed Ctrl(⌘)+P, to my surprise, I got my wrist slapped <g>! Photoshop pops up a warning every time you try to print something that will run off the page.

Figure 8.20   Choose to cancel printing if you get this warning.

Now, there's an easy way to make this chrome guy picture print without changing a pixel of the visual content. Photoshop is capable of resampling an image, but this means you change the number of pixels, interpolation takes place, and you're printing a fuzzy image.

The solution lies in the first math formula in this chapter: If you increase the resolution of the image, you decrease the physical dimensions. Choose Image, Image Size to access the options for changing the resolution of the image. This means that you are resizing, and not resampling; there's an important distinction here.

What happens when you pour a quart of water into a 12 oz. glass? You get a spill, and this is sort of what happens when you decrease the dimensions of the image to the extent that the resolution is now far higher than your printer can print.

This is *okay*, though—the excess printing information is simply discarded during printing time, and you've lost perhaps 15 seconds on a print job by doing this. But I feel it's better to waste a little print spooling time than to go changing the visual content of the image forever. Check out Figure 8.21. Notice that I've decreased the dimensions so that the image will print to an 8 ½" by 11" page, oriented in landscape. You do *not* check the Resample image box in the Image Size command.

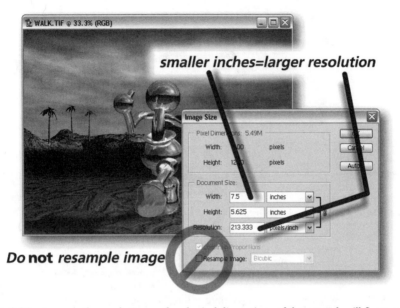

Figure 8.21   Increase the resolution so the physical dimensions of the artwork will fit on a page.

If you're printing to a PostScript device, you will want to choose File, Page Setup prior to printing. We can't go into every printing option within the span of one chapter, but how about the two most important ones?

In Figure 8.22, you can see the Print dialog box. When you press Ctrl(⌘)+P, you arrive at the Print with Preview dialog box. It is here that you get to decide some important things:

- To decide on a portrait or landscape orientation for the image to be printed, you click on Page Setup (marked as item 1). You also choose your printer here by clicking on Printer (many people have a laserjet for business and an inkjet for wallet photos).

- You also have your last chance here to resize the image by dragging on the bounding box in the upper left of this screen. You also can change the print size by entering percentages and units of measurement (item 2).

- If you're creating a camera-ready piece of art, you will want to click Screen (item 3), which we will get to in a moment.

- Finally (at least in *this* book <g>) in the lower-right area of the dialog box, you can choose to have Photoshop add crop marks and other markings that come in handy when building product mock-ups or package design. Or if your print is one of four CMYK composite prints and you really want registration marks, click item 4. (Hint: Many print shops strip off your own crop marks and put on their own. And this is because they know their presses better than you do.)

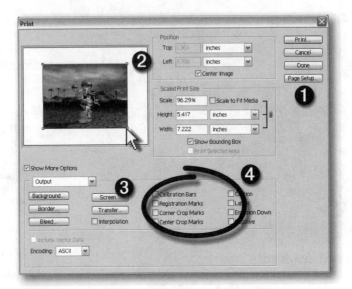

Figure 8.22   Photoshop has printing options galore, but you might need to use only a few of them.

Let's take a look at what you'll see when you click on the Screen button. In Figure 8.23, I make my recommendations for a 600-dpi PostScript printer. 85 lpi is correct for a 600-dpi printer, and the use of diagonal screens (such as 45°) has been a long-standing tradition among physical plate-making experts. It seems that when you run a diagonal screen, folks notice the individual dots of ink less. Try running a 90° screen on a print, and you'll see what I mean.

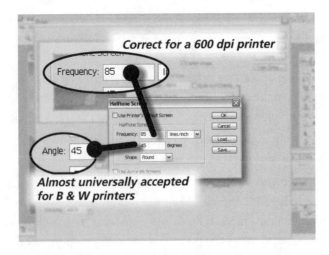

Figure 8.23   A 45° angle has been a favorite with printing experts.

Ah, at last we arrive at my favorite part of Photoshop imaging. It's called *film recording*, and it might or might not even involve Photoshop, unless the service bureau you use owns Photoshop. Film recording is sort of the opposite process to scanning. With film recording, you're taking a digital image and turning it into a 35mm slide (or another film format). The results are breathtaking, and the steps you need to know are just around the corner.

Film Recording

Film recording from digital media is not a new process. If you hear a lot about it these days, it's simply because the price has come down on film recorders so much that if you've got two grand in your pocket, you could own a decent film recorder. Film recording has been fed by PowerPoint users for the past decade, but increasingly, fine artists have taken to putting images on a slide—it's an eminently portable medium, and the colors are usually to die from!

Steps to Film Recording

Pick up the telephone book and find a *slide service bureau*. Regular service bureaus do imagesetting work and set type and do layouts, but it's the slide service bureau that owns the expensive machinery that will turn your Photoshop work into a pocket-sized wonder. You can expect to pay around $4 per slide, and if you've got a lot of work, you might negotiate a discount.

The first step to film recording your work is to make certain that the image has the correct *aspect ratio*. Fine—what's an aspect ratio? Your image is going from data on a disk to a 35mm slide, let's say. Chances are pretty good that your image does not have the 3:2 aspect ratio that belongs to a 35mm slide. And a service bureau is not responsible for adding a background or creatively cropping your image. You don't want this to happen, the service bureau doesn't exactly welcome a request for clairvoyance, and it's really very simple to whip your image into the proper aspect ratio.

To give you an example of the best way to discover how far off you are with the image, press Alt(Opt)+click the Document sizes area of the workspace, as shown in Figure 8.24. My telephone picture isn't even close to having a 3:2 aspect ratio.

Figure 8.24   It's your call on how your image is turned into film. Try to make it easy on the service bureau and invest some time in getting the proportion the same as 35mm film.

In my opinion, the easiest way to get an image properly formatted is to add a background to both the horizontal and vertical aspect of the image. In Figure 8.25, you can see the failsafe method for picking out a background color that will not clash with the image. You press Alt(Opt)+click with the Eyedropper tool to pick up a background color that already exists in the image. How more harmonious can you get?

Figure 8.25   Alt(Opt)+click over a neutral area of the image to set the background you'll soon create.

Let's pay another trip to the Image Size dialog box. This time, we are deliberately going to change the dimensions with absolutely no regard to the resulting resolution of the file. Why? Because film recorders don't care about image resolution—only image size matters, measured in MB.

In Figure 8.26, the Resample image box is unchecked; and I've typed 1.7 (inches) in the height field, and the Width field changes to 2.267 (inches). This is good—this means that we can stop by the Canvas Size command and add to both the vertical and horizontal measurement of the image.

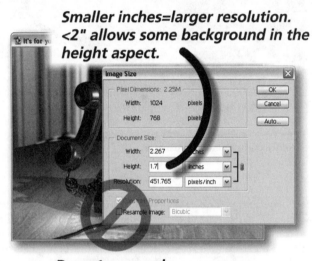

Figure 8.26   Keep the Width under 3 and keep the Height under 2, and then you can add background color to both aspects of the image.

Now, choose Image, Canvas Size, and type **3** in the Width field and **2** in the Height field. Now you've got a 3:2 image! See Figure 8.27. Click OK.

Figure 8.27   The aspect of the image is now ideal for film recording, simply because
you added background to the image.

Note

Aspect Ratio Follows an Order   When we speak of aspect ratios, the first number
before the semicolon is the width, and the following number is the height. Therefore, a
2:3 aspect ratio is *not* the same as a 3:2 ratio. And most service bureaus would prefer
that you give them a wider-than-tall image, because the film recorder that's writing the
film, line by line, has fewer transverses to make if the image is wide.

In Figure 8.28, you can see that I've added a little texture to the background areas of the
image. You can do this too, by filling the background area with a texture. Later in this
book, Scott Hamlin shows you how to add clouds to an image, and all I did was fill an
alpha channel with clouds and then use the Texture Channel feature in the Filter, Render,
Lighting effects feature. The whole procedure is in the Trick 5 section of Chapter 22,
"Gary Cauldron and Photoshop Tricks."

Figure 8.28   Get the image onto a Zip disk and truck it on over to your slide service bureau.

I never really mentioned what size is a good image size for film recording. I've had 900K images written to slides and the subject matter was simple enough that you never noticed the lack of image information. After experimenting for about a year with my slide service bureau, I've found that a 4.5MB image renders pretty well to film.

Here's a secret: most RIPs (Raster Image Processors—the software that enables a film recorder to render to film) will interpolate an image that is smaller than 18MB or so. This means that unless your image is 18MB, do not perform any interpolation by yourself with Photoshop. Interpolation once is bad enough, but if it happens twice to your image before it is recorded, you might notice a resulting fuzzy 35mm slide.

Summary

We have covered a vast amount of information in this chapter. You now know there are more ways of getting your data into your computer and onto hard copy than you can shake a stick at—if stick-shaking is your idea of a good time. This chapter covered literally the ins and outs of Photoshop. With newer, faster, and more powerful image-input devices coming out almost daily, you can take some comfort that the information in this chapter still offers solid basic instruction that does not and will not change.

Part IV

Photoshop for Photographers

Chapter 9

Basic Picture
Editing

After you have a picture in a file on your
computer, you can use Photoshop to
change it in an almost unimaginable number of ways. In this chapter, you discover

how to do the basics—those common tasks that serve as the foundation for editing photographs. You also learn how to use Photoshop's new File Browser, which enables you to find the files you want easily and view, sort, and organize them. Additionally, you learn those small, but necessary tasks like opening, rotating, and resizing photos (you want them to fit in your email messages, don't you?). Finally, you learn a few things about saving digital pictures and taking home a few other goodies.

Pretend that you've just returned from a two-week vacation from some far away place (with a strange sounding name) or from your favorite (rich) uncle's fifth wedding. Because you had your new digital camera, you took a lot of photographs—so far, so good. If you took pictures with a film camera, you'll need to use a scanner to get the photographs into your computer (you may want to review Chapter 8, "Input, Output, and Resolution," if that's the case). Now it's time to see what those photos actually look like, because the view of a photo in the low-resolution LCD of your digital camera gives only a hint of what the image really looks like.

Over time, you will start to accumulate many photos and images on your hard disk—and you'll need a way to locate the files you want to see. Basically, there are two ways to find a photo in your computer: by name or visually. And this is a good place to begin your first exercise…

Tip

Shortcuts   Many of the basic shortcut keys used in this chapter apply to all Windows applications, not only Photoshop. For example, the infamous Ctrl(⌘)+C for copy and Ctrl(⌘)+V for paste is used universally in all applications (Windows or Macintosh) including Microsoft Word, CorelDRAW, Illustrator, and even your web browser and email. The point is that keyboard shortcuts are real timesavers and you should get in the practice of using them.

Opening Pictures by Name

Before Photoshop 7, you could open a photo file only by choosing its name. Alternatively, you could invest in PicaView or use Windows natively supported Thumbnail view of a file, but opening an image directly from Photoshop was hit or miss—if the last person to use the file had activated Save Thumbnail in Preferences, cool; but if not, you were gambling on the filename being a really descriptive one. Although opening an image is really simple, give the procedure a quick read and discover what can go wrong. Here is how it's done:

Opening an Image

1. With Photoshop running, use the keyboard shortcut Ctrl(⌘)+O (you also could choose File, Open, but I encourage you to get in the habit of using the shortcut keys). Either way results in the Open dialog box appearing as shown in Figure 9.1.

Figure 9.1   Photoshop's Open dialog box offers a quick way to open an image—if you remember its name.

2. All the graphics files in the currently selected folder are shown if All Formats appears in the Files of type box. A folder can have hundreds of files in it but appear empty if none of them are graphic files. This is true in all programs. The Open dialog box will display only the files that can be opened or imported for *that* program. Also, when you change the Files of type setting to a specific file format (TIFF for example), you will see only the files in the folder with the format you selected. So if you suddenly discover that many of your files are missing, check the Files of type setting before you panic.

3. Click the file you want to open. Depending on the type of file it is, a preview thumbnail may appear in the Image information and preview area. This applies only if the file format you selected has a preview capability—and not all formats do. Photoshop also allows you to turn the preview capability on or off when saving a file (you do this in the Preferences, File Handling dialog box). So if this feature was turned off at the time the file was saved, a preview will not be available. (You can read more about this in Chapter 2, "Optimizing and Customizing Photoshop Preferences.")

4. Click the Open button and the image appears in the workspace.

If you have only a few photos, remembering the name of an image file might not be too difficult. But what if you have several hundred—or worse—several *thousand*? In previous versions of Photoshop, you could find a file only by opening many of them at once and looking at them individually, or by slowly going through the files and looking at their previews in the Open dialog box. You also could go to the File, Automate, Contact Sheet II and generate previews of images from a folder onto contact sheets for viewing later, but all of these methods are time-consuming.

In this release, Adobe has added a File Browser that enables you to search for a file using the thumbnail previews. The Browser not only lets you search for files quickly and easily, but it also adds a few additional features that can be very handy for photographers and hobbyists alike.

Using Photoshop's New File Browser Feature

Adobe did an excellent job of creating a File Browser that (at first glance) is easy to understand and simple to use. But for all of its simplicity, the File Browser has many hidden features as well. Let's take the File Browser for a spin:

You can launch the File Browser three ways:

- Choose File, Browse.
- Choose Window, File Browser.
- Use the keyboard shortcut Ctrl(⌘)+Shift+0.

Depending on the screen resolution you've selected on your system, the File Browser may open in its own window in the center of the workspace, or it may appear as one of the palettes in the palette well, as Figure 9.2 shows.

Figure 9.2   The File Browser is a really great new tool that lets you locate and work
with photos easily.

If the File Browser appears as part of the palette well and you have a ton of pictures to
search through, this default setting may seem limiting. You can give yourself more space
by clicking the File Browser tab and dragging it to the workspace; then click the arrow in
the upper-right corner of the palette and choose Expanded View. The File Browser
enlarges to fill the workspace, and you can see more images in the display area.

Note

Expanding Your File Browser Horizons   Expanded View is also available when the
palette is in the palette well, but it's a little less obvious—the arrow is located on the
right side of the File Browser tab when the File Browser is active. The palette menu also
provides an option to Show in Separate Window or Dock to Palette Well, which enables
you to move the File Browser in and out of the workspace.

Use the Explorer-style interface on the upper-left side of the File Browser to select the
folder containing the pictures you are searching for. Click the folder to see its contents.

In the right side of the File Browser window, thumbnails of images in the chosen folder
appear. The first time you open a folder in the File Browser, Photoshop takes a few
moments to create a file (called a *cache*) that contains all the thumbnails. After the cache

file is created, the thumbnails appear instantly the next time you open the folder. Because the cache is a file, Adobe gives you the option of exporting or importing it, which can save you a significant amount of time regenerating thumbnails when you move photo file folders to other systems.

After you find the file you want to open, double-click the thumbnail to load the picture. You also can open the file by dragging the image thumbnail into the workspace. If you have removed the File Browser from the palette well, it will remain open until you close it or return it to the well.

File Browser Tips and Features

The *Inside Photoshop 7* gang loves the File Browser. If you work with a lot of images, you will find these File Browser hints helpful.

Getting Comfortable with the File Browser

If you need to look through a large quantity of photos, first open the File Browser using any of the methods previously described. Click the triangle in the upper-right corner of the palette to access the flyout menu. Choose either the Medium Thumbnail or Large Thumbnail setting. Maximize the File Browser window and press Tab (this toggles off the other palettes in the Photoshop workspace). Now you have a screen full of thumbnails, as shown in Figure 9.3.

Figure 9.3   The best way to review a large number of images is to maximize the File
Browser window and press Tab to turn off Photoshop's palettes.

Picture Data and More

Many digital cameras attach data to each photograph taken. This information is called *metadata*. The File Browser displays this information in the main preview window (on the left in Figure 9.3). Depending on your camera, the information can range from the date the picture was taken to each of the camera settings used at the time the picture was taken. This camera captured *much* more data than I needed; in fact, I wouldn't be surprised to find out it recorded the current selling price of the camera's company stock at the time the photo was taken.

In addition to all the information the camera adds, the File Browser also lets you rank the images using one of six different levels (A–F). This ranking is helpful for sorting photos by projects. You might, for example, assign a rank of A to all images in your first-priority project and assign a rank of B to images in a project that's a little less pressing. To rank a photo, you simply right-click (Macintosh: hold Ctrl and click) the image thumbnail and pick a rank from the context menu.

Tip

Rank, File (Browser), and Serial Number   If you don't see the rank listed beneath the image in the File Browser window, click the options flyout button (in the upper-right of the File Browser window) and choose Large Thumbnail with Rank. The images will be displayed in the large thumbnail size, and the rank you assigned will be listened beneath the photos.

Several DAM Things to Consider

As great as the new Photoshop 7 File Browser is, it is not intended to be a replacement for Digital Asset Management (DAM) software. If you are trying to manage a few hundred favorite photos, Photoshop's File Browser may be just the ticket. If you have a more serious collection of images, you will need a product that can let you assign keywords, keep track of photos that are on CDs or in other locations, and offer other database management features as well. Several products are out there doing this. I am currently managing a library of over 25,000 photos (not all of them are gems—but even external FireWire and the long-awaited USB 2 multi-Gigabyte hard disks are inexpensive these days, so why toss away images?). The two leaders in the DAM software field are Portfolio 6 by Extensis (http://www.extensis.com) and Cumulous by Canto (http://www.canto.com). Portfolio 6 wins the vote here because it's easy to use and doesn't require that you become network certified to install or configure it.

Rotate—The Best File Browser Feature

Here's a feature you'll love—you can rotate photographs directly in the File Browser. Well, actually it rotates only the thumbnail, and only for the moment; but the feature enables you to see how the image will look if you rotate it to fit in composition before you actually place it, which is convenient enough for me.

To rotate an image, right-click (Macintosh: hold Ctrl and click) it and find the rotation options in the context menu. After you rotate the thumbnail, a warning dialog box appears to inform you that at this point the rotation applies only to the image thumbnail, but Photoshop will automatically apply the rotation to the image when it is opened. (You can turn off the warning dialog box by clicking the Don't show again checkbox, but I advise leaving it unchecked; the reminder may keep you from inadvertently rotating images sometime in the future.) When you choose to open the image, Photoshop rotates the original image file to match the thumbnail displayed in the File Browser.

> **Note**
>
> **Portrait and Landscape**   Two terms commonly used in the printing and computer industries (and frequently seen in a Print Properties dialog box) are the terms *portrait* and *landscape*. These terms have confused many people because both terms can have other meanings. For example, "landscape" means "Mow your lawn for $50," to a gardening customer. When talking in terms of the *computer* industry, these terms are describing the orientation of the page. Portrait brings to mind a painting or photograph of a person. Usually this painting or photo is of an individual sitting or standing; therefore, the canvas usually is taller than it is wide. So in terms of page orientation, portrait is used to describe a page positioned so it is taller than it is wide (similar to the way you print a business letter). Landscape brings to mind an image of, well…a landscape, which tends to be an image that is wider than it is tall. In landscape mode, an image is displayed or printed horizontally on the page or monitor.

Rotating a Picture

Now that you know how to rotate images, let's cover how you might need to rotate an image and how you can to do this directly in Photoshop's workspace. One of the most common operations performed on digital photographs involves rotating the image. Why? Because all images taken with a digital camera are in a landscape orientation, so if you rotated the camera to take the picture using a portrait orientation you must also rotate the image so that it appears correct. Rotating an image is simple. Here's how it is done:

Quick Rotation Refresher Course

1. Press Ctrl(⌘)+O or double-click an empty area of the workspace to open an image.

2. From the File menu, choose Image, Rotate Canvas and choose the amount and direction of rotation (CW on the menu option means a clockwise direction and CCW means a counterclockwise direction).

Rotation Facts

Be forewarned: Rotating an image at any angle that is *not a multiple of* 90° (that is, 180°, 270°) may result in a loss in image quality, depending on the size of the image. For example, with a 55K JPEG image, rotating the image by, say, 14° will mess it up almost beyond recognition. You *can* rotate a 15MB image in less than 90° increments, however, without too much loss of focus. The reason files suffer quality loss is that digital images are made up of rectangular *pixels*, neatly aligned in rows and columns. When you try to rotate rectangular pixels, the bitmapped image is distorted.

Wait. This is an important concept, and I'm going to expand upon it. Read on…

In other places in this book, you've probably heard talk of these tiny squares that make up raster images called *pixels* (short for *pi*cture *el*ements). Each pixel is assigned a color. When the computer rotates an image at 90° increments, it needs only to change the order of the pixels on the screen; the actual pixels remain unchanged. When an image is rotated at an angle that is more or less than a 90° increment, the computer must recalculate the color of each pixel to give the appearance of rotation. Although the mathematical process used to make these calculations (called *interpolation*) is very sophisticated math, the image quality still suffers. The amount of perceptual loss is determined by the subject matter and overall image size. For example, if an image mostly shows natural subjects, such as clouds, rocks, trees, and even in some cases, people—the loss from rotating an image can be imperceptible. If the same amount of rotation is applied to a photograph of a building or text—the loss in image detail can be more noticeable.

Tip

Setting Up Your Shots   Most pictures are to capture a moment. It might be a birthday, a wedding, or your toddler's first steps; or you might take your photos to capture an object, texture, or place that captures something your composition is meant to convey. Whatever the reason for your photo, take the time to set up your scene the way you want it. When you consider what you're shooting and how it will look best (landscape or portrait? With a busy background or zoomed in on the photo subject?), you have a better chance of taking a quality photo you'll be likely to use.

Always Work on a Copy

Before you do any photo editing, it's always a good idea to make a working copy of the image so that you can work on the copy and keep the original intact. Here's how to make a copy of the image in Photoshop:

Working on a Copy

1. Press Ctrl(⌘)+O to open an image.

2. Go to the Image menu and choose Duplicate. In the Duplicate Image dialog box, choose either the name that appears as the default or give the copy a different name and click OK (see Figure 9.4).

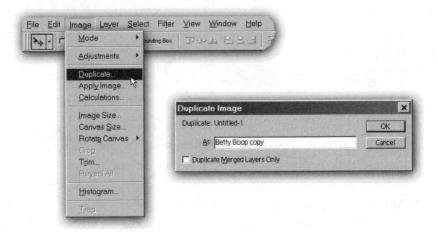

Figure 9.4   The Duplicate command provides a quick and easy way to create a working copy.

Tip

Naming Your Copy   When it comes to naming a working copy, I recommend keeping the word *copy* at the end of the original name. In Figure 9.4 for example, the original file name is *Betty Boop* and the duplicate is named *Betty Boop copy*. This makes looking for these files easier and keeps both filenames together in the listing.

Cropping a Photograph

Many photographs can benefit from being cropped, but we get so excited about an image's visual content that we often forget how much better an image could look if a few parts were lopped off. Cropping a photograph can improve its overall appearance by removing elements in the picture that distract from the subject. Most magazines and books do not use entire images when they print a photograph. In most cases, a small detail has been isolated from a larger image. This also means that a single photograph actually can provide many individual images.

You can crop an image when scanning it, but you also can crop it in Photoshop by using the Crop tool. Drag a marquee selection around the part of the picture that you want to keep. The result is a bounding box provided by the Crop tool that you can move or resize—proportionately or disproportionately—if you need to fine-tune the selection. When you are satisfied with the results, either double-click inside the bounding box or press the Enter (Return) key. If you change your mind and don't want to crop after all, press the Esc key. Here are some advantages of cropping:

- Cropping an image helps reduce the file size, which is a particularly important consideration if you are saving an image for the web because smaller file sizes minimize page load time.

- You can show off the detail in your image by using a well-placed crop to zoom in on a particular area.

- Cropping a picture removes distracting material and makes a better picture.

- Sometimes you can, and should, get more than one picture out of a single image. You often can produce a series of pictures by cropping different parts of the same image.

Figure 9.5 shows a picture of the crest located at the top of one of the oldest churches in Austin, Texas. As you can see, even at the maximum zoom setting, it was still a small part of the overall photograph.

Figure 9.5   You cannot see the intricate detail of the crest in the photo on the left. The cropped crest on the right really brings the detail into focus.

By cropping the crest on the church building, I created a close-up effect. This shows off the details of the crest, and viewers can easily see them.

Image Resolution and Cropping

Keep the image resolution in mind when you crop for a zoom effect. If you right-click (Macintosh: hold Ctrl and click) on the document title bar in Photoshop and choose Image Size, a dialog box appears that gives you some very useful information about the image (see Figure 9.6). The Pixel Dimensions section (at the top of the dialog box) gives a height and width measurement that indicates the size of the image when viewed on your monitor. The Document Size portion tells you the dimensions of your image when printed.

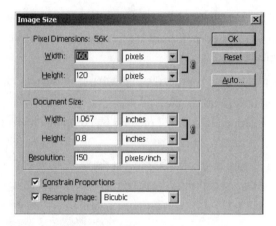

Figure 9.6   The Image Size dialog box enables you to track and control the resolution of images you crop and resize.

Say for example that you have an image that has a large Pixel Dimension; in other words, the image fills your workspace (with room to spare) when viewed at the normal zoom level. But the same image has a small Document Size. For the sake of making this point, let's say the Document Size is only a 1"×2" image. The image appears huge on the screen, but not very big on paper, eh? If you crop this image to view the details of a smaller part within the image, onscreen the image is still large enough to give you a zoomed effect of the details. But when you print this image, you will have an image less than 1"×2", which is the original printed dimension minus the subtracted amount. This image might be more appropriate for the web, a passport ID, or a situation in which the image will be viewed on a monitor and can be displayed at a larger size if needed.

Cropping Suggestions

You can crop an image in other ways to make it more interesting. Some cameras enable you to crop the image *before* you snap the picture. Here are some cropping ideas to consider before taking a photograph:

- The center of interest doesn't always have to be located in the physical center of the print. With some images, you may want to position the center of interest slightly to the left or right or even a little below or above the physical center of the image area.

- Consider the horizontal and vertical lines of an image. Think about whether you want the horizon in a photograph to be absolutely horizontal or the vertical lines of buildings absolutely vertical.

- Don't worry about not being able to fit the whole subject into your camera's viewfinder. Allowing the viewfinder to show only part of the main subject can give you some compositional freedom.

- Crop a scene so that people or animals shown in profile (or near profile) appear to be looking into the picture, not out of it. In other words, subjects should have more picture area (or space) in front of them than behind them.

Changing Perspective with the Crop Tool

Here is a little something about the Crop tool you may not know: you can change the perspective of a photograph with it. (Or maybe you *did* already know this since it was in the heading. Still, you probably didn't know it before you read it, right?)

This feature is handy for correcting the distortion introduced when you photograph subjects at angles. Called *keystone distortion* (named after its similarity in shape to the keystone used in constructing an arch), this technique can be used quickly and easily. Here are the steps to show you how:

Using the Crop Tool to Change Perspective

1. Open the cabinet.psd file in the Examples/Chap09 folder on the Companion CD. As you can see in Figure 9.7, the picture of the furniture is distorted due in part to the angle at which it was shot.

Figure 9.7   This furniture appears crooked because of an angle distortion.

2. Choose the Crop tool from the toolbox. Drag a marquee around the cabinet. Align the marquee with the edges of the cabinet, as shown in Figure 9.8. The entire piece won't fit, but that's OK—you're going to adjust it in the next step.

Figure 9.8   The crop marquee roughly surrounds the furniture you are going to transform.

3. In the Options bar, check the Perspective option. Now move the corner control handles so that the edges of the marquee match the edges of the cabinet, as shown in Figure 9.9. With the edges of the marquee aligned with the cabinet, Photoshop now knows the perspective of the cabinet with respect to the edge of the document window. However, do not apply the crop at this point because you still need to make adjustments to include the subject fully within the bounding box selection.

Figure 9.9   Align the marquee with the edge of the cabinet.

4. Use the middle handles now to drag the sides of the bounding box away from the cabinet until most of the image is visible, as shown in Figure 9.10. Double-click the image (or press the Enter (Return) key) to apply the crop and have Photoshop correct the keystone distortion.

Figure 9.10   Move the middle handles to include most of the image in the perspective crop.

5. The results left some unwanted empty space along the edges as shown in Figure 9.11. Crop the image once again (with Perspective unchecked) to clear away the unwanted edges.

Figure 9.11   The distortion is gone, but now you need to use the Crop tool again to clear away the resulting debris.

Figure 9.12 shows the final corrected image. No distortion and no more rough edges.

Figure 9.12   Now the cabinet is on the level.

The Anatomy of a Digital Picture

Working with digital pictures is much easier if you understand a few things about them. After you read and understand the concepts in this section, working with digital images and all of their techno jargon will make more sense. It isn't brain surgery (it isn't even hard) and it involves very little math. Ready? Here we go.

Pixels

As you *gotta* know by now, all bitmap images are made of the building blocks called *pixels*, a term used to describe the smallest part of a raster (bitmap) image. Pixels have two characteristics you need to remember: they are rectangular and they can be only one color. This means that a digital picture is like a mosaic picture made from colored square tiles.

Two common devices used to produce bitmap pictures are scanners and digital cameras (which both operate in a remarkably similar fashion). So where do the pixels come from? How do we get the mosaic of colored tiles from these devices? Digital cameras contain millions of tiny light detectors that are all jammed together to form a sensor that produces the digital picture when the shutter is opened. If you consult your camera's documentation, you'll be able to tell how many millions of pixels (megapixels) are produced by the camera's sensor. (Hopefully, you already *know* this before you buy a digital camera!) Simply put, when you push the camera's button, the shutter opens and light strikes each of the millions of little light detectors that make up the camera's sensor. Each light detector in the sensor produces a digital value representing the color of the light that struck it. The camera combines all of these values to produce a digital picture containing the millions of pixels.

> **Note**
>
> **Getting Our Megapixels Straight**   The term *megapixel* is used only to describe the size and number of the sensors in a digital camera; it is never used to describe the size of a digital image. A digital picture is described by its width and height in pixels or by its saved file size. For example, you can see the size of an open image in the Document Sizes area of the status bar in Windows or on the bottom scroll bar in Mac OS. But when you look at the Image Size dialog box, the Pixel Dimensions might display the Width as 2048 (pixels) and the Height as 1536 (pixels). Because the sensor of the camera is described as being 3.36 megapixels, you might expect to be able to multiply the height by the width and get 3.36 million pixels. But the *real* math says the picture contains only 3,145,728 pixels. False advertising? No. The sensor is designed to register more pixels than needed to produce the image. Designing the sensor to cover a larger area helps avoid the problem of possible gaps near the edge of the image (because it's not always known at what angle the light will come in and hit the sensors).

The answer to the sometimes-asked and often-misunderstood question, "Hey, how big is a pixel?" is both simple and complex. The fact is that a pixel has no fixed dimensions unless spoken about in relation to a unit of measurement. For example, *30 pixels* is meaningless in size. It's like saying, "This car gets 50 miles." Fine. Per what? A pixel's relative size becomes meaningful when it gets a denominator and the resolution is described as a fraction, such as 35 pixels/inch—which is *really* low resolution!

One common mistake is to confuse *samples per inch* (the resolution fraction used to describe digital media) with *dots per inch*, which is the standard printing resolution. Now, a dot is *not* a sample or a pixel—we're talking apples and oranges here—but the scanner manufacturers have historically labeled the measure of a scan, "120dpi", for example. But *we* know better! The manufacturer *means* 120 samples (or pixels) per inch—ppi for short, and *not* dpi. Let's do a brief exercise to try to understand the relationship between screen and document pixels.

Screen Versus Printout (Add a Pinch of PPI)

1. Press Ctrl(⌘)+N to open a new document. In the New dialog box, set Width to 4 inches, Height to 2 inches, Resolution to 72 pixels/inch, Mode to RGB Color, and Contents at White (see Figure 9.13). Click OK.

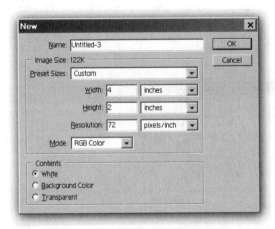

Figure 9.13   Create a new image that is 4×2 inches with a resolution of 72 ppi.

You aren't actually going to use this file to create an image, only to create a point. Just pretend for now that this file contains a really dynamic image. What do you know about this file? Well, you know that when viewed at actual pixel size (screen resolution or 100% zoom level), that this image is not very large on the monitor. You also know that if you print this masterpiece (just play along, OK?), this lovely image will print 4 inches wide and 2 inches tall—but at a really crummy printing resolution, because most inkjets require at least 200 pixels per inch rendering resolution. You know the dimensions as sent to the printer because you set those dimensions when creating the file. Let's move on.

2. Right-click (Macintosh: hold Ctrl and click) the title bar of the image and choose Image Size. What do you see? You see that the Document Size is 4"×2" as expected. The Pixel Dimension (the screen representation) is 288×144. This also is expected because you know the resolution is 72 ppi—so if you do the math and multiply 72×4, you get 288 (and similarly 72×2=144). With me so far?

3. Now we'll cheat a little. Instead of opening up another new document, let's play with the numbers in this Image Size dialog box to see what happens if the image had been created at a different resolution (more pretending on your part). In the Image Size dialog box, change the Resolution to 600 pixels/inch. Wow! Figure 9.14 shows a comparison of the Image Size information of the same images if they were created at different resolutions.

Note

Resolution Isn't Always Easy to Calculate!   600 pixels per inch is a tad large for printing to a resolution that is even of today's magazine quality. Traditionally, 266 pixels/inch suits the resolution of magazines, but the math in this set of steps becomes sloppier, and besides, there are now scanners that scan to a bit depth of 48 (16 bits per channel, which is twice the 8 bits per channel that we are accustomed to). These higher resolution images are gorgeous to look at when printed—but this affects the overall file size…so let's play it simple for now and work through the traditional math.

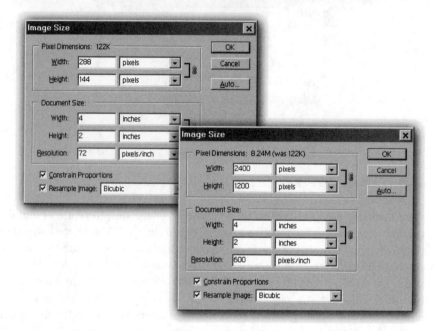

Figure 9.14   A comparison of Image Size information dialog boxes shows the difference resolution makes.

4. Just for fun now, click OK to apply the changes to the Image Size dialog box and watch the document window become too big to view entirely on your monitor, even at 100% zoom level.

So what did we learn here? You don't think I'm going to answer that *for* you, do you? Oh, okay. Read on…

Resolution Quirks and Characteristics

At first glance you may have noticed only the obvious. When you increase the resolution of the file, it becomes really huge on the screen. But that's only part of the story. Did you notice that the printable (or document) size remained the same? The image still prints at dimensions of 4"×2". This means that more pixel information will be packed into the same size image, offering more detail and clarity than the image that was printed at 72 ppi. You'll also notice in the comparison in Figure 9.13 a jump in file size. The 72 ppi file had an estimated file size of 122K and the 600 ppi file would take up 8.24MB of hard disk space.

So, assuming that you want to create an image from scratch, how do you determine which resolution to use?

Here are some guidelines to help you make this decision. You first need to consider what you want to do with the file. If the image is intended for monitor-viewing only, such as for the web or sending via email to Aunt Bertha, you want 72 ppi. If you want to print the image to an inkjet or a relatively high-resolution laser printer and get a fairly nice result, shoot for somewhere between 150–200 ppi. If you plan to send the image to a professional printer, you can't go wrong with a resolution of 300 ppi.

Changing the Size of the Picture

In the previous exercise, you compared two identical images at different resolutions. Now let's see a real example of that. From the Examples/Chap09 folder on the Companion CD, open Pixels72.tif and Pixels300.tif. Looking at the Image Size information for both files, you discover that the Pixels72.tif file (as you might guess) has a resolution of 72 ppi and the Pixels300.tif file has a resolution of 300 ppi. Both files have the same printable size. If you compare these images side-by-side in Photoshop, the Pixels300 image opens at a zoom viewing level of 25%, whereas the Pixels72 image opens at the 100% zoom level.

Viewing Pixels300 at a lower than 100% zoom level, it appears to be less sharp when compared to the Pixels72 file (which is at 100% zoom level). Click the title bar of the Pixels300 document to make it active and press Ctrl(⌘)+plus sign until the image is displayed at 100%. You'll notice two things. First, because this is a higher resolution file, the document window doesn't easily fit into the workspace at 100% zoom level. Also, the edges and clarity within the image are now becoming more apparent at this zoom level. If you really want to do an in-depth comparison, print both files and compare them side-by-side. This is where you will see a huge difference. The edges of the letters and the specular highlights will appear jagged in the 72 ppi file, but the 300 ppi file shows a flawlessly smooth transition in these areas.

When you apply this to your digital camera pictures, imagine the sharpness in detail you may be losing if you keep your quality settings on low. Always shoot for quality and keep those settings on the highest resolution setting. You may not be able to fit as many images on a digital camera memory card, but if you do capture a wonderful moment on film (or in this case, on a memory card), it has a better chance of looking great when you print it.

> **Note**
>
> **JPEG Isn't the Same as *Today's* JPEG**   Many digital cameras automatically compress images using the new JPEG compression. In past editions, we said a lot of nasty things about lossy compression (a term used to describe the technique of conserving data space by discarding some relatively unimportant image information), but today new algorithms are finding their way onto the camera circuitry, and 10-to-1 compression means two things:
>
> - You can store a 9MB image on a memory card in the space of about 1.13MB. Hey, this means you can save more images before you have to download or swap the memory card.
>
> - The image qualities that are lost by JPEG compression really don't matter in a 9MB image. Traditional film has film grain, and digital images can sometimes display noise in large, solid areas such as a clear sky, but on the whole, JPEG is A-OK. Many of the images in the color signature of this book started their lives as JPEGs. Can you detect anything that shouldn't be there in the images?

You can use the Image Size dialog box to change a file's resolution or its printable and pixel dimension size. But what happens when you do this? First, let's consider two options at the bottom of the Image Size dialog box.

The Constrain Proportions option is an option that is checked by default. I recommended that you leave it checked because there is rarely a time when you don't want to resize proportionally, which is what this option does. When this option is checked and you change the width of an image, you will see the height automatically adjust to keep the document proportional. If the Constrain Proportions is unchecked and you change the width of the document, the height will *not* automatically adjust and the results can look as though you stretched the document in one direction but not the other. This creates a kind of a funky image as though you were working with silly putty and pulled only in one direction. Try experimenting on the Pixels300.tif file to see the results for yourself. Press Ctrl(⌘)+Z to undo when you're done.

You use the Resample Image option to help Photoshop guess at size changes made to the file. If you read Chapter 2, you found out that the Bicubic option is the recommended choice for resampling. Let's talk about what happens when you resize or change the resolution of a file when this option is checked. When you increase or decrease the resolution or size of an existing file, the result will be a loss in clarity. Why? When you're increasing the file's resolution, you're asking Photoshop to guess at pixel information that was never there. The result might be acceptable if the increase is not significant, but don't expect perfection. When you decrease the resolution, you lose sharpness and detail because Photoshop now needs to guess at which pixel information to discard. However, you can correct (or at least improve) downsampling by using the Filter, Sharpen, UnSharp Mask filter. You cannot correct an upsampled image, however, short of disguising it by using, say, the Filter, Artistic, Dry Brush filter.

When the Resample Image option is unchecked, Photoshop's goal is to maintain the same number of pixels, which means that the file's clarity is not affected. You no longer have the option to adjust the pixel dimensions. If you change the resolution, the printable size of the document will automatically adjust to whatever size is needed to keep the pixels in the same order and the same quantity. If you adjust the printable dimensions (or Document Size), similarly, the resolution will automatically adjust to a number that also maintains the pixel order and quantity (the same file size gives you a clue as to this). Let's test this out.

Resampling an Image

1. If the Pixels300.tif is not already open, open the file from the Examples/Chap09 folder on the Companion CD. Right-click (Macintosh: hold Ctrl and click) the title bar of the image and choose Image Size. Make sure that the Constrain Proportions option is checked.

2. Uncheck the Resample Image option. Change the Resolution to 72 pixels/inch (as seen in Figure 9.15). You will notice that the Pixel Dimensions are unavailable and remain a constant. The Document Size numbers, however, made a huge leap in size. Click OK to apply the change in resolution and you won't notice any change to the file onscreen.

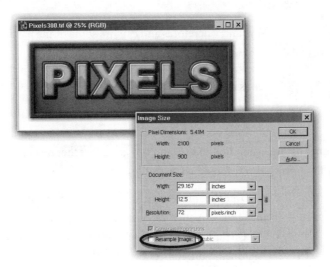

Figure 9.15 With the Resample Image option unchecked, any changes to resolution affect Document Size and vice versa.

On your own, play with the options and numbers in the Image Size dialog box until you feel you understand the concepts thoroughly. Simply close the file without saving changes when you are finished. No harm done.

So if the file is the same on the screen, what did you change? Well, as noted before, the Document Size numbers took a huge leap in size. This file will now require a surface of over 29 inches in width and 12.5 inches in height if you want to print this image. When you changed the pixels per inch, the printable size needed to adjust to keep the same amount of pixels onscreen (and to maintain image quality). What you've essentially changed is the way Photoshop thinks about the same 2100×900 pixels that you originally started with.

Types of Graphic Files

At some point, you will need to save your image and make a decision about the file format you want to use. You save an image in Photoshop in the same way you save a letter in your word processor or any other program. What makes it seem more complicated is your range of choice: you can save your image files in many—almost 30— different formats. If you are new to computer graphics, looking at the list of supported graphic formats can almost take your breath away; yet, there are only a few formats you will actually need on a regular basis.

Don't let all of these format names confuse you. The formats can essentially be categorized into three groups: Internet formats, graphic-standard formats, and Photoshop-native format.

Let's dig deeper into the whys and wherefores and explore some of the particulars of each group of file formats.

Internet Formats

The Internet formats are most commonly used to send images attached to emails or within web pages. They are used because most Internet browsers recognize and display them. JPEG and GIF are examples. PNG is another good Internet format. It's not widely accepted, but Photoshop can read and write this format.

The size of graphic files sent over the Internet must be as small as possible so they can be downloaded quickly. To make files smaller, *compression* is applied to the files. The two most popular formats that have built-in file compression are GIF and JPEG. The following table summarizes the significant differences between the two formats:

Feature	GIF	JPEG
Compression	Lossless: Fixed compression. No loss of image quality.	Lossy: User-selected compression. Loss of image quality depends on amount of compression.
Compression results	Moderately reduced file size.	Greatly reduced file size.
Color depth	256-colors only.	24-bit color or grayscale.
Best used with	Low-color cartoons, line drawings, logos.	Photographs.
Allows transparency?	Yes.	No.

Graphic-Standard Formats

You use graphic-standard formats when you need to be sure someone else can open your files. Two good examples are TIFF and TGA (or Targa) files. Both formats can retain an alpha channel, but unfortunately, only TIFF can retain resolution information (TGA reverts to 72 ppi when saved regardless of what *you* want!). PICT files are a Macintosh standard—they come in 16-bit and 32-bit color (24-bit color with an alpha channel), but nobody outside the Macintosh community really uses them. Similarly, no one outside the Windows community uses BMP files. They do not hang onto specified resolution settings, and they are limited to 24-bit color. (About five years ago, Macromedia demonstrated that a BMP could hold an alpha channel with their X-Res product, but no other company has duplicated that and X-Res is currently in hibernation.) My advice is to use only PICT and BMP files for desktop wallpaper.

When you need to send an image to a service bureau or a printer, you will most likely need to send it in a format that has become the *de facto* standard. Its official name is *Tagged Image Format File* but everyone refers to it by its initials, *TIFF* or *TIF*—they're both pronounced the same. TIFF files offer several lossless compression options, and Photoshop 7 allows you to save the TIFF file with a Zip option to help reduce file size. But be warned—when the Zip option is used and the file is sent to someone else, the person on the other end is likely to have trouble viewing the file unless they have Photoshop. They can open the file in Photoshop and resave it as a TIFF file (without the Zip compression) to be able to view it in another image viewer program.

Warning

Leave Your PICT at Home   If you're working with a service bureau or printer, don't even think about bringing along a PICT format image. Although they are common among Macintosh users, PICT files are responsible for rendering failures to (PostScript and Scitex) image setters, and you will not win friends at the bureau or printer by using these files. Bring a TIFF instead.

JPEG is another common format, and not just for Internet files. As mentioned previously, it uses a lossy compression method, which scares off a lot of people. But when it comes to color photographs, JPEG loses far less information than GIF. As a general rule of thumb, if I have an image that is important to me and I want to preserve the best possible image quality, I will save it as a TIFF file first, and then save another copy as a JPEG for purposes of sending to friends, because the JPEG format is significantly smaller than its TIFF counterpart (and therefore easier to upload and download in email attachments).

The real disadvantage of lossy (JPEG) compression is that repeated editing and saving of the file causes a small but progressive loss of image quality each time it is saved. This is another good argument for saving two versions of the same file. If you need to open the file for more edits or adjustments, open the TIFF and then resave as a JPEG after the edits are made.

Native File Format

The Photoshop PSD format is the best format to use when you are saving images that contain layers or other Photoshop-specific features. The Photoshop native format is basically a TIFF format file—with extras. It compresses the image with a lossless compression.

Confession time: Truth be known, in many cases, I save the same file in three separate versions. The file might start out as a TIFF file, but if I altered the file in Photoshop and have made use of layers or other Photoshop features, I will save a PSD version of the file. This enables me to come back to the file at any time to make changes easily. I also keep a flattened JPEG version for the reasons mentioned earlier—it's lower in file size and easier to share with friends.

Summary

Now that you have learned to locate, open, twist, and save your photos, let's move on to the next chapter where you learn the basics of image color and tonal correction.

Chapter 10

Color and Tone Correction

There are 1,001 things that can make your
photograph a clunker. You could have
accidentally sheared Aunt Bessy's forehead
off when you framed through the lens,

or someone in the photo could have their eyes closed, or *you* could have moved and blurred the picture.

Even with today's high-tech image editors, such as Photoshop, there's not much you can do about visual information that is completely missing from a picture (except take the picture again). But—here comes the good news—there are a *lot* of features in Photoshop that can clean up a picture that's too dark or too light, or whose colors are cast in an unflattering direction (for those times when everyone in the image has the complexion of a smoked sausage or an icicle).

In this chapter, we start at the root of color and tone corrections that computers enable us to do, and then quickly rise, taking this knowledge with us, to some practical examples of how to perform what folks on the street would call "miracles." Because tones are found in both color and black-and-white images, we explore tones and tonal correction first.

Working with Tones

Before talking about correcting tones, it might be nice to explain what a tone *is*! *Tones* are the brightness values of an image. When you view an image using a computer monitor and adapter card, what you see is generally broken down into three components— three channels of additive color: red, green, and blue (hence the phrase *RGB monitor*). A combination of 100% intensity from all three guns in the cathode tube of your monitor builds a white tone; and when there is no signal through any of the guns, the monitor displays a black tone.

But RGB color is more than what your monitor displays; it is also a color mode in Photoshop, called a *color space*. A color space describes the limits to which any particular mode can express color. For example, all Indexed color mode images, such as the GIFs people put on the web, have a color space of 256 unique colors. If you want to add a color that's not in the color space, you need to first lose a color (and this process is called "messing up a perfectly good image"). You can do nothing about the limitations of the color space. Fortunately, RGB color has a color space of 16.7 million possible unique colors. And because it's a fact that the human eye can perceive only a handful of colors at one time, the RGB color space ain't too bad.

Note

Colors Are Not Immune to a Computer's Mathematical View   Because computers calculate colors digitally, all color components are measured in whole, discrete, limited numbers. Huh? Okay—Photoshop's convention is to give 256 levels of intensity to each of the 3 color channels (red, green, and blue) that make up the RGB color space. So the number 256 pops up a lot in calculations.

Why 256? Because to a computer, this number is a nice, neat amount. It's actually expressed as 2 (on or off, in binary terms) to the 8th power (there are 8 bits in a byte of info), and 2 to the 8th power is 256. And because there are 3 channels, the number 256 to the 3rd power is 16.7 million and some change.

RGB Equals HSB

The bad news (it's not all that bad, actually) is that if you work with colors in the RGB color space as combinations of red, green, and blue, you'll immediately find it almost impossible to define a color that you want. And if you have trouble finding the right *color*, you will almost surely find it impossible to tack down a specific *tone* and correct it.

One of the first people to see this problem is Dr. Alvy Smith (the founder of PIXAR). He, too, wanted a more convenient way to define colors as we see them, so he co-invented the HSB color space, which corresponds exactly to the RGB color model. In other words, every color you can define using amounts of red, green, and blue can be identically expressed as degrees of hue, amounts of saturation, and amounts of brightness: *HSB*.

Tip

Brightness by Any Other Name   For the same reason that no two people speak identically, it seems as though no two computer engineers will call the Brightness component of HSB color by the same name. Alternative names for Brightness are Lightness, Value, and Luminance.

What is the practical difference between these terms? Answer: None!

Defining a Tone

Okay, I feel like a fool illustrating the different mechanics of RGB and HSB color in a black-and-white book, but bear with me. Suppose that you want to define 41% black to use in image retouching. Figure 10.1 shows how you'd do it in RGB color—with a lot of guessing and a lot of math. This figure also shows how you'd define 41% black using the HSB color model—not the same chore, eh?

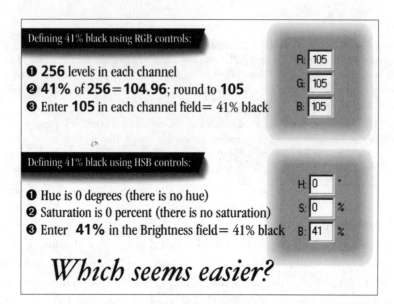

Defining 41% black using RGB controls:

❶ **256** levels in each channel
❷ **41%** of **256** = **104.96**; round to **105**
❸ Enter **105** in each channel field = 41% black

R: 105
G: 105
B: 105

Defining 41% black using HSB controls:

❶ Hue is 0 degrees (there is no hue)
❷ Saturation is 0 percent (there is no saturation)
❸ Enter **41%** in the Brightness field = 41% black

H: 0 °
S: 0 %
B: 41 %

Which seems easier?

Figure 10.1   When you are looking for the tonal value of a color, why waste time calculating equal amounts of three colors? Instead, use the HSB color space to define the shade.

Being able to define a percentage of black is a good skill to have. Someday, someone is bound to call you on the telephone to ask you for art that has a certain tone in it, and you're now prepared to spec a tone. But the larger issue here is that brightness can be isolated from the other HSB components, which means that you can adjust the tones in an image without mucking up the saturation of colors or the hues. In the following section, first you'll correct the tones in a grayscale image, and then you'll try the same techniques on a color image. In both instances, what you'll be doing is a small sample of exactly what the pros do using Photoshop.

Examining an Image's Histogram

A *histogram* is a map. The map tells you at which brightness point pixels are located. For example, Figure 10.2 shows an image and a histogram of the image. Let me explain what the histogram says about the image…

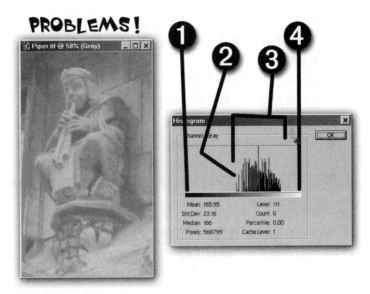

Figure 10.2   A histogram tells how many pixels are located at each point of the 256 brightness levels. In this image, there are too many pixels occupying neighboring values— and the neighborhood is crowded!

1. At level 0 (zero), there are no pixels. That means that there is no true black in the Piper image (which you can also see simply by looking at the picture).

2. Very few pixels are shown in the midtone region. A tip you can learn from a photographer (or from this book) is that the midtones are the location of most of the detail you see in many pictures. If there are not enough midtone pixels, or if they are bunched together, you are missing much of the image's content.

3. Most of the pixels in this image are bunched around the upper midtones, which isn't necessarily a bad thing—but there is little or no contrast between adjacent levels. In other words, level 112 should be markedly different in pixel count than, say, level 113. By staggering the amount of pixels at every other level (this is sometimes called *combing*), you increase the contrast without messing up image detail.

4. No white pixels are used in this picture, which accounts for a lot of the dullness of the image.

What can you and Photoshop do to correct this image? You can make the changes using tools of varying sophistication, which you'll check out in the following section, beginning with the Brightness/Contrast command.

Adding Contrast to a Photograph

Brightness and contrast do not need a fancy definition in this book. You adjust them in an image in Photoshop in much the same way you adjust the controls on your computer monitor. We're particularly interested in the Contrast control on the Brightness/Contrast dialog box because there's so little contrast in the Piper image.

When you add contrast to an image, it's almost as though you're commanding the pixels in the image to make a decision. You're telling the pixels in the lower end of the range to choose a value even darker than the current value. The converse is true with lighter pixels—by adding contrast, you force lighter pixels to become lighter. This is why the Brightness/Contrast command is

- The simplest of the tone controls in Photoshop.
- The only tool you might ever need if your images have poor (but not disastrous) separations of tones.

Let's see what adding contrast alone can do for the Piper:

Using the Brightness/Contrast Command

1. From the Examples/Chap10 folder on the Companion CD, open Piper.tif in Photoshop.
2. Choose Image, Adjust, Brightness/Contrast, and the dialog box floats above the workspace.
3. Drag the Contrast slider to +59, as shown in Figure 10.3. As you can see, the Piper image definitely improves when contrast is created.

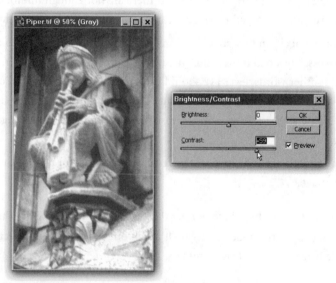

Figure 10.3   Increasing the contrast gives you a quick fix for a dull image.

4. Save the image in Photoshop to your hard disk as Piper1.tif in the TIFF file format. Keep it open; you can delete it from your hard disk later.

So what does this improved image have in terms of pixel distribution? Let's check into the Histogram feature and find out. Choose Image, Histogram, and you'll see a graph that looks like Figure 10.4. It's not a bad distribution of pixels. But your eyes and the histogram will tell you that you need something more sophisticated to push those pixels into the right levels!

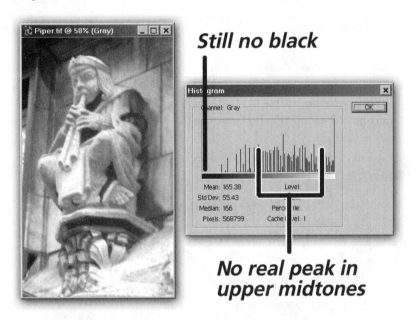

Figure 10.4   The histogram (and your eyes) tells you that the picture still has no black point and that the upper tones are still bunched together, obscuring image detail.

You can close the Piper1.tif image now, and load the original Piper.tif again from the Companion CD. In the following section, we'll work with the Levels command (sounds ideal for setting brightness levels, huh? <g>) and see whether we can make this picture, um, "picture perfect."

Using the Levels Command

Photoshop's Levels command divides the histogram of an image around three distinct points: the *black point* (level of 0 brightness), the *white point* (level of 255 brightness), and a *midpoint* (level of 128 brightness). Although you can make manual adjustments to an image, often you will find that clicking the Auto button in the Levels command's dialog box dramatically improves an image—so much so that after one step, you can call it quits!

Before you touch anything, try to envision the original histogram of an image as having an elastic band that encompasses all the levels. You can then stretch the band to make the levels proportionately spread out to the extent of the elastic band.

The Levels command dialog box consists of an Input area and an Output area, although even some pros (including *moi*) don't notice at first the controls at the bottom of the screen. In a moment I'll discuss these Output controls, whose sole purpose is to create *less* contrast in an image.

Let's test the Levels command now.

How the Levels Command Works

1. With Piper.tif as the current image in the workspace, press Ctrl($\mathcal{H}$)+L to display the Levels command dialog box. Note in the current histogram that the Levels command is showing. It's very similar to the histogram shown for the original image a while ago.

2. Click Auto, as shown in Figure 10.5. Wow! The image really snapped up, tonally, didn't it?

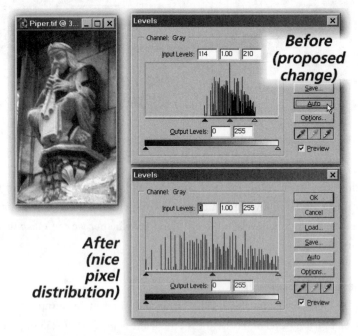

Figure 10.5   Using the Auto button usually corrects the tones in color and grayscale images quite well.

3. You can click OK to apply the changes and close the image without saving.

Let's review exactly what the Levels command did. Refer to Figure 10.5, if necessary:

- The Auto feature by default clips the upper- and bottom-most pixels by five percent on the histogram. So when Photoshop defines the lightest and darkest pixels in the image, it ignores the first five percent of either extreme. This is done to eliminate any lone, errant pixel at an unrealistically high or low brightness value in the image, such as a reflection—a single pixel—off a far-away car. By the way, you *can* change and customize the Auto feature's five percent clipping range by clicking the Options button (in the Levels dialog box) and making adjustments to the default settings.

- After the lightest and darkest pixels in the image have been defined as white and black, respectively, Photoshop redistributes the intermediate pixel values proportionately. If you look at the "after" histogram in Figure 10.5, you'll see that Photoshop has not only stretched the area of pixels in the image to cover the whole tonal spectrum of levels, but also has gently increased contrast in the midtones by staggering each neighboring pixel's value. This is the *comb* effect I mentioned earlier, and it makes midtone detail easier to view.

The Auto feature is not a 100%, use-it-all-the-time panacea for poorly exposed images, however. In some cases, you will want to increase or decrease contrast in the image selectively (in other words, by hand).

To do this on a muddy picture, follow these steps:

1. First, drag the black point slider (the far-left slider) to where there is a small number of pixels at the left of the histogram. Currently, the black point of your muddy image probably has no pixels at the absolute black point. This action redistributes all the pixels in the image (along a proportionate scale), so expect some differences in the overall shape of the histogram.

2. Next, drag the white point slider (the one on the far right) from its current position under no pixels to a position under several pixels (on the histogram). You've just added a lot of snap to the image, but you have one more control to adjust.

3. Take the midpoint slider (the middle slider under the histogram) and drag it slightly to the left so that the middle of the three Input fields at the top of the Levels dialog box reads about 1.2 or so. You've opened up the midtones by decreasing contrast, and now you might see more detail in the image's most critical zone: the midrange.

4. If, on the other hand, the midtones in the image look wimpy and washed out, drag the midpoint slider slightly to the right until the middle Input value box reads .9 or so. It doesn't take a lot to change the midtone values dramatically.

Note

What Is Gamma?   Descriptions of *gamma* by manufacturers, a lot of educated people, and sometimes the author, are usually imprecise. So don't get buzzed about the term.

The midpoint slider is sometimes called the *gamma* control, a mildly inaccurate term used to describe the contrast in midpoint areas. Gamma actually is the nonlinearity of the monitor; as more voltage is supplied, the brightness of an image does not increase linearly—there's a dip in the 50% brightness area, and this "sag" in signal versus brightness is the true definition of gamma. We correct the sag by increasing the gamma.

Understanding the Output Controls in the Levels Command

You may never need to use the Output controls in the Levels dialog box unless you're making a camera-ready laser print (or film print) for a commercial printer.

Essentially what happens when you drag to the right with the Output Levels black point slider is that you tell Photoshop, "No, no—the black is too black in this image; only allow the lowest value to be (something such as) 95%. The converse is true of the white point Output slider. When you drag it to the left, you're telling Photoshop to ignore any information around the top percentile of the image and to define absolute white beneath the new point. Why would you decrease contrast in an image? Isn't contrast good?

Hold the Presses

Yes, and no. For the human eye looking at an inkjet or laser print of your work, you want an image to be crisp and well balanced, tonally. But commercial printing presses don't use ink jets or dots of toner to make an image. Commercial presses roll ink onto a very absorbent paper, and this ink *bleeds*. So to correct this problem, pressmen usually will tell you that their presses can hold 7% or 10% black and about 240% white.

The math is simple and you will get a positively crummy-looking, washed-out print from your laser printer that, in turn, will make a plate which will reproduce your work beautifully off of a commercial press. Here's a translation of what the pressman says:

Pressman: *I can hold 10% black.* 10% of 256 (the number of levels of brightness in an image) is 25.6 (call it 26). So you need to set the Output black point slider to 26 for the image.

Pressman: *I can hold 95% whites.* This is the lightest area that is screened onto the newspaper. Anything higher results in no ink on the paper (and a glaring highlight is visible). You figure out that 95% of 256 is 243.2 (243) and then drag the white point slider to 243. Then press Enter (Return), and save your image as one that is destined for the commercial presses.

What Do a Good Color Picture's Tones Look Like?

In the Examples/Chap10 folder of the Companion CD is a picture called 3Folks.tif. Open it in Photoshop; you're not going to do anything with it because it's already a good picture. You're only going to look at the color image's histogram.

Choose Image, Histogram now. As you can see in Figure 10.6, the histogram tells you that the zones are well-defined and separated. Your eyes naturally tell you this too, but it's important to be able to read a histogram.

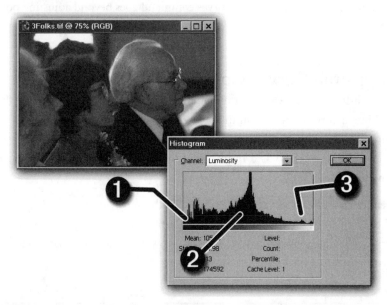

Figure 10.6   Color images have hues, certain amounts of saturated color, and brightness values. The Brightness (also called Luminosity) affects the other two properties.

Let me explain the items called out in Figure 10.6:

1. There is a true black in the image's pixels—not only that, but there's a good amount of true black and dense-colored pixels. We can see this in the image in the middle woman's hair and the gentleman's jacket. Notice that there isn't a lot of detail to this navy blue jacket. This density is reflected in the histogram by the fact that there seems to be an even number of neighboring pixels in the low tones—there's no combing going on.

2. The midtones show a fairly steep peak, and the midrange is where many pixels are located. This is good; this is where flesh tones are located, and this means that there's plenty of flesh tone value in the image. This is to be expected with a close-up picture of people's faces.

3. The picture has very little pure white, but there are some pixels in the upper register of this histogram, and that, too, is good. The man in the picture has a starched collar, and sunlight is streaming through the windows in the background.

Notice that throughout this section, I've referred to tones as midpoints, black points, and so on. When you use the Levels command, you're really only moving these three points; Photoshop interprets the rest of the pixels to make smooth falloffs in the image.

In the following section, you work with the Curves command, the most sophisticated of the three tonal-correction tools. The Curves command goes beyond adjusting points on a tonal map.

Examining the Curves Command

Instead of a histogram, the Curves command presents you with a diagonal line that you can mold into a curved line, and in the process, redistribute *groups* of pixels to reshape the tonal landscape of an image. You can lay down as many as 15 "anchors" on the Curves graph, reposition them, and as a result, bend the curve until it makes an image look tonally perfect.

As I mentioned earlier, the Curves command is the most sophisticated tonal tool in Photoshop. As you begin your independent adventures with the program, the Curves command might be something you want to grow into, not necessarily charge into head-first.

Tip

Reset the Dialog Box   Anytime you get in over your head in these dialog boxes and want to try again without canceling and then redisplaying the dialog box, hold down the Alt(Opt) key, and the Cancel button becomes a Reset button. When you click Reset, every modification you made in the box returns to its original setting.

The left-to-right axis on the Curves graph is the original position of all tones in the image. The top-to-bottom axis represents the changes you propose, so naturally the graph looks like a diagonal line when you begin. The left-to-right display goes from shadows to highlights that you can manipulate.

Here's a brief, hands-on experiment using the Curves command:

Correcting Image with Curves

1. Open the Bride.tif image from the Examples/Chap10 folder on the Companion CD. It's a pretty crummy picture, as you can see in Figure 10.7. The comment in this figure explains the problem areas in the image. Press Ctrl(⌘)+M to open the Curves dialog box.

Whites are dirty, midtones lack contrast, blacks aren't truly black.

Figure 10.7   The midtones have no snap, and there is no true white or black in this image, but the Curves command will shake down this picture.

2. Choose the Black Point Eyedropper tool from the eyedropper tools in the Curves dialog box, and then click an area you feel should be the darkest tone. I'd choose the shadow of the gentleman's tie or a piece of shrubbery in the background that is shaded for the target point for the tool.

3. Choose the White Point Eyedropper tool, and then click in the image where you think pure white should be. The bride's veil is an excellent place to click. In both Step 2 and this one, the Curves dialog box changes the preview image to reflect your changes, but the diagonal line will not change because you've not yet specified a point on it.

4. Click a second time on the White Point Eyedropper button to unselect it. Now you can use this tool to examine the tones in the image, and it won't cause changes in the image.

5. Ctrl(⌘)+click the gentleman's cheek. This should be the midpoint of the image's tones. A marker appears on the diagonal line on the graph.

6. Click and drag directly left in the graph. This increases contrast in the image without making the overall image brighter or darker. See Figure 10.8 for the locations of the cursor in this example.

Figure 10.8   You can change an image's brightness and contrast at up to 15 points with the Curves command. Or you can use the command exactly like the Levels command, and use the eyedropper tools to set white and black points.

7. Click OK to apply the change. You then can choose to save the image, or close it without saving.

We've spent some time taking bad images and turning them into well-behaved ones, but in the following section, you'll see how to take a lousy photo, make it *worse*, and then use certain areas of the picture to make an artistic element in a different photo. It's fun! C'mon…

Working with the Threshold Command

The Threshold command works only on the tones in an image. Expect all color to be lost in a picture when you use this command. The Threshold command forces pixels into one of two camps: black or white. This command can be very useful for determining the edge in a copy of an image or for cleaning up a black-and-white drawing. However, we're going to use the Threshold command shortly as an artistic filter—to create silhouettes.

Here's the story: Suppose that you have a nice sunset picture, but the photo lacks visual detail. The obvious thing to do would be to add elements; but be mindful that because it's a sunset, these elements should have little or no detail—the lighting's too poor. Toss in text as an element; and before you know it, you've got a greeting card that'll floor Mr. Hallmark. The first step is to modify a crummy picture.

Working to Further Degrade a Poorly Exposed Photo

As I mentioned earlier, the Threshold command changes the image information to black or white at any given pixel, and there's a "break point" feature that enables you to control (to a certain extent) which pixels wind up being black or white. The Threshold command works best when there is a clear, unambiguous separation between light and dark areas, and the image you will work with—Candid.tif—is *nearly* perfect for the assignment.

The couple in the picture is definitely not illuminated (I think a flash didn't go off), and the background is. Unfortunately, medium-to-dark areas are scattered through the photo. These areas need to be painted white to reinforce the edge of elements; and if you want to save time duplicating this example, make certain that the foreground elements are in the clear from a light background.

Here's how to prep the image for the Threshold command:

Retouching a Photo for the Threshold Command

1. Open the Candid.tif image from the Examples/Chap10 folder on the Companion CD.

2. Choose the Brush tool, and choose white as the foreground color. On the Options bar, choose the hard round 9-pixel brush tip. The Opacity and Flow should be at 100% and the Mode set at Normal. The goal is to separate the foreground detail of the couple from the background. For example, the man in the photo has the ceiling molding running through his head, and it's a medium color. Paint around his silhouette. Also, you can lose the side of his glasses to the far left (nobody wants a nice silhouette of themselves with glasses!). The bride's veil can be deleted, as shown in Figure 10.9. Bridal veils are not an everyday piece of apparel (although women get *married* every day), and we want a "generi-card," not one linked to weddings.

Figure 10.9 Paint with white around certain areas of the couple's silhouette to make selecting the foreground easier when you use the Threshold command.

3. Choose Image, Adjustments, Threshold. The Threshold dialog box appears; by default, the Threshold Level is set to 128 as the "break point."

4. Drag the slider in the dialog box to about 126, as shown in Figure 10.10. It does *not* matter whether the interiors of the people are completely black or the room is entirely white. What you want is to be able to see the couple's *edges*, and 126 seems to help you do that. Press OK when you've tuned the Threshold command.

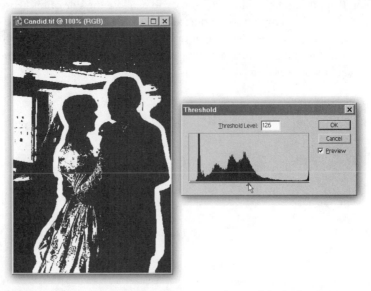

Figure 10.10 Use the Threshold command to create edge work in the image.

5. With the Brush tool and the same tip you used last, start with white and paint away the areas that lie outside the couple.

6. After you've cleaned away the background, switch to black foreground color and fill in areas of the silhouettes that didn't quite qualify to be turned to black, as shown in Figure 10.11. More than likely, you'll find that the bride's white sleeve contains many areas of white among the shading.

Figure 10.11 Use the Brush tool and white and black to retouch the photo so that it truly is a silhouette image.

7. Open the Palm_set.tif image from the Examples/Chap10 folder on the Companion CD. You might not have an image exactly like this in your collection of pictures (mostly because I asked a professional photographer to get me some coverage when he vacationed in Hawaii!), but surely you will come across a breath-taking sunset (and you should take a picture of it) regardless of where you live (except parts of Finland, and Syracuse, NY).

8. With both images in the workspace and a clear, unobstructed view of both windows, use the Move tool to drag a copy of the Candid scene into the Palm_set.tif image, as shown in Figure 10.12. You can close the Candid.tif image now. Save the file to your hard disk if you want (or close without saving changes).

> **Tip**
>
> **Use the Same Scale**   If you want to do this with your own pictures, make sure that all the elements are the same scale. I was careful to blow up the Candid picture after I received the Palm_set image.
>
> In this case, it doesn't matter that you lose visual detail when you enlarge a digital image because the Threshold command is going to further mess up the image detail, anyway.

Figure 10.12   Move a copy of the silhouettes to the Palm_set.tif image.

Now we have two problems: we need to horizontally flip the image because the man's head is too tall and is sticking into the palm tree, and we need to get rid of the white in the Candid layer of the image. The following steps solve these problems:

9. Double-click the Layer 1 title and rename this layer **Candid**. Press Enter (Return) to apply the new name. Choose Edit, Transform, Flip Horizontal, and only the contents of the Candid layer (and not the background) are flipped.

10. With the Candid layer as the active layer on the Layers palette, choose Multiply from the drop-down modes list on the upper left of the palette. Everything that is darker than 128 on a brightness scale will remain the same, but anything lighter will disappear. This is not a permanent state and you can switch back to Normal layer-combining mode anytime you want (but doing this is not part of the plan here).

11. Open the Message.tif image from the Examples/Chap10 folder on the Companion CD. With the Move tool, drag a copy of the message into the Palm_set image, and then choose Screen from the modes drop-down list (on the Layers palette). With Screen mode, lighter colors remain and darker colors drop out, as shown in Figure 10.13. Double-click the Layer 1 title, rename this layer **Message**, and press Enter (Return) to apply the change.

Figure 10.13   Use different layer modes for combining elements whose background is a solid, contrasting color.

12. Last step! Click the Candid layer, and then choose Filter, Blur, Blur. This takes the hard pixel edge off the couple's silhouette. The Threshold command doesn't know squat about anti-aliasing!

13. Either save the layered image as **Bon Voyage** in Photoshop's native format or flatten the image and save it in the TIFF file format. You're finished! Close the image any time now.

Admittedly, the preceding example is more of a design issue than the demonstration of a Photoshop principle. But you did use Photoshop in a creative way (this is good), and the end product of your little experiment is nothing short of a professional creation. I would not be ashamed at all to print a copy of this picture and sneak it into the card rack at the supermarket.

Selective Tonal Adjustments

All we've done with tone shifting up 'til now has been made with a global approach, which means it affects the entire image. But all images are not 100% crummy. Sometimes only *parts* of an image are underexposed or generally less than wonderful.

You can use the Quick Mask feature to encompass only part of an image (and then change only that part of the image). In the steps that follow, you'll work with an image of a child, the right side of whose face is obscured by shadow. You'll create an extremely subtle transition between selected and masked areas, and then use the Levels command to even out the image.

Selectively Restoring an Image

1. Open the Smiley.tif image from the Examples/Chap10 folder on the Companion CD. As you can see in Figure 10.14, it's a well-exposed image, and one side of the child's face is fine. It's the right side of the picture that falls into shade.

Figure 10.14   What do you do when only a part of an image is wrong? You only partially correct it!

2. Press B to switch to the Brush tool. On the Options bar, choose the soft round 100-pixel brush tip, click the Airbrush icon, and set Flow to 50%. The brush size depends on the size of the image you're fixing: 100 pixels for the airbrush works in this example.

3. Press D (default colors), and then click the Edit in Quick Mask Mode icon on the toolbox, as you have so many times before. Everywhere you paint will be selected when you switch back to Edit in Standard Mode.

Fortunately, the Airbrush doesn't leave lines, so your selection work will be based on how you move the cursor around to apply the Quick Mask to areas heavily in shade, tapering off your application of Quick Mask toward the edges of the shaded area where the least selecting needs to happen. Now, in Figure 10.15, I've specified a light white for my Quick Mask tint color. Do not be confused and think I'm whitewashing the image with actual color—it's purely for visibility's sake: you can use the default red tint if you like.

Figure 10.15   Apply Quick Mask tint overlay to the areas that need lightening. The outer edges of the child will need less Quick Mask than her face.

4. Click and drag around the area of the child's face that is most deeply in shadow, and then work your way outward to include the child's apparel and part of her hair (refer to Figure 10.15 as a guide).

5. Press Q to exit Quick Mask mode (or click the Edit in Standard Mode icon to the left of the Quick Mask Mode icon). At the bottom of the Layers palette, click the Create new fill or adjustment layer icon and choose Levels. The selection created earlier automatically limits the area that the Levels command will be applied to (on the new adjustment layer). The "marching ants" selection disappeared, but you can see that it was replaced with the black and white filled areas on the Levels 1 layer mask that now represents the selection.

6. In the Levels dialog box, drag the white point Input slider to about 144, and then drag the midpoint (okay, okay—the *gamma*) slider to about 1.4, as shown in Figure 10.16. Then drag the black point Input slider to about 10 to subtly goose up the blacks in the picture. The whites are whiter on the child, and the midtones show more detail because you're lessening the contrast in the midtones. You know, I didn't even know which relative of mine this was until I performed these steps!

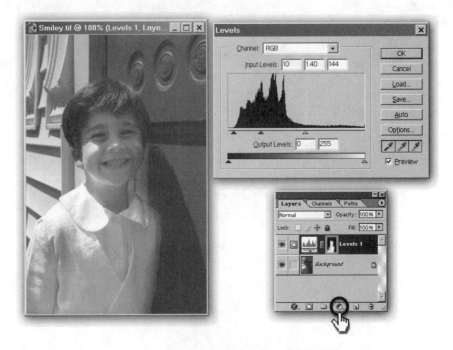

Figure 10.16   Lighten the selected area by using the Input Levels sliders.

7. Press Enter (Return) to return to a beautifully retouched image. Folks who don't use computers don't realize exactly how valuable and powerful tone and color manipulation is with Photoshop. You can save this image if you like or close it without saving changes.

By using an Adjustment layer for the Levels command, you have the flexibility to adjust your selection if it is less than perfect. If you'll look at the Levels 1 layer, you will see a mask thumbnail to the right of the Levels thumbnail. With this mask thumbnail active, use the Airbrush tool to paint additional black color to mask the areas to which you do not want to apply the Levels adjustment. Conversely, paint white in the areas that you want the Levels adjustment to show through.

Tones, tones, tones! Everything has been about correcting tones and we've not yet talked about *color correcting*. We'd better get busy on that topic before we run out of chapter…

Colors, Color Shifting, and Color Correcting

First off, forget everything you learned as a child in school about the "color wheel." This wheel was based on a Mr. "Roy G. Biv," which stood for "red, orange, yellow, green, blue, indigo, and violet." But within the context of our early education, this color wheel worked only for calculating color opposites (blue on the wheel is the opposite of yellow, for example), and basically told us nothing if we wanted to blend these colors together as subtractive pigments or additive colors. The progression of the spectrum was correct; I'll hand our teachers that much.

Ready for some new, improved color wheel stuff? Take a look at Figure 10.17. Aside from the fact that this is a black-and-white plate rather than color (sorry about that), you'll notice some new names for occupants of the color wheel. The spectrum progression in this plate is counter-clockwise—the narrowest frequency is red (as measured in degrees), and cyan is the farthest away from red at 180°; then the color wheel decreases by degree to offer us blue and magenta as we travel counter-clockwise back to red.

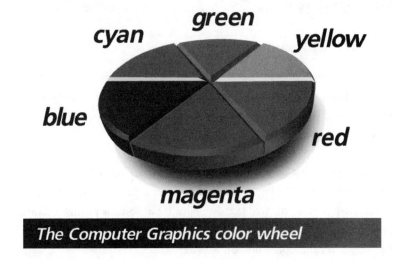

The Computer Graphics color wheel

Figure 10.17   In addition to the traditional color wheel that most of us did not understand in grade school, I offer the computer graphics color wheel, which will make eminent sense in a moment or two.

Every color on the computer color wheel has a complementary color; this is the color's opposite (and what you'd get if you painted a color, marquee selected it, and then pressed Ctrl(⌘)+I to invert the chroma of the color). Also, if you want to produce blue, you mix the neighboring (secondary) colors, cyan and magenta. Cyan, magenta, and yellow are secondary additive colors; and red, green, and blue (as in RGB color) are primary additive colors.

What does this mean to image color correction? Everything! If a color is casting way too much red in an image, you introduce some cyan—the color opposite of red—to neutralize the red.

But enough theory. Let me guide you through color shifting a photograph whose colors are uniformly wrong.

Wielding the Hue/Saturation Command

The Hue/Saturation command is an excellent resource for changing one of the three properties of HSB color. In this experiment, a little thought needs to back up your actions. Here's the story:

I deliberately messed up the Croquet1.tif image. *How* I did it is unimportant, but how to correct it *is* important.

> **Note**
>
> **Detect Before You Correct**   When retouching, find out what's wrong with the image before you dig into your arsenal of tools. The more you learn about the image, the more precisely you can correct it.

What do you see in the image?

- The grass is brown instead of green.
- You can't know this one, so I'll help you here. The light blue ball farthest to the left is greenish cyan, and the ball to the right of the other one is red instead of yellow.

This strongly suggests that all the colors in this image are off. But by how much? Well, let's see. If the color wheel in Figure 10.17 is to serve a purpose, we must use it for the basis of a calculation. Each pie wedge is 60°. Now if pale blue is posing as cyanish-green in this picture, this means that there is (approximately) a 40° to 60° positive shift in the hue of the image. Try this correction on for size:

Hi! How Are Hue Doing?

1. Open the Croquet1.tif image from the Examples/Chap10 folder on the Companion CD.
2. Press Ctrl(⌘)+U to open the Hue/Saturation dialog box. Position the box so that you have a clear view of the image.
3. Drag the Hue slider to about 40°, as shown in Figure 10.18. Figure 10.18 shows nothing of the hue shift, but on your screen you will see a fantastic transformation. The image becomes "correct." You can try 60° if you like, but basically, you've corrected a lousy picture in one step.

Figure 10.18   Take a look at the colors in the image, envision what the correct colors should be, and then rely on the computer color wheel to guide you in correcting the hues.

4. Click OK to apply the change, congratulate yourself several times, and then close the image without saving it, unless you're really into croquet and my wife's foot (hint: you're not).

There's more mayhem afoot as I've goofed around with another version of the same photo. This time, only one color is really off in the image. Oh, what tool to use? Read on!

Using the Variations Command

You probably will use the Variations command often in future color correcting, because this command puts at your fingertips and eyeballs variations on how an image should look, based on hue and range of tone. The command even has an amount slider for subtle changes and a clipping feature.

Tip

Clipping Defined   *Clipping* is used by Adobe in the Variations command context to mean, "The pixels have 100% color, there's no room for any more color, you've gone off the scale, and a fat, monochrome color now takes the place of what used to be tonal subtlety." There are other places in Photoshop where "clipping" is used, but there it describes something other than color overload.

Let's walk through what to do with the Variations command and Croquet2.tif:

Working with Variations

1. Open the Croquet2.tif image from the Examples/Chap10 folder on the Companion CD. As you can see, the grass is either totally browned out or the developing liquid used on this picture was from 1954.

2. Choose Image, Adjustments, Variations. To give you a clue on to how to correct this image, crank the Fine/Coarse slider all the way up to exaggerate the colors in the examples in the dialog box.

We can see two possibilities here for color replacement, and we might use both. Notice that the More Cyan thumbnail comes closest to a realistically lit outdoor picture. Cyan, if you treat the thumbnails like our color wheel, is the opposite of red, and red certainly predominates in the image.

3. Now drag the Fine/Coarse slider about one click to the right of the middle of the slider. Click the More Cyan thumbnail. Surprise! The picture with the title Current Pick looks a lot more attractive, but the More Blue box looks better still. This happens because you need to get rid of not only some red but also some yellow in the image. See Figure 10.19 to learn where this is leading.

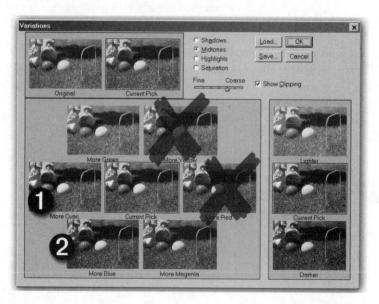

Figure 10.19 Got a color casting problem? Solve it by introducing color opposites into the photo.

4. Click on the More Blue thumbnail. The picture looks pretty perfect now, so click OK to apply the changes.

5. Now you can save the image or simply close it without saving.

You've experienced the thrill of hue shifting and color opposite replacement so far. It's time now to introduce the third color casting control feature in Photoshop.

Working with the Color Balance Command

Okay, the final color-correcting feature is called the Color Balance command. Unlike other color features in Photoshop, you can go back and undo a color shift with this command. Why? Because you're changing the relationship between opposite colors—you're adding a little of this by subtracting an equal amount of that. So although this command might not be as intuitive as the Variations command, it has some good points:

Note

Pixel Color Changes   All changes you make to pixel color are *progressive* changes. In other words, there's no way back to an original image to which you've applied three or four changes, except by using the History palette. Pixels by their nature cannot be restored by using an equal amount of opposite color. It's all change based on change, as you saw in the previous section with the Variations command. You didn't know that you'd need to add blue until you'd first subtracted red (added cyan).

1. There are fewer controls to mess with.

2. Adobe gave us a hot key to display the command's dialog box immediately.

So without further ado:

Working with the Color Balance Features

1. Open the Croquet3.tif image from the Examples/Chap10 folder on the Companion CD. Unlike Croquet2.tif, this image appears to have been left near a sunny window for a decade, until there's no pigment left except shades of magenta.

2. Press Ctrl(⌘)+B to display the Color Balance dialog box.

3. Examine (*detect*) which tonal range is most affected by this bad color casting. The problem appears to be in the midtones; and by default, the Midtones button is already clicked, so this one's gonna be a breeze. This allows the highlight and shadow areas to be unaffected while you experiment (*correct*).

4. Drag the Magenta/Green slider way to the Green end, to about +95. The image looks a lot better now, but after removing this ton of magenta, we can see that the image also is too green.

5. Drag the Yellow/Blue slider to about –73, as shown in Figure 10.20. You'll see that on your screen the image is looking very natural, very freshly taken, instead of being mired in colors best suited for bicycle safety helmets.

Figure 10.20   Use the Color Balance sliders to shift a particular color in a particular range of
tone toward its color opposite on the computer color wheel.

6. Click OK to apply the changes, and then either save the image to your hard disk
or close it without saving.

This color and tone stuff wasn't too hard to understand, was it? As long as you understand *why* computer displays behave (or misbehave) the way they do, everything you
need to change revolves around the RGB color space. And as we've gleefully ignored that
color model in favor of HSB color space, we are assured that because RGB and HSB
engender the same color space, we're not making weird demands of Photoshop or the
system, and we're making large strides toward improving the quality of poorly taken pictures. Do you smell a career in here someplace? You should!

Summary

Colors are as important as selections when it comes to digital imaging. Manipulation of
both can lead to stunning photographic retouching work. In the next two chapters, you
will put what you've learned in this section of the book to work by restoring and enhancing an heirloom photograph—you will see how to perform the digital equivalent of a
craft that formerly required years of experience.

Chapter 11

Restoring an Heirloom Photograph

Traditional photographic retouching was

an art on the wane before the advent of

digital sampling of images and Adobe

Photoshop. At its best, traditional image

restoration was performed by a gifted craftsman with a background in both illustration and photography, whose tools included a magnifying glass, a collection of brushes, and semitransparent dyes. And the price commanded for such work could set your family back an amount equivalent to a new fridge or an air conditioner. At its worst, image restoration could ruin the original photo or make the photo's subjects look as though they were created from shiny plastic. Airbrushes, in the wrong hands, tend to do this kind of stuff.

In this chapter and Chapter 12, "Retouching an Heirloom Photograph," you work through the restoration, retouching, and enhancement of an image that a traditional photo retoucher would probably dismiss as damaged beyond repair. If you have an image of your own, get it out of the shoebox. You will see shortly that image recovery is well within your grasp, because the word *traditional* simply doesn't apply to the power found in Photoshop.

The image you will work with in this chapter is Lee.tif, found in the Examples/Chap11 folder on the Companion CD. The original image—photographed more than 30 years ago—fell victim to a house fire, subsequent water damage, somewhat less-than-optimal care during the salvage process after the fire, and has perhaps suffered least of all from aging through the passing years.

The first thing to do when you take on an assignment as demanding as the restoration of an image is to acquire a digital copy of it. In the case of Lee's picture, there was no image negative, and therefore the print had to be scanned. If you *do* own the film negative or positive (color slide) of a photo you want to restore, you should make arrangements with a photo-finisher to get it scanned and copied to a CD-ROM—pronto. The scanned image then becomes one generation closer to the original image, and you have more image content to use. *Reflective scans*—those performed with flatbed scanners—cannot capture from a photograph all the original image information that is contained in a negative or positive. Negative-scanning hardware (called *film scanners*) used to be very expensive. Like the rest of the scanner hardware market, their prices have fallen dramatically, and even top-end film scanners, such as Nikon's CoolScan series, can be purchased for a very reasonable price. One last note on this subject: several of today's film scanners offer a built-in powerful feature called Digital ICE[3] (pronounced *ice-cubed*), which provides powerful and automatic restoration of some of the worst slides and negatives imaginable.

Scanning Modes and Resolution

Regardless of whether a photo is color or grayscale (or a sepia tone image), you should acquire the digital sample of the image in RGB Color mode. RGB Color mode parallels the color capability of human vision, and you need as much original image information sampled as possible to restore the digital copy of the photo.

Image resolution—the number of pixels (*picture elements*)—should be defined as the greatest amount of digital information your system can handle. The fewer the samples (pixels) per inch at which you scan, the less original information is translated to digital image format—and you want every pixel you can get to mend the photo. The Lee.tif image is a modest 1.8MB in size, and the authors do *not* recommend that you scan to achieve this small file size unless your system has modest RAM and processor specs. The techniques shown here are valuable ones, and we were a little skimpy on the Lee.tif image's saved file size to enable you—no matter what the capabilities of your computer might be—to follow along.

Generally, you should scan an image so that it will be at the correct physical size for the final resolution of the piece as printed. Image restoration is an *exception* to that rule, however; scan at a resolution with which you can work comfortably in Photoshop. You then can make a copy of the retouched piece at different resolutions for output as necessary in the future. For photo restoration work, we recommend that you consider having the scanner scale for your photo to be 200% of whatever is to be the final size. When you are finished with the restoration, it is a simple matter to resample the image to the correct size.

Become a Detective Before Retouching

The term *re-creation* often is used to describe an event in which actors play out an historic scene from the American Revolution, or a monologue delivered by someone in makeup and clothes patterned after information about Mark Twain. Clearly, to preserve the fidelity of the image being conveyed, re-creation requires some research.

Because image restoration depends upon adding to areas of the original image that are beyond recovery, you should thoroughly examine the original before you pick up the Brush tool. Where are the problem areas? Which areas of the image can you resample to mend damaged areas? In essence, the details that are not damaged in the current image should give you an indication of the style needed for areas that *are* damaged.

In Figure 11.1, you can see two views of the Lee image. Open the file in Photoshop, and take a good look at different viewing resolutions. A superficial examination shows a crease running through the little girl's hair, water stains that have discolored her skirt, and many pinholes (dots of pure white) that are a combination of careless original printing (you're supposed to clean negatives before you print them), and dust that could not be removed because of the fragility of the print.

Figure 11.1   Examine the image you want to restore first for obvious problems and then for not-so-obvious ones.

Certain areas of the image are simply missing—areas of the hair, the background, and Lee's skirt need to be added to blend not only with the image content, but also with the grain and the focus of the photograph. In the following sections, we examine these issues more closely and reveal how to deal with each restoration challenge.

A Shallow Plane of Focus Was Used

If you look carefully at the image, you can see that Lee's face is in near-perfect focus, but the focus of the image drops off severely toward her hair and her hands. This lack of focus in image areas could have been done as an artistic effect or it could have been caused by the lack of light and the type of camera used. For example, the *f-stop*—the depth of field used to capture an image—was not easy to define with focal plane (also called *portrait*) cameras in the 1950s.

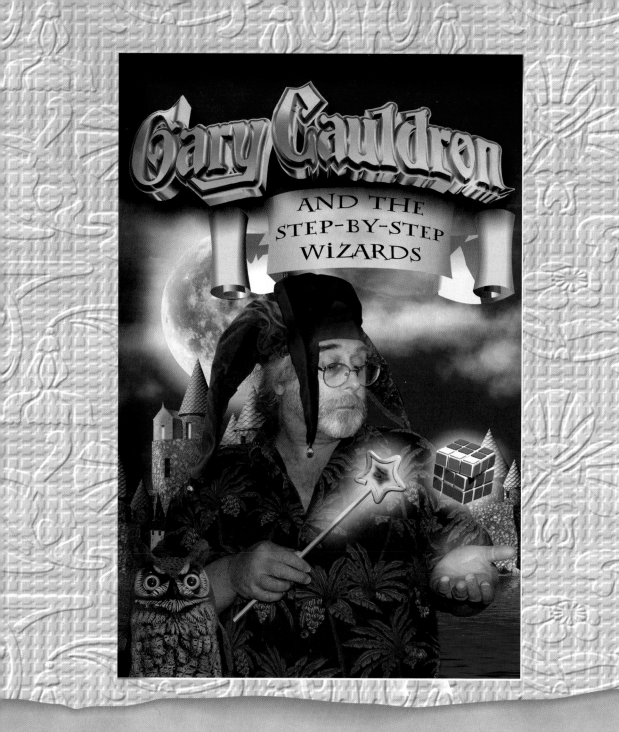

"Gary Cauldron" In Chapter 22, "Gary Cauldron and Photoshop Tricks," you'll find not one, but 10 whole sets of tricks you can perform in your work, all of which go way beyond simple retouching. Gary explains the retouching that goes behind the most professional imaging efforts.

Artist: Gary David Bouton

"Roswell" Imagine a little green man who lands on earth from another planet in 1947 and an ensuing cover-up. Sounds like a great idea for a retro comic book! Chapter 15, "Out of This World A.R.T (Advanced Rendering Techniques)" covers advanced techniques for painting the alien named Roswell, with a surprisingly small amount of actual painting. (In other words, you don't need to be da Vinci to try this chapter.)

Artists: Robert Stanley and Bill Morrison

"Picnic"   Chapter 1, "Getting Creative When You Have No Idea What You're Doing," takes you to a mysterious and funky picnic where *a lot* of things look wrong. Don't panic! The characters don't know what they're doing, and neither do you. We offer suggestions on how to retouch—this is your initiation to the world of Photoshop tools.

Artist: Gary David Bouton

"Restoring and Retouching an Heirloom Image" In Chapter 11, "Restoring an Heirloom Photograph" and Chapter 12, "Retouching an Heirloom Photograph," you gain first-hand experience from the masters of Photoshop in bringing a ruined heirloom photo back to life and making it even *better* than new! These chapters contain the techniques to use the most if you want to make a career out of photo-restoration.

Artist: Gary David Bouton

"We Come in Peace"   This image has absolutely nothing to do with the book, except that you can find cool Alien Skin plug-ins on the CD, and the Alien Skin Software staff goes to work in attire you *wish* you could wear to the office. Find out more in Appendix A, "The *Inside Photoshop 7* CD-Rom" and see Alien Skin's ad in the back of the book.

Artist: Gary David Bouton

"Splash" In Chapter 14, "Bringing Out the Artist in You," Robert Stanley shows you how to paint over photographs. If you freeze at the thought of creating a painting in Photoshop, this chapter is for you! Art ability isn't needed, but by the time you're finished, you may feel so creative that you might be tempted to cut off your ear (but let's *not* and say we did).

Artist: Robert Stanley

"Dave and Dave, Gare and Gare"   Guess what? This chapter isn't in the book! The mysterious and tantalizing Chapter X, "Creating Impossible Images" is a free sample of the books contents, and you can find it on the web at the *Inside Photoshop 7* page of http://www.newriders.com. By the way, these are *not* images of twins!

Artist: Gary David Bouton

"Lysander Park" Aww, some reprobate put graffiti on Lysander Park's statue commemorating how much pollination goes on in town. No problem. In Chapter 6 "Using the Clone Tool, Healing Brush Tool, and Patch Tool," you learn how to remove Mars (and Venus...I'm *kidding*) and repair images in a whole new way with version 7 tools.

Artist: Gary David Bouton

"Piper" Ever want to reach out and grasp a particularly inviting color scheme and save it as your own? Well—you can! In Chapter 22, Trick 2:"Borrowing an Image's Color Palette," you create a palette from an image and then apply it to a different image!

Artist: Gary David Bouton

"Everything that has to do with water
in your back yard"
—Since Early 1998

"Spare Me! Lanes and Paul's Pools"   In Chapter 17, "Special Effects with Type," you'll learn how to scale, bend, and generally make a special effect out of a short phrase. This is the stuff that award-winning headlines are made of, dear reader, so put a bookmark somewhere at the two-thirds point in this book!

Artist: Gary David Bouton

Pearing off.

There has been an age-old argument over which is the better snack fruit: it's apples versus pears. I personally like pears more, and I'll tell you why. My grandmother had a pear tree, and my father had an apple tree. Every summer, my grandmother told me to pick up a pear and eat it, while my father told me all fall to pick up the apples that had fallen in the back yard.

"Pearing Off"   In Chapter 17, "Special Effects with Type", you'll learn how to perform a text wrap around the pear in this image—usually something you can only do with a desktop publishing program. Photoshop's type features have vastly improved, and the authors have vastly improved—do yourself a favor and check out Chapter 17.

Artist: Gary David Bouton

"Lucky Star"   This image might look like a painting, but it began as a modeled photorealistic scene. If you want to turn a photo into a painting, it's easy in Photoshop 7. Just follow the guidelines created for you in Chapter 22, Trick 5: "Making a Painting from a Photo."

Artist: Gary David Bouton

"Lemon" Believe it or not, this is a painting done in Photoshop—all the geometry is derived from paths you can create. Chapter 13, "Using Paths," goes beyond paths. Paths are great—but what are they great for? Find the answers in Chapter 13.

Artist: Mara Zebest Nathanson

"ImageReady Animation" Without a doubt, J. Scott Hamlin is the master of web effects and elements. In Chapter 20, "Animation," you get a totally fresh outlook on how to create small gems of animation using the new version of Photoshop and ImageReady.

Artist: J. Scott Hamlin

"Photoshop Scripting Art" Yes, you can create these spirals and a whole lot more with the scripts provided on the Companion CD for Chapter 21, "Scripting and Actions." Scripting is new to Photoshop, but it has a very powerful beginning. Let Scott Balay take you on a guided tour of the new capabilities in Photoshop for scripting, and oh yes...actions!

Artist: Scott Balay

"Julian Floats" Chapter 22, Trick 1: "Julian Floats" is a humdinger. We've found that approximately 48% of our audience wants to know how to do head transplants and 43% want to know how to make a person or object fly. Hey 43%, here's your wish come true! Check out Chapter 22, and yes that is Gary and Barbara's nephew.

Artist: Gary David Bouton

This lack of focus will make areas of Lee's hair difficult to restore, and the course of action in Photoshop will be to add strands of hand-painted hair to the finished image.

It's Not a Color Image

When an image is damaged as severely as Lee's image was, it's difficult to tell whether the color in the image is natural or was added to the photo. Certainly, you can see some color in this image if you open Lee.tif in Photoshop. But was this a color image or a grayscale image that was hand-tinted?

If you zoom the image to more than 300%, you can see that the edges of Lee's profile are indistinct, suggesting that a tinted wash of color dye was used to color a grayscale version of this photo. Additionally, it seems suspicious that a 3-year-old in the 1950s would wear makeup. When asked whether she had put lipstick on her child for the photographic session, Lee's mom said, "No."

This is wonderful news, at least pertaining to the reconstruction of the image. To retouch a grayscale image, you need to match only 256 tones (max), compared to the 16.7 unique colors possible in a color image. The color content of this image will be discarded in the restoration technique.

Inconsistent Noise Is in the Image

There are three reasons for *noise*, which we'll define as the uneven dispersal of random-colored pixels in the digital image. The first is the hand-tinting. The dyes used became separated either because of age and abuse or were not mixed evenly. There are particles in some areas on the surface of the photo, but other areas are unaffected.

Scanning itself can produce noise in an image. When you are scanning at high resolutions (usually greater than 600 dpi), the particles in photographic emulsion sometimes can reflect off the scanning element at an odd angle, producing noncontiguous zones of shading in the digitally acquired image. Also, the age of the photograph plays heavily into the noise present in the file of the scan. Scanners are extremely sensitive to changes in surface brightness, and the emulsion used in photographic imaging ages inconsistently. As you can see in Figure 11.2, a close-up of Lee's right cheek shows noise caused by at least two of the factors described. Although noise might not be apparent at 1:1 viewing resolutions, it will interfere with the process of restoring image areas. The trick is to decide how much noise to filter from the image, and how much remain to preserve photographic integrity.

Lee.TIF @ 200% (RGB)

Lee.TIF @ 700% (RGB)

Noise from age and from scanning

Figure 11.2   An uneven amount of noise in the digital image makes it difficult to blend
new areas into the photograph.

The sections that follow in this chapter demonstrate different techniques for restoring
the image. You will learn more about the overall process if you work through this chapter from start to finish. Many examples in this book illustrate a principle; and with the
Lee.tif image, we recommend that you actually follow (which means *do*) the steps to
build your Photoshop technique in addition to your knowledge.

Different Approaches for Different Problem Areas

Obviously, the first target in this image is Lee's hair. Thanks to a noticeable crack in the
original photo's emulsion, her hair seems to be parted horizontally. Additionally, the pinholes in the image distract terribly from the image content, and the water stains in the
image force the viewer to look at the surface of the picture instead of looking *into* it, to
see the pretty girl. Each flaw in the image requires a different set of steps, a different
Photoshop tool here and there, and a different conceptualization of what should appear
in the finished image.

Changing Color Modes, Edgework, and Restoring the Hair

As mentioned earlier, the camera focus threw edges of Lee's hair into a blobby mass on photographic paper. Notice that the edge between her hair and the backdrop is actually a gradual transition between foreground and background. A soft-tipped tool can address the problem of restoring the edges, and Photoshop's Clone Stamp tool can make quick work of cloning areas of Lee's hair into the damaged areas.

Here's how to remove the crease from Lee's hair:

Stamping Out Photo Flaws

1. Open the Lee.tif image from the Examples/Chap11 folder on the Companion CD if you have not already done so.

2. Maximize the window area for the document, and then type **200** in the Zoom text box at the lower left of the status bar (Macintosh: the bottom left of the scroll bar) and then press Enter (Return). If retouching looks okay at 200%, it will surely look fine at Actual Pixels setting (100%), normal viewing, and lower resolutions.

3. Press the spacebar to toggle to the Hand tool, and pan your view of the image so that Lee's hair is centered onscreen.

4. Choose Image, Mode, Lab Color. Press F7 to display the Layers\Channels\Paths palette if it isn't already onscreen.

5. Click the Channels tab and then click the Lightness channel title. Choose Image, Mode, Grayscale from the menu, and click OK in the attention box that tells you that the other channels will be discarded. You have a faithful grayscale represen-tation of the original image now. The document is also ⅓ the original file size.

6. Choose the Clone Stamp tool from the toolbox. On the Options bar, make sure that Opacity is set to 100%, painting mode is Normal (from the modes drop-down list), and the Style for the tool is set to Clone (aligned). Choose the soft 21-pixel tip brush from the Brushes palette (right-click) or from the Options bar.

7. Press Alt(Opt) and click in an undamaged highlight area of Lee's hair to specify the sample area in the image from which you will clone into damaged areas. In the Clone (aligned) style, the sampling point travels as you apply the Clone Stamp tool to different image areas.

8. Drag the Clone Stamp tool across an area damaged by the crease (see Figure 11.3). You should definitely follow the angle of the strands of Lee's hair. In other words, if you sample from the highlight area where the strands arc clockwise, apply this area only to an image area in which strands also arc clockwise.

Figure 11.3   Damaged hair can be restored by using a good conditioner...or the Clone Stamp tool.

9. You'll eventually run out of sampling areas with the Clone Stamp tool; with the Clone (aligned) Option, the sampling point travels in tandem with the cursor. At that point, press Alt(Opt) and click a different area from which to sample the hair; then continue melding the cloned strokes with the undamaged hair areas.

10. When the curve of the hair strands changes direction, resample the Clone Stamp tool in an area that shows similar curves; then stroke into the damaged area to restore it.

11. When you reach the edge where the hair meets the backdrop, press Alt(Opt) and click an undamaged hair area on the edge between hair and backdrop. Make certain that this sampling point is very similar to the damaged area; otherwise, the curve of the hair silhouette will not be correct. Instead of dragging in this small area, simply click the tool over the damaged area. The Clone Stamp tool provides a circular "burst" of replacement cloning, and you eliminate the problem of cloning into an area you do not want to change.

12. Choose File, Save As, and save the image to your hard disk as Lee.tif in the TIFF file format.

Clone Stamp tool corrections are much easier to make in Grayscale mode than in a color image. Hair, for example, often contains many shades of color, but you can retouch hair successfully in Grayscale mode by using only similar brightness values. In your own work, scout around for an image to find similar patterns for replacements. In a surprisingly large number of images, you can mend a not-so-perfect area by copying a perfectly good image area to it.

Advanced Editing with the Clone Stamp Tool

The water stains on Lee's right cheek are easy to correct when the image is in Grayscale mode. One problem in retouching skin is that the human body is composed of many different types of skin, each with a unique coloration. Additionally, the shading caused by light striking human skin is usually fairly steep in transitional areas such as the cheeks and the nose or anywhere the topology of a face curves and twists. But wait—there's more bad news. Because there's noise in the affected area, simply painting over the stain with the Brush or Airbrush option is out of the question. You need to match the tone *and* the noise to fix the stained area.

The authors tried several techniques to remove the water stain, and finally arrived at a novel solution. We measured the brightness value near the stained area and then defined the Clone Stamp tool's sampling point at an identical brightness area in the image. This technique requires using incredibly short strokes, but it also gives you the opportunity to experiment with the usefulness of Photoshop's Info palette.

Here's how to get the toughest stains out of an image:

Calculating Brightness with the Info Palette

1. The easiest way to zoom to 300% viewing resolution in the image is to click once with the Zoom tool in the document window. Next, hold the spacebar to toggle to the Hand tool, and pan your view so that you can see Lee's left cheek centered in the window.

2. Press F8 to display the Info palette. Click the eyedropper flyout on the upper-left field of the palette, and choose Grayscale from the flyout menu (see Figure 11.4). The Info palette offers dual displays so that you can see pixel colors displayed simultaneously in different color modes (RGB and CMYK, for example). Because all you need now is Grayscale information, adjusting both areas on the palette is not necessary in this example.

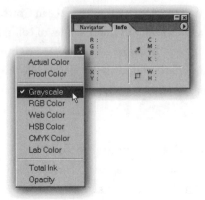

Figure 11.4   The color mode you specify on the Info palette determines the pixel color
displayed under your cursor at all times.

3. Move the cursor to an area extremely close to (but not directly on) the water
   stain in the image. Figure 11.5 shows a good target location for the cursor. You
   can use any tool to get color information. (The Eyedropper tool was used in this
   figure to visually reinforce a point.) You'll see that 12% to 13% black seems to
   be the tone surrounding the water stain that obscures the image area.

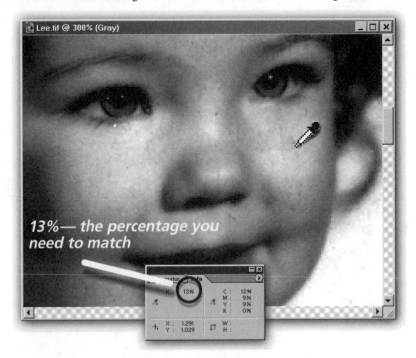

Figure 11.5   The Info palette indicates the brightness of the location over which
your cursor is located.

4. Choose the Clone Stamp tool; then, with the same Options palette settings you used earlier, hover the cursor over Lee's right cheek. Although the lighting is slightly different, the same general geometry and the way light casts on the cheek make it a suitable cloning source location. When the Info palette tells you that your cursor is over a location that is within one or two percent of 12%, press Alt(Opt) and click to define the sample point.

5. Click, don't drag, the water stain area (see Figure 11.6). The water stain is replaced by a sampled area of the same brightness as surrounding image areas, and it also contains the same type of image noise. Notice that three or four separate water stains appear on Lee's left cheek. Take a brightness reading from the other areas close to the water stains, sample other areas on Lee's right cheek, and restore these water-stained areas.

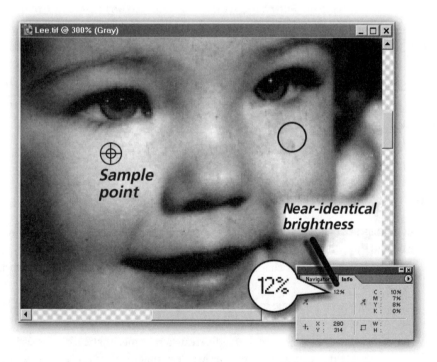

Figure 11.6 Match the Clone Stamp tool's sampling point to the brightness near the stained image areas.

6. Press Ctrl(⌘)+S to save your work.

The Clone Stamp tool is terrific for mending small areas of detail in an image, but a different strategy must be adopted when there are small flaws in a larger image area. The next section addresses solutions for reducing noise in the image.

Tip

Alternative Mending Procedures…Sometimes In addition to the Clone Stamp tool, you also can restore areas using the Patch tool. The Clone Stamp tool produces better results than the Patch tool for the restoration in this example. Always leave yourself open to multiple solutions for single problems, however.

Using the Dust & Scratches Filter

The name *Dust & Scratches Filter* suggests that this filter is a magic tool for removing pinholes and other areas of sudden pixel color changes in a digital image. In fact, the Dust & Scratches filter can *introduce* noise to an image; what the filter does depends on the type of image area in which you work, and the settings you specify for the filter. The Dust & Scratches filter is used in the following set of steps to soften the noise on the left side of Lee's face, but not to eliminate the noise completely, because a smooth, flawless area looks artificial next to other areas that display some degree of noise. The trick is not to highlight a perfectly corrected area, but to restore an image to the highest quality displayed in the original.

Here's how to tone down the noise on Lee's left cheek:

Averaging Brightness Differences

1. Press Ctrl(⌘)+– (minus key) to zoom the document to 200%. (This is the third method described in this chapter for zooming in and out; use the one that works best for you.)

2. Hold the spacebar to toggle to the Hand tool, and then drag in the document to pan your view to the right cheek area.

3. Choose the Lasso tool, and then drag to create a marquee that encompasses Lee's temple, the right cheek, and the part of her neck that displays noise. Peek ahead at Figure 11.7 to see the location and shape of the marquee selection.

4. Right-click (Macintosh: hold Ctrl and click), and then choose Feather from the context menu. In the Feather selection box, type **5** in the Feather Radius field; click OK to apply the feathering to the selection. Depending on the overall image size in your own retouching work, you might need a higher or lower amount for the Feathering. The number 5 works in this example to make a gradual transition between the interior of the marquee, which will be filtered, and the exterior of the marquee, whose pixels will not be changed.

5. Choose Filter, Noise, Dust & Scratches.

6. Type **2** in the Radius field. Photoshop will search by 2 pixels in distance to sample and reassign pixel brightness to bring the out-of-place, noisy pixels back to a brightness displayed by most of the other pixels in the selection.

7. Drag the Threshold slider to about 6 (see Figure 11.7). The Threshold determines how similar in brightness value pixels must be to qualify for filtering. The higher the value, the more subtle the filtering effect, because more original brightness values are included in Photoshop's calculations. Lower Threshold values produce posterization (ugly, banded areas instead of smooth photographic tone transitions) in the selected image area.

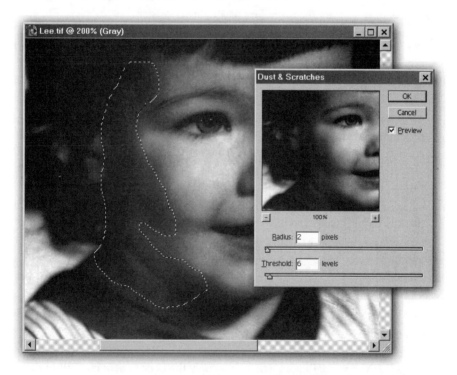

Figure 11.7 Use the Dust & Scratches filter to reduce, but not totally eliminate, noise in the selected area.

8. Click OK to apply the filter, press Ctrl(⌘)+D to deselect the marquee, and then press Ctrl(⌘)+S to save your work. Keep the image open in Photoshop.

One or two other areas in the Lee.tif image can benefit from the technique described in the preceding steps. Look around the image, and reduce the noise in selected areas to blend them into the original image areas.

Using Different Selection Techniques

Restoring this image has led the authors to conclude that the way in which a selection marquee is defined is as important as the steps used to retouch or replace the selections. In the steps that follow, the pinholes on Lee's skirt and the water stains at the bottom of the image are removed by first *partially* selecting the affected areas. The Dust & Scratches filter and the Clone Stamp tool then are used to mend the selected areas.

Photoshop's Quick Mask mode gives you the opportunity to *partially select* areas—that is, to make a selection of partial opacity. When you then apply the effect, it only partially affects the image area. The result is a subtle retouching effect with some of the noise in the image retained to keep the overall image quality consistent.

Here's how to restore the pinhole areas in the image:

Using Quick Mask to Define Areas

1. You want the areas you mask over to be selected areas. Therefore, if the Quick Mask icon on the bottom of the toolbox looks like a filled circle inside an empty rectangle, just click it—you're all set to go. If the Quick Mask icon looks like an empty circle inside a filled rectangle, however, Alt(Opt)+click it. Doing this reverses the selection/masking state of the feature and puts you in Quick Mask mode.

2. Click the foreground color selection box on the toolbox, and choose a medium black from the color picker. In the B field of the HSB area on the color picker, type **40** (a value that will work in this example). Press Enter (Return) to close the color picker.

3. Press **B** (Brush tool), and then click the hard 13-pixel brush tip on the Brushes Options bar.

4. Hold the spacebar and drag upward in the document window to pan your view so that you can see the skirt area of the image.

5. Click areas in the image where you see pinholes (see Figure 11.8). You have more latitude in the strength with which you apply the Dust & Scratches filter; the selections made in Quick Mask mode are only a little more than half-strength, which means that you can apply stronger filtering while retaining some of the original image content.

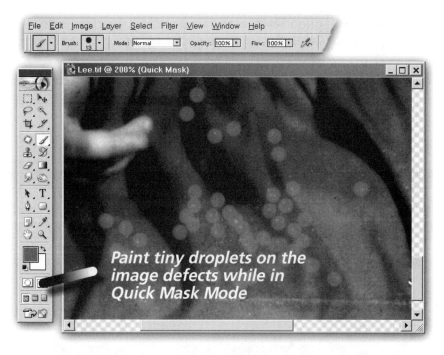

Figure 11.8   The percentage of black with which you define Quick Mask overlay determines the opacity of the selection area.

6. When you are finished painting all the pinhole areas, click the Edit in Standard Mode icon to the left of the Quick Mask mode icon to display onscreen the selections you have created as a marquee ("marching ants").

7. Press Ctrl(⌘)+H to hide the marquee. In the filter dialog box, in preview, you need to compare the areas to be filtered with the original image areas—and marquees are generally a visual distraction. The hidden marquee is still active; you simply have no onscreen reminder of it.

8. Press Ctrl(⌘)+Alt(Opt)+F to access the dialog box for the last-used filter—the Dust & Scratches filter—without actually launching the last-used filter settings.

9. Drag the Radius slider to 3, and then drag the Threshold slider to 11. Look at the preview window in the Dust & Scratches dialog box. Play with the controls here; now is the time for experimenting on an image that you're not getting paid to retouch! When the pinholes have vanished in the preview window, click OK to apply the effect.

10. Press Ctrl(⌘)+D to deselect the marquee selection, press Ctrl(⌘)+S to save your work, and keep the image open in Photoshop.

Using the Clone Stamp tool, you can clone over the water stains at the bottom of the image. Here's how to approach this restoration area:

Replacing Water-Stained Areas

1. Scroll the document window to the bottom, and click the Edit in Quick Mask Mode icon (or press Q); then, with the Brush tool, apply Quick Mask to the stained areas (peek ahead to Figure 11.9 to see which areas to select). Press Q to exit Quick Mask mode and view the marching ant selections.

2. Choose the Clone Stamp tool, find an area close to one of the selected areas, and then press Alt(Opt) and click to define the sampling point of the Clone Stamp tool.

3. Drag in the selection area to replace the stained area (see Figure 11.9). Each stain obscures different tones in the image. Before moving to a different, isolated selection, be sure to resample with the Clone Stamp tool an area that is close in color tone to the selection area.

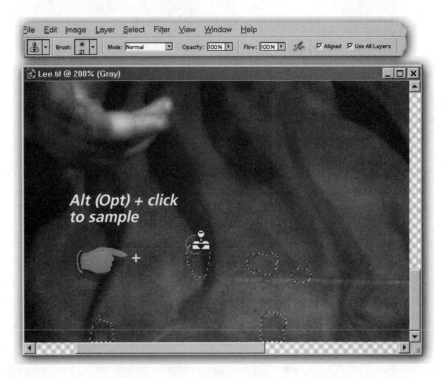

Figure 11.9 Sample areas close to the area you're working to ensure tonal consistency as you restore the image.

4. Press Ctrl(⌘)+S to save your work; keep the document open in Photoshop.

As you work toward the bottom of the image, you will see a horizontal streak running the width of the image. Some areas do not require retouching, but the more obvious streak areas pose a problem. There is much variation in image detail, and none of the techniques you have used so far will mend the streak invisibly. So, it is now time to bring out the Healing Brush.

Copying Image Areas

The Healing Brush tool essentially serves as a local copying tool; you pick and apply samples by using a kind of onscreen paintbrush. You might find, however, that simply copying an image area and pasting it into a damaged area can be quicker and can provide results that other techniques don't provide.

Tip

Healing Brush Versus Clone Stamp   The main difference between the Healing Brush and the Clone Stamp tools is that the Healing Brush adds the lighting and texture of the scene to the painted-over area; the Clone Stamp tool does not. Also, the Healing Brush is good for strips of offending image areas, but not for large, wide image areas.

In the following set of steps, you'll repair the streak in the image using the Healing Brush tool.

Applying the Healing Brush tool

1. Choose the Healing Brush tool from the toolbox. Locate the far left end of the streak and Alt(Opt)+click to sample just below the line formed by the streak.
2. Now click and drag the Healing Brush tool over the streak.
3. Press Ctrl(⌘)+S to save your work, and then close the image.

Fortunately, the folds in the skirt help disguise any repeating pattern in the replacement work. If the skirt itself had a pattern, you would need to carefully align that pattern, as well as the folds in the fabric.

Replacing the Image Background

If you've read this far, you have at your disposal many of the methods for image restoration and can use them with your own images or on client images. In this example, however, you have reached a crossroad—how should you handle the backdrop in Lee.tif, which still shows signs of age and abuse? Should you invest the time in retouching an area that amounts to a blank space? Or would it be easier to replace the background instead of cloning, blurring, and finessing this nonessential area?

The next sections show you how to create an accurate selection around the silhouette of Lee. You then can separate the background from the areas you have modified and add a suitable replacement image to the picture.

Becoming a Virtual Hair Stylist

Hair is perhaps the most difficult photographic detail to define accurately, because its appearance on film is inconsistent—in highlight areas it appears sharp, and as light on it diminishes, it loses clear focus. To compound the restoration challenges in Lee.tif, the edges of her hair have been further thrown out of focus by the camera.

Because much of the general shape of the hair will be masked in the image, our approach to defining the hair from the backdrop is unique—we separate the image from the backdrop. In Chapter 12, strands of hair are painted along the selection outline to replicate the soft appearance of hair falling out of focus at the edges. A possible stumbling block in the retouching work is that the grayscale copy of Lee contains less visual information than the color original, especially around the edges of her hair. To avoid this potential problem, you begin the selection definition work by opening a copy of the *original* color image from the Companion CD. Because Photoshop enables you to copy a mask from one image to another, provided that the two files have identical pixel dimensions, you define the selection on the image that shows the clearest detail, and then copy the saved mask to the grayscale image.

Here's how to begin the selection definition:

Quick Masking at Different Opacities

1. Open the Lee.tif image from the Examples/Chap11 folder on the Companion CD. Save the color image to your hard disk in the TIFF file format, as Original color image.tif.

2. Zoom to 300% viewing resolution in the document, and maximize the document window so that it takes up the full screen. Hold the spacebar to toggle to the Hand tool, and pan your view so that you can see clearly the right side of Lee's hair.

3. Click the Quick Mask icon to put the image into Quick Mask mode, choose the Brush tool, and then choose the 13-pixel soft tip on the Brushes palette of the Options bar. Press D (Default Colors) to ensure that the current foreground color is black.

4. Drag the Brush along the outside edge of Lee's hair. Don't hesitate to overlap the edge, traveling toward the inside of the hair. Because the edge of the tip is soft and anti-aliased, and the hair is out of focus, areas at the edge that display Quick Mask are partially selected (see Figure 11.10).

Figure 11.10   Work toward the inside edge with the Brush tool. The edges of the hair are soft, as is the Brush tip.

5. When you finish Quick Masking the edge as far as you can with this view of the document, hold the spacebar and drag upward in the document window to see additional unmasked areas.

6. Continue painting the outside edge of the hair. When you reach the area of soft, out-of-focus hair to the right of her eye, press **5** on the numeric keypad to decrease the opacity of the Brush tool to 50%. Each keypad number represents 10% increments of Opacity on the Options bar, and zero equals 100% Opacity. Stroke the faint areas of Lee's hair. Hair that is light and out-of-focus should be partially selected, using the Opacity setting for the Brush tool, because you want only part of this hair to be visible after you replace the original backdrop with a new image.

Tip

Entering Opacity   If 20%, 30% and so on don't cut it in Step 6, and you want to get really fussy with the opacity for the brush, type any *two* numbers—for example, typing **53** will change the opacity to 53%.

7. Continue to partially select the hair in Quick Mask mode. Remember that there are different opacities of hair in the image, and that Quick Mask represents the inverse areas of the image you want to keep. Therefore, use low Brush Opacity (such as 20%) for darker fringe areas of the hair and high opacity (such as 80 or 90%) for masking lighter areas of the hair. Although this is the opposite of what intuition tells us, it makes more sense when you see the finished Quick Mask.

8. After you finish masking around the hair next to Lee's right eye, choose the Smudge tool from the toolbox, set the mode to Darken on the Options bar, and then set the Strength to 50%.

Because the 10% increments for opacity have left hard demarcation in zones of the Quick Mask, you need to soften the transitions between, say, 70% opaque Quick Mask and 20% opaque Quick Mask. Although Quick Mask is only a preview mode for selection marquees, it can be affected by Photoshop's paint and editing tools.

9. Drag from a more opaque area of Quick Mask to a less opaque area. This action smears the Quick Mask and softens the transition between regions with a different opacity.

10. Press Ctrl(⌘)+S; keep the file open.

Unlike other image-editing programs, Photoshop writes an alpha channel to hold Quick Mask information and presents the channel selection information as a Quick Mask when you reopen a document saved in this state. You can close this document at any time, but do not try to open it in *another* image editor. Many image editors cannot interpret a Quick Mask saved selection as an alpha channel. Quick Masks are meant as non-permanent masking, but you can indeed save an image in Quick Mask mode from session to session. If you choose to turn it into a Standard Editing mode marquee and then deselect the marquee—you've lost the Quick Mask forever. The moral? If you love your Quick Mask, save any Quick Mask selections that have been saved as marquee (Standard Editing mode) selections to the alpha channels.

In the following steps, you continue to refine the Quick Mask selection, but use the Navigator palette to help you move around the edge of Lee in the image. The Navigator palette works faster than the Hand tool and is ideal for design situations in which an irregular outline wends through the entire image.

Using the Navigator Palette

1. Choose Window, Navigator. In the palette, the current view is framed with an outline.

2. Drag the highlight box down until you can see onscreen areas that have not been painted with Quick Mask.

3. With the Brush tool as the active tool, press **0** on the numeric keypad to set the Opacity to 100%, and then continue masking the edge of Lee. The masking procedure goes faster in areas of her dress and arm because they display better focus around the edges.

4. After you finish the right edge of the mask, drag the highlight box in the Navigator palette to the top left, and continue masking the edge (see Figure 11.11).

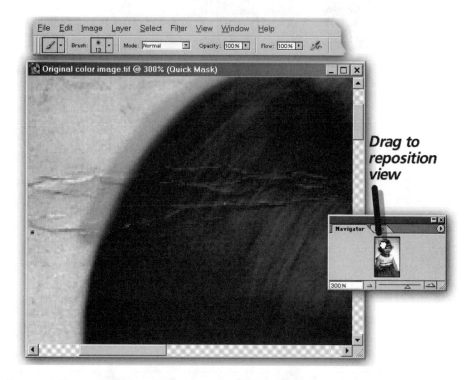

Figure 11.11   The Navigator palette provides a quick way to zoom and pan to the area in which you need to work.

5. When you reach the curly hair on the left of the image, use the partial opacity/keypad shortcut to mask the hair (as you did on the right side of the image in the preceding example).

6. When you finish the edge outline, double-click the Hand tool to zoom out to full image without scroll bars.

7. Choose the Polygonal Lasso tool from the toolbox. On the right side of the image, carefully click points that fall within the width of the Quick Mask edge work you created. Close the Polygon Lasso path to encompass the backdrop by clicking once on the beginning point of the selection you defined. When the

marquee appears, press Alt (Opt)+Delete (Backspace) to fill the selection with foreground black color (Quick Mask tint); then press Ctrl(⌘)+D to deselect the marquee selection (see Figure 11.12).

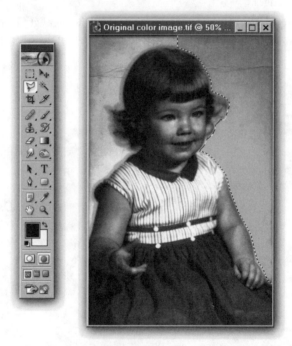

Figure 11.12   You can add to or subtract from a Quick Mask by filling a selection marquee with the current foreground color.

8. Perform Step 7 with the left side of the image.

Warning

Make Sure You Have a Good Selection   If you're not certain that your Polygonal Lasso definition falls within the width of the Quick Mask edge, close the marquee selection, and fill the area anyway; and then press Ctrl(⌘)+D.

Then zoom into the area in question; and if you have violated the original Quick Mask outline, press X to reverse the foreground/background colors on the toolbox. Choose the Brush tool, medium tip, hard, and then erase the offending areas.

Finally, pick up that Lasso tool and get back to selecting the large areas.

9. Click the Edit in Standard Mode icon to the left of the Quick Mask icon (or press Q). If the Channels palette is not onscreen, press F7 and click the Channels tab to display it. Then click the Save selection as channel icon at the bottom of the Channels palette.

10. Press Ctrl(⌘)+D to deselect the marquee, and press Ctrl(⌘)+S to save your work.

11. Open the Lee.tif grayscale image you worked on earlier (it's on your hard disk), and then click the Original color image.tif title bar to make this document the active document in the workspace.

12. On the Channels palette, right-click (Macintosh: hold Ctrl and click) the Alpha 1 title, and choose Duplicate Channel from the context menu.

13. In the Duplicate Channel dialog box, choose Lee.tif from the Document Destination field (see Figure 11.13), and click OK to add the channel to Lee.tif.

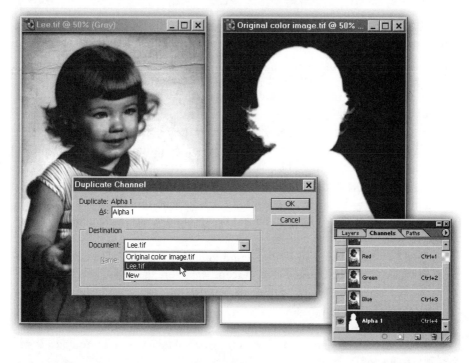

Figure 11.13   Duplicate saved selections in alpha channels across documents that are of equal size.

14. Press Ctrl(⌘)+S to save the Lee image with the new channel. Close the Original color image.tif file.

Creating a Rough Sketch for a Client

If you were to add a new backdrop to the Lee image right now, the picture would not represent a finished image. The hair needs some refining (as mentioned earlier), and the grayscale image lacks a certain warmth—precisely because it's still a grayscale image!

As we conclude the restoration process, it would be nice if you could walk away with a rough sample of what you can accomplish and an idea of where this image is going. If you were retouching this image for a client, all you would need to do now is a little cleanup, and you could show it around as a "work in progress."

The following steps will not alter the image in such a way that will affect anything you want to do in the future. You add an impromptu backdrop (one that you will use to replace the original in Chapter 12) so that you can compare the original to your work and see the dramatic change you have made in image quality.

Adding a Proxy Image Background

1. Press Ctrl(⌘) and click the Alpha 1 title on the Channels palette to load as a selection marquee the alpha channel you duplicated in the previous section.

2. If your view is of the Alpha 1 channel, click the Layers tab to view the Layers palette, and click the Background layer to make it active. Choose the Gradient tool.

3. Hold Alt(Opt) and click at the top of the backdrop in the image. Your cursor toggles to the Eyedropper tool, and the current foreground color for the gradient is the color you clicked in the image.

4. Press X to switch foreground and background colors, and then press Alt(Opt) and click over an area of the backdrop toward the bottom of the Lee.tif image. Press X now to switch foreground and background colors, making the darker tone the foreground.

5. On the Options bar, choose Foreground to Background from the Gradient drop-down list. Click the Linear Gradient icon. Make sure that Opacity is 100% and that the mode for the Gradient tool is Normal.

6. Drag from the top to the bottom of the image with the cursor. This adds a transitional blend of tones to replace the background (see Figure 11.14), whose brightness values were sampled from the original image content. You have kept the feeling of the original lighting in the image.

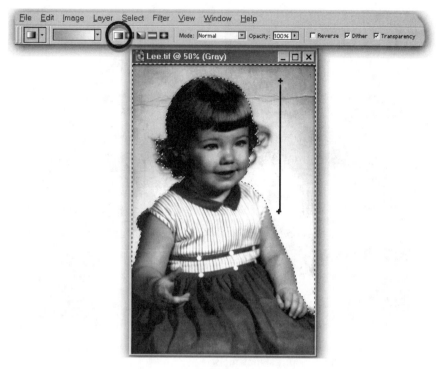

Figure 11.14   Add a gradient fill in the selection area to replace a damaged backdrop with a fresh Photoshop creation.

7. Press Ctrl(⌘)+D to deselect the marquee, and press Ctrl(⌘)+S to save your work. You can close the image at any time now.

In Figure 11.15, you can see the result of this chapter's efforts to restore life to the image. Does the Lee image require more work to bring it to completion? Definitely. But right now is a good time to pause and reflect upon what you have accomplished so far.

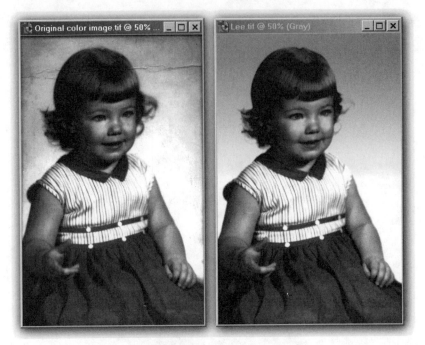

Figure 11.15   Image restoration is part detective work, part selection work, and much inspired use of Photoshop's painting tools.

Summary

This chapter has shown you most of the tools for restoring monochrome images. Restoration involves working with both image content and the "feel" of the image. For best results, always begin restoration work by examining what is beneath the surface and try to figure out how to copy undamaged image areas to fill areas that have been obscured. A "worst-case scenario" image was used in this chapter to give you real-world experience in restoration and an opportunity to learn not one, but several restoration techniques. Hopefully, images you want to restore will never be in such poor condition as Lee's.

In Chapter 12, "Retouching an Heirloom Photograph," you will learn how to put color back into the image, make the image look more dimensional, and in short, take about 20 years of grime, neglect, and wear-and-tear off the photo. Let's give the little girl something to *really* smile about.

Chapter 12

Retouching an Heirloom Photograph

In Chapter 11, "Restoring an Heirloom Photograph," you learned some techniques that transformed a water- and fire-damaged picture from an unacceptable image to a pleasing one. You also can perform some important post-restoration steps on this or another image to *enhance* the picture and bring it to nearly new condition. This chapter shows you how to add lifelike color tones, replace the background, and add dimension to the image. When the distractions of the current background and surface flaws have been retouched away, the audience will discover the content and emotional qualities within the image.

Adding Original Colors and Tonally Correcting the Image

In Photoshop, everything you paint and every selection you composite with other image areas is performed in a mode. Modes specify how layer pixels and the pixels you paint into an image are combined with existing image pixels. The Layers palette and the Options bar feature a Mode drop-down list that allows you to choose how a foreground element is merged to a background element. Understanding modes is the key to making photographic corrections in Photoshop and each mode is explained in great (but not dry and dusty) detail in Chapter 2, "Optimizing and Customizing Photoshop Preferences."

In the following sections, you learn how, by merging a copy of the original color Lee.tif file into the grayscale image you created in Chapter 11, to produce a color image without restoring the surface damage and noise that you removed. You do this by assigning the Color mode to the original image when it is added as a layer to the retouched image. Modes also play an important part in the addition of elements that help bring out the dimensional quality of this photo.

Using Modes and Image Layers

1. Open the Lee.tif image you saved in Chapter 11. If you didn't complete the steps in that chapter, you can open the Lee12.tif image from the Examples/Chap12 folder on the Companion CD. Go to the Image menu and choose Mode, RGB Color.

2. Open the Original color image.tif you saved in Chapter 11 or use the Lee.tif image found in the Examples/Chap11 folder on the Companion CD. The color image should now be the current foreground image in Photoshop.

3. Holding the Shift key, click and drag the Background title of the Original color image.tif from the Layers palette, and drop it into the document window of Lee.tif (see Figure 12.1). The Shift key makes the new layer centered on the image. Now that you have added the color image as a new layer in Lee.tif, you can close the Original color image.tif document at any time.

Figure 12.1   Drag the Background title of the color image to the retouched image. This adds the color image as a new layer.

4. With the new layer as the current editing layer in the Lee image, choose Color from the Mode drop-down list on the Layers palette. The image springs to life. The new layer contributes only color information to the composite image. Information about cracks and water stains is not included because these flaws are composed primarily of brightness and saturation—not color (hue)—information. Double-click the Layer 1 title, the title becomes a text entry field. Rename this layer **Color** and press Enter (Return) to apply the new name.

5. On the Channels palette, hold the Ctrl(⌘) key and click the Alpha 1 channel, which contains the saved selection area you created in Chapter 11. Doing this loads the Channel information as a selection marquee.

6. Press Delete (Backspace). The background areas outside the selection have been removed (see Figure 12.2), and with them, the discoloration on the backdrop in the image.

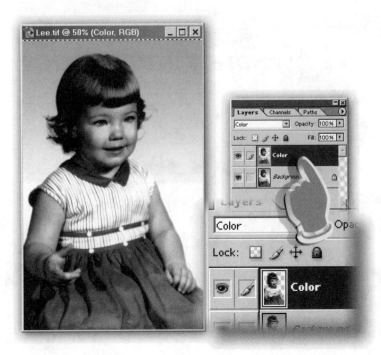

Figure 12.2   On the top layer of the image, keep only the color areas that represent the final colors you need.

7. Press Ctrl(⌘)+D to deselect. Choose File, Save as, and then save the image as Lee in Color.psd, in the Photoshop file format.

Adding a color copy of the original image to a layer in Color mode is a pretty neat trick, although the previous steps don't add even shading of color to the image because color is not evenly distributed in the original image. In the following sections, you learn to modify the grayscale background image to produce more interaction between the Color mode layer and the background one, and modify the color content of the Color layer to produce more even, consistent color values in the image.

Mapping Tonal Levels in the Image

Color mode doesn't touch the brightness values in the underlying layers; it simply adds the hues found in the source layer to create in the image a composite of layer color and background tone. The brightest and darkest tones in the background image of Lee fail to display color, however. Color mode cannot add color to areas in the tonal extremes of an image.

The solution to adding original color to these areas is to redistribute tones—brightness values in the background image—so that every area in the background has enough neutral tone to mix with the Color mode layer information. Actually, professionals who hand-tint grayscale photos make a photographic copy of an image that lacks contrast so that the physical tints are displayed more predominantly. What you will do in the following steps is the virtual equivalent of preparing a "duller-than-life" version of the background image to bring out the colors on the Color layer.

Modifying Tones with the Levels Command

1. Click the Background layer on the Layers palette, and press Ctrl(⌘)+L to display the Levels dialog box.

2. Drag the midpoint slider to the left until the Input levels center field reads 1.08. This reduces the contrast in the midtones of the background image. Keep the Levels dialog box open for the next few steps. The most important controls in the Levels dialog box are labeled in Figure 12.3.

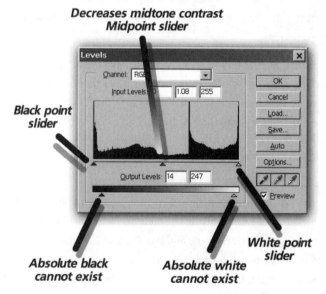

Figure 12.3   The controls in the Levels dialog box change the tonal distribution of pixels in an image.

3. In the Output Levels area, drag the black slider to the right until the value in the left Output Levels field is 14. This action reduces contrast in the image by specifying that absolute black (0 on a brightness scale of 0–255) doesn't exist in the Lee image. The darkest tone in the image will now be 14, which will enable some of the color on the Color layer to show through at the darkest points in the image.

4. Drag the white slider to the left until the corresponding Output Levels field reads 247. You've now specified that absolute white is not reached in the image—247 is the brightest area in the image in a range of tones whose maximum is 255. By increasing the white point, the colors in highlight areas in the image mix with neutral tones and become apparent when the layers are eventually merged in the document. The changes that appear in the layer are subtle but necessary.

5. Click OK to apply the tonal changes, and press Ctrl(⌘)+S to save your work.

The terms *Input* and *Output* in the Levels command might not adequately describe their function. Some of Photoshop's controls don't have explicit names that indicate their purpose because some of the features have no real-world equivalent. Think of the controls for the Levels Input sliders as options that compress the dynamic range of tones in an image. By dragging the black point slider to the right and the white point slider to the left, you add contrast to the image because you are compressing the breadth of all tones that can appear in an image to a narrower range. The midpoint slider also affects contrast, but it does so in the isolated area of midtones in an image, where much of the visual detail in a picture is located. By dragging left, you decrease midtone contrast, and by dragging right, you increase it.

The Output Levels controls enable you to *expand* the dynamic range of tones in an image. In the preceding steps, you created less contrast, thus allowing a greater range of tones at the upper and lower tonal limit of the image. By decreasing the *absolutes* (the extremes in tonal regions), you allow the headroom for color to become noticeable in these areas.

Evening Out the Colors in the Image

The color copy layer in the document is only a "primer coat" of color for the finished, retouched image. The colors are unevenly distributed on Lee's skirt because the original image colors were partially destroyed by age and handling of the image. The solution to retouching this area is to sample the original colors, and then simply paint them into areas that appear too dark, light, or washed out. Because the Color mode active on this layer doesn't display tones—the aspect of color that creates image detail—you can pour it on using the Brush tool without fear of losing image detail. The detail of Lee is on the Background layer.

Here's how to even the color distribution in the image's skirt area:

Applying Flat Color in Color Mode

1. Click the Color layer title on the Layers palette to make it the current editing layer. Uncheck the eye icon for the Background layer if you find tinting the Color layer with an image underneath distracting.

2. Choose the Brush tool, and on the Options bar, choose the tip at the far right of the second row on the Brush Preset picker (27-pixel, soft), and then hold Alt(Opt) while you click over an area of the skirt that contains the greatest amount of color. This Alt(Opt)+click action momentarily changes the brush into an Eyedropper tool so that you can sample the color in the dress. You might need to click two or three times and check the foreground color selection box on the toolbox to confirm that the color you have sampled is the most colorful.

Tip

Brighten Up Your Color Palette   You might even want to goose up the sampled colors saturation while visiting the color picker to attain more pronounced colors on the Color layer. It's *not* cheating; the person who tinted the original photograph was using an artistic call, and umpteen years later, so are you!

3. Release Alt(Opt) and begin painting over the skirt (see Figure 12.4). Remember that it is color you need on the Color mode layer (and not the details of the skirt). Work carefully around Lee's left hand, and change to a smaller tip to get into the smaller areas.

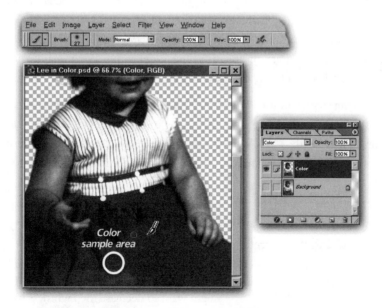

Figure 12.4   Fill the skirt area with a solid color, which will then be composited with the grayscale background image.

4. At regular intervals, click the Eye icon on the background layer to (Indicates layer visibility icon) to see how the color you're adding to the Color layer composites with the background image.

5. When you have completely painted over the skirt, press Ctrl(⌘)+S to save your work. Keep the document open in Photoshop.

Although the authors did not find other areas in the image where the preceding steps were necessary, you might want to scout around the image yourself. Perhaps the collar of Lee's dress could stand some color renewal, and areas of her hair might benefit from adding flat color.

Applying color is only phase one of the retouching process. The next section shows you how to control the saturation of color in the picture.

Purity of Color: Saturation

Humans have created many user-friendly descriptions for the components of color, which enables us to pinpoint a specific color. The Hue, Saturation, Brightness (HSB) color model consists of three components through which we can accurately describe colors we see. *Hue* is the wavelength of light that gives a color its distinguishing characteristic. *Brightness* is the amount of light reflected in proportion to the amount absorbed by a material. Highly reflective objects are bright, whereas rough objects absorb light and are seen as dark. *Saturation* is the relative purity of an individual hue. Most objects we see are composed of several hues, and the hue *strength* is what determines whether we say something is bluish-green or greenish-blue, for example. When many hues are present in near-equal amounts, the color of an object is dull and grayscale in content.

In the following steps, you use Photoshop's Hue/Saturation command to alter the saturation of the Color mode image layer. By exaggerating the hues in the layer—emphasizing existing hue strengths—you blend the layer with the background image in such a way that the colors make a more significant contribution to the image detail.

Strengthening Hues

1. Press Ctrl(⌘)+U to display the Hue/Saturation dialog box.

2. Click and drag the Saturation slider to about +33, (see Figure 12.5).

    By default, the Preview box is checked in all Photoshop adjustment and filter dialog boxes so that you can see your changes before you apply them. If the image looks fine, click OK. You might want to decrease the Lightness by –2; use your own artistic taste. By decreasing the Brightness you make the colors on the layer look richer and slightly duller.

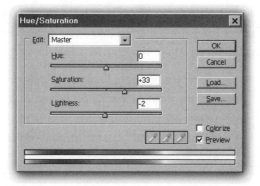

Figure 12.5   The Hue/Saturation command enables you to adjust color properties
independently of one another.

3. Press Ctrl(⌘)+S to save your work.

The color and tonal properties of Lee's image have now been optimized. As discussed in
Chapter 11, you might want to go into the Background layer now and remove pinholes
that are not covered by the Color layer information. In the next sections, you add a new
background to the image and evaluate the composition as it comes together to see which
other areas need to be addressed.

Introducing New Image Elements

Take care when adding a new element to an heirloom photograph. Clearly, you don't
want to add to the image something that does not fit the time period—a digital clock,
for example, would be a giveaway that something in the Lee.tif image has been
retouched. Equally important when you add something to an image is not to disturb the
balance—the amount of visual interest the new element creates versus the original image
area. The backdrop in Lee's image is stark and plain. To keep the little girl as the center
of attention, you can afford only marginal improvements to the background.

Because a truly photographic image would detract from Lee in the picture, the authors
created a large image of some wispy clouds for you to use in the following steps. The lens
and the focus of the original image could not compete for visual attention against a digitized photo, and there is simply something nice and abstract about a backdrop of
"painted" clouds. The colors complement the subject in the image. You can experiment
with textures and filters in your own work to produce stylized backdrops.

And you will add a drop shadow to the image by copying the selection defined by Lee's outline. The drop shadow helps bring out the interaction between the foreground and background in the image and forces the viewer to look *into* the image.

For every solution, however, there is a problem. Because Lee's current backdrop is white, the introduction of a darker color (through the use of the sky image and drop shadow) causes fringing to appear around Lee's image. The fringing occurs because of a slightly imprecise definition of the selection around her. Don't worry—we'll fix it.

Here's how to add layers of interest to the heirloom image:

Adding Depth to the Image

1. Open the Clouds.tif image from the Examples/Chap12 folder of the Companion CD.
2. Hold down the Shift key and drag the Background title on the Layers palette into the LeeinColor.psd image (see Figure 12.6). You can close the clouds image at any time to conserve Photoshop and general system resources.

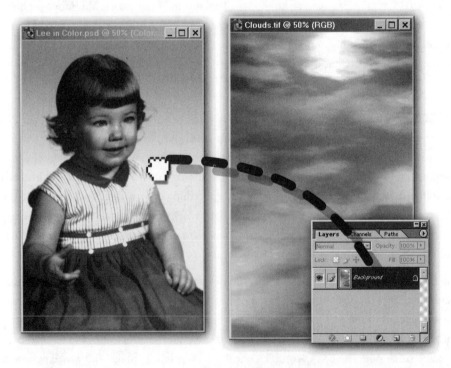

Figure 12.6   Drag the cloud image into the Lee in Color.psd image to add a new background.

3. Double-click the Background title on the Layers palette for the Lee image and rename the layer **Black and White** in the New Layer dialog box. Click OK.

The Background is now a Photoshop layer, and as such, you can erase the layer's pixels to transparent. Background layers cannot be erased to transparency, which is why the conversion needs to be made.

4. Double-click the Layer 1 title (this layer contains the cloud image), type **Clouds** to rename the layer in the text field that opens up, and then press Enter (Return) to apply the new name.

5. On the Layers palette, drag the Clouds layer so that it is below the Black and White layer.

6. With the Clouds layer active, Alt(Opt)+click the Create a new layer icon at the bottom of the Layers palette and name the layer **Shadow**. Click OK.

7. On the Channels palette, Ctrl(⌘)+click the Alpha 1 channel to load the selection. On the Layers palette, click the Black and White layer to make it the active layer and press the Delete (Backspace) key to remove the backdrop from this layer (which was created in Chapter 11). You should now be able to see the Clouds layer background.

8. Click the Shadow layer to make this the active layer. Press D (Default colors). Press Ctrl(⌘)+Shift+I to invert the selection. Press Alt(Opt)+Delete (Backspace) to fill the current selection with black foreground color. Change the Mode of this layer to Multiply.

9. Press Ctrl(⌘)+D to deselect. Hold down the Ctrl(⌘) key to toggle to the Move tool and drag the Shadow layer contents down and to the left of Lee by the amount shown in Figure 12.7.

Create a new layer

Figure 12.7   Use the Move tool to drag the Shadow layer to the position shown here.

10. Go to the Filter menu and choose Blur, Gaussian Blur. In the Gaussian Blur dialog box, type **19** in the Radius field and click OK. Figure 12.8 shows that the fringing from the original backdrop, displayed along the selection edge of Lee, is painfully obvious against the dark background.

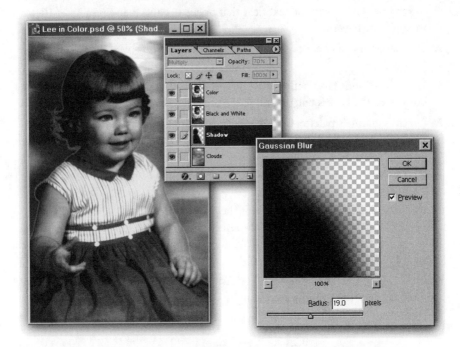

Figure 12.8 Apply the Gaussian Blur filter at a high level to create a subtle shadow and lower the Opacity of the Shadow layer to 70%.

11. Drag the Opacity slider for the Shadow layer to 70% and then press Ctrl(⌘)+S to save your work. Leave the file open.

Now is a good time to remove the fringe from Lee's image. You might want to take a soda break before we finish up the last details of this image and polish it off.

Removing the Fringe

1. Click the Black and White layer to make this the active layer. Click the Add layer mask icon at the bottom of the Layers palette.

2. Press B to switch to the Brush tool. On the Options bar, choose the soft round 17-pixel brush. The mode should be Normal, and Opacity and Flow should be at 100%. If Black and White are not the current colors, press D for the default colors.

3. Zoom in close and press the spacebar to get to an area along Lee's edge where there is fringing. Start painting the fringe away. If you make a mistake, press X to switch white to the foreground and paint back over the error. Then press X to switch to black again and continue on.

4. You might notice that some color information from the Color layer still remains in the removed fringing areas. Here's a quick fix for that. Ctrl(⌘)+click the layer mask thumbnail (on the Black and White layer) to load (display) your mask as a selection. If you see the marching ants around the outside edge of the document, press Ctrl(⌘)+Shift+I to invert the selection. Click the Color layer to make it active and press the Delete (Backspace) key (see Figure 12.9).

Ctrl (⌘) + click to
load mask selection

Figure 12.9   Use a layer mask on the Black and White layer to remove the fringe and use the layer mask selection to remove additional fringe on the Color layer.

5. Press Ctrl(⌘)+D to deselect. Right-click (Macintosh: hold Ctrl and click) the layer mask thumbnail and choose Apply Layer Mask.

6. Click the Create a new layer icon. Use this new layer to paint in a few wispy strands of hair. Because you are using a new layer, you can discard the layer easily if you are not happy with the results. Choose the Smudge tool from the toolbox. On the Options bar, choose a soft round 17-pixel brush, set the mode at Normal, Strength at 40%, and make sure the Use All Layers option is checked.

To avoid using the Shadow and Cloud layers as color sources for your smudge work, turn off the visibility for the Shadow and Clouds layers. Pull color from inside the hair area and make brush strokes outward to simulate wisps of hair strands (see Figure 12.10).

Don't forget to use Ctrl(⌘)+Z or Ctrl(⌘)+Alt(Opt)+Z to undo any smudge strokes you don't like. If you like a stroke but want to refine or remove a portion of the stroke, use a layer mask on the layer with the Brush tool to refine your strokes.

Figure 12.10   Use the Smudge tool to create wispy hair strands.

7. When you are satisfied with the final touches, turn on the visibility for the remaining layers and press Ctrl(⌘)+S to save your work. See Figure 12.11 for the final image.

Figure 12.11   The final results for the Lee in Color image.

Hopefully, you've learned more than how to use Photoshop's tools to restore and enhance an heirloom photograph in these two chapters. Every picture is different, and an approach to each damaged, worn, or faded photograph must be designed before anyone touches the image. The best approach is usually based on examining the hows and whys of the photograph's appearance in the here and now, and at the time it was taken.

Clearly, different circumstances cause damage to the photographs you need to restore, and you might need to use tools other than those presented here. But although the tools may change, the procedure remains the same: uncover, discover, and then retouch and enhance.

Summary

Whether the Photoshop assignment ahead of you is to restore an image or integrate a new image with an old one, continuity is the key to successful image integration. Allow some of the original image's areas to blend with new ones, and you will find that as a professional-level retoucher, your best work is that which goes unnoticed. If you provoke a smile through your work, consider yourself artistically rewarded.

Part V

Photoshop
for Artists

Chapter 13

Using Paths

There are two categories of digital graphics;

good art and bad art. I'm *kidding*—the type

categories are bitmap and vector graphics.

Bitmap graphics, also called *pixel-based* or

raster graphics, are created using rows and

rows of rectangular pixels of different colors. A *pixel* is simply a placeholder for a value (a color). Viewing a scene through a wire mesh screen door is a fair, real-world visual analogy of bitmap graphics. Photoshop is primarily an image-editing program that is bitmap-based. If you have ever painted a diagonal line that appears jagged, this is bitmapping at its worst. Photoshop uses anti-aliasing to help minimize the jagged-edge effect. *Anti-aliasing* is the placement of transitional colors between neighboring pixels of different colors.

Open a document in Photoshop and with the Line tool (found on the Shapes tool flyout on the toolbox), draw a diagonal black line on a white background. The line appears smooth at the 100% zoom level (normal view). Now magnify a section of the line to 700% or more, as shown in Figure 13.1. You'll notice that the transition between the black line and the white background is made up of black pixels at different brightness values. A major disadvantage to having an image that relies on pixel information becomes apparent when you attempt to modify the size or resolution of the image. The pixels become more noticeable, resulting in a loss of focus and poor display of image detail.

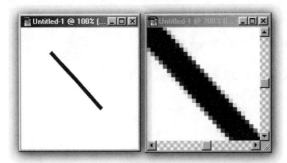

Figure 13.1   Bitmap programs use anti-aliasing to keep edges looking smooth (at normal view on the left). When magnified (view on the right), the transition of pixels that contributes to this smooth appearance becomes more apparent.

Vector-based graphics are on the other side of this computer graphics coin. Any line drawn in a vector program such as Illustrator, CorelDraw, or Xara is defined for the computer in mathematical terms. Because the computer has a mathematical interpretation for a line, this allows resizing in any direction and to any magnitude without the loss of resolution or clarity. All the computer is doing is multiplying or dividing math equations that constitute the line. Fortunately for you and me, the mathematical equations generated by drawing a line are transparent to the user. We never have to get into the math, and for most of us (including the author), this is a good thing. We need concern ourselves only with what we are drawing onscreen—hey, we're artists and not mathematicians, right? Okay, some of us actually *are* mathematicians…

Note

Visual Interpretations   So if our monitors are raster in nature, how can they show vector images? Good question. Vectors, being math-based, are a little ephemeral. You can't exactly display a line formed by the equation $x=y^2$.

What really is happening when you use vector tools is that a raster interpretation is being shown on-screen, constantly updating as you refine your work. Only when you go to print a vector masterpiece do you see that the information being sent to the printer is telling the printer to render lines as smoothly as the resolution of the printer can produce.

But for all intent and purposes, when you see a vector line onscreen, you—the artist—accept it as a vector and not a bitmap.

When drawing vector-based lines, you need to be aware of certain rules. Once you understand these rules, creating lines and curves will become easy with practice.

Photoshop has two Vector tools: the Pen tool and the Path Selection tools. The Pen tool gives you the power to create vector-based lines within Photoshop. Lines drawn with the Pen tool are referred to as *paths*. These paths are referenced on the Paths palette. When you are using the Paths palette, the paths themselves are not printable, but you can make the paths into *selections* for use in the image document. Furthermore, the paths can be permanently saved for reuse. Paths also can be filled and saved in a format such as Acrobat (PDF) so that when printed, the vector outlines and fills print as crisp and clean as is physically possible. They're as clean as vector (Type 1 and TrueType) fonts. Paths can even be transferred and used in other Photoshop files or between other programs such as Illustrator (and PageMaker, which can treat a path as a *clipping path*—a "peek-a-boo" in an image whose areas outside the path are invisible).

Note

You Must Name a Work Path If You Want to Save It   When you draw a path in Photoshop, it is represented on the Paths palette as a work path. This work path is only temporary. If you deselect the path and later draw a different path, the new path will replace the old path with the work path title.

If you want to save the path for future use, you need to name the work path. Naming is easily accomplished; just double-click the work path title (or click the arrow in the upper-right corner of the Paths palette and choose Save Path from the context menu). In the Save Path dialog box, type a name for the path or accept the default path name, and click OK.

Figure 13.2 shows the flyout menus for the Pen tool and Path Selection tools. Adobe has made it easy to access most of these tools with modifier keys, instead of clicking the flyout menus to switch tools. When the Pen tool is active, pressing the Alt(Opt) key toggles to the Convert Pen tool, and pressing the Ctrl(⌘) key toggles to the Direct Selection tool. Additionally, if the Auto Add/Delete checkbox is checked on the Options bar, the Add Anchor Point tool will automatically toggle on when the Pen pointer is over a path. Similarly, the Delete Anchor Point tool will automatically toggle on when the Pen pointer is over a point on the path.

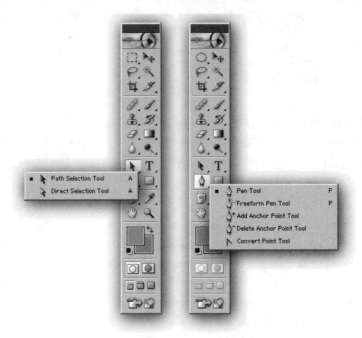

Figure 13.2   The tool lists for the Pen tool and Path Selection tools.

Note

Finding Tools Hidden in the Toolbox   You will be using many tools from the toolbox in this chapter. If you've been exploring the workspace before reading this, you might have changed the top-facing icon on an icon flyout on the toolbox. A good example of this is the Paint Bucket tool, which shares a space with the Gradient tool.

If, in any set of steps, you're asked to choose a tool from the toolbox and it's not visible, click and hold on the tool to reveal the flyout and make the selection of tools you need.

Understanding the Pen Tool Rule—Think of Points

In order to understand the Pen tool, think back to early math lessons in grade school. You might remember a time when your teacher tried to convey the concept that, "At least two points are required to define a line or line segment." Never will that be truer than when using the Pen tool.

The Pen tool creates points, which define the way a line segment looks. Adobe calls these *anchor points*, and so shall we. In a sense, you don't actually draw a line with the Pen tool; you define the points that make up the line. There are three *main* anchor point types:

- Corner
- Smooth
- Sharp

Using the Corner Anchor Point

The corner point is the easiest to draw. With the Pen tool selected, click a spot and click again in another spot (remember, two points make a line). The line segment created between the two anchor points is a straight line. When several connected lines make up a shape, we call the shape a *path* and the lines are called *path segments*. Again, this is Adobe verbiage, so we are using it to synch with Adobe documentation.

In the following set of steps, you practice the creation of useful corner points by drawing a simple triangle. Hopefully, a few concepts will become clearer along the path. Sorry…

Note

The Rubber Band Option Want to preview path segments as you draw them? When the Pen tool is active, the Option bar has a Rubber Band option that enables you to see the path segments as you move your pointer in the image. The segments are not permanent until you click the following point. To preview path segments as you draw, click the inverted arrow next to the shape buttons in the Options bar, and select Rubber Band.

Using Corner Point

1. Open Practice.psd in the Examples/Chap13 folder on the Companion CD.

   The file has an active layer, titled Practice, and a few hidden layers. Leave them hidden for now (we'll get to those later).

2. Press P to switch to the Pen tool. If the Paths option is not already selected on the Options bar, click it (refer to Figure 13.2). Click once in the document near the bottom-left side to make your first of three anchor points for a triangle.

   Whenever the Pen tool is selected, the Paths option on the Options bar—the middle of the three funny little icons shown in Figure 13.3—should be selected for the remainder of this chapter, unless otherwise noted.

3. Hold down the Shift key (to constrain the movement of the Pen tool to vertical) and click near the bottom-right side of the document.

There should now be a straight horizontal line near the bottom of the document, as shown in Figure 13.3. So far, the line you created is considered an open path segment.

Figure 13.3   Click once in the lower-left side of the image, and then hold the Shift key and click again on the lower-right side of the image to create an open horizontal path near the bottom.

4. Click a third point at the top middle of the document, forming another straight path segment.

5. Close the path by clicking the last point at the same location as the first point created.

A teensy circle appears to the bottom right of the Pen pointer, indicating that the path is about to be closed (see Figure 13.4).

The wonderful thing about paths is that they can be modified at any time. If you are not satisfied with the location of any of the three points that make up the triangle, you can make changes easily:

6. Hold down the Ctrl(⌘) key to toggle to the Direct Selection tool (the pointer changes to a hollow arrow), and then click and drag a point to move it to a different location.

Notice that the path segments associated with the point move to reflect the changes being made. The anchor point that is selected is solid, and the unselected points are hollow.

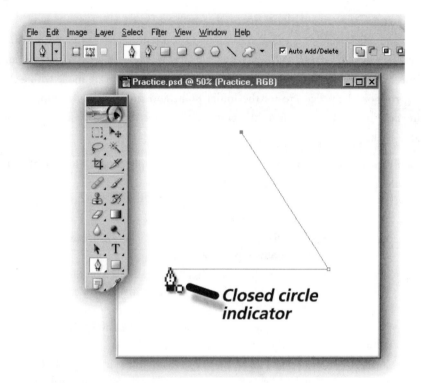

Figure 13.4   Use the circle indicator on the Pen pointer to help determine when to click and close the path.

7. Hold down the Ctrl(⌘) key and nudge the selected point using the arrow keys on your keyboard.

When you press the arrow keys, you nudge the anchor point by one screen pixel—the farther your viewing resolution, the greater a distance one keyboard nudge will do. A whole new world of control and precision should start to become apparent. Let's try one more experiment.

8. Hold down the Ctrl(⌘) key to continue accessing the Direct Selection tool, and then click and drag a path segment instead of an anchor point.

You can change either the position of the segments that make up a path or the individual anchor points.

9. Click the Path tab on the Layers/Channels/Paths palette to view the Paths palette (or choose Window, Paths). Double-click the work path title and in the Save Path dialog box type **Triangle**. Click OK. Hide the path by clicking an empty area below the path title on the Paths palette. Click the Layers tab to return to the Layers palette. Press Ctrl(⌘)+Shift+S to save your work (navigate to a place on your hard disk where you wish to save the file). Keep the document open for the next adventure.

Creating Curves with the Smooth Anchor Point

A smooth anchor point is called smooth because a path segment that passes through it doesn't change direction at all. Therefore, the area of the path segment surrounding the smooth anchor point is, well…*smooth!* Smooth anchor points are made with a click and drag motion. The click creates the initial point and the dragging motion creates the direction lines that extend from the point. These direction lines are used to control the curve of the path segment.

Again, we will use a practice exercise to make a simple shape. This set of steps uses smooth anchor points to create a circular shape.

Using Smooth Points to Create Curves

1. Open Practice.psd in the Examples/Chap13 folder on the Companion CD if it is not already open in Photoshop's workspace.

2. Click the eye icon to the left of the Circle Template layer on the Layers palette to view this layer. The template guides you along in this example.

3. Press P to select the Pen tool from the toolbox, click the green dot next to the number 1, and then drag upward until you reach the end of the red template handle (see Figure 13.5).

   Notice as you drag that a direction line is made in the opposite direction (indicated by blue handles on the template). The direction line will extend beyond the blue handle length, but don't worry about that now. We'll come back and fix it later.

4. Click and drag the number 2 green template dot until reaching the end of the second red direction line.

5. Continue the same technique on dots 3 and 4, dragging in the direction of the red direction lines. To close and finish the circle, move the Pen pointer over the first green dot, and when you see a circle appear next to the pointer, click once (see Figure 13.6). This closes the path. No dragging is required when closing the path, as shown in Figure 13.6.

   You should now see a circle path that is a similar shape to the template. We will fine-tune some of the direction lines to make it a perfect match

6. Hold down the Ctrl(⌘) key to toggle to the Direct Selection tool. Click point 1 on the path to view this point and the direction lines associated with this point. Click the end of the direction handle near the blue template handle and drag it until it matches the same length as the template. Repeat this process for the remaining points if any adjustments are needed for them. The path should now look identical to the template.

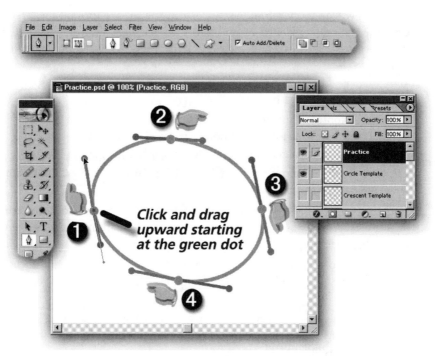

Figure 13.5   Click item 1 in the template and drag upward until you read the red template handle. A direction line will automatically extend in the opposite direction near the blue template handles.

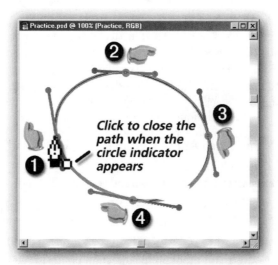

Figure 13.6   A circle appears near the Pen pointer to indicate when the path is about to be closed. Just click to close the circle path.

7. Click the eye icon to the left of the Circle Template layer to turn off the layer. Click the Paths tab to view the Path palette. Double-click the Work Path and in the Save Path dialog box, type **Circle**. Click OK. Press Ctrl(⌘)+S to save your work.

Next, we will experiment with the points on the circle path. Worried about ruining that circle? Don't be. Because you saved your work, you can experiment to your heart's content in the following steps. The File, Revert command in the last step puts the path back to its condition when you last saved it.

8. Press Shift+A until the Direct Selection tool is active (the hollow arrow tool). Click anywhere on the circle path to display the points. Click any curved path segment of the circle and drag.

Notice that the curved path segment responds to the dragging, and the direction lines associated with the curved path segment adjust according to the curve you modify by dragging.

9. Click a point to see both direction lines associated with that point (the anchor point will have a solid fill). Click the end of one of the direction lines and drag in any direction.

Notice that you also can change or control the shape of the curve this way as well. If you drag up and down on the end of the control handle, the opposite handle responds like a seesaw.

10. Click the point and drag it to a different spot. Nudge the point by using the arrow keys.

The points, direction lines, and path segments can all be changed using similar techniques.

11. If you saved the work as instructed in Step 4, you can return to the circle shape by choosing File, Revert. Or, if you prefer, you can get in some additional practice by turning the Circle Template layer back on and adjusting the direction points and lines to return to the circle shape of the template. Leave the document open for the next steps.

Working with the Sharp Anchor Point—The Point with Two Independent Handles

The *sharp anchor point* is a point with two independent direction lines. As you noticed in the previous steps, the direction handles on a smooth point respond with a seesaw effect. With a sharp point, the direction lines respond independently. This type of point is most commonly used when you have a sharp peak connected to curved lines in a path. You can use the Convert Point tool on the direction points to redirect the direction line and create a sharp anchor point.

In the following steps, the emphasis is on sharp anchor points, the Convert Point tool, and the Direct Selection tool. You will make changes to the circle-shaped path to create a crescent-shaped path. You can select the Convert Point tool or the Direct Selection tool from the tools list. In most situations, however, it is more efficient to keep the Pen tool selected and toggle to the Convert Point and Direct Selection tools using modifier keys. You will use these modifier keys as you create the crescent shape from the circle.

Using the Convert Point Tool and Sharp Points to Change a Path Shape

1. If the Circle Template layer is showing, click the eye icon on the Layers palette to hide it. Click the eye icon to the far left of Crescent Template layer title to turn on this layer.

2. Click the Paths tab to display the Paths palette and click the Circle path to make this path visible. On the Paths palette, click the triangle in the upper-right corner of the palette and choose Duplicate Path from the flyout menu. When the Duplicate Path dialog box appears, rename the path **Crescent** and click OK.

3. Press Shift+A until the Path Selection tool is active (the solid arrow tool). Click the circle path and move it down until it rests close to the Crescent template, as shown in Figure 13.7. Click an empty space in the document to deselect the path points.

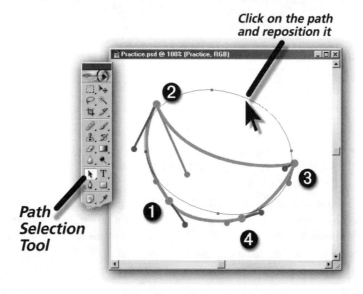

Figure 13.7   Use the Path Selection tool to move your path closer to the Crescent Template.

4. Press P to switch to the Pen tool. Hold down the Ctrl(⌘) key to toggle to the Direct Selection tool and click anywhere on the path to make the anchor points visible. Continue to hold down the Ctrl(⌘) key, and click the anchor point near the number 1 green dot and drag the anchor point to reposition it onto the number 1 green dot location (see Figure 13.8). Click the end of each handle (for this anchor point) and adjust the direction lines to match the template for point number 1.

Note: Because this is still a smooth point, dragging on one handle end will make the opposite handle follow in a seesaw fashion.

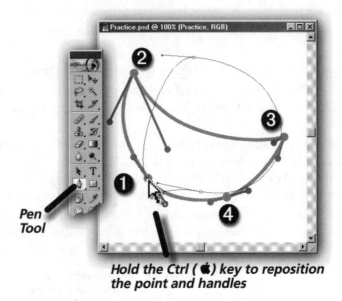

Pen
Tool

**Hold the Ctrl (⌘) key to reposition
the point and handles**

Figure 13.8   Toggle to the Direct Selection tool with the Ctrl(⌘) key, and then click the anchor point and drag to match the position of number 1 on the template. Also make the necessary adjustments to the handles associated with this point.

5. Continue to hold down the Ctrl(⌘) key to toggle to the Direct Selection tool, click the anchor point near the number 4 green dot, and drag the anchor point to reposition it onto the dot location (see Figure 13.9). Click the end of each handle (for this anchor point) and adjust the direction lines to match the template (for point number 4).

6. Continuing to hold down the Ctrl(⌘) key to toggle to the Direct Selection tool, click the anchor point near the number 2 green dot and drag the anchor point to reposition it on the dot location. Click the end of the left handle (for this anchor point) and adjust it downward to match the blue direction line of the template (for point number 2).

7. Hold down the Alt(Opt) key to toggle to the Convert Point tool, click the end of the (opposite) right handle, and drag this direction line into position over the red line on the template, as seen in Figure 13.10.

   You just created your first sharp point (two curved lines that meet at a sharp anchor point).

   To complete the crescent shape, you need to alter the anchor point near point 3 on the template.

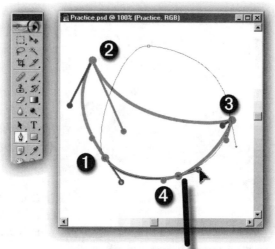

Hold the Ctrl ( ) key to reposition this point and handles onto the template

Figure 13.9   Repeat the previous step for the anchor point closest to the number 4 green dot in the template.

Hold the Ctrl ( ) key to reposition this point

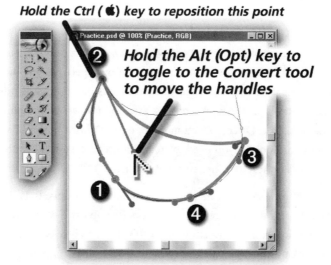

Hold the Alt (Opt) key to toggle to the Convert tool to move the handles

Figure 13.10   Hold the Ctrl(⌘) key to move the anchor point and the Alt(Opt) key to move the direction lines (by dragging their direction handles) to match the template.

8. Repeat Steps 6 and 7 (for the anchor point near point 3 of the template). Hold the Ctrl(⌘) key to move the point into position. Hold the Alt(Opt) key to convert the handles at an angle to match the template, as shown in Figure 13.11.

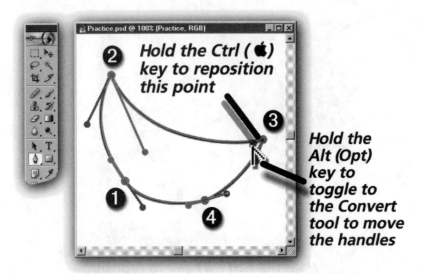

Figure 13.11 Hold the Ctrl(⌘) key to toggle to the Direct Selection tool and reposition the remaining anchor point onto point 3 of the template. Hold the Alt(Opt) key to toggle to the Convert tool to reposition the direction lines to match point 3 on the template.

9. Press Ctrl(⌘)+S to save your work. Keep the document open for the next phase.

Using Paths to Help Paint an Image

Paths are forever changeable in a variety of ways. As you've seen thus far in this chapter, anchor points and path segments can be moved and reshaped. Keep your goal in mind when working with paths. You may need to switch tools often—that is quite common. The Path Selection tools, as the name implies, are used for selecting a point or portion of the path (as with the Direct Selection tool) or the entire path (as with the Path Component Selection tool). If you need to create or alter a part of the path, the Pen tool and the related tools on the tools list are what you need.

Paths are non-printing vector objects. Paths are not made up of pixels. Paths remain separate from the bitmap image. Once you create a path, you can save it and later use it in a number of ways, including converting the path's shape to a selection, filling the path with color, or stroking the path (adding color to the border of a path). So the concept here is that paths are useful tools that help you arrive at various painting and editing goals with a specific piece.

Also keep in mind a few concepts about *altering* a path. So far, you have used the Convert Point tool to change the property of an anchor point from smooth to sharp, and in the process, you changed a direction line so that it moves independently of its opposing direction line. You also can perform some tricks with an anchor point that work independently of the anchor's direction lines. For example, if you toggle to the Convert Point tool and click a smooth point, the point will instantly convert to a corner point—and the direction lines disappear. Similarly, you can click and drag a corner point with the Convert point tool to change this type of point to a smooth point. It is also common to add points or delete points as needed to change the shape of a path.

Using path geometry as the basis for a selection is demonstrated in the following steps. You will add color and life to this image by using the circular and crescent-shaped paths that were created. You've heard the saying, "When given a lemon—make lemonade." In this case, we first need the lemon. So let's make one.

Adding Color to a Path

1. With the Practice.psd document open, click the Paths palette and click the Circle title to make the circle path visible. Hold down the Ctrl(⌘) key and press the Enter (Return) key to load the path as a selection (and hide the path).

2. Click the Layers tab to view the Layers palette. Double-click the Practice layer to rename the layer. The name will now be highlighted. Type **Lemon Top**. Click the foreground color selection box on the toolbox and choose a pale beige color (R:243, G:235, B:217). Click OK. Press Alt(Opt)+Delete to fill the crescent shape with this color.

3. Press B to switch to the Brush tool. Click the foreground color selection box on the toolbox and choose a yellow color (R:238, G:214, B:86). Click OK. On the Options bar, type **20%** for Flow. Click the Brushes tab to show the Brushes palette and choose a large, soft brush such as the 65-pixel tip. The object is to paint a yellow circle, leaving the beige color as a border near the outer edge and also on the inside center (as shown in Figure 13.12). If you feel the yellow looks too pale, paint a little more. Press Ctrl(⌘)+D to deselect when you are pleased with the results.

   If you do not like the first stroke and want to try again, press Ctrl(⌘)+Z to undo the last stroke, or use the History palette to go back as many strokes as needed.(Alternatively, you can press Ctrl(⌘)+Alt(Opt)+Z to perform multiple undos.) Deselect the marquee when you are happy with your changes.

4. Hold down the Alt(Opt) key and click the Create a new layer icon at the bottom of the Layers palette. In the New Layer dialog box, name the layer **Top Slices**. Click OK.

   In the interest of time, some extra paths were created in advance and saved in the file for use. The next step will make use of some of these paths.

5. Click the Paths tab to show the Paths palette. Ctrl(⌘)+click the Lemon Centers path title to load these paths as a selection. Click the foreground color selection box on the toolbox and choose a yellow color (R:237, G:196, B:34). Click OK. Press Alt(Opt)+Delete (Backspace) to fill the selection with the yellow color.

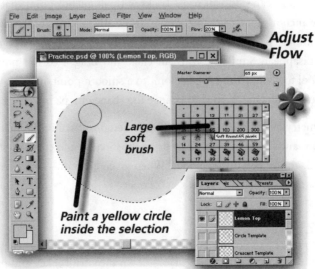

Adjust Flow

Large soft brush

Paint a yellow circle inside the selection

Right-click (⌘+click) when the Paintbrush is chosen to access the Brushes palette right underneath your cursor!

Figure 13.12   Use a large, soft brush at 20% flow to add some yellow color to this circle selection.

6. Click the foreground color selection box on the toolbox and choose an orange color (R:212, G:109, B:33). Click OK. Press B to switch to the Brush tool. On the Options bar, choose the soft-round 65-pixel brush and keep Flow set at 20%. Paint the orange color around the outside edges of the slice selections, as shown in Figure 13.13. (Tip: Keep some of the brush size outside the selection area when painting.)

7. Click the Brush preset picker on the Options bar and choose the soft round 21-pixel brush. Continue to leave the Flow set at 20%. Paint some orange color along the remaining edges of each slice, as shown in Figure 13.14. When you're satisfied with the results, press Ctrl(⌘)+D to deselect.

8. Click the Add a layer style icon at the bottom of the Layers palette and choose Bevel and Emboss. In the Layer Style dialog box, choose a smooth Inner Bevel with Depth 75%, Size 5 (px), Soften 0 (px), Angle 120°, Altitude 30°. Leave the Highlight mode at the default settings. Click the black color swatch for the Shadow mode and choose a brown color (R:123, G:55, B:5). Click OK (see Figure 13.15).

9. Hold down the Alt(Opt) key and click the Create a new layer icon at the bottom of the Layers palette. In the New Layer dialog box, type **Lemon Peel** for the name. Click OK.

10. Drag the new layer down below the Lemon Top layer on the Layers palette (or press Ctrl(⌘)+[twice) to move this new layer down two positions on the Layers palette.

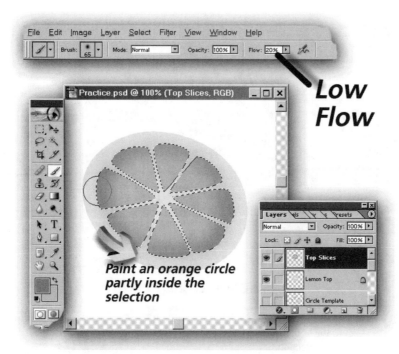

Figure 13.13   Fill the Top Slices selection with yellow. Paint an orange color on the outer edges of the slices. The goal is to have a yellow color that blends into an orange color at the outer edges of the selection slices.

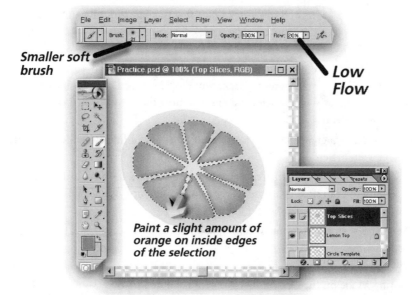

Figure 13.14   Use a smaller brush to paint along the inside-edge selections (with orange color). It might be helpful to let the brush rest between two slices at a time as you apply paint in small amounts on the inside edges.

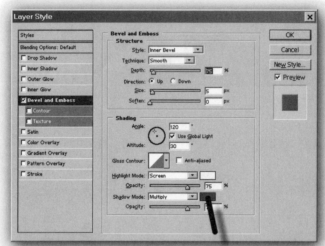

**Click on the color swatch and
change color to a brown tone**

Figure 13.15   Use the settings shown above to give a subtle Bevel and Emboss
effect to the lemon slices.

11. Click the Paths tab to show the Paths palette. Ctrl(⌘)+click the Crescent path
     title to load this path as a selection. Click the Layers tab to return to the Layers
     palette. Click the foreground color selection box on the toolbox and choose a yel-
     low color (R:238, G:214, B:82). Click OK. Click the background color selection
     box on the toolbox and choose the orange color used previously (R:212, G:109,
     B:33). Click OK.

12. Press G to switch to the Gradient tool. On the Options bar, choose Linear
     Gradient and the Foreground to Background options. Drag a gradient starting at
     the inside-right area of the selection and end near the left edge of the selection,
     as shown in Figure 13.16.

     The gradient is a great start and looks great. But we can fine-tune the results to
     make it even better.

13. Press B to switch to the Brush tool. Choose a soft round 65-pixel brush. Press X
     to switch the orange color to the foreground. Paint some orange along the right
     side of the selection, as shown in Figure 13.17.

     The next few steps show you a technique for painting a peel-like texture for this
     lemon.

14. Click the Create a new layer icon at the bottom of the Layers palette. Change the
     painting Mode on the Options bar from Normal to Dissolve. Paint over the
     orange areas again in this new mode to create a rough texture. Press X to switch
     to the yellow color. Paint over the yellow areas into the orange areas (to
     contribute to this rough texture look).

Experiment until you like the results, pressing X to switch between the two colors. If you are unhappy with a paint stroke, press Ctrl(⌘)+Z to undo and try again (or use the History palette to go back as many paint strokes as you wish).

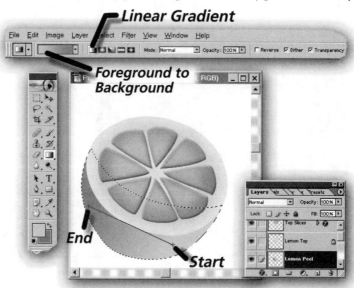

Figure 13.16   The above figure happens to show the desired gradient results when you drag a gradient as demonstrated in this figure. However, you won't see the results on your image until after you complete the gradient drag and release the mouse button.

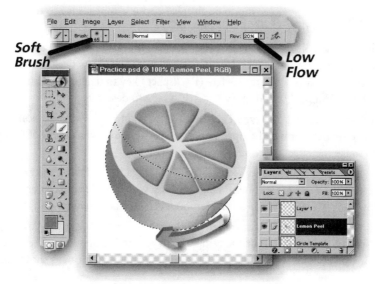

Figure 13.17   Paint orange along the right edge, keeping a small portion of the brush inside the selection as shown above. Stroke more than once if needed until you are pleased with the results.

15. Optional: Click the foreground color selection box on the toolbox and choose a pale yellow color (R:247, G:239, B:184). Click OK. Paint more texture with a stroke or two in the center of the yellow color, as shown in Figure 13.18.

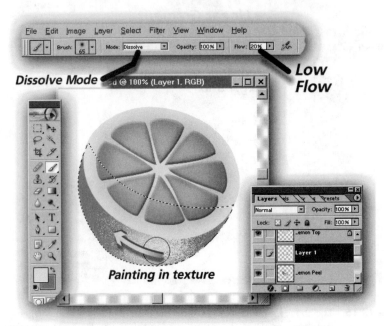

Figure 13.18 Paint additional texture with a pale yellow color in the area shown here.

Painting with the Dissolve mode might give a rough appearance to the outside edge of the selection. Here's how to fix this.

16. If the Lemon Peel is not selected, press Ctrl(⌘)+click the Lemon Peel layer to select it. With Layer 1 still highlighted as the active layer, press Ctrl(⌘)+Shift+I to invert the selection. Press the Delete (Backspace) key to delete the texture outside this lemon peel selection. Press Ctrl(⌘)+D to deselect.

17. Double-click Layer 1 and type **Peel Texture** to rename this layer. Optional: On the Layers palette, lower the opacity of the Peel Texture layer to 65% if you prefer to make the effect more subtle.

One last detail will help you keep all the layers organized. Taking the extra steps now to organize layers will help make working with the file easier later on. Follow the next step to keep all the lemon layers in one layer set.

18. Click the Lemon Peel layer and then on the Layers palette, click the Link icons to the right of the eye icons for the remaining layers above the Lemon Peel layer. This action enables you to link the layers that create the lemon, as shown in

Figure 13.19. Click the arrow in the upper-right corner of the Layers palette and choose New Set From Linked. In the New Set From Linked dialog box, type **Lemon** for the name. Click OK.

Layer sets allow for easy organization of compositions. A layer set is analogous to a folder that holds all the separate layers within it. Remember what a pain it used to be in Photoshop to scroll the Layers palette when you had 25 layers on the palette? To access the individual layers, simply click the arrow on the layer set title (on the Layers palette). The folder opens to reveal all the layers inside. Click the arrow again to close the folder.

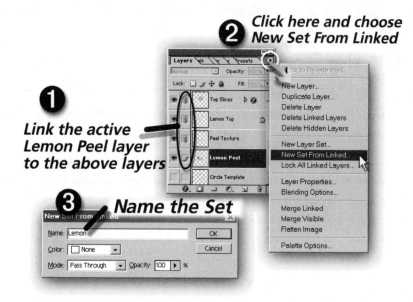

Figure 13.19   Create a layer set for the lemon layers by linking the layers and choosing New Set From Linked from the context menu on the Layers palette.

  19. Press Ctrl(⌘)+S to save your work. Keep the document open for the next phase.

Adding Details to the Design

This lemon looks attractive enough so far, but our canvas still is rather big and empty. You need some additional design elements to spark more interest for the eye. Because the main topic of this chapter is paths, the remaining design elements will give you additional practice for creating paths and making use of paths as selections for painting.

Don't worry—we've created templates to help guide you along in this process. Just to let you in on a secret, I often rely on some sort of template myself to create paths and illustrations. Templates can take many forms (other than the neat outlines that appear in the exercises of this chapter). For example, a template could be a pencil sketch (of an idea) scanned into the computer or a photograph you want to use as a template for creating paths.

This next construction phase will add two leaves to the design. As you draw the paths for the next example, you will find it easier to draw if you keep one hand on the mouse and the other near the Ctrl(⌘) and Alt(Opt) keys for easy access to the modifier keys. This enables you to quickly toggle to the Direct Selection or Convert Point tools, respectively, as the need for these tools arise.

You will want to toggle to the Convert Point tool while creating a smooth point to move one of the control handles slightly. This instantly changes the attributes of the smooth anchor point to a sharp point, which allows you to adjust the handles independently (giving you greater control of the path curves). This technique will be used consistently, endlessly, and mercilessly in the "Leaf Path Practice" example.

This next set of steps is intended to give you additional practice with the Pen tool. The Leaf Template that is provided in the file for this exercise has two leaves drawn. The exercise will walk you through drawing the first leaf. Apply the same steps to draw the second leaf (on your own). Remember to toggle to the Direct Selection tool and click outside the path area (an empty space of the document) to deselect the current path you're working on—before starting to create a new path.

If you feel secure and confident in your skill with the Pen tool, you have the option of skipping to the "Painting with Path Selections" example. On the Paths palette, there is a path titled Leaves. In the following example, you can choose either to use the paths on the Leaves title or the paths you create yourself for the exercise, which shows how to use these paths for painting.

Leaf Path Practice

1. Open the Practice.psd file if it is not already open. On the Layers palette, click the eye icon to the left of the Lemon layer set title to hide the lemon. Click the square to the left of the Leaf Template layer to toggle the eye icon (or layer visibility) on.

2. Press Ctrl(⌘)+spacebar to toggle to the Zoom tool and drag a marquee selection around the leaf templates to magnify the area for better viewing. If you need to zoom in closer, press Ctrl(⌘)+the plus key to increase the magnification. Press the spacebar to toggle to the Hand tool and scroll until the top leaf area of the document is in view.

> **Tip**
>
> **Set Up Keyboard Zoom to Automatically Resize Windows**   Ctrl(⌘)+the plus
> key and Ctrl(⌘)+the minus key increase or decrease the zoom level of your image.
> When adding Alt(Opt) to these keyboard shortcuts (for example, Ctrl+Alt+the plus key
> (⌘+Option+the plus key)), the image window will resize to accommodate the new
> zoom level.
>
> You can make it the default response to have the window resize by toggling a preference
> for it in the Preference dialog box. Press Ctrl(⌘)+K to open the General Preference
> dialog box and click the Keyboard Zoom Resizes Windows checkbox. Click OK to exit
> the dialog box. Now Ctrl(⌘)+the plus key will resize the window *and* increase zoom
> simultaneously. Adding the Alt(Opt) key now has the reverse function of increasing or
> decreasing the zoom level *without* resizing the window. Check out Chapter 2,
> "Optimizing and Customizing Photoshop Preferences," for more details on Photoshop
> preferences.

3. Choose the Pen tool from the toolbox. On the lower-left corner area of the leaf,
click and drag a short distance to create the control handles for the first point.
Before releasing the mouse button, press the Alt(Opt) key and drag the top
handle slightly to convert it to an independent handle, as shown in Figure 13.20.

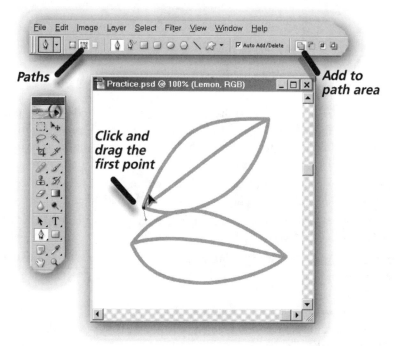

Figure 13.20   Click and drag to create the first point near the bottom-left corner
of the top leaf. Press the Alt(Opt) key and move the top handle
toward the direction of the next curve.

4. Working in a clockwise direction, click and drag a second point along the curve on the top leaf template line (see Figure 13.21).

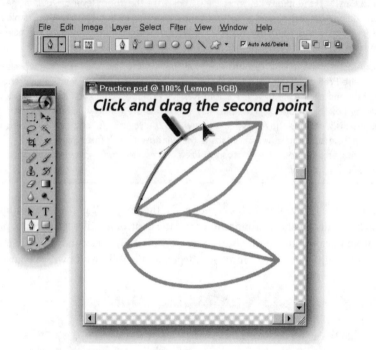

Figure 13.21   Click and drag to create the second point near the top-center leaf line.

5. Click and drag a third point at the leaf corner (at the right side). Again, press the Alt(Opt) before completing the drag and move the control handle slightly downward to conform to the start of the bottom curve, as shown in Figure 13.22.

   Don't worry if the curves of the path do not match the leaf template precisely. You will adjust the direction lines and fine-tune the path after completing it.

6. Click and drag a fourth point along the middle curve of the bottom edge of the leaf template (see Figure 13.23).

7. When you reach the starting point, place the pointer over the first point created, and when a circle appears next to the Pen pointer, click to close the path (see Figure 13.24).

8. Press Shift+A until the Direct Selection tool is the active tool (the hollow arrow). Click the path to view the points. If you see places where the path needs adjusting, click the point to view the direction lines for that point. Drag the direction point (at the end of the direction line) to adjust the direction line (and path) to match the curves of the sketch. If needed, drag and reposition the points. Continue to adjust the direction lines until the curves for the path match closely to the curves on the leaf template (see Figure 13.25).

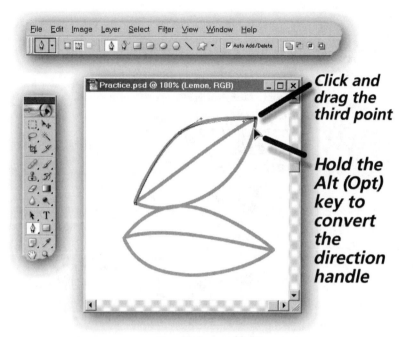

Click and drag the third point

Hold the Alt (Opt) key to convert the direction handle

Figure 13.22   Click and drag to create the third point near the right corner of the top leaf. Press the Alt(Opt) key and move the top handle toward the direction of the bottom curve.

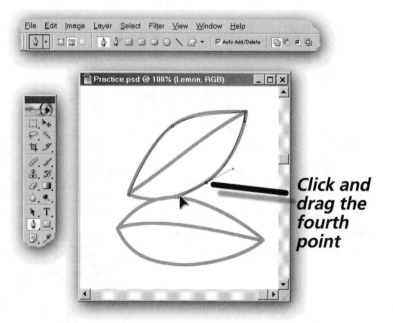

Click and drag the fourth point

Figure 13.23   Click and drag to create the fourth point near the bottom- center leaf line.

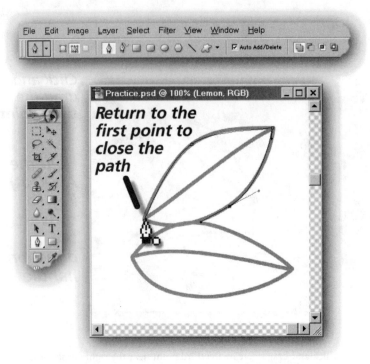

Figure 13.24   When you position the pointer on the first point, a circle will
appear, indicating that the next click will close the path.

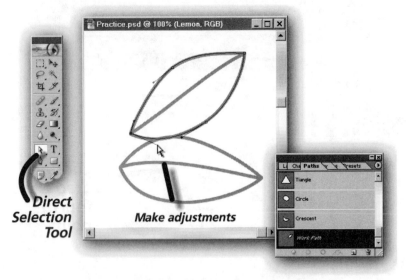

Figure 13.25   Use the Direct Selection tool (hollow arrow) to select points and
direction lines to adjust the shape of the path further (to match
the template).

You'll need to start a new path to represent the center curve that runs down the middle of the leaf. We will show you later how the path will be useful for a nice coloring effect of the leaf. Only the curvature of the centerline is important for the next path; the remaining path can be anywhere outside the leaf to close the path. Don't worry about the placement of points outside the leaf. We will show you later how to make ingenious use of this path.

9. Click with the Direct Selection tool somewhere in the document—away from the path—to deselect the current path. Press P to switch to the Pen tool. On the Options bar, click the Add to selection icon if it is not already chosen. Click and drag the first point outside the lower-left corner of the leaf's center. Hold down the Alt(Opt) key before completing the drag to alter the direction line slightly (see Figure 13.26).

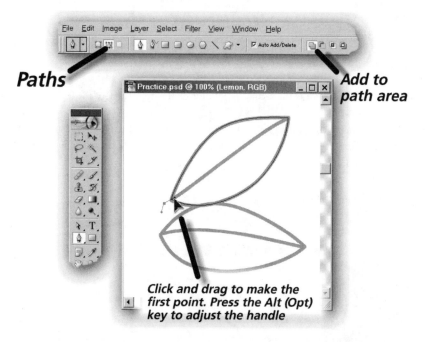

Paths

Add to path area

Click and drag to make the first point. Press the Alt (Opt) key to adjust the handle

Figure 13.26   Click and drag the first point of the new path outside the lower corner of the old path. Press the Alt(Opt) key and drag the upper direction point (on the direction line) in the direction of the leaf's centerline curve.

10. Click and drag your second point outside the leaf area near the top V-shape of the leaf. Again, hold the Alt(Opt) key to move the direction line downward (see Figure 13.27).

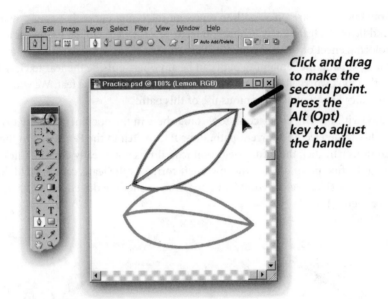

Figure 13.27   Click and drag the second point outside the upper area of the leaf.

11. Click points (without dragging) along the outside of the lower leaf area until you reach the first point created. Click the first point to close the path, as shown in Figure 13.28.

Figure 13.28   Click points along the outside-bottom leaf area. Click to close the path when back at the first point created.

12. Hold down the Ctrl(⌘) key to toggle to the Direct Selection tool. Click the centerline to view the direction lines for this path segment and make any necessary adjustments to the direction handles to match the centerline curvature of the Leaf Template.

13. Press the Ctrl(⌘) key to toggle to the Direct Selection tool and click in an empty area of the image window to deselect the current path. On your own, repeat Steps 2–12 to create the second leaf on the template. Press Ctrl(⌘)+S to save your work. Keep the document open for the next set of steps.

Using Paths in Other Programs

Hopefully the Practice.psd lessons in this chapter have helped you understand the Pen tool. If you have never used programs such as Illustrator but would like to start, you'll be glad to know that all this Photoshop Pen tool stuff applies to Illustrator as well as many other vector-based drawing programs.

Another important thought to keep in mind is that paths created in Photoshop can be copied and pasted into Illustrator and similarly, paths created in Illustrator can be pasted into Photoshop. When you select and copy a path in Illustrator and open a document in Photoshop to paste this path, a dialog box will appear and Photoshop will ask whether you want to paste as pixels or paste as a path. The "paste as pixels" option will immediately create a bitmap version of the path resulting in a pixel representation of the path, at the size at which it exists in Illustrator. And as pixels, the design is carved in stone (to mix metaphors). The "paste as path" option (hint: always choose this) will not only paste the path information into the document but will also have the path located on a Work Path title in the Paths palette. Renaming the path title enables you to permanently store the path information for future use.

Reinforcing Your Understanding of Path Selection Techniques

Creating paths for a large project can be a tedious task. With patience, however, the task can be accomplished easily and the results will be well worth the effort, because paths provide a smoother and more precise selection than pixel strokes.

Keep in mind how you plan to use a path (for future projects). As demonstrated with the leaf path you created, you will use the curvature information of the centerline paths, but the remaining part of that path is of no importance.

There is no dazzling filter work involved in the upcoming steps. The main ingredients involve the repetition of choosing a path, making the path a selection, and applying color to the selection. Before you know it, your work will pay off as you start to see a finished product.

In the next exercise, you will make use of the Leaves path title, but if you have completed the previous work and would like to use the paths you created for the leaves instead, please don't hesitate to substitute your work path title in place of the Leaves path title. Let's get started on polishing off the leaves.

Painting with Path Selections

1. With the Practice.psd document still open, click the Paths tab to view the Paths palette. Click the Leaves title to view the leaf paths. Hold down the Ctrl(⌘) key to toggle to the Direct Selection tool and click the upper leaf path. Click the Load path as a selection icon at the bottom of the Paths palette (see Figure 13.29). Click an empty space below the path titles to deselect the path (if necessary, stretch the palette up until the palette has an empty space).

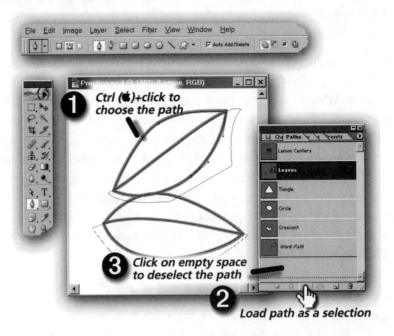

Figure 13.29   Click the Load path as a selection icon at the bottom of the Paths palette to make the selected path into a selection. Clicking an empty space on the palette will deselect the paths, leaving only the selection.

2. Click the Layers tab to return to the Layers palette. Hold down the Alt(Opt) key and click the Create a new layer icon at the bottom of the Layers palette. In the New Layer dialog box, type **Leaf 1** for the name. Click OK. Press Ctrl(⌘)+[to move this layer below the Lemon layer set. Click the eye icon next to the Leaf Template layer to turn off this layer.

3. Click the foreground color selection box on the toolbox and choose a green color (R:77, G:130, B:42). Click OK. Click the background color selection box on the toolbox and choose a darker-green color (R:5, G:32, B:19). Click OK.

4. Click the Gradient tool. On the Options bar, click the Linear gradient icon and choose the Foreground to Background gradient on the drop-down list. Drag a gradient from the inside-bottom edge of the selection to the upper edge of the selection at an angle that matches Figure 13.30. Press Ctrl(⌘)+D to deselect.

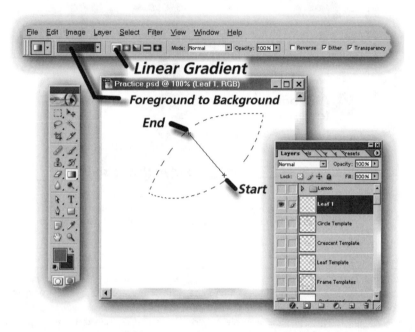

Figure 13.30 If you can imagine the face of a clock, drag a gradient (inside the leaf selection) at an angle starting near 4 o'clock (at the bottom of the leaf) and ending near 10 o'clock (at the top of the leaf).

5. Click the Paths tab to view the Paths palette. Click the Leaves title to view the paths. Hold down the Ctrl(⌘) key to toggle to the Direct Selection tool and click the path that creates a center line for the upper leaf. Click the Load path as a selection icon at the bottom of the Paths palette and click an empty space below the path titles to deselect the path (see Figure 13.31).

6. Click the Layers tab to return to the Layers palette. On the Layers palette, click the Lock transparent pixels icon near the top of the palette. A lock icon will appear on the Leaf 1 layer to indicate that no painting will be applied to the transparent portion of this layer.

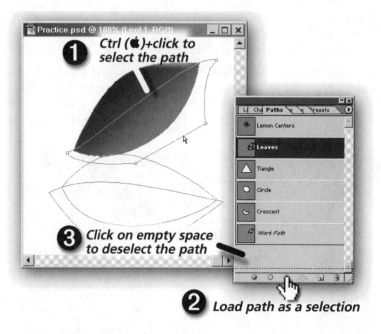

Figure 13.31   Select the path that will give a centerline definition to the leaf and turn the path into a selection to prepare for additional painting.

Note

Protecting Transparent Areas of a Layer   The Lock Transparent Pixels option on the Layers palette (as the title implies) keeps the transparent areas of a layer transparent. You might think of this feature as a paint repellent or an automatic way to mask transparent pixels. This option is available only on layers that contain transparent pixels. When more than one layer in an image contains transparent pixels, each layer can have its own setting; that is, two layers could use the Lock transparent pixels feature while others don't. In the image you're working on now, the transparent area in the image is the area around the leaf. With the option enabled for this layer, the leaf area is now the only area to which color can be applied, because that is the only part of the layer that has nontransparent pixels.

The advantage of preserving transparent areas will soon be apparent because the centerline selection extends outside the leaf area. Keep in mind that it is all right to have a portion of the brush outside the leaf area when painting. With the transparent areas protected, no paint will be applied outside the leaf.

7. Press B to switch to the Brush tool. On the Options bar, make sure that painting Mode is set back to Normal and the Flow is set to 20%. Choose a large, soft brush (65-pixel). Press X to switch the dark-green color to the foreground. Keep a small portion of the brush in the selection area, stroke dark-green tones along the top-center edge of the leaf selection (see Figure 13.32).

Use your own artistic judgment whenever asked to stroke color in these steps. Stroke more than once if it seems to be needed. The low Flow setting on the Brush tool allows for color to be added in a subtle fashion, layer upon layer, in a manner of speaking.

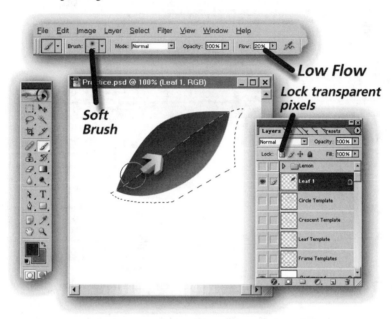

Figure 13.32   Lock the Leaf 1 layer and paint the dark-green color along the inside centerline selection.

8. Press X to switch Color Selection boxes again. Click the foreground color selection box on the toolbox and choose a lighter yellow-green color (R:184, G:204, B:59). Click OK. Stroke a small amount of this color along the bottom edge of the selection (with only a fraction of the brush portion inside the leaf area) to add additional form and color (see Figure 13.33).

9. Click the foreground color selection box on the toolbox and choose the green color again (R:77, G:130, B:42). Click OK. Press Ctrl(⌘)+Shift+I to invert your selection (or Shift+F7; same deal) to add form to the upper half of the leaf now. Add the green color along the centerline of the upper leaf (keeping a small portion of the Brush above the centerline area), as shown in Figure 13.34.

   Even though the selection may appear to be the same if you have scrolls on the image window and can't see the edges of the image (where there are indeed selection marquee lines scampering about), the selection is now the inverse of its original shape. Color is now being added to the upper half of the leaf area, with green near the upper centerline.

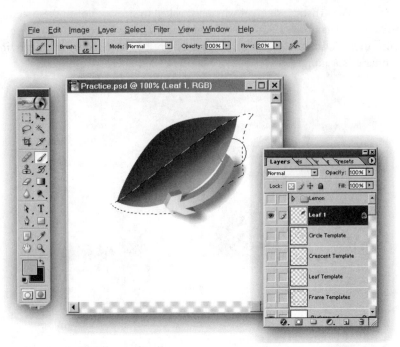

Figure 13.33   Add a little more form to the lower edge with a lighter yellow-green color.

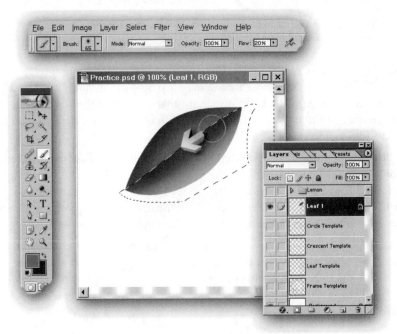

Figure 13.34   Invert the selection and paint green along the upper centerline area to add form to this leaf.

10. Optional: Click the foreground color selection box on the toolbox and choose the lighter yellow-green color again (R:184, G:204, B:59). Click OK. Stroke a small amount of this color along the upper centerline area to add additional form. When satisfied, press Ctrl(⌘)+D to deselect.

11. Press Ctrl(⌘)+S to save your work. Keep the document open for the step to follow.

12. Repeat Steps 1 through 11 to paint in the second leaf with the following changes. In Step 2, when you create a new layer for the leaf, title it Leaf 2 (instead of Leaf 1) and position the Leaf 2 layer below the Leaf 1 layer. Substitute the lower leaf paths (for the upper leaf paths mentioned in the remaining steps) and continue to follow the directions in the same manner. In Step 4, drag the gradient (to color the leaf) in a more vertical angle for Leaf 2 (rather than the previous angle used for Leaf 1).

Using Custom Shapes to Obtain a Path Selection

Not only can paths be saved for future projects, altered in unlimited ways, and transferred between documents and illustration programs, but paths can also be useful in another way by making use of a Photoshop feature: custom shapes.

Remember, paths are mathematical—therefore they can be sized in any direction and still retain a crisp edge for selections or painting. For example, you might find it very useful to create a company logo using paths, and then save that logo path as a custom shape. You then can quickly access the custom shape and drag the company logo (path shape) to any size needed (such as a small version for a business card design or a larger version for a letterhead design).

Creating a custom shape is easy. Using the Path Selection tool, click a path that you've created and choose Define Custom Shape from the Edit menu. Name the shape in the Shape Name dialog box. The new shape will now appear in the Custom Shape pop-up palette. To permanently save the new custom shape as part of a new collection, select Save Shapes from the pop-up palette menu on the Custom Shape palette (and then name your custom shape file). Chapter 4, "Enough Selections! The Layers and Shapes Chapter," has provided additional information on this topic if you would like to know more.

For the next exercise, we created shapes in advance (with the Pen tool) to make a framework design for the lemon image. These frames were saved in a custom shape file provided for you on the Companion CD.

Custom Shapes and Background Design

1. Open the Practice.psd file if it is not already open. On the Layers palette, turn on the Lemon set layer visibility by clicking the square to the far left, which enables the eye icon for this layer. Click the Frame Templates layer to toggle on the visibility for this layer and to make it the active layer.

   The Frame Templates layer is provided as a guide to aid in placement of the frame paths (the custom shape paths). If you would like additional practice with creating paths, however, you can use the Frame Templates as a guide and create the paths on your own. Just remember to compare them to the paths used for the custom shapes, because we all may have different ideas of where to place points along a path.

2. Choose the Custom Shape tool on the toolbox (or press Shift+U until the Custom Shape Tool is active). On the Options bar, choose the Paths mode for the custom shapes tool. Click the arrow next to the Custom shape picker to display the Custom Shape palette. Click the arrow at the upper-right corner of the Custom Shape palette and choose Load Shapes (see Figure 13.35). In the dialog box, navigate a path to the Examples/Chap16 folder on the Companion CD and choose FrameShapes.csh.

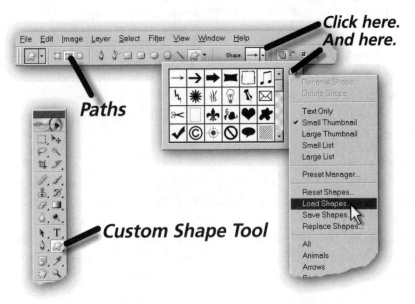

Figure 13.35   This figure shows the Options bar and the options you need to select for the Custom Shape tool. Choose Load Shapes to load the sample file for this example.

Note

Managing the Shape Palette   When you selected Load Shapes in Step 2, you added these two frame shapes to the palette you currently have loaded. If you switch palettes by choosing Reset or Replace Shapes, the two frame shapes will be lost from the current palette.

If you don't want the frames on your current shapes palette, the safest way to banish them is to right-click (Macintosh: hold Ctrl and click) over the unloved shape and choose Delete Shape.

3. Scroll down on the Custom Shape palette and choose the Inner Frame. On the Options bar, click the arrow next to the Custom Shape Tool icon to view the Geometry options and choose Fixed Size. Type **574 px** for Width and **618 px** for Height (see Figure 13.36).

Tip

Specifying Units of Measurement   If you do not type a unit of measurement, such as "in" (for inches) or "px" (for pixels), Photoshop will default to the unit of measurement specified in the Units & Rulers section of Preferences. You can press Ctrl(⌘)+K to high-tail it to Preferences when needed. You can also quickly make a change to your default units of measurement by clicking the plus sign on the lower-left corner of the Info palette and choosing a measurement from the context menu that appears.

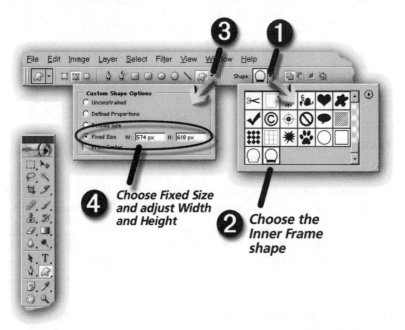

Figure 13.36   Choose the Inner Frame custom shape and type the fixed size amounts for width and height in the Geometry options.

Tip

Don't Forget to Reset the Default   The default Geometry option is
Unconstrained. This option allows you to click and drag to any size. By holding down the
Shift key as you drag, the custom shape will size proportionally. However, the author
took the time to drag the shape to the desired size and used the Info palette to view
the correct (height and width) size so that you could benefit. It also provides an opportunity to use the Fixed Size option to see how cool it can be if you know the size in
advance.

4. In the document, click and drag the Inner Frame shape until it lines up with the
   inner frame template lines, as shown in Figure 13.37.

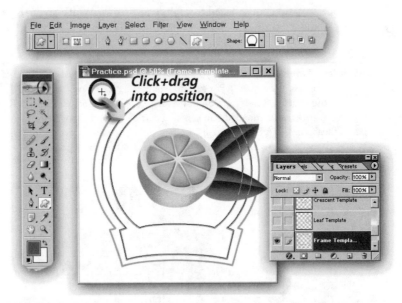

Figure 13.37   With the Fixed Size option, just click and drag to position the
custom shape path into the desired location.

5. Hold down the Alt(Opt) key and click the Create a new layer icon at the bottom
   of the Layers palette. In the New Layer dialog box type **Inner Frame** for the
   name. Click OK.

6. Press Ctrl(⌘)+Enter(Return) to turn the custom shape path into a selection.
   Click the foreground color selection box on the toolbox and choose a blue-green
   color (R:2, G:99, B:101). Click OK. Press Alt(Opt)+Delete (Backspace) to fill the
   selection with this color. Press Ctrl(⌘)+D to deselect.

7. On the Options bar, click the Custom Shape palette and choose the Outer
   Frame. Click the Geometry options and type **630 px** for Width and **665 px** for
   Height (see Figure 13.38).

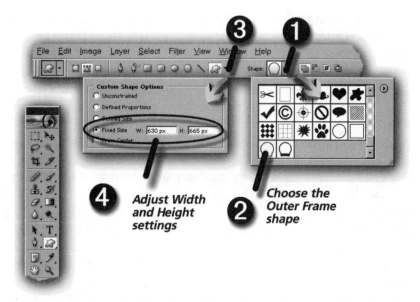

Figure 13.38   Change the custom shape to the Outer Frame. Adjust the Width and Height amounts in the Geometry options palette.

8. In the document, click and drag the Outer Frame shape until it lines up with the outer frame template lines, as you see in Figure 13.39.

Figure 13.39   Click and drag to reposition the outer frame shape with the template lines. The goal is to allow the outer frame shape overlap a little onto the inner frame shape.

9. Hold down the Alt(Opt) key and click the Create a new layer icon at the bottom of the Layers palette. In the New Layer dialog box, type **Outer Frame** for the name. Click OK.

10. Press Ctrl(⌘)+Enter(Return) to turn the custom shape path into a selection. Click the foreground color selection box on the toolbox and choose a yellow color (R:234, G:208, B:70). Click OK. Press Alt(Opt)+Delete (Backspace) to fill the selection with this color.

    On the Options bar, you may want to switch the Geometry options back to the default of Unconstrained for future use of the Custom Shape tool. Otherwise, it might be a real shock when you try to access a simple heart shape for a future project, and Photoshop will allow you to use only one size—the size of North Dakota.

11. Press X to switch the yellow color to the background. Click the foreground color selection box on the toolbox and choose an orange color (R:212, G:109, B:33). Click OK. Press B to switch to the Brush tool. On the Options bar, set the size to a soft-round 65-pixel brush, Mode to Normal, and Flow to 20%. With a small amount of the brush size inside the selection area, paint orange around the outer edges of the frame to add form to its appearance (see Figure 13.40). When satisfied, press Ctrl(⌘)+D to deselect. On the Layers palette, click the visibility icon to turn off the Frame Templates layer.

    Don't worry about a steady hand or perfection. Just paint until it looks appealing. The Flow setting is low, so color can be added using more than one stroke (if more color is needed). If you decided you added too much orange in a particular area, press X to switch to the yellow color, paint over that area. Press X again to switch to orange again and continue where you left off. You also have the option of using the History palette to undo brush strokes you don't like.

12. Click the Add a layer style icon at the bottom of the Layers palette and choose Bevel and Emboss. In the Layer Style dialog box, make Depth 300%, Size 5 px, and Soften 3 px. Leave most of the remaining settings at the default, except click the color swatch for the Shadow Mode and select a maroon color (R:84, G:1, B:3). Click OK (see Figure 13.41).

13. Click the Inner Frame layer to make it the active layer. Hold down the Alt(Opt) key and click the Create a new layer icon at the bottom of the Layers palette. In the New Layer dialog box, type **Outer Frame Shadow** for the name. Click OK.

14. Ctrl(⌘)+click the Outer Frame Layer to load the frame shape as a selection. Go to the Select menu and choose Transform Selection. On the Options bar, click the Maintain aspect ratio icon and type **95%** for Width. Press Enter(Return) twice to exit the Options bar and commit the changes (see Figure 13.42).

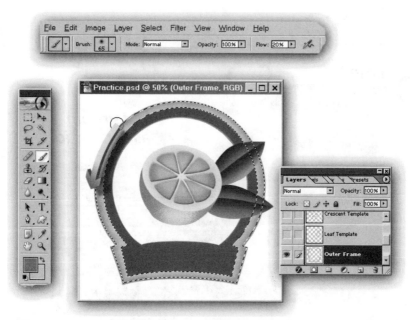

Figure 13.40   Add form and dimension to the outer frame by painting orange on the outer edges. The low Flow setting allows you to add a subtle amount of color. Stroke more than once if more color is needed.

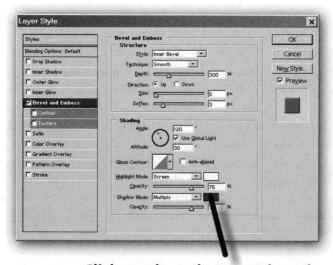

Click on the color swatch and change color to a maroon color

Figure 13.41   Use the settings shown above to apply a Bevel and Emboss effect for the Outer Frame. Adjust the Shadow color to a maroon.

Let's create a custom-sized shadow between the two frames. Here's how:

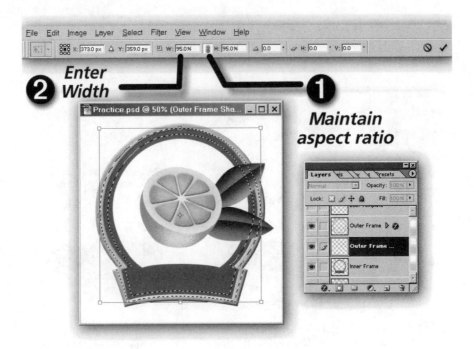

Figure 13.42   Use the Option bar to help reduce the size of the selection proportionally.

15. Press D to get the default color of black as the foreground. With the Outer Frame Shadow layer still the active layer, press Alt(Opt)+Delete (Backspace) to fill the selection with black. Press Ctrl(⌘)+D to deselect.

16. On the Layers palette, change the Layer mode from Normal to Multiply. Lower the Opacity to 60%. Go the Filter menu and choose Blur, Gaussian Blur. In the Gaussian Blur dialog box, choose 4.0 for the Radius. Click OK (see Figure 13.43).

    Uh-oh. There seems to be some shadow showing in a few areas outside the frames. Here's how to fix this...

17. Press W to switch to the Magic Wand tool. Click the Outer Frame layer to make it active. Click anywhere in the white background color outside of the frame (see Figure 13.44). A selection should now appear around the outer frame area. Click the Outer Frame Shadow layer to make this selection active and press the Delete (Backspace) key to delete any shadow that appears within this selection area (outside of the frame). Press Ctrl(⌘)+D to deselect.

18. Press Ctrl(⌘)+S to save your work. Keep the document open for the next exercise.

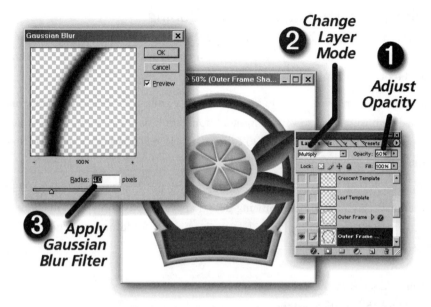

Figure 13.43   Use the Gaussian Blur filter along with Layer palette options to create a soft shadow effect.

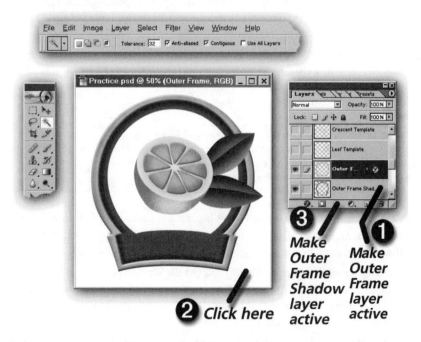

Figure 13.44   Make the Outer Frame layer active to create a selection outside the frame area with the Magic Wand tool. Then make the Outer Frame Shadow layer active again and press Delete (Backspace).

A Ton More Path Talk—Only Kidding

Whew! Get a cold beverage and take a break. The truth is we have covered a lot of territory—hopefully enough to give you the ground work for understanding paths and the related tools.

Speaking of groundwork—we do have some extra ground to cover in finishing up the image design we started so very long ago. I don't know about you, but I've watched my kids graduate from high school, go to college, and get married since I began writing this chapter.

The next steps will show how to add color and some finishing touches to the remainder of the image, giving it a more enticing design appeal. Even though this may not relate directly to the topic of paths, it may be your inspiration for future projects that, like this image, started with paths.

Finishing Touches to the Background

1. Open the Practice.psd file if it is not already open.

2. Hold down the Alt(Opt) key and click the Create a new layer icon at the bottom of the Layers palette. In the New Layer dialog box, type **Circle Backgrd** for the name. Click OK. Press Ctrl(⌘)+[twice to position this layer below the Inner Frame layer (on the Layers palette).

3. Press Shift+M until the Elliptical Marquee tool is selected. Drag a circular selection that remains within the frame area but includes all the white area in the center (behind the lemon), as shown in Figure 13.45.

Note

Moving a Marquee While in the Progress of Creating One   When using the Marquee tools to make a selection, you can reposition the selection—as you drag—by holding down the spacebar while creating your selection and dragging to move the selection into the desired position.

4. Click the foreground color selection box on the toolbox and choose a deep red color (R:121, G:0, B:0). Click OK. Click the background color selection box on the toolbox and choose a brown color (R:48, G:2, B:6). Click OK.

5. Press G to switch to the Gradient tool. On the Options bar, select Foreground to Background and click the Radial Gradient icon. Click in the center of the lemon and drag a gradient down just below the frame area, as shown in Figure 13.46. Press Ctrl(⌘)+D to deselect.

    Optionally, you can hold down the Shift key as you drag a gradient to constrain the drag to a vertical line.

Hold spacebar while dragging to reposition selection as it is created

Figure 13.45   Make an elliptical shape selection that covers the inner-white area (without going outside the frames).

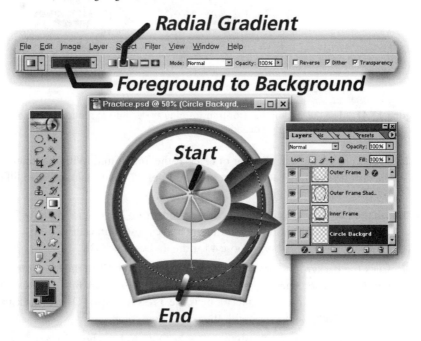

Figure 13.46   Drag a Radial Gradient starting at the lemon center and ending before reaching the outer edge of the selection.

6. Hold down the Alt(Opt) key and click the Create a new layer icon at the bottom of the Layers palette. In the New Layer dialog box, type **Inner Frame Shadow** for the name. Click OK.

7. Ctrl(⌘)+click the Inner Frame Layer to load the frame shape as a selection. Go to the Select menu and choose Transform Selection. On the Options bar, click the Maintain aspect ratio icon and type **93%** for Width. Press Enter(Return) twice to exit the Options bar and commit the changes (see Figure 13.47).

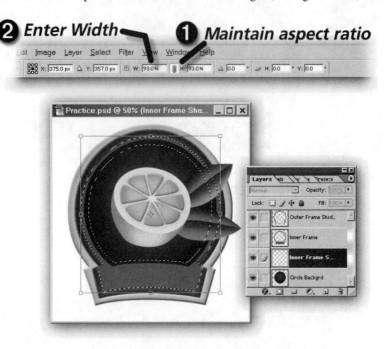

Figure 13.47   Use the Options bar (for transforming a selection) to reduce the size of the selection proportionally.

8. Press D to get the default color of black as the foreground. With the Inner Frame Shadow layer still the active layer, press Alt(Opt)+Delete (Backspace) to fill the selection with black. Press Ctrl(⌘)+D to deselect.

9. On the Layers palette, change the Layer mode from Normal to Multiply. Lower the Opacity to 60%. Go the Filter menu and choose Blur, Gaussian Blur. In the Gaussian Blur dialog box, choose 4 for the Radius. Click OK.

10. Click the Background layer to make it the active layer. Click the foreground color selection box and choose a pale-yellow color (R:245, G:233, B:163). Click OK. The background color should still be white. Press Alt(Opt)+Delete (Backspace) to fill the Background layer with the pale-yellow color

11. Press B to switch to the Brush tool. On the Options bar, choose a large, soft round 200-pixel brush. Change the painting Mode from Normal to Dissolve. The

Flow should still be at 20%. Place the pointer near the lower-right corner edge of the document. When you see a double arrow, stretch the size of the document window out far enough to give you some working room.

12. Press X to switch white to the foreground color. Paint in white around the inner edges of the document window. The goal is to have a circle center of pale yellow dissolving into white at the edges (see Figure 13.48).

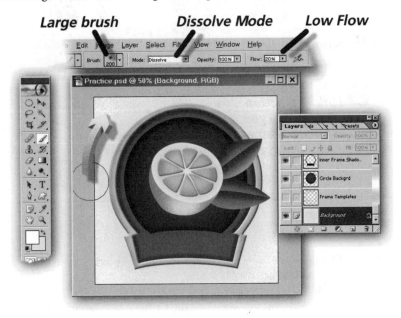

Figure 13.48   Paint a circular border of white in Dissolve mode.

If necessary, press X to switch back to the yellow color to touch up areas you feel need more yellow. Press X again to switch to white again. Use your artistic judgment. When satisfied, don't forget to return the painting Mode back to Normal on the Options bar (so that funky things don't happen the next time you reach for the Brush tool).

Let's clean up the Layers palette a little in the next step.

13. Click the Circle Backgrd layer to make it the active layer. Click the linked layer squares to the left of the four frame layers above the Circle Backgrd layer, as shown in Figure 13.49. Click the arrow in the upper-right corner of the Layers palette and choose New Set From Linked. In the New Set From Linked dialog box, type **Frames** for the Name. Click OK.

14. Drag the Template layers to the Delete layer icon (the trash can) in the bottom-right corner of the Layers palette.

Here's an optional idea. If for some reason you prefer to keep these layers, you can link them and create for them a layer set called Templates. Remember to click the Layer visibility icon to turn off this layer set.

We created shadows for the frames—but what about the lemon and leaves? Let's give those items a shadow too.

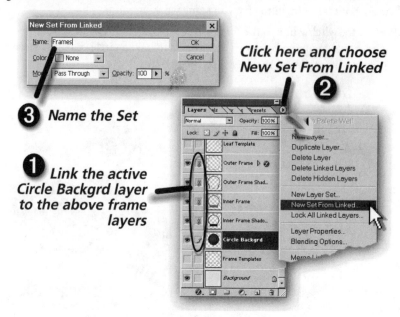

Figure 13.49   Link the frame layers to the Circle Backgrd layer and create a
new set from the linked layers.

15. Hold down the Alt(Opt) key and click the Create a new layer icon at the bottom of the Layers palette. In the New Layer dialog box, type **Lemon/Leaf Shadow** for the name. Click OK.

16. Ctrl(⌘)+click the Leaf 2 layer to load a selection. Ctrl(⌘)+Shift click the Leaf 1 layer to add this leaf to the selection. Click the arrow next to the Lemon layer set to open the set, and Ctrl(⌘)+Shift click the Lemon Top and the Lemon Peel layers to add the lemon to the selection area (see Figure 13.50).

Note

Using Boolean Modifiers with Layer Selections   Pressing Ctrl(⌘) while clicking a layer will turn any image information resting on that layer into a selection. Adding other modifier keys allows you to control the selection by adding, subtracting, or intersecting with other layer information.

To be more specific, pressing Ctrl(⌘)+Shift allows you to add other layer information to the selection. Ctrl(⌘)+Alt(Opt) subtracts other layer information, and (if you have the dexterity) Ctrl(⌘)+Shift+Alt(Opt) allows the intersection of layer information when creating layer selections.

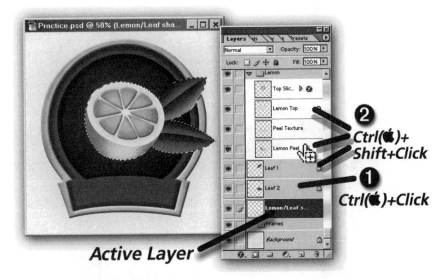

Figure 13.50   Ctrl(⌘)+click the first leaf layer. Then Ctrl(⌘)+Shift+click additional
layers to add to the selection to select the lemon and leaves. The new
Lemon/Leaf Shadow layer should still be the active layer and resting
below the Lemon and Leaf layers.

17. With the Lemon/Leaf Shadow layer still as the active layer, press D to make black
the default foreground color. Press Alt(Opt)+Delete (Backspace) to fill the selection with black. Press Ctrl(⌘)+D to deselect.

18. On the Layers palette, change the layer mode from Normal to Multiply and
change the Opacity to 60%.

The Transform tool will be used to modify the shadow (which is not visible at
the moment because it rests behind the Lemon and Leaf layers). In transforming
the shadow layer, I chose the Distort command off the context menu (and pro-
ceeded to play with the bounding box handles). This is the same context menu
that can be viewed if you right-click (Macintosh: hold Ctrl and click) inside the
bounding box area of the Transform tool. You get to benefit from my trials and
tribulations, however, because I found the perfect numeric sequence that yields
the desired results (without having you suffer through the same sequence of tug-
ging and dragging on the bounding box handles). This formula is passed on to
you in the next step.

19. Press Ctrl(⌘)+T to activate the Transform tool. On the Options bar, use the
numeric values seen in Figure 13.51. Type **455** for the X coordinate, **359** for the y
coordinate, **103.9** for Width, **99.7** for Height, set rotation at **–4.4**, set Horizontal
skew at **–9.2**. Press Enter (Return) twice to exit the Options bar and to commit
the changes.

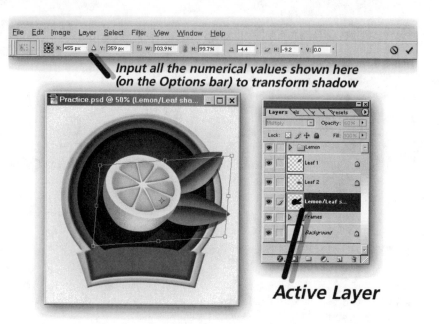

Input all the numerical values shown here
(on the Options bar) to transform shadow

Active Layer

Figure 13.51   On the Options bar, use the options shown above to transform the shadow to the desired shape and position.

20. Go to the Filter menu and choose Blur, Gaussian Blur. In the Gaussian Blur dialog box, choose 4 px. Click OK.

Let's create a layer set for the Shadow and Leaf layers.

21. On the Layers palette, click the Link layer squares to the left of the Leaf 1 and Leaf 2 layers. Click the arrow in the upper-right corner of the Layers palette and choose New Set From Linked. In the New Set From Linked dialog box, type **Leaves/Shadow**. Click OK.

Just one last detail to add and then we can call it a wrap. Let's add some text to label the image. A file has been prepared in advance so that you can accomplish this quickly and easily. Here's a quick overview of how the text file was created: The font used was Bremen Bold BT. A slight arc was applied using the Warped Text feature. The text was rasterized (Layer, Rasterize, Type) and a gradient of colors was applied. Each letter was separated onto its own layer so the layers could be positioned to overlap each other. Additional layers were created for the shadow of each letter (all the layers are provided so that you can study them). A Bevel and Emboss layer effect was applied to the individual letters. For the shadow layers, layer options such as Mode and Opacity were applied (along with a Gaussian Blur filter using a 1.8 radius).

22. Open LemonText.psd in the Examples/Chap16 folder on the Companion CD. Press V to switch to the Move tool. Resize and position both documents so that

they both can be viewed. Click the title bar of the LemonText.psd document so that this is the active document and (on the Layers palette) drag the Lemon Text layer set into the Practice.psd document. Drag the text to position it on the lower part of the inner frame area as shown in Figure 13.52.

Figure 13.52   Drag the layer set from the LemonText.psd file into the Practice.psd file. The layer set will now appear in the Practice document (with all the layers included in the set). Position the text as shown in the figure.

23. Press Ctrl(⌘)+S to save your work.

Tip

Brushing Up on Path Creations   This chapter is part of a section on Art and Photoshop. If you ever feel that you want to brush up on the particulars of path creation without recreating this chapter's design, check out Chapter 5, "Working with Channels and Paths," in the "Photoshop Core Concepts" section of this book.

Summary

This chapter involved a mixture of painting and path work. Hopefully you learned an important lesson: how to make paths become useful design and selection tools. The finished product shown in Figure 13.53 is rather striking—don't ya think?

Figure 13.53   The final image has an impressive polished look when you consider
the simple basic shapes that were the beginning point.

The quality of art is directly proportional to the earnest amount of work you put into it.
The lemon was not merely a "Here's how to draw an ellipse" tutorial, but through effort
and understanding, you arrived at something magnificent.

Let's continue, shall we? Turn this page!

Chapter 14

Bringing Out the Artist in You

Lots of people rely on Photoshop purely as a means of retouching photos. These people never venture near any of the paint tools because they've decided that they aren't "artistic" (whatever *that* means). Many people accept the fact that they aren't Ansel Adams; and that's the very reason they rely on Photoshop. They need a means to correct their technical weaknesses in photography. But because they "can't draw a straight line without a ruler," they never consider Photoshop as a means for painting. Why should they? They can't paint! If you are one of those people who think you "can't paint," this chapter is for you!

This chapter discusses painting in Photoshop for the non-painter. We'll use the term *non-painter* because you won't need any particular level of artistic skill to create images that emulate real paintings. Non-painters aren't either good or bad at painting; they've just never really made the effort before.

Painting for the Non-Painter

As with everything else in life, you have to make some effort to get good results; but for this chapter, you don't need to know the technical side of how to draw or paint. You don't need to know about color or composition, either, because a full treatment of these topics is outside of the range of this book. If you are familiar with the various concepts of art, that's great, but it's not a prerequisite for our work here. For now we will be focusing on converting photographs into images that look like traditional paintings. You may want to consider this the "training wheels" chapter because in the following chapter you explore more advanced painting techniques.

The first step is examining how to get past that "Photo-that's-just-been-filtered-to-look-like-a-painting-but-ain't-foolin'-anybody" look. We'll use the Art History brush to create painterly images (complete with the usual spins you've come to expect from the *Inside Photoshop* books). We'll also discuss when you should consider making an image into a painting instead of just letting it stand on its own as a photo, image requirements you want to allow for, and finally, thoughts about outputting your "paintings."

Applying Artistic Filters

The easiest way to turn a photo into something that resembles hand-painted art is to apply a filter to the image. If you choose Filter, Artistic you will find a boatload of filter choices. Some allow different settings, and some don't. What all of these filters have in common is that once you've applied them they look exactly like what they are— "canned," the way Spam looks like meat. Most of the time that's not going to be the effect you want.

So how do you make an image look less processed and more natural? It's elementary, my dear Watson. You let the filter do the bulk of the work and then add the human element (namely, you) to the mix by adding your own brush strokes. The result can be very effective.

Setting Up Your Mini Art Studio

1. Open the Rocky.tif image from the Examples/Chap14 folder on the Companion CD.

   The image is a medium-format shot of the Arizona desert taken by Charles Hage. As you can see in Figure 14.1, the author is ready to apply the filter to the image. The point of this particular exercise isn't about applying filters *per se*, so we're skipping past that part. The image you will begin with is pre-filtered. Keep in mind that you can use the following technique with any filter you choose; the sky's the limit!

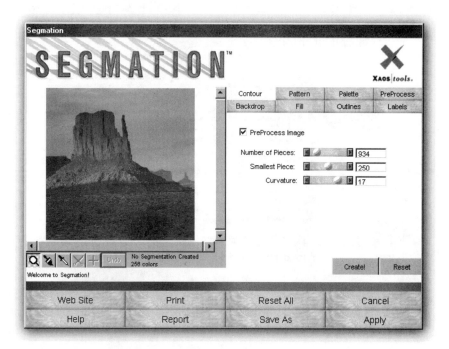

Figure 14.1   These are the Segmation settings that were used for the photo you work with in this example (the filter hasn't been applied yet).

The image you've just opened is acceptable as it is—it's a great foundation to build on—but it still looks "computerized." Let's move in to transform the image into something that appears to look more hand-painted.

Note

Segmation   Just in case you're interested, the filter that was applied to the Rocky.tif image was a third-party plugin, Xaos Tools' Segmation filter (www.xaostools.com). This filter was chosen over one of Photoshop's native filters because the author feels Segmation does a better job than most filters of making the image look hand-drawn, and the applied filter lends itself well to the stylized end result that we want to achieve.

2. In the top right of the Layers palette, click the right-facing triangle to open the flyout menu. Choose New Layer.

3. When the New Layer dialog box appears, name this layer **Sky** and click OK.

4. Double-click the Zoom tool (also known as the magnifying glass) so that the Rocky.tif image is zoomed to 100%.

5. Choose the Brush tool from the toolbox (If the Pencil tool is visible, click and hold your cursor in that particular toolbox cell until the flyout menu appears and then choose the Brush tool).

6. Next, move to the Options bar, and click the Brush Preset picker (as shown in Figure 14.2). Then click the right-facing triangle to open the context menu; choose Calligraphic Brushes.

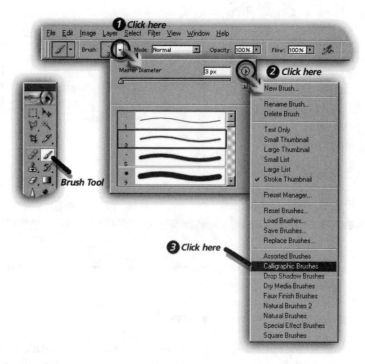

Figure 14.2   To load the Calligraphic Brushes, you'll need to navigate through these menus.

7. Another dialog box appears asking whether you want to replace the current set of brushes. Choose OK.

8. On the Options bar, click in the Brush Preset picker to open the drop-down menu and choose the 7-pixel Flat brush (see Figure 14.3). Press Enter (Return) to close the menu.

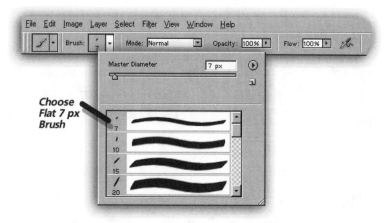

Figure 14.3   Choose the very first brush in the row of brushes. The remaining Option bar settings should be as shown.

Ok, now that we're finished setting up our brush requirements and giving ourselves a decent view of the image, we're ready to roll. Again, keep in mind that you don't need to be Micro-angelo to create cool artwork here; you just need a bit of creativity and the willingness to use it.

Note

Mouse or Graphics Tablet?   For all of the tutorials in this chapter, the author used a mouse. Of course you can also use a graphics tablet if you own one. Some folks can't live without their Wacoms, and there are additional advantages to using a tablet (such as pressure sensitivity, which creates realistically tapered strokes). The point is, don't feel completely left out if you don't own a tablet; it's not as necessary as you might think.

Adding the Human Touch to a Filtered Image

The concept behind removing the "computer look" from filtered images is a simple one. Using another layer (or two), we are going to build upon the base created with the filter by adding strokes via hand. We don't have to paint completely over the underlying image. We only have to insert enough new strokes to give the illusion that a person did the entire image.

Enough talk, let's get in there and paint like Picasso...Elmer Picasso, the barber.

Painting in Some Soul

1. The Brush tool should currently be active. Press Alt(Opt) to temporarily access the Eyedropper tool and sample the light cloud color, as shown in Figure 14.4.

Figure 14.4   First you sample the color.

2. Now move the Brush in a squiggly line to disrupt the nice neat line made by the Segmation filter, as you see in Figure 14.5.

Tip

Remember Undo   Don't forget that if you make a squiggly line that you're not so crazy about, you can always press Ctrl(⌘)+Z to undo (or go to the Edit menu and choose Undo Brush). If you make a number of strokes that you aren't happy with, you can always use the History palette to click around and find a previous state you like.

Now paint in some areas for the rest of the sky. Simply add some squiggly lines around the solid shapes that represent the cloud patterns. Another artistic trick in this area is to sample from one area and paint in another.

3. Press Alt(Opt) to access the Eyedropper tool and click in the cloud shape shown in Figure 14.6. This samples the cloud's color values. Release the Alt(Opt) key, move your cursor into the sky area, and make a squiggly shape.

Figure 14.5   Then stroke along the edge of color to disrupt the solid lines.

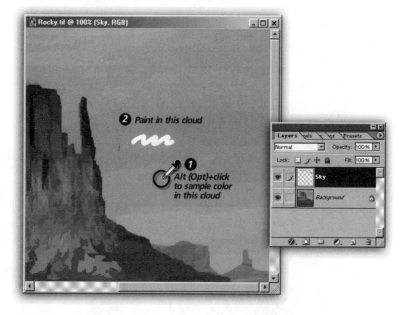

Figure 14.6   First you sample the color from one cloud…and then you paint the sampled color into another cloud area.

You can paint as little or as much as you want here. The idea is to simply break up the hard shapes made by the computer. You can even press the right bracket key (]) three times to increase the brush size to 10 pixels; then paint in a couple of spots to break up the size of your lines even more. Once you feel you've painted enough, you can move on to do the rest of the image.

4. Alt(Opt)+click the Create a new layer icon found at the bottom of the Layers palette, and name this new layer **Ground**.

Tip

Use a Safety Net   You don't have to make a new layer to continue painting but if you're an absolute beginner, look at the new layer as a valuable safety net. You may get the sky exactly the way you want it, but you might not like the way the paint strokes on the ground turn out. If you save your work on individual layers, you have more control over what you keep and what you redo.

As you may have noticed by the name of the layer, next you're going to work on the image areas that represent the rock shape and the ground. You will focus on the rock first, so adjust the window sliders so that the mountain is located dead center in the image window.

5. Press the Alt(Opt) key to toggle to the Eyedropper tool and sample some of the bright orange. Make a few vertical strokes, as you see in Figure 14.7. If you were using the larger brush while painting in the sky area, press the left bracket key ([) until you have the 7-pixel brush again.

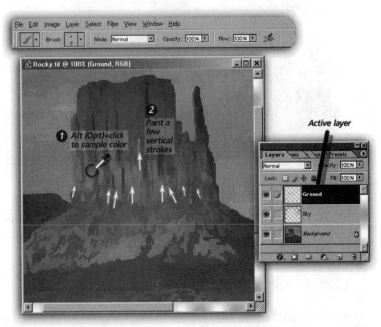

Figure 14.7   This area doesn't need a lot of work. The strokes you see were the final ones applied to this particular area.

A good rule of thumb when doing this type of painting is to follow the natural lines of the image. In this area, the rocks are lined up vertically, so for the most part the author's lines are also drawn in the same direction.

Now look at the base of the rock formation. Here the filter is very obvious, but not for long! Many of the shapes are really plastic-looking; they remind the author of a paint-by-numbers image. The goal is to make these shapes appear more natural by breaking them up, as you've been doing.

6. Again, you'll want to sample color from the image and then apply your own strokes in roughly the same direction, as shown in Figure 14.8.

Figure 14.8   The lines on the left side of the base of the rocks move diagonally toward the top right, the center lines move more directly up, and the lines on the right move diagonally toward the top left to mimic the natural lines of the image.

It's not necessary to add an excessive number of lines in these areas. A few strokes go a long way toward "selling" the illusion that the entire image has been done by hand. Make sure to sample a number of colors, though; using just a single color can give the "trick" away.

There is a small dark area to the right that is part of the rock slope; and on the left, the line intersects with the ground. Using the same technique, apply additional lines to this small section.

Finally, apply your own painterly strokes to the ground area (if you feel especially shaky you can always make another layer before you begin). This area requires the most painting of the entire image; but as with the rest of the areas you've painted, it doesn't require a lot of artistic skill.

7. Press Alt(Opt) to toggle to the Eyedropper tool and sample the ground color. Paint in horizontal strokes into the ground area, as shown in Figure 14.9.

Figure 14.9   The idea hasn't changed; follow the natural lines of the ground to paint out that filtered look. The arrows indicate a suggested method of applying strokes right to left, but the author is left-handed. You may find that a left-to-right method works better for you.

Paint the ground with as many or as few strokes as you see fit. You may want to go to the Examples/Chap14 folder on the Companion CD and open the finished version of the file, Rocky-final.psd. In this file, you can see exactly how the author applied his strokes. You can hide individual layers to see how the lines were painted. In fact, if you look closely, you'll notice that the author cheated and painted some lines going in the opposite direction in the ground lines. Not only that, you may notice some strokes are not really stokes at all, more like dabs of digital paint.

At this point some of you have created your very first digital painting! Congrats, folks! You may want to save this new file as Rocky.psd.

Now let's look at another semi-automatic way of creating an image that uses a different approach to creating this "painting" illusion. Instead of using a filtered image, we'll apply the Art History brush to a vacation photo.

Becoming One of the Great Painters in Art History

The Art History brush has been around for a while now, but it's one of those tools that people don't seem to discuss much. It's even possible that some of you may not even know where to find this tool. (Hint: Look in the same toolbox cell as the History Brush tool.) Or perhaps you found it, took a couple of cursory swipes (in whatever image you had open at that moment), and decided that the Art History brush didn't do too much and haven't given it a thought since. Well, the Art History brush does need a little bit of set up, and it can be a bit finicky sometimes; but armed with proper knowledge (namely, this book), you can create a very realistic painted image.

Note

A Brief History Lesson   Shortly we'll be using the Art History brush, which is a variation of the History brush. To better appreciate the Art History brush, you need to understand how the History Brush works.

What is the History brush? Imagine undo attached to a brush so that you can recover small areas of an image. The Art History Brush works exactly like the History Brush except that it adds painterly effects to the mix.

A *state* is the condition of the image at a particular instance. The first instance occurs when you open the image (it's unaltered state), then you make a paint stroke (which makes another instance), then you make another paint stroke (which makes the next instance). This goes on as History continues to note each image change until you finish the image. You can click on various states in the History palette to jump around in "time."

You can choose what point in History you want to paint with by clicking in the box to the left of any of the History states found in the History palette. By default, Photoshop draws from the initial Snapshot it makes when you open an image—note the Paintbrush icon in the Snapshot of the Rocky image if it's still open.

What is a Snapshot? As you can imagine, Photoshop can remember only a finite number of History states (you can choose how many states you want Photoshop to remember in Preferences). If you have 20 states chosen and you make 21 strokes of paint with the Brush tool, the first state disappears to be replaced with the 21st stroke. It's gone with no way to go back. You can click on the initial Snapshot, but that takes you to the very beginning, which may be too far. Clicking the Create new snapshot icon on the History palette creates a state that you can access as long as your Photoshop session lasts. Unfortunately, Snapshots are not saved; but if you make three Snapshots of an image in the History palette, you can click on each Snapshot and then save each version of the same file with a unique name to preserve the variations that have been created.

So let's dive in by opening our working image and adjusting the Art History brush settings based upon our image size.

Prepping the Image and Work Area

The first thing you need to do to get started is to open the image that you'll be using. Find the Splash.tif file in the Examples/Chap14 folder on the Companion CD. Open this image, and let's talk about it for a moment before moving on to the tutorial.

The original photograph was shot a few years ago in Hawaii and might actually look nice in a decent frame, save for the one problem that drives the author nutty. If you zoom the image to 200% or look at the detail image (see Figure 14.10), you may notice that the face is not tack sharp. Through the viewfinder, everything looked crystal clear, but an 8×10 print proved otherwise so all this time the image has been put away. If you have a couple of photos that are "not quite there" in the focus department (and who doesn't?), you might want to use one as a good candidate for the following techniques.

Figure 14.10   Because we're going to turn this image into a painting, the fact that the original image isn't totally sharp is unimportant; it'll give you a reason to tell people you're an impressionist. No, please—you don't have to show me your Jack Nicholson, really!

One more thing to point out before we begin: If you open the Image Size dialog box (Image, Image Size) you'll see that this image is 200 ppi. It is possible to work on images as small as 72 ppi if these images are without people (which would really only be good for desktop wallpaper or web images). But images that contain people shouldn't have a resolution less than 150 ppi.

Creating an Impressionist Painting Using Art History

The Splash.tif image should be open from the previous section. (If it's not, go ahead and open it now.) Double-click the Hand tool to make the image fill the workspace.

1. Click the tab of the History palette, and drag it away from the group of other palettes. If the History palette isn't visible for some reason, go to the Window menu and choose History.

For this tutorial, you're going to be using both the History and Layers palettes quite a bit, so pulling the palettes apart instead of continually clicking back and forth makes sense. It would also be a good idea to minimize or even close the other palettes and place the History palette above the Layers palette to maximize workspace.

2. Click the Layers palette to pull the palette to the front if it's not already there.

The first thing you're going to do is to prepare the image for your artistic creation. The Art History brush samples the state you instruct it to draw from (just as the History brush does). The concept is to give the Art History brush a state with exaggerated color (also known as *artistic license*).

3. Press Ctrl(⌘)+M to open the Curves dialog box. Click the Load button, navigate to the Examples/Chap14 folder on the Companions CD, and click the BlueSky.acv file to load the pre-fabricated values into the Curves dialog box, as shown in Figure 14.11). Click OK.

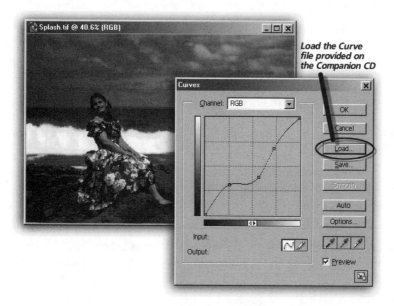

Figure 14.11   The cool thing about Curves is that you can save and load them for later use. This is a fairly radical curve for this image; and as you can see, it provides plenty of color for any painting.

4. Move to the History palette, press the Alt(Opt) key, and click the Camera icon located at the bottom of the palette (that's the Create new snapshot icon for those of you playing along at home). The New Snapshot dialog box opens; enter the name **Blue sky**, as shown in Figure 14.12. Click OK.

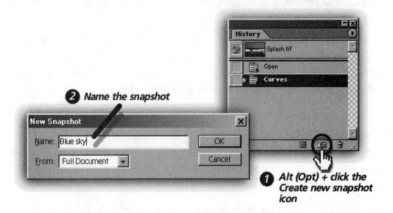

Figure 14.12   Name the New Snapshot **Blue sky** because naming it **Holy Zoo** wouldn't make a lick of sense.

5. Press Ctrl(⌘)+Z to Undo the Curves you just applied.

As noted, the Blue sky curves are sufficient for creating a very good painting; but this is the *Inside Photoshop* book you're reading, and we don't do anything halfway. So let's kick everything up a notch…*or two*. The next set of steps is no glitch in the Matrix, folks. We're going to make a very different snapshot from which we will also be drawing.

6. Press Ctrl(⌘)+M to open the Curves dialog box again. Click the Load button, navigate to the Examples/Chap14 folder on the Companions CD, and double-click the RockBright.acv file to load the prefabricated values into the Curves dialog box (as shown in Figure 14.13). Click OK.

7. Move back to the History palette, press the Alt(Opt) key, and click the Create new snapshot icon located at the bottom of the palette. The New Snapshot dialog box opens; enter the name **Rock bright**. Click OK to close the dialog box.

8. Press Ctrl(⌘)+Z again to Undo these curves, too.

9. On the Layers palette, click the right-facing triangle to open the flyout menu, and choose New Layer. In the New Layer dialog box, type the name **Ground.** Click OK.

Now that you've organized your palettes, let's set up the Art History brush.

10. Press and hold the pointer on the History Brush cell until the flyout appears; then choose the Art History brush.

Figure 14.13   This is a fairly different set of curve values compared to the last ones.

11. On the Options bar, click the Brush Preset picker, click the right-facing triangle to open the flyout menu, and choose Natural Brushes, as shown in Figure 14.14. When the dialog box appears asking whether you want to replace the current set of brushes, choose OK.

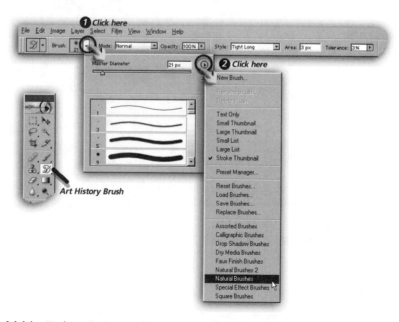

Figure 14.14   You're going to acquire a new set of brushes, just as you did in the first tutorial. This time the choice will be the Natural Brushes.

This is the way the tutorial is structured: Start with a larger brush and work your way down to smaller brushes for the details. As with some fine art, some areas of the image are heavily worked, and other areas remain sketchy. These techniques go a long way toward adding to the realistic look you're after—no filter is able to do what you'll do here.

> **Tip**
>
> **Reset Your Brushes**   Don't forget to reset your brushes by choosing Reset Brushes from the Brush Preset picker after you've completed this tutorial.

12. On the Options bar, set the Style to Tight Long, Area to 50px and the Tolerance to 50%; then from the Brush Preset picker, choose the 59-pixel Charcoal brush, as shown in Figure 14.15.

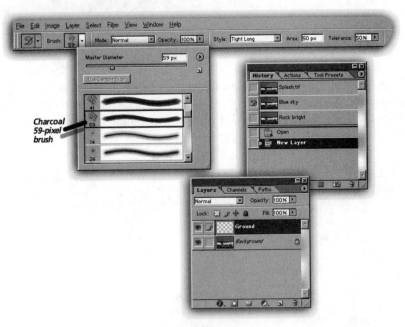

Figure 14.15   This larger brush will be used to emulate sketchy under-painting as would be found in traditional art.

Ok, you've got your entire workplace set up; all you need to do now is use it!

Strokin' Up a Storm

The first thing you need to do is to try to cover up as much of the original photo as is possible. The Ground layer should still be the active layer in the Layers palette.

Laying the Foundation of the Painting

1. In the History palette, click in the far left box of the snapshot named Blue sky to make it the History state (the History Brush icon will appear in the box), and then drag your large brush all over the entire image, as shown in Figure 14.16.

Figure 14.16   Try to cover as much of the image as is possible. There will be small sections the Art History brush will not cover, but that's not a problem.

You may have been somewhat surprised to see the colors leap out of your pointer the way they did. As you'll see, that was intentional; you'll be giving the Art History brush a tighter leash as you progress. The result should be roughly blocked in color, as though Mr. Magoo were painting without his glasses.

Tip

Art History Brush Settings   The Art History brush has a number of unique settings, so let's take a moment to discuss them. The Style option sets the length of the stroke (short, medium, or long) and the type of stroke coming from the brush (loose or tight). The Area option sets how far the pixel strokes stretch from the Art History brush. Tolerance controls how varied the color of the stroke will be from the original sampled area.

2. Next, on the Layers, palette click the right-facing triangle to open the flyout menu, and choose New Layer. In the New Layer dialog box, type the name **Medium.**

The layer is named Medium so that you can recognize instantly which layer is holding the medium level details. You're painting on multiple layers for a number of reasons. You may have noticed that the Art History brush doesn't fill some areas completely; an odd quality about the Art History brush is that you might see that an area doesn't have any "paint" in it, and yet the Art History brush will do nothing when dragged over that area. However, one can gain the ability to paint in areas where the Art History brush has "frozen" (just stopped working) by moving to a new layer.

If you make a bad stroke you can always press Ctrl(⌘)+Z to Undo it, or you can click the History palette list (as discussed in Chapter 2, "Optimizing and Customizing Photoshop Preferences") to move back to a state you liked.

3. From the Brush Preset picker menu choose the 19-pixel Stipple brush. In the Options bar, change the Style to Tight Medium, the Area to **15** px and the Tolerance to 15% (see Figure 14.17).

Now your "painting" should start to take shape. In fact, for the most part, you won't be doing anything else to the clouds. They look just fine as they are, which is kind of on the rough side. Now let's zoom in and "work up" the details of some very specific areas.

4. Click the Create a new layer icon at the bottom of the Layers palette. Double-click the layer's name (the name should be Layer 1), and rename the layer **Patch.** Press Enter (Return) to set the new layer name.

5. Zoom the image to 100% by choosing View, Actual Pixels (or by pressing Ctrl(⌘)+ the plus key until the Zoom factor is 100%).

Tip

Going in for a Closer Look   You may want to zoom in further for a closer look (to find those holes) and maneuver around the image by pressing the spacebar (to toggle to the Hand tool) whenever you find it necessary to move your view to a different section of the image.

6. In the Options bar, choose the 12-pixel Stipple brush.

Figure 14.17   As with the color that was applied to the last layer, you should be able to cover the entire Medium layer in a single pass or two.

On the Layers palette, click the eye icon to the left of the Background layer to toggle the visibility off. You should see many small holes of transparency in your art. You're going to "plug those holes" next.

7. Using the Art History brush, paint over any gaps where you can see all the way through to Photoshop's checkerboard pattern, as shown in Figure 14.18.

Patching your work this way may not have really been necessary for this particular image because the background layer should be well covered; but if you ever come up against this type of problem with your own images, you'll be set.

It is important to keep the file open for the next exercise. Closing the file now will cause you to lose the snapshots saved on the History palette.

The Devil Is in the Details
From this point forward you'll be focusing on painting in the necessary details to make this image really pop. Let's begin by tightening up the horizon line. This is the home stretch.

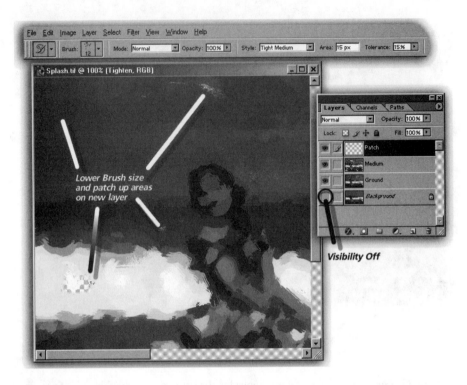

Figure 14.18   Because of the way the Art History brush works there may still be some very tiny transparency holes that cannot be patched. They can always be filled in with a small bit of sampled color, using the Paintbrush if necessary.

Tightening Up Your Image

1. On the Options bar set the Opacity to 80%. Press the left bracket key ([) until the Stipple brush is 4 pixels set the Area to 5 px and the Tolerance to 5%.

2. Create a new layer, and name it **Tight**. Then click and drag the Art History brush along the horizon line, as shown in Figure 14.19.

3. Next, run the Art History brush along the edges of the white wave, over all of the rocks, and over the subject. Use Ctrl(⌘)+plus sign to zoom in if necessary, and don't forget to make use of the spacebar (to toggle to the Hand tool) when you need to move around in the document window.

4. Make a new layer, and name it **Details**.

5. Drag the Art History brush over the subject's hair, face, and skin only.

6. Drag the Art History brush over the subject and all the rocks, as shown in Figure 14.20.

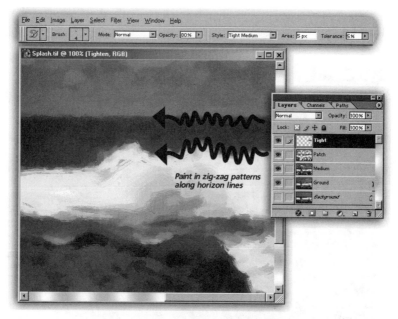

Figure 14.19   Run the Art History brush along the line that makes up the horizon. Moving the brush over the line in a small zig-zag pattern might work best for some folks.

Figure 14.20   Drag the Art History brush over the dress, over all of the rocks, and even a little into the water area if you want. You may not want to hover for very long over the dress area, but come up with a look you like.

7. Now set the Style back to Tight Short, and go over the dress again, as shown in Figure 14.21.

Figure 14.21   The dress should show an unusual effect at this point.

Earlier, you set the dress up to look a certain way, and this last step should have changed the look a bit more.

Next let's put the last touches on the face.

8. Create a new layer, and name it **Face**, then click in the box to the left of the Splash.tif thumbnail in the History palette to draw from that state.

9. Switch to the History brush from the toolbox. Press the right bracket key (]) until the brush is about 20 pixels. Make sure that the opacity is 100%.

10. Apply the History brush to the face area and only, slightly into the hairline.

11. Go to the Edit menu, and choose Fade History Brush. Lower the opacity to 44%, as shown in Figure 14.22.

12. Switch to the Art History brush from the toolbox. Press the left bracket key ([) until the brush size drops down to 2 pixels, and set the style to Tight Long. Drag quickly through the white area of the wave to add a small amount of color. Also drag the brush through all the water and over the horizon as well as over the dress and all of the rocks.

Figure 14.22   Using the History brush with Fade gives the face a slight boost in sharpness while holding on to the painterly look we're after.

Now that you've added some texture to the water and the rocks, and added a bit more detail to the dress, you're almost done.

13. In the History palette, click the box to the left of the Rock bright thumbnail to make it the History state. Bet you forgot you even made that one, huh?

Well, we're finally at the end, and we've saved the best for last.

14. Drag the Art History brush thoroughly over the rocks and through the darker parts of the water, as shown in Figure 14.23.

That's all, folks! Congratulations! You're done with this tutorial. This last bit of added texture should look fairly striking. If you're a non-painter, you may find your "artistic" friends asking you to show them a thing or two.

Note

Signing Your Work   The best way to acknowledge your artistic endeavor is by signing the finished piece. If you're using a tablet this should be no problem, but if you're using a mouse your best option is to make a scan of your signature and then drop that into your completed paintings. Many artists save their signatures as EPS files so the signature can be scaled up or down as needed.

Figure 14.23   The Rock bright state adds nice texture to the rocks and water; dragging the Art History brush quickly over the subject's dress may yield some satisfying results also (hint, hint).

The concept of making several different curves to draw from using the History palette, and then using these contrasting states to make an even more colorful "painting" is a new one. Up until this chapter, the idea has always been to work from a single History state where the color has been pumped up. But then, that's the kind of thing that's expected of the *Inside Photoshop* series!

We'll wrap up this chapter by attempting to squeeze the last drop of realism into our "hand-painted" work of art. You'll want to keep the image open for this final short exercise.

Adding to the Illusion Using Extra Texture

An additional way to add to the illusion of hand-painting is by adding the look of canvas to your images. A very effective way of doing that is to print your image on canvas-textured paper. A number of manufacturers make this type of paper for home inkjet printers. Although the paper is more expensive than plain paper, it's still pretty reasonable.

> **Tip**
>
> **Finding the Hard to Find**   Even if you don't have access to a wealth of stores in your area, you don't have to be left out in the cold when it comes to items like canvas-textured paper, as long as you're connected to the Internet.
>
> Online stores like Buy.com, OfficeDepot.com, and OfficeMax.com sell canvas-textured inkjet paper as well as hard-to-find stuff like photo-quality paper in legal size.

Photoshop also provides a couple of faux textures that can be printed onto whatever types of paper you may have on-hand. The results may be a little less impressive than those gained by using textured paper, but you might also be surprised by how many people you fool.

Touching Tiny Tutorials Teaching Tactile Tricks

As just mentioned, you can generate your own painterly textures in Photoshop. If you'd like to add the look of canvas to a *flattened* version of the Splash image, it's as simple as 1-2-3, only there's no two or three. Er, anyway, from the Filter menu, choose Texture, Texturizer. When the Texturizer dialog box opens, choose Canvas from the drop-down menu, adjust Scaling to 143%, Relief to 1, and the Light Direction should be Top, as shown in Figure 14.24.

Figure 14.24   Enter all the Texturizer values you need by typing them in.

Our final tutorial for this chapter demonstrates how to apply the Emboss filter to all of the strokes generated by the Art History brush to convey the 3D look of impasto (the thick application of pigment to a canvas) paintings.

The newly saved Splash.psd file from the last tutorial should still be open, so let's get moving.

Applying Paint Thickness to Your Masterpiece

1. If you haven't already flattened the image to apply the canvas texture mentioned above, click the Layers palette context menu, and choose Flatten Image.

2. Drag the Background layer onto the Create a new layer icon at the bottom of the Layers palette. This creates a copy of the Background layer, to which you will apply your filter effects.

3. Go to the Image menu and choose Adjustments, Desaturate to drain all of the color out of the layer.

4. From the Filter menu, choose Stylize, Emboss.

5. The Emboss dialog box opens; set the Angle at –45°, the Height at 1 pixel, and Amount to 500%, as shown in Figure 14.25.

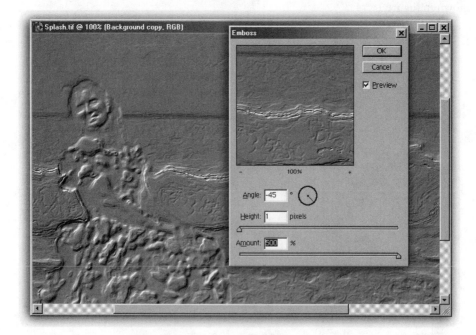

Figure 14.25   Enter the Emboss values to set up the effect.

6. Now change the Blending mode (on the Layers palette) for the Background copy layer to Overlay.

7. Everything looks pretty good except for the embossed modeling, which makes the subject's face look kind of funky. Using a layer mask will clear that right up.

8. Go to the Layers menu, and choose Add Layer Mask, Reveal All (or drag the Background copy layer into the Add layer mask icon at the bottom of the Layers palette).

9. Press D for default colors (black should now be the foreground color). Click the Brush tool to make it active. Click the arrow next to the Brush Preset picker, then click the arrow at the upper-right corner of the picker dialog box, and choose Reset Brushes off the menu. When the message asks whether you want to replace the brushes, click OK. Choose the 13-pixel soft edge brush. Drag the Brush over the subject's face, as shown in Figure 14.26.

Figure 14.26 Apply paint to the layer mask by painting all over the subject's face and slightly into the hairline.

Now the face looks a bit out of focus because of the removal of the emboss effect. We can rectify that.

10. From the Edit menu, choose Fade Brush and lower the opacity to 44%.

Now everything looks peachy-keen! Hoo hah! If you want to save all this work, press Ctrl(⌘)+S and save your creation as a PSD file.

Summary

And that, as they say in Hollywood, is a wrap! Coming up in the next chapter—advanced rendering techniques. Translation: harder art stuff. Hey, don't run off anywhere, all of you non-artistic people. You lived through this; you should give the next chapter a shot. You may actually (shudder) like it! The next chapter doesn't demand a lot in the way of artistic skill. The only real requirement being that you know Photoshop fairly well— which should be expected in a chapter that features advanced material.

Chapter 15

Out of This World A.R.T. (Advanced Rendering Techniques)

One of the things that the *Inside Photoshop* books have been emphasizing from the very first edition has been to think outside the box. This chapter is completely about thinking outside of the box. In fact, toss that box out. Strap yourself in and get ready for blast-off because, folks, we are going to places no Photoshop book has ever gone before.

> **Warning**
>
> **Before You Begin**   Because this chapter deals with more advanced techniques, it is expected that you have a thorough knowledge of Photoshop (you need to be an inter-mediate-level user). If you're just learning the program you *will* get lost; ya gotta learn to crawl before you can walk the walk, kiddo. If you've skipped ahead to this chapter, I strongly suggest you go back and read the chapters leading up to it in detail. Minimal painting skills are needed, knowledge of art and lighting are pluses. See our ad in the Sunday edition.
>
> Although this chapter includes a lot of instructions, you won't always be told every little thing like when to zoom in or out (though you'll find some of those instructions occasionally, too). This chapter is meant to make you think about choices; we all have to grow up sometime…Ok, now, let's talk about comic books!

Rendering: What Is It? How Much Does It Cost?

In this chapter, we color a simple cartoon character using what we'll refer to as *advanced rendering techniques*. Many commercial artists refer to areas that have been painted with shading and texture details as being *rendered*. In this chapter, we explore some of the tips and tricks the pros use to achieve these same effects.

First you learn timesaving shortcuts for painting in flat color, and then you explore the mechanics of lighting the flat color you just painted. Finally, you take a peek at applying texture. All of these tutorials are geared to take your images from the ordinary to the out of this world.

Coloring Stellar Artwork

In this initial exercise, you set up the image and discover how the pros color black-and-white art using flat areas of color. Later in the chapter, you'll tackle even more advanced pro stuff like where to order the best late-night pizza to munch on as you work.

One thing that separates a pro from an amateur is the amount of time each spends to accomplish the same thing. Many pros rely on a lot of shortcuts to move their projects along, so we'll touch on a number of those throughout our journey. Some pros also rely on their personal arsenal of tricks to give their images a unique look; toward that end, we'll discuss the author's own rendering tricks.

Flatly Coloring Line Art

1. Open the Roswell.tif image from the Examples/Chap15 folder on the Companion CD.

This image is what is commonly referred to as line art. Simple black-and-white lines with no shading whatsoever. This type of artwork is the foundation for comic strips, comic books, web art, and many forms of animation.

The subject of the image, a lovable alien named Roswell, is the title character from the comic book "Roswell" by Bill Morrison.

Our master plan is to separate the black lines from the white background for coloring and painting. There's a great trick for that!

2. Go to the Image menu and choose Mode, Lab Color, as shown in Figure 15.1. You're going to go into Lab mode for just a moment.

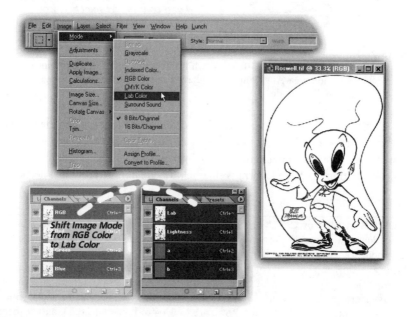

Figure 15.1 Just a hop and a skip into Lab Color for a moment...

3. Click the Channels tab to view the Channels palette. Then, click the Lightness channel and drag it onto the Load channel as selection icon. Marching ants appear all over the place, as you see in Figure 15.2. Head back to the Image menu and choose Mode, RGB Color. Ah, you're back in the world of RGB!

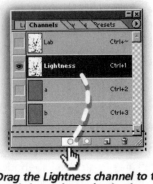

**Drag the Lightness channel to the
Load channel as selection icon**

Figure 15.2   Dragging the Lightness channel into the Load channel as selection
icon turns the light (in this case, white) information of the image into
a selection area. After you see you have a selection, change the image
back to RGB mode.

If you Ctrl(⌘)+click on the Red, Green, or Blue channels without making the jump to Lab
mode, you will get a selection that seems identical. But when it comes time to paint, there
will be a more apparent fringing in the results. By making the jump to Lab mode, and then
making the selection from the Lightness channel, you get a more accurate selection.

Tip

Why RGB Instead of CMYK?   Comic books are printed in CMYK, so why aren't
you working in that mode? Because you are just getting your feet wet, that's why! In a
real production environment, coloring and painting would be done in CMYK mode,
which has a smaller palette of colors (blue suffers most in CMYK), so by working in
RGB your first image can be a bit brighter, color-wise. Also, CMYK files are 20% larger
(because there are four channels as opposed to three in RGB), so you are taxing your
system resources less in RGB mode. If you are looking to break into the industry, there's
no reason why you need to work in RBG after you've worked your way through this
chapter, okay?

4. Click the Layers tab to view the Layers palette. Double-click the Background title to
convert the Background to a layer. Rename the layer **Sketch** in the New Layer dialog box that opens (see Figure 15.3), and change the Mode to Multiply. Click OK.

Now we'll be able to use the Sketch layer as our template, and we'll be placing new layers above and below this layer.

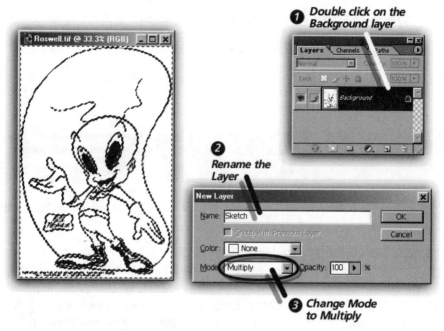

Figure 15.3   We're converting the Background into a layer for our devious purposes.

5. Press the Delete (Backspace) key to remove the white areas from the Sketch layer. Now you're ready to paint. Press Ctrl($\mathcal{H}$)+D to deselect.

6. Press Ctrl($\mathcal{H}$)+Shift+N to create a new layer and open the New Layer dialog box. Name the new layer **Color** and click OK. Then drag the Color layer below the Sketch layer in the palette list, as shown in Figure 15.4.

Figure 15.4   Drag the Color layer below The Sketch layer.

7. Double-click the Zoom tool to zoom the image to 100%. Press W to switch to the Magic Wand tool. On the Options bar, choose New selection from the group of selection options (next to the Magic Wand icon). Set the Tolerance to 32 and check the Contiguous and Use All Layers boxes, as shown in Figure 15.5.

Figure 15.5   Use these Magic Wand settings to become a Photoshop magician.

Tip

Smarter Navigation   Don't forget that you can navigate easily around the image by using the Hand tool. You can access the Hand tool at any time by pressing and holding the spacebar.

Even though the Color layer is now the active layer, you'll be able to use the black edges from the black Sketch layer to trap your selections. Sneaky, huh?

8. Click with the Magic Wand inside Roswell's head to turn the area into a selection. Press the Shift key (to add to the selection) and click in Roswell's left ear.

Ok, we have a selection, but there's a problem because of that pesky thing called Tolerance. Sometimes the Magic Wand isn't totally accurate (*What?!* A gasp is heard through the crowd.) When Tolerance isn't set correctly, the color won't butt up against the line art properly in all areas. This happens all the time, but it shouldn't. Perhaps you've seen comics (the worst offenders) that have white in areas that should've been colored (assuming the color registration is fine—if the printing is correct then it's the colorist's fault)—now you know why. We could play around with the Tolerance setting, but even that might need to be changed within any given drawing, unless you only work in flat color. Ugh! But don't panic, there is a solution!

Note

Remember Your Selections   Selections are the electronic equivalent of friskets used by traditional airbrush artists. These artists cut little areas into frisket paper and then spray the color onto their boards, using the friskets as their masks.

Throughout this chapter, you'll want to make sure that selection tools are always set to the New selection option on the Options bar. Some people find Adobe's marching ants distracting; if you're among them, you can turn the ants off by pressing Ctrl(⌘)+H. You'll need to remember, however, that you've made a selection. If you find yourself unable to paint in a given area, that's probably why.

You may notice that this chapter doesn't include many instructions telling you to deselect (Ctrl(⌘)+D). If you deselect an area when there is no instruction to do so, you will probably make a mistake.

Generally, the chapter works this way. Something is selected (let's say the head), and then you are instructed to make a new selection (let's say with the Magic Wand) on the leg. The first time you click in the leg, the leg doesn't get selected. Instead, Photoshop "deselects" the head selection. You must then click again to select the leg. This is *much faster* than having to reach for Ctrl(⌘)+D a zillion times, and is a timesaver. But then, you already know the selection tools exhibit this type of behavior if you are an intermediate user.

Just assume, for this chapter, that after you begin painting there should always be a selection somewhere. If you need to confirm your selection, simply press Ctrl(⌘)+H to redisplay the ants.

9. Click the Actions tab to view the Actions palette. Click the right-facing triangle (at the upper-right corner of the Actions palette) to open the context menu and choose Load Actions. Navigate to the Examples/Chap15 folder on the Companions CD and click on the Roswell.atn file to load the pre-fabricated action. Click Load.

If you move the Action palette slider to the bottom of the list, you'll see the Action set named Roswell, as shown in Figure 15.6.

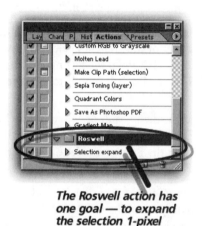

The Roswell action has one goal — to expand the selection 1-pixel

Figure 15.6   The Roswell action set contains a simple action to expand selection areas by 1 pixel on each side. This action is assigned a hot key combination.

Note

Returning to Normal   After you've finished the exercise you can go back to the default action sets by simply choosing Reset Actions from the same context menu that you used to load the Roswell action. Or click on the Roswell action and choose Delete from the same menu to remove the Roswell action only.

An alternative to using Roswell.atn is to go to the Select menu and choose Modify, Expand from the menu, enter the 1-pixel value in the dialog box, and click OK. You would need to make the trip through this menu sequence each time you want to make sure the selection is covering everything you need to be covering, however. By using Roswell.atn, you eliminate the need for all those trips to the Select menu—but even with this action there will still be areas where you will need to go in and paint small spots of color with a small brush (usually in tight corners). Hey, life is rough!

Note

Using Actions   Pros use Actions for a good reason; they greatly speed up productivity when dealing with repetitive work.

Make sure that you check out Chapter 21, "Scripting and Actions," to learn more about how Actions can help you with your workload. Though Chapter 21 discusses creating actions for web images, after you learn how to create your own actions the feature can be used to automate anything.

10. Press Shift+F12 to expand the selection area using the Roswell action.

Okay, now that you've got your new and improved selection, we probably need to color this baby! Well, this leads to the next trick of the pros; they save their palettes so that they can pull them out again the next time they work—"What color was that cola logo, again? Oh, I'll just use any color red; they won't care,"—or so they can keep colors consistent when multiple people are working on the same project.

11. Click the Swatches tab to view the Swatches palette. Click the right-facing triangle in the upper-right corner of the Swatches palette to open the context menu and choose Load Swatches. Navigate to the Examples/Chap15 folder on the Companions CD and click the Roswell.aco file to load the color swatch file. Click Load.

What we've done here is added a small group of colors (10, to be exact) to the default swatches. As with the Roswell action, after you're finished with this tutorial you may delete the Roswell swatches from the Swatches palette by using the context menu that you used to load them (simply choose Reset Swatches and click OK).

12. Hover your cursor over the lime green swatch located at the bottom of the Swatches palette. An Eyedropper tool appears and the tool tip should display the swatch's name, *Face*, if you hover long enough (as seen in Figure 15.7). Click the Face swatch to choose this color as our foreground color.

Figure 15.7   Applying the correct colors will be a snap because the tool tip shows the intended area to be colored.

Tip

Creating Color Swatches   You can make your own set of Swatches from any image you have. Go to the Image menu and choose Mode, Indexed Color to convert the file down to 256 colors or less. Then go to the Image menu and choose Mode, Color Table. In the Color Table dialog box, you can name your customized color table and save the file out as an *.ACT file (for this example, let's name the swatch **Hoffman.act**).

From the Swatches palette context menu, choose Replace Swatches. When the dialog box opens choose *.ACT from the Files of Type drop-down menu (otherwise, you'll never see the Hoffman.act file you created). Navigate to the place your hard drive where the file is stored. After the Swatches are loaded into the Swatches palette, you can rename the individual colors as I have done. Save the renamed colors out as a *.aco file using the Save Swatches option from the Swatches palette context menu.

13. With the sampled color from the *Face* swatch as the Foreground color, press Alt(Opt)+Delete(Backspace) to apply the green to the face and ear areas.

Okay, the hard part has been properly setting up the image and the workspace. Coloring the rest of the image with flat color should be a walk in the park.

Let's take a moment to see where all the additional colors are going to be placed, as shown in Figure 15.8.

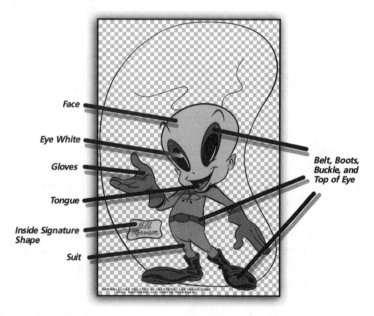

Figure 15.8   Refer to this figure to see which colors go where. The callouts list the swatch name for each color.

You'll use shortcuts to apply color to Roswell's spacesuit in the following steps.

14. Next, you need to paint the suit blue. Press W to choose the Magic Wand tool (if it is not still the active tool). Click inside Roswell's right arm. Hold down the Shift key and click the Magic Wand inside Roswell's leg to select the bottom part of the suit. Still holding down Shift, click inside Roswell's left arm, his tummy, and where the suit shows through on the chest insignia (while making sure not to select the insignia). When you're through, you should see marching ants in the same areas, as shown in Figure 15.9.

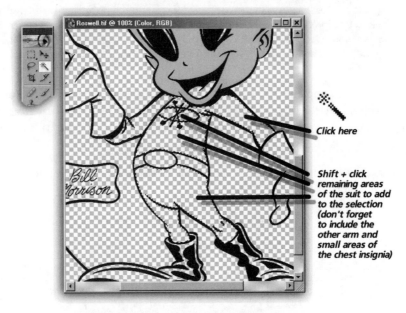

Figure 15.9   Most of the spacesuit areas have been selected quickly using the Magic Wand.

15. Press Shift+F12 to expand the selection. Click the blue color swatch named *Suit*. Press Alt(Opt)+Delete (Backspace) to fill the spacesuit with blue. Press Ctrl(⌘)+D to deselect. Leave the document open and read on for instructions to finish coloring.

Upon inspection of the spacesuit, you may notice that there are still small areas that aren't colored (see Figure 15.10). That is to be expected. The most important thing is to color the large areas of color first; then you'll go through with a small hard-edged brush and touch up the problem areas.

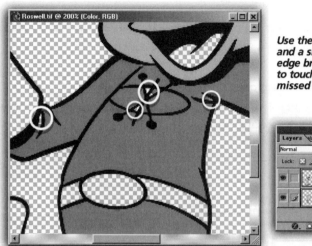

Use the Brush Tool and a small hard edge brush size to touch up the missed areas

Figure 15.10   It's faster to use the Magic Wand for dropping in gross color than to use the Brush tool; small corners can always be touched up after with a small hard-edged brush.

The boots make up one area where you can pretty much expect to use the Brush tool; many of the spaces between the lines are too fine for the Magic Wand to select properly. The emphasis of this tutorial is on speed, so when you select the areas of the boot, do the best you can while trying to maintain a quick pace (make it your personal challenge). Try to balance speed with accuracy, and when you find yourself hitting the wall of diminishing returns, that's your cue to drop the Magic Wand, pick up the Brush, and paint the area in, because now *that's* the fastest method.

At this point, the steps for coloring the rest of Roswell are repetitive, so go ahead and finish coloring only the character. The colors in the swatches are arranged in the order you should color Roswell, and again, the correct destination for each color will appear when you hold your pointer over each swatch. When you reach the swatches with the prefix BG:, the Roswell character should be completely painted.

When you reach a yellow swatch named Inside Signature Shape, use it to color the area within the curvy shape where Bill Morrison's signature resides. Use the Magic Wand tool to select the bulk of the area inside the signature shape (and expand the selection). Again, because of the finer lines in the signature, you'll want to paint part of the yellow using the Brush tool. After you're done, the image should match Figure 15.8 (of course, yours will be in color and we're limited to grayscales in this book—but you'll get the idea). Finally, we'll wrap up by putting the background colors onto a new layer (in the next exercise), so come back to this spot after you've finished painting Roswell and the signature shape color onto the Color layer.

Adding Color to the Backing

In this very short section, we wrap up the exercise by making a new layer and coloring the bean shape that will make up the background behind Roswell.

Finishing Touches to the Background

1. Press Ctrl(⌘)+Shift+N to create a new layer and open the New Layer dialog box. Name the new layer **Backing** and click OK. Then drag the Backing layer below the Color layer in the palette list, as shown in Figure 15.11.

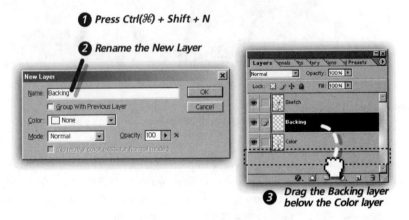

Figure 15.11   Paint the background colors on a layer separate from the character's coloring. This enables you to create realistic lighting and shading behind Roswell later in the chapter.

2. Press W to switch to the Magic Wand tool. Click inside the bean shape around Roswell. Hold down the Shift key and click in the area between Roswell's legs to also color that area.

3. Press Shift+F12 to expand the selection.

4. On the Swatches palette, locate the BG: Inside Bean Shape swatch, click this color swatch to make it the foreground color.

5. Press Alt(Opt)+Delete (Backspace) to fill the bean shape with color. The background should look like Figure 15.12.

Figure 15.12   Except for a few small empty areas, the inside of the bean should be colored.

6. With the Magic Wand still the active tool, click in the outer area around the bean. At this point, you should know the routine well: Expand the selection (choose the BG: Outside Bean Shape color swatch) and fill the selection until your image matches Figure 15.13.

Figure 15.13   Finally, the image should be completely covered with flat color.

Now would be a good time to save this file to your hard drive as Roswell.psd. You may have noticed that there was one swatch that we haven't used yet, a dark blue swatch named Bean Outline. We'll save the Bean Outline for later in the chapter.

If at the end of this exercise you find yourself scratching your head and thinking, "That didn't seem any faster than if I'd have just painted everything with a brush—" simply keep in mind that as you're learning you go slower than you will when this technique is second nature. If you find yourself in a fast-paced position, you'll appreciate those short-cuts.

That does it for painting in flat color. Next, we tackle light and shadow. In the next sections, you make your cartoon character look more realistic than he currently does. You'll do that using two devices: lighting and texturing.

Adding Modeling for Dimension

In art, the way that light and shadow play upon any given character or object is referred to as *modeling*. The field of animation has seen a dramatic change in modeling most recently. For years, adding any kind of shadows to animated characters rested squarely in the domain of feature films, and even then shadows were usually saved for the "realistic" characters, and even then very sparingly. There were no shadows drawn on the Flintstones; the cost of time and money was too high. Character modeling has always been a luxury in animation, but adding roundness and depth to flat art provides valuable additional information that sells the illusion that the unreal is real.

The creator of Roswell, Bill Morrison, painted many memorable Disney movie posters in the late 80s (including the infamous Little Mermaid poster of urban myth). Initially, when he began submitting his paintings, the Art Directors loved them because of all the modeling he added using his airbrush. But word got back to Bill that the Disney animators also hated the look because Bill's characters didn't match the flatly painted Disney characters. That all changed once Disney began to employ their CAPS system (developed by those kooky cut-ups at PIXAR). Bill began to notice that the animation started to be created the way he had been painting his movie posters from the start.

Painting Light and Shadow

We'll dive into our Roswell image shortly, but before we do, let's discuss the lighting principles Bill followed to ensure his characters always appeared fully dimensional. A breakdown of Bill's principles is provided in Figure 15.14.

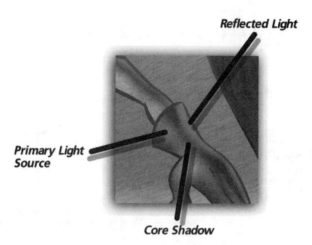

Figure 15.14   The specific technique of modeling that you'll be trying involves painting three specific elements.

Let's explore the finer details of these three modeling rules of thumb:

- **Primary Light.** The primary light is the equivalent of a key light in photography. This should usually be the hottest light source in the image (unless the colorist is going for mood).

- **Core Shadow.** The core shadow always separates the primary light from the reflected light.

- **Reflected Light.** Reflected light is always colored light from a secondary light source that is always shown on shadow areas.

By abiding by these rules, characters will always have a more believable look and feel to them.

Enough theory, eh? Let's light Roswell. Assuming that the Roswell.psd image is open— you did save the file as a Photoshop document, right?—let's begin.

Adding Roundness Through Modeling

1. In the Layers palette, click the Color layer to make it the active layer. Press the Alt(Opt) key and then drag the Color layer to the Create a new layer icon. This actually creates a duplicate of the Color layer which you should rename **Modeling**, as shown in Figure 15.15.

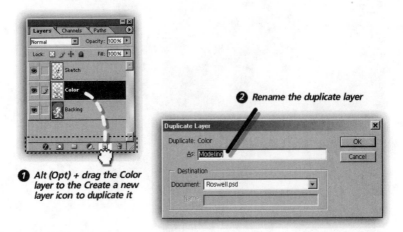

Figure 15.15 You will use the Color later after you've painted lighting effects on the Modeling layer.

2. Next, you need to protect what you've done up to this point. On the Layers palette are four Lock icon options. Click the Modeling layer to make it active and click the Lock transparent pixel icon. Go through and click each of the other layers and each time click the Lock all icon to lock all attributes of the other layers. Your Layer palette should match Figure 15.16.

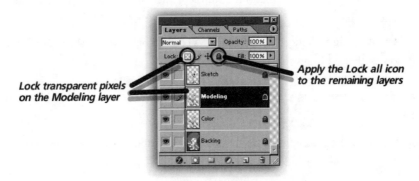

Figure 15.16 The Modeling layer has only Lock transparent pixels activated; every other layer should have Lock all attributes activated.

Now you're going to start by adding the core shadow to Roswell's head. Double-click the Zoom tool to view the image at 100%.

3. Click the Modeling layer to make this the active layer. Press W to choose the Magic Wand tool. On the Options bar, uncheck the Use All Layers option. Click the green color of Roswell's head, as shown in Figure 15.17.

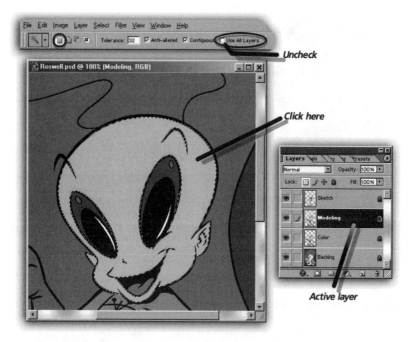

Figure 15.17   Use the Magic Wand to select the green color.

To achieve the lighting effects you need, you're going to treat all of the colors applied in the first section of this chapter as mid-tones (which they are). So to create the effect of roundness, you begin by painting in all of your shadow areas on Roswell, starting with his bulbous head. You won't be using the Brush tool to paint in these areas… Surprise! Surprise! Surprise! You'll use the Dodge tool!

 Note

Where to Start and Where to Focus   If this were a traditional airbrush painting, Bill's instructions would be to work from light to dark areas (which means that you would begin with the boot areas instead of Roswell's head), but because of the flexibility of Photoshop, you can start pretty much wherever you choose.

One thing you'll want to keep your eye on when creating shadows (and also when adding highlights) is to try to keep the lighting consistent throughout the character. The shadow on the arm should match the shadow on the head or the leg. As a beginner, it's easy to forget about the bigger picture, but the lights and shadows should all be consistent in value.

4. Choose the Burn tool from the toolbox (or you can press Shift+O to cycle through the tools until the Burn tool is active). On the Options bar, choose the 65-pixel soft-edged brush, and then press the right bracket (]) key to increase the brush size to 70 pixels. Set Range to Shadows and Exposure to 100%. Drag the Burn tool around Roswell's head, as shown in Figure 15.18.

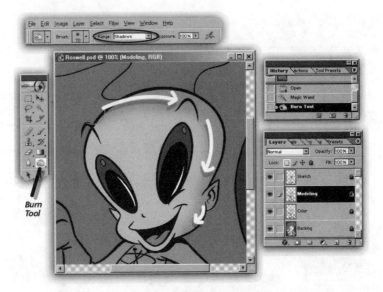

Figure 15.18   Stroke the back of Roswell's head as illustrated to create a deep green color. If you go too slow and the color becomes too dark, or if the color looks uneven, or you simply don't like the result, press Ctrl(⌘)+Z and try again.

Your next move is to add to Roswell's face a small amount of shine from the primary light.

5. Choose the Dodge tool from the toolbox. On the Options bar, choose the 300-pixel soft-edged brush, set the Range to Highlights and the Exposure to 30%. Click the Dodge tool just once in the face, as shown in Figure 15.19.

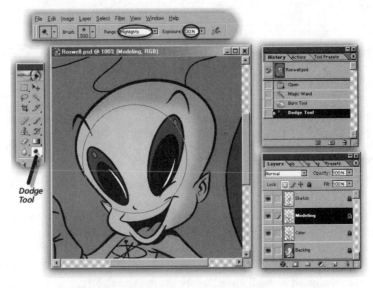

Figure 15.19   One click with the Dodge tool adds a subtle amount of shine.

That's all you'll do to Roswell's face for the time being. Now you can move on to the spacesuit.

6. Press W to choose the Magic Wand tool and click in the blue area of the space-suit top. Hold down the Shift key and click in the bottom area; the entire spacesuit area should be a selection. Press Ctrl(⌘)+H to hide the marching ants.

7. Choose the Burn tool from the toolbox (the settings should still be the same as from when you added shadows to the head) and begin a sweep, starting with Roswell's shoulders all the way down the right side. Curve the shadows to indicate small muscles, as shown in Figure 15.20.

Figure 15.20   You are adding volume and weight (and muscle tone) simply by adding core shadows. The marching ants were left visible so you can see which areas should be selected.

8. Press the left bracket ([) key twice to lower the brush size to 50 pixels. Make another sweep along Roswell's right side, starting under the armpit and continuing down to the boot, as shown in Figure 15.21.

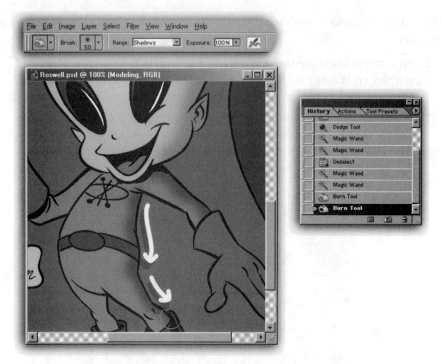

Figure 15.21   You are adding volume to the potbelly and the small muscles of the alien.

So far, you've been able to do a fair amount of work without a lot of specific masking, but to paint in the other areas of Roswell's shadow, you're going to need to block off some additional areas.

   9. Choose the Polygonal Lasso tool and select Roswell's left arm, as shown in Figure 15.22. Hold down the Shift key to add to the selection area and select the left leg, as shown in the same figure.

When making this selection, just click within the black outlines of the areas shown in Figure 15.22. The other areas outside the outlines don't have to be exact (they are protected by the layer's Lock option). The goal is to prevent shadowing from being applied to neighboring areas, such as the glove, boot, face, chest, and stomach.

Figure 15.22   We're throwing a selection double-whammy on this layer! The selection protects the chest and groin area from Shadow "overspray," and the Lock Transparent pixel option on the layer protects the rest of the area from getting damaged.

10. Choose the Burn Tool to add shadows, as shown in Figure 15.23.

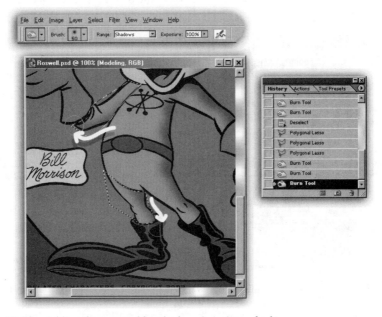

Figure 15.23   Adding the arm and leg shadows is a piece of cake now.

What is "overspray?" Well, when using a traditional airbrush, any time paint goes into an unwanted area it is referred to as overspray. We've got the shadows looking the way we want them to look on the spacesuit, but the highlight areas are going to be a bit trickier. Because of the shadowing, you can no longer use the Magic Wand to make selections easily… or can you?

11. Press W to choose the Magic Wand tool. Click the Color layer in the Layers palette to make it active. Then click in the spacesuit top, hold down the Shift key, and click the spacesuit bottom areas. Roswell's entire spacesuit should be selected, just as it was back in Figure 15.20

12. Click the Modeling layer to make it the active layer. Click the Create a new layer icon at the bottom of the Layers palette. You're not going to name this layer; it's not going to be around very long.

13. Press B to switch to the Brush tool, and on the Options bar set the Brush size to 50-pixel soft-edged, with Opacity and Flow set at 100%. Press D for the default colors. Press X to switch white to the foreground color.

Note

A Note About Brush Size   The default brush set comes with 45- or 65-pixel choices, but if you use the bracket keys to increase or decrease brush size, the brush picker moves in 10-pixel increments (10-, 20-, 30-, 40-, 50-pixel brushes). If you choose directly from the Brush Preset picker starting with the 45-pixel brush, it is not a big deal.

14. Paint the highlights as shown in Figure 15.24. When you reach the knee areas, press the left bracket ([) key until you lower the brush size to 20 pixels.

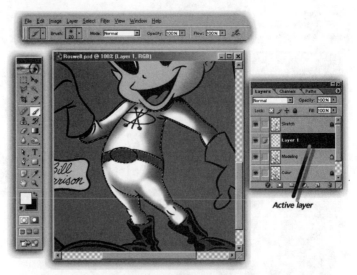

Figure 15.24   Try to match the highlights as shown in this figure. The stomach was painted with the 50-pixel soft-edged brush, but areas such as the knees required the 20-pixel soft brush. Use the bracket keys to quickly change brush size to the required area.

The highlights are pretty dense and they don't blend very well with the rest of the suit's "lighting" at the moment, but that's an easy fix.

15. Go to the Filter menu and choose Blur, Gaussian Blur and apply a setting of 7.5 pixels. Click OK.

16. Lower the Opacity of Layer 1 to 60%. Now the highlight should match the rest of the lighting, as shown in Figure 15.25.

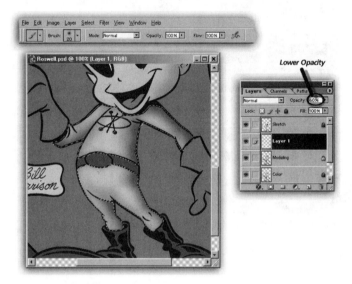

Figure 15.25   The light areas of the spacesuit should now match the other lighting.

17. Press Ctrl(⌘)+E to merge Layer 1 down onto the Modeling layer.

By applying the highlight effect on a separate layer, you could very quickly dial down the opacity to just the right level. This method is much faster (and more flexible) than simply lowering the opacity on the Brush and painting on the Modeling layer. Another advantage gained by using a separate layer is that you are able to get a very nice, wide blur that would have been difficult to achieve without time-consuming brush dynamics modifications.

Note

Advanced Shading   Because this image is quite complex, we're not able to discuss every nuance of the shading. However, you should feel free to compare your work with the gallery image and use the techniques here to add a subtle touch to your work.

For instance, you could add more subtle lighting effects to Roswell's face beyond what this chapter covered by painting additional highlights and shading on a temporary layer. You would then merge the effect with the rest of the Modeling layer.

Let's move on to Roswell's gloves now. Before we begin, make sure that Modeling is the current active layer.

18. Press W to choose the Magic Wand. Click in the blue color of one glove. Press Shift and click again on the other glove to add this glove to the selection.

19. Choose the Burn tool from the toolbox and use the 50-pixel soft-edged brush to apply strokes to the left glove, as indicated in Figure 15.26.

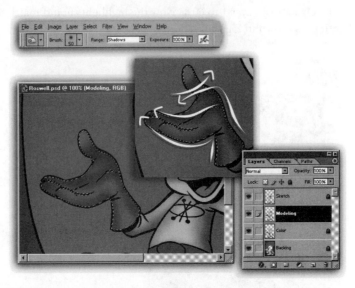

Figure 15.26   The core shadow should be added using these stokes.

20. Now apply strokes to the right glove, as you see in Figure 15.27.

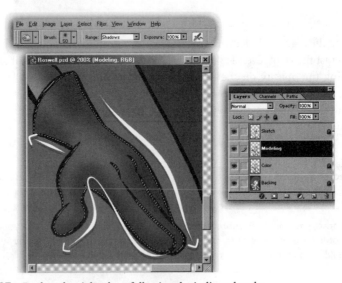

Figure 15.27   Darken the right glove following the indicated paths.

21. Click the Create a new layer icon at the bottom of the Layers palette. This gives you a blank layer titled Layer 1. The glove selections should still be the active selection. Press Ctrl(⌘)+H to hide the marching ants.

As you've probably guessed, you're going to paint highlight areas into the glove area now.

22. Press B to switch to the Brush tool. Set the brush size to 40 pixels and using white (which should still be the default foreground color), paint in the larger areas of solid white as shown in Figure 15.28. Press the left bracket key ([) to lower the size to 20 pixels, and then paint the thumb tip areas and some of the fingers. Lower the brush's Opacity to 60% and paint in the softer white areas to match the figure.

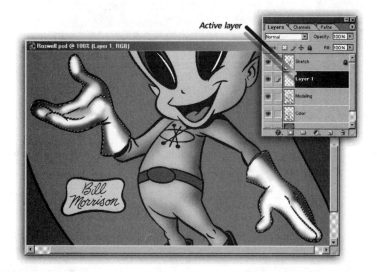

Figure 15.28   You'll rely on several brush sizes and opacities to match your work to this figure.

23. Because Gaussian Blur was the last filter you used, you can press Ctrl(⌘)+F to apply the filter again. The same setting (7.5 pixels) will be applied, which works great, as shown in Figure 15.29. On the Layers palette, lower the Opacity on Layer 1 to 30%.

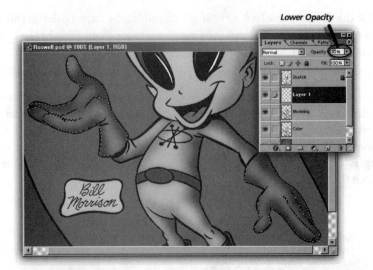

Lower Opacity

Figure 15.29   A Gaussian Blur setting of 7.5 pixels works well on the glove highlights and looks perfect when the layer Opacity is lowered to 30%.

24. Press Ctrl(⌘)+E to merge Layer 1 with the Modeling layer.

Next, you'll quickly paint in a highlight for the tongue. At this point, the Modeling layer should be the active layer once more.

25. Press W to choose the Magic Wand tool, and click in the red area of the tongue. Click the Create a new layer icon to paint safely on ever-temporary Layer 1.

Note

Why Flatten?   Why do we keep flattening Layer 1 into the Modeling layer? Because you can't simply paint all our lighting effects onto a single layer like that, or when you change the opacity of your latest effect, you would also lower the opacity of the effect that looked just right with a different opacity applied earlier. Besides, we're trying to keep the number of layers to a minimum, and an image with as many effects as this one could balloon quickly with a lot of layers.

Why don't we just paint on the Modeling layer and use Fade to soften the effect? Because we are usually doing multiple things, Fade won't work. Fade affects only the last command. See? There is a method to our madness.

26. Choose the Brush tool and use the left bracket ([) to lower the brush size to the 8-pixel soft-edged brush. The Brush tool's Opacity should be at 60%. Make a "J" shape inside Roswell's mouth, as shown in Figure 15.30.

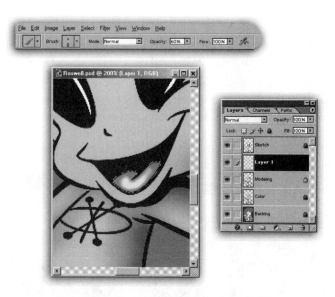

Figure 15.30   Make progressively shorter strokes so that the curved area of the tongue is the whitest.

27. Go to the Filter menu and choose Blur, Gaussian Blur. Lower the Radius to 2 pixels. Click OK.

28. From the Filter menu choose Noise, Add Noise. In the Add Noise dialog box, enter a value of 9.75% in the Amount box, choose the Uniform option under Distribution, and check the Monochromatic option. Click OK. Lower the Opacity on Layer 1 to 80% in the Layers palette.

This breaks up the highlights on the tongue to mimic random light falloff on a real tongue.

29. Press Ctrl(⌘)+E to merge Layer 1 down onto the Modeling layer.

At this point, it's been a while since you've saved the file, so do that by pressing Ctrl(⌘)+S. You've got a few more things to model so you might also want to get up and take a break or at least stretch a little.

Making Your Image Shine

We've still got a bit more to do to Roswell as far as modeling goes. In this section, you'll be applying gloss to Roswell's boots and belt and adding your reflected light to Roswell. You're basically adding all the shine to the little, green man. You'll also add some lighting effects to the background elements and then move on to texturing effects. As you can see, this is a lot more ground to cover so let's go...starting with Roswell's boots!

Shine! Shine! Shine!

1. Press W to choose the Magic Wand tool and click in the blue area to select the left boot. Then hold down the Shift key and click in the blue area of the other boot.

2. White should still be the foreground color. Choose the Brush tool from the toolbox and raise the Opacity to 100%. Press the right bracket key (]) until the brush size is 50 pixels. The brush should still be soft-edged, so stroke both boots as shown in Figure 15.31.

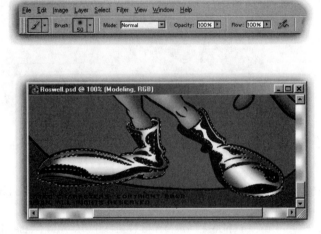

Figure 15.31   Just one quick swipe in each boot should add enough shine for the time being.

Moving on to Roswell's belt now…

3. Press W to choose the Magic Wand. Click in the appropriate areas to choose the belt and buckle (pressing Shift to add to the initial selection if necessary). Right-click (Macintosh: hold Ctrl and click) inside the selection to bring up the context menu and choose Layer via Copy to move the selection to a new layer.

4. From the Styles palette, choose the gray style (third row from the top, and the third style from the right) named *Bevel Edge*, as shown in Figure 15.32.

Tip

Adding Styles   If you have only the default styles loaded, you may not see this style on your palette. Not a problem—click the arrow in the upper-right corner of the Styles palette to access the context menu and choose the Photographic Effects to load these styles onto your palette. You can choose Append in the dialog box to add the styles to your current list (or click OK to simply replace your current list of styles).

5. Press Ctrl(⌘)+E to merge Layer 1 down onto the Modeling layer.

Now that you have the bulk of Roswell modeled, let's paint in the infamous reflected light.

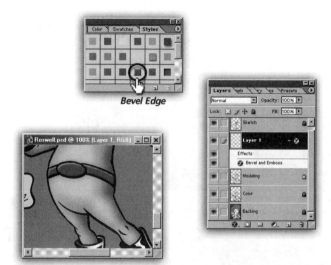

Figure 15.32   You used a simple layer style to "model" Roswell's belt. Of course, you can always make the belt fancier if you want to, but don't be afraid to consider the simplest solution.

6. Click the Create a new layer icon at the bottom of the Layers palette.

7. Click on the Color layer to make it active, and then choose all of the modeled areas of Roswell. (This leaves out his eyes because we haven't modeled them. We will in the texture section. Also leave out the tongue.) Then click on Layer 1 to make it the active layer, as shown in Figure 15.33.

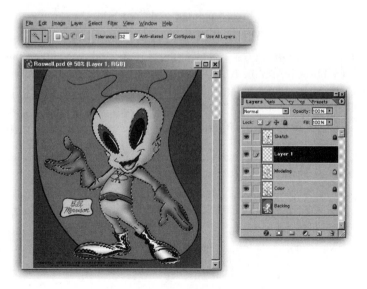

Figure 15.33   All of the modeled areas of Roswell should be selected.

8. Click the foreground color and choose a hot pink color (R:215, G:120, B:160). Click OK.

9. Choose the Brush tool, the 50-pixel soft-edged brush should be the current brush. Stroke the image as illustrated in Figure 15.34.

Figure 15.34   Stroke the hot pink reflected light color as illustrated.

The stroke to add reflected light also painted pink color into the tummy and right leg, which we don't want, so we need to erase that.

10. Press E to choose the Eraser tool from the toolbox, and then choose the 13-pixel soft-edged brush from the Brush Preset picker and erase the pink "overspray" from the groin area, as shown in Figure 15.35. Finish your cleanup by erasing small areas where color goes "past" the outlines.

Next you combine Layer 1 back with the Modeling layer as you've been doing...

11. Press Ctrl(⌘)+E to merge Layer 1 down onto the Modeling layer.

Let's now add shadows and light to place Roswell in his environment.

12. Ctrl(⌘)+click the Modeling layer in the Layers palette (this selects everything on the Modeling layer). Next, press Shift+ Ctrl(⌘)and click the Sketch layer. This adds to the selection. At this point all of Roswell should be selected (which is what we want), as shown in Figure 16.36.

Figure 15.35 Use a small soft-edged brush to remove the pink from the groin area and for any additional cleanup. We've used Ctrl(⌘)+H to hide the marching ants for clarity; don't deselect anything yet.

Figure 15.36 The focus should be on whether all of Roswell is selected or not; don't worry about anything else.

We want to select only the Roswell character, so this selection gives us a bunch of stuff we don't need: the bean shape outline and the legal line at the bottom of the art, telling us who owns the copyright. Don't worry about any of it for the moment.

13. Click the Create a new layer icon at the bottom of the Layers palette. Drag Layer 1 above the Sketch layer.

14. Press I to choose the Eyedropper tool and click in the darkest blue color in one of Roswell's gloves to sample the color. Press Alt(Opt)+Delete (Backspace) to fill the selection, as shown in Figure 15.37

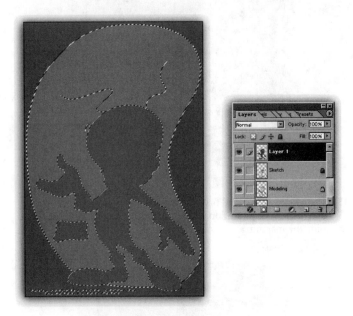

Figure 15.37   Now we've filled the selection with blue; this will be Roswell's shadow.

For best results, zoom in close when performing this next step, and press the spacebar (to toggle to the Hand tool) when you need to move your view as you work around the image.

15. Press Ctrl(⌘)+D to deselect (for once!). Press E to choose the Eraser tool. Choose a 21-pixel soft-edged brush and erase everything that isn't the Roswell character, as shown in Figure 15.38. When you're finished, you might want to press Ctrl(⌘)+minus key to zoom out to 33% (to check for any missed spots).

16. After you're done erasing, drag Layer 1 so that it's above the Backing layer, as shown in Figure 15.39. Double-click in the layer's title to rename the layer **Shadow**. Press Enter (Return) to set the name.

17. Press Ctrl(⌘)+minus key to zoom out to 33% and drag the document edge out to give yourself some working room. Go to the Edit menu and choose Transform, Scale and use Scale to distort the shadow, as shown in Figure 15.40. Press Enter (Return) to accept the transformation when you're done.

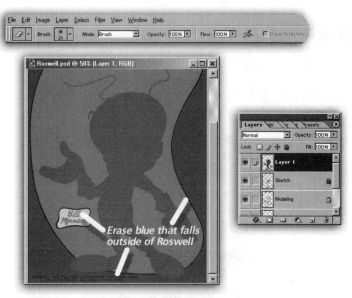

Figure 15.38   Erase everything that isn't Roswell. Don't forget to scroll up to get all of the bean shape outline if you are zoomed in as you work.

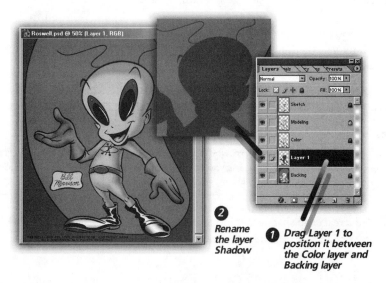

Figure 15.39   Drag the layer down the list to a point just above the Backing layer.

You can get the same distortion by simply pressing Ctrl(⌘)+T and typing in the Options bar the numbers shown in Figure 15.40.

Use the numbers shown on the Option bar to help achieve a similar transformation

Figure 15.40   Squish Roswell's shadow as shown.

If you missed some spots with the Eraser or even the Brush tool (as the author did) go back in and remove them now. They'll be pretty easy to clean up. At the minimum, you should zoom in to 100% and check your work.

   18. Change the Shadow's layer mode to Darken. From the Filter menu, choose Blur, Gaussian Blur. Enter a Radius of 7.5 pixels and click OK.

Note

Why a Shadow Layer?   Okay, so why does the Shadow layer merit its own layer? Putting the shadow on its own layer protects it in case you need to tweak the shadow's opacity once some of the other lighting effects are in place.

We've added a real drop shadow behind Roswell (the way artists did in those prehistoric days before version 5). Let's add a few more effects to "sell" the illusion that Roswell is standing in 3D space.

   19. Press Alt(Opt) and click the Create a new layer icon at the bottom of the Layers palette. Name the layer **Backing light effects**.

   20. Press B to choose the Brush tool. Choose the 80-pixel soft-edged brush (start with the 65-soft brush and press the right bracket key (]) twice to move up to 80). Press D for the default colors. Press X to switch white to the foreground color. Click on one side of the backing and then hold down the Shift key and click on the other edge to make a horizontal line, as shown in Figure 15.41.

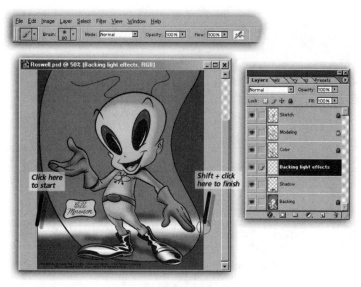

Figure 15.41   This quick straight line helps define the horizon.

21. Lower the opacity of the Backing light effects layer to 40% and change the layer mode to Overlay to make the effect a subtle one. This will be the last lighting effect you create before you learn about textures and other effects.

22. Press Ctrl(⌘)+minus key to zoom out to 33%. Press X to switch black to the foreground color. Press the right bracket (]) key until your brush is 175 pixels; then make a single stroke to the foreground area of the image, as illustrated in Figure 15.42. Go to the Edit menu and choose Fade Brush. In the Fade Brush dialog box, lower the Opacity to 70%. Click OK.

Wow! What a ride! Now save your work! The image should be looking pretty decent; it's taken us only a few pages and a couple of screen captures to get to this part of our rendering journey.

Next you'll be dealing with texturing and effects, but let's take a moment to discuss working methods—which will explain why this chapter is structured the way it is. Normally, you'll want to create your textures right after you've applied modeling to your selection so that you don't have to reselect the same area and do all the work twice. But in the preceding examples you didn't do things that way. Instead, this chapter has instructed you to paint all the modeling first, and now you're going to add texturing. We are doing it this way because one of the biggest mistakes a beginner makes is not keeping the lighting consistent from one area to the next. Even Bill (the creator of Roswell) said he was guilty of this mistake, and he emphasized that one can properly learn to gauge consistent lighting only through experience. By focusing initially purely on the lighting, you've already learned an important lesson.

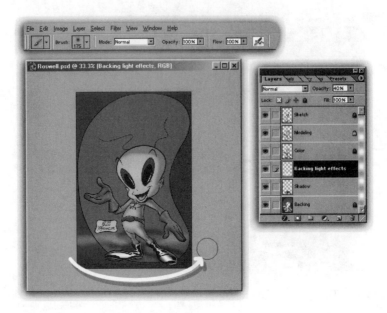

Figure 15.42   Another quick swipe of black will create the illusion of primary light falloff.

Applying Textures and Other Effects for Added Realism

Finally in our journey, we address the use of texture to add an extra touch of realism to the Roswell image. Another common mistake Bill Morrison mentioned was that many beginners make everything look like it's *all* made from the same fake plastic material (like you see in bad 3D animation). Part of that plastic look has to be addressed through lighting, and the rest can be enhanced using various textures and effects to reinforce the illusion.

If you've looked at the finished color Roswell image in the color signature, you may notice that there are many textures. Well, we're going to let the cat out of the bag right away by revealing a big, juicy secret to start off this section: almost all of the textures you see here are variations of only the Noise and Blur filters!

For the backing, you'll be adding lighting effects and textures just as artists do in a working environment.

Adding Texture to the Backing

1. Click the Backing layer to make it active, and then press W to choose the Magic Wand and click the inside bean shape color to make it the selection. Then hold down the Shift key and click the inside bean shape color between Roswell's legs, as shown in Figure 15.43.

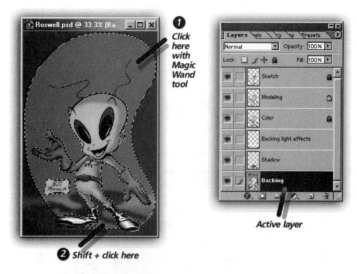

Figure 15.43   Don't forget to select the inside bean color between Roswell's legs.

2. Click the Lock all icon to unlock the Backing layer. Press B to choose the Brush tool. Hold down the Alt(Opt) key to toggle to the Eyedropper tool and click in the hot pink area of Roswell's head to choose that color. Choose the 300-pixel soft-edged brush from the Brush Preset picker. Press Enter (Return) to dismiss the brush picker. Stroke the bean shape as indicated in Figure 15.44. Go to the Edit menu and choose Fade Brush. In the Fade Brush dialog box, lower the Opacity to 66%. Click OK.

Figure 15.44   After painting the area as indicated, use the Fade Brush dialog box to lower the opacity of the effect.

3. Stretch out the document window to give you room for this next stroke. Press the Alt(Opt) key to temporarily access the Eyedropper and click in the yellow signature shape to sample that color. Sweep the bean, as illustrated in Figure 15.45. Go to the Edit menu and choose Fade Brush; then lower the Opacity to 66%. Click OK.

Figure 15.45   You'll only get this instruction once in your life: Sweep the bean!

4. From the Filter menu choose Noise, Add Noise and enter a value of 9.75% (if it's not already entered), Gaussian Distribution, and check the Monochromatic option (see Figure 15.46). Click OK.

Figure 15.46   Let's add a whole lotta noise here.

5. Go to the Filter menu and choose Blur, Motion Blur and then enter a value of 24° for Angle, and a Distance of 4 pixels, as shown in Figure 15.47. Click OK.

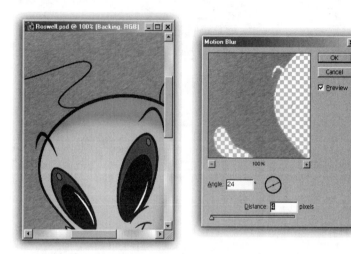

Figure 15.47 This motion blur setting gives the look of brushed metal.

Let's move on to the outside bean shape now.

6. Press W to choose the Magic Wand and click to select the outside purple color. From the Filter menu, choose Texture, Texturizer. In the Texturizer dialog box, choose Sandstone for Texture, Scaling of 100%, Relief of 4, and Light Direction from the Top. Click OK.

7. Choose the Custom Shape tool from the Toolbox (or press Shift+U until the Custom Shape tool is active). When the Custom Shape tool is active, the Custom Shape picker appears on the Options bar. Click the right-facing triangle to open the context menu and choose Load Shapes (as shown in Figure 15.48). Navigate to the Examples/Chap15 folder on the Companions CD and click on the Roswell.csh file to load the file; click Load.

This shape is actually one of Gary's custom shapes that he created for a previous book. You'll find a complete set of nifty new ones on the Companion CD, so look for them!

8. Scroll down the Custom Shape picker and find a shape named Twirl (the last available shape). Click the icon to choose it. On the Options bar, choose the Fill pixels option (on the left side of the bar), and enter an opacity value of 30%. Hold down the Alt(Opt) key to access the Eyedropper and sample some of the hot pink color off of Roswell's head.

At this point, you simply want to make some random shapes along the "flat wall" behind the alien. After you come to the white horizon line you created earlier—that's your signal to start making the shapes more scrunched to simulate the foreshortening you see in 3D (this technique is called *forced perspective*).

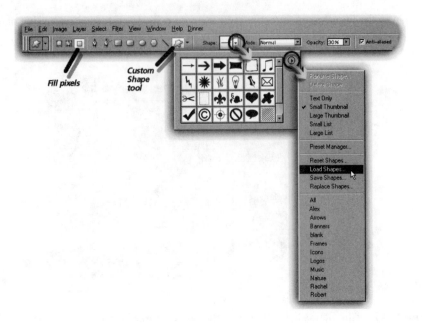

Fill pixels

Custom Shape tool

Figure 15.48   For this next effect, you'll need to load a custom shape.

9. Drag out a custom shape, as shown in Figure 15.49. If you want to relocate the position as you drag, hold down the spacebar while you readjust the location of the shape and release the spacebar to continue dragging. If you make a shape you don't like, press Ctrl(⌘)+Z and do that one again.

Figure 15.49   Make the shapes different sizes but still proportional over all until you get to the "horizon" line; then squish the shape more and more. Because of the "shadow" you painted on the ground earlier, you also see a color shift between the wall and the image bottom.

After looking at the completed effect of all of the background texturing, the blue of the Shadow layer looks a little distracting—so let's lower the opacity for that layer. Before doing this, we'll combine all of the background layers—our work in that area will then be complete—and then move on to the business of texturing Roswell.

10. Click the Shadow layer and lower the Opacity to 50%. Click on the Backing layer to make it the active layer. Then link this layer to the other background effects layers (Backing light effects layer and the Shadow layer) and press Ctrl(⌘)+E, as shown in Figure 15.50.

Figure 15.50 Merging completed layers helps keep the file size low if you don't have much in the way of system resources, but the trade off is that you lose editing flexibility.

We're getting very close to wrapping everything up now; you need only to texture Roswell and add some additional special effects to the eyes.

Adding Alien Skin and Effects

Since we're in the home stretch, let's skip the chitchat and get straight into the tutorial. We'll begin by texturing Roswell's head.

Alien Dermatology and Other Stuff

1. Double-click the Zoom tool and move the window sliders until you have a clear view of Roswell's head.

2. Click the Color layer and press W to choose the Magic Wand. Click in the green area of Roswell's head to make it a selection, and then click the Modeling layer to make this layer active.

3. From the Filter menu choose Noise, Add Noise. Enter a value of 12% for Amount, and keep the Gaussian and Monochromatic options checked. Click OK.

4. Going back to the Filter menu choose Blur, Gaussian Blur and enter a value of 2 pixels, as shown in Figure 15.51. Click OK.

Figure 15.51   This Gaussian Blur setting creates a nice mottled look to the alien's skin.

For the spacesuit, we're going for a sparkly look. Don't all spacesuits use that same material?

5. Click the Color layer and press W to choose the Magic Wand. Click in the top blue area of Roswell's spacesuit to make it a selection, hold down the Shift key and select the bottom of Roswell's suit. Finally, click the Modeling layer to make this layer active.

6. From the Filter menu choose Noise, Add Noise. Enter a value of 7% (leave the Gaussian and Monochromatic options) and click OK.

7. Head back to the Filter menu to choose Blur, Gaussian Blur and enter a value of .5 pixels, as shown in Figure 15.52.

Finally, wrap up with the gloves. We'll leave the belt with that matte color just for simplicity's sake.

8. Click the Color layer and select Roswell's gloves (you know how by now). Click the Modeling layer and go back to the and enter an Angle of –69°, and a Distance of 10 pixels, as shown in Figure 15.53.

9. From the Edit menu, choose Fade Motion Blur and lower the opacity to 69%.

Now you've painted everything on Roswell except for his eyes and his outline (which includes his insignia). To address both of these items, you're going to need paint above the Sketch layer.

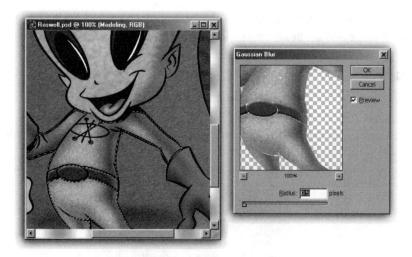

Figure 15.52   Without the Gaussian Blur the noise is a little too much, but you want to add only a touch.

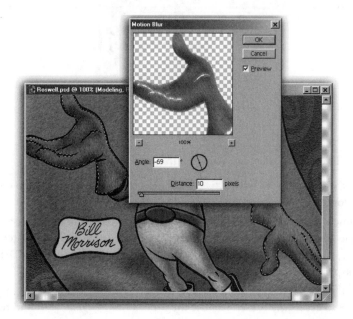

Figure 15.53   These Motion Blur settings create a nice texture for the gloves.

Crossing the Line for Effect

Up until now, you've been working only in the area below the outline, but in order to really polish this image, you need to do a few things above the original Sketch layer.

You'll color Roswell's insignia, add specular highlights and reflections to his eyes, and soften the black outline. Ready to go? Good! We'll start with the insignia.

And Now for Something Completely Different

1. Click on the Sketch layer to make it the active layer.

2. Choose the Lasso tool from the toolbox and draw a selection around the insignia, as shown in Figure 15.54. Don't worry about an exact selection; the goal is to make sure the entire insignia is within the selection area.

Figure 15.54   A down and dirty selection works in this instance.

Before you can copy the selection, you need to disable Lock all attributes.

3. Click the Lock all icon to deactivate this function. Press Ctrl(⌘)+J to copy the selection to a new layer.

4. Rename the layer **Insignia** and activate Lock transparent pixels to act as a psuedo-selection. Change the blending mode to Normal. On the Swatches palette, click in the swatch labeled Tongue, and then press Alt(Opt)+Delete (Backspace) to fill the insignia with red, as shown in Figure 15.55.

5. Click the Lock transparent pixels icon to unlock this attribute on the layer and press E to access the Eraser. Choose the 5-pixel hard-edged brush and remove anything that isn't the insignia, as shown in Figure 15.56.

Now you need to soften the outline. With all of the subtle painting you've done up to this point, the black line work looks a bit too harsh.

6. Click the Sketch layer to make it active, and then hold down the Alt(Opt) while dragging it to the Create a new layer icon at the bottom of the Layers palette. Name this duplicate layer **Outline** and then change the blending mode to Normal, Opacity to 85% and click the Lock transparent pixels icon.

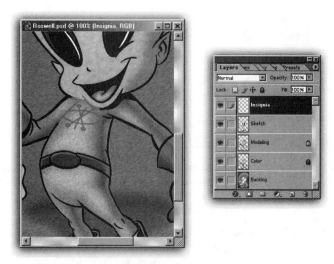

Figure 15.55   With a little maneuvering, you've got a red insignia.

Figure 15.56   Use the Eraser to clean up the area.

7. Press B to access the Brush tool. Choose the 9-pixel hard-edged brush to start.

8. Paint the outline as labeled in Figure 15.57 using the Swatches palette (these colors are available in the default palette, as well as in the swatch file you loaded earlier). The proper names are displayed by the tool tips. Roswell's pupils, boots, and mouth should be left black. Increase or decrease your brush size as needed.

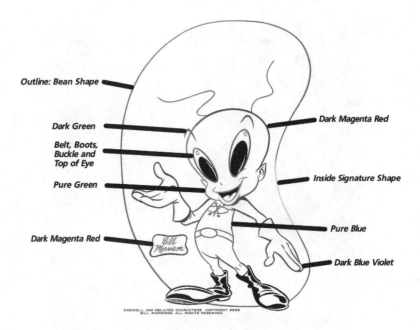

Outline: Bean Shape

Dark Green

Belt, Boots, Buckle and Top of Eye

Pure Green

Dark Magenta Red

Dark Magenta Red

Inside Signature Shape

Pure Blue

Dark Blue Violet

ROSWELL AND RELATED CHARACTERS COPYRIGHT 2002
BILL MORRISON. ALL RIGHTS RESERVED.

Figure 15.57   All of these colors are listed in the Swatches palette.

Some areas of the outline need to be painted with a hard-edged brush, but there are some areas where you will have a gradient; for example, the area where Roswell's green color gradually changes into the hot pink or the touch of yellow on the bean outline. Use the 60-pixel soft-edged brush to achieve these subtle effects.

All that's left to paint are the eyes (the windows of the soul). The first item on our agenda will be to paint over the ovals meant to represent specular highlights (the shiny part), you didn't paint them when you painted the other shiny stuff because you hadn't crossed over the outline yet. It's important to realize that a professional like Bill Morrison draws in these ovals purely as a reference for the colorist. Bill may be unaware of whether the lighting will be hard or soft, but he knows that regardless, the eyes still need specular highlights.

Tip

The Eyes Have It   If you ever want to know how many lights were used to shoot a portrait (as well as where the lights were placed and whether they were hard or diffused light sources) simply look in the subject's eyes. All of the photographer's arsenal (that was in front of the subject) will be revealed in the specular highlights of the subject. As an artist you can use this knowledge to paint more realistic looking eyes.

As for this image, we've painted Roswell to look as if he is lit with soft lights—so there should actually be a couple of additional soft-light sources reflected in the specular highlights of his eye. (You can add the correct lighting if you want,, but because this is a very stylized rendering we're cheating a little.)

Because the rest of the lighting is soft, you'll want the specular highlight to also have a soft edge. To do that, however, you need to first paint out those reference ovals.

9. Click the Create a new layer icon, and then press Ctrl(⌘)+the plus key to zoom in to 100% or more.

10. Press B to choose the Brush tool and choose the 9-pixel hard-edged brush. Hold down the Alt(Opt) key to access the Eyedropper and sample the blue inside Roswell's eye; then paint out the reference ovals in both eyes, as shown in Figure 15.58. When finished, click the eye icon next to this layer to turn off the visibility.

Figure 15.58   First sample the eye color, and then paint out the ovals.

After you've painted out the ovals, turn off the layer's visibility by clicking the eye icon. Now you're going to access the reference ovals to generate a soft-edged specular highlight.

11. Click the Outline layer to make it active, and then press W to choose the Magic Wand tool and click in one of the reference ovals. Then hold down the Shift key and select the other oval.

To see the ovals properly, you'll want to zoom in to 200%.

12. Click Layer 1's visibility icon to make the blue cover over the ovals below and then click the Create a new layer icon at the bottom of the Layers palette.

We're good to go except for one thing—you need to have solid speculars, not small doughnuts, which means you need to fill in those holes.

13. Press Q to go into Quick Mask mode. If only the ovals are filled with red tint, then Alt(Opt) click on the Edit in Quick Mask Mode icon (below the background color swatch on the Toolbox). The tint should now fill everything except the ovals. Press X to make white the foreground color. Press B to switch to the Brush tool and choose a 5-pixel hard-edge brush. Paint out the holes in the selection to make them slightly larger, as seen in Figure 15.59.

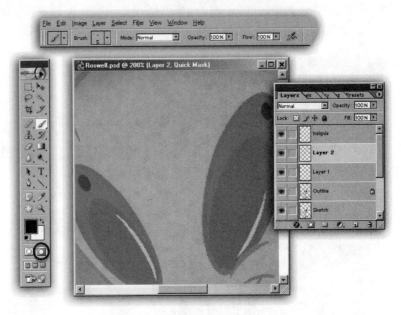

Figure 15.59 Use Quick Mask to make a solid oval selection.

14. Press Q again to exit Quick Mask mode, then Press D for the default colors and then press X to make white the foreground selection.

15. Press Alt(Opt)+Delete (Backspace) to fill the selection with white, and then press Ctrl(⌘)+D to deselect the ovals.

16. From the Filter menu choose Blur, Gaussian Blur and enter a value of 3 pixels, as shown in Figure 15.60.

Okay, you may not believe this but all you have left is to add a small amount of reflected light to the eyes and you're done! And you thought this was the never-ending chapter...

17. Click the Create a new layer icon at the bottom of the Layers palette.

18. The Brush tool should still be the active tool. Choose the 35-pixel soft-edged brush. Hold down the spacebar (to access the Hand tool) and move over to an area of hot pink color; then hold down the Alt(Opt) key to access the Eyedropper, sample the hot pink color, and hold down the spacebar again to get back to the eyes.

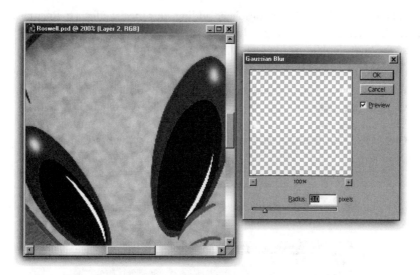

Figure 15.60   3 pixels worth of blur is all you need.

19. Make two slightly curved strokes, as shown in Figure 15.61.

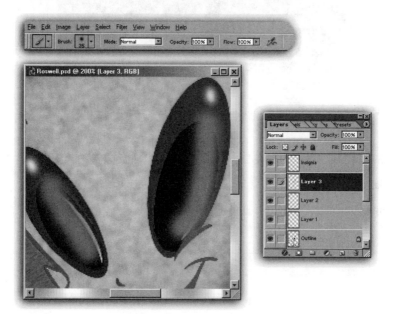

Figure 15.61   You should see two "i"s in the eyes now.

20. Lower the Opacity of the layer to 45%.

21. Press Ctrl(⌘)+E twice; all the layers should now be combined onto Layer 1. Rename the layer **Eyes**.

That's all there is to show! You've completed adding your special effects to Roswell… but wait, one last step comes hurtling in from an alternate universe! Let's try a simple trick to make the boots look more like leather (you know, from those alien cows).

22. Click the Create a new layer icon at the bottom of the Layers palette. Choose the Smudge tool from the toolbox and select the 9-pixel soft-edged brush. In the Options bar, make sure Use All Layers is checked and Strength is at 60%. Then smudge away, as shown in Figure 15.62. If you make a mistake, press Ctrl(⌘)+Z—or if you make a really big mistake, use the Eraser tool.

Figure 15.62   Use the Smudge tool on an empty layer and you can't mess up!

Some people prefer to leave the original line work; the choice is up to you. You also can lower the opacity of the smudged layer for a more subtle effect.

And finally, we come to the most important step of all…

23. Sign your name under the signature shape.

Figure 15.63   The time to personalize your work has come.

You can now combine all of your layers and save your completed work!

And that is how we do it *downtown*. Of course, this is a very stylized type of rendering; we could have explored ways to make Roswell look relatively photo-real, but that topic is so *huge* that this chapter would have been the only one in the book.

The key concepts to remember are to keep your lighting consistent and your textures varied—they shouldn't all look like plastic (unless they're supposed to *be* plastic). And one more thing needs to be said: If you're doing your own line art, make sure that it is dynamic. If it doesn't work in black and white, no amount of texturing and lighting is going to make it better. The end result won't be worth the time and effort if the initial image isn't strong.

Part VI

Typography and Special Effects

Chapter 16

Typography

Like geography (the study of land) and mythology (the study of unicorns and stuff), typography is the study of the style and appearance of typeset words. Like its printed counterpart, electronic type—the sort you use in Photoshop—is specifically designed to communicate, provoke, look sloppy or tidy, and portray about a dozen other properties. This chapter helps you understand the emotional impact of the typeface you use and see how it is laid out on a page. You also learn about the robust controls Photoshop offers that affect the appearance of text.

Let's start at the beginning with a few observations about text. Creating a printed page or a web page with text that really provokes and stimulates is not as easy as you'd think. Come along!

Type is all about communication. Communication means relaying information about our logic and emotions to others. The better you become at communicating, the more others will understand you, and the more you'll come to know yourself because logic, emotion, and about 98% water are what you're made of.

Although you may never have thought about type before, perhaps never even noticed it, you have seen so many zillions of letters, billions of words, millions of pages, that if you really stop and think about it, you already know something about type—how to read it. What you need to learn now is the how to choose and use it.

Considering how important type is, it's strange that it has been so neglected. The typeset word is one of the few ways to communicate precisely—and for posterity.

You will notice that the figure captions in this chapter are a little different than in the other chapters (see Figure 16.1). In addition to the description of the figures they accompany, the captions also contain the name of the typeface, the foundry (creator of the font), and the ESP (refers to the EsperFonto™ "impression" or mood of the typeface). When no foundry is listed for a font, it means that multiple foundries create and distribute that font.

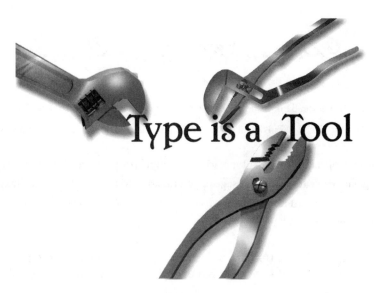

Figure 16.1   Type isn't the end result. Even with the best type tools, if you don't use them properly, the end result won't be good.

Typeface: ITC Charter (ITC); ESP: Formal, Modern, Cool, Serious, Official.

The ESP, or EsperFonto Impressions system (www.will-harris.com), assigns predefined attributes to a font. EsperFonto was developed (and has a patent pending on the system) by yours truly, Daniel Will-Harris. Its purpose is to help people choose an appropriate font(s) for a project by matching up a font's ESP attributes to the message they want their document to convey to readers.

Type Is Your Personality on Paper

If you're not taking advantage of the wide, wide variety of typestyles available today, you're not getting the most out of your documents—the most style, the most attention, the most personality, the most professional image. Figure 16.2 shows two very different typefaces, Bank Gothic and Cezanne. Which one would you use to invite your friends to a birthday party, and which one would you use to summon a person to a hearing? If in doubt (which is doubtful), check the font's ESP for a hint.

TYPE IS YOUR

Personality on Paper

Figure 16.2   Typeface: Bank Gothic (Bitstream); ESP: Formal, Modern, Cool, Serious, Official. Typeface: Cezanne (P22); ESP: Formal or Casual, Traditional, Warm, Personal, Friendly, Antique.

Using the appropriate (the best) typeface can compel people to read your message. The wrong typeface can cause your message to go unread or to be misinterpreted. Take a look at Figure 16.3 to see just a few of the tens of thousands of typefaces available and some of the messages they can help to convey.

1 **If you use the same typefaces as everyone else, you'll *look* just like everybody else. Yawn.**

2 Typefaces have personality

3 Casual to Formal

4 Silly to Serious

5 Staid to *Stylish*

6 OLD FASHIONED TO **Modern**

Figure 16.3   Typeface 1: Arial (yawn); ESP: Formal, Modern, Cold, Internal Revenue, Boring.

Typeface 2: Oz Handicraft (Bitstream); ESP: Casual, Traditional, Warm, Friendly.

Typeface 3: Oz Handicraft (see above). Followed by Bodoni; ESP: Formal, Modern, Cool, Serious.

Typeface 4: Remedy (Emigre); ESP: Casual, Modern, Warm, Friendly, Fun. Followed by ITC Galliard; ESP: Formal, Traditional, Cool, Serious, Elegant.

Typeface 5: Arial (see above). Followed by ITC Galliard Italic (see above).

Typeface 6: ITC Rennie Mackintosh; ESP: Casual or Formal, Traditional, Warm, Friendly, Elegant, Art Nouveau. Followed by Univers/Zurich Bold Extended; ESP: Formal, Modern, Cool, Serious.

Presented with two documents side by side—one well written but ugly in its presentation because it uses boring or inappropriate typefaces, and the other rambling but attractively presented—which do you think people will read first? They'll read the one that looks more professional and appealing. The amateurish ugly one gets put at the bottom of the pile—unread no matter how well written the message is.

Type Is Emotional and Subliminal

Typefaces reach the audience on a number of different levels. For example, if you use one of today's "grunge" fonts, you are saying—and without the subliminal approach—that you're "happening," "rebellious," "hipper than thou." The sort of type the talking head appears to be speaking in Figure 16.4 here would be delivering a message in a rough, coarse voice that commands conscious attention; hence the font. On the other hand, if you want to read a different part of a reader's conscious, you'd opt for something with flourish and a softness that embraces the words themselves and makes them easy to digest.

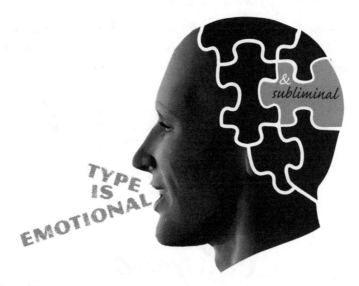

Figure 16.4   Typeface (right): Caflish Script (Adobe); ESP: Casual, Traditional, Warm, Friendly, Personal.

Typeface (left): Magnesium Grime (MVB Design); ESP: Formal or Casual, Modern, Cool or Hot, Distressed, Angry, Aged.

Throughout our reading experience, we associate the way text looks with not only the message the text is likely to carry, but also the *emotion* that the author or designer wants to elicit. Without even reading the words, you know that something creepy or frightening is going on if the poster you're looking at uses a font with sharp, jagged points and dripping blood. Conversely, you may think you're looking at a love note if the text is set in open, curly script with hearts used to dot the "i"s. Your brain just automatically makes these associations and sets your expectations and emotions accordingly.

A good typeface causes people to anticipate what your message will say, entices them into reading your message, and may even cause them to *like* your message. A well-chosen typeface can make people take your message *more* seriously. Of course, a bad typeface can work against you and make people take your message *less* seriously.

Another way to think about type is to liken it to the background music in a movie. If it's good, you probably don't even notice it. If it's bad, it's distracting. If the music is good, it makes you feel differently about the action on-screen. Turn off the sound next time you're watching a movie and see how it loses excitement. Without music, a chase scene isn't as exciting. A love scene isn't as lovely.

Imagine the wrong music: Picture *Psycho* with *The Sound of Music*'s soundtrack. Think of *The Sound of Music* with *Psycho*'s soundtrack.

Likewise, if you bought a ticket to a movie based only on the title of the movie and the typeface the title was set in, you'd probably be very disappointed with the movie you chose if the typefaces used were the ones shown in Figure 16.5

Really grotesque examples of how the message fights the messenger (and loses!)

Figure 16.5   These typefaces don't fit the movies they're referring to.

Typeface (*Sound of Music*): Sabeh (GarageFonts); ESP: Casual, Modern, Cool, Friendly or Serious, Distressed, Wild.

Typeface (*Psycho*): Shelley Allegro; ESP: Formal, Traditional, Warm, Elegant.

Now, swap the fonts used in the titles to the ones shown in Figure 16.6, make your selection, and you'd be right on the money.

*These fonts with these titles would make
Julie Andrews and Alfred Hitchcock a lot happier.*

Figure 16.6   Now *these* typefaces *look* right. They *feel* right. They convey the same message and mood as the movie. All that's changed is the typeface, but it's made a world of difference.

Type Is the Messenger, Not the Message

You might want to tack Figure 16.7 up on the wall, because it's a truism that is often lost in the plethora of fonts easily available in electronic and web publishing today.

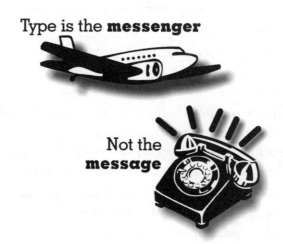

Figure 16.7   The true purpose of type is to enhance the message, not merely carry it.

No matter how much we like to play with the emotional value different typefaces have or toy with each letterform as an element of artistic expression, a typeface's most important job is to facilitate communication.

Type *can* be used as art to decorate the page, but when a typeface distracts and interferes with the reader's comprehension of the content, the page designer has failed. The art of typography used to be the domain of specialists, but computers and digital type have now given you the ability to do things with type that even the most seasoned typographer of yore would find difficult. This chapter's aim is to give you an understanding of what constitutes good typography and to raise your level of "fontish" sensitivity so that you use the gift of digital type to its fullest.

Top Type Tips

Type doesn't have to be intimidating if you think about it like this: You've been looking at type for years. You've been reading it since you were a kid. You know what it looks like. When it's hard to read, you know it.

- **Get to know type.** Short of taking it out for dinner and dancing, the best way to get to know type is to use it. Pay attention to type (you'll see that it's everywhere once you start to notice it). Experiment with it. Play with it. Don't be afraid to make a mistake or do something ugly—we all learn from our mistakes.

- **Make your type readable.** If people can't read your type, they won't get the message in your text. That's a simple rule, but a lot of people seem to forget it. And choosing type with that rule in mind is not hard to do—you'll find some simple rules for ensuring readable type later in the chapter (in the section, "Body Text: Important, Invisible, Substantial, Subtle").

- **Use appropriate typefaces.** Make sure that the typeface you choose markets the message and matches the mood. To help you choose, read this chapter, and visit www.will-harris.com to use the EsperFonto system.

- **Make your type interesting.** Don't use the same typefaces for everything—it's boring for your audience and bad for business because you don't get across the full impact of your message. There are more typefaces available now than ever before in history. They are more affordable and easier to use.

- **In case of emergency: Break Rules!** Remember that there are simply times to go with your gut and let the message determine what font you choose—whether or not it fits with the plan you had for your design.

Types of Type

Typographers (sometimes affectionately known as *font freaks*) developed a standardized way to describe a typeface by analyzing how the characters are formed, their intended use, and whether the individual elements in the typeface are letters or elements that make up words, pictures, or decorations. The most important and useful categories for type are these:

- Serif and Sans Serif
- Body and Display
- Picture, Symbol, or Pi Fonts

Most font catalogs, online or paper, use these characteristics to organize their collections. You need to know what these types of type are and when you use them. Luckily, these points are easy to learn.

Serif Versus Sans Serif

A *serif* typeface is a typeface that has serifs (how surprising). A *serif* is the small cross-bar (or finishing stroke or "doo-jiggie") that ends the main stroke of letters.

Sans serif is a typeface "sans" (French for "without") serifs. Oi? Oy. The circles in the first line of Figure 16.8 point out where the serifs are on two different typefaces. The second line of type is set in two different sans serif typefaces.

Figure 16.8   Notice that the serif fonts have small protrusions (marked with solid circles behind them), whereas the sans serif typefaces don't (marked with circle outlines behind them).

Typeface (Serif Roman): PMN Caecilia (Adobe); ESP: Formal, Modern, Cool or Warm, Friendly, Forward-looking.

Typeface (Serif Gothic): Bodoni; ESP: Formal, Traditional, Cool, Serious, Elegant.

Typeface (Sans Serif Roman): PMN Caecilia (Adobe); ESP: Formal, Modern, Cool or Warm, Friendly, Forward-looking.

Typeface (Sans Serif Gothic): Bodoni; ESP: Formal, Traditional, Cool, Serious, Elegant.

Note

Gothic Versus Roman   It's worth mentioning here that there is a sub-class to fonts—whether they are Roman or Gothic. If you take a look at Figure 16.8, you will see that the fonts that are called out with the Roman tag are made of thick and thin lines. In contrast, Gothic fonts have characters made up of uniform strokes and even widths.

A good rule of thumb is to use serif type for body text and sans serif for headings. Should you always follow this convention? Well, most of the time. Using a serif typeface for both body and display is also perfectly acceptable. In some situations, especially those that include publishing technical data, it is appropriate to use sans for both body text and headings.

As to which is easier to read, the scientific answer is—*Whatever you grew up reading.* Most Americans grow up reading serif type. Many Europeans grow up reading sans serif type. That doesn't mean that Americans freak out up when forced to read sans serif or that Europeans recoil in horror if presented with serifs. But when you ask what is easy for someone to read, the answer depends on where they grew up.

Setting your body text (the small type) in a serif face is almost always a safe bet.

Sans serifs can be difficult to read over long stretches because they are monotonous. This is the polite way to say that many sans serif faces can be boring—not just emotionally but also artistically—the characters are all the same weight, all over, and this actually bores the eye and makes you think about other things, such as lunch or unfinished laundry.

The mechanics of serifs may make them easier on the eye. The little serifs are said to help lead the reader's eye from character to character. Serifs also give letters a more distinctive appearance and shape. And because we read as much by the shape of words as by the letters alone, shapes are an important ingredient in making serif typefaces easier to read.

The exception: When your text is being read on a low-resolution device, such as a computer screen or fax, sans serif type can sometimes be clearer for body text, especially if the text is sized at 10 points or under.

If you choose to use sans serif type for your body text, you can make it easier to read by shortening the line lengths and using more leading (the distance between lines of type). More on this later.

Body Faces Versus Display Faces

We have yet another category of typefaces to explore: Body faces and display (often called "headline") faces. Let's take a look at the characteristics of these font types and consider how you can use them effectively to communicate a feeling or an idea, or to sell something.

Take a look at Figure 16.9. Can you see how each font "belongs" to a different family? Can you also see how some fonts make better body text than others? The display fonts on the right are great for headlines, but not much else. I can't imagine having to read a paragraph set using Croissant (fourth display font in the list), for example.

Figure 16.9   Typeface (Body upper): Goudy Old Style; ESP: Formal, Traditional, Warm, Friendly, Elegant.

Typeface (Body lower): Bookman; ESP: Formal, Traditional, Warm, Open, Antique.

Typeface (Display 1): ITC Anna; ESP: Formal, Modern, Cool, Friendly, Art Deco, Stylish.

Typeface (Display 2): Longhand (LetterPerfect); ESP: Casual, Modern, Warm, Friendly, Personal.

Typeface (Display 3): Celestia (Adobe/MVB Design); ESP: Formal, Traditional, Warm, Friendly, Antique.

Typeface (Display 4): Croissant; ESP: Ornamental, Modern, Cool, Stylish.

Typeface (Display 5): Gallia; ESP: Ornamental, Traditional, Garish, Antique.

Display faces are used for headlines and headings over 14 points in size. They tend to arrest attention, but the meat (or if you're a vegetarian, the *germ*) of most messages is contained in the body text. The best headlines (the ones in which the fonts are selected to best carry the feeling and tone of the content) catch the reader's attention and direct it to the body text long enough for the meaning to work its magic.

Unless you're creating marketing flyers, body text will probably represent the bulk of text in your publications. The stories and articles—the main text readers read—are known as the *body* of your publication. In contrast, headlines and subheads are not body copy, they're *display* type.

Although you often can use body text faces for display work, it's rare that you can use display faces for body text—they're too busy, distracting, and hard to read, as you can see in Figure 16.10. A typeface such as Times Roman (I know, I *know*—one of the most common fonts on the face of the earth) could indeed serve as *both* a display text (in a bold face, most likely) and as body text (in sized 8 points and larger).

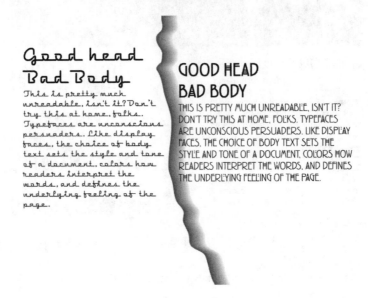

Figure 16.10   Display faces are useful, beautiful, and fun—but only when used correctly. Here you can see two wonderful display faces that work great as headlines and abysmally as body text because it's difficult, and even painful, to read them in small sizes.

Typeface (Left): Neon (Font Bureau); ESP: Casual, Modern, Warm, Friendly, Art Deco.

Typeface (Right): ITC Rennie Mackintosh; ESP: Casual or Formal, Traditional, Warm, Friendly, Elegant, Art Nouveau.

Body Text: Important, Invisible, Substantial, Subtle

Body text is like wallpaper or paint color. Even when people don't notice the typeface, it colors the way they look at the page. Superficial? Perhaps. Important? You betcha.

Body text is really quite small, with each letter of normal body text being about one-third the size of the average ladybug. And yet, these tiny little letters can contain all the knowledge of humankind—thoughts, feelings, hopes, fears, warnings, discoveries, and dreams.

The most important job of body text is to serve the text—not decorate the page or distract the reader. Body text faces are specially designed to be easy to read over long stretches.

Well-done body text (as opposed to *medium rare*—sorry!) is "invisible" body text. You read right through it to the words. If you *notice* the body text typeface, you are interrupted in your thinking, and the text has distracted you from receiving the message. That's not body text's job.

Most people don't consciously notice type, but it can strongly affect the way we feel about what we read. Body text is an unconscious persuader—it changes the tone of a document without you knowing it. Experiment with the typefaces in Figure 16.11 to see what I mean. Feel yourself tense up reading some paragraphs and relax reading others?

Figure 16.11   These are some popular "hidden persuaders" of the body text families.

As you begin to choose fonts for the body text in your publications, remember these rules:

- **Set the body text between 10 and 12 points.** 11 points is the best choice for printing for laser or ink jet printing. Use the same typeface, type size, and leading for *all* your body copy.

- **Use at least 2 points leading.** For example, use 12-point leading with 10-point type.

- **Watch your line lengths.** Make the lines in your publication longer than 30 characters and shorter than 70.

- **Make paragraph beginnings clear.** Use *either* an indent or block style with white space between paragraphs. Don't use both.

- **Use only one space after a period, not two.** Period.

- **Don't justify text unless you have to.** If you justify text, you must hyphenate. Justification also adds character spaces as necessary to align both the left and right margins, which can make your body text look odd.

- **Never underline anything! Use italics instead.** Don't put lines under headlines or subheads. Ruling lines only *separate* them from the text with which they belong. Lines go *above* headings. Also, be sure to leave more space above headings than below.

- **Don't set long blocks of text in italics, bold, or all caps.** They're harder to read. We read by the *shape* of entire words as much as by individual letters.

Display Faces: Attracting Attention

Display faces are meant to attract attention—that's what they are there for. (When you started looking at this chapter, didn't you read the chapter title and a few headings before you started on the text?). Because display faces are so dramatic, they have the strongest personalities. You have to be especially careful about the feeling a face conveys and be sensitive to what it reminds the reader of.

Display faces are fun, exciting, and different. They are meant to be used in large sizes and read over short stretches. *Short* is a relative term: the most outrageous display faces work for only a word or two at most—after that, they drive you up the wall (see Figure 16.12).

Display faces are ordinarily used for the following:

- *Subheads* are usually at least 20% larger than body text and can be as large as 18 points. Subheads should be bold or italic so that they stand out from the body text. It's a good idea to use headings and subheads liberally to help readers find what they're looking for.

- *Headlines* should be *at least* twice as large as body text. Headlines are normally between 20 and 36 points.

Some display faces are specifically designed to be easy to read, but for many display faces, legibility takes a back seat to punch. If you find you are working with a simple display font and want to try using it for body text, test a couple of paragraphs, but don't plan on using it for an entire page.

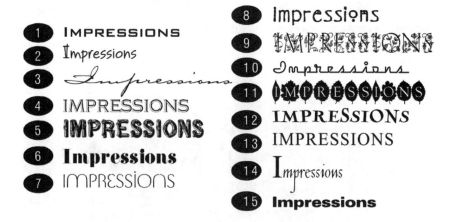

Figure 16.12   You can see how you could wear yourself out staring at these fonts too long. Check out the "Display Fonts" sidebar for a full breakdown of the ESPs used here.

Typeface 1: Bank Gothic; ESP: Formal, Modern, Cool, Serious, Machine-age.

Typeface 2: ITC Bruno; ESP: Casual, Modern, Warm, Friendly, Personal, Fun.

Typeface 3: Carpenter; ESP: Formal, Traditional, Cool, Serious, Elegant, Antique.

Typeface 4: ITC Citation; ESP: Formal, Traditional, Cool, Serious, Classical, Carved in Stone.

Typeface 5: Fetch Scotty (Intecsas); ESP: Casual, Traditional, Warm, Friendly, Rustic

Typeface 6: Florence; ESP: Formal, Traditional, Warm, Friendly, Art Deco.

Typeface 7: Jensen Arabique (Jason Castle Design); ESP: Formal or Casual, Modern, Warm, Friendly, Elegant, Soft.

Typeface 8: Glasgow (Architect Fonts); ESP: Casual, Traditional, Warm, Friendly, Antique, Art Nouveau.

Typeface 9: Lilith Initials (Intecsas); ESP: Formal, Traditional, Warm, Friendly, Art Nouveau, Drop caps.

Typeface 10: Neon (Font Bureau); ESP: Casual, Modern, Warm, Friendly, Art Deco.

Typeface 11: Leaves (Judith Sutcliff, Electric Typographer); ESP: Formal or Casual, Traditional, Warm, Friendly.

Typeface 12: Manka's Hand (Will-Harris House); ESP: Casual, Traditional, Warm, Friendly, Quirky.

Typeface 13: Rasta Rattin Frattin (Intecsas); ESP: Casual, Traditional, Warm, Friendly, Rustic, Art Nouveau.

Typeface 14: Tagliente (Judith Sutcliff, Electric Typographer); ESP: Formal, Traditional, Warm, Friendly, Elegant, Antique.

Typeface 15: Univers Extended Black; ESP: Formal, Modern, Cool, Serious.

In Figure 16.13, you can clearly see that legibility—the vessel of the thought being presented—is of secondary importance, and that creating art from the arrangement of specific ornamental fonts comes first.

Figure 16.13   For some projects, you can think of display faces as art. You can create entire designs using only type.

Typeface (Insects): Insecta; Picture Font.

Typface (Leaves): Leaves (Sutcliff Electric Typographer); Picture Font.

Typeface (Leonardo): Leonardo (Sutcliff Electric Typographer); ESP: Formal, Traditional, Warm, Serious, Antique.

Typeface (Dear Diary): Daly Hand (Sutcliff Electric Typographer); ESP: Casual, Modern, Warm, Friendly, Personal.

Typeface (Electric Typographer): Greene & Greene (Sutcliff Electric Typographer); ESP: Casual, Traditional, Warm, Friendly, Craftsman.

Figure 16.14 gives another example of how text can lead you through a dialog box or stimulate your artistic mind with the creative use of font faces, size, alignment, and the use of color.

Figure 16.14   The message takes the back seat to a well-dressed and inventively thought-out idea of the messenger.

Typeface (upper): Glasgow (Architect Fonts); ESP: Casual, Traditional, Warm, Friendly, Antique, Art Nouveau.

Typeface (middle): Stamped (Architect Fonts); ESP: Casual, Traditional, Warm, Friendly, Rough.

Typeface (lower): Scribble (Architect Fonts); ESP: Casual, Modern, Warm, Friendly, Personal.

Finally, a piece of freeform prose is enhanced by ornamental text and the creative arrangement of the elements on the page. You probably would not stop and gawk over this piece if it were typed in Courier (a monospaced font in which all characters are assigned the same width) in Microsoft Word, but in Figure 16.15 (and especially in color!), the text is suitable for framing and hanging.

Figure 16.15   Jazz is the motif for the content of this message and so is the arrangement and choice of fonts. The fonts are riffing off of each other in a way that is both stimulating and provoking.

Typeface (body upper): Rasta-Rattin-Frattin (Intecsas); ESP: Casual, Traditional, Warm, Friendly, Art Nouveau.

Typeface (body middle): Lilith (Intecsas); ESP: Formal, Traditional, Warm, Friendly, Elegant.

Typeface (body lower): Harting (Intecsas); ESP: Casual, Modern, Warm, Friendly, Typewriter.

Typeface (Rakowski-intecsas): Bunny Ears (Intecsas); ESP: Casual, Modern, Warm, Friendly, Fun.

Typeface (background): Dwiggins 48 (Intecsas); ESP: Formal, Modern, Warm, Friendly, Drop Caps.

Typeface (right column, top to bottom): Lilith Initials, Harting, FetchScotty, Tenderleaf Caps.

Sometimes, what comes out of your keyboard aren't characters at all, but instead are tiny pictures. Pi fonts are our next area of exploration—the type of font that's actually clipart *disguised* as a font!

Picture, Symbol, Pi Fonts

Some fonts don't even contain letters and numbers—they contain symbols or pictures. The most well-known of these fonts are Wingdings and Zapf Dingbats (see Figure 16.16).

Figure 16.16   Wingdings and Zapf Dingbats are two of the most popular Pi (Picture) fonts.

Many symbol fonts are specific to certain sciences, such as equation fonts, or to certain industries, such as electronics schematic fonts.

And there's a whole range of fonts that are like self-contained collections of clip art in a single consistent style (see Figure 16.17). ITC has a large selection of "Design Fonts" with art in a wide range of styles, from cool to professional to downright funky.

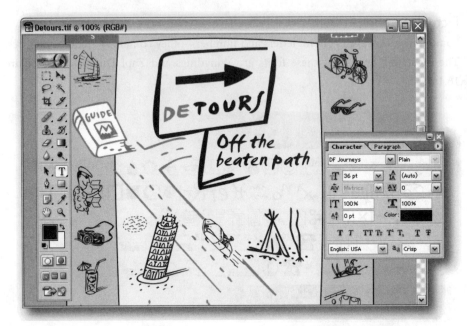

Figure 16.17 This cover is made entirely of fonts. Every picture is part of the DF Journeys font. This gives them a consistent style that makes the whole design come together. Even the ink spatters under the Tower of Pisa are a font—Smudger Alternates.

Typeface (pictures): DF Journeys (ITC); ESP: Casual, Modern, Warm, Friendly, Fun.

Typeface (text): Smudger (ITC); ESP: Casual, Modern, Warm, Friendly, Personal.

Hey, with a few bucks in your pocket today, you can be very choosy about what makes up your font collection, which brings us to a little creative, virtual window-shopping. How do you choose the right font from the combination of typefaces that are as expressive as the way you dress in public?

Choosing Type

If you think of typefaces as representing you, you're on the right track. When you're with friends or family, you act more casually than you do when you're with business associates. With friends, you're more likely to be personal, informal, sometimes even goofy—you long ago stopped trying to make a good impression. On the other hand, with business associates you're more reserved, professional, official—you're always trying to make a good impression.

Of course, how you present yourself—in person or in type—all depends on you. But how you want to relate to other people and how you want them to see you are the basis for choosing typefaces (see Figure 16.18). If you want to deliver a certain message in a certain way to a certain audience, you need the right font to do the trick.

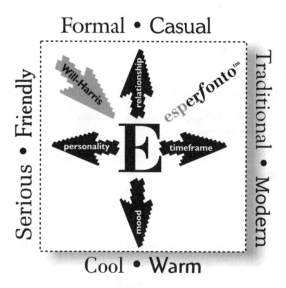

Figure 16.18   EsperFonto helps you easily choose the typefaces that are appropriate for your job.

Typeface (sans serif): Gill Sans; ESP: Formal or Casual, Modern, Warm, Serious or Friendly, Elegant.

Typeface (serif): Walbaum; ESP: Formal, Modern, Cool, Serious, Official.

Tip

Try EsperFonto   If you aren't sure what feeling a font conveys, try my online EsperFonto system, at www.will-harris.com. EsperFonto walks you through choosing faces by feelings and helps you choose the most appropriate font for your job.

You are fast becoming a connoisseur of typefaces. By learning the hows and whys of type before you begin creating it, you are starting things right. But now that you've learned the rules, it's time to kick out the jams and *break* a couple.

Everything's Relative

Formal doesn't always mean *business,* just as *casual* doesn't always mean *personal. Formal* also doesn't necessarily mean *tux or evening gown.* Think of formal as being *proper, conventional,* or *traditional.*

Casual doesn't always mean *sweats or blue je*ans. Think of casual as *friendly, easygoing, or insouciant.* (Don't you just love that word? Just so you don't have to drag out the dictionary, *insouciant* means unconcerned, carefree, or nonchalant.)

Some fonts can manage to be both formal and casual, depending on how you use them. And because everything really *is* relative, there are degrees of both formality and informality—it's a continuum. The trick is finding just the right point of balance and choosing the feel that's appropriate for the moment.

Moods, Feelings, and Impressions

Once you've established the relationship between your text and the reader, the next step is to figure out what you want readers to feel. What kind of impression or mood you want to convey?

The basic categories:

- **Formal or Casual.** What's your relationship to the reader? Formal tends to be more "official, proper, conventional, traditional, classic." Casual tends to be "friendly, easygoing, individual, traditional, unique, fresh."

- **Traditional or Modern.** You can tell this just by looking at the type. Does the type look new? If so, it's modern. Does it look like it came from some time in the past? Then it's probably traditional.

- **Warm or Cool.** This category is not about temperature, it's about emotions. Blue is considered a cool color, and red is a warm one. Typefaces have that same kind of cool or warm feeling. Cool faces tend to be those that look more official and businesslike. Warm faces are those that tend to look more personal. That said, there are formal faces that also are warm and friendly, such as Cheltenham or Goudy Old Style, and casual faces that are cool, such as Futura or Serifa.

- **Serious or Friendly.** I find that faces with softer edges tend to look more friendly, while those with sharper edges look more serious.

Take a look at Figure 16.19. Do you see how the letterforms give you an impression?

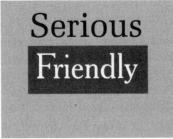

Figure 16.19 Every typeface gives a certain impression, such as Formal, Casual, Traditional, Modern, Warm, Cool, Serious, or Friendly.

Typeface (Formal): ITC Galliard; ESP: Formal, Traditional, Cool, Serious, Elegant.

Typeface (Casual): ITC Souvenir; ESP: Casual, Modern, Warm, Friendly.

Typeface (Traditional): Goudy Old Style; ESP: Formal, Traditional, Warm, Friendly, Elegant.

Typeface (Modern): PMN Caecilia (Adobe); ESP: Formal, Modern, Cool or Warm, Friendly, Forward-looking.

Typeface (Warm): ITC Highlander; ESP: Casual, Modern, Warm, Friendly.

Typeface (Serious): Melior / Zapf Elliptical; ESP: Formal, Modern, Cool, Serious.

Typeface (Friendly): Original Cheltenham (Bitstream); ESP: Casual or Formal, Traditional, Warm, Friendly.

How would you want your reader to feel about your message? The answer should be reflected in the font you select.

Depending on how far you want to take this, there's an endless number of more specific adjectives, such as "hard or soft," "smooth or rough," "exciting or sedate," "elegant or hard-working," "businesslike or childlike," "plain or fancy," "classic or cute," "charming or brusque," "tacky or trendy…" When you think of the feeling you want to convey, choosing the most appropriate typeface becomes easier.

What's the Message You're Trying to Convey?

You would be amazed by the number of people who forget to ask this. They just plunge right into designing without considering what they want the outcome to be. If you ask this question, you will immediately start off on the right path. The message tells you emotional things, such as what kind of mood you want to present, as well as mechanical things, such as how much type you'll have, what kind of font you need (body text or display), and how much space you have to fill.

Knowing Your Medium

An important aspect of understanding the message you want to convey is knowing your medium. The first question to ask is whether your type will be used in print or on the web.

If you're creating a design for print, you need to test it on paper—type looks different in print than it does on-screen. If you're using it on-screen, you need to test it at the most common resolutions to make sure that it's clear and easy to read.

Will you be using the type in small or large sizes? Type you'd choose for a magazine can be very different from type you'd choose for a poster; and certain typefaces, both on and offline, are more legible at some sizes than others.

Will your readers be viewing the text close up or far away? Are viewers holding the page with text in their hands, viewing it on a monitor 18 inches away, or seeing it from a distance on a billboard?

Knowing Your Market

For your message to be effective, you have to choose type styles based on your market. One of the best ways to know what your market expects is to look at magazines for that specific industry area. People get used to certain looks, so although a typeface like Souvenir is really a casual face, for a while it was used in upscale, elegant advertisements and was considered a formal, elegant face (it isn't anymore).

Don't talk up or down to your audience. Avoid using fonts that your audience will find pretentious, but also avoid fonts they'll find childish or crass. For best results, reach your audience in visual language they will understand.

Tip

It's All Subjective   Remember that taste is a matter of opinion and familiarity, as we discussed earlier. What one person finds "elegant," another person may consider "stiff." Although you can't account for everybody's taste (and, as they say, you can't please all the people all the time), getting to know what your audience likes is half the battle to choosing fonts effectively.

Okay, gang, let's fire up Photoshop and put all this typeface theory into practice. Our main tools in the next section will be the Character and Paragraph palettes, which you access from the Options bar when the Type tool is chosen. You also can display the palettes by picking them from the Window menu. This first exercise helps you size things up.

Using Type

Type is *always* measured in "points," and there are 72 points per inch, as mentioned in Chapter 2, "Optimizing and Customizing Photoshop Preferences."

You might think it's odd that type isn't measured in inches or millimeters, but when you think about it, many things have their own sizes. A bucket of water, a flagon of mead, a fortnight, a metric liter—you get the idea. The true size of any given font is coded into the font file. Some fonts will look smaller at 72 points (1") than others because the font creator has left a given amount of headroom space to the font. So at 72 points, the capital letters might be only 50 points. Besides adding this padding so that the font leading isn't too tight, foreign accent marks usually go above characters, and the accents make up the difference between the capital character and a true measurement of 72" points being exactly 1". Figure 16.20 gives you an example of this.

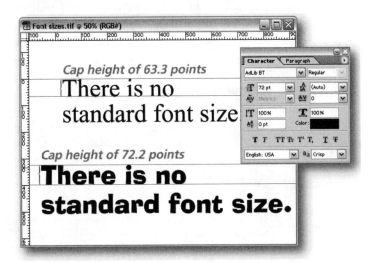

Figure 16.20   Even though you enter the same point size for two different fonts, there's no guarantee that their size will be consistent.

Creating 5" Type

1. Open the 2-face.psd document from the Examples/Chap16 folder on the Companion CD.

2. Right-click (Macintosh: hold Ctrl and click) the title bar of the document and choose Canvas Size. In the Canvas Size dialog box, middle Anchor should be chosen by default. You want to expand this canvas, leaving the logo at the far left, so click the anchor to the left of the middle square. Then enter a Width of **20** inches, a Height of **6**, and click OK.

3. Choose the Type tool from the toolbox and click the icon to view the Character and Paragraph palettes (on the right side of the Options bar). Choose Arial as the font, set the Style to Bold, and point size at 360 points. Press D for default colors (black should be the foreground color). Click in the new document and type **2FACE**, as shown in Figure 16.21.

Figure 16.21   The height of the logo is about 5 inches tall. If 72 points equal an inch, 360-point type should theoretically be the same height as the logo.

You need some guides to help judge the bottom and top spacing for the text height. These guides will aid in the following steps. Here's how to create the guidelines.

4. Press Ctrl(⌘)+R to display the rulers. Click in the top ruler, drag a guide down, and position it at the lowest edge of the logo. Drag another guide from the top ruler and position it at the highest edge of the logo (peek ahead at Figure 16.22

to see where the guides have been placed). Press the Ctrl(⌘) key to toggle to the Move tool and position your text near the logo so that the lower edge of the text is aligned with the bottom guide.

5. The Text tool should still be active. Highlight the text and scrunch the width of the text by typing **50%** in the Horizontal scale option on the Character palette (see Figure 16.22), and press Enter (Return) to apply the change. Press Ctrl(⌘)+Enter (Return) to set the text.

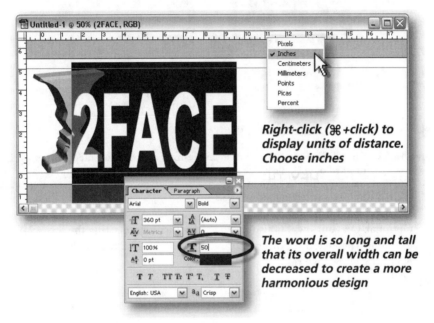

Right-click (⌘+click) to display units of distance. Choose inches

The word is so long and tall that its overall width can be decreased to create a more harmonious design

Figure 16.22   The Horizontal scale of type can be adjusted to complement and balance the vertical appearance of a design.

Now let's stretch the text so that it reaches the top guideline.

6. Press Ctrl(⌘)+T to bring up the Transform tool. On the Options bar, click the Maintain aspect ratio icon (it's the chain icon that links width to height proportionately). Click and drag the upper-right corner of the bounding box to scale the text so that it meets the upper guideline, as shown in Figure 16.23. When you're satisfied, press Enter (Return) to apply the transformation.

Figure 16.23   Click the Maintain aspect ratio and resize the text. Press Enter (Return) when finished or click the check mark on the far-right side of the Options bar. (Clicking the "no" sign, next to the checkmark, is equivalent to pressing the Esc key and cancels out any changes.)

7. Optional: On your own, polish off the assignment by selecting the text with the Text tool. Then choose a different font to give the logo a new look and feel. See Figure 16.24 for inspiration.

Figure 16.24   With a little more polish (using Adobe Viva multi-master font) we're done.

Ascenders and Descenders

In the last section, you learned that choosing the same size type in different typefaces might display type that looks dramatically different in size, depending on whether the font designer built in added leading with the characters. Ascenders and descenders are additional characteristics that affect the way same-sized typefaces appear. Type is measured from the bottom of the *descenders* to the top of the *ascenders.*

Descenders are the bottoms of lowercase letters that fall below the *baseline* (or the bottom of most letters). The only letters that have descenders are g, j, p, q, and y. Ascenders are the tops of lowercase letters that rise above the *x-height.* The letters with ascenders are b, d, f, h, k, l, and t.

Typefaces with a small x-height, such as Bodoni, look smaller than typefaces with a large x-height, such as Caecilia. The x-height of a typeface is simply the height of the lowercase x. Most lowercase letters are the same height as the lowercase x (with the exception of letters with ascenders or descenders). Figure 16.25 illustrates all of this clearly.

Figure 16.25   Different fonts can appear larger simply based on the measured distance from the descenders to the ascenders. X-height can play a factor in this illusion, too.

Vertical and Transparent Type

You can type text at any time one of the Text tools is active by simply clicking in a document and typing. You also have the option to drag a marquee selection with the Type tool before typing. This allows you to create a text box for the type. When you use a text box, the type automatically wraps within the confines of the box. If you need to resize the box, you use the handles on the bounding box to do the trick. In addition to resizing, you also can rotate the box.

You'll find four different Type tools on the toolbox flyout menu. The Horizontal Type tool and the Vertical Type tool will create text (as their name implies) either in a horizontal or vertical direction. These tools also automatically generate their own layer on the Layers palette. The two remaining text tools on the Toolbox flyout are the Horizontal Type Mask tool and the Vertical Type Mask tool. Like the first two tools listed on the flyout, these tools also lay text in a horizontal or vertical direction, respectively. The main difference is that these tools do not create their own text layer. Instead, they create a selection of the text on the current active layer. This selection then can be used to fill with a color, a gradient, or anything you might care to do with any other selection. You can think of the result as rasterized text, since this text can no longer be edited once you've accepted or committed the "masked" text to make it a selection.

Now that we've run through the differences of the Text tools available to you, let's try another exercise to put some of these tools to work.

Vertical Type

1. Load the Kibbutz font from the Examples/Chap16 folder on the Companion CD or use your own heavyweight font. Open the Hotel.tif in Photoshop from the Examples/Chap16 folder on the Companion CD.

2. Press D for the default colors. Press X to switch white to the foreground color. Choose the Vertical Type tool from the toolbox and open the Character palette from the Options bar (or from the Window menu). Choose the Kibbutz font (or any heavyweight font), and set the font size to around 90 pt. Click at the top of the empty sign area in the image and type **HOTEL** (all uppercase letters), as shown in Figure 16.26. If the individual letters are vertical, as you shown in Figure 16.27, click the arrow in the upper-right corner of the Character palette and choose the Rotate Character command on the flyout menu. This rotates the individual characters so that they appear one above the other.

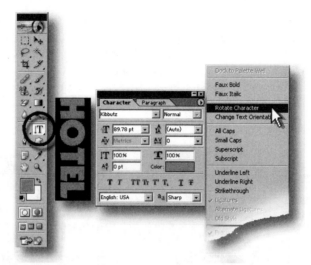

Figure 16.26   Use the Vertical Type tool to type text in a vertical direction. Additionally, you can use the flyout menu found on the Character palette to further control the orientation of the individual characters.

3. You need to tighten up the spaces between characters to make the letters fit the sign. Press Ctrl(⌘)+A to select all the letters, and on the Character palette set tracking to **–200**, as shown in Figure 16.27. Remember, this value sets the character space between letters, even though they are stacked vertically.

Figure 16.27   There is too much space between characters. The letters don't fit the sign. Tighten up the space by adjusting tracking. A negative number brings characters closer together, and a positive number increases the distance between the characters.

4. With the text still highlighted, you can adjust text size to find the magic number that makes this text appear as though it were made for the sign in this image (70 pt seems to work well). When you are satisfied with the text, press Ctrl(⌘)+Enter (Return) to set the text. From any point in your workflow, you can always turn text on its sides. Press Ctrl(⌘)+T to use the Transform tool and rotate the text, as shown in Figure 16.28. Holding the Shift key while rotating restrains rotation to 15° increments.

Hold Shift to constrain Free Transform Rotate

Figure 16.28   Ctrl(⌘)+T allows you to rotate text with the Transform tool. You can also choose the orientation for the text. Press Enter to exit the Transform tool and apply changes. Press Esc to cancel the Transform tool, along with the changes you've made.

The goal of this exercise is to get you comfortable with the Text tool features. So experiment a little on your own with the text. I'm goofing around with the finished results in Figure 16.29.

Figure 16.29 Onnnnly kidding! This sign doesn't look right.

5. If you would like to experiment with a glow for your text, try this trick. Click the Add a layer style icon at the bottom of the Layers palette and choose Outer Glow. In the Layer Style dialog box, click the color swatch to choose a color for your glow. Play with the sliders, especially the Spread and Size sliders, until the results look appealing. By contrast, Figure 16.30 shows what you can do with the right font for the right occasion. I used a Neon font, rasterized the text (Layer, Rasterize, Type), and used the Free Transform Distort tool to finesse the shape of the text. Then I put a Gaussian Blur behind the neon (another method to obtain an Outer Glow effect).

Figure 16.30   A perfect example of how an unusual font can suddenly become "just the right font" for the right situation.

Fills for Text

One of the great things about Photoshop is its built-in flexibility. If you can imagine a design concept, you can find a way to make it happen in Photoshop. When you're designing text, it helps to think of it as more than text. When you are creating text in Photoshop, chances are that the text is more than just letters that form words—text here is art and, as such, it's an important part of your overall design.

But with all designs, and text is no exception, don't lose sight of the power of simplicity. The effects you can create for text can be wild and zany, but many times the simplest of ideas can be the most effective. Just the right font with the right color may be all you need to complete the look you are after. If you need something fancier, you may find a style in the Styles palette that gives you just the look you want.

Here's a quick exercise to get you acquainted with experimenting with color and styles.

Color with Style

1. Press Ctrl(⌘)+N to open a new document. Make a 400-pixel square document, 72 ppi, RGB Color, and click OK. Press D for default colors (black should be the foreground color).

2. Choose the Horizontal Text tool from the toolbox. Make sure the Character palette is showing, and use the Kibbutz font loaded in the previous exercise, (or any heavyweight font). The font size or tracking isn't important. This is just practice, but go ahead and set the font size to 170 pt. Set the tracking to 100 so that some space is added between letters.

3. Click near the left center of the document window and type the word **FILL**. Press the Ctrl(⌘) key to toggle to the Move tool if you want to reposition the text in the center of the document window. Press Ctrl(⌘)+A to highlight all the letters. Now here's a little trick that many people forget to use: press Ctrl(⌘)+H to hide the reverse coloring that occurs when you highlight the text. You can now view the normal color of the text even though you have the text highlighted. Click the Color swatch located on the Character palette and choose a new color. You can see the color fill update live on the text (because we are no longer captive to that pesky highlighting problem). When you find a color you like, click OK (see item 2 on Figure 16.31). Press Ctrl(⌘)+Enter (Return) to commit the text.

4. Now click the Styles tab to view the Styles palette (or go to the Window menu and choose Styles). Click the triangle at the upper-right corner of the Styles palette to see the context menu for this palette. Adobe has provided you with some cool choices for Styles. You should see a list of these Styles on the menu, one of which is titled Text Effects 2. Choose this one and click OK to replace your current set. Don't worry. You can get your current set back by choosing Reset Styles off the same menu when you're done.

5. Item 1 on Figure 16.31 shows that I have chosen the Double Turquoise Border style. Your text layer should still be active on the Layers palette so simply click this style to apply the style to your text. That's it.

Have fun experimenting with other styles. After applying a style, you will see a list of the layer effects that make up the style. This list appears under the layer (on the Layers palette). You can double-click any of the effects and tweak the settings in the Layer Effects dialog box to change the effect. This affects only the layer to which you have applied the style and doesn't change the original style.

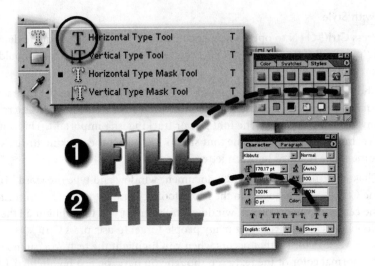

Figure 16.31   Applying a new fill or a specific style is easy.

Hmmmm! Now, how about the Type Mask tool? Like I said before, enough theory; let's jump into another quick exercise to give this tool a tryout.

Mask Type

1. Open the rose granite.tif image from the Examples/Chap16 folder on the Companion CD. Use Kibbutz as the font (or any heavyweight font) at 300 points, and set the tracking back to 0. Choose the Horizontal Type Mask tool (not the Vertical). Click in the document window and type the word **FILL** (all capital letters). Everything appears as a sort of Quick Mask.

2. Hmmm, the tracking is off, causing two of the letters to appear too close together. Highlight the letter after which you need to add space—in this case, highlight the letter I and change Tracking to **75** (see Figure 16.32).

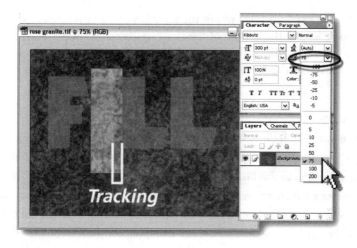

Figure 16.32   You can adjust tracking on an individual character basis.

3. You can press Ctrl(⌘)+Enter (Return) to change to Quick Mask mode, or as
    soon as you choose a tool other than the Type Mask tool, the Quick Mask text
    becomes a selection marquee. (You have no special layer here, so there's no way
    to save this except as a channel.) Choose the Brush tool from the toolbox and
    pick a weird brush (the Chalk 60-pixel brush is the brush chosen in Figure
    16.33). On the Options bar, set a low flow (7%), and choose a light color to
    make a rough, chalky design as you paint in the word-as-selection. Press
    Ctrl(⌘)+H to view the text without the "marching ants."

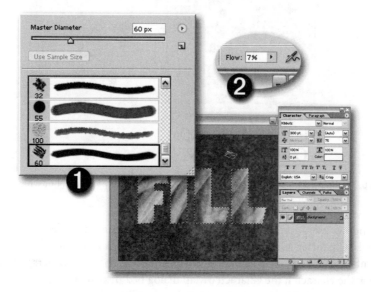

Figure 16.33   Paint across the selection to add finishing touches to a text selection created
    with a Type Mask tool.

4. Optional: Press Ctrl(⌘)+J to put the selection on its own layer. Click the Add a layer style icon at the bottom of the Layers palette and choose Bevel and Emboss. In the Layer Style dialog box, choose Pillow Emboss from the Style drop-down list at the top of the dialog box options. Click OK.

Picking Extended Characters

How do you enter something like a cents symbol? For Window users, a good place to start is the Character Map (found under Programs, Accessories, System Tools). I actually like having a shortcut to this little utility on my desktop because I frequently use it to see what kind of unusual characters might exist within a particular font. The Mac OS uses the Art Director's Toolkit. Here's a brief exercise to show how you can use these utilities to help type unusual characters that are not displayed on your keyboard.

Typing Extended Characters

1. Open the two cents.tif from the Examples/Chap16 folder on the Companion CD. As you can see in Figure 16.34, you need to type **2¢** at the bottom of this image.

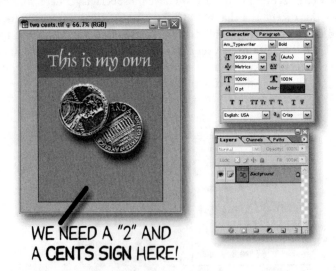

Figure 16.34   We need to add the text 2¢. The number 2 is easy enough, but what about the ¢ symbol?

2. Windows users go to the Start menu and choose Programs, Accessories, System Tools, Character Map. In the Character Map dialog box, locate and choose the symbol you need (most standard fonts will display these characters). When you click the character, the Character Map dialog box displays in the lower-right corner the extended keyboard command for "cents." Look at the bottom right of

Figure 16.35, and you can see that if you hold down the Alt key while you type
0162, the result will be a cents symbol. You also can double-click the symbol to
place it in the Characters to copy box. Then click the Copy button. Back in
Photoshop, you can paste the symbol into the document using the Text tool.

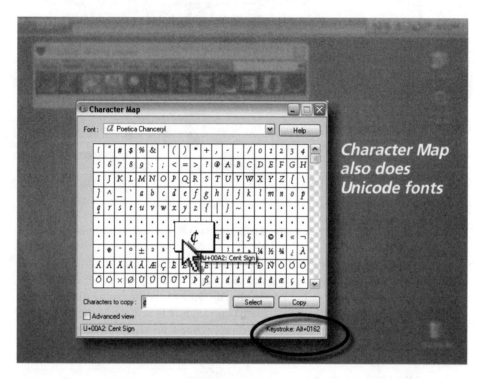

Figure 16.35   In Windows, use the Character Map to locate the character and use either the
Character to copy option or note the extended keyboard command for typing
the character.

3. The Mac OS X, shown in Figure 16.36, licenses the Art Director's toolkit, which
   does what the Character Map does and more.

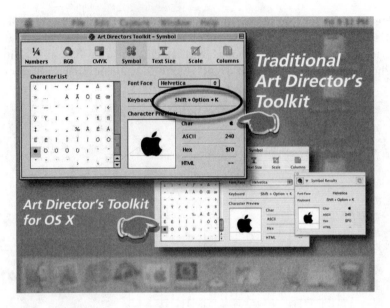

Figure 16.36   Use the Art Director's Toolkit on the Mac OS to access the extended characters.

4. Pick a foreground color for your text. Choose the Horizontal Text tool from the toolbox. Choose a font and font size and type **2**. Then choose either Ctrl(⌘)+V to paste the character or hold down the Alt(Opt) key while typing **0162** to type the cents symbol. If the symbol doesn't appear, it may be because the font you choose doesn't support that symbol. Simply choose another font that will. See Figure 16.37 for the finished image.

Figure 16.37   Finito. Makes cents to me!

Exploring the Character Palette

In Photoshop 7, Adobe has added some new icons to the Character palette that are worth explaining. Take a look at Figure 16.38 and follow along as we identify and explain these new icons, located near the bottom of the Character palette.

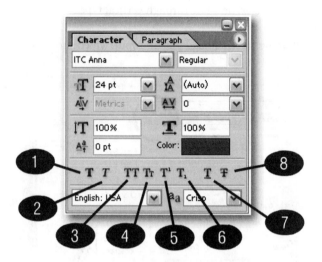

Figure 16.38   The new icons in Photoshop 7's Character palette are as follows:

1. **Faux Bold.** This is helpful if the font you have chosen does not provide a bold font style option. The Faux Bold icon can aid in producing a bold effect.

2. **Faux Italic.** Similar to the Faux Bold, if there is no italic option for the particular font you have chosen, this icon can simulate an italic style in its place.

3. **All Caps.** This icon is pretty much self-explanatory. When turned on, it will format the text in all uppercase characters, as though you had pressed your Caps Lock key.

4. **Small Caps.** This icon formats type in small caps but will not change characters that were originally typed in uppercase. If there is a small caps designed into the font, Photoshop uses the font's small caps; otherwise, Photoshop generates a faux small caps when you choose this option.

5. **Superscript.** This option reduces the text in size and shifts it above the type baseline of the normal text. If the font does not support superscript, Photoshop generates a faux superscript.

6. **Subscript.** This option reduces the text in size and shifts it below the type baseline of the normal text. If the font does not support subscript, Photoshop generates a faux subscript.

7. **Underline.** This option applies a line under horizontal type, or a line to the left or right of vertical type. Underline Left or Underline Right options are available only on the menu when vertical text is used.

8. **Strikethrough.** This option allows you to apply a horizontal line through horizontal type or a vertical line through vertical type.

Figure 16.39 shows the Character palette flyout, which shows you the names of the new icons.

Figure 16.39   The flyout menu options from the Character palette spell out the icon options for you. The Underline option gives you a choice of Underline Right or Underline Left when you have vertical type active. You have only one Underline choice when horizontal text is used.

Figure 16.40 shows you the result of each of these different icons.

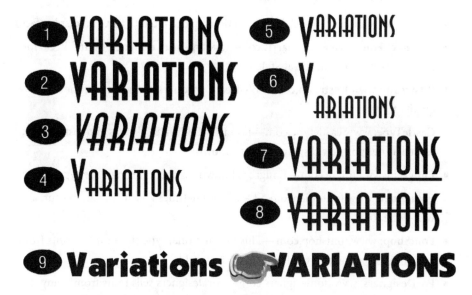

Figure 16.40   The new Character options in Photoshop 7 give you a number of variations for the way your text is displayed.

Summary—Have Fun with Type!

When you start to notice and work with type, it's kind of like being a kid again. You perceive things you've seen for years but never really *noticed*. It opens a whole new world to explore. You'll be surprised by how much type you see all around you.

You can be a type-spotter (someone who finds it challenging to figure out the typefaces you see) as well as a typesetter (someone who actually gets down and dirty, rolling around in all those letters). You may even get to the point where, like me, you look at a restaurant menu and try figure out what font it's in before you figure out what you're going to order.

So, if at all possible, have fun. You'll be more creative if you're not bored, and your readers will be more attentive if they remain amused and awake.

Experiment. Play. Type can surprise you—faces you thought you'd never use can "look just right" for certain things. Sometimes the unexpected seems fresh. Sometimes it's just unexpected and looks inappropriate—but you'll never know unless you try.

Where to Buy Fonts on the Web

Literally thousands of web sites sell fonts. Here are the sites I find most useful:

- **Adobe**: www.adobe.com—A large selection of high-quality text and display faces.
- **Architect Fonts**: www.will-harris.com—Six typefaces designed by architects for anyone wanting architectural-style type.
- **Bitstream**: www.bitstream.com—Bitstream produces a large line of the highest-quality fonts.
- **CastleType**: www.castletype.com—Jason Castle revives classics and lost classics, as well as designs new display faces of his own.
- **Emigre**: www.emigre.com—Emigre is known for their cutting-edge type designs.
- **FontDiner**: www.fontdiner.com—Quirky, sometimes kitsch, and always fun and well-done fonts.
- **FontShop**: www.fontshop.com—This international type store carries fonts from large foundries and individuals around the world.
- **ForDesigners**: www.fordesigners.com—ForDesigners sells fonts from many foundries and commissions new faces that are exclusive to them.
- **GarageFonts**: www.garagefonts.com—Many designers contribute to this collective of cutting-edge type designs.
- **Intecsas**: www.will-harris.com—David Rakowski is a Pulitzer-prize nominated composer who also loves to revives classic display faces.
- **ITC**: www.letterspace.com—Garret Boge designs fonts ranging from the classics to fresh new faces.
- **MVB Design**: www.mvbdesign.com—Mark Van Bronkhorst designs beautiful display and text faces that run the gamut from classical to striking new designs.
- **MyFonts**: www.myfonts.com—A collective of many different foundries and designers, MyFonts offers unique online services, such as "What the Font," a system that can analyze font samples and tell you their typefaces.
- **P22**: www.p22.com—A wonderful selection of period display faces.
- **PrecisionType**: www.precisiontype.com—With one of the largest collections of typefaces anywhere, PrecisionType is a great place to find hard-to-find fonts.

- **Scriptorium**: www.fontcraft.com—The place to find historically inspired script faces.

- **Sutcliff Electric Typographer**: www.will-harris.com—A large assortment of warm, hand-drawn display faces with unique personalities.

- **TypeQuarry**: www.typequarry.com—Distinctive faces by talented independent type designers.

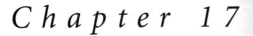

Chapter 17

Special Effects with Type

Now that Daniel Will-Harris has taught

you about the proper use of text, Bouton is

going to muck it up and show you how to

create special effects—and a lot of them are

un-kosher. Text in Photoshop is either a bunch of pixels or a vector, and both media can be modified just as you would modify a photograph.

If there's a special something you've been yearning to do with text in Photoshop, you have at least a one-in-four chance that I cover it in this chapter (because, as you will see, there are four parts).

Pleasing Clients with Multiple Versions of Text Handling

My first inclination was not to write this part, because if you are like me, you have the secret conviction that a client is owed *one* revision of a concept, and that's it! But my heart is as soft as my head, and the following steps will show you exactly how flexible text and styles can be—which is a real career-saver and personal-worth enhancer, in my book.

Spare Me Lanes—A Lesson in Bowling and Client Coddling

The fictional bowling alley Spare Me! Lanes needs a new logo. Let's pretend that you slaved over the graphic, which is (do you need to guess?) a bowling ball striking pins. For the text, use the Ol'54-tt font in the Examples/Chap17 folder on the Companion CD. You'd best install this font in your system font folder now, or there won't be much of a show here. (Thanks to J.S. Smith for allowing us to offer free use of the font and for allowing me to make the necessary conversion for the Mac platform.)

Okay, if you've got the font installed now, let's continue. Suppose that the client basically likes the logo, but wants the S in "Spare me!" to be bigger and narrower.

Note

More Fonts   As long as you are installing the font Ol'54-tt, you might as well install Frankfurter Plain and Kibbutz because these fonts will come into play later in the chapter. I wanted to provide you with really bold fonts because they are more easily turned into graphics than a font like Courier New.

And so begins our special-effects-with-type chapter...

Creating Variations on a Theme that Was Perfect in the First Place

1. Open the Spare Me Lanes.psd file from the Examples/Chap17 folder on the Companion CD. Open the Layers palette (press F7 to summon it). You'll notice that on the Layers palette the S in "Spare Me" is on a different layer than the rest of the text. This was done for this reason: the lout that owns the place is probably going to want to mess with the S, and unfortunately, you cannot modify one character in a sentence without some constraints. This means that you can turn this "S" into a left-handed screwdriver—if he likes—without totally compromising the text already present.

Also notice that in Figure 17.1, the Layer Effects applied to the top text layers have their little list extended on the Layers palette. This shows you that the effects have been applied equally to both S and "pare me." You can close these drop-downs if they annoy you.

All characters have same style, but "S" is on separate text layer.

Figure 17.1   I don't know; the logo looks pretty spiffy to me. But the client doesn't share my excellent taste in graphics.

2. The client says, "I want the S to be taller than the bowling ball and almost equal the height of them cylindrical things...*um*, oh yeah, the pins. And squoosh the S a little. Perfect." Click the S layer title on the Layers palette, and then press Ctrl(⌘)+T to put the S into Free Transform mode. Drag up on the center top box handle, and then drag left on the center left box handle. Stop when the S looks like the one in Figure 17.2, and then press Enter (Return) to confirm changes.

Figure 17.2   Text can be stretched using (some of) the Free Transform tools.

3. Indulge your creative instincts and, with the Move tool, move this misshapen S beside the rest of the text (see Figure 17.3).

Figure 17.3   After you put the stretched S beside the pins, you know something's not right…

Note

Character Palette Can Restore a Font   Did you know that even when you distort text, the Options bar and the Character palette still keep track of the size and width of a character? In practice, then, you can undo a really messed up font completely by entering values in number fields—no Free Transform box required.

4. You turn to the client, and he says, "Em, nahhhh. What do you think? Can we change it back?" (This guy makes Danny DeVito's typical characters look sophisticated and sensitive!) Sure, you can undo the stretched letter; press Alt(Opt)+Ctrl(⌘)+Z (which is the History Backwards shortcut) until you're back at your original (fantastic) design.

5. Next? "Can you somehow make the S bolder?" Yeah, I'll go get a bicycle pump right now. Seriously, this means you have to convert a copy of the S to an uneditable outline. And you know what the very first thing you need to do is? Save the style you created for the logo to the Styles palette! How else are you going to apply the current style to a new character/outline? Do this: on the Layers palette, double-click the encircled "f" on the S layer. This brings up the Layer Style dialog box. Click the New Style button, and name this style **Bowling Alley**, as shown in Figure 17.4. Click OK, and click OK again to get out of the Layer Style menu, and you've got a new style at the end of the current Style palette if you press F6.

We saved this style as Bowling Alley to show you how you can save style settings that you may want to reuse for future projects. You also can find the Bowling Alley style by loading the Text Effects 2 styles and using the Double Turquoise Border style from that palette.

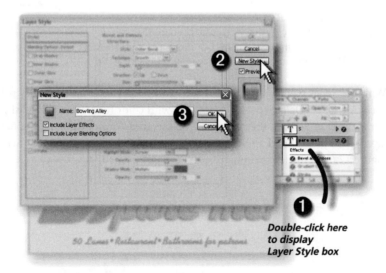

Double-click here
to display
Layer Style box

Figure 17.4   Save the style of the current lettering when some dimwit wants to see the font in a weight you don't have—which means—you have to create it yourself.

6. Alt(Opt)+click the Create a new layer icon at the bottom of the Layers palette to create a new layer on top of the S design. When the New Layer dialog box pops up, name the new layer **Fat "s"** and click OK. Ctrl(⌘)+click on the thumbnail of the S on the Layers palette. This loads the S as a marquee selection. Now choose Select, Modify, Expand, and type **12** in the Expand field and click OK (see Figure 17.5).

Figure 17.5   Clients like "variations" the way that ants like a picnic. Be prepared with the legendary Alt(Opt)+Ctrl(⌘)+Z move. (And for Heaven's sake, make sure that Undo states in General Preferences is set to at least 20!)

7. With the Styles palette open, click the Bowling Alley style on the Styles palette. Press Alt(Opt)+Delete (Backspace) to fill with color (any color will work). Press Ctrl(⌘)+D to deselect the marquee. You see, there was nothing on the new layer—you filled it and applied the style in one fell swoop. Clever, eh? See Figure 17.6 for the latest monstrosity the client wanted.

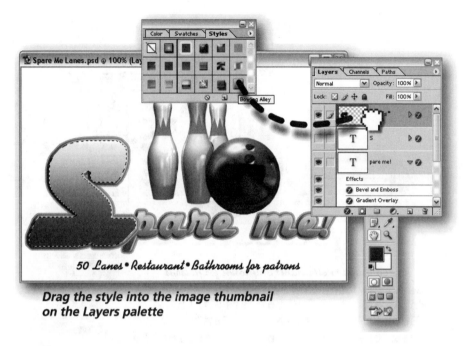

50 Lanes • Restaurant • Bathrooms for patrons

Drag the style into the image thumbnail on the Layers palette

Figure 17.6   Create an expanded selection, and then fill it with "style"!

8. Click the eye icon next to the Fat "s" layer to hide it. Uh-oh. The client has seen the Styles palette onscreen and naturally wants you to play with it. "Mighty narrow selection there—you got any other palettes?" Yes, you do. Click the flyout button on the Styles palette, and then choose Text Effects. And then tell the client, "Mr. Schnorer, I've researched Photoshop's palettes, and the style we have right now is the best."

   "Nah," he says. "Let's see what the Text Effects palette has. We *are* using text, right?" What do you do? You load the Text Effects to the Styles palette.

9. "Oooh, oooh. That one says "Chrome–Polished"—I read the tool tips. Try that one," the clients says in an unbridled ecstatic moment. You can drag the chrome style from the palette right into the thumbnail window to apply it (did you know that?). Try this technique first for S and then for "pare me" (see Figure 17.7). The design still doesn't quite cut it, does it?

Figure 17.7   There are styles that improve a typeface, and there are styles that just lay there like a lox.

10. The client agrees that the original design was the best, and to make your trip and your client/server relationship (!) worthwhile, he offers you a lane in the afternoons (off-peak hours, of course), and a free sandwich (except the deli style specials) from the chalkboard in the restaurant section of Spare Me! Lanes. You drag the Fat "s" layer to the trash icon on the Layers palette, save the client a flattened copy of the work (File, Save As, and then choose TIF and uncheck the Layers checkbox so that he can't have someone else mess with your design), and go get your sandwich. On the ride home, you swear to take up golf.

I know the preceding was unrealistic (for *some* of us, anyway), so next I'm going to toss you a really easy client with modest typographic needs. Meet Paul and Paul's Pools, on Route 57 next to the Dunkin' Donuts. In fact, some people park at Dunkin' and walk over, just to see Paul.

Working with the Create Warped Text Tool

Finally, Adobe got hip to what CorelDRAW has offered since 1989—the capability to warp text—to *envelope* it. Unfortunately, you have to work in a proxy box and cannot distort text directly with a tool or anything, but hey, I'm happy that we now have this feature (and you should be, too); it saves us the hassle of running out to XARA or DRAW to get the effect.

Check out Figure 17.8. Paul's got a bee-yoo-ti-ful image of a beach ball; it's very appealing. Paul wants his company name to arc around the top of the beach ball.

Figure 17.8   Paul's beautiful sign needs an equally neat logo.

Fair enough. Ready to outdo yourself?

Life's a Beach

1. Open the Paul's pools.tif image from the Examples/Chap17 folder on the Companion CD. Now, you have Frankfurter Plain installed as a font—right? Good. You'll be using it.

2. Choose the Type tool, and then on either the Character palette (I prefer this) or the Options bar, click the color swatch and in the color picker, choose a nice light purple (R:126, G:115, B:239). Click OK. On the Character palette, choose Frankfurter Plain at about 50 points (I guessed this one, but sizing text is trial and error—and easy, because you've got the Free Transform tool workin' for you these days). Click at the top of the document image and type in all caps (Frankfurter Plain has only caps; I'd like to see you do lowercase!) **PAUL'S POOLS,** as shown in Figure 17.9.

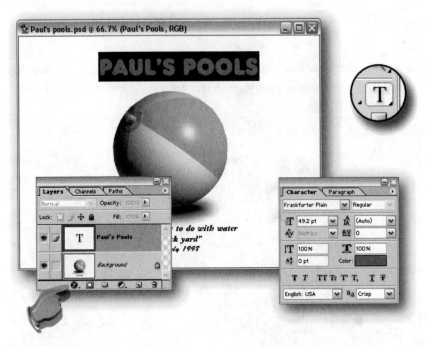

Figure 17.9 Type the name of the company. Embellishing the name will come next.

3. To fancy-shmancy up the type, at the bottom of the Layers palette, click the Add a layer style icon, and choose Stroke. The Layer Style box pops up. Add 5 pixels of yellow (R:255, G:246, B:109) outside the purple text (click the Color field to change the color). Click OK to exit the color picker. While you're still in the Layer Style dialog box (as shown in Figure 17.10), why not add a soft drop shadow? Click the Drop Shadow title on the Styles list at the far left of this box. Lower Opacity to 65%, 100° for Angle, 20 (px) for Distance, 15% Spread, and 20 (px) for Size. Click OK to close the box, and apply your special text effect.

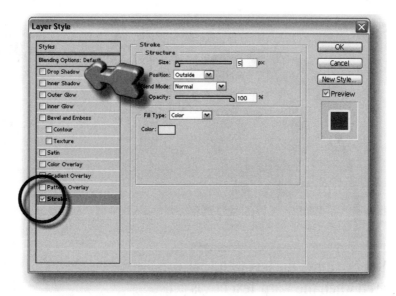

Figure 17.10   Add some perk to the lettering before you arc it.

4. Paul's wife walks by and ooohs and aahs at your craftsmanship. She says, "Paul can't get squat out of that computer. We bought it two years ago, and he's still trying to make sense out of Excel 95. Makes nice pie charts, though." Now, you kick into full gear (mostly because you were flattered). Click the Create warped text icon on the Options bar.

The warped text feature will apply to all the text on the active type layer. Figure 17.11 shows highlighted text for emphasis, but it is not necessary to highlight the text to apply a warped text feature.

5. In the Warp Text dialog box, click the Style drop-down list and choose Arc. Take a look at Figure 17.11 and use the same settings you see there. By the way, you *can* step out of the dialog box, and reposition the text in the image window. I *love* modeless dialog boxes!

Note

Modeless Operations   A modeless dialog box lets you mess around on the screen and will not inhibit user activity. A modeful dialog box insists that you click OK or Cancel to close the box before you make any changes in the original document window. The nerve!

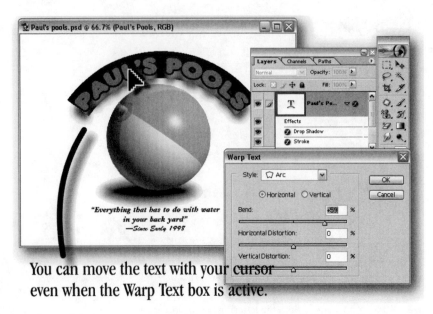

Figure 17.11   You do not want to curve the text totally around the beach ball. Let it suggest a curve that is *simpatico* with the curve of the ball.

6. Paul moseys by after selling a skimmer to a customer, and both Paul and his wife love the logo, as shown in Figure 17.12.

Figure 17.12   Text that conforms to the "flow" of a design is easier on the eyes overall and suggests that the designer really handles expert equipment expertly and knows his or her design stuff.

7. Paul writes you a check for a million dollars and asks whether that's enough (hey, this is a tutorial file, not a newspaper). You ask him to do one last thing. "Paul, can you have someone inflate all 200 of your beach balls and put them in a rusting red VW in the parking lot at Spare Me! Lanes? The owner says he's fond of the ocean…"

Building the Typical (But Charming) Travel Postcard

My friend Ron Pfister lent me the Hawaii image used in this upcoming tutorial because he and his wife go to Hawaii every year on their anniversary and take pictures. That's about the time I'm removing rocks from our backyard for Barbara's garden. Okay, I hear no sympathy, so I'll continue…

The sunset, in glorious shades of maroon and orange, with the sea lapping at the shore and a palm tree in silhouette is familiar to almost everyone who's ever seen a postcard. But how do they get the text on there, and how do they do that thingy where a sunset pokes through the letters of the word *Hawaii*? Well, at least in this book, you follow these steps!

Creating a Tropical Postcard

1. Open the Hawaii.tif image from the Examples/Chap17 folder on the Companion CD. It's okay to *ooh* and *aah* a few times. Also notice that in Figure 17.13, I've got the Character palette set to Frutiger Ultra. Do you need to own this font? No, not really. You simply need something blocky and heavy, and Futura Knockout, Olive Antique Heavy, and yes, Kibbutz (which you installed earlier) will all fit the bill.

Figure 17.13 You're going to fit a huge "Hawaii" at the bottom of the image. So huge, in fact, that you'll be able to put a scene inside the lettering.

2. Type **HAWAII** at about 130 points in the image. Um, it would help to define a light color first, on the Character palette or the Options bar. Click the Color tab and choose a yellow color (R:255, G:210, B:0) and click OK to exit the color picker. If you have substituted a different font, you may find it necessary to highlight the text and adjust the point size amount. The goal is to keep the text as large as possible but still maintain a comfortable fit within the image window.

3. Click the Warp Text button and then choose Arc as the Style, but look at Figure 17.14. The Warp Text controls are interactive (you see onscreen what you're defining as values). I've warped the arc so that the left side is larger than the right. Interesting, huh? You do this, too.

Figure 17.14   Warp the text both in an arc direction, but also in 3D. Make the left closer to us than the right side.

4. Click the Add a layer style icon at the bottom of the Layers palette and choose Inner Shadow, accept the defaults, and click OK. Now, open aloha.png from the Examples/Chap17 folder on the Companion CD. With the Move tool active, drag the contents of the aloha image into the Hawaii.tif window. Center the word above HAWAII (see Figure 17.15).

Inner Shadow

Figure 17.15   Drag the "Aloha" text into the Hawaii window and position it using the Move tool.

5. Save the piece to your hard disk as Hawaii.psd, in Photoshop's native file format so that the layers can be preserved.

Note

Layered TIFFs   Photoshop TIFFs have the capability to save layers, but I do not endorse or encourage it unless you are a video-type professional and need layered TIFFs. For the rest of us, you simply annoy your client when you send them a layered TIFF because you forgot to flatten it, and the client can't open the file with Windows, the Mac OS, or a pair of pliers.

Here's where some weird, wild, and fun stuff begins.

6. Open Sunrise.tif from the Examples/Chap17 folder on the Companion CD. It's a synthetic image, by the way (see Figure 17.16).

Figure 17.16   You will add the sunrise picture to the inside of the HAWAII text.

7. Using the Move tool, drag the sunrise image into the Hawaii.psd image, and then drag its title down on the Layers palette's list until it is directly above the HAWAII text. Now you're going to make a clipping group.

8. Hold Alt(Opt) and then place your cursor right between the text layer and the sunrise layer. Your icon turns into two circles. Click at the line between the two layer titles, and *surprise*—the sunrise picture goes inside the base clipping group, which is the lettering. Take a look at Figure 17.17, and c'mon—you *gotta* admit that this is cool.

Want to know a quick keyboard shortcut for creating the clipping group? Press Ctrl(⌘)+G. To undo the grouping, simply press Ctrl(⌘)+Shift+G. You might want to practice these two keyboard shortcuts to toggle the grouping on and off and see for yourself. It's also worth mentioning that with the sunrise layer (Layer 2) and the Move tool active, you can move the sunrise image around to position it anyway you want through the letters in this grouping. For example, in Figure 17.17 the sun is positioned between the first two letters of the word HAWAII.

Base layer   clipped image

Figure 17.17   A clipping group enables everything above the Base layer to show though.

9. Inkjet a copy of this card to friends, write something smart-alecky on it, and then don't answer the telephone for a week when your friends discover that the cancellation mark says Wisconsin.

Ready for the *piece de resistance* (that's French, I think) for the type effects chapter? I'm going to teach you something you thought could only be done in Quark or PageMaker—you will wrap text around an object in a picture.

No, I'm not kidding.

Wrapping Text

The whole secret to text wrapping in Photoshop is this:

1. Type periods in front of a line to push it flush with an already established border.

2. Hide the periods.

Okay, it's not as simple as it sounds. That's why I have a job.

In the upcoming steps, you copy a short paragraph from a text editor, drop it into an image window, set the type specs, and then wrap the text around a (modeled) picture of a pear. I can tell that you're excited already…

Wrapping Text in Photoshop

1. Open the pear.psd image from the Examples/Chap17 folder of the Companion CD. The Background is on a layer to facilitate copying parts of the background later in this tutorial.

2. Open Pearing off.png from the same folder, and then with the Move tool, drag its visual contents into the pear.psd document window. Place the text neatly to the left, as shown in Figure 17.18. Close the Pearing off.png file.

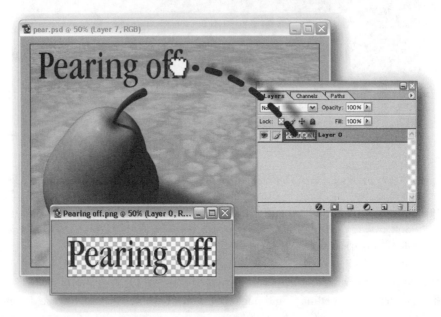

Figure 17.18   Use the Move tool to drag the text layer into the pear.psd file and position it in the upper-left corner of the document.

Okay, here comes a big tip that applies to your text endeavors in Photoshop:

Tip

Using Microsoft Word   Buy (or have it bought for you) Microsoft Word. In your typesetting experience with Photoshop, you will find no greater helper. Why? Because people put hard breaks (in other words, they press Enter (Return)) in copy, and if this body copy is too wide or two narrow, you can spend a seeming eternity stripping breaks out of text. Word, on the other hand, can put in soft or hard breaks and if you change the column width, the paragraph breaks go away and re-establish themselves with no user intervention (which means less work for you).

You can then copy your text to the clipboard, make an insertion point with Photoshop's Type tool cursor and press Ctrl(⌘)+V and *the breaks are preserved*. This is how I did the Pear.txt copy you'll be using.

Teamed with a good word-processing program, you'll be happy to find that Photoshop all of a sudden becomes a fairly decent PDF maker and mini-DTP program.

3. Open the pear.txt file from the Examples/Chap17 folder on Companion CD into a text editor (see Figure 17.19). Select all the text, and then press Ctrl(⌘)+C to copy the text to the clipboard.

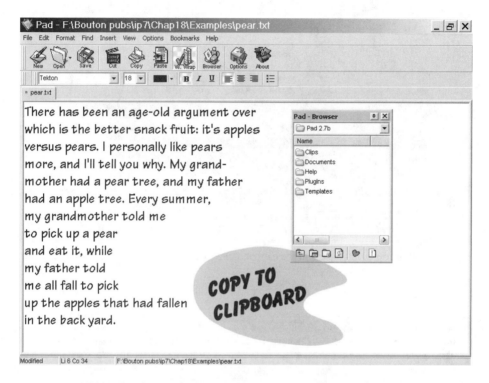

Figure 17.19   Hey, this is a true story in the Pear.txt file, and it probably accounts for why I became a messed-up adult and took up computing.

4. In Photoshop, press Ctrl(⌘)+R to expose the rulers, and then drag a guide out of the right margin and place this vertical guide about one-half of a screen inch from the right border. Then press Ctrl(⌘)+R again because you do not need to see the rulers.

5. Press D for the default colors (black should now be the foreground color). Choose (what else?) the Type tool and then on the Character palette, set the text to Times New Roman and to 8 point. I know this seems small, but you can make it larger later, and we have a lot of type on the clipboard. The picture is a decent size, too, when measured in typographic points. On the Options bar, set justification to Left align text. (Here you want a left word wrap, so you use left justification; for right wrapping, it's vice versa. Trust me on this one.)

6. Click an insertion point to the right of the stem of the pear, and then press Ctrl(⌘)+V. Wow, instant text (see Figure 17.20)!

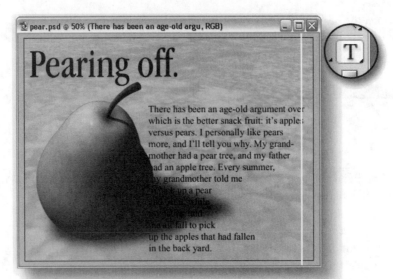

PASTE TEXT WHEN TYPE TOOL IS CHOSEN

Figure 17.20   You can copy text to the clipboard, and when you insert it into Photoshop, the line breaks are preserved.

TIP

Correct "Straight Quotes"   If you use a text editor to bring in spell-corrected type (hey, Photoshop has a good spell-checker, but why check spelling in Photoshop when word processors and text editors can do it more quickly?), chances are that you will lose what's known as *Typesetter's quotes* (also called *curly* or *smart* quotes. No problem. Go into the placed paragraph text with the Type tool, highlight the straight quote, and then use the keyboard commands to replace the quote marks with curly quotation marks.

7. Now, the text is an unformatted mess as far as our text wrapping dreams go, so the first thing you do is choose the Move tool and drag the text toward the pear until parts of some long words and all of short words encroach on the pear and shadow.

8. Click the Create a new layer icon at the bottom of the Layers palette and choose a bright color. Press B to switch to the Brush tool and choose a 19-pixel hard-edged brush. Drag a gutter around the right of the pear, as shown in Figure 17.21. This paint line is used as a temporary guide for where your text will start on the left side.

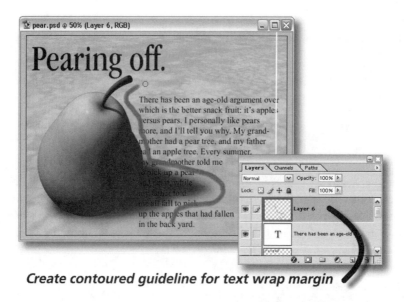

Create contoured guideline for text wrap margin

Figure 17.21   You can't have the text on the left kissing the edge of the fruit. You just *can't*. Create a guideline for where the text will begin, and make the guide a consistent distance from the pear.

9. With the Type tool, click at the beginning of each line and type periods until that line touches the guide at the right (see Figure 17.22). You see where this is leading?

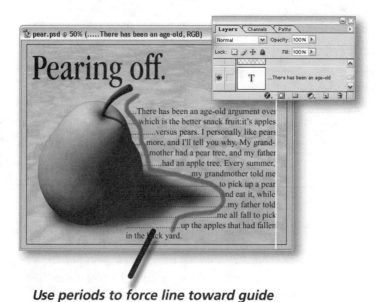

Use periods to force line toward guide

Figure 17.22   Push the text so it appears to align right, using periods at the beginning of each line.

> **Tip**
>
> **Shifting Words to Adjust Line Length**   By the way, if there is too much space on a line between the pear and the beginning of the text, put your cursor in front of the first word on the next line, and press Delete (Backspace) to bring the second line up to the first line, and then put a space between the last word of the top line and the first word of the bottom line. Then position the cursor where you believe the line should end, and press Enter (Return) to move the unwanted, remaining text on the first line down to the next line. Believe me, it is *much* easier to do than it is to describe!

   10. When you are satisfied with the text, press Ctrl(⌘)+Enter (Return) to commit the changes to the text. You also can click the eye icon to the left of the "word wrap" layer to turn off the visibility of the painted brush line you made earlier. On the Layers palette, Ctrl(⌘)+click the Text layer icon (the cute T in a box to the left of the Layer title) to load the text of that layer as a selection marquee (see Figure 17.23).

Figure 17.23   Load the text as a selection.

   11. Click the Channels tab to view the Channels palette. Alt(Opt)+click the Save selection as channel icon at the bottom Channels palette and name the new channel **dots**, as shown in Figure 17.24. It's always a good practice to name layers and channels in a multi-channel and/or multi-layer document. Press Ctrl(⌘)+D to deselect.

12. Switch to the Eraser tool in Block mode from the Options bar. Erase the text; be very careful that you do not erase the periods (see Figure 17.24).

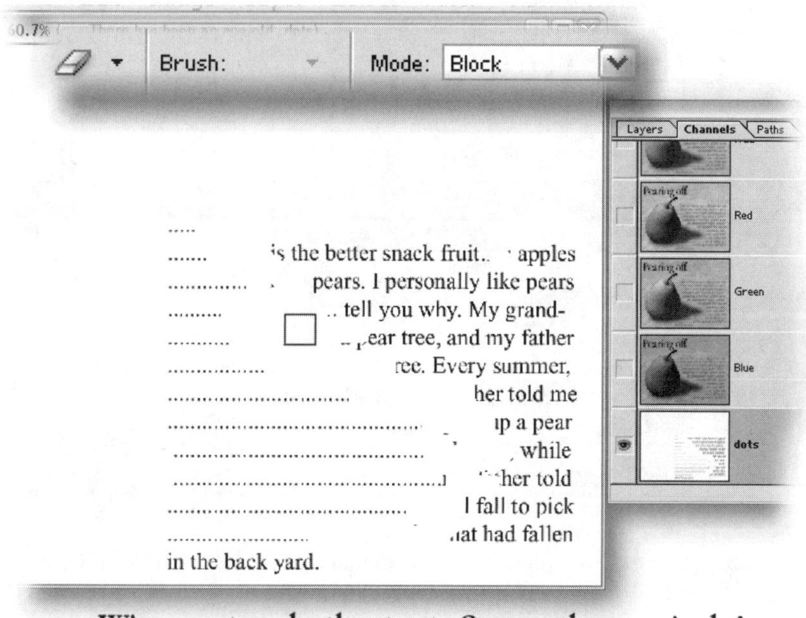

Wipe out only the text. Spare the periods!

Figure 17.24   We only need the dots. Erase all the text and for Heaven's sake *be careful!*

13. When the periods are all that remain, Ctrl(⌘)+click the dots title to load them as a selection, and then on the Layers palette, click the Background layer to make it the active layer.

14. Choose Select, Modify, Expand. Type **3** in the number field and click OK. Do you know why the periods needed to have their selection expanded? The goal is to use this background selection to *cover* the periods on the Type layer by placing a new layer on top of the text (see Figure 17.25).

Figure 17.25   This new layer will contain Background layer image content and is going to get rid of the unwanted periods on the text layer. Period.

15. Press Ctrl(⌘)+J to copy the selection from the Background layer to a new layer.

16. Drag the Text layer below this new layer (between the new layer and the Background layer). The goal is to have the new background dots layer above the text, but below the pear and shadow. Check out Figure 17.26.

Is that a neat trick, or what? Can I take a bow now?

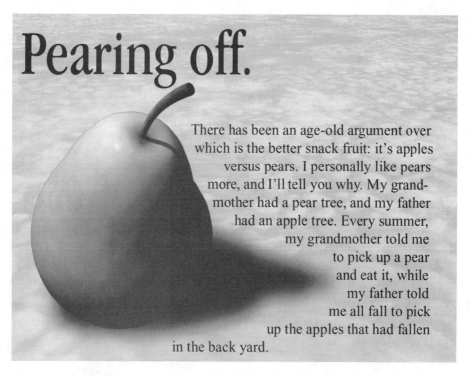

Pearing off.

There has been an age-old argument over which is the better snack fruit: it's apples versus pears. I personally like pears more, and I'll tell you why. My grandmother had a pear tree, and my father had an apple tree. Every summer, my grandmother told me to pick up a pear and eat it, while my father told me all fall to pick up the apples that had fallen in the back yard.

Figure 17.26   Paragraph wrapping is easier than gift wrapping. Or at least it takes fewer steps to get it right!

You're the master. Now you know not only how to handle type, but to distort it, customize it, and—excuse me for a moment. A VW just pulled up on our driveway, crammed with beach balls…

Summary

Thinking of text in Photoshop as simply another type of shape helps to expand your type-bending experiences. True, the shapes contain a message, but the message isn't always of primary importance. Take, for example, the word *lobster*. Now, would the word better convey a lobster if the type were red and its shape looked like a lobster? You will learn as you experiment with type that there is a real synergy between text and graphics. I see no reason why one can't masquerade as another—and vice versa.

I've been doing this stuff for years!

On deck, right around the corner, is Scott Hamlin's ode to creating mind-blowing web effects, using text, graphics, animation, and some duct tape I loaned him last month. Don't miss out—find out what "cutting edge" *really* means!

Part VII

Photoshop
for the Web

Chapter 18

Creating Interface Elements

If users visit your web site and can't find their way around, chances are, they are not going to come back. How can you make sure your web visitors have a pleasant experience, one that they want to repeat?

You make sure that you've designed the interface elements in such a way that visitors find your site easy to use, interesting, and inviting. You may not have thought of Photoshop in relation to web work before, but in this chapter you'll learn to create interface elements that your site visitors will appreciate.

Interface Design 101

What are *interface elements*? Well, if you've searched the Internet, you've seen them on every web page; they are any of the graphical elements—buttons, links, tabs, and other items—that allow you to maneuver on individual pages and move from web page to web page. In addition to providing a navigation method for users, interface elements also add style to the page—hopefully a style that gives the visitor an instant positive feeling and not one that scares the user away.

Designing interface elements for the web is like designing for any industry. You need to create visual appeal; but you also need to balance that with purpose and function. As you've seen over and over again in this book (it has probably become a mantra by now), you need to have your *concept* firmly in mind before you begin designing anything.

Many people consider the navigation bar to be the most important interface element on the web because it serves as the map for your web site. Navigational elements usually include a link to your site's home page (so if your users get lost, they can find their way back home—come along, Toto…), a Contact page (so they know how to reach you to complain about the design), and content pages with information specific to your site goals.

When you begin to think about designing interface elements for the web, there's one major question you should ask yourself as you begin your design endeavor. Who is the target audience? If you're designing for children, making your interface colorful and simple is a good idea. Of course, if you are designing for the teenage crowd, a video game interface might work better. If the target audience is a professional crowd, then a simple, efficient, and to-the-point design should be your goal. Those are just a few suggestions, but you get the idea.

Another suggestion: Be observant and try to analyze what it is that works in the designs that *you* find appealing. Maybe you like designs that have a tab system at the top of a web page—or maybe you like buttons down the side. Whatever your preferences, Photoshop can help you to unleash that creativity in web design, just as it can in any other aspect of designing.

Creating interface elements in Photoshop boils down to form, structure, depth, color, and texture. Adding depth and color in Photoshop is very easy. Creating form, shape, or structure is not necessarily difficult, but it may require more effort. Photoshop gives you all the tools to create and modify your ideas. And for some reason, I have the urge to quote the famous *Field of Dreams* line: "Build it and they will come!" Let's get started, okay?

Creating an Interface from Scratch

Aside from developing a design concept for an interface, the real challenge to creating an interface from scratch in Photoshop is coming up with the shapes. Although Photoshop has all the tools to create basic shapes—such as the rectangle, rounded rectangle, ellipse, and various polygonal shapes—there still may come a time when you want a particular shape you don't have ready-made. After all, you can't expect Photoshop to have a separate tool for an infinite number of possible shapes. But what Photoshop may lack in tools for creating unusual shapes, it makes up for by giving you the flexibility to use Boolean operations, filters, and other tools to create the shapes you want. Ready to have some fun?

Getting Started: Setting the Guides

I. Press Ctrl(⌘)+N to open a New Document. Set the Width to **550** (pixels) and the Height to **410** (pixels). Make the Resolution **72** pixels/inch and set the Mode to RGB Color. Leave White selected in the Contents section and click OK (see Figure 18.1).

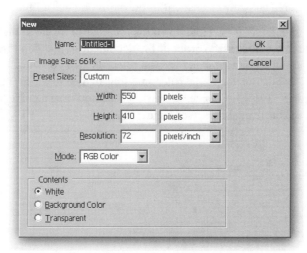

Figure 18.1 Open a new document 550 pixels wide by 410 pixels high.

2. Press Ctrl(⌘)+R to view the rulers. If the units aren't already set to pixels, double-click inside one of the rulers. This displays the Units & Rulers Preferences dialog box. In the Units section, change the Rulers setting to pixels. Click OK. You'll be setting up a lot of guides for this chapter, and you will need to set them at exact pixel increments (using the rulers).

An alternative method for quickly switching your default units of measurement is to view the Info palette. Click the plus sign at the lower-left corner of the palette to display a unit measurement drop-down menu, and choose which units of measurement you prefer.

Note

Pixel Preference   Whenever you are planning a design for use on the web, it is a good idea to choose pixels as the unit of measurement. Why? Because web pages are viewed on monitors and monitors are based on pixels. If you've ever set the resolution for your monitor, you know that you are given setting choices based on pixel measurements. Typically the setting choices are 640×480 pixels, 800×600 pixels, 1024×768 pixels, and so on.

Many people use the 800×600 setting for their monitors because this often is the default display setting that comes with the system, and many people leave their monitors set to the factory defaults.

You can use this information to your advantage when designing. If you design for the lowest common denominator (or the average resolution setting), you might want to set the width of the web page to 600 pixels or less (preferably less to allow for the space needed for the scrollbars).

If you have made it this far into the book, you probably know that the Ctrl(⌘)+ plus or minus keys allow you to zoom in or out of your document quickly. Remember these shortcuts if they aren't already permanent impressions on your mind.

3. Zoom in to at least 700%. Hold down the spacebar to toggle to the Hand tool, and move to the upper-left corner of the document so that you can view the number 5 on the horizontal and vertical rulers. Press V to switch to the Move tool. Click inside the horizontal ruler and drag a guide to the 5-pixel mark on the vertical ruler. Then click inside the vertical ruler and drag a guide to the 5-pixel mark on the horizontal ruler (see Figure 18.2).

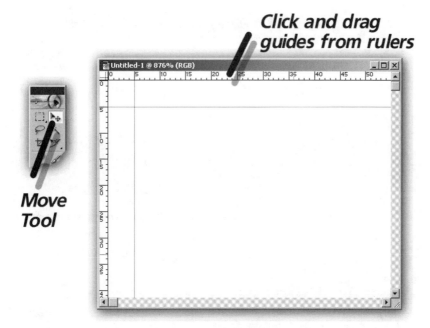

Figure 18.2 Place a horizontal and a vertical guide.

4. Hold down the spacebar to toggle back to the Hand tool (or use the scroll bars on your document window) and move your view of the document to the lower-right corner of your document. The goal is to be able to view the 405 mark on the vertical ruler and 545 mark on the horizontal ruler. Click and drag a horizontal guide (from the horizontal ruler) and place it at the 405-pixel mark on the vertical ruler. Similarly, click and drag a vertical guide (from the vertical ruler) and place it at the 545-pixel mark on the horizontal ruler.

5. Zoom out to 100%. Go to the View menu and choose New Guide. In the New Guide dialog box, set the Orientation to Vertical and enter **140** pixels for the Position. Click OK. Choose View, New Guide again. Set the Orientation to Horizontal and enter **80** pixels for the Position (see Figure 18.3). Go to the View menu and make sure there is a check mark next to the Snap option (if the Snap option is not checked, select it).

   If you know exactly where you want a guide to be, the New Guide feature is the quickest way to position it. Your guides won't be of much use, however, if the Snap option isn't turned on.

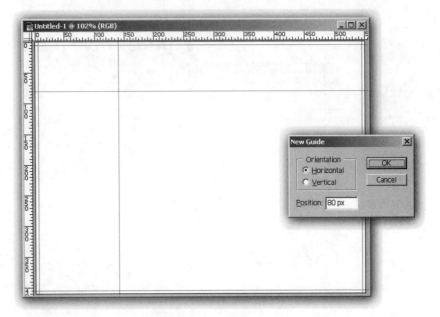

Figure 18.3   Use the New Guide feature to place guides.

6. Press Ctrl(⌘)+Shift+S and save this file as MyIFace.psd in the native Photoshop format. Keep the file open for the next exercise.

Now that the guides are set in place, you can start creating some basic shapes for your interface.

Creating the Vertical Interface Components

First you'll work on the vertical components of the interface, which will be the foundation for such elements as the navigation buttons and logo screen. Let's start by building the basic shapes.

Creating the Button Base

1. Press D for the default colors (black should now be the foreground color). Alt(Opt)+click the Create a new layer icon at the bottom of the Layers palette and name the new layer **Button Base**. Click OK.

2. Choose the Rounded Rectangle tool from the toolbox (or press Shift+U until the Rounded Rectangle tool is the active tool). On the Options bar, choose the Fill pixels icon and change the Radius to **20** pixels. Draw a rounded rectangle extending between the vertical guides at 5 and 140 pixels and down to the horizontal guides at 5 and 405 pixels, as shown in Figure 18.4.

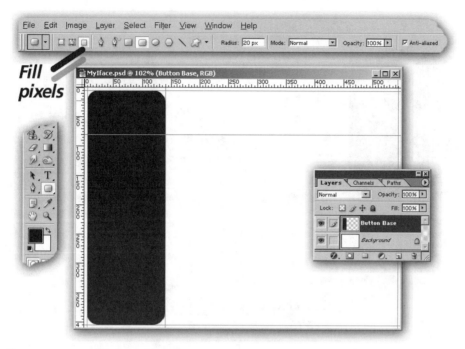

Figure 18.4   Draw a rounded rectangle using the guides for positioning. The rectangle shape easily snaps into place along the guides.

This rectangular shape will be the basic bar for the interface platform, which will later contain the navigation buttons. The rounded rectangle, by itself, is not a very interesting shape. Let's see if we can make it more interesting.

3. Drag the Button Base layer to the Create a new layer icon at the bottom of the Layers palette twice (this makes two copies of the Button Base layer). Choose the duplicate layer that is directly above the Button Base layer and double-click the layer name; then rename the selected layer to **Vertical Bracket**. Double-click the name of the duplicate layer above the Vertical Bracket layer, and rename this layer **Cutout**. Click the Vertical Bracket layer to make it the active layer. Press the slash (/) key on your keyboard to toggle the Lock transparent pixels option on. Open the Edit menu and choose Fill. Select 50% Gray from the Use pop-up menu and click OK (see Figure 18.5).

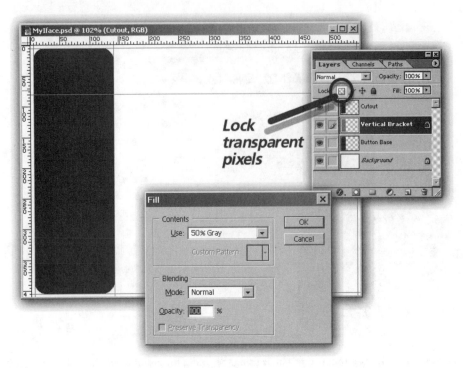

Figure 18.5   Make two copies of the Button Base layer and rename them **Vertical Bracket** and **Cutout**.

Don't be alarmed if you don't see the results of the gray fill in your document window. This happens because the Cutout layer contains a black fill and is covering up the changes made to the Vertical Bracket layer. The Cutout layer is only a temporary layer. In the following steps, you will use it to cut a shape out of the Vertical Bracket layer. You will also change the color of the Vertical Bracket layer so that you can later see the results clearly.

4. Click the Cutout layer to make this layer active. Press V to switch to the Move tool. Hold down the Shift key and press the up arrow on your keyboard twice. This moves the rounded rectangle on the Cutout layer up 10 pixels. Release the Shift key and press the up arrow two more times. This moves the rounded rectangle on the Cutout layer up two pixels. Now press the right arrow five times to move the rounded rectangle on the Cutout layer to the right five pixels (see Figure 18.6).

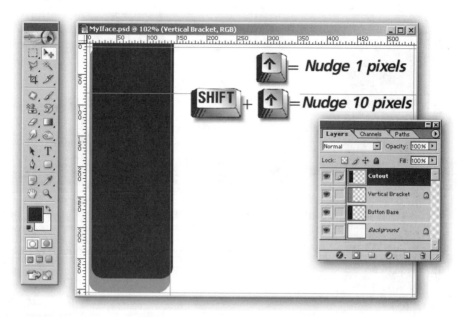

Figure 18.6   Use the arrow keys on the keyboard to reposition the rounded rectangular shape on the Cutout layer.

5. Hold down the Ctrl(⌘) key and click the Cutout layer. This loads the rounded rectangular shape on the Cutout layer as a selection. Now click the Vertical Bracket layer to make this the active layer and press the Delete (Backspace) key. Press Ctrl(⌘)+D to deselect. You can delete the Cutout layer now, so drag the Cutout layer to the trashcan icon at the bottom of the Layers palette. Press Ctrl(⌘)+S to save the changes and leave the image open for the next exercise.

As you can see in Figure 18.7, you use the Cutout layer to trim away a portion of the Vertical Bracket layer. Using the image information from one layer to cut out or trim from another layer is one way that you can achieve Boolean shape operations in Photoshop.

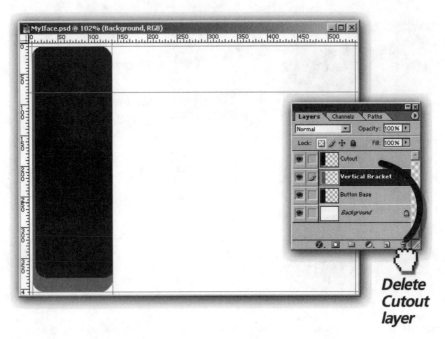

Figure 18.7   Use the image on the Cutout layer to cut away from the Vertical Bracket layer. Discard the Cutout layer when it has served its purpose.

Now you have the makings of something a little more interesting. However, let's get rid of our white background and add a little texture. Here's how…

Adding Background Texture

1. Press Ctrl(⌘)+N to open the New dialog box. This is a temporary document, so don't worry about naming it. Set the Height and the Width to 400 pixels. Set the resolution to 72 pixels per inch and set the Mode to RGB Color. Leave Contents set to White and click OK. Go to the Filter menu and choose Noise, Add Noise. Change the Amount in the Add Noise dialog box to 150, set Distribution to Gaussian, and turn on the Monochromatic option. Click OK (see Figure 18.8).

   The Add Noise filter is a random texture, so there's no need to worry about doing anything special to it to turn it into a seamless texture.

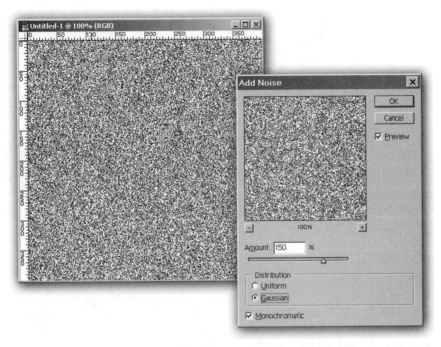

Figure 18.8   Create a new 400×400 document and apply the Add Noise filter settings
shown here.

2. Go to the Filter menu and choose Blur, Blur. Next go to the Filter menu and
   choose Stylize, Emboss. In the Emboss dialog box, set the Angle to 135°, Height to
   1, and Amount to 50%. Click OK. Right-click (Macintosh: hold Ctrl and click) the
   title bar and choose Image Size to open the Image size dialog box. Change the
   Height and Width to 200 pixels, and click OK. (If you have checked the Constrain
   Proportions option, changing the Width measurement will cause the Height measurement to automatically adjust.) Press Ctrl(⌘)+A to select all. Go to the Edit
   menu and choose Define Pattern. Change the name to **MyIface Background
   Pattern** in the Pattern Name dialog box and click OK (see Figure 18.9).

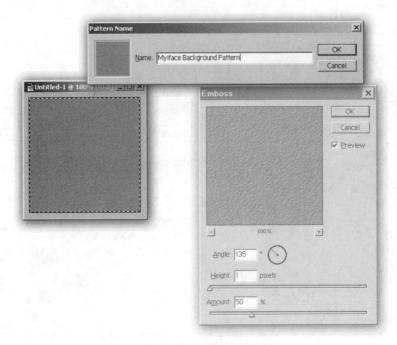

Figure 18.9   Select all and define the document as a pattern.

We created this texture in a second document so that you could shrink the effects of the Add Noise, Blur, and Emboss filter combination. The bumpy texture that results from the combination of those three filters is a little overbearing. Resizing the final effect down to 50% makes the texture more subtle.

3. Close the temporary document without saving changes. In the MyIface.psd document, click the Background layer to make this the active layer. Go to the Edit menu and choose Fill. In the Fill dialog box, select Pattern from the Use menu. Open the Custom Pattern menu and select the MyIface Background Pattern that you created in the previous step. Click OK to apply (see Figure 18.10). Press Ctrl(⌘)+S to save the changes and leave the image open for the next exercise.

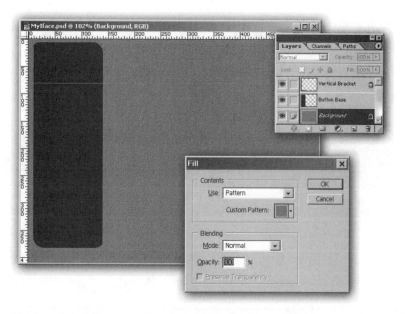

Figure 18.10   Fill the Background layer with the newly created pattern.

Now that you have a nice texture background, you need to add some depth to the shapes. Layer Styles will help you add instant depth and dimension to flat shapes. Let's get started.

Adding Color and Depth

1. Click the Button Base layer to make this the active layer. Double-click to the right of the Button Base name to open the Layer Style dialog box. Click the Gradient Overlay option under Styles, as seen in Figure 18.11.

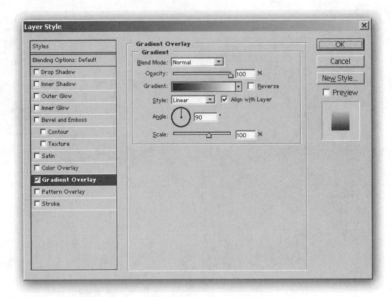

Figure 18.11   Open the Layer Style dialog box for the Button Base layer and select the
Gradient Overlay option.

Warning

Avoid Accidents in the Layer Style Dialog Box   You need to be careful when
working in the Layer Style dialog box. You can easily turn on a layer style without making
its properties visible. For example, in this instance the Blending Options: Default title
was highlighted when the dialog box opened. If you click the checkbox to turn on the
Gradient Overlay style without clicking on the actual Gradient Overlay title, you still will
be viewing the Blending Options: Default settings (*not* the settings for the Gradient
Overlay options). You need to make sure that the style you want to edit is highlighted or
you will be editing either the default options or the options of another style (whichever
style is currently highlighted).

2. Click the small gradient preview (under the Opacity slider) to open the Gradient
   Editor. Click the lower-left Color Stop (below the gradient bar), and then click
   the color swatch next to the Color option to open the color picker. Change the
   color to R:80, G:80, B:80. Click OK to apply. Click the lower-right Color Stop,
   and then click the color swatch to open the color picker. Change the color to
   R:145, G:145, B:145. Click OK.

3. Click OK to exit the Gradient Editor. In the Layer Style dialog box, change the
   Angle to 180° and leave the remaining Gradient Overlay options at their default
   (see Figure 18.12). Click OK to apply the results.

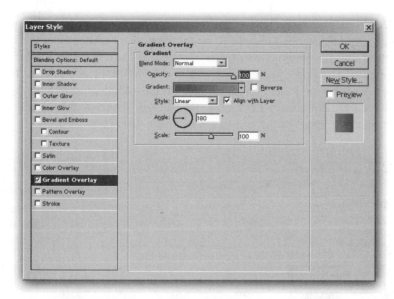

Figure 18.12   Change the Angle in the Gradient Overlay to 180 degrees. The settings should now appear as they do here.

Looking at the results in Figure 18.13, you can see that it doesn't matter what the original color was for the rounded rectangle on the Button Base layer. The Gradient Overlay overrides the color and fills the rounded rectangle with the gradient. If you remove the layer style, the rounded rectangle will revert back to its original color (black).

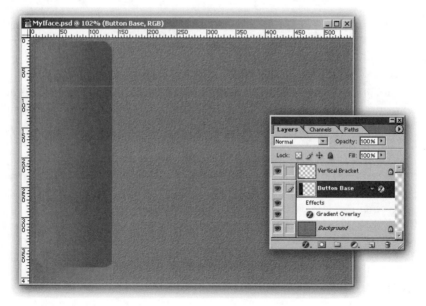

Figure 18.13   Apply the Gradient Overlay style and observe the results.

5. Double-click the Add a layer style icon (Hint: It looks like an "f") to reopen the Layer Style dialog box. Click the Bevel and Emboss style (remember to click the title to view the options for this style). Set Style to Inner Bevel and Technique to Smooth. Leave Depth at 100% and set Direction to Up. Enter a value of **15** px for Size, **16** px for Soften, **120°** for Angle, **30°** for Altitude, and turn off the Use Global Light option. Leave the rest of the Shading options at their default settings (see Figure 18.14). Leave the Layer Style dialog box open.

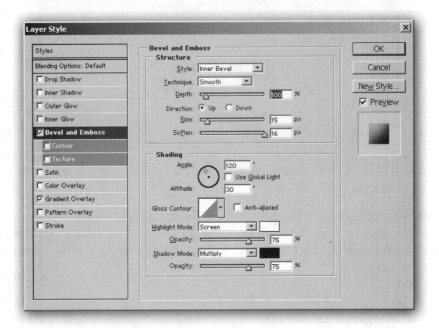

Figure 18.14   Apply a Bevel and Emboss layer style.

6. Now click the Drop Shadow style title. Change Distance to 0, Spread to 10, and Size to 10. Turn off the Use Global Light option and use the remaining default settings (see Figure 18.15). Click OK to apply.

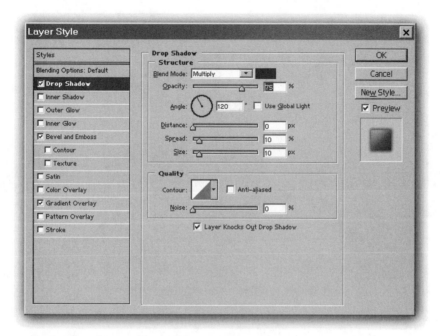

Figure 18.15   Apply the Drop Shadow layer style settings shown here.

Now that you've added some color and depth to the Button Base layer, let's do the same for the Vertical Bracket layer.

7. Double-click to the right of the Vertical Bracket layer title to open the Layer Style dialog box. Click the Gradient Overlay option title under Styles. Click the gradient preview to open the Gradient Editor. Click the lower-left Color Stop (below the gradient bar), and then click the color swatch to open the color picker. Change the color to R:128, G:128, B:128. Click OK. Click the lower-right Color Stop, and then click the color swatch to open the color picker for this setting. Change the color to R:190, G:190, B:190. Click OK to exit the color picker (see Figure 18.16). Click OK to exit the Gradient Editor.

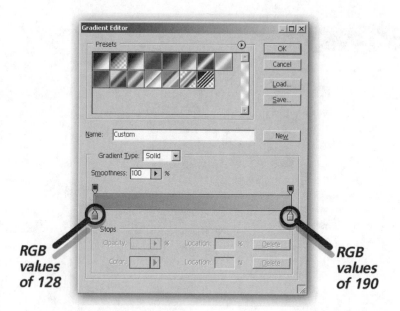

RGB values of 128

RGB values of 190

Figure 18.16   Make changes to the Gradient Editor to apply a gradient from RGB values of 128 to RGB values of 190.

8. Change the Angle to **180°** and leave the remaining options for the Gradient Overlay at the default settings.

9. Now select the Bevel and Emboss style title. Change Size to **3** px, Soften to **5** px, and turn off the Use Global Light option. Leave all of the remaining options at the default settings (see Figure 18.17).

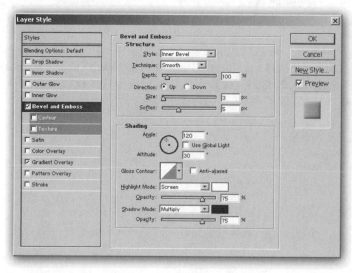

Figure 18.17   Apply a Bevel and Emboss style. Change only the Size and Soften options and turn off the Use Global Light option.

10. Click the Drop Shadow style title. Once again, leave most of the default settings as they are, except turn off Use Global Light, set Distance to **0** px, Spread to **5%**, and Size to **5** px (see Figure 18.18). Click OK to apply the results. Press Ctrl(⌘)+S to save the changes and leave the image open for the next exercise.

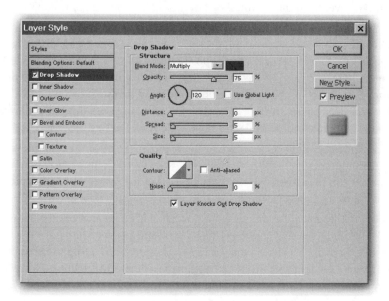

Figure 18.18   Apply a Drop Shadow style using the settings shown here.

Now you're getting somewhere. Your shapes have depth, which makes them much more interesting. You still have a way to go before you have a polished navigation interface, however. Let's start adding components to the interface design.

Note

The Global Light Option   You've probably noticed that we keep turning off the Use Global Light option for the various layer styles. When the Global Light option is on, editing the lighting for one layer style affects any of the other layer styles that have the Global Light option turned on. In other words, if you change the lighting direction for one style, the other styles will automatically update their settings whether you want them to or not. To have more control over where we want the lighting to be applied on the different style components, turn off the Global Light option so that you won't inadvertently mess up your lighting when you're working on a layer style for another component.

Creating the Screen Base

1. Click the Button Base layer, and then click the square next to the Vertical Bracket layer to link this layer to the Button Base layer. With the Move tool active, press the right arrow key 5 times to move both layers over 5 pixels. Unlink the Vertical Bracket layer from the Button Base layer. Drag the vertical guide that's positioned at 140 pixels back onto the vertical ruler to remove it.

2. Go to the View menu and choose New Guide. In the New Guide dialog box, set the Orientation to Vertical and the position to 150 px and click OK. Go to View, New Guide again and set the Orientation to Horizontal, position to 140 px; then click OK. Go to View, New Guide once more and set the Orientation to Horizontal, position to 40 px, and click OK. You won't use this last guide for a while, but you might as well set it now while you're setting the others.

3. Click the foreground color swatch from the toolbox to open the color picker. Change the color to R:160, G:160, B:160. Click OK. Click the Vertical Bracket layer to make this the active layer and Alt(Opt)+click the Create a new layer icon at the bottom of the Layers palette. Name the new layer **Screen Base** and click OK.

4. Select the Rounded Rectangle tool again. The Fill pixels icon on the Options bar should still be selected and the radius should still be set to 20 px. Draw a rounded rectangle between the vertical guide at 5 and 150 px and between the horizontal guides at 5 and 140 px, as shown in Figure 18.19. Press the slash (/) key to toggle the Lock transparent pixels option on for the Screen Base layer. Press D for the default colors of black and white.

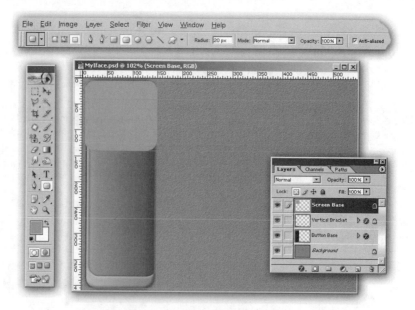

Figure 18.19   Draw a rounded light gray rectangle on the Screen Base layer using the new guides.

5. Double-click to the right of the Screen Base title to open the Layer Style dialog box. Click the Gradient Overlay option under Styles. Click the gradient preview to open the Gradient Editor. Click the lower-left Color Stop (below the gradient bar), and then click the color swatch to open the color picker. Change the color to R:100, G:100, B:100. Click OK. Click the lower-right Color Stop, and then click the color swatch to open the color picker. Change the color to R:160, G:160, B:160. Click OK (see Figure 18.20).

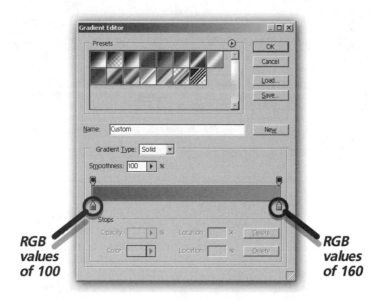

Figure 18.20   Select the Gradient Overlay style, and change the gradient from RGB values of 100 to RGB values of 160.

6. Click OK to exit the Gradient Editor. Change the Angle to 180° and leave the remaining options for the Gradient Overlay at the defaults. Click the Bevel and Emboss style. Change Size to 10 px, Soften to 5 px, turn off the Use Global Light option, set the Opacity for the Highlight Mode and Shadow Mode to 50%, and leave the remaining options at the default settings (see Figure 18.21).

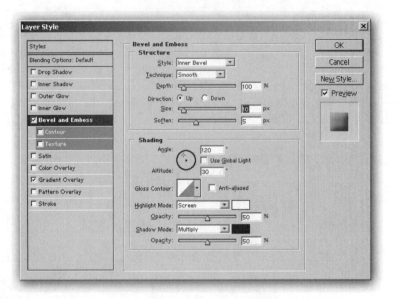

Figure 18.21   Apply the Bevel and Emboss style.

7. Click the Drop Shadow style title. Once again turn off the Use Global Light option, set Distance to 0 px, Spread at 6%, Size at 6 px, and leave the remaining options at the default settings (see Figure 18.22). Click OK to apply the results.

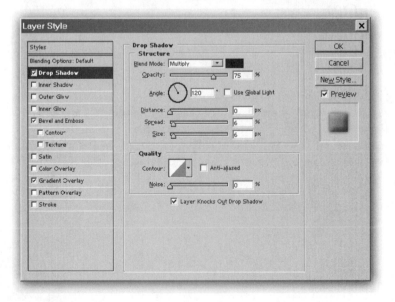

Figure 18.22   Apply the Drop Shadow style with the settings shown here.

8. Press V to make sure the Move tool is active. Drag the vertical guide at 150 pixels and the horizontal guide at 140 pixels back onto the ruler to delete these guides. Go to the View menu and choose New Guide to add vertical guides at 15 and 165 pixels. Then use the New Guide feature to add horizontal guides at 15 and 125 pixels.

9. Alt(Opt)+click the Create a new layer icon at the bottom of the Layers palette and name the new layer **Screen**. Click OK. Select the Rounded Rectangle tool and draw a rounded rectangle between the vertical guides at 15 and 165 pixels and the horizontal guides at 15 and 125 pixels, as shown in Figure 18.23.

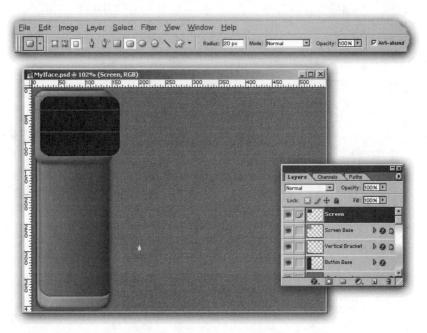

Figure 18.23   Set guides and draw a rounded rectangle on the newly created Screen layer.

10. Double-click to the right of the Screen layer title to open the Layer Style dialog box. Select the Drop Shadow style. Turn off the Use Global Light option, set Distance at 0 px, Spread at 6%, Size at 6 px, and leave the remaining options at the default settings. Click OK. Press Ctrl(⌘)+S to save the changes and leave the image open for the next exercise.

We're not adding the Gradient Overlay or Bevel and Emboss styles to this layer because this is the actual screen area. You will use the Screen layer to create a window. You then will add all those layer styles to the window, but the goal is to have a flat area in the center of this window area for placing a company logo.

Creating the Logo Screen Window

1. Drag the Screen layer to the Create a new layer icon at the bottom of the Layers palette to create a duplicate layer. Double-click the name of the duplicate layer to rename this layer **Screen Window** and press Enter (Return) to set the new name. If the layer styles are not showing on the Screen Window layer, click the small arrow on the Add a layer style icon to display the layer styles. Drag the Drop Shadow effect to the trash icon at the bottom of the Layers palette to delete that layer style.

2. Press the slash (/) key to turn on the Lock transparent pixels option for the Screen Window layer. Go to the Edit menu and choose Fill. In the Fill dialog box, select 50% Gray from the Use menu and click OK (see Figure 18.24).

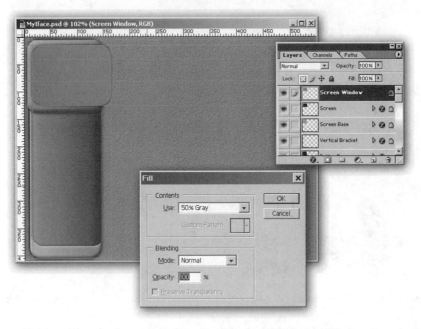

Figure 18.24   Make a duplicate of the Screen layer and name it **Screen Window**. Remove the Drop Shadow effect, and fill with 50% Gray.

The 50% gray fill for the Screen Window layer wasn't really a necessary step. So why take the time to fill the layer content with this color? Coloring the layer helps you differentiate the Screen Window layer from the Screen layer, which will also allow you to see the results of the next step more clearly.

3. Ctrl(⌘)+click the Screen Window layer to load the layer's contents as a selection. Click the Channels tab to view the Channels palette (or go to the Window menu and choose Channels). Alt(Opt)+click the Create new channel icon at the bottom of the Channels palette and make sure that Masked Areas is selected in the Color Indicates section of the dialog box. Click OK. You should now have

a new channel titled Alpha 1 that is filled with black. White should be your current background color. Press Ctrl(⌘)+Delete (Backspace) to fill the selection with white background color. Press Ctrl(⌘)+D to deselect. Go to the Filter menu, choose Other, Minimum, and change the Radius to 10 (pixels). Click OK (see Figure 18.25).

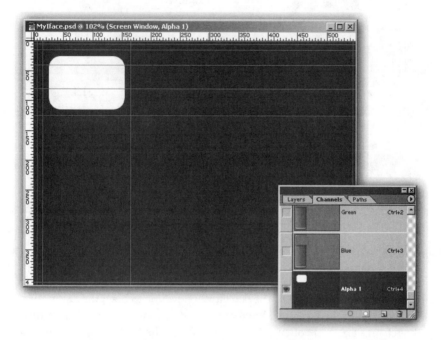

Figure 18.25   Load the Screen Window as a selection, create a new channel, fill the selection with white, deselect, and apply the Minimum filter with a Radius of 10.

The Minimum and Maximum filters are useful for resizing shapes. In this case, you used the Minimum filter to reduce the size of the rectangle. Similarly, you could use the Maximum filter to expand the size. Both filters perform a sort of shape-contouring function—which is another common vector-shaping tool usually listed among the Boolean shaping tools.

4. Return to the Layers palette and select the Screen Window layer. Press Ctrl(⌘)+Alt(Opt)+4 to load the Alpha 1 channel as a selection. Press Delete (Backspace). Press Ctrl(⌘)+D to deselect. Select the Move tool and delete the vertical guides at 15 and 165 pixels and the horizontal guides at 15 and 125 by dragging them off the document (see Figure 18.26).

Figure 18.26   Load the Alpha 1 channel as a selection and delete the selection area. Clean up the document by removing some of the guides.

5. Double-click to the right of the Screen Window title to open the Layer Style dialog box. Select the Bevel and Emboss style. Leave most of the default settings, but change Size and Soften to 5 px. Turn off the Use Global Light option and change the Opacity of the Highlight Mode and Shadow Mode to 50%.

6. Below the Altitude setting is a Gloss Contour thumbnail (see Figure 18.27). Click the down arrow next to the Gloss Contour thumbnail to open the contour picker. Select the Ring Contour (bottom row, second from left). Click OK. Press Ctrl(⌘)+S to save the changes and leave the image open for the next exercise.

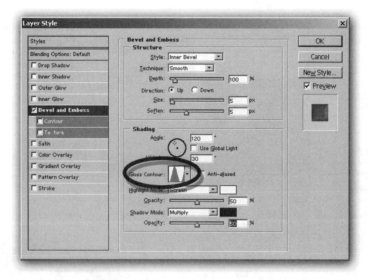

Figure 18.27   Use the Ring Gloss Contour and the settings shown here to apply a Bevel and Emboss layer style on the Screen Window layer.

In this exercise, you're making the Bevel and Emboss style a little different to set it apart. As mentioned previously, this screen area is where a company might want to put its logo, so the distinctive screen shading helps draw attention to it.

Creating the Horizontal Interface Components

Now you have a base for the buttons and a screen for the logo—you need to add a horizontal component. A horizontal component provides a place for buttons and logos, but what about a place for titles, headings, and (heaven forbid) banner ads? Move on to the next exercise to see how to resolve this dilemma.

Creating the Header Bar

1. Click the Channels tab to view the Channels palette. Click the Alpha 1 channel and press Alt(Opt)+Delete (Backspace) to fill with the black foreground color. Use the View, New Guide feature to add a vertical guide at 220 pixels. Choose the Rectangular Marquee tool from the toolbox. Draw a rectangular selection between the vertical guides at 5 and 220 pixels and the horizontal guides at 5 and 80 pixels. Press Ctrl(⌘)+Delete (Backspace) to fill with the white background color (see Figure 18.28). Press Ctrl(⌘)+D to deselect.

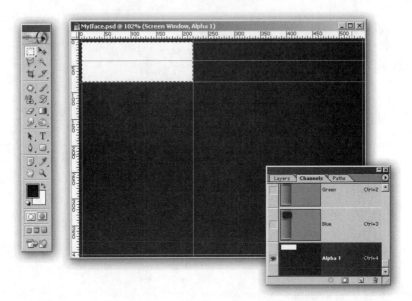

Figure 18.28   On the Channels palette, fill the Alpha 1 layer with black, add a vertical guide, and create a rectangular marquee to fill with white.

2. With the Rectangular Marquee tool still selected, draw a rectangular selection between the vertical guides at 5 and 545 pixels and the horizontal guides at 5 and 40 pixels. Press Ctrl(⌘)+Delete (Backspace) to fill with white background color. Press Ctrl(⌘)+D to deselect (see Figure 18.29).

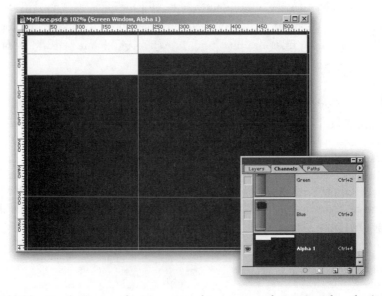

Figure 18.29   Use the Rectangular Marquee tool to create another rectangular selection using the guides and fill with white.

It doesn't yet look like much, but this is the basis for a portion of the header component. You're going to use another method to create shapes in Photoshop and, believe it or not, this method involves using the Gaussian Blur filter and the Levels command.

3. Go to the Filter menu and choose Blur, Gaussian Blur. Set the Radius to 15 pixels and click OK. Press Ctrl(⌘)+L to open Levels. Enter **119** in the far-left Input Levels field and enter **129** in the far-right Input Levels field, as shown in Figure 18.30. Click OK.

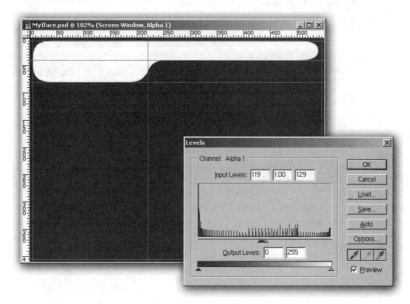

Figure 18.30   Apply the Gaussian Blur filter and use the Levels command to redefine the shape.

Now you have a nice S-shaped transition between the taller rectangle and the shorter rectangle. Notice that all of the corners have been rounded. The results of this technique aren't always ideal, however. For instance, the curve on the far right is a little too pronounced. You can fix this easily, though, as you'll see in the next exercise. It doesn't matter what the left corners look like because the Screen Base layer will cover this area.

Note

What Just Happened?   When you used the Gaussian Blur filter, you introduced a large number of grayscale values to the channel. The Levels command was able to throw out most of those grayscale values. The result is that all the corners have been rounded by the blur effect from the Gaussian Blur filter and the integrity of the shape was smoothed out by the Level values applied. Of course, all that mumbo jumbo doesn't have to make sense—you can just be satisfied that it works.

4. Use the View, New Guide feature to set a vertical guide at 528 ps. The Rectangular Marquee tool should still be selected. Draw a rectangular selection between the vertical guides at 220 and 528 pixels and the horizontal guides at 5 and 40 pixels. Press Ctrl(⌘)+Delete (Backspace) to fill with the white background color (see Figure 18.31). Press Ctrl(⌘)+D to deselect.

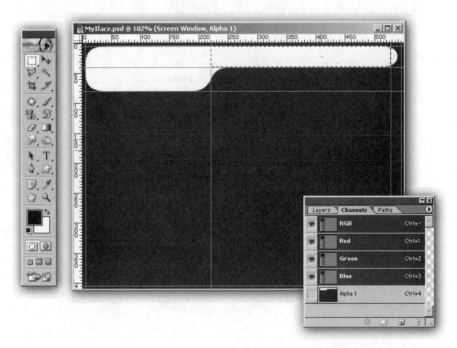

Figure 18.31   Make a rectangular selection at the guides shown here and fill with white.

5. Press Shift+M to cycle to the Elliptical Marquee tool. Zoom in to the upper-right corner of the document (the goal is to get a close view of the guides and the curve area at the far-right side). Hold down the Shift key and draw a circular selection. Start at the intersection of the horizontal guide at 5 pixels and the vertical guide at 545 pixels. Drag down and to the right until you get to the horizontal guide at 40 pixels. It might help to press the spacebar while keeping the mouse button pressed to reposition the selection in place as you drag. Press Ctrl(⌘)+Delete (Backspace) to fill with white background color (see Figure 18.32).

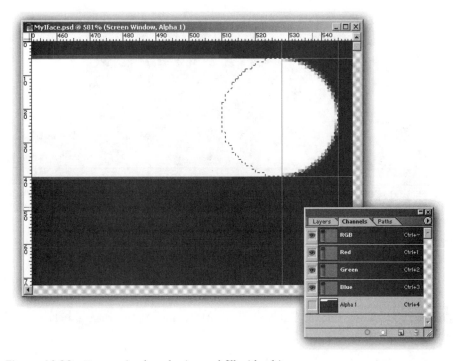

Figure 18.32   Draw a circular selection and fill with white.

6. Press Ctrl(⌘)+D to deselect. Press Ctrl(⌘)+ minus until you are back at a nor-
    mal viewing level. Click the Layers tab to return to the Layers palette. Click the
    Vertical Bracket layer to make it active. Alt(Opt)+click the Create a new layer
    icon at the bottom of the Layers palette and name the new layer **Header Bar**;
    click OK. Press Ctrl(⌘)+Alt(Opt)+4 to load the Alpha 1 channel as a selection.
    Press Alt(Opt)+Delete (Backspace) to fill with black. Press Ctrl(⌘)+D to dese-
    lect (see Figure 18.33). Use the Move tool to drag the vertical guides at 528
    pixels off the document and into the ruler. Press Ctrl(⌘)+S to save the changes
    and leave the image open for the next exercise.

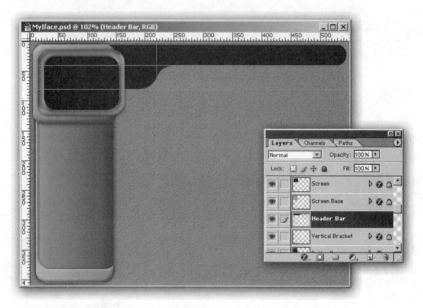

Figure 18.33   Create a new layer named Header Bar, load the Alpha 1 channel and fill with black.

Whew! How about a soda and snack break before we move on? Now that you have the basic shape of the header bar, it's time to give it depth. You should be familiar with the routine by now… ready? Finish that soda and let's go.

Fleshing Out the Header Bar

1. Double-click to the right of the Header Bar text to open the Layer Style dialog box. Now click the Gradient Overlay option under Styles. Click the gradient preview to open the Gradient Editor. Click the lower-left Color Stop (below the gradient bar), and then click the color swatch to open the color picker. Change the color to R:100, G:100, B:100. Click OK. Click the lower-right Color Stop, and then click the color swatch to open the color picker. Change the color to R:160, G:160, B:160. Click OK (see Figure 18.34).

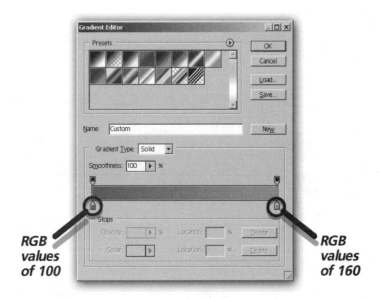

RGB
values
of 100

RGB
values
of 160

Figure 18.34 Apply the Gradient Overlay style and edit the gradient to go from RGB values of 100 to RGB values of 160.

2. Click OK to exit the Gradient Editor. The default 90° Angle is exactly what you want this time around, so let's move on. Select the Bevel and Emboss style. Change Size to 10 px, Soften to 5 px, turn off the Use Global Light option, set the Opacity for Highlight Mode and Shadow Mode to 50% Opacity, and leave the remaining options at the default settings (see Figure 18.35).

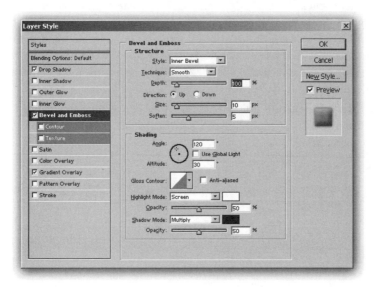

Figure 18.35 Use the settings shown here to apply a Bevel and Emboss layer style.

3. Select the Drop Shadow style. Turn off Use Global Light option, set Distance to 0 px, Spread to 5%, Size to 5 px, and leave the remaining options at the default settings (see Figure 18.36). Click OK to apply the results.

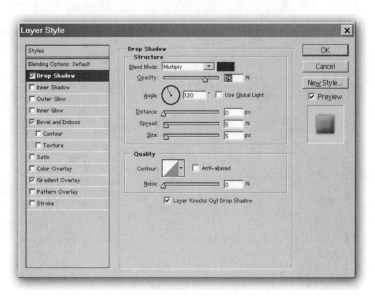

Figure 18.36   Apply the Drop Shadow style with the settings shown here.

4. With the Header Bar layer as the active layer, Alt(Opt)+click the Create a new layer icon at the bottom of the Layers palette. Name the new layer **Header Bar Bracket** and click OK. Ctrl(⌘)+click the Header Bar layer to load its contents as a selection. Go to the Edit menu and choose Stroke. In the Stroke dialog box, set the Width to 5 px, leave the color black, set Location to Inside, and leave the rest of the defaults as they are. Click OK. Press Ctrl(⌘)+D to deselect. With the Move tool, drag the vertical guide at 220 and the horizontal guides at 40 and 80 off the document onto the rulers to delete them (see Figure 18.37).

The Header Bar component is a little bland by itself, so we'll use this stroke to add a little flair. However, you don't want the entire stroke. You need to cut some of it away to make it more interesting.

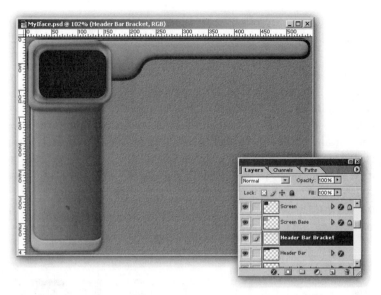

Figure 18.37   Apply a stroke on the Header Bar Bracket layer using a selection of the Header Bar layer contents.

5. Use the View, New Guide feature to place horizontal guides at 15 and 95 pixels and vertical guides at 50 and 530 pixels. Select the Rectangular Marquee tool and draw a rectangular selection between the horizontal guides at 15 and 95 pixels and vertical guides at 50 and 530 pixels. Press the Delete (Backspace) key (see Figure 18.38).

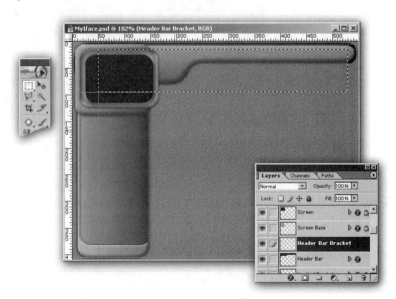

Figure 18.38   Set guides to help make an easy rectangular selection, and delete it from the Header Bar Bracket layer.

6. Use the Move tool to remove the horizontal guides at 15 and 95 px and vertical guides at 50 and 530 px. Zoom in on the far-right end of the stroke on the Header Bar Bracket layer. Use the View, New Guide feature to place horizontal guides at 26 and 44 px and a vertical guide at 528 px.

7. Choose the Polygonal Lasso tool from the toolbox. The goal is to make a triangular selection, as shown in Figure 18.39. You need only to click at the corner points along the intersection of guides. With the Snap option turned on, the tool automatically snaps to the guides. So click the intersection of the horizontal guide at 26 px and the vertical guide at 528. Click again at the intersection of the horizontal guide at 44 px and the vertical guide at 545. Click again on the intersection of the horizontal guide at 44 px and the vertical guide at 528. Click once more at the intersection of the horizontal guide at 26 px and the vertical guide at 528 to complete the triangular selection. Press the Delete (Backspace) key.

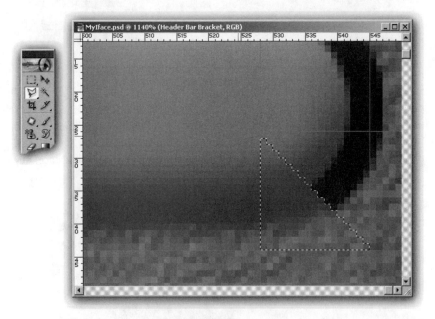

Figure 18.39   Use guides to make a triangular selection easy, and use this selection to delete more area from the Header Bar Bracket layer.

8. Zoom out to a normal view. Press Ctrl(⌘)+D to deselect. Use the Move tool to remove the horizontal guides at 26 and 44 px and the vertical guide at 528 px. Right-click (Macintosh: hold Ctrl and click) on the Header Bar layer and choose Copy Layer Style. Right-click (Macintosh: hold Ctrl and click) on the Header Bar Bracket layer and choose Paste Layer Style (see Figure 18.40). Press Ctrl(⌘)+S to save the changes and leave the image open for the next exercise.

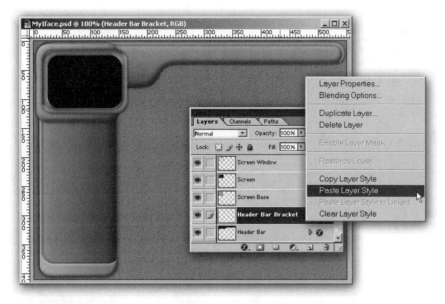

Figure 18.40   Copy Layer Style from the Header Bar layer, and paste it to the Header Bar
Bracket layer.

Now the Header Bar looks more interesting. Let's add one more component to the
Header Bar to complete it. Next you're going to finish things off, using a technique similar to the one you used on the Button Bar.

Finishing the Header Bar

1. Click the Vertical Bracket layer to make it the active layer. Atl(Opt)+click the
   Create a new layer icon at the bottom of the Layers palette. Name the new layer
   Header Base and click OK. Use the View, New Guide feature to place horizontal
   guides at 20 and 95 pixels and vertical guides at 50 and 520 pixels. Select the
   Rounded Rectangle tool and draw a rounded rectangle between the horizontal
   guides at 20 and 95 pixels and vertical guides at 50 and 520 pixels on the Header
   Base layer, as shown in Figure 18.41.

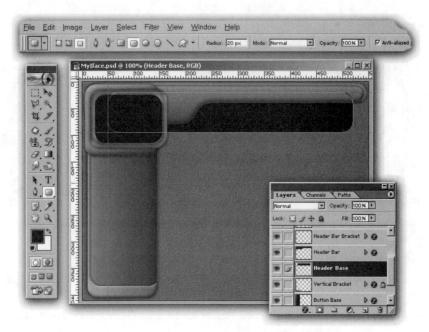

Figure 18.41   Draw a rounded rectangle on a new layer named Header Base.

2. Go to the View menu and choose Clear Guides. Right-click (Macintosh: hold Ctrl and click) on the Header Base layer and choose Paste Layer Style (see Figure 18.42).

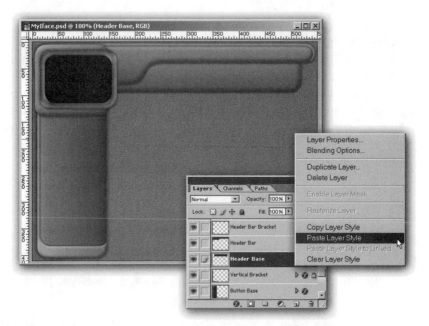

Figure 18.42   Clear the guides and paste the layer style onto the Header Base layer.

3. Drag the Header Base layer to the Create a new layer icon at the bottom of the Layers palette to create a duplicate. Double-click the title of the duplicate and rename the layer **Header Base Bracket**. Press Enter (Return) to set the new name. Drag the Header Base Bracket layer to the Create a new layer icon and rename this duplicate **Cutout**. Press Enter (Return) to set the new name. Right-click (Macintosh: hold Ctrl and click) on the Cutout layer and choose Clear Layer Style (see Figure 18.43).

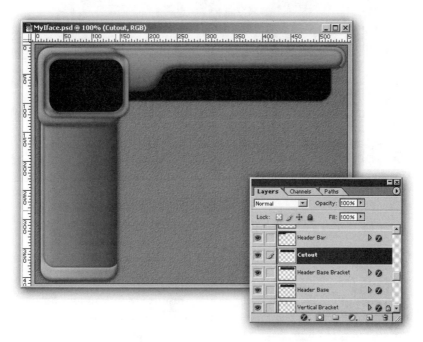

Figure 18.43   Create two duplicate layers based from the Header Base layer. Rename the duplicate layers and remove the layer style from the Cutout layer.

4. Press V to switch to the Move tool. With the Cutout layer as the active layer, hold down the Shift key and press the left arrow on your keyboard two times. This will move the rounded rectangle on the Cutout layer 20 px to the left. Release the Shift key and press the up arrow on your keyboard 5 times to move the Cutout layer up 5 px.

5. Ctrl(⌘)+click the Cutout layer to load its contents as a selection. Select the Header Base Bracket layer and press Delete (Backspace). Delete the Cutout layer and press Ctrl(⌘)+D to deselect. Drag the Cutout layer to the trash icon at the bottom of the Layers palette to delete this layer (see Figure 18.44). Press Ctrl(⌘)+S to save the changes and leave the image open for the next exercise.

Figure 18.44   Reposition the Cutout layer to use this layer's contents to remove a portion of the Header Base Bracket layer. Delete the Cutout layer when it has served its purpose.

Finishing the Interface

Now the header component looks very nice. We just need some buttons for our interface and we're done. We've put a lot of mileage on the Rounded Rectangle tool so far, but we're not done. The Rounded Rectangle tool is excellent for making pill-shaped buttons.

Creating the Buttons

1. Use the View, New Guide feature to place vertical guides at 25 and 165 pixels and horizontal guides at 150 and 178. Click the Screen Window layer to make it active. Alt(Opt)+click the Create a new layer icon at the bottom of the Layers palette and name the new layer **Button 1**. Click OK. Select the Rounded Rectangle tool and draw a rounded rectangle between the horizontal guides at 150 and 178 pixels and vertical guides at 25 and 165 pixels on the Header Base layer (see Figure 18.45).

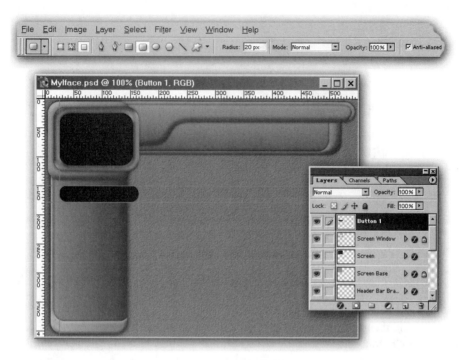

Figure 18.45   Set four guides and use the Rounded Rectangle tool to draw a pill-shape button.

Now you can take advantage of a useful aspect of the Rounded Rectangle tool. You have the radius set to 20 px (for each corner of the rounded rectangle). Because this button is less than 30 px high, you get nicely rounded ends on the rounded rectangle, creating a perfect pill shape for the interface buttons.

2. Go to the View menu and choose Clear Guides.

3. Right-click (Macintosh: hold Ctrl and click) the Header Bar Bracket layer and choose Copy Layer Style. Right-click (Macintosh: hold Ctrl and click) the Button 1 layer and choose Paste Layer Style.

4. If the list of layer styles is not showing on the Button 1 layer, click the arrow next to the Add a layer style icon to view the list. Double-click the Bevel and Emboss style to open this Layer Style dialog box. Open the pop-up menu for Gloss Contour and select the Rolling Slope – Descending contour (bottom row, fourth from the left). See Figure 18.46.

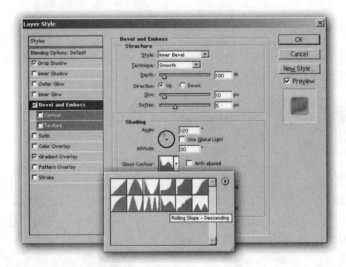

Figure 18.46   Copy the layer style from the Header Bar Bracket layer to the Button 1 layer and edit the Gloss Contour.

Copying and then editing a layer style is a great way to save a little time. In this case, the new Gloss Contour setting goes a long way toward making the shading look very unique from the rest of the elements on the interface.

   5. Now select the Drop Shadow Style and change the Distance setting to 2 px (see Figure 18.47). Click OK to apply the changes.

The button is starting to look pretty nice, but there's still a small detail you can add to make it even more interesting.

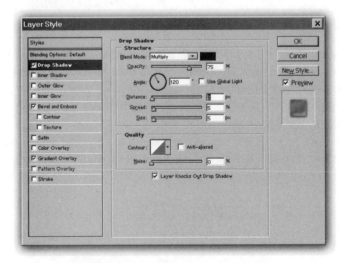

Figure 18.47   Edit the Drop Shadow style for the button.

6. With the Button 1 layer selected, Alt(Opt)+click the Create a new layer icon in the Layers palette and name the new layer **Button 1 Bracket**. Click OK. Ctrl(⌘)+click the Button 1 layer to load the contents as a selection.

7. Go to the Edit menu and choose Stroke. Change the Width to 4 pixels (color should still be black) and press OK to apply. Press Ctrl(⌘)+D to deselect. Use the View, New Guide feature to place a vertical guide at 35 px. Select the Rectangular Marquee tool. Starting to the right of the stroke, draw a selection around the stroke or button that ends at the vertical guide at 35 pixels (see Figure 18.48).

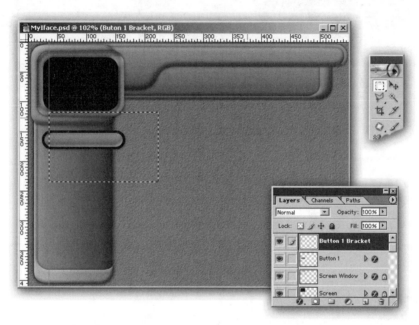

Figure 18.48   Use the contents from the Button 1 layer to make a selection and add a stroke. Create a rectangular selection as shown to prepare this side of the stroke for deletion.

8. Press the Delete (Backspace) key, and then press Ctrl(⌘)+D to deselect. Right-click (Macintosh: hold Ctrl and click) the Vertical Bracket layer and choose Copy Layer Style. Right-click (Macintosh: hold Ctrl and click) the Button 1 Bracket layer and choose Paste Layer Style (see Figure 18.49). Go to the View menu and choose Clear Guides. Press Ctrl(⌘)+S to save the changes and leave the image open for the next exercise.

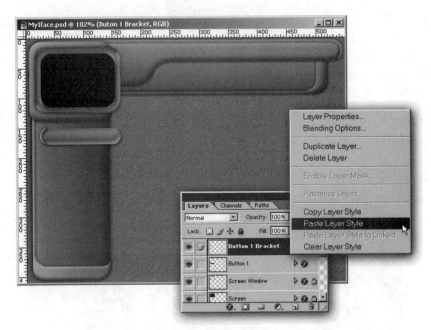

Figure 18.49   Copy and paste the layer style from the Vertical Bracket layer to the Button 1 Bracket layer.

Much better. Now all you need to do is create some copies of the button and its associated bracket, and you've got yourself an interface. To avoid having to mess with making multiple copies of two separate layers, we'll use layer sets to simplify the process.

Populating the Interface

1. The Button 1 Bracket layer should still be the active layer. Click the link icon next to the Button 1 layer to link these two layers. Click the arrow on the upper-right corner of the Layers palette and choose New Set From Linked. Name the new set **Button 1 Set** and click OK.

2. With Button 1 Set selected, click the arrow in the upper-right corner of the Layers palette again and choose Duplicate Layer Set. In the Duplicate Layer Set dialog box, rename the set **Button 2 Set** and click OK.

3. With the Move tool and the Button 2 Set selected, hold the Shift key and press the down arrow key on your keyboard 4 times to move the Button 2 Set down 40 pixels (see Figure 18.50).

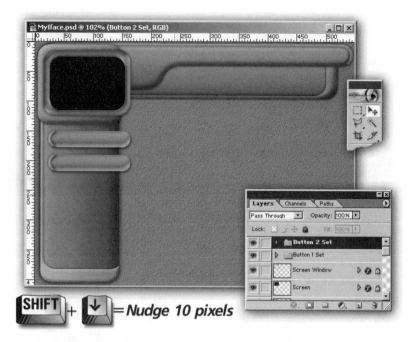

Figure 18.50 Create a layer set for the Button layers and duplicate the set. Then nudge the duplicate set down 40 pixels.

Aren't layer sets great? They enable you to treat a group of layers like one layer. You can nudge, align, and distribute the layer sets—and do just about anything else you can do with a single layer. Now you need only to create and position a few more layer sets, and you're done.

4. Create four more duplicate sets, and name them appropriately. Nudge each duplicate down 40 pixels. When you have six sets of buttons, link them all together, and nudge them up 4 pixels by pressing the up-arrow key (see Figure 18.51). Press Ctrl(⌘)+S to save your document.

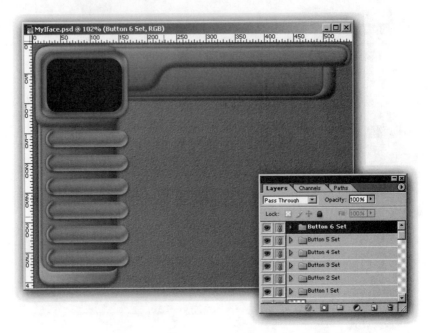

Figure 18.51   Create four more duplicate sets and nudge them into position.

Presto! We have an interface. Add some text and a logo, and you're in business. By the way, the text for the buttons in Figure 18.52 were done quickly using the Pillow Emboss option from a Bevel and Emboss Layer Style (with a Size of 1 px, Soften at 0 px, and the remaining options at their defaults). And if you don't recognize that spiral logo, here's a hint: Gary Bouton provides this little gem as a custom shape on the Companion CD (and it has made its share of appearances in previous chapters). Now that you know the basics, you can build from here. Remember to experiment and have fun as you use Photoshop to create new looks for the web.

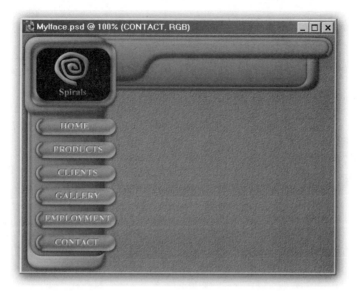

Figure 18.52   You can add text any way you like it and plop in a logo—and you've got a ready-made interface.

Summary

You might have noticed that some of the features covered in this chapter actually create interesting and useful shapes that would be more time-consuming to create in a vector application. Creating imagery in Photoshop from scratch is a lot of fun. Features like layer styles and layer sets add dimension and aid you in positioning pieces easily. Where would we be without Photoshop? I don't even want to think about it.

Chapter 19

Rollovers, Slicing, and Optimization

Photoshop is more than a good program—

it's a *great* program. But even the best pro-

grams have certain limitations. For all its

power and flexibility in graphic design and

creation, one of Photoshop's limitations is *movement*. When it comes to making things move on your web pages—for example, creating effects like rollovers and animations—Photoshop needs a little help. And that's where ImageReady comes in.

Before programs like ImageReady were available, web designers who wanted a highly graphic site with slick rollovers had to hand-code and optimize everything. This process could take 5 to 15 hours or more, depending on the complexity of the project and the designer's attention to detail. With ImageReady, these same tasks can take a fraction of the time. After you are familiar with the process, you could easily slice and optimize a web interface in as little as 20 minutes.

It's important to bear in mind that ImageReady's HTML scripting capabilities are limited. For instance, you cannot use ImageReady to create a dynamic scrollable text field, a pop-up menu, or a dynamically expanding menu.

Here are some of the things you *can* do with ImageReady:

- **Slice up an image and/or interface.** This feature is helpful when you are working with a large image. You can slice the image into a number of pieces, and then reassemble the pieces in an HTML table to download the image faster. (In reality, the download times of the individual pieces may not be "faster," but because they are loading at one time, our brains "fill in the blanks" and grasp what the image is before it completely appears.)

- **Create simple rollovers.** You see rollover effects on nearly every web site. A rollover effect is one in which an object "does something" when the mouse pointer moves over it. For example, an item on a menu may appear highlighted when pointed to; an image might display a tooltip or a caption when the pointer is positioned over it. As your mouse rolls over an object or link, the object somehow changes to show the effect of the mouse.

- **Multi-region rollovers.** A multi-region rollover is a variation of the simple rollover, with the difference being that when your mouse rolls over an object or link, the result is that text or graphics become highlighted or visible on the page (not necessarily in the same location as the position of the mouse). You might use this effect, for example, when you want to show a series of submenu choices when the user points at a menu on the screen. When the user points to the menu, a submenu appears. When the user moves the mouse pointer off the menu, the submenu disappears. It is this cause-and-effect action that takes place on different areas of the screen that make it a "multi-region" rollover.

- **Image maps.** An image map is a graphic that is broken up into clickable areas. For example, you click a portion of a graphic and are taken to a specific page of the web site. Image maps are made by "mapping" the coordinates of an area in the graphic that you want to use as a link.

- **Animations.** This concept should be a fairly familiar one, especially after you read Chapter 20, "Animation." Animations need to convey motion and timing, and are typically generated as .gif files in dynamic HTML, or in Flash file format.

- **Optimize imagery.** Designing for the web is all about balance, and it's often a trade-off between bandwidth and beauty. The skilled web designer walks a fine line between appearance and functionality, and the goal is always to craft good pages that display quickly, which is what optimizing basically does.

Preparing an Interface for ImageReady

Typically, you will begin to work with ImageReady about the time you've finished designing your latest interface masterpiece in Photoshop. By that point, you often have numerous layers, possibly including layer styles, adjustment layers, and so on.

The best strategy for working with ImageReady is to prepare your file while you're still in Photoshop. There are several reasons for this. First, ImageReady's approach to creating animation frames and rollovers is to take a picture of the current visible state of the document. This means that a well thought-out plan for layer management will help make the process in ImageReady much easier and less prone to error.

Be forewarned, however; ImageReady is also a system resource hog. If you are currently running other applications, you might have trouble opening ImageReady when you launch it from Photoshop. For best results, do everything you can do in Photoshop before you switch to ImageReady, but when you're ready to make the switch, close all other programs (including Photoshop) so that ImageReady can run as efficiently as possible.

The examples you'll use in this chapter begin at the point in Photoshop where an interface has been completed and is ready to be sliced, diced, and optimized. The interface featured in the following example is taken from Photoshop Web Foundry—a collection of over 120 customizable interfaces that's available from my company, Eyeland Studio (**www.eyeland.com**).

The starting file on the Companion CD has been reduced to 10 layers but was originally composed of 44 layers (see Figure 19.1). Why so many layers? As you learned in earlier chapters, creating numerous layers gives you the flexibility and freedom you need to make adjustments to your images without affecting things you don't want to affect. For example, you can change the texture of an element. Or, if you have created the different elements on separate layers, adjust the opacity of an element without reducing its depth perception.

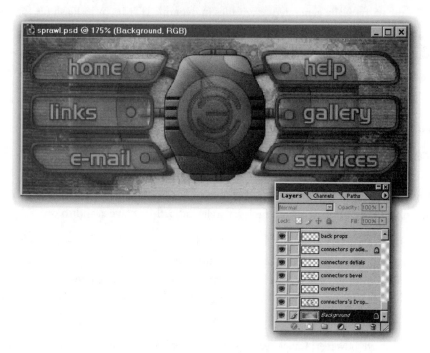

Figure 19.1   An interface with many, many layers.

Creating the Rollover Layers

When we get to ImageReady, we will set it up so that when the pointer rolls over a button, a change will occur in the button and in the center screen area. In other words, two portions of the interface will change when there is a rollover event on a button: the button text will change color and the art for the center screen area will also reflect a change.

The example file is set up so that there are separate layers for the interface in what will be the normal state. The *normal state* is the state of the interface when there is no rollover action being applied. In addition to the normal state layers, there are layers that will be turned on and used as the rollover state. The *rollover state* is a state showing the effect you want the viewer to see when the mouse pointer rolls over the object.

Creating Image Slices

When you slice an image, you typically do it for one of three reasons: to integrate rollovers, to integrate animations, or to optimize the file size of an image by combining .jpeg and .gif images. Images saved in .gif format are usually at their best quality when an image is limited in the amount of colors it contains (256 or less). Graphics saved in .jpeg format look best when the image is more complicated in the range of colors (such as a color photograph, for example). A color photograph might provide a good example for slicing in both formats because it could allow you to isolate parts within the same image. In other words, one section of the photo might contain a lot of colors, which means .jpeg would be your best choice, while another area of the same photo could be saved in the .gif format because it contains only a few colors. Now let's talk about slicing for integrating rollovers and animations.

You use at least two images to implement a rollover. Every time you create a slice for a rollover, you are specifying an area that will have twice the download requirements because two images will be downloaded for that area instead of one.

For the sake of optimization, you want to make the slices as small as possible. The smaller the slice, the less pixel information you need. Logic tells us that two 100×100 images will usually download faster than two 200×200 images. And even though keeping download times short is important, you don't want to make the slices so small that your site's visitors have trouble finding the area of the slice that is used as a clickable link or button. So your goal is to minimize the size of the slices, while still maintaining a usable size for links.

It's important to be as consistent as possible. If you have a series of buttons all with a similar shape and size, you can make your slices all the same size and shape as well. Photoshop's guides are a big help for keeping slices consistent. They also help optimize your time because they make creating slices quite literally a snap.

In the exercises that follow, you will often see the instruction to hold down the Shift key when positioning the guides. Holding down the Shift key positions the guides at the intersection of pixels. If you do not have the Shift key down when you position a guide, the guide could end up in the middle of pixels, as shown in Figure 19.2.

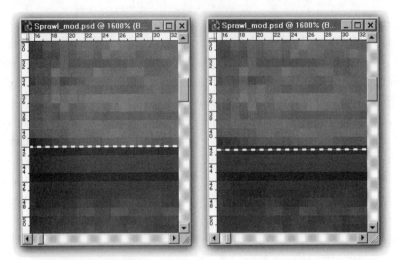

Figure 19.2   The document on the left shows a guide positioned at the intersection of the pixels, but the guide in the document on the right is positioned over the top of the pixels.

The problem with guides being placed in the middle, rather than at the intersection of the pixels, is that this can result in imprecise selections and slices (see Figure 19.3). Selections and slices automatically snap to the intersection of pixels. If you have Snap to Guides turned on as well, you may not be getting the snap you want. A selection or slice will tend to snap to the intersection of pixels that is closest to the guide. So, for best results, hold down the Shift key when placing the guide to avoid any confusion.

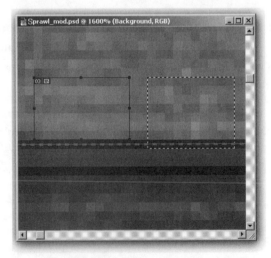

Figure 19.3   The slice on the left snapped to the pixel intersection above the guide. The selection on the right automatically snapped to the intersection of pixels that occurred below the guide.

This may not seem like a very big problem when your image is zoomed out, but it can result in your slices or selections being off by 1 pixel, which can cause a big problem later. If you notice that things don't quite line up when exporting your final interface, this is most likely the problem.

In the file for the following exercise, the buttons are different sizes and shapes. Nevertheless, you can set up the slices so that each button behaves in a similar fashion. Let's get started and see how this works.

Setting the Guides

1. Open the Sprawl_mod.psd file from the Examples/Chap19 folder on the Companion CD. Press Ctrl(⌘)+R to toggle on the rulers. Go to the View menu and make sure the Snap option is checked. If it is not, select it to toggle the Snap option on. You also can use the Ctrl(⌘)+Shift+; key combination to toggle the Snap option on and off (see Figure 19.4).

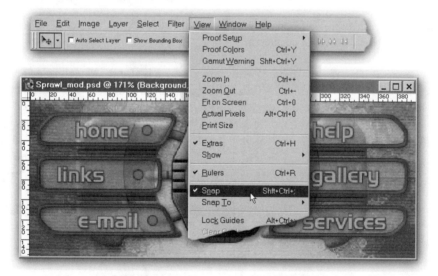

Figure 19.4   To prepare for slicing, enable Rulers and Snap.

2. Press Z to switch to the Zoom tool and click twice over the Home button to zoom in a little. Press V to switch to the Move tool. Press and hold the Shift key while you click inside the horizontal ruler and drag a guide down from the ruler. Position the guide just below the black line (on the inside of the top portion) of the Home button (see Figure 19.5).

Figure 19.5   Place a horizontal guide just below the black outline within the inside top portion of the Home Button.

3. Optional: There's a lot of blue in this image, which is also the default color for the guides. If you would like to change the color of the guides to make them easier to see, press Ctrl(⌘)+K to view the Preferences dialog box. In the Preferences dialog box, choose Guides, Grid & Slices from the top drop-down menu. Change the color for Guides (I used the light gray). While you're there, notice also that the default Line Color for slices is also Light Blue. Try choosing yellow for the Slices Line Color (see Figure 19.6).

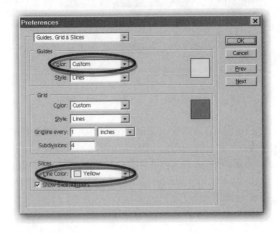

Figure 19.6   Edit Preferences to change the Guides and Slices Line Color options so that the guides will be easier to see.

4. Zoom in close to a button for the placement of your guides. Press and hold the Shift key and drag a guide down from the horizontal ruler. Position the guide just below the black line on the inside of the bottom portion of the Home button. Add four more horizontal guides (two each for the Links and E-mail buttons) by positioning the guides as described in Step 2. Position the guides just below the black line on the inside top of the button and just above the black line on the inside bottom of the button (see Figure 19.7).

Figure 19.7   Position horizontal guides for the rest of the buttons.

When you are finished, double-click the Hand tool to zoom out. Notice that the guides you've positioned for the Home, Links, and E-mail buttons are also perfectly positioned for the Help, Gallery, and Services buttons. Ain't symmetry grand?!

5. Now we need to place two more horizontal guides for the center screen area. Press Z to switch to the Zoom tool and click twice in the center of the interface to zoom in on this area. Now Shift+drag two horizontal guides from the horizontal rulers and place one on the top of the circle and one on the bottom, as shown in Figure 19.8.

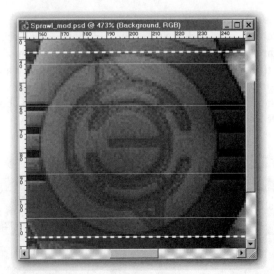

Figure 19.8   Place horizontal guides at the top and bottom of the circle for the center screen.

Now you need to place the vertical guides. Because describing the position for these vertical guides is a bit more difficult, we'll use pixel coordinates here. If your unit of measurement is not already set at pixels, you can change them in this next step.

6. Double-click inside one of the rulers, and the Preferences dialog box appears. The Units & Rulers options should be showing. In the Units section, change Rulers to pixels, as shown in Figure 19.9. Click OK. Now your rulers will show pixels.

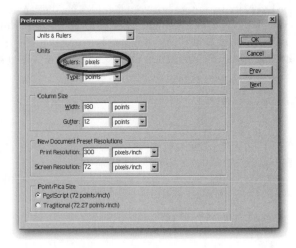

Figure 19.9   Ensure that the units for your rulers are set to pixels.

7. Now you need to position eight vertical guides. To do this, you drag each guide out from the vertical ruler and place it in the correct position, but you'll use an alternative method to simplify the process. Go to the View menu and choose New Guide. In the New Guide dialog box, choose Vertical Orientation and type **11 px** for Position. Click OK. Repeat the View, New Guide command to position the remaining Vertical guides at the pixel coordinates of 133, 147, 160, 239, 252, 266, and 387 (as shown in Figure 19.10).

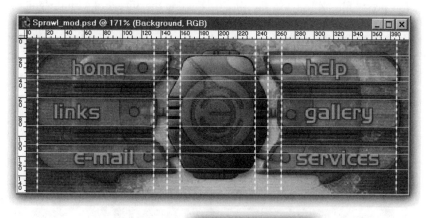

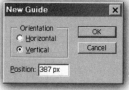

Figure 19.10   Place eight vertical guides using the New Guide command. These guides help isolate the buttons and central screen area.

8. Press Ctrl(⌘)+Shift+S and save this file to your hard drive using the same file name. Keep the file open for the next exercise.

Now that all the guides are set, you're finally ready to slice. You probably can already see how you're going to optimize the slices. You're going to make all the button slices inside the blue bars that help define the button. Then you need to set up the slices for the rest of the buttons in the same way so that when site visitors see how one button works, they will know how all the other buttons work.

Slicing the Interface Buttons

1. Choose the Slice Select tool from the Slice tool flyout menu on the toolbox. At the far right of the Options bar is a toggle switch for Show Auto Slice and Hide Auto Slice. This may seem counterintuitive, but if the button reads Show Auto Slice, the Auto Slice layer is hidden. If it says Hide Auto Slice, the Auto Slice layer is visible. You want the Auto Slice layer to be visible, so click the button if necessary to turn the feature on.

2. Now press Shift+K to select the Slice tool. Using the Slice tool with the guides, draw a slice for the Home button. Start at the intersection of the guides at the upper left of the Home button and end at the intersection of the guides at the lower right of the Home button (see Figure 19.11).

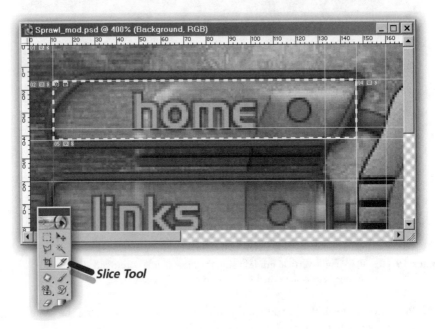

Figure 19.11   Draw a slice over the Home button.

Notice that several slices adjacent to the slice for the Home button are automatically generated. Auto-generated slices have a gray flag in the upper-left corner of the slice. Slices you create have a blue flag. If you switch to the Slice Select tool and try to select one of the auto-generated slices, you will see that you cannot select these slices. You can select only slices you create. You can, however, "promote" an auto-generated slice to a "user slice" by selecting Promote to User Slice from the Options bar (when the Slice Select tool is active or when you right-click (Macintosh: hold Ctrl and click) on the gray slice flags).

3. Right-click (Macintosh: hold Ctrl and click) on the blue flag in the upper-left corner of the slice you just created and choose Edit Slice Options. In the Slice Options dialog box, change the name to Home and enter a URL. Click OK (see Figure 19.12).

You also can get to the Slice Options dialog box from the Options bar when the Slice Select tool is active. Simply click the slice to choose the active slice and then click the Slice Options button on the Options bar. For the purpose of this exercise, enter any URL in the Slice Options dialog box. When preparing images for your own web site, you will want to insert the web site URL for the link that applies to the active slice for this section of the Slice Options dialog box.

Figure 19.12   Change the name of the slice to Home and add a URL.

Note

Slice Option Dialog Box   If you leave the Name field showing the default slice name, the result will be many slices generated with the document file name and some appended nonsense. When you enter your own slice names, you have the benefit of being able to easily identify the slices again later. Photoshop and ImageReady will use those slice names as the filenames. If you leave the URL field blank, nothing will happen when the user clicks the button. The Target field is used when you are working with HTML frames. The rest of the fields are not important unless you want to add Alt tags. The Slice Options dialog box also gives you the option of sizing and positioning the slide numerically, using the fields in the Dimensions section.

4. With the Slice tool still active, create slices for each of the buttons and for the screen area, as shown in Figure 19.13. Right-click (Macintosh: hold Ctrl and click) the flags in the upper-left corner of each slice and choose Edit Slice Options to give the each slice a name that corresponds to the button name and a URL. Name the screen area slice **Screen**. Do not add a URL to the Screen slice, however. The screen area will not be a button and it will not have a rollover event assigned to it.

Notice that the Links and Gallery buttons are not as wide as the rest of the buttons. Do not make the slices for the Links and Gallery buttons as wide as the slices for the other buttons. A file titled sprawl_mod3.psd is provided in the Examples/Chap19 folder on the Companion CD for your reference.

Figure 19.13   Create the remaining slices and use the Slice Options dialog box to change the name for each slice.

5. Press Ctrl(⌘)+S to save your changes and keep the document open for the next exercise.

Wrapping Up in ImageReady

Now you're finally ready to move into ImageReady. Before you launch ImageReady, be sure to save the document (Ctrl(⌘)+S). Because ImageReady and Photoshop use resources heavily (when launched together), it is always wise to save the file so that nothing is lost if resource levels become a problem. All that aside—it's just good practice in general to save your work frequently. Now let's create some rollovers.

Creating Rollovers

Creating a rollover effect is so easy it should be a crime. You use the Rollovers and Layers palettes to create this effect. You simply designate a new rollover state in the Rollovers palette and then turn on the visibility for the layers that produce a rollover effect. It really is that simple. But seeing is believing, so let's rollover into the next exercise to show you how easy it can be.

Creating the First Rollover

1. With the Sprawl_mod.psd document still open (or sprawl_mod3.psd, if you cheated) press Ctrl(⌘)+Shift+M to launch the document in ImageReady. Choose the Slice Select tool from the toolbox. Click the Home button slice to make this the active slice. Click the Slice tab to view the Slice palette. If the palette is not open, go to the Window menu and choose Slice (see Figure 19.14).

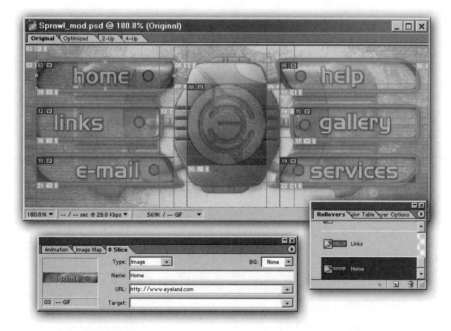

Figure 19.14   Open the interface document in ImageReady and view the Home Slice information using the Slice palette.

Tip

The Slice Info Is Still There   Notice that the slice information you entered in Photoshop appears in ImageReady, just the way you entered it. You also can edit the slice information in ImageReady and see the changes reflected when you jump back to Photoshop.

2. Click the Rollovers tab to view the Rollovers palette (or go to the Window menu and choose Rollovers). Scroll down to the Home slice.

Notice that the names used in the Rollovers palette are those that were set in the Slice Options (previously in Photoshop). Here is another great reason for taking the time to name your slices—the default names would be far less descriptive. Additionally, the thumbnails in the Rollovers palette are usually too small to tell one similarly shaped button from another, so naming the slices really does help.

Note

New Rollover Palette for ImageReady 7.0   If you familiar with ImageReady 3 (shipped with Photoshop 6), you might notice that the Rollovers palette has been over-hauled. In ImageReady 3, you could see only one rollover at a time. In ImageReady 7, you can view all the Rollovers together. This is an especially nice because it makes managing slices much easier and makes it a little harder to mess things up.

3. With the Home slice selected in the Rollovers palette, click the Create rollover state icon at the bottom of the Rollovers palette (next to the trash icon). A new thumbnail named Over State is appended to the Home slice in the Rollovers palette. Click the Over State for the Home slice. Now turn on the visibility for the Home Rollover Button layer in the Layers palette (see Figure 19.15).

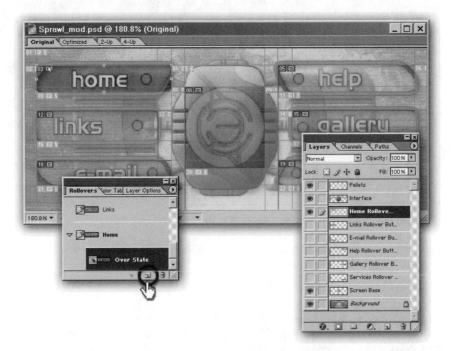

Figure 19.15   Add a rollover state to the Home slice layer and turn on the Home Rollover Button layer visibility.

That's it! You just created a rollover state for the Home button. ImageReady basically reflects on the Over State of a button any changes you make in the Layers palette. In fact, the program does this not just for the Home slice alone, but will also reflect the changes (made to the Layers palette) in any other slices as well. For instance, if you're working on the Over State for the Home slice and make a change to the Screen slice in the Layers palette, both slices will be changed on rollover. That is how you get your multi-slice rollover.

We have a problem, however. Have you noticed it yet? Some of the layer contents (on the Layers palette) are covering the changes you need to make in the screen slice area. We did this on purpose to illustrate how to make edits for situations like this in ImageReady. Let's fix the problem.

Making an Emergency Edit in ImageReady

1. Go to the View menu and choose Show, Slices to temporarily hide the slices. Press Ctrl(⌘)+; to toggle the Snap option off. On the Layers palette, turn off the visibility for all the layers except the Interface layer.

2. Click the Interface layer to make it the active layer. Choose the Polygonal Lasso tool and make a selection around the center object on the Interface layer. (Be careful to include the shadow for the center artwork, but exclude the button bars and their shadows.) The selection should look similar to the one in Figure 19.16. The selection should be close to the left edge of the center object (to avoid the button shadows) and farther away from the right and bottom edge of the center object (to include the shadow for the center object). Press Ctrl(⌘)+J to put this center object selection on its own layer. Double-click the Layer 1 title and rename the layer **Central Platform**. Press Enter (Return) to apply the new name.

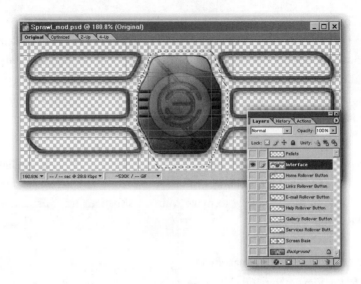

Figure 19.16   Select the central component on the Interface layer. Then Ctrl(⌘)+J will move the selection to a new layer.

3.   Turn off the visibility for the Central Platform layer and click the Interface layer to make this the active layer. Press Ctrl(⌘)+Shift+D to reselect the last selection used. Press Delete (Backspace) to delete the center object from the Interface layer, as shown in Figure 19.17. Press Ctrl(⌘)+D to deselect.

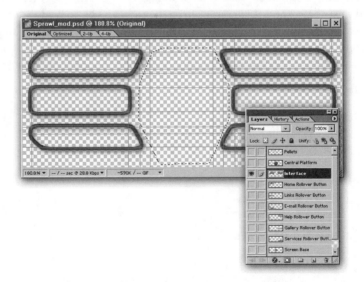

Figure 19.17   Select and delete the center component on the Interface layer.

4. Double-click the Interface title, rename this layer **Button Bars,** and press Enter (Return) to apply the new name. Drag the Central Platform layer below the Screen Base layer. The Over State should still be active on the Rollovers palette (see Figure 19.18). Turn on the visibility for the Background, Central Platform, Screen Base, Home Rollover Button, Button Bars, and Pellets layers (leave the visibility off for all other layers).

The Home state on the Rollovers palette should still have all the same layers visible, with the exception of the Screen Base and Home Rollover Button.

Figure 19.18   Return the visibility to the desired layers for the Home Over State on the Rollovers palette.

The little detour shown in the preceding exercise is unfortunately indicative of how things tend to work when you're doing a real job. No matter how much you prepare in Photoshop, sometimes things crop up. Fortunately, ImageReady can handle most of the basic edits you might need to do.

Now the Over State of the Home button reflects a change both on the Home button itself, and over the screen area. Although you can't see any indication of it in the Over State, you've just implemented a multi-slice rollover. When you export the interface, ImageReady will generate the HTML/JavaScript code so that both the Home slice and the Screen slice will change when someone rolls over the Home button.

Creating the Remaining Rollovers

1. Go to the View menu and choose Show, Slices to toggle the view of the slices back on. Press Ctrl($\mathcal{H}$)+; to toggle the Snap option on again.

2. Click Links in the Rollovers palette to make this the active slice. Click the Create rollover state icon at the bottom of the Rollovers palette. With the Over State thumbnail for the Links slice active on the Rollovers palette, turn on the visibility for the Links Rollover Button and Screen Base layer (see Figure 19.19).

Now you've created the rollover for the Links button. Notice that when you went from the Over State for the Home slice to the Links slice in the Rollovers palette, the layers changed. ImageReady automatically reverts the visibility of the layers according to how they are set for each slice or Over State. This makes it very easy for you to check your work. You can go back through the Over State for each slice and make sure that you have set up each Over State correctly.

Figure 19.19   Add a rollover state to the Links slice and turn on the visibility of the Links Rollover Button and Screen Base layers.

3. Repeat Step 2 for all of the remaining button slices. Click the slice title in the Rollovers palette, add an Over State, and then turn on the visibility of the Screen Base layer and the Rollover Button layer that corresponds to the slice title. For example, to create the Over State for the E-mail slice, click the E-mail slice in the Rollovers palette. Click the Create rollover state icon at the bottom of the Rollovers palette. With the Over State thumbnail active for the E-mail slice, turn on the visibility for the E-mail Rollover Button and Screen Base layers.

When you are finished, each of the slices that correspond to the six buttons should have Over State assigned to them in the Rollovers palette. This process should be very simple. It's here where all the work in preparing a file pays off. It is not necessary to wade through a bunch of layers to create the rollovers. Our layers are clearly named and easy to track so you can identify the layers to turn on very easily.

Before we move ahead and export the interface, let's take a quick look at optimizing the file sizes of the slices so that they will all download faster.

Optimizing Files

In the next exercise, you learn about some of the optimizing options available to you in ImageReady. If you click an image slice and then click the Optimized tab near the top of the document window, the status bar at the bottom of the window displays information about the file and the image slice. The status bar information provided is as follows (see Figure 19.20 for callouts of this area):

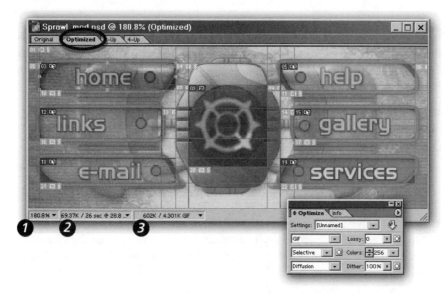

Figure 19.20   The status bar provides information about the file and the current slice.

- The first section on the left is merely the current Zoom level for the document (marked as item 1 in the figure).

- The second section tells you ImageReady's best guess as to what the total file size will be for all of the images in this interface when the image is exported (and the slices and rollovers are generated). Notice that ImageReady estimates that this file will be 69.37K with the current image settings (item 2). Furthermore, it tells you approximately how long it will take for these images to download for a target connection rate. ImageReady uses 28.8Kbps as the default setting (for the average connection rate), but these days 56.6Kbps is probably a more accurate average.

- The third section, over to the right, is another Image Information box that provides information about the selected image slice. The first number is an approximation of the overall *unoptimized* file size. The second number is the *optimized* file size. You should pay attention to this number when you change the image setting for the slices. Notice in Figure 19.20 that the Home button's slice size is 4.301K when it is set to .gif format.

Reducing File Sizes

1. Click the Optimize tab to view the Optimize palette (or go to the Windows menu and choose Optimize). Choose the Slice Select tool from the toolbox and click the Home slice. Click the Optimized tab near the top of the document window (refer to Figure 19.20).

When a slice is selected, the Optimize palette shows you the image settings for that slice. In this case, the image setting defaulted to .gif format. This format is great for solid colors; but for more photographic images or images like the example interface, .jpeg compresses much better.

Before you change the image settings for the Home slice to .jpeg, let's determine whether switching to .jpeg will make a difference.

2. Use the information in the status bar to help you make the choice (refer to Figure 19.20). With the Home slice still selected, change the image settings from GIF to JPEG in the Optimize palette and compare the file sizes. You can see that ImageReady's default JPEG settings are excellent, so you can leave those settings at their default options.

3. Now look at the far right Image Information box and notice that the slice's size dropped from 4.301K to only 1.895K. Changing the image to JPEG cuts the files down to less than half their earlier size.

4. On your own, click the remaining slices and change the GIF option for each one to JPEG in the Optimize palette. Using the Slice Select tool, click one of the auto-generated slices and change it from GIF to JPEG. ImageReady will automatically convert all of the other auto-generated slices to JPEG.

5. When you are done, look at the middle Image Information box. Notice that ImageReady now estimates the final total file size at 31.95K—this is a savings of over 50% from the original estimate of 69.37K. As you can see, optimizing images for download over the Internet is extremely easy in ImageReady.

If you have a target size that you need to hit (let's say, for example, a client tells you the overall download needs to be under 50K), just adjust the image settings for the images and monitor the Image Information boxes until you get to the size you need. When you've achieved the desired size, you're done. There is a little problem with this that you need to keep in mind, however. In these figures, ImageReady actually fails to account for the rollover images. What you are actually getting is information on only the default states of all the slices. The only way to accurately determine the overall download requirements for the page is to export the interface and check the results yourself.

Now all that is left for you to do is export the interface and test it out.

Exporting the Interface

1. Go to the File menu, choose Save Optimized As, and save the Interface to your hard drive. You will see a progress bar as ImageReady goes through and processes the files (which includes generating the HTML and Javascript code). Everything is saved to your hard drive.

2. When ImageReady is done, find and open the HTML file that was generated so that you can preview the interface in a browser. Rollover the buttons and see how they work. Every time you rollover a button, the title should change color and you should see the central screen area reflect a change.

3. You can preview the code in your current browser by going to the View menu and choosing Source. You can also press Ctrl(⌘)+Alt(Opt)+P from inside ImageReady to preview the code in a browser. When you do this, ImageReady shows you both the interface and the HTML/Javascript code (see Figure 19.21).

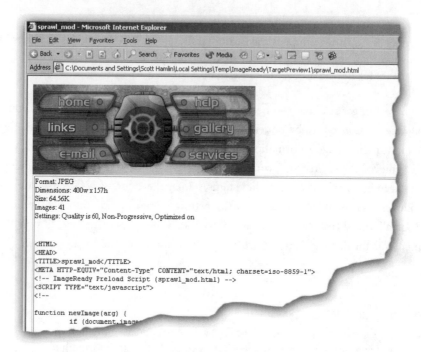

Figure 19.21   Using the Preview in a default browser shows the interface and the HTML/Javascript code.

Summary

As you've seen in this chapter, good preparation in Photoshop makes working in ImageReady almost an afterthought. ImageReady is capable of doing a lot of what Photoshop can do; but when you are working in ImageReady, you want to focus on what it does best—rollovers, animations, image maps, and so on. Take the time to set things up correctly in Photoshop because Photoshop offers a more robust feature set for the actual designing aspect of your graphics. After you set things up, you can focus on creating rollovers and optimizing image slices, export the results, and then easily be done with the ImageReady side of preparing files for the web.

Chapter 20

Animation

To those who see Photoshop as a tool for editing static images, using Photoshop to create animation might seem like using a backhoe to flip a pancake. When used in tandem with ImageReady, however,

Photoshop is actually an excellent tool for creating short animations for the web. In this chapter, you'll get first-hand experience in making three different kinds of exciting, dramatic GIF animations for a web site. For each animation, you will use Photoshop to create the graphics that compose the animation and then switch over to ImageReady to assemble the images into a compact, eye-catching file.

Also in this chapter, you'll have the opportunity to learn how to make text dissolve before your very eyes. Then you'll move on to using Photoshop's largely overlooked displacement mapping capability to create a sequence of images for use in a GIF animation. You'll finish out the chapter by learning how to animate seamless tiling textures to create the effect of fog drifting by a porthole window.

But before we get into creating a specific animation, let's take a look at a list of dos and don'ts for creating web animation.

Animation Guidelines

When approaching an animation project, keep these guidelines in mind:

- **Minimize the dimensions of the animation by animating only what you have to.** Don't try to animate the whole screen. Several small animations on a page work much better than one huge, undownloadable-in-your-lifetime animation.

- **Limit the number of colors you use.** Just as with non-animated GIFs, the fewer colors you use, the smaller the file size.

As you work your way through the chapter, you will see how to put these guidelines into use.

Creating Animated Dissolving Text

In movies and on TV, the dissolve is one of the classic visual special effects used to get your attention or to signal a change of scene. In a dissolve, the image simultaneously breaks up into small pieces and fades. Dissolves are effectively used in all kinds of multimedia, web, and video projects.

The fundamental concepts and processes that go into making dissolve animation are universal—only the details differ from project to project and medium to medium. After you've had a chance to get your feet wet creating the GIF animation we've cued up for you, you'll be able to approach with confidence almost any animation project that involves something melting away into nothingness.

Remember that this is a *learning* experience. Do not adjust your dial, and read on to the first exercise.

Preparing Channels and Layers for Animation

As you get more experience creating web animations, you'll realize that there is a lot of preparation involved. This section walks you through the process of creating the channels and layers you'll need to get the animation effects you want.

Tip

Planning Is the Key to Creating Fast Loading or Downloading Animations
Whenever you are working with animation, web animation in particular, keeping an animation's finished file size as small as possible is of paramount importance. Large animations download slowly, play jerkily, and annoy viewers so much that they will probably start muttering unkind things while they impatiently click the Stop button—or a link to any other site they can find.

Beginning a Dissolve-Type Animation

1. Open the Dissolve.psd image from the Examples/Chap20 folder on the Companion CD, and save it to your hard disk using the same name and file type. Double-click the Hand tool to maximize the view of the file in Photoshop.

   If you right-click (Macintosh: hold Ctrl and click) on the title bar and choose Image Size, you'll notice that the image is 190 by 56 pixels by 72 pixels per inch in resolution. We've purposely kept the dimensions small to ensure that the finished animation will download quickly. Click Cancel to close the Image Size dialog box.

   A quick look at the Layers palette shows two layers—the Background layer and a layer named Window. The Background layer contains a texture with a gray rectangular shape in the middle. The space occupied by the Background layer will contain an animation of dissolving text that you will create. The dissolving text animation will be framed by the static Window artwork on the Window layer.

2. First, you need to create channels for the different stages of the dissolve effect. Click on the Channels tab to open the Channels palette. Notice that in addition to the Red, Green, and Blue channels, there's already a channel called Alpha 1, which you will use a little later. Alt(Opt) and click the Create a new channel button at the bottom of the Channels palette. Name the channel **Base** in the New Channel dialog box, and then press Enter (Return) to create the new channel (see Figure 20.1).

   In the New Channel dialog box, two options are listed in the Color Indicates portion—Selected Areas and Masked Areas. The resulting new channel will either appear all white or all black, depending on which of these options is chosen. You will be selecting a different color to fill the channel in the next step. Do not be concerned about which option is selected or if your new channel does not look exactly like the one shown in Figure 20.1.

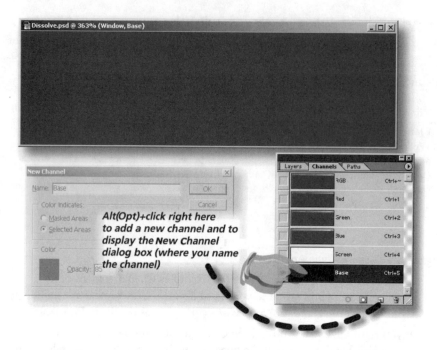

Figure 20.1   Add a channel called "Base" to the Dissolve image.

3. From your view of the Base channel in the image window, go to the Edit menu and choose Fill. In the Fill dialog box select 50% Gray from the Use pop-up menu, and click OK to fill the channel with a neutral gray. Go to the Filter menu and choose Noise, then Add Noise with an Amount of 100%, select a Gaussian Distribution, and be sure Monochromatic is checked (see Figure 20.2). This noisy pattern will serve as the basis for the dissolve effect.

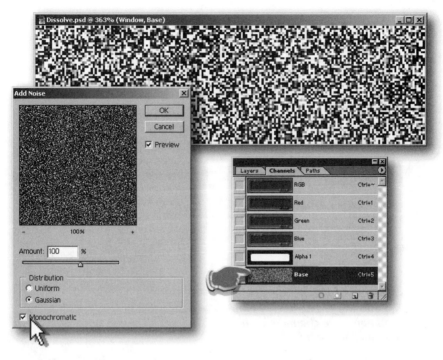

Figure 20.2   Add noise to the Base channel. This is the basis for the dissolve effect.

Now the objective is to create six masks that we will use to generate the dissolve effect. Of course you can create as many or as few masks as you want, but six is adequate to show the dissolve effect without inordinately adding to the saved file size.

4. Make a copy of the Base channel by dragging it to the Create a new channel icon in the Channels palette while holding the Alt(Opt) key. In the New Channel dialog box, name the channel **Phase 1** and then click OK. Make five more copies of the Base channel by pressing Alt(Opt) and dragging them to the Create new channel icon at the lower right of the Channels palette. Name the new channels **Phase 2** through **Phase 6**. When you're finished, you should have six phase channels (see Figure 20.3). Note that it is very important that the channels for each phase come from the same Base channel. If you apply the Add Noise filter to each channel separately, the dissolve effect will not work.

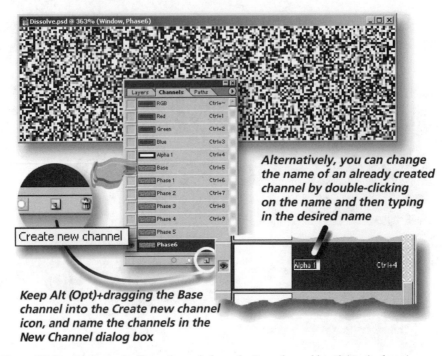

Figure 20.3   Create six duplicate channels from the Base channel by Alt(Opt)+dragging the Base channel into the Create new channel icon on the Channels palette.

5. Click on the Phase 1 channel. Now open the Threshold command (Image, Adjustments, Threshold). Change the Threshold Level to 36, and click OK to apply the setting to the Phase1 channel. Repeat this process for the channels Phase 2 through Phase 6, applying Threshold levels of 72, 108, 145, 181, and 218, respectively. At this point, you should have seven new channels: the Base channel and six channels named Phase 1 through 6. The Phase 1 through Phase 4 channels should look similar to the channels shown in Figure 20.4. As you can see, each channel has a different random distribution of black pixels.

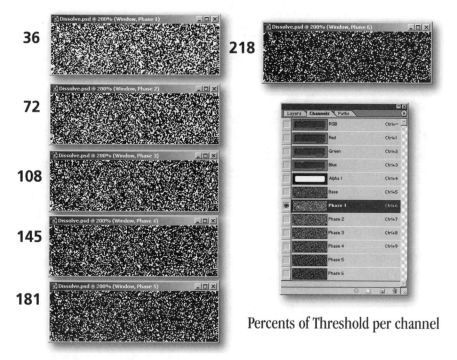

Percents of Threshold per channel

Figure 20.4 The distribution and frequency of black pixels in each channel changes as the value of the Threshold command is increased for each successive channel.

6. Now open the Layers palette. Click the Background layer to make it the active layer. Choose the Type tool from the toolbox. Click in the document and type **PHOTOSHOP** in big bold letters (20-point Arial Black was used for the example). Use all caps so everyone can see the effect better. If you can't see all of the text, hold down the Ctrl(⌘) key to toggle to the Move tool and center the text. When finished typing, press Ctrl(⌘)+Enter (Return) to commit the text to a layer. If needed, press V to choose the Move tool, and move the text roughly over the center of the screen so that no part of the text goes off the edge of the visible area of the document window. In the Layers palette, right-click (Macintosh: hold Ctrl and click) the layer with the text, and choose Rasterize Layer from the context menu (see Figure 20.5).

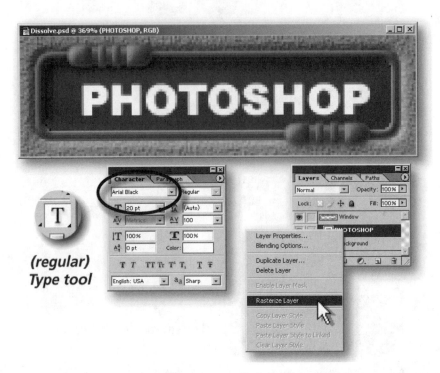

Figure 20.5   Create the text and then convert it to pixels using the Rasterize Layer command.

7. Now press Ctrl(⌘)+A to select all, press Ctrl(⌘)+X to cut, and then press Ctrl(⌘)+V to paste. These editing moves center the rasterized text on the layer. Don't worry about the layer's name for now; you name the layer in the next step.

8. Click the Background layer, and then press Ctrl(⌘)+Shift+N to create a new layer. Change the Name in the New Layer dialog box to **Phase 1** and click OK. Now press Ctrl(⌘)+Alt(Opt)+4 to load the Alpha 1 channel as a selection. Click the Foreground Color selection box (on the toolbox) to open the color picker box, and change the Foreground color to R:60, G:60, B:140. Click OK. Now press Alt(Opt)+Delete (Backspace) to fill the selection with the foreground color (see Figure 20.6). Press Ctrl(⌘)+D to deselect. Now click the PHOTOSHOP (text) layer title on the Layers palette and press Ctrl(⌘)+E to Merge Down (the chosen layer) to the Phase 1 layer.

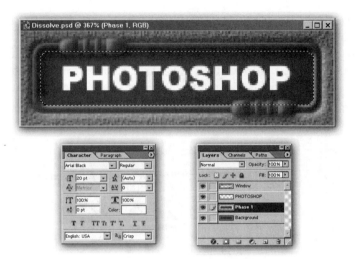

Figure 20.6   Fill the selection marquee with the color you specified in the color picker.

9. Alt(Opt)+drag the Phase 1 layer to the Create a new layer icon in the Layers palette. This makes a duplicate layer and displays the New Layer dialog box. Name the duplicate **Phase 2** and click OK. Repeat this process four more times, naming the duplicates **Phase 3**, **Phase 4**, **Phase 5**, **Phase 6,** and **Phase 7**. When you are done, the Phase 7 layer should appear above the Phase 6 layer, which in turn, should be above the Phase 5 layer, and so on (see Figure 20.7).

Figure 20.7   When you finish creating the duplicates, you should have layers through Phase 7.

10. Return to the Channels palette. Delete the Alpha 1 channel and the Base channel. Deleting these two channels allows you to use keyboard shortcuts to load all the Phase channels as selections. Go back to the Layers palette and click the Phase 1 layer title. Press Ctrl(⌘)+Alt(Opt)+4 to load the Phase 1 channel as a selection for the Phase 1 layer (see Figure 20.8). Press the Delete (Backspace) key. Press Ctrl(⌘)+D to deselect (turn off the visibility for the Phase 2 through Phase 7 layers if you would like to view the results.

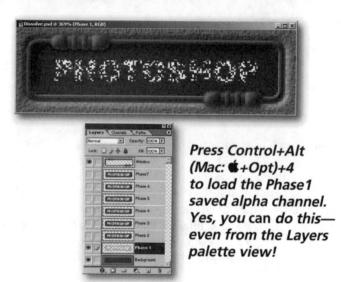

Press Control+Alt (Mac: ⌘+Opt)+4 to load the Phase1 saved alpha channel. Yes, you can do this— even from the Layers palette view!

Figure 20.8 Load a channel without even seeing it on the Channels palette by using the keyboard shortcut.

11. Click the Phase 2 layer. Press Ctrl(⌘)+Alt(Opt)+5 to load the Phase 2 channel for the Phase 2 layer. Press Delete (Backspace). Continue by choosing the Phase 3 layer and loading the Phase 3 channel by pressing Ctrl(⌘)+Alt+6. Repeat this process for each of the Phase layers so that when you get to the Phase 6 layer you will be pressing Ctrl(⌘)+Alt(Opt)+9 to load the Phase 6 channel (see Figure 20.9). Each time, delete the contents within the selection. Notice that you don't have to deselect each time you move on to the next layer—this is a new Photoshop nicety. The new selection *replaces* the previous selection. Now you have everything you need to create the animation. The next step moves you to ImageReady.

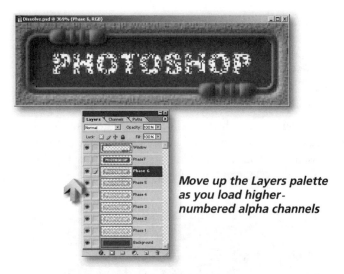

Move up the Layers palette as you load higher-numbered alpha channels

Figure 20.9   Work your way up through the layers—and the saved selections—to delete different parts of each layer.

12. Press Ctrl(⌘)+S to save. Now press Ctrl(⌘)+Shift+M to open ImageReady 7. The Photoshop file you were working on is automatically brought into ImageReady. Now all you need to create the animation is the Animation palette and the Layers palette. Close all other palettes. If the Animation and/or Layers palettes aren't visible, choose them from the Windows menu, or press F7 to reveal the Layers palette and F11 to display the Animation palette (see Figure 20.10). On the Layers palette, turn the visibility off for all of the Phase layers by clicking their eye icons.

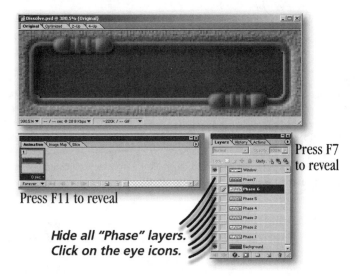

Press F7 to reveal

Press F11 to reveal

Hide all "Phase" layers. Click on the eye icons.

Figure 20.10   Hide the layers by clicking the eye icons.

13. The first frame, which automatically appears on the Animation palette, should show the Background layer and the Window layer. Click the Duplicates current frame icon at the bottom of the Animation palette (it looks like a page icon). This duplicates the selected frame of animation. Now turn on the visibility of the Phase 1 layer. Notice that the second frame on the Animation palette now reflects the change you made on the Layers palette.

The key to understanding the ImageReady Animation palette is to know that the currently selected frame displays the current state of the document window. In other words, the contents of the visible layers are reflected in the current frame of the animation, as pointed out in Figure 20.11.

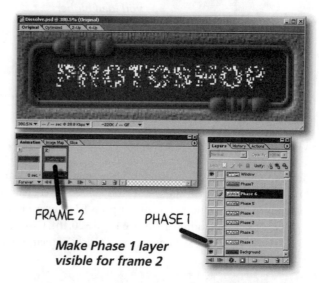

FRAME 2   PHASE 1

Make Phase 1 layer visible for frame 2

Figure 20.11   The top visible layer is shown in the current frame on the Animation palette.

Warning

Avoiding ImageReady Messes   It's easy to inadvertently mess up your animation in ImageReady. If you are not careful, you can select and change the wrong frame in the Animation palette. For that reason, it's best to have your layers well organized and clearly named before you get to the animation stage. The more tinkering you have to do, the more likely it is that you will accidentally mess things up. Corrections are easy to make unless you delete layers you need, but animation is time-consuming enough as it is—so make it easy on yourself and get organized.

14. Make sure the second frame is selected and click the Duplicates current frame icon on the Animation palette to duplicate the selected frame. Then, with the third frame on the Animation palette highlighted, turn on the visibility of the Phase 2 layer. You do not need to bother with the Phase 1 layer because the content of the Phase 2 layer covers the content of the Phase 1 layer.

15. Repeat this process until you have eight frames in your animation. On the eighth frame, the Phase 7 layer should be visible.

Each time you create a new animation segment during this process, you need to select the last frame you created when adding a new frame from the Layers palette. This means, for example, that to generate the next frame, you would choose frame 3, click the Duplicates current frame icon (the button with the Page icon on it) at the bottom of the Animation palette to duplicate the frame, and then make the Phase 3 layer visible. You then would continue on to create frame 4, and so on (see Figure 20.12).

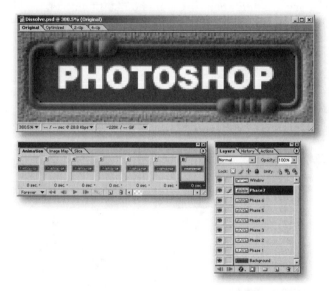

Figure 20.12   The animation at this point includes eight frames and eight configurations of what is visible on the Layers palette.

Now you're finished with the first part of this process. Take a breather, get a cold beverage from the icebox, and then come on back to complete the animation!

Round and Round We Go: Creating Loops

To create an animation that loops—that begins again at the ending point—we must now add the frames currently on the Animation palette to the palette in reverse order. It's sort of like inflating and deflating a balloon. And there should be no surprises for you, because we're only reverse-ordering and adding to the palette in the same way you built the beginning half of the animation.

Let's get to it!

Reversing the Dissolve Effect

1. Choose frame 8 on the Animation palette, and click the Duplicates current frame icon at the bottom of the Animation palette to duplicate the frame. Click the eye icon to toggle the visibility off for the Phase 7 layer. As you can see, we're not reversing the process yet—this is a pause in the animation. You're now going to make the phase layers invisible sequentially as you add frames to the animation.

2. Make each successive Phase layer invisible as you add frames, as shown in Figure 20.13. For example, create the next frame by clicking frame 9 and clicking the Duplicates current frame. Then turn the visibility for the Phase 6 layer off. Continue doing this until you arrive at frame 14. At frame 14, the Phase 1 layer should still be visible. You won't create a frame 15 because the animation will loop back to frame 1 after frame 14.

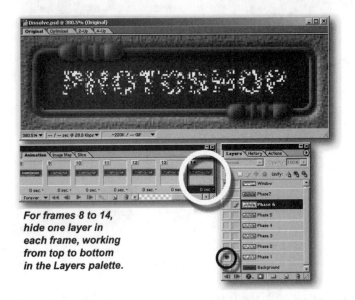

For frames 8 to 14, hide one layer in each frame, working from top to bottom in the Layers palette.

Figure 20.13   To make a looping animation, have the last frame make a transition to the first frame.

3. Now choose frame 8 on the Animation palette, click the Selects frame delay time arrow (the tiny arrow just below the thumbnail), and choose Other from the pop-up menu. Enter the number **3** in the Set Frame Delay dialog box, as shown in Figure 20.14, and click OK. You've just set the frame delay for frame 8 to 3 seconds. Therefore, when the animation gets to frame 8, it will display for 3 seconds before moving on. Choose frame 1, and change its Frame Delay to **3** seconds, too.

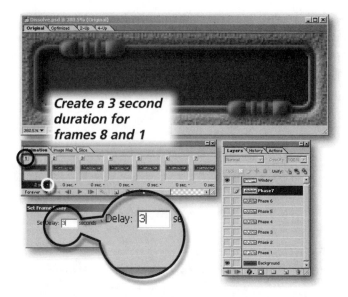

Figure 20.14 Create short pauses in the animation by increasing the display length for frame 1 and frame 8 to 3 seconds.

4. You're finally ready to export the animation. Choose Save Optimized As from the File menu. Name the animation and save it to your hard disk. View the animation with a browser or any utility you have that can preview GIF animations.

When you play the animation, it should pause on the first frame for a few seconds. Then the word *PHOTOSHOP* should appear gradually over a blue background. Next the animation should pause for a few seconds while the word is fully visible. Finally, the text and blue background should dissolve out of view and loop back to start all over again.

It's worth noting that ImageReady does an excellent job of optimizing this animation. You might expect this animation to have a large file size. The GIF format uses a compression scheme that works best when there are contiguous strings of pixels with the same color. With the dissolve effect, the pixels aren't scattered all over the frame; instead, many pixels remain static from one frame to the succeeding frame, which makes compression easier and results in more manageable file sizes.

ImageReady employs interframe transparency optimization on the frames. Basically, only the pixels that have changed from one frame to the next are visible on each frame. The rest of the pixels are turned invisible. This allows the GIF format to compress the animation to just under 15Kb.

You might see this using a GIF animation utility, such as GIF Movie Gear (**www.gamani.com**). In Figure 20.15, most of the frames are almost entirely gray (which is the color for transparency in GIF Movie Gear). Only the pixels that have changed from the previous frame are visible. ImageReady makes all the other pixels on that frame invisible automatically.

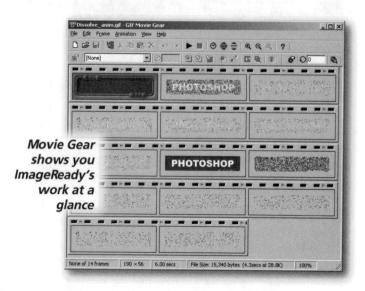

Movie Gear shows you ImageReady's work at a glance

Figure 20.15   ImageReady compresses an animation file so that pixels that appear onscreen more than once appear in the file *only* once.

The key to the dissolve animation is the Threshold filter. You created a base noisy texture, and then used Threshold to set high contrast at six points along the grayscale from 1 to 255 (Threshold goes from 1 to 255, not 0 to 255 like the Levels command does). Essentially, you leveraged the unique characteristics of the Threshold filter after the results of the Noise filter to create an animation effect. There are many such vertical (unique, seldom fully used) commands in Photoshop—you simply need a book like this one to point them out! Ready for another example? In the following section, the Displace filter is used in a novel way to create a fun animation.

Creating a Bulging Pipe Animation

Most of us who have ever watched a cartoon have seen Popeye or some other totally malleable character move through a pipe—the funny part being that metal pipes usually don't give way and take on a bulge for sailors real or imagined.

Because a cartoon is a form of animation, there's no reason a bulging pipe cannot be a GIF animation. You just have to know a little about displacement mapping to displace the ordinarily unyielding form of a pipe.

Using Displacement Maps for Special Animations

In the steps coming up, you'll use a file from the Companion CD and learn how to make the Displace command come to life, although we admit that it's a command that gathers dust in most Photoshop books. You simply need to see the results to get hooked. Check out Figure 20.16. The comedy mask is bent, according to the tones in a displacement map.

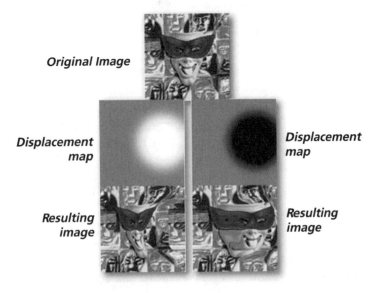

Figure 20.16   Now *this* is a funny picture of a comedy mask!

The top image is an original, undistorted version. Each copy of the image at the bottom has been distorted, using the displacement maps above them. In both examples, the Displace filter was set to Horizontal 70% and Vertical 0%. Because the example on the left used the displacement map with white that gradiates into medium gray, the image was displaced to the left. Conversely, the example on the right moves from black to gray, so the image is distorted to the right. Had the Displace filter been set to Horizontal 0% and Vertical 70%, the image that used the white to gray displacement map (on the left) would have been distorted upward and the image that used the black to gray displacement map (on the right) would have been distorted downward.

Digging into the Whys and Wherefores of Displace

Any non-layered Photoshop file can be used as a displacement map, which means that anything that is flattened and has the *.psd tag is fair game for displacing another, different image. The key to using the Displace filter is to understand how it uses displacement maps. A *displacement map* is an image that controls the way a selection is distorted. The Displace command works according to the brightness values in displacement maps, as you saw a small example of in Figure 20.16. A value of white (255) corresponds to the maximum positive displacement which translates to up vertically and/or left horizontally. A value of black (0, zero) corresponds to the maximum negative displacement, which translates to down vertically and/or to right horizontally.

This means that brightness values of 129 and higher result in displacement up and/or to the left, and brightness values of 127 or less result in displacement down and/or to the right. Values that are 128 result in no displacement. Because displacement maps use only brightness information, it's a good idea to create them in RGB mode using black, white, and grayscale tones. Keeping the image in RGB mode is also a good idea, because many of Photoshop's filters don't work in Grayscale mode. Because judging how colored images will convert to grayscale is a difficult task, it's usually best to work with grayscale colors.

The Displace filter allows you either to stretch a displacement map to fit your image or tile it to fit. If you use a displacement map that is the same size as the image, which is your best choice, it renders either of the options inconsequential.

So if you're ready to have some fun and create something entertaining for others, without further adieu, here's how to begin the bulging pipe effect:

Getting Started Using the Displace Command

1. Open the Bulgepipe.psd image from the Examples/Chap20 folder on the Companion CD, and save it to your hard disk using the same name and file type. Notice that this file has three layers.

   The top layer is called Top Pipe Drop Shadow. Beneath the Top Pipe Drop Shadow layer is a layer named Pipe, and then you'll find the Background layer. You will be creating an animation by distorting the visual contents of the Pipe layer.

First you need to make a displacement map to use with the Displace filter. The image we'll use for this example file is 180 pixels square. You can view this information if you right-click (Macintosh: hold Ctrl and click) the title bar of the Bulgepipe.psd file and choose Image Size.

2. Open a new document and make it a 180-pixel square RGB document (72 ppi). Select Fill from the Edit menu and choose 50% Gray from the Use flyout menu. Save this file as a Photoshop (PSD) file and call it **Bulgedmap.psd**.

3. Now we need to do a little setup. Press Ctrl(⌘)+R to toggle on the rulers. Make sure the Snap option is on in the View menu (a checkmark will appear next to this option if it is turned on). If it is not on, select it or press Ctrl(⌘)+Shift+; (semi-colon) to toggle it on. Finally, double-click either ruler to display the Units & Rulers preferences. Change the Rulers units to pixels, as shown in Figure 20.17.

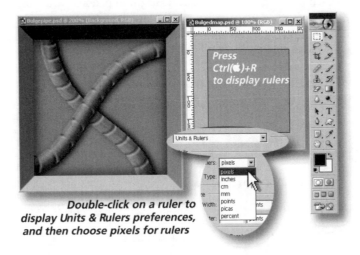

Figure 20.17 Choose pixels as the unit of measurement for Photoshop's rulers.

4. Press Ctrl(⌘)+Shift+N to open the New Layer dialog box. Name the layer **White** and click OK. Drag a vertical guide from the vertical ruler and position the guide at 90 pixels. Next, drag a horizontal guide from the horizontal rulers down to 90 pixels. On the Layers palette, click on the eye icon to the far left of the Background layer to toggle the visibility off for this layer. In the next step, you're going to make a selection and it's often hard to see the crosshair icon for the Marquee tool over 50% gray. Save the file and name it **DispMapBase.psd**. Keep Photoshop open.

Creating Displacement Map Visual Content

It's now time to apply brightness values to the current image. Watch (um, and partici-pate!) how easy this is to accomplish now that the guides are at your command…

Toning the Displacement Map

1. Choose the Elliptical Marquee tool from the marquee flyout on the toolbox. Make sure your Info palette is visible. If not, click the Info tab or go to the Window menu, and choose Info. Use the intersection of the guides as a starting point; place the cursor crosshair on this intersection. Hold down the Shift+Alt keys (to make the circular selection drag outward from the center point), and drag a circular selection. Make the circle selection approximately 130 pixels in diameter. You can see this information in the lower-right corner of your Info palette, which will display the Width and Height in pixels as you drag. The measurement does not have to be exact, but the circular selection should not be so large that it fills the entire document. Turn on the visibility of the Background layer, as you see in Figure 20.18.

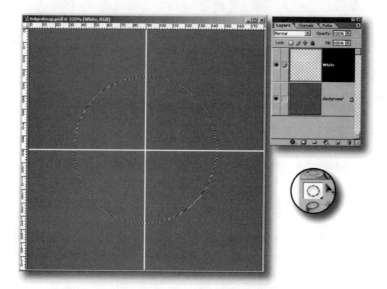

Figure 20.18   Create a circle selection in the middle of the image window, about 130 to 150 pixels across.

2. Choose Feather from the Select menu, or right-click (Macintosh: hold Ctrl and click), and choose the Feather command from the context menu. Change the Feather amount to 10 pixels, and click OK to apply the feathering, which softens the edges of the image area. Press D (default colors). Press Ctrl(⌘)+Delete (Backspace) to fill the selection with white as the background color. Press Ctrl(⌘)+D to deselect. On the Layers palette, Alt(Opt)+drag the White layer to the Create a new layer icon, and name the new layer **Black**. Press Ctrl(⌘)+I to Invert the non-transparent areas on the Black layer. At this point you should have three layers in your document: the Background layer filled with solid gray, the White layer, and the Black layer, as shown in Figure 20.19.

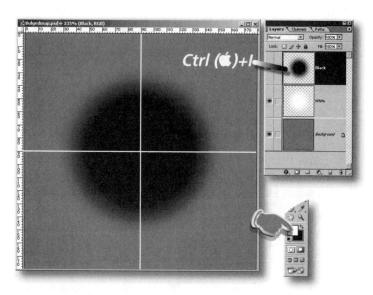

Figure 20.19   Choose the Invert (not Inverse) command to reverse the tonal chroma
of the non-transparent contents of the Black layer.

3. Select the Black layer. Now choose the Move tool and drag the black fluffy ball to
   the bottom right so that only the upper-left quarter of it is visible (the rest is cut
   off by the edges of the document). Optional: You can hold down the Shift key as
   you drag to constrain movement to a perfect 45° angle. Choose the White layer,
   and drag to the bottom left so that the upper-right quarter of the ball is visible
   (see Figure 20.20). Press Ctrl(⌘)+A to Select All, go to the Edit menu, and
   choose Copy Merged. Press Ctrl(⌘)+D to deselect. Press Ctrl(⌘)+N to open a
   new document, and click OK to accept the default options in the dialog box.
   (Photoshop senses the size and other attributes of the image information on the
   clipboard and should have this size information automatically in the New
   Document dialog box.) Press Ctrl(⌘)+V to paste the image in the document.
   Press Ctrl(⌘)+E to Merge Down—a good shortcut to remember. Save this file as
   a Photoshop (PSD) file, and call it **dismapfile1.psd**.

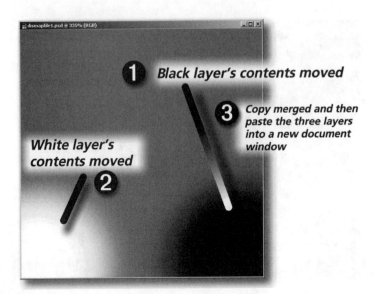

Figure 20.20   Make a flat copy of your work so far. Guess what this file will be used for.

Now you have created the first of a series of displacement maps for the animation. For the rest of the displacement maps, you'll move the White and Black layers in the DispMapBase.psd file progressively upward.

4. Click the title bar of the DispMapBase.psd document to make it the current editing document in the workspace. On the Layers palette, click the Black layer title. Now link the White layer to the Black layer by clicking in the link column to the left of the White layer. With the Move tool still active, hold down the Shift key and press the up arrow on your keyboard five times. Release the Shift key and then press the down arrow five times. This action nudges the White and Black layers up 10 pixels—five different times (holding Shift nudges by increments of 10), minus five pixels (the single strokes without holding Shift)—for a total move of 45 pixels. Press Ctrl(⌘)+A to Select All. Press Ctrl(⌘)+Shift+C to Copy Merged. Press Ctrl(⌘)+D to deselect. Press Ctrl(⌘)+N to open a new document, and click OK to accept the default size (the size will document to the size of the image on the clipboard). Press Ctrl(⌘)+V. Press Ctrl(⌘)+E to merge. Save this file as a Photoshop (PSD) file and call it **dismapfile2.psd**.

5. Repeat this process three more times, naming the files **dismapfile3.psd**, **dismapfile4.psd**, and **dismapfile5.psd**. Now you have all the displacement maps you need to create the animation. Check out Figure 20.21. You can close these displacement files at this point, but leave the Bulgepipe.psd file open.

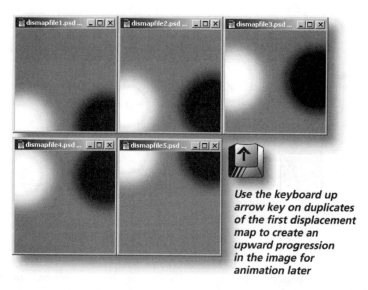

Use the keyboard up arrow key on duplicates of the first displacement map to create an upward progression in the image for animation later

Figure 20.21   Next you will move these colored layers upward, creating the movement that will correspond to the bulge in the pipe in the animation.

6. Click the title bar of the Bulgepipe Photoshop file to make it active. On the Layers palette, Alt(Opt)+drag the Pipe layer to the Create a new layer icon to make a copy of this layer. Rename the copy **Bulge 1** and click OK. Go to the Filter menu and choose Distort, Displace. Set the Horizontal scale to 10% and the Vertical scale to 0%.

    As mentioned earlier in this chapter, as long as a displacement map is the same size as the current image, it doesn't matter whether you choose Stretch To Fit or Tile from the Displacement Map options. Similarly, if the map is the same size as the image, it usually will not matter whether you choose Wrap Around or Repeat Edge Pixels for the Undefined areas.

7. Click OK and you will see the Choose a Displacement Map dialog box. Navigate and select the dismapfile1.psd file you created earlier and click the Open button. Make the Pipe layer invisible (by clicking the eye icon to the far left of this layer) to make it easier to see the results. Or look at Figure 20.22!

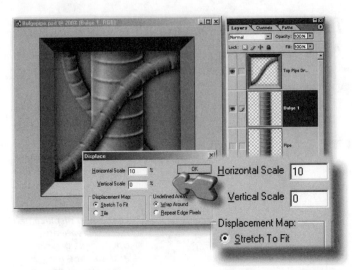

Figure 20.22   The applied displacement map creates a bulge effect in the lower portion of the pipe.

8. Create four more copies of the Pipe layer, and drag them above the Bulge 1 layer. Rename them **Bulge 2, Bulge 3, Bulge 4,** and **Bulge 5**, and place them in stacked order: Bulge 5 above Bulge 4, Bulge 4 above Bulge 3, and so on.

9. Now go through and apply the Displace filter to each layer using the corresponding displacement map in each case. For example, click the Bulge 2 layer to make it active, and apply the Displace filter using the dismapfile2.psd file; click the Bulge 3 layer, use the dismapfile3.psd file, and so on (see Figure 20.23). Now you have everything you need to create an animation.

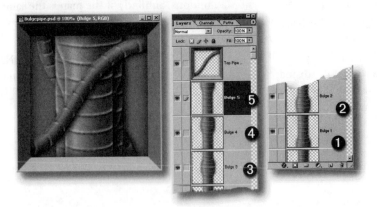

Five layers, each with a different bulge point

Figure 20.23   You now have a progression upward of the bulge in the pipe, and the PSD file is now ready for ImageReady. Um, you don't want to *know* what the bulge in the pipe really is…

10. Press Ctrl(⌘)+S to save. Now press Ctrl(⌘)+Shift+M to open ImageReady 7. The file you were working on is automatically brought into ImageReady. Now all you need to create the animation is the Animation palette and the Layers palette. Close all other palettes. If one or both of the palettes aren't visible, choose them from the Windows menu. In the Layers palette, toggle off the visibility for all the Bulge layers by clicking their eye icons. The Pipe layer visibility should be turned on (make sure the eye icon is showing for this layer).

11. Click the Duplicates current frame icon at the bottom of the Animation palette to duplicate the selected frame—in this case, frame 1. Now turn on the visibility of the Bulge 1 layer, and turn off the visibility of the Pipe layer. Repeat this process by clicking the Duplicates current frame icon, turning on the visibility of the Bulge 2 layer, and then turning off the visibility of the Bulge 1 layer. Each time you create a new frame, turn on the visibility of the next Bulge layer and then turn off the visibility of the previous Bulge layer (see Figure 20.24). Why? Because otherwise you would be able to see a bulge on an underlying layer.

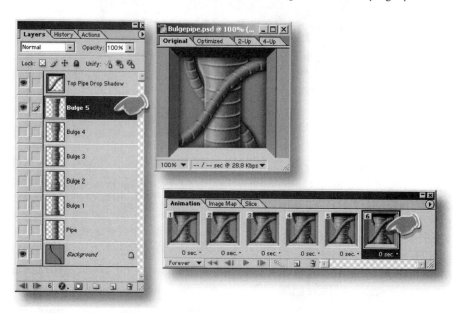

Figure 20.24   Progress up the Layers palette, making the previous layer invisible as you add frames to the Animation palette.

When you are finished, you should have six frames in the Animation palette. The first frame should show the Pipe layer and the remaining five frames should show each of the Bulge layers in sequence.

12. Choose frame 1 in the Animation palette, and click the Selects frame delay time arrow just below the small thumbnail. Select Other from the pop-up menu. Enter the number **3** in the Set Frame Delay dialog box, and click OK. Now repeat this step for frames 2 through 6, and change the frame delay to **0.1** seconds.

You've just set the frame delay for frame 1 to three seconds. This means that there will be a three-second pause at the beginning of the animation and every time it loops. We changed the frame delay for the rest of the frames to 0.1 seconds so that the sequential bulge frames won't go so fast that you can't see it (see Figure 20.25).

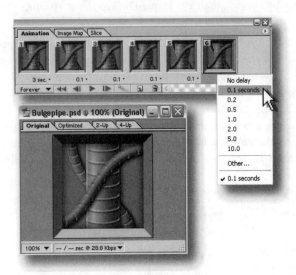

Figure 20.25   Give the poor pipe a rest at frame 1. The other frames carry the motion and should be set to .1 seconds.

Now you're ready to export the animation. Select Save Optimized As from the File menu. Name the animation, and save it to your hard drive. View the animation with a browser or any utility you have that can preview GIF animations.

The animation should start off with a short pause, and then the bulge in the pipe will move upward out of sight. The whole thing repeats every three seconds. Looking at this animation using a GIF animation utility, such as GIF Movie Gear (**www.gamani.com**) shows that, once again, there is a lot of gray area in the frames after frame 1. Once again, ImageReady has optimized the animation to show only the pixels that change from frame to frame (see Figure 20.26).

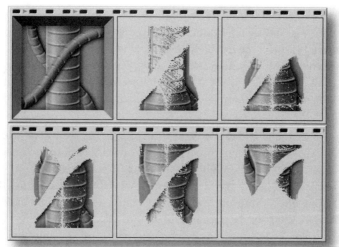

Optimizing= ImageReady only writes pixels that change from
frame to frame into the GIF animation

Figure 20.26   Once again, ImageReady intelligently discards redundant visual information
to make a really compressed file.

We'll make this chapter a trilogy of special effects animations with our conclusion, the
"rolling fog over the ocean" trick. The railing is just to your right in case you get sea-sick...

Animated Fog/Scrolling Texture

For this animation, you learn two useful techniques: creating a fog texture and animating a seamless texture. Creating an animation out of any seamless texture is fairly easy,
and Photoshop has seamless texture generators, among them (and the ones you will use)
are the Clouds and Difference Clouds filters.

Getting Your Hands on Some Clouds

First, you need to generate a seamless tile with the Difference Clouds or Clouds filter. The
Difference Clouds and Clouds filters automatically generate seamless tiles if the file size
is 512. (Tip: The Adobe engineer who created the Clouds effects made the fractal
texture—the clouds—terminate and repeat at 128 pixels or a multiple of such.)

The Difference Clouds filter is a little more versatile than the plain Clouds Filter, Render
effect. For example, you can apply the Difference Clouds filter multiple times and get an
effect that progresses in a geometric fashion, while the Clouds filter simply exchanges the
previous application of the command with a new rendering of clouds.

C'mon. Let's get started:

Creating Seamless Tiling Clouds

1. Press Ctrl(⌘)+N to open a new document. In the New dialog box, make the dimensions a 512-pixel square RGB, 72-dpi document. Click OK. Press D to set the default colors of black and white. Go to the Filter menu and choose Render, Difference Clouds or Clouds filter. Now you have a seamless tile that you can resample to any size you want. In fact, let's begin the next step by resizing the texture.

2. Go to the Image menu and choose Image Size. Resize the file to 140 pixels square by making sure the Constrain Proportions option is checked in the Image Size dialog box and changing the Width for the Pixel Dimensions to 140 (the Height will automatically adjust to the same measurement). On the Layers palette, Alt(Opt)+drag the Background layer to the Create a new layer icon and title this layer. Click OK. Click on the Background layer to make it active. Click on the foreground color, and choose a nice rich medium blue (0, 0, 255). Click OK. Press Alt(Opt)+Delete (Backspace) to fill the Background with the blue color. Next, select the Fog layer, and change the Blend mode to Lighten. At this point, the texture looks like light clouds on a sunny day, but as you will see it's not hard to convert the effect to fog (see Figure 20.27).

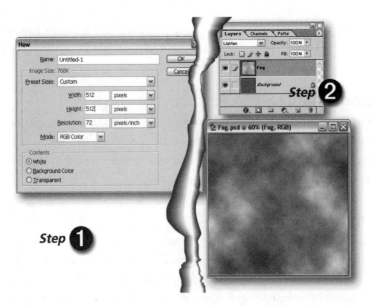

Figure 20.27   Create an image whose dimensions enable you to create a seamless Clouds tile. Then resize the image (we'll explain why shortly).

3. Open the Porthole.psd image from the Examples/Chap20 folder on the Companion CD, and save it to your hard disk using the same name and file type. Double-click the Hand tool to maximize the view of the file in Photoshop. The Porthole.psd file has two layers: the Background layer, which contains simple

artwork for a sky/ocean scene, and the Porthole layer, which contains artwork that looks like a porthole and provides a hole looking through to the Background layer. There is also a Channel named Window in the Channels palette that you'll use shortly (see Figure 20.28).

Figure 20.28   Open the Porthole! The image, that is!

4. Return to the document you created in Step 1, and select the Fog layer. Press Ctrl(⌘)+A to Select All. Press Ctrl(⌘)+C to copy. Now click the title bar of the Porthole.psd file to make this the active document. On the Layers palette click the Background layer title to make this the active layer. Press Ctrl(⌘)+V to paste. Double-click the name to rename the new layer Fog, and press Enter (Return) to set the new name. Change the Blend mode from Normal to Lighten (see Figure 20.29).

Figure 20.29   The layer you copy from the original window needs to be in Lighten mode so that the viewer can see its effect on the Background layer.

5. Press Ctrl(⌘)+A to Select All. Press Shift+Ctrl(⌘)+C to choose Copy Merged. Press Ctrl(⌘)+D to deselect. Press Ctrl(⌘)+N to open the New Document dialog box. The dimensions of the new image should default to 140 pixels width and height. Change the name to **Fog_anim**. Click OK. Press Ctrl(⌘)+V to paste. Double-click the Layer 1 name, rename the layer **Fog 1**, and press Enter (Return) to set the new name. Save the file as a Photoshop (PSD) document (see Figure 20.30).

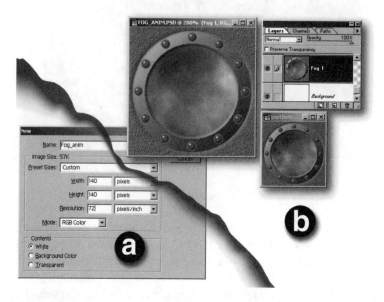

Figure 20.30   Create a new image and then use the Copy Merged command to copy a composite of the porthole scene to the new window.

6. Return to the Porthole.psd file, and click the Fog layer (on the Layers palette). Go to the Filter menu and choose Other, Offset. Change the Horizontal to 14 and Vertical to 0 in the Offset fields. Make sure that the Wrap Around option is checked, and click OK to apply the transformation. Press Ctrl(⌘)+A to Select All. Press Shift+Ctrl(⌘)+C to choose Copy Merged. Press Ctrl(⌘)+D to deselect. Click on the Fog_anim.psd document to make this the active document. Press Ctrl(⌘)+V to paste. Rename the new layer **Fog 2** (see Figure 20.31).

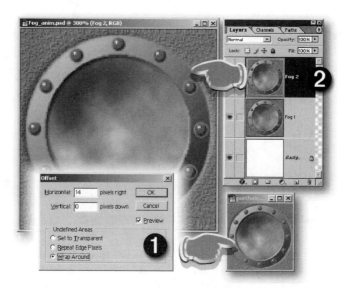

Figure 20.31   Use the Offset command to make the fog roll across the porthole.

7. Click the Porthole.psd title bar to make it the active document. The Fog layer should still be the active layer. Press Ctrl(⌘)+F to reapply the Offset filter (without opening the dialog box—since this will apply the last filter used). Press Ctrl(⌘)+A to Select All. Press Shift+Ctrl(⌘)+C to choose Copy Merged. Press Ctrl(⌘)+D to deselect. Make the Fog_anim.psd the active document in the workspace and press Ctrl+V to paste. Rename the new layer **Fog 3**.

8. Repeat the preceding step seven more times. Each time, press Ctrl(⌘)+F with the Fog layer selected in the Porthole.psd file. Then Select All, Copy Merged, and paste into the Fog_anim.psd file. Rename the layers sequentially. For instance, the next layer in the Fog_anim.psd document should be Fog 4. When you are finished, you should have 10 layers named Fog 1 through Fog 10, as shown in Figure 20.32.

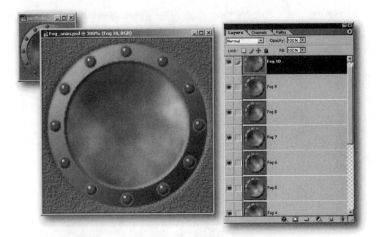

Figure 20.32   The Offset amount is 14. There are 10 frames. If you do the math, 10×14=140, you'll find that it's the exact width of the image window. Looks like the fog will seamlessly repeat a full cycle in 10 frames, at least from where I'm sitting.

9. With the Fog_anim.psd document active, press Ctrl(⌘)+S to save. Now press Ctrl(⌘)+Shift+M to open ImageReady 7. The file you're working with is automatically brought into ImageReady. Again, all you need to create your animation is the Animation palette and the Layers palette. Close all other palettes.

10. Toggle the visibility to off for every layer except the Fog 1 layer. Now click the Duplicates current frame icon at the bottom of the Animation palette to duplicate the selected frame of animation—in this case, frame 1. Now make the Fog 2 layer visible, as shown in Figure 20.33.

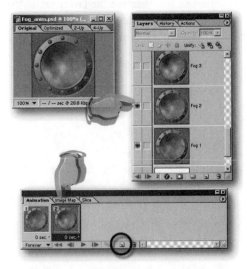

Figure 20.33   Replace the view by one layer every frame to make an animation of wafting fog.

11. Repeat the process from the preceding step by selecting frame 2, clicking the Duplicates current frame icon in the Animation palette to duplicate the frame, and then, with the newly created frame 3 selected, make the Fog 3 layer visible. Repeat for the various layers, each time duplicating the last frame and turning on the visibility for the next Fog layer. When you are done, you should have 10 frames. On frame 10, you should be making the Fog 10 layer visible. Keeping track of the layers should be easy because the frame number should match the number on the Fog layer. This means that the Fog 4 layer should be on frame 4, the Fog 5 layer should be on frame 5, and so on (see Figure 20.34).

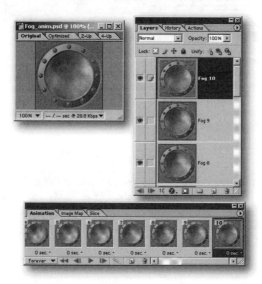

Figure 20.34   Assign each layer to the animation frame to which its number corresponds.

12. Select frame 1 in the Animation palette, click the Selects frame delay time arrow (the tiny arrow just below the small thumbnail), and choose 0.1 seconds from the pop-up menu. Assign frames 2 through 9 the same duration. Setting each frame to 0.1 seconds keeps the animation from running so fast that you can't see the fog.

13. Now you're ready to export the animation. Choose Save Optimized As from the File menu. Name the animation, and save it to your hard disk. View the animation with a browser or any utility you have that can preview GIF animations.

The animation will loop continuously. After a loop or two, it will be hard to determine which frame is the beginning and which is the end. The texture loops endlessly. Looking at the animation in GIF Movie Gear, you can see which pixels changed from frame to frame (see Figure 20.35).

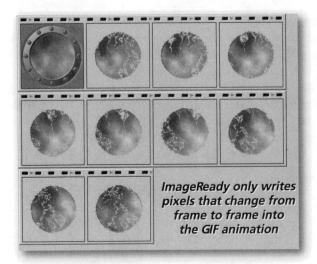

ImageReady only writes pixels that change from frame to frame into the GIF animation

Figure 20.35   The animation is written to file with the porthole only once because it is a recurring element.

Tip

Filtering Selected Layers   Although ImageReady has an Offset filter, you didn't use it in this lesson. Why not? Because unlike Photoshop, ImageReady applies effects to all layers, while Photoshop filters only the target layer. This observation was made at the pre-release date of Photoshop 7, and it might change, but be aware!

Summary

Photoshop and ImageReady make a great combination for creating GIF animations. In this chapter, we've looked at only a few of the possibilities, but they demonstrate the fact that Photoshop has plenty of potential for creating animations and that creating animations with ImageReady is a simple task. Also, isn't it great to know that ImageReady does such an excellent job of optimizing the animation when it comes time to export?

Post Script (Pun Intended)

You also might want to look into the Filter, Liquify command as a means for distorting frames. If you use this filter, you must stop adding new frames at some point and then reverse the remaining frames until you've "ping-ponged" the total animation. This is necessary because the Liquify filter doesn't have a multiple undo feature. Check out Figure 20.36, and see what a lousy thing we've done to one of our relatives!

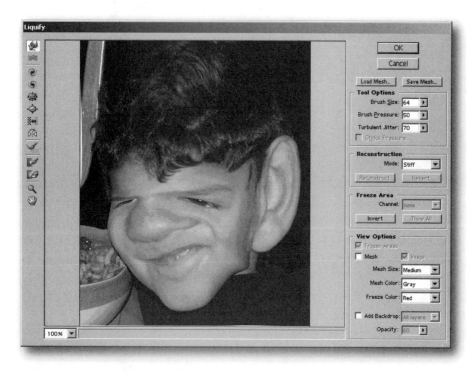

Figure 20.36   The Liquify filter is somewhat like the Displace filter, except the results are messier. And funnier.

Stay tuned for "Scripting and Actions," coming up in the next chapter.

Chapter 21

Scripting and Actions

As your experience with Photoshop grows, you will find that you do some tasks repeatedly and often. Wouldn't it be nice to be able to automate those often-used tasks so that you can carry them out with a simple key combination or selection? Good news—you can do just that using *actions*, a method of recording keystrokes and command sequences that enables you to automate tasks. Both Photoshop and ImageReady include a number of preset actions, and you can use either program to create additional actions you want to use.

Photoshop 7 introduces a new automation feature that allows you to use scripting languages to control the functionality of actions. So when should you use actions for automation, and when should you write a script? The answer comes down to how much flexibility and precision you need. In this chapter, you'll learn about both methods, but we'll tackle the action approach first.

Splitting Images with Actions

Let's look at an example. Suppose that you want to split an image into small pieces to be used for a sliding puzzle game or an animation in which the pieces come together to form the complete image. Using a 4×4 grid of images, the action should be able to create all 16 images automatically.

Splitting Images with Actions

1. Open an example image to record the action with (any image that have lying around on your hard drive will do). I'm using a photo of a strange car on display in Le Centre Pompidou in Paris (see Figure 21.1).

Figure 21.1   Open an image you can use to record the action. The image I used is 400×400 pixels.

2. Click the Actions tab to view the Actions palette (or go to the Window menu and choose Actions). Click the Create new action icon at the bottom of the Actions palette. In the New Action dialog box, type **4×4 image split** as the name of the action, and click Record (see Figure 21.2).

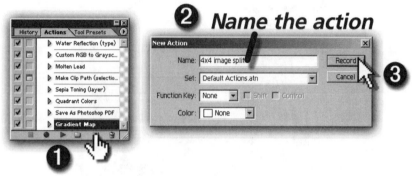

Figure 21.2   Create a new action named 4×4 image split, and start recording.

3. At this point, Photoshop begins recording the operations you perform on the image until you click the Stop button at the bottom of the Actions palette. Press Ctrl(⌘)+R to view rulers (if they are not already on). Drag guides into the document to define the dividing points between the images. My image is 400×400 pixels, so I created horizontal and vertical guides at every 100-pixel mark (see Figure 21.3).

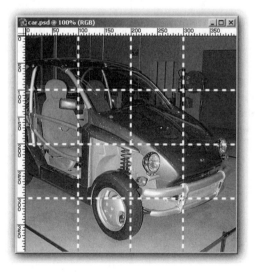

Figure 21.3   Place guides at dividing points in the image.

4. Go to the View menu and make sure that the Snap option is enabled. Choose the Rectangular Marquee tool from the toolbox. Select the top-left corner portion of the image, using the guides as an aid. The selection will snap into place (see Figure 21.4).

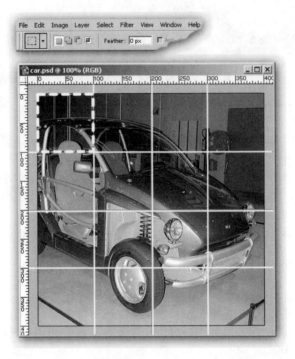

Figure 21.4   Select one of the image pieces.

5. Press Ctrl(⌘)+C to copy the image piece to the clipboard. Press Ctrl(⌘)+N to create a new image document. The New dialog box automatically shows the size of the clipboard image, which in this case is 100×100 pixels. (The settings in your New dialog box may appear differently than the one shown in Figure 21.5. That's fine—Photoshop uses the information on the clipboard for the image you are using, so the differences don't matter.) Click OK to accept the default settings for the new document.

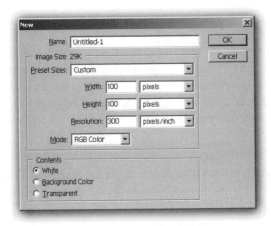

Figure 21.5   Create a new image document to store the selected image piece.

6. Press Ctrl(⌘)+V to paste the clipboard image into the new document. Press Ctrl(⌘)+E to merge the layer with the background (see Figure 21.6). Now you're ready to save the file.

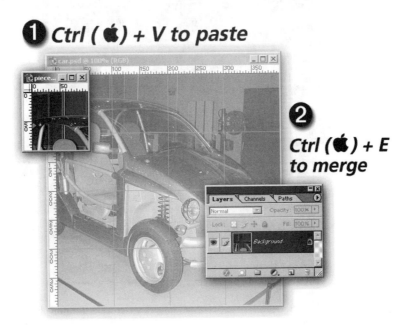

Figure 21.6   Paste the image piece into the new document and merge its layers.

7. Choose File, Save As, and save the file as **piece1.tif**. Now that the image piece has been saved, close the image piece and return to the original image document.

8. The first image piece is done, so let's continue with the rest. You want the action to handle the creation of all 16 images. Do not stop the recording yet. Select the second image piece in the first row as you did previously in Step 4. Repeat Steps 5–7 (copy and paste the selection into a new document and save, then close). Name the second piece **piece2.tif** and so on. Repeat this process until you have taught the action to create and save all 16 images. When you're done, press the Stop button on the Actions palette.

To verify that the action works, you can delete the piece1 through piece16 TIFF files, and run the action again to see that it does, in fact, re-create the desired files (see Figure 21.8). Aside from the tedious bit of work needed to train the action for each of the 16 images, it only needed to be done once, and now the action will do all the work whenever you need an image split in the same fashion.

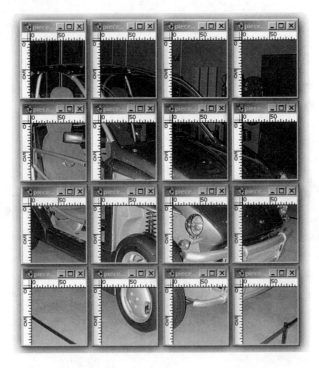

Figure 21.8   When the action is run, 16 small images are created from one large image.

But is this the best way to accomplish this task? Actions record exactly what you do, so if you create a selection sized 100×100 pixels starting at the coordinate x=300 and y=200, it will remember those specific values. The action isn't smart enough to realize that what you're *really* trying to do is divide the image into a 4×4 grid of equal-sized images. So what's the difference?

Try running the action on an image sized 2000×500 and you'll see that the 16 images created will only come from the upper-left 400×400 pixel portion of the image. The action was created under the assumption that the source image is 400×400 and a 4×4 grid of images should be created. This limitation may or may not be an issue for you. You could even adjust the action to resize the image to 400×400 at the outset, before it begins creating the different images. But what if you want to split that 2000×500 image without resizing, and maybe you want to use a 5×5 grid without creating an even more tedious action? This is one of many problems best solved with scripting.

Splitting Images with Scripting

Photoshop 7's new scripting feature supports three scripting languages: AppleScript, Visual Basic, and JavaScript. All three languages provide the same support within Photoshop, but the "external" languages, AppleScript and Visual Basic, do provide the ability to interact with other applications. For example, you can use an external script to perform operations on all files in a given folder or set up an interaction between Adobe InDesign and Photoshop, in which Photoshop scripts can be triggered from within InDesign. In this chapter, however, I focus on JavaScript, because it is the one you're most likely to be familiar with if you've done any web design. Coming from a web design background, I was already experienced with JavaScript, so getting acclimated to scripting with Photoshop was easy.

For those of you who have programmed with JavaScript before, Photoshop has incorporated the language's syntax and core objects, such as Math and String. This means that you really need to learn only how to access objects in Photoshop and the methods attached to them.

Enough talk! Let's look at an example script that splits an image into small pieces and saves them, without the limitations of the action we created earlier. In the Examples/Chap21 folder on the Companion CD, you will find the imagesplit.js file. Open it in your favorite text editor or look ahead to Figure 21.9. Save a copy of the file to the Presets\Scripts folder under your main Photoshop application folder.

Tip

Where's the Scripts Folder? If you do not find a Scripts folder on your system, you probably need to install this from your Photoshop 7 CD. Simply close all applications as you would do with any installation process. Put the Photoshop 7 CD in and browse to the Scripting folder. When you find the ScriptingSupport.exe file, double-click it to install the Scripting Support feature, and you'll be ready to follow along with the rest of this chapter.

I've tried to comment the code so that the general idea of the script will be apparent even if you are new to JavaScript. Also, if a line of code must break because of the width of the printed page but should not break in your actual code, the break is indicated with a code continuation, or carriage return, character (➥). The first few lines are as follows:

```
// image splitter:
// separates an image into a series of equal-sized pieces and saves them.
var rows = 5;  // number of image divisions in the y direction (# of rows)
var cols = 5;   // number of image divisions in the x direction (# of
➥columns)
var piecename; // name of the current piece
var piecefile; // file to save current piece to
var piecedoc;   // reference to the document containing a single image
➥piece
```

```
// image splitter:
// separates an image into a series of equal-sized pieces and saves them.
var rows = 5;   // number of image divisions in the y direction (# of rows)
var cols = 5;   // number of image divisions in the x direction (# of columns)
var piecename;  // name of the current piece
var piecefile;  // file to save current piece to
var piecedoc;   // reference to the document containing a single image piece

if (documents.length > 0){
    // there is a document open, so there is an image that can be split.

        preferences.rulerUnits = Units.PIXELS;   // make sure that pixel units are used
        var doc = activeDocument;                // get a reference to the current image
        var piecewidth = doc.width / cols;       // determine the width of each piece
        var pieceheight = doc.height / rows;     // determine the height of each piece
        var piecepath = new Array();             // array to hold selection coordinates

        for (var y=0; y<rows; y++){              // loop through each row
            for (var x=0; x<cols; x++){          // loop through each column in each row

                // determine the current piece's name (left-to-right, top-to-bottom):
                piecename = "piece" + ((y*cols)+x+1);
                piecefile = new File (doc.path + "/" + piecename + ".tif");

                // record the coordinates of the current piece's corners:
                piecepath[0] = new Array (x*piecewidth, y*pieceheight);
                piecepath[1] = new Array (x*piecewidth+piecewidth, y*pieceheight);
                piecepath[2] = new Array (x*piecewidth+piecewidth, y*pieceheight+pieceheight);
                piecepath[3] = new Array (x*piecewidth, y*pieceheight+pieceheight);

                // select the piece:
                doc.selection.select (piecepath, SelectionType.REPLACE, 0, false);

                doc.selection.copy ();                  // copy piece to clipboard
                // create a new document to hold the current piece:
                documents.add (piecewidth, pieceheight, 300, piecename, NewDocumentMode.RGB,
DocumentFill.TRANSPARENT);
                piecedoc = activeDocument;              // reference to the new document
                piecedoc.paste();                       // paste from clipboard

                // save the piece:
                piecedoc.saveAs (piecefile, new TiffSaveOptions(), false, Extension.LOWERCASE);
                piecedoc.close();                       // close the piece document
                doc.selection.deselect();               // all done!  deselect the piece and loop
            } // end x loop
        } // end y loop
} else {
    // there are no documents open!
        alert ("This script requires an open document to work.");
}
```

Figure 21.9   Some example Javascript code for you.

Here you can see the imagesplit.js script in its entirety. The first two lines are comments that simply provide a short note about the script's purpose. The variables rows and cols are used to define the total number of images to be generated and can be adjusted independently. For example, if you want to split an image into 2 rows of 4 images each, for a total of 8 equal-sized images, you would edit these two lines so rows equals 2 and cols equals 4. The script then automatically adjusts the sizes based on these values. The next three variables are used to keep track of the name, file, and document associated with each piece that will be created. Let's move onto the next part of the script.

```
if (documents.length > 0){
    // there is a document open, so there is an image that can be
    ➥split.

    preferences.rulerUnits = Units.PIXELS; // make sure that pixel
    ➥units are used
    var doc = activeDocument;                // get a reference to the
    ➥current image
    var piecewidth = doc.width / cols;       // determine the width of
    ➥each piece
    var pieceheight = doc.height / rows;     // determine the height of
    ➥each piece
    var piecepath = new Array();             // array to hold selection
    ➥coordinates
```

The majority of the script lies within the if statement on the first line of this code block. If there are any documents loaded in Photoshop, the code continues with the image-splitting process. First, the rulers are set to use pixels as the unit of measurement. Setting the units is a good idea because operations, such as creating a new document or making a selection, are done using the current units. You wouldn't want the script to create an image sized at 300×300 *inches*, when you meant pixels! A reference to the current document then is assigned to the doc variable, so that you can easily access it throughout the script. Variables for the width and height of each piece are determined by dividing the current document's width and height by the number of columns and rows, respectively. Finally, an array is declared which will contain the coordinates of each piece's boundaries. Let's continue on to the real *core* of the script:

```
for (var y=0; y<rows; y++){           // loop through each row
    for (var x=0; x<cols; x++){       // loop through each column in
    ➥each row

        // determine the current piece's name (left-to-right,
        ➥top-to-bottom):
        piecename = "piece" + ((y*cols)+x+1);
        piecefile = new File (doc.path + "/" +
        ➥piecename + ".tif");
```

The script is ready to start working on each individual piece, so you begin with a nested loop. First, I set up a loop that iterates through each row. Each time, the y variable takes on the value of the current row (the values begin with 0 and go through rows-1). Within the y loop is a loop that does the same thing for each column and uses x as the counting variable. By placing the column loop within the row loop, the inner block of code will execute once for each piece you need to create. The piecename variable is set with a name for the current piece, numbered from left-to-right and top-to-bottom. The `piecename` variable then is used to create a reference to a new .tiff file in the source image's directory path.

```
// record the coordinates of the current piece's
➥corners:
piecepath[0] = new Array (x*piecewidth,
➥y*pieceheight);
piecepath[1] = new Array
➥(x*piecewidth+piecewidth, y*pieceheight);
piecepath[2] = new Array
➥(x*piecewidth+piecewidth, y*pieceheight+pieceheight);
piecepath[3] = new Array (x*piecewidth,
➥y*pieceheight+pieceheight);

// select the piece:
doc.selection.select (piecepath,
➥SelectionType.REPLACE, 0, false);
```

Photoshop keeps track of selections as arrays of coordinates that make up the selection path. The coordinates themselves are represented by arrays consisting of an x and a y value. In these first four lines of this code segment, four elements of the `piecepath` array variable are set to the coordinates of the corners that make up the current piece, starting with the top-left corner and going clockwise. Then, the `doc.selection.select()` method uses the `piecepath` array to select the current piece. The other three parameters to the method are the type of selection (used for adding to, subtracting from, intersecting with, or replacing the current selection), feather radius, and whether to anti-alias the selection.

```
doc.selection.copy ();              // copy piece to
➥clipboard
// create a new document to hold the current piece:
documents.add (piecewidth, pieceheight, 300,
➥piecename, NewDocumentMode.RGB, DocumentFill.
➥TRANSPARENT);
piecedoc = activeDocument;           // reference to the
➥new document
piecedoc.paste ();                   // paste from
➥clipboard
```

Continuing on, you can see that the next phase of the script copies the selected piece to the clipboard. Then, a new document is created, using the specified width and height, resolution, name, color mode, and fill color (background color, transparent, or white). After a reference to the new document is assigned to the `piecedoc` variable, the current piece is pasted from the clipboard into the document.

```
// save the piece:
piecedoc.saveAs (piecefile, new
➥TiffSaveOptions(), false, Extension.LOWERCASE);
piecedoc.close();              // close the piece
➥document
doc.selection.deselect();          // all done!  deselect
➥the piece and loop
```

To finish off the work for the current piece, the image is saved using the default TIFF options and the file reference set up at the beginning of the loop. The document is then closed and the marquee on the source image is deselected, ready to start on the next piece of the image.

```
        } // end x loop
    } // end y loop
} else {
    // there are no documents open!
    alert ("This script requires an open document to
    ➥work.");
}
```

The two curly braces close the x and y loops. The third curly brace closes the if (documents.length > 0) statement. The else statement executes only if there are no documents, alerting the user that the script is intended to be used *only* if a source image is already open.

Go ahead and try the script by opening a document in Photoshop. Go to the File menu and choose Automate, Scripts (again, if the option is not available, you need to install Scripting Support from the Photoshop 7 CD). Choose imagesplit from the Scripts list and click Run Script to run the script on the active image (see Figure 21.10). After a flurry of activity, the script will complete, and the source image's directory (the same folder that the image was opened from) should contain the new "piece" .tiff files created by the process. Beware that the script does not check for existing files when the .tiffs are saved, files with those names in the target directory are overwritten automatically.

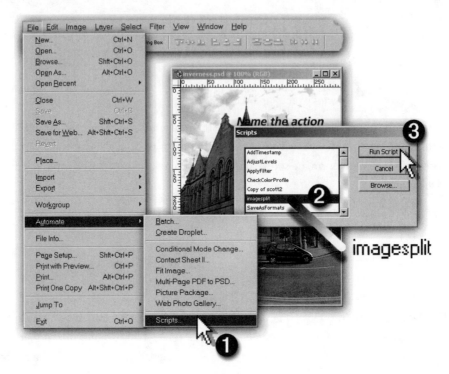

Figure 21.10   I ran the *imagesplit.js* script on this photo from Inverness, Scotland as a test.

Figure 21.11 shows the results of running the imagesplit script on my test image of Inverness, Scotland. The imagesplit script, unlike the action you created, will work on images of any dimensions, even if the image is not square. Additionally, a simple change to two variables in the imagesplit.js file (rows and cols) allows for a quick adjustment to the way in which the image is divided. Note that changing a .js file doesn't require a restart of Photoshop—simply save the .js file and run it again via File, Automate, Scripts.

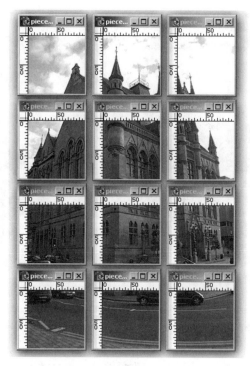

Figure 21.11   My test image was 300×400 pixels, not square like the car image. I still wanted
square pieces, however, so I set *rows* to *4* and *cols* to *3* before running the script.

Scripting for Complex Tasks

The preceding section showcased the benefits of automation in batch-processing tasks.
Actions and scripts both provide valid solutions, but scripting allows for greater control
and flexibility. So what about doing something a little more complicated—something
that can't even be done with an action?

Plotting Patterns with Lens Flares

I came up with an idea to "draw" lens flares onto a document by plotting them in spi-
raling paths (see Figure 21.12). It may not be the most practical use of scripting, but the
images are fun and they look cool, so why not?

Figure 21.12   Here are four lens flare pattern images that were created by a single script.

A single script created all four of these images, requiring only minor changes to parameters to create the different patterns. The color of each image was not scripted, but added after the script ran by using Photoshop's Image, Adjustments, Variations feature.

Let's deconstruct the script to find out how the images are drawn! In the Examples/Chap21 folder on the Companion CD, you will find the spiral.js file. Open it in your favorite text editor. Save a copy of the file to the Presets\Scripts folder under your main Photoshop application folder.

```
// spiral:
// generates spiral patterns by plotting lens flares
var docwidth = 500;
var docheight = 500;
var totalnum = 100;
var rotations = 3;
var outerradius = 200;
var innerradius = 50;
var radiusspan = outerradius - innerradius;
var currentradius;
var x, y, radians;
```

The code begins by setting up some variables and editable parameters. The `docwidth` and `docheight` variables determine the size of the entire image—change these values to create a larger or smaller document. The `totalnum` value sets the total number of lens flares to be plotted. Don't get too crazy with this number, because choosing something very large could take a very long time to run! Set `rotations` to the number of full rotations the spiral pattern will go through. The `outerradius` and `innerradius` variables set the radius of the outermost and innermost edges of the spiral, respectively. The remaining variables keep track of the span of the radii, the radius of the current lens flare from the document's center, and temporary variables for x and y coordinates of the lens flares and their amount of rotation (radians) through the spiral.

```
// make sure that pixel units are used:
preferences.rulerUnits = Units.PIXELS;
documents.add (docwidth, docheight, 300, "Spiral", [sr]
➥NewDocumentMode.RGB, DocumentFill.TRANSPARENT);
var doc = activeDocument;
```

Like the imagesplit.js script, this one begins by setting the active units to pixels, which allows you to assume that any values for coordinates and dimensions used in the script will be treated as pixels. The next part of the script creates a new document with the specified dimensions and assigns a reference variable to the new document.

```
// fill the layer with black:
var fillColor = new SolidColor();
fillColor.rgb.red = 0;
fillColor.rgb.green = 0;
fillColor.rgb.blue = 0;
doc.selection.fill (fillColor);
```

Lens flares always add light to an image, so to ensure that they show up, place them on a dark image. This portion of the script creates a new solid color object, which is an RGB color where each component color is 0 (creating solid black). The `fill()` method is called with the new color object to perform the fill, like Photoshop's Edit, Fill feature. At this point, we've completed all the needed setup—we can now start to *draw* lens flares on the canvas.

```
for (var n=0; n<totalnum; n++){
    radians = (n/totalnum)*(2*Math.PI)*rotations;
    currentradius = innerradius + radiusspan*(1-
    ➥(n/totalnum));
    x = docwidth/2 + (currentradius * Math.cos(radians));
    y = docheight/2 + (currentradius * Math.sin(radians));
    doc.activeLayer.applyLensFlare (40*(n/totalnum), new
    ➥Array(x,y), LensType.PRIME105);
}
```

Yes, I'm afraid there is some math used here, but it isn't as hard to understand as you might think (although, admittedly, staying awake during high school trigonometry might have helped). I'll break it down and explain each part of this section in detail. First, notice that the code is encapsulated in a loop where the n variable starts at 0 and goes up until it is one less than the total number of lens flares. Essentially, the loop runs once for each lens flare, so each execution of the loop focuses on one lens flare, which means that you can think of the n variable as that flare's number.

If you are unfamiliar with trigonometry (or are scared by five-syllable words), I'm here to help. I'm using trig functions as just another way to draw. You are probably familiar with using x,y coordinates, in which your drawing surface is created on a grid. If you number the lines horizontally and vertically, you can use two numbers (x and y coordinates) to uniquely identify any point on the graph.

In trig, instead of x and y, you have a radius and an angle. Using the center of your drawing surface as a reference, you can represent any point as the distance from the center (its radius) and its angle from the horizontal. This angle is represented in radians, not degrees. A full-circle rotation in radians goes from 0 to 2×Pi, while a circle in degrees goes from 0° to 360°.

```
radians = (n/totalnum)*(2*Math.PI)*rotations;
```

The loop begins by calculating the angle of the current lens flare. Because 2×Pi is a full circle, you multiply that by the total number of rotations that the spiral will complete. Then, you multiply that by the percentage of how many lens flares have been drawn (n/totalnum). For example, if rotations is set to 1, totalnum is 100, and you are currently working on the 25th lens flare (n=24), you can see that plugging in all the values gives you Pi/2 radians, or 90°. When writing math in loops, it often helps to mentally "plug in" values to make sure that you get what you expect. This is especially useful when checking the smallest and largest values that the counting variable (n) will contain. Sometimes, however, you can discover cool and unexpected results if you run something that has "bad math" in it. Don't be afraid to experiment or even modify an equation at random!

```
currentradius = innerradius + radiusspan*(1-(n/totalnum));
```

This line calculates the other component that you need to draw the lens flare: its radius (distance) from the center of the document. You start with innerradius to ensure that none of the lens flares will be closer to the center than this inner edge. You can set innerradius to 0 if you want the spiral to converge on a single point. You then add the total span of radius values multiplied by the percentage of lens flares that have been drawn. Note that this percentage is subtracted from 1 to reverse the direction that the radius changes. As it is written now, the first lens flare is drawn at the outermost edge, and the last one is at the innermost edge. See Figures 21.13 and 21.14 for a comparison of the different radius directions. Later in the script, the intensity of the lens flares is adjusted based on the percentage done, so the change in direction here actually adjusts whether the intense lens flares appear on the inside or the outside.

Figure 21.13   This is the result of running the spiral.js script in its current form.

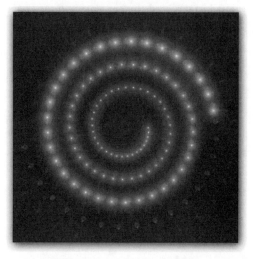

Figure 21.14   After adjusting the *currentradius* calculation by reversing its order, the spiral looks different, drawing the inner flares first and finishing on the outside.

```
x = docwidth/2 + (currentradius * Math.cos(radians));
```

You may find it easy to think about plotting these lens flares in terms of trig coordinates, but unfortunately, Photoshop doesn't understand them. So, we have to do a conversion back to the more "friendly" x and y coordinates before we can place the lens flare. Let's start with the x coordinate. The trig cosine function allows you to convert an angle (in radians) to a relative x coordinate between −1 and 1. If we multiply this relative value by the `currentradius` value that was calculated in the preceding line of code, we'll get an actual pixel distance from the document center (docwidth/2) in the x direction.

```
y = docheight/2 + (currentradius * Math.sin(radians));
```

Coming up with the conversion for the x coordinate leads to a simple solution for the y coordinate. The important change in this equation is the use of the sine function. Like cosine, the sine function converts an angle to a relative coordinate, this time in the y direction. Also note that the center of the image in the y direction is half of the document's height, not its width.

```
doc.activeLayer.applyLensFlare (40*(n/totalnum), new
➥Array(x,y), LensType.PRIME105);
```

It's the moment we've all been waiting for—finally placing a lens flare. The `applyLensFlare()` method calls Photoshop's Filter, Render, Lens Flare filter using the provided parameters. The first parameter is the intensity of the flare. Because the script places many flares, I wanted to make them rather faint so they don't brighten everything to the point that the image is washed out. To make it interesting, I didn't use a constant value for the intensity, but instead used the percentage done (n/totalnum) times 40 to get flares that will gradually "ramp up" in intensity from 0 to 40.

Again, calculations done with the counting variable (n) are often easier to understand if you substitute example variables into the equation to see whether you're on the right track. The filter requires a minimum intensity of 10, so using 0 for this parameter results in a flare of intensity 10. In any case, the flares will grow stronger toward the center of the spiral. The next parameter is an x,y coordinate, so I just provided the values converted in the previous step. Finally, the type of lens flare is specified. The other two types are LensType.PRIME35 and LensType.ZOOMLENS. See Figures 21.15 and 21.16 for examples of these other lens types, with all other settings left at their defaults.

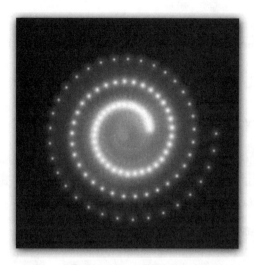

Figure 21.15   Changing the lens type to LensType.PRIME35 provides a more colorful result.

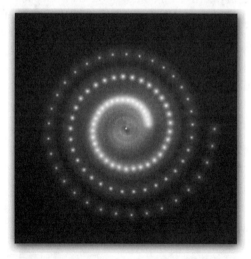

Figure 21.16   Using the LensType.ZOOMLENS option leads to another style with a heavy red tone.

Go ahead and run the spiral.js script by selecting it from Photoshop's File, Automate, Scripts dialog box. Depending on the speed of your machine and the number of lens flares set with the `totalnum` variable, running the script could take a little while, but don't panic if you don't see anything happen on the screen until it finishes. By the way, you may not see anything in the document or on the Layers palette, but if you open the Channels palette before running the script (you won't be able to open it *while* the script is running), you will be able to get a glimpse into the action on the thumbnails of the

Channels palette. Because the script creates its own image document, it isn't necessary to check for active documents the way we did with the imagesplit.js script. Because of that, we don't need to burden ourselves with any assumptions about the current state of Photoshop, since the script creates a specific working environment.

Adding Random Variation

The spiral.js script showcases only a few of the possibilities you have available when you are using a script to do something artistic. For example, you can use JavaScript to generate random values for some settings, creating a unique pattern each time the script runs. Let's try some modifications that add some random variations to the pattern.

Modifying the Variables

1. Open the spiral.js file in Notepad or any text editor program. First, change the `rotations` variable statement to the one in the following code segment. The `random()` function returns a random number between 0 and 1. By multiplying it by 9, rounding it to the nearest integer, and adding 1, I have effectively generated a random whole number between 1 and 10, inclusive. You could run the script once and a spiral would be generated with 2 full turns; if you run it another time, it might generate a spiral with 7 turns (see Figure 21.17).

```
var rotations = Math.round(Math.random()*9)+1;
```

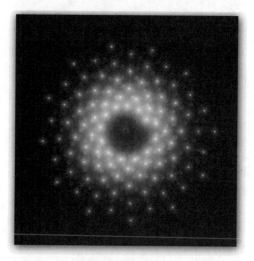

Figure 21.17   With a randomized number of rotations, the script generated this tightly wound spiral pattern.

2. Find the `innerradius` variable declaration and change it to the line shown in the following code segment. This code, similar to the randomized rotations in the preceding step, picks a random inner radius between 0 and 180 each time the script runs (see Figure 21.18).

```
var innerradius = Math.random()*180;
```

Figure 21.18   Randomizing the inner radius and the number of rotations allowed the script to create this variation.

3. As I mentioned before, three different kinds of lens flares are available: PRIME105, PRIME35, and ZOOMLENS. Why not randomize those too? Add the following code to the script, after the declaration for the x, y, and `radians` variables. Locate the line that says, var x, y, `radians`; place your cursor at the end of this line and press Enter (Return) to type the following code segment on the next line.

```
var lenstypes = [LensType.PRIME105, LensType.PRIME35,
➥LensType.ZOOMLENS];
var currentlenstype = lenstypes[Math.round
➥((lenstypes.length-1)*Math.random())];
```

The first line creates an array containing the types of lenses available to us. Then, a `currentlenstype` variable is defined and set to a random element in the `lenstypes` array. Notice how the length of the `lenstypes` array is used to govern the values the random number generator will create.

4. The code needs to take advantage of the new `currentlenstype` variable, so you need to find the last line in the code (loop), and change the last parameter LensType.PRIME105 to `currentlenstype` as shown in the next code segment. Now, each time the script runs, it will randomly choose one of the three lens types. See Figure 21.19 for an example of this random effect.

```
doc.activeLayer.applyLensFlare (40*(n/totalnum), new
➥Array(x,y), currentlenstype);
```

Figure 21.19   The rotations, inner radius size, and lens type are now randomized each time
the script is run.

5. For a more "organic" look, try moving the currentlenstype declaration into
   the body of the loop, just before the applyLensFlare() method is called. Can
   you see what will happen now? The lens flare type will be randomized every
   time a lens flare is plotted, not just once at the beginning of the script. This
   change makes interesting designs like Figure 21.20 possible.

Figure 21.20   By moving the lens type randomization into the body of the loop, each lens
flare will potentially be different.

The version of the script with these randomizations added is available on the Companion CD in a file called spiral2.js. As you can see, these kinds of randomizations can be applied to almost any part of this script. So what's the goal here? That's up to you, but one of the interesting by-products of using random values is that you don't know what you're going to get—surprising results can emerge in unexpected ways. Sometimes the most interesting things emerge when you think of programming graphics as an *exploratory* process. Sometimes I change an addition operation to a subtraction or replace a multiplication with a division without having the slightest clue about what the change means. The thought of making arbitrary changes to a mathematical equation might make you uneasy, but what could go wrong? It's not like smoke is going to come pouring out of your computer if you make a mistake. Of course, it *is* possible that you divide by zero and create an error or send invalid input into a Photoshop filter, which might even cause the application to crash, so just make sure you don't have anything really important open. Figure 21.21 shows a few examples of images created after making arbitrary changes to some of the math equations.

Figure 21.21   These images were made by arbitrary changes to some of the math in the script—changes that were actually illogical and done experimentally.

Summary

The use of looping, conditional logic, and complex math in a script provides many powerful benefits over simple actions, but scripting is not without its limitations. For instance, you cannot use scripts to draw lines, gradients, or use other tools from Photoshop's toolbox. The ability to draw a line or edit pixels directly would be very helpful, but I guess everything can't be automated. For now, some things still need the human touch—or should at least be done the old-fashioned way. In this chapter, you've seen how you can record actions for often-used tasks and create scripts that produce varied, interesting, and sometimes surprising effects.

Part VIII

Photoshop Tricks and Closing Thoughts

Chapter 22

Gary Cauldron and Photoshop Tricks

"Well," the author muttered gruffly to his Version 7 pupils, "I reckon thar ain't no harm in tellin' ye wot's in store once you pass through the introductory paragraph to this chapter." With that, Gary reached into his coat, which appeared to contain several thousand pockets.

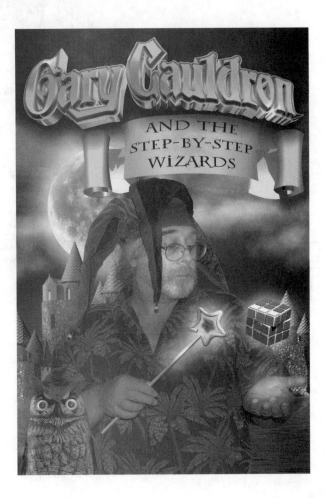

Figure 22.1

"Hmmph. A drubin…not much use in Photoshop. Let's see here—a gollywop, not fully house-broken, either, by the feel of things. Aye, here it is; the manuscript for Chapter 22…before the editors got to it." The room went silent—the news from Gary made the pupils stop using the Free Transform tool and sit waiting with baited breath for the author's next words.

On unraveling the chapter, Gary announced, "Within these pages, ye will find Photoshop tricks and tips about which almost no one in the regular world knows. Why, once ye have read this, you'll be smarter and more talented than, than…Robert Stanley!" The class oohed and aahed.

Suddenly there was a beeping from one of Gary's coat pockets. "Oh, it's jes' me cell phone," and with that he drew it to his ear, past the tousled hair and a beard that seemed to have been groomed with a lawn rake. "Ello," Gary spoke into the phone. The room was a dead silence; the Version 7 students could only hear, "Yes, this is Gary. I'm sorta busy right now…oh, Mr. Stanley's *lawyer*! Um, no…I dinna' mean that las' part. Ooooh, I shouldn't said that." A mild laughter rippled through the classroom.

Okay, I'm done messing around now. What I said a paragraph ago is true. You see, when I write a chapter, I usually wind up contriving a picture that you, dear reader, can modify. This essentially means that I've tricked up a photo or an illustration before you learn how to trick it up. So I think the best gift I can include in this, my 2,000th book on Photoshop, is a closer look and some tips from "behind the scenes." Some tricks are extended, while others are short, but not obvious.

How about a visit to my virtual classroom?

Trick 1: Making Julian Float

Besides putting one person's head on someone else's body, one of the most entertaining and captivating Photoshop tricks is to make a person weightless, be it a super hero or in this example, my nephew Julian. As you can see from the way he glides across thin air in Figure 22.2, Julian wants immediate, physical gratification from meditating.

Figure 22.2 Julian learns to float and mom is ecstatic. Now, he won't track mud into the house.

There's a trick you should learn before you even hire a model or put film or a chip in your camera. And this trick has to do with perspective (technically, one could call it one object's *orientation* in relation to another). Let's take a quick look at what goes into a photo-fantasy before it hits Photoshop.

Creating the Right Eye Level

This floating fantasy is easy to disassemble mentally. Perhaps you think you've got it figured out: "Yeah, you took a picture of the kid, and then trimmed around him and pasted him into a sky picture." Well, not exactly; there are nuances and touches that are small but critical to sustaining a believable (but weird) final picture.

First, if you're going to make Julian float at eye level, you must be at eye level when his picture is taken. Julian is sitting on our back deck, which means that for this great fantasy composition, photographer Barbara had to get down on her tummy and elbows to be at Julian's eye level.

Okay, let's get you in on the fun. The next section shows you how the masking of Julian was done using the least possible effort.

Using the Right Tools for Masking

Open Julian.tif from the Examples/Chap22 folder on the Companion CD. We (Julian's mom, Barbara, and I) tried to keep the background as neutral in tone as possible. Why? Because if you make a background too dark, you'll see cringing when you move the selection to a different image window. The same thing happens when the background is too light.

Let's walk through some beginning steps and useful techniques for carving Julian out of his surroundings.

Masking Around a Kid in Blue Jeans

1. On the Layers palette, double-click the Background layer title and press Enter (Return) to accept the default new name of Layer 0 when you see the dialog box. Click the Add layer mask icon on the bottom of the Layers palette.

2. Press D for the default colors. Choose the Brush tool, and then choose the 19-pixel hard-edged tip (Opacity and Flow should be set to 100% with Mode at Normal). Through trial and error, this seems to be not only the best size tip for creating a "gutter of transparency" around Julian, but the hardness characteristic is good for most of his silhouette.

Note

Three Favorite Selection Tools In my own selection work, there are three different tools/techniques that I always use for selecting a complex outline out of the background layer. First, a hard-edged tip isn't really totally hard—it uses anti-aliasing, which means that there's always a one or two pixel "spread" outward from where I make my stroke. This "play" with the true extent of the brush tip produces realistic, natural boundaries.

Second, the Pen tool is best used when you have a visual item that is smooth and well-defined, such as Julian's sneakers. Creating a path and then converting the shape into a selection also produces a minute amount of anti-aliasing, so even the smoothest of objects still have a slightly soft outline. This is a very photorealistic selection technique for the right objects.

Finally, as you will see in this example, you can use the Lasso tool to select concave areas around the outline of a selection. You need nerves of steel and a talent for the "deft stroke" to use this technique, but with practice, you can switch tools when you come to an outline concavity, flood the selection with foreground color in Layer Mask mode, and resume work easily with other selection tools.

3. Start at the bottom, if only because *I* did, and zoom in to at least 300% to perform most of the masking work. I'm showing you Figure 22.3 only because this is the way I began the task. I zoomed in, worked the edge with the Brush tool, and just to blow off steam (to reduce any possible tedium while masking), I made the "gutter of transparency" extend away from Julian, so there would be less "grunt masking" (the talentless practice of removing large chunks of image from the picture).

In Layer Mask mode:
•*Use small hard brush for silhouette*
•*Use Polygon Lasso tool and Alt(Opt)+ Delete(Backspace) to remove large areas*

Figure 22.3 Ya gotta start someplace in your masking endeavors. Why not start the way I did?

4. Here we go with a little advice and a little unattended work on your part. There's no reason why you can't attack the clothes first, and leave the masking of the hair until I explain how to *do* it! Make a stroke on (stage right) of Julian's sweater, as shown in Figure 22.4.

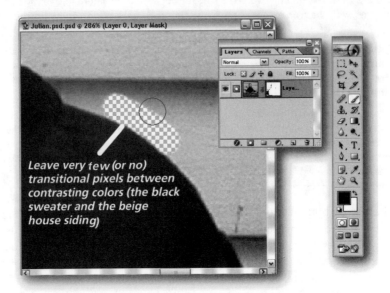

Figure 22.4   Stroke slightly inside the border between the image foreground and background to hide the transitional pixels at the edge of the sweater.

Now, here comes the proverbial dilemma: when you make a cut on a line, do you do it from the middle, the outside, or the inside of the line? In Photoshop masking, you mask from a little inside those transitional edge pixels composed of a mix of foreground and background image color. Why? Because the brush anti-aliases the edge—it moves your stroke's effect slightly outward, so your recourse is to mask slightly inside the line.

Masking toward the inside of the dividing line is such an important concept, I'm tossing in another screen figure here, illustrating how and where to make masking strokes (see Figure 22.5).

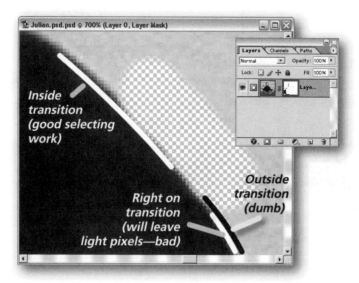

Figure 22.5   Mask the background away by stroking slightly inside the selection.

5. Continue masking down (stage right) of Julian. You will notice very little difference in the smoothness and the transitional pixels on Julian's pants when compared to his sweater. This means that you can use the same brush tip and technique here. In fact, mask right down to Julian's sneakers and then stop.

Switch to a smaller brush if you feel the need, but for most of the work, the current brush size should do just fine. If you make a mistake, press X to switch to white and correct the mistake. Press X again to go back to black and continue.

6. Press Ctrl(⌘)+S; name the file Julian.psd, and save it to your hard disk.

By virtue of this chapter being at the end of this book, I'm sorta making the assumption that you've already read my chapter (Chapter 5, "Working with Channels and Paths") and Mara's chapter (Chapter 13, "Using Paths") on using the Pen tools to make paths. If you did not read those chapters, we suggest you go back and by all means practice a little before continuing here.

Super-Smooth Image Areas Demand the Pen Tools

You will find practically no way to efficiently create a mask area around the laces on sneakers and sneakers themselves without using the Pen tool(s) to define the foot area in the image. A small brush tip is inefficient (you will waste time), and c'mon—doesn't everyone have some experience with XARA, Illustrator, or CorelDRAW? The tools are not hard—in fact, Photoshop 7 enables you to use only the Pen tool plus keyboard modifiers to access every Pen tool worth accessing. Here's a short recap on the Pen tool from earlier in the book:

- The Pen tool makes anchor points. The line that passes though the points is straight if you click only points and it's a smooth curve if you click and drag after the point is set.

- Holding Alt(Opt) toggles the Pen to the Convert Point tool, which enables you to turn a smooth curve anchor into a cusp (the line passing through the anchor veers in direction after it has passed though the point).

- Holding Ctrl(⌘) toggles the Pen tool to the Direct Selection tool, so that you can tug on anchor point direction line points (the very end of a direction line has a point by which you can steer the associated path segment), and to reposition anchor points.

Feel ready? Let's get moving with some vinyl and dirty sneakers:

The Pen Tool Rules

1. With the Pen tool active, first click the Paths icon (the middle of the three icons at the top-left of the Options bar so that you are creating a plain path and not a shape layer. Click a point where you left off masking with the 19-pixel hard tip. You should probably zoom into about 700% viewing resolution on the sneakers (see Figure 22.6). The sneaks are well defined, but you cannot mark the division between sneaker and wood planks using the Pen tool from a distance.

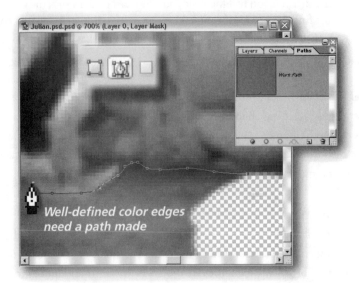

Figure 22.6   Select the Paths icon and zoom the display up to 700% so that you can see clearly where the individual pixels change color. You'll be creating a path along that dividing line.

Get into a rhythm here. Look for sudden changes in direction that the outline of the sneakers show, and then click (or click and drag) anchors at these sudden direction changes. In either selection technique, Photoshop puts the path segments between the anchors.

Work clockwise around Julian; create a path, or several paths that can be selected with a selection marquee, and then fill the marquee with black, thus hiding the selection area's visual contents.

2. Creating one long path around the sneakers and then closing the path inside the sneakers is not your end goal. You want to create an outline along the sneakers, loop it *outside* the sneakers to close it, and then click the Load Path as a Selection icon on the bottom of the Paths palette. (Pressing Ctrl(⌘)+Enter (Return) also will accomplish this step.) When you fill (Alt(Opt)+Delete (Backspace)) the selection marquee with black, the layer mask hides the filled-in area, and you deselect the marquee and move on. I myself did the sneaker outline in about three different paths. Again, tedium is something to be addressed and conquered, so if you grow weary of a routine, start chipping away at this picture in a different area.

The more you practice, the more natural selecting stuff becomes, which means you are not bored and tedium doesn't enter the picture!

3. After you have cleared away the sneakers, work clockwise up Julian's (stage left) side with the Brush tool again, until only his bushy hair remains to be addressed.

4. Press Ctrl(⌘)+S; keep the file open.

Hair: Taming, Trimming, and Masking It in an Image

The first technique you will learn here is how to use a really tiny brush tip to trim around Julian's wind-tousled hair. This might seem overly finicky when there's Extensis and Corel products out there that claim to automate the procedure. My response is that everyone's hair looks different in an image, and therefore there cannot be a single solution.

Believe it or not, I use three different masking techniques for hair, and not one of them is Corel KnockOut Pro. KnockOut is a fine product, but you spend almost as much time setting it up as you will spend finishing the masking with the technique I show you in this section.

Let's get you a small brush tip, and see whether we can't give Julian a rough haircut:

Trimming Hair with a Tiny Brush

1. Scroll the window so that you have a clear view of at least part of Julian's hair.

2. Choose the 5-pixel, hard brush from the Brushes palette. You can right-click (Macintosh: hold Ctrl and click) to display the Brush Preset picker and press Enter (Return) to dismiss it.

3. Go to work on the hair, and as usual, keep to the inside of the hair to eliminate the anti-aliased border between hair and the siding of the house. If an area has only a strand or two of hair, lop it off. You'll restore some sort of random combing of the hair using other techniques coming up soon. Take a look at Figure 22.7 for a good idea of what hair-trimming looks like, Photoshop-style.

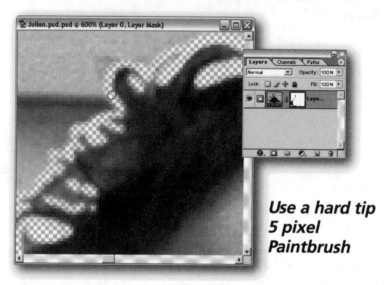

Figure 22.7   Get into the hair's nooks and crannies with the tiny brush tip, and erase as much as you feel makes a reasonable effort. There are more techniques to solve the hair problem shown shortly.

4. After you've created a "transparency gutter" around Julian's hair, leave it, and survey the rest of the gutter. You won't finish the hair until you have moved Julian to new surroundings. You can't really see where you haven't trimmed enough of the image element-border until it contrasts against a new background.

Ooops. The author, upon surveying the gutter around Julian, notices that he has missed a concavity in the border. We talked about this before, and now's a good time to show you how to address an oversight of this kind.

5. Choose the Lasso tool, and then slowly and carefully make a loop that includes the concavity area, as shown in Figure 22.8. Make the selection marquee shape, press Alt(Opt)+Delete (Backspace) to flood the area and hide it in Layer Mask mode, and then press Ctrl(⌘)+D to deselect.

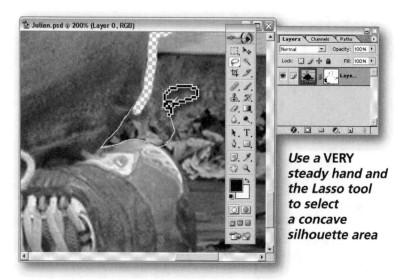

Use a VERY
steady hand and
the Lasso tool
to select
a concave
silhouette area

Figure 22.8   Congratulations. You now have three different selection techniques at your disposal. And the fun hasn't even started yet <g>!

6. Press Ctrl(⌘)+S; keep the file open.

Getting Rid of Everything Except Julian in the Image

Before I discovered a new trick, I used to go through the tedious (but emotionally satisfying) process of deleting large chunks of the background in an image by working the Lasso tool in Polygon Lasso mode up through the "transparency gutter," looping to the outside of the selection as far as the extent of the image window, and then slam a decisive "good riddance" Alt(Opt)+Delete (Backspace) on the keyboard. Which is why I get a new keyboard every few months (my new Logitech iTouch is quite nice, by the way).

Let's briefly run through the old-fashioned way of masking an image before introducing the modern way.

Wending Around and Outside the Selection to Broaden (and Complete) It

1. Survey before you excavate. In Figure 22.9, the image is zoomed out, and you can see all around Julian. Does the gutter completely run around him? Good.

Figure 22.9   Now, from any direction, you can start a Lasso segment in the gutter
and complete it on the outside—*way* on the outside—of Julian.

2. Zoom to 200% viewing resolution. With the Polygonal Lasso tool, make a few
clicks inside the transparency gutter so that you've traveled quite a distance in
the gutter; then move the Lasso tool toward the image window border, and close
the selection marquee. Figure 22.10 shows the "hard" part of this removal
technique.

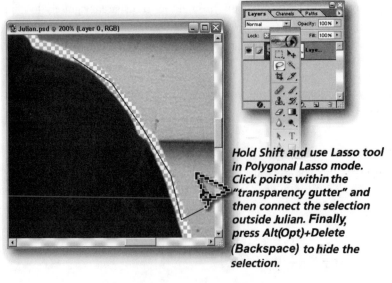

Figure 22.10   Get the tool in the gutter, hold Shift and click points down the gutter. Then,
move the tool to the extremes of the image window and close the selection.

3. Press Alt(Opt)+Delete (Backspace), and deselect the marquee, and soon, your image will look like Figure 22.11. This is a valid method for totally masking the kid from the background, but soon you will see something more efficient.

SEE HOW YOU REMOVED A HUGE CHUNK OF BACKGROUND?

Figure 22.11   You can remove large chunks of the background, one selection at a time, but isn't there a better way?

I can hear the sound of another tutorial coming around. Yesssssss…

The Ridiculously Simple Way of Completing a Mask

1. On the Layers palette, drag the layer mask into the trash icon, and click Apply when the confirmation dialog box pops up. Everything you hid up to this point has now been deleted from the image file.

2. Ctrl(⌘)+click on the thumbnail of Julian on the Layers palette. Doing this loads the non-transparent areas of the layer as a selection marquee.

3. On the Channels palette, Alt(Opt)+click on the Save selection as channel icon on the bottom of the palette. In the New Channel dialog box, choose the Selected Areas option and click OK.

It makes no difference whether the boy is black and the gutter is white, or vice versa. What you can see in the new alpha channel is boy and gutter, and that's the important thing. But if you want to go inverting selection colors in an alpha channel, before you save the channel, Alt(Opt)+click (as you did in the previous step) on the Save selection as channel icon. The New Channel dialog box will appear and offer you the choice of Mask Areas or Selected Areas (see Figure 22.12).

Figure 22.12   Save Julian's outline to an alpha channel.

4. Click the Alpha 1 channel to view it in the document window. Choose the Magic Wand tool from the toolbox, and then on the Options bar, set the tolerance to 32, and the method of selection to Contiguous. What you've done here is tell the Wand, "Choose just about everything in the area where I click, except white and off-white areas." This is what a low Magic Wand Tolerance does. A high Tolerance number will select into the border colors. The default setting of 32 works nicely in this case. Now click on the black area *outside* the gutter, as shown in Figure 22.13.

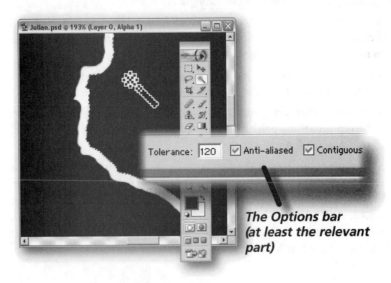

Figure 22.13   Choose, with the Magic Wand tool, the outside of the Julian's silhouette.

5. *Really important step here.* Go to the Select menu and choose Modify, Expand. Type **1** in the Expand By field, and then press Enter (Return). What you've done is negate any of the effect of anti-aliasing that is in the gutter of the alpha channel. In other words, you have selected everything except Julian. With white as your background color, press Delete (Backspace). As you can see in Figure 22.14, you now have a perfect selection defined for Julian.

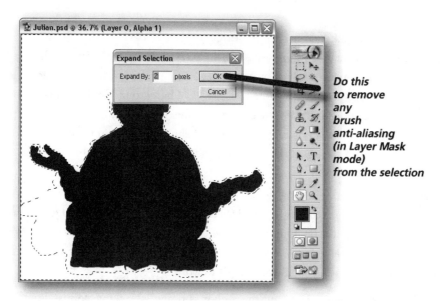

Figure 22.14   A perfect definition of Julian's silhouette means that you can now select only Julian and move him to greener pastures (literally. You'll see).

6. Ctrl(⌘)+click the Alpha 1 Channel to load the Channel as a selection. Press Ctrl(⌘)+Shift+I to invert the selection (pressing Shift+F7 does the same inversion). Click the Layers tab to view the Layers palette. Click Layer 0 to view the image in the document window and press Delete (Backspace). Press Ctrl(⌘)+D to deselect.

7. Press Ctrl(⌘)+S; keep the file open.

Now we're going to shift gears (actually, shift *pictures*) and go to work tidying up the host image for the floating boy.

> **Note**
>
> **Always at Eye Level**   When Aunt Barbara took the photo of the fence that will ulti-
> mately be behind our floating Julian, she was careful to photograph it at eye level, the
> same as she did with Julian. Remember that if you want a trick to work, you need to
> match orientations, match lighting—think of everything you can to make the two images
> appear happily as one after Photoshopping them.

What You Can Make of a Picket Fence

Photographer Barbara and I were exceptionally pleased that the picture of Julian came
out (hint: digital cameras enable you to preview what you've got in the camera before
your talent scoots off to a soccer game). We needed a background in the dead of winter,
and found a patch of grass and a fence close to home. We did not need a sky in the picture—we could add one later. Besides, the clutter behind the fence in the picture made it
necessary to mask off the top of the image, expand the canvas size, and then drop in a sky.

A Really Easy Task: Masking a Fence

What is a fence? If you read Frost's, *The Mending Wall*, you know that good fences make
good neighbors. If you listen to Bouton, good fences are easy to mask, because they are
roughly linear along all edges. This step in making Julian float does not need a set of
steps; just read about it here and you can get to work.

As you can see in Figure 22.15, all the author is doing is clicking points along (and
slightly to the inside) of the fence geometry. To complete this part of the exercise, open
FenceAndGrass.tif from the Examples/Chap22 on the Companion CD and double-click
its thumbnail on the Layers palette to make the Background a layer. Choose the Pen tool
and click away at the fence. Start at the left edge of the image and work your way across
to the right edge. When you make it to the edge, press Ctrl(⌘)+minus to reduce the size
of the image and drag the window out to give yourself room. Then complete the selection by clicking outside the edge (up and around the top) until you loop back around to
the right edge fence and close the path. Press the Delete (Backspace) key to remove the
upper part of the image.

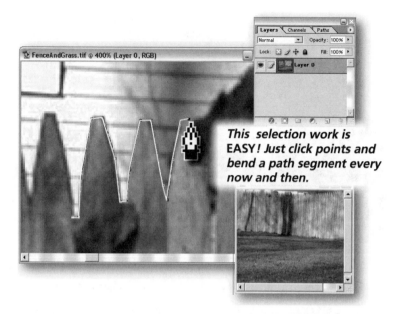

This selection work is EASY! Just click points and bend a path segment every now and then.

Figure 22.15   Click, click, click…and before you know it, you've handsomely masked the non-fence and non-grass areas of the image.

Hey, I think it's time we put Julian on some winter grass.

Moving Julian and Working Further on His Coif

Getting a copy of the now perfectly masked Julian into the FenceAndGrass image is as simple as drag and drop. But, in the steps that follow, you learn how to make even the finest detail about his hair look natural in the new scene. (By the way, notice that Julian and the fence's lighting conditions are both overcast. Try to match light sources when you do photo-trickery along these lines).

Integrating Julian with the New Picture

1. Choose the Move tool and with Julian.psd in the workspace, take the layer title on the Layers palette, and drag the title into the FenceAndGrass.tif image window (see Figure 22.16). You can close the Julian.psd file now.

Figure 22.16   Wow. This is a lot easier than when I was a kid and used to hop fences!

Note

> **Who Says There's No Shortcut to Success?**   You're only cheating yourself if you want to get on with the composition but didn't go through all our pages of selection advice. But the *Inside Photoshop* 7 authors (lovingly known as "Ocean's 11") aim to please and if you want to start participating right now, you can use the file in Examples/Chap22 called Julian.psd, which has our kid already masked.

   2. On to the hair. Sub-trick #1: Zoom into the locks of hair, Ctrl(⌘)+click on the Julian thumbnail on the Layers palette to load him as a selection (press Ctrl(⌘)+H if it helps to hide the selection). Choose the Brush tool. Set the size to a 13-pixel hard edge brush. Press Alt(Opt) to toggle to the Eyedropper tool. Sample a darkish area of Julian's hair, set the painting Mode (on the Options Bar) to Darken, and then stroke the very tips of his hair, as shown in Figure 22.17. Doing this perfectly ends the *actual* selection of Julian's hair. Press Ctrl(⌘)+D to deselect when you're satisfied with the results.

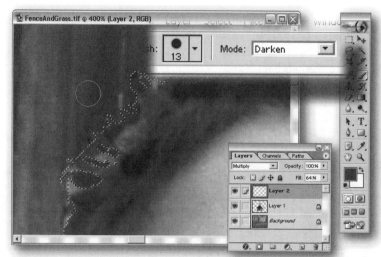

SUB-TRICK #1: LOAD OPAQUE AREAS, EYEDROPPER SAMPLE A HAIR COLOR, AND THEN
STROKE THE EDGES.

Figure 22.17 The selection marquee, like everything else in Photoshop, has a little
anti-aliasing to it. Fill in those intermediate spots with a dark hair color.

Note

Anti-Aliasing Gosh, the term "anti-aliasing" has been tossed around in this chapter
an awful lot, without a definition, eh? Okay, here's what it means:

Anti-aliasing is the use of different colored pixels at the edge of an image to make up for
the fact that most computer programs cannot resolve a screen pixel color when the
sampling range gets very small.

For example, think about a black-and-white checkerboard extending into the distance. At
some point in the distance, the monitor, your eyes, the program—or all three—cannot
truly see the color of the checkerboard when an area takes up less than one pixel. The
problem here is that technically, the pixel should be black or white. But you cannot have
both black and white in a single pixel. So the program does one of two things: it shows
you, for example, a white pixel. But there's a 50% chance that this should be a black
pixel...and so the white pixel in this example is traveling under the alias of a black pixel.

Anti-aliasing splits the difference through the use of different colors. Anti-aliasing will
make the pixel in question here 50%, a mix of what the true colors should be in a single
pixel. The results usually look quite pleasing. Although anti-aliasing is necessary for
sophisticated computer graphics, equally sophisticated techniques must be used to get
rid of anti-aliasing (or at least to change the anti-aliasing colors) to make a good composite image.

3. Sub-Trick #2: Use the Smudge tool, a small brush size (13-pixel soft brush), and mild pressure (60% Strength) to blend your painted strokes with the actual pixels that make up the image of Julian's hair. Also make sure the Use All Layers option (on the Options bar) is not selected. Try it and you'll get the concept immediately (see Figure 22.18).

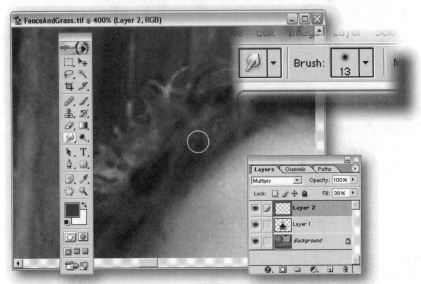

SUB-TRICK #2: USE THE SMUDGE TOOL TO BLEND YOUR PAINTED HAIR WITH ACTUAL HAIR PIXELS IN THE IMAGE.

Figure 22.18   Smudging areas can make color you've added to the current color in an image blend in a natural way.

4. Sub-Trick #3: Creating stray hairs. Press B to choose the Brush tool. On the Options bar, change Mode to Normal and click on the Brushes palette icon (it looks like a page icon at the far right of the Options bar). In the palette, click on the Brush Tip Shape option on the left side and create a new brush that is 2 pixels in diameter and 86% hard. Press Alt(Opt) to toggle to the Eyedropper tool, and then choose a darker color from Julian's hair. Then stroke to make occasional loose hairs here and there (see Figure 22.19). You might also want to use the Blur tool on your painted hairs to make them more photographic in appearance.

SUB-TRICK #3: CREATE A 2 PIXEL, 86% HARD BRUSH, SAMPLE DARKER HAIR STRAND COLORS, AND THEN PAINT IN STRANDS OF HAIR. YOU MIGHT WANT TO USE THE BLUR TOOL OVER THE NEW HAIRS JUST A LITTLE.

Figure 22.19   Paint strands of hair on Julian's head. Experience has taught me that 3 pixels is too wide and that 1 pixel is too narrow to imitate hairs on images that range between 5 and 10MB in size.

5. Press Ctrl(⌘)+S; keep the file open.

Well, Julian looks totally blissed out, but he's still on the ground. Let's continue and skyrocket the kid.

Adding Space, Adding a Sky, and Levitating Julian

First, you're going to need to add some headroom in this photograph so that you can add a sky and levitate Julian. This is not hard stuff, so let's mosey back to Photoshop now…

Concluding the Magic Trick

1. Right-click (Macintosh: hold Ctrl and click) on the title bar to FenceAndGrass and choose Canvas Size. As you can see in Figure 22.20, we anchored the current picture at bottom center (you do this by clicking on the bottom-center square under Anchor in the interface) and then entered 2520 pixels in the Height field. The number is pure guesswork, but it works. Click OK to make the change.

SOME SKY WOULD BE NICE.
IT MAKES IT EASIER FOR THE KID TO FLOAT...

Figure 22.20   Increase the size of the empty area at the top of the image by
using the Canvas Size command.

2. Now we may or may not have a problem here. You see, a 3.3 megapixel digital
camera takes images that are around 9MB in file size. The last time I took a pretty
picture of the sky (this is Syracuse, NY, second only to Seattle and Buffalo for
crummy skies), I had an analog camera, and I had my nice sky pictures written to
PhotoCD—which has a non-interpolated (a true) picture resolution of 4.5MB.
Guess the image won't take up the whole area we need it to. Open NiceClouds.tif
and with the Move tool, drag the image into FenceAndGrass. See the problem in
Figure 22.21? Close the NiceClouds.tif image; it's no longer needed.

Figure 22.21   It's actually pretty funny. How many people have the problem of the sky being too small?

You can, however, scale the clouds image to the size you need without much fuss because unlike intricate pictures of the Hubble space telescope, a sky basically has a few clouds that are very diffuse at their edges. The image also needs to be cropped to eliminate the edges of the lawn, as you can see in Figure 22.22. Choose the Crop tool and do this step on your own. It might help to move Julian to the center of the image before you crop it.

1 The sky image is way too small.

2 The image needs cropping along the vertical sides.

Figure 22.22   Fantasies are more fun to experience than they are to create, huh? <g>

3. On the Layers palette, drag the cloud layer (Layer 2) below the lawn layer (Layer 0) so that the clouds layer is tucked behind Julian *and* the lawn and fence. Press Ctrl(⌘)+T to put the cloud image in a Free Transform box, drag on a corner handle (or two) to make the sky fit the opening you created for it. When done, press Enter (Return) to accept the transformation. With the Move tool, choose the Julian layer, and lift him into the sky.

4. In Figure 22.23, I'm getting super-picky. The clouds look fine, except that they show film grain after being enlarged, and digital images in this picture do not show grain (they show noise occasionally, but that's not our problem today). Also, a shadow beneath Julian might not be totally realistic (he is lit flat—no part of him shows strong lighting and shadows), people expect to see shadows in a photo, so let's oblige our audience.

Figure 22.23   It's looking good, except for some minor details.

5. Click the cloud layer (Layer 2) to make this the active layer. Zoom into Julian's right hand to observe this neat sub-trick. Go to the Filter menu and choose Pixelate, Facet. As you can see in Figure 22.24, the clouds, (only on close inspection) look marginally less realistic...but the grain is gone!

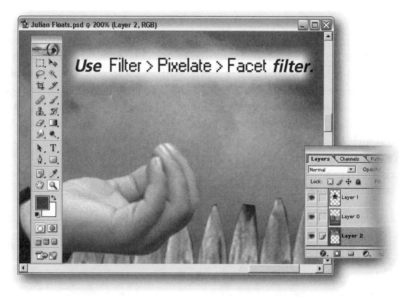

Figure 22.24   If there were a fabric-softener for clouds, it would be the Facet
command in Photoshop.

6. I'm going to digress here for a moment. Open the duck.psd image from the
Examples/Chap22 folder on the Companion CD. Just drag the little fellow into
the FenceAndGrass image with the Move tool, and you have a heightened
sense that Julian is actually floating high enough to greet a migrating duck (see
Figure 22.25). Close the duck.psd file.

Figure 22.25   What do you think that duck is thinking right now?

7. Last step. Press D for the default colors. Click on Layer 0 (the lawn layer) to make it the active layer. Alt(Opt)+click on the Create a new layer icon at the bottom of the Layers palette. Name the new layer **shadows** and click OK. With a large (200-pixel) soft tip brush, in Quick Mask mode (press Q), and with black as the foreground color, paint a shapeless blob beneath Julian. Switch back to Standard editing mode by pressing Q again. If the marching ants surround the outside edges of the image, press Ctrl(⌘)+Shift+I to Invert the selection. Press Alt(Opt)+Delete (Backspace), assuming the current foreground color is black. Press Ctrl(⌘)+D to deselect. Decrease the Opacity on the layer until a harmonious and subtle blend of artificial shadow and real grass co-exist in the picture. Check out Figure 22.26.

*Paint in faint, shapeless shadows. The sun is **not** strong in the image(s).*

Figure 22.26   The perfect day, the perfect altitude, and mom has to spoil it with her meatloaf surprise.

8. Save this image as Julian Floats.psd in Photoshop's native file format, and you can keep it open as long as you like, or until the screensaver kicks in.

You *did* it! Yay, you!!!

Trick 1 Summary

Creating illusions is a fun endeavor; however, getting the details right from the get-go is crucial to your image-making success. Take with you the hair tricks we covered, and most importantly, when taking photos of scenes you want to blend, *make sure the height of the camera is agreeable for both images.*

Trick 2: Borrowing an Image's Color Palette

Actually, you will learn how to *steal* an image's colors in this trick, because the word *borrowing* strongly suggests that you will put something *back* when you are done.

Okay, here is the scenario—first, you cannot copyright or trademark the use of certain colors. You can get in a lot of trouble borrowing corporate colors for your own logo, but I'm talking about a beautiful autumn day, or in this case, a poster that uses such nice colors together, you'd like to sample and re-purpose the color combination.

Sampling and Downsampling a Bunch of Colors

We're going to make this trick as simple, as ideal, and as unrealistic as possible because we want you to understand what's going on. So let's suppose that the Getaway.psd image has the colors you want, located neatly on a layer. Here's how the tune goes:

Copying and Downsampling Colors

1. Open the Getaway.psd image from the Examples/Chap22 folder. Take a look at Figure 22.27, and more pragmatically, you'll get a nice idea of the colors on your screen or, at least, in the color section of this book.

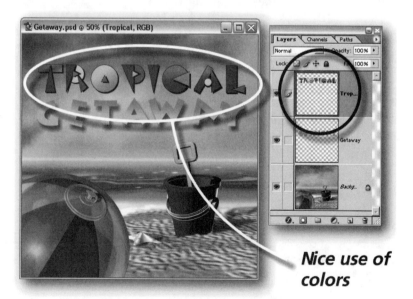

Figure 22.27   There are about 2,275 unique colors in the word "Tropical," but this is mostly due to the blends between colors. Actually, there are only about 20 striking colors in the text. And you *want* them!

2. Right-click (Macintosh: hold Ctrl and click) the thumbnail of the Tropical layer (on the Layers palette), and then choose Duplicate layer. In the Document field of the Duplicate Layer dialog box, choose New as the target for the text. The text then appears in an image window (the same size as the Getaway.psd document). Crop the image and Flatten it.

3. Go to the Image menu and choose Adjustments, Posterize. Now, I read the Photoshop documentation, and it says that the Posterize command will take as many colors as you enter in the number box, multiplied by the bits per channel. So as you can see in Figure 22.28 (you should be doing this, too, by the way), a Posterize amount of three will yield an image that has, um…24 colors!

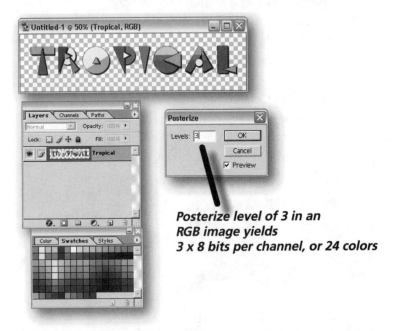

Posterize level of 3 in an RGB image yields 3 x 8 bits per channel, or 24 colors

Figure 22.28   Notice that you still retain a lot of the original colors, even though some colors shift, when you apply Posterize to a 24-bit, RGB image.

Note

The Hard Way   I consider this the hard-but-more-accurate way of color sampling—you start with a blank Swatches palette (provided as Blank.aco in the Chap22 folder), and use the Eyedropper tool to sample a color, drop it on the Swatches palette, and then name the color (you haven't yet learned how to turn this feature off).

But then again, the trick here is to glom sample colors you like in one fell swoop, so these steps are legit and worth knowing.

4. Choose Image, Mode, and then choose Indexed Color. Accept the Exact setting in the dialog box, and then click OK. You might notice that the exact number of colors Photoshop reports can be anywhere from 16 to 24 or so. This technique is an inexact practice, and the colors you wind up with depend upon the color profile you have set for Photoshop. But you've still sampled a bunch of colors you like, and now it's time to save them.

5. Choose Image, Mode, Color Table, and then save the color table as getaway.act.

6. To load the color table, click the menu flyout on the Swatches palette (press F6), and then choose Replace Swatches. Make sure that you choose Color Table (*.ACT) in the Files of type box. Then navigate to where the Getaway.act file was saved. Click Load.

7. Press Ctrl(⌘)+S; keep the file open.

You might think to yourself, "Terrific, Gare. Now what can I do with this color table?" Glad you asked. You can now posterize a grayscale image and then apply the colors you glommed in Step 5.

Creating a Posterized Poster

One of the wonderful things about New York City is the architecture. No two building are alike, and some of the whitestones and brownstones have gargoyles "protecting" the entranceway.

Piper.tif is a fine architectural image, the type that, sadly, no one except Disney resorts does anymore. I wanted to hang the picture on the wall, but because it's a monotone, almost grayscale image, I figured the only way to make this a less depressing wall ornament was to colorize it.

And to do that, dear reader, we'll return to this color palletization stuff:

Creating the Posterized Piper

1. Open the Piper.tif image from the Examples/Chap22 folder on the Companion CD. As a grayscale image, it has 256 possible tones, but you want only seven tones to replace with this nifty color palette.

2. Go to the Image menu and choose Adjustments, Posterize, and then enter 7 in the number field. Click OK. This amount is 7 samples multiplied by one channel, or 7. In Figure 22.29, you can see a copy I made to compare the posterized piper to the original. It's not too bad, considering all the visual information it has lost.

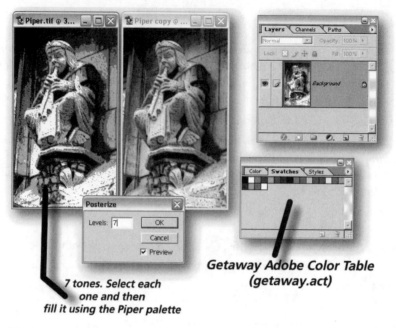

**7 tones. Select each
one and then
fill it using the Piper palette**

**Getaway Adobe Color Table
(getaway.act)**

Figure 22.29   These are the steps necessary for creating a color version of the
posterized, greyscale piper.

3. With the posterized piper in the foreground in the workspace, choose Select, and then Color Range.

4. Because the Fuzziness slider goes from 0 to 200 and you want the seven colors you will add to be perfectly anti-aliased and smooth, drag the slider to 29 (about 1/7th of 200), and then click an area of the piper. I suggest you work from dark to light (selecting the seven tones). Click the darkest tone and then click OK (a selection appears). Click a color from the Swatches palette and press Alt(Opt)+Delete (Backspace) to fill. Press Ctrl(⌘)+D to deselect.

5. Repeat this step six more times and you've got the color palette you like applied to an image that *I* like!

6. Press Ctrl(⌘)+S; keep the file open.

I refuse to insult your intelligence and show a black and white picture of the finished color piper. Instead, check out the color gallery in this book, and it wouldn't hurt my feelings in the least if I heard some "ooooohs" and "ahhhhs"—even in my imagination.

Trick 2 Summary

Palletizing the colors in an image is easy. The hard part is knowing what to do with the colors when you're done! You can use gradients to command attention by using a color "set" like the one you've created. Frankly, there's a lot of mediocre black-and-white art—at least in *my* shoebox under the bed—that would benefit from having new life pumped into it with an interesting color palette.

Trick 3: Creating a Photoshop Book Cover

This might at first seem a little self-serving—I do most of my own book covers, including the *Inside Photoshop* ones, and I want to show you, step by step, how one is created. We step outside of Photoshop for some image areas and textures and stuff, but as you will soon see, Photoshop is absolutely necessary to integrate the diverse and unusual image parts.

The Hand and Bulb Cover

The "Hand and Bulb Cover," was the name I gave an illustration idea for *Inside Adobe Photoshop 5:* Limited Edition. This illustration, of course, followed my all-important rule:

You always begin with a concept. If you do not start with a concept, regardless of how skilled you are with Maya, Poser, or Photoshop, the piece is still going to look like cyber-doodles, instead of art that has a point. If you remember only one thing from this book, remember that *the concept* comes before anything else.

My concept was to use the cliché of a light bulb expressing an idea, but the bulb isn't real—it's unfinished without the input from the artist, which is expressed by a hand with a brush looming over the bulb. Additionally, the filament in the bulb is an exclamation point, signifying (I hope!) that a *good* idea has punch!

First Stop: Some Organic Texture

I used Painter to create a seamless, tiling background that looks as though it has been worked on for a month or two. I set Painter to create a seamless tile, and then used the scratchboard rake pen with the Distorto family of canvas messer-uppers, and as you can see in Figure 22.30, the result is a very natural-looking piece of glop. I wanted a seamless tile, because often with Photoshop layers, a finished 6MB image on a book cover bloats up to 60MB or more. By making a tile, I could repeat the design with less processing overhead than a single 6MB image.

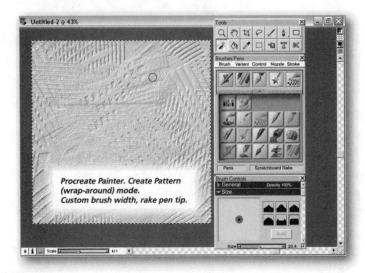

Figure 22.30   Painter is not exactly for photographers, but its procedural textures and fractal patterns make it ideal for the photorealistic artist.

I Turned to trueSpace

To get the images I needed, I used both Poser—for the hand—and trueSpace version 3 (at the time) for the other elements, including lighting reflection tracing and framing of the scene. In Figure 22.31, you can see a wireframe setup of the scene. I throw this in only because some fellow Photoshoppists aren't into the strange-but-rewarding world of modeling applications.

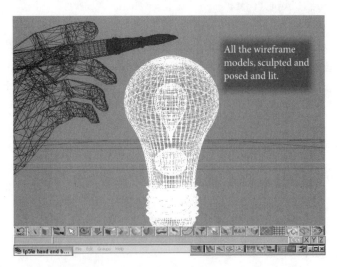

Figure 22.31   Create a setup scene in wireframe mode instead of trying to real-time render the whole scene as you tinker with it.

In Figure 22.32, you can see the rough idea coming out. Unlike a lot of my modeling chums, I decided it was better to break up the scene and do seven or eight individual renderings with the lighting I want instead of fussing until 2009 on one perfectly lit scene. Like Photoshop, trueSpace renders alpha channels for plucking only the object out of an image window.

Figure 22.32   The scene requires special lighting for each object, even when the finished image will display spotlighting. Sometimes you have to cheat backstage to make the actors look good.

Lighting and Filtering the Book Cover Art

Often, you will see two shadows near you, and they overlap because two light sources are near each other. This lighting technique is intriguing to me, so I lit the light bulb from two closely positioned sources. After I had test rendered the scene, I was able to get two mathematically correct shadows. I copied the shape of the shadows using the Pen tool, and added them to the scene at partial opacity, like real shadows are prone to project.

In Figure 22.33, you also can see the background I created in Painter. The difference in this scene is that I applied Photoshop's Chalk and Charcoal filter to a shred of the top of the background, and I reduced part of the light bulb to a line drawing to suggest that the composition isn't yet complete, and there are "rough-out" areas in the painting/mock photo.

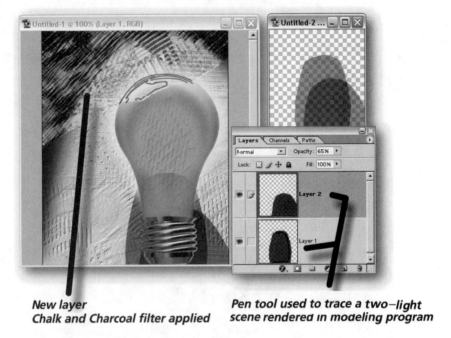

New layer
Chalk and Charcoal filter applied

Pen tool used to trace a two–light
scene rendered in modeling program

Figure 22.33   A lot of artificiality goes into making a scene look real!

Reflection Maps Galore

Although trueSpace is perfectly capable of calculating reflections, I needed only one or two actual, calculated reflections in this piece. I needed the hand to reflect into the brass exclamation "filament" in the bulb, and I needed accurate shadows.

Instead of processor-intensive calculations, I used two carefully built reflection maps to apply to the filament and the base of the bulb, shown in Figure 22.34. By the way, the filament was placed on a layer in front of the bulb; it became too hazy when the filament was actually inside the bulb.

You can't see it in black in white, but the filament has a forest and a ravine reflected into it. I created the scene in Bryce and then messed with it, rather severely, in Photoshop until I got the right level of detail. I had Photoshop and trueSpace open at the same time so that I could instantly update the reflections.

The Vienna Street is a real image of Vienna I found someplace. I removed the color and blurred it, and the location and combinations of black and white made the bulb base look credible.

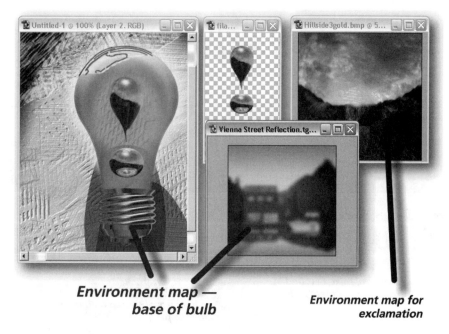

Environment map —
base of bulb

Environment map for
exclamation

Figure 22.34   You can map an image onto the surface of a model to make it look
as though it's reflecting something. Almost everything you see in
real life has some sort of reflection.

Creating Fleshtones and Passing Them Through a Model

This is going to sound silly, but it's darned near impossible to accurately map a sample of
flesh tone to the model of a hand. There is an incredible amount of geometric complexity
to a hand—even a model of one.

My solution to putting a finish on the hand (again, this was lit and rendered separately
from the light bulb) was to use "pass through" surface mapping. In other words, the texture was projected through the model, and what landed on the surface was in pretty
good focus without much distortion. The important trick, as shown in Figure 22.35, is
that to get the best flesh tone on the hand, I scanned my own arm, and then messed with
it in Photoshop to get a seamless tiling texture that had nice variation (everyone's skin
has tone variation).

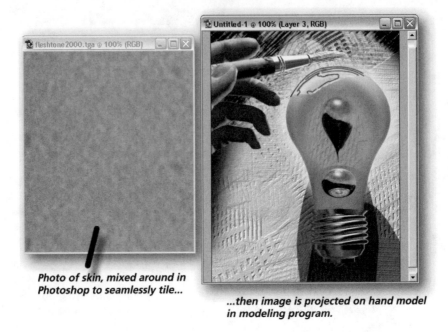

Photo of skin, mixed around in
Photoshop to seamlessly tile...

...then image is projected on hand model
in modeling program.

Figure 22.35   The skin texture was applied to the hand during the rendering phase.
I'm only showing the two images here as a point of information.

Last Minute Touch-Ups

A reasonable person would call it a wrap and send the cover off to Indianapolis. But
Noooooooooo. I saw a number of small touches that would hopefully go a long way in the
creation of this scene.

First of all, models imported from Poser usually have bumps and dents in them when DXF
is the exchange format. I had no choice—the only conduit between Poser and trueSpace
was DXF at the time this was created. So in Figure 22.36, you can see a small example of
what I did a *lot*: I used the Pen tools to create even, rounded vertices, loaded the path as a
selection, and then used the Clone Stamp tool to fill in the gaps in the structure of the hand.

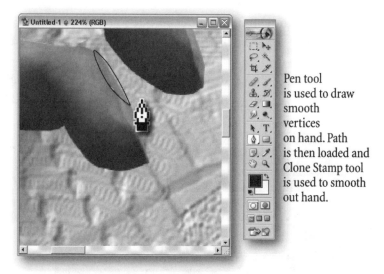

Pen tool
is used to draw
smooth
vertices
on hand. Path
is then loaded and
Clone Stamp tool
is used to smooth
out hand.

Figure 22.36   Ecch! Yuck! This hand needs some smoothing out, and it's
beyond the help of Jergen's.

During one of the renders, I caught the hand in the reflection from the exclamation
point filament. This was terrific, but it also distended the arm reflection and made it
look unnatural. After all, I did not have an entire Poser model in the modeling scene; I
only imported a hand. So in Figure 22.37, you can see this gaffe before I took a dark color
and the airbrush mode of the Paintbrush tool and eased the reflection into nothingness.

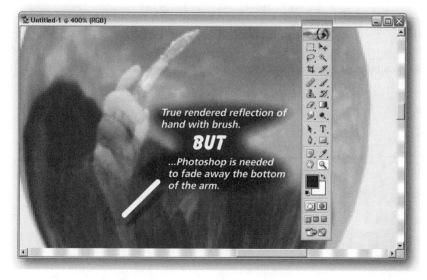

True rendered reflection of
hand with brush.

BUT

...Photoshop is needed
to fade away the bottom
of the arm.

Figure 22.37   Sometimes you want only part of a calculated reflection a modeling
program produces. No problem; Photoshop's got the art tools to fix things.

Poser (especially now with version 4 Pro) can provide you with invaluable props and even whole people, but there's one thing it doesn't provide: fingernails. Yeah, that's pretty picky, but when it's close-up time, you want the hand to look as natural as possible. In Figure 22.38, I used the Pen tool to draw the missing thumbnail and then airbrushed inside the selection marquee that was loaded based on the path. Much better, eh?

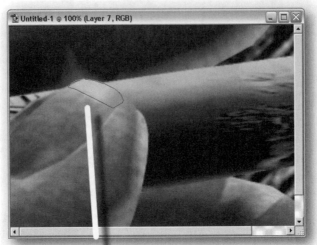

Poser doesn't do fingernails! Use the Pen tool to make the shape and then load the selection and fill it.

Figure 22.38   Hey, Poser models do *not* bite their nails. At least not as long as I was looking...

In Figure 22.39, you can see both the finished art as it was delivered to New Riders and the book cover. Hopefully, this book cover will be familiar to some of you. I wanted to show you all the loving care I put into my work for myself and for my audience.

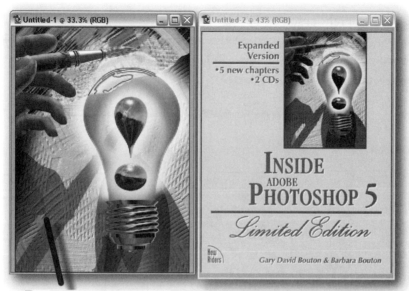

Two light sources copied from the modeling render, and added beneath the hand.

Figure 22.39   "So what you're trying to say is that this assignment was easy, right, Gare?"

Trick 3 Summary

It's not easy taking 100% synthetic imagery and turning it into something that looks just a tad short of real, but really makes an impression—and has a point. None of this would be possible if we didn't have Photoshop and a few image creation programs that were the province of SGI workstations only a decade ago. Let's hear it for the *personal* computer!

Trick 4: Removing Fringing from Leaves

This trick might sound a little reminiscent of Trick 1, in which you filled in Julian's hair selection marquee right to the edge. But this trick is different, in that it is nearly impossible to accurately select the tops of trees to replace a hum-drum (Syracuse-based) sky with something more interesting. There are too many thicknesses and colors of leaves and branches.

So I brewed up this simple-to-do method for getting a better sky into a picture while maintaining 99% of the visual integrity of the surrounding treetops.

Welcome to Henderson's Mill

Henderson's Mill is one of those wonderful upstate parks where you can bring a picnic basket and eat undisturbed—I think folks have chased all the wildlife away with their *own* wild lives decades ago (see Figure 22.40).

Henderson's Mill, fall 2001. Unretouched photo.

Figure 22.40   Henderson's Mill is a nice, secluded place—without almost any flies.

So I snapped a few pictures, nothing particularly interesting, to get the trees and the sky so that you can see how to separate them and then replace the sky.

Select Only What Needs Selecting

The first step to image improvement is to select only the areas that you need to let the Color Range command do its thing. This means you really want to select only the tree-tops and the area a little lower to catch where the blah sky is poking through some branches.

Here's how to commence with the first step in clearing away blah sky from the nice trees.

Using the Rectangular Marquee Tool in Addition Mode

1. Open the ParkWow.tif image from the Examples/Chap22 folder on the Companion CD. About 30% viewing resolution is good for the selection work. Double-click the Background layer on the Layers palette. Click OK to accept the default settings.

Tip

Using the Resize Field   You can change an image's viewing resolution to 30% easily by entering that amount in the Resize field (in Windows, this is on the far left of the Status bar; on the Macintosh, it's on the far left of the bottom image window scrollbar). Then you press Enter (Return) and life is good.

2. Choose the Rectangular Marquee tool from the toolbox, and marquee an area where trees meet monochrome sky. Hold Shift (this enables you to add to the current selection), and then create more rectangles until the sky looks somewhat like that shown in Figure 22.41. Add any remaining marquee selections necessary to include all the sky areas.

With the Rectangular Marquee tool, hold Shift to add to the selection and mark off the problem areas where leafy trees meet blah sky.

Figure 22.41   Try to encompass all the "problem areas" with an additive succession of rectangular selections.

3. Choose Select, Color Range, and then click the Eyedropper tool into the sky, as shown in Figure 22.42. I set the Fuzziness to 31. My goal was to toy with the Fuzziness slider until I reached the point where the leaves are not selected, but neither do they display spindly or missing components, such as branches.

    Oh, yes. If looking into that dinky preview box doesn't cut it for you, you can have Photoshop lay a matte down over the image itself to show you what's going to be selected. To do this, choose Black or White Matte from the Selection Preview drop-down list in the Color Range command.

Figure 22.42   Choose the appropriate amount of fuzziness with which to select
sky tones. By the way, don't worry about the black areas to the left
and right top of the Color Range window. This is a variation in
sky that you can easily delete later on.

4. After exiting the Color Range command, delete the sky—Delete (Backspace)
ought to do it. The next wise thing to do is to click the Edit in Quick Mask
mode icon and see, through the Quick Mask's tinting indicator, exactly how
close you got to neatly trimming away the sky from the leaves (see Figure 22.43).
If the tinting is showing the trees instead of the sky, Alt(Opt)+click on the Edit
in Quick Mask mode icon to reverse what is tinted.

Okay, the figure shows that we are not dead on with separating the leaves from the
sky, but that's the whole point of this trick. You don't try to tighten the selection;
instead, you paint into the gap that the selection marquee left. Click the Edit in
standard mode icon to exit Quick Mask mode, and press Ctrl(⌘)+Shift+I to
invert the selection. Go to the Channels palette and click the Save selection as
channel icon at the bottom of the palette to save the selection for later.

Figure 22.43   It's actually better to have a gap in the selection than to have
the selection eat into the trees because when you delete the
sky, the treetops look like a locust fest was there.

5. Get out the Brush tool, right-click (Macintosh: hold Ctrl and click) and choose
the 21-pixel soft-edged brush from the palette. Press Enter (Return) to hide
the Brushes palette. The saved selection should still be loaded. Hold down the
Alt(Opt) key to toggle to the Eyedropper tool, and click a color really close to the
selection edge. Choose Darken for the painting Mode on the Options bar (better
to go darker than lighter when mating a new sky with an image), and then make
brisk strokes that go all the way to the edge of the selection marquee, as shown in
Figure 22.44. Resample (use the Eyedropper) *often*; the color of the treetops
varies wildly from pixel to pixel!

Eyedropper sample from around here

Figure 22.44   You are filling in the areas that through the Color Range's anti-aliasing feature kept the selection you made from actually touching the treetops. In simpler terms, the gap in the selection consists of non-transparent pixels of only 3-4% opacity. You're driving the opacity up to an amount that looks real, in context.

6. Spend a few more minutes painting in the gap around the leaves. Now, it's time for the acid test—to drop a new sky into the background. When you're satisfied with the results, press Ctrl(⌘)+D to deselect.

7. Press Ctrl(⌘)+Shift+S; keep the file open and name it ParkAbsurd.psd (in Photoshop's native file format) and save it to your hard disk.

Mating the New Sky to the Treetops

Regardless of how thoroughly you think you painted the treetops, when you put in a more lush, darker sky, *drat*—the fringes to the trees pop up again—see Figure 22.45 (which you have yet to create, but take a look at it anyway). No problem, though. Here's a little secret to go along with the tricks here. Remember how you load an anti-aliased selection? You can paint the edges of the selection in RGB mode twice or even three times, and you will see that you are encroaching further and further out of the selection marquee. Why? Because repeated applications around an anti-aliased border will eventually prevail, because the brush tips, too, are anti-aliased.

Move the sky into the image so you can better see the problem areas

Figure 22.45   Aha! Aha! You painted perfectly, but not enough to mate the treetops with the sky.

Let's get the new sky into the image, and then get to work on this pestilence that's called image fringing.

New Sky; New Problems

1. Now, Bouton goofed again, and the sky isn't large enough for a 9MB picture, but humor me and open the DramaticClouds.tif picture from the Examples/Chap22 folder on the Companion CD.

2. With the DramaticClouds.tif in the foreground, drag the Background layer on the Layers palette into the ParkWow.psd scene. Close the DramaticClouds.tif image. On the Layers palette, drag Layer 1 (the clouds layer) below Layer 0 (the park layer).

3. Press Ctrl(⌘)+T to display the Free Transform box, and then drag by the corners the sky image until it's lower than the top of the trees and extends full left and right in the image window. Press Enter (Return) to apply the transformation. Man, oh, man, that fringing is an eyesore, isn't it?

Note

Avoiding the Defringe Command   Usually, you should resist the temptation to use the Layer, Matting, Defringe command. This command replaces edge pixels with pixel colors found within the selection.

But more often than not, unless you are working with a 10MB+ image, the Defringe command will make a mess out of the edges of a selection. And the result will look like a deckled edge book.

4. Let's spring into action! Ctrl(⌘)+click on the Alpha channel you saved earlier to load the selection of the trees. If the sky is selected instead of the trees, press Ctrl(⌘)+Shift+I to invert the selection. Press Ctrl(⌘)+H to hide the selection. The Brush tool should still be active with a 21-pixel soft brush size. Let's ease back on the Opacity to 74% (on the Options bar for the Brush tool) to give you a chance to mess with different colors before an area becomes 100% painted. Keep the Mode at Darken.

Get into this rhythm: Alt(Opt)+click with the Eyedropper tool close to where you want to paint. Release Alt(Opt), and then make short strokes from the trees into the sky. Naturally, your strokes will end because the selection marquee is still active, but check out Figure 22.46. Even though the image is in grayscale, you can still see that the trees are blending neatly into the sky area. And that's at 200% viewing resolution; imagine how subtle your artistry will be at 1:1 viewing.

Figure 22.46   Keep sampling and resampling and then make short strokes toward the edge of the selection (okay, wherever you *think* the edge is!).

5. Do all the retouching you can do around the treetops, and then keel over. Press
Ctrl(⌘)+S; keep the file open.

Other Selection Techniques

I'd like to share one or two other moves with you, because although the image looks a lot
more natural now, some things can help it along even farther. Let's work while we talk,
okay?

Completing the Binding of Treetops and Sky

1. There are bound to be areas within the trees—not just the treetops—that have a
blah sky in them, and if you remove these areas, the replacement sky can poke
through. With the Rectangular Marquee tool, drag an area where there are really
offensive blah sky areas, as shown in Figure 22.47. Choose Select, Color Range,
and see whether you can pick at a blah sky area with the Eyedropper tool. When
you are satisfied with the Fuzziness (I used a setting of 54), click OK and return
to the scene.

**Mark off smaller areas within the trees
for use with the Color Range command**

Figure 22.47   Select the tiniest of flaws in the trees.

2. Pick a very neutral shade of green (R:115, G:131, B:96 is good), and then press
Alt(Opt)+Delete (Backspace) and then Ctrl(⌘)+D to deselect the marquee
selection. Now, all those blah sky holes are filled with foliage.

3. You will need to load the selection again (Ctrl(⌘)+click Layer 1 on the Layers palette). Now, keep painting, but when you come to some twigs and some purple foliage in the image, sample those colors and paint with them. Remember; use short strokes and sample often.

4. As mentioned in Step 3, working from left to right, you will eventually hit some purple foliage—it was probably the outdoor lighting, because plants don't usually grow to 40 feet tall. But respect what the camera has provided, and sample new colors and paint away (see Figure 22.48).

Figure 22.48   Sample often, and keep the strokes short. Do I sound like a broken record? (A record was an analog music archiving device before the CD.)

5. Finally, with the Magic Wand tool, with Contiguous unchecked and Tolerance set to about 16, click in a blah sky area. Doing this will drag out all the blah sky pixels because non-contiguous means "doesn't have to be neighboring to," so the whole image layer gets the treatment. Choose Select, Modify, Expand, and then expand by two pixels, and then press Ctrl(⌘)+Alt(Opt)+D to Feather the selections by two pixels. Then, very carefully choose a bland green which will work in all selection areas and press Alt(Opt)+Delete (Backspace) to fill the selections. Press Ctrl(⌘)+D to deselect (see Figure 22.49).

Figure 22.49   Plug up the last of the ugly holes with pleasing green, and you are finished!

You're home free, and the picture looks terrific!

Trick 4 Summary

As you can see in Figure 22.50, everything at Henderson's Mill looks both pretty and plausible. And it's all because you've learned five different techniques for getting rid of the fringing between original sky and treetops. We are a little concerned, however, that the bumble bee from Chapter 1 might have eaten through the pages of this book to land in this figure.

Figure 22.50   Hey, if you wanted a "dry" book, I've got plenty upstairs from college Calculus.

Trick 5: Making a Painting from a Photo

This trick is at the top of my bag, because it just dawned on me a week or so ago that the new Photoshop brushes could indeed be used with the Lighting Effects filter to produce painting-like compositions from photos, models, or other photorealistic endeavors. "Just like Painter does," I exclaimed to myself upon gleaning the similarity in approach between my idea and what Painter does with the Apply Surface Texture command.

We use a fanciful poster instead of a photograph in the steps to come, because until you get a real grasp on the technique here, you can make loved ones look hideous with a minimal amount of effort.

You Need Layers to Make Different Paint Strokes

Unlike Procreation's Painter (okay, I finally gave away Corel's alias), where you can paint and try out different brushes and then apply the resulting textures on a copy of the art-work using the Clone command, Photoshop doesn't work on clones of images. Therefore, if you want different areas with unique textures that look like you have painted them with a real paintbrush, you need to compose your piece in layers.

Let's begin by unfolding this mysterious new property that Photoshop offers:

Setting Up Your "Painting" Brush

1. Open Fat_Star.psd from the Examples/Chap22 folder on the Companion CD.
2. Press Ctrl(⌘)+N to create a new document, about 200 pixels by 200 pixels. This is where you test the flow amount of different brush tips. Choose the Brush tool and set the Flow to 5%. If you changed the painting Mode in the last exercise, set it back to Normal. Choose the Chalk 60-pixel "novelty" brush that's shown in Figure 22.51 (near the end of the default brushes list).

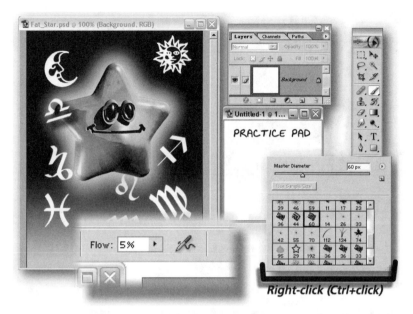

Figure 22.51   These are more or less the things you need before trying to make this silly astrology poster into a fine painting.

3. Get a feel for the brush's characteristics using the doodle pad image window. Click the Fat_Star.psd title bar to make this the active document. Click the Background layer on the Layers palette to make this the active layer.

4. Press D for the default colors. Double-click the Edit in Quick Mask mode icon and make sure that the Colored Indicates option is set to Selected Areas (or Alt(Opt)+click on the Quick Mask icon until the circle is colored and the rectangle isn't on the face of the icon). Your work is in Quick Mask mode now, and now's your chance to paint all over the place. The more "character"—random, uneven strokes—the better for the finished painting (see Figure 22.52).

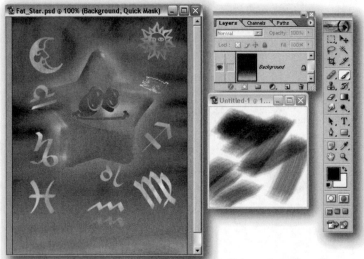

**Make strokes all over the place, in
Quick Mask mode, on the Background layer**

Figure 22.52   Knock yourself out. This is about as much fun as is legally possible!

5. Press Q to exit Quick Mask mode. Click the Channels tab to view the Channels palette and click the Save selection as channel icon at the bottom of the palette to save the selection as an alpha channel. Click the Alpha 1 channel to switch your view to the alpha channel.

You do not want this willy nilly texture to dominate anything except the blue background. So now you have to remove the star, the glow, and the horoscope symbols from the alpha channel.

6. First, Ctrl(⌘)+click the star title on the Layers palette. Press X to switch white to the foreground. From a view of the alpha channel, press Alt(Opt)+Delete (Backspace) to flood the selection area with white (see Figure 22.53). Press Ctrl(⌘)+D to deselect.

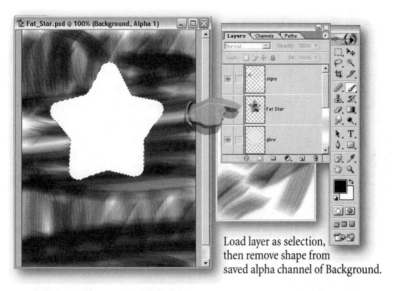

Load layer as selection, then remove shape from saved alpha channel of Background.

Figure 22.53   Remove the star's silhouette from the alpha channel, and it will show no brush strokes when the Lighting Effects filter is applied.

7. Repeat Step 6 with the glow layer, the signs, and especially that straggler Leo, just above the background (see Figure 22.54). Does your image look like this? You can quickly select the remaining layers by Ctrl(⌘)+clicking the Leo layer, and then Ctrl(⌘)+Shift click the glow and signs layers to add them to the selection.

Remove glow and signs from alpha channel

Figure 22.54   Remove all silhouettes that you do not want "paint textured."

8. Return to the Layers palette and click the Background layer to make it the current editing layer. Go to the Filter menu and choose Render, Lighting Effects. As shown in Figure 22.55, choose Directional for the Light type and the Alpha 1 channel for the Texture Channel. The setting for the Height slider is minimal— you're making paint strokes, not trying to rival the Mariana Trench. Dispense with the fancy options below the lighting boxes (in other words, use the settings shown in the figure to keep Metallic, Shiny, and other settings minimal). Drag that point on the end of light in the proxy window toward and then away from the center until the exposure of the proxy window looks the same as the color in the Background layer. Click OK to apply.

Figure 22.55   Use the Lighting Effects Texture controls to apply the paint strokes saved in an alpha channel to the Background layer.

9. Save your work as Fat Star.psd. Keep the file open for the next exercise.

More Fun with Pseudo-Painting

Things are going to liven up from here on out. The hero, the fat star, needs to be treated with a lot of delicacy simply because it is the hero of the picture and you don't want to totally demolish it with paint strokes. So you make a copy, apply the Artistic...*wait a second*. I should be telling you this in the following *tutorial*!

When You Brush Upon a Star

1. Switch active layers on the Layers palette so the Fat Star is chosen. Drag the Fat Star layer onto the Create a new layer icon on the bottom of the Layers palette. You now have a duplicate of the star layer. The Fat Star copy should be the active layer on the Layers palette. Go to the Filter menu and choose Artistic, Dry Brush. See Figure 22.56 for the settings to apply. Then click OK to apply the Dry Brush effect and return to the workspace.

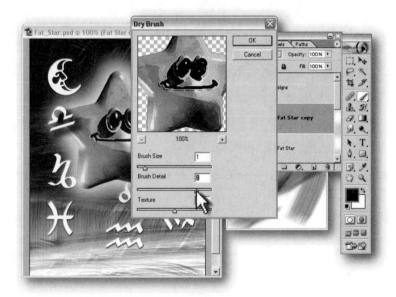

Figure 22.56   Add some pre-conceived artistic excitement to a copy of the star by using the Filters menu.

2. Okay—follow me closely now. You've got the Brush tool selected, right? Right-click (Macintosh: hold Ctrl and click) and then click the Brushes palette's flyout menu and choose Natural Brushes; click OK to replace (as opposed to adding to the current list of brushes) in the ensuing dialog box. Choose the tip from the top row that says "29" (pixels) and looks as though someone sneezed on a windshield. Crank the Flow up to 20%, and click on the Quick Mask icon. Make sure black is the foreground color (if it's not, press X to switch).

3. Paint away on the star, as shown in Figure 22.57. It helps verisimilitude ("realness"—I learned that word from Daniel Will-Harris) to paint more heavily, that is, repeat strokes more often, in the darker areas of the fat star, with fewer strokes and perhaps some empty places, in the Fat Star's lighter areas.

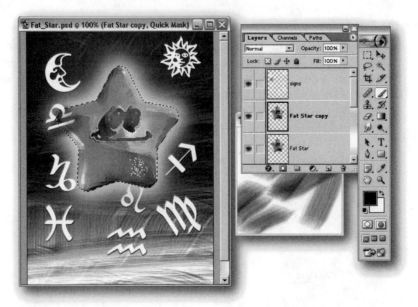

Figure 22.57   Paint back and forth or in any direction you might paint a star on a blank canvas.

4. Repeat the process of switching back to Standard Editing mode (press Q). Save the selection as Alpha 2 on the Channels palette, and press Ctrl(⌘)+D to dese-lect. Click the Fat Star copy layer in the Layers palette to make it the active layer. Then it's off to the Lighting Effects filter for texturizing, using the same settings as the previous exercise (except make Alpha 2 the Texture Channel and adjust the point in the proxy window again until the color matches the star color from the document window). Click OK to apply settings.

5. When the fat star has been textured on the copy layer, try turning the Opacity down on this layer to achieve a blend of unfiltered and filtered versions (30% gives a subtle effect). This is a swell way to control the amount of "paint strokes" after you've applied them (see Figure 22.58).

You have the option
to mix amounts of original star
and painted, bumped copy

Figure 22.58   Just "dial up" the amount of effect you want for the finished, painted star.

6. Optional: On your own, get creative with the strokes you apply in Quick Mask
   mode to the glow layer (see Figure 22.59). Me? I painted back and forth around the
   circumference of the glow to strongly suggest the emanations are traveling outward. Go ahead and experiment using the same techniques we've applied so far.

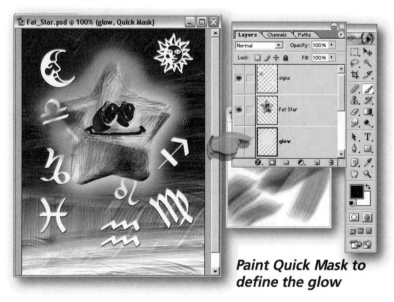

Paint Quick Mask to
define the glow

Figure 22.59   Paint in Quick Mask mode on the glow layer until you achieve the
effect you want.

7. Whoa, Nelly! Let's take a break for a moment to contemplate final strategies for making the horoscope signs look painted.

Be sure to choose the Brushes flyout and choose Reset Brushes before continuing with the tricks!

The horoscope signs will not withstand the radical type of filtering you've just applied to everything else. Instead, let's try a different approach and filter—so that you can make the symbols both legible and interesting.

The Minimize Command and the Spatter Effect

The horoscope symbols are too frail to be filtered with something as strong as the Spatter Effect. You can beef up their outlines with a command that apparently very few people use; the Filter, Other, Minimum command. Contrary to its name, the Minimum command actually adds to the outline of a selection or image area.

Come on. Let's do it...

Minimum, Then Spatter

1. Ctrl(⌘)+click the signs layer to load the signs as a selection, and then on the Channels palette, click the Save selection as channel icon (Alpha 3). Click the Alpha 3 layer to view the Alpha 3 channel. Press Ctrl(⌘)+D to deselect.

2. Go to the Filter menu and choose Other, Minimum. Set the Amount to 2 pixels, and as you can see in Figure 22.60, the symbols look beefy and can stand up to some serious distortion.

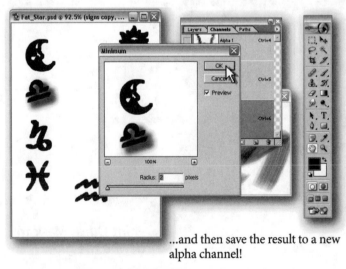

...and then save the result to a new alpha channel!

Figure 22.60   The Minimum command is sort of a combination between Expand Selection and filling the expanded selection.

3. Click OK to apply the beefiness. Choose Filter, Brush Strokes, and then Spatter. Use the settings shown in Figure 22.61, and then click OK to apply the effect.

Figure 22.61   Not all artists are tidy with their strokes. It makes you more of a synthetic virtuoso to apply both straight and spattered strokes to a work.

4. Ctrl(⌘)+click Alpha 3 to load the spattered symbols. Click the Layers tab to view the Layers palette. Click the Fat Star copy layer to make this layer active, then click the Create a new layer icon at the bottom of the palette to put the new layer below the signs layer. Choose a pale blue color and press Alt(Opt)+Delete (Backspace) to fill the selection with color. Press Ctrl(⌘)+D to deselect. Lower the Opacity of the signs layer so that you can see the spatter effect and still make out the symbols. Come to think of it, you should probably add an effect to the signs layer by clicking on the encircled "f" icon on the bottom of the Layers palette; then choose Bevel and Emboss. Then add to the signs a Pillow Emboss (from the Style drop-down list). Click OK.

5. Repeat Steps 1–4 for the Leo layer so that it doesn't feel left out.

6. Look at Figure 22.62. This has got to be one of the most robust paintings never painted!

Figure 22.62   Is it a painting? High art? Nope—it's Photoshop, pushed just a little!

Trick 5 Summary

So there you have it—a simple way to make your friends and loved ones look hideous. You're probably beginning to get the idea that you can use Photoshop tools for all sorts of things—not just the tasks the box tells you about.

Because this is a multi-trick chapter, we'd best get moving on to another thing Photoshop can do to match Painter features.

Trick 6: Fun with Fractals: Creating Seamless Tiles

Fractal math, when plotted to the screen, can be an absolutely wonderful thing. There is no simple way to describe fractal math (at least not in this book), except to say that fractals are so complex that they cannot be plotted with a mere curve. Fractals are a seemingly random set of fluctuations that apparently cannot be represented by an equation. But many fractals *are* generated through simple mathematical equations.

Fractals come in two types: terminating and non-terminating. We are interested in the terminating type of fractal because more often then not, a fractal is written so as to form a seamless tile. And the good news is that Photoshop's Clouds and Clouds Difference filters both terminate at 128 pixels.

> **Note**
>
> **What Is a Fractal?**   Ken Musgrave (active Terragen list member and part of the team that re-engineered Bryce) probably summed up the answer to, "What is a fractal?" most elegantly (and if you still have a little high school geometry left in you like I do, it makes queer sense), to wit:
>
> "If we accept a number to the second power as a square, and a value to the 3rd power as a cube, then fractals lie somewhere in between."

So let's get busy creating something that looks organic:

Creating a Seamless Fractal Tile

1. Create a New document, 128-by-128 pixels in dimension, and RGB in color.
2. Create an alpha channel. Click the Create new channel icon on the bottom of the Channels palette (press F7 if the palette isn't already open onscreen).
3. Make sure that your toolbox colors are black and white. Do this by pressing D.
4. Choose Filter, Render, and then choose Clouds. Press Ctrl(⌘)+F a few times until you think you've rendered something interesting.

Because the Clouds filter generates a random fractal result each time it is used, pressing Ctrl(⌘)+F merely repeats the last filter applied (in this case—the Clouds filter), and allows you to try the filter repeatedly until you have a result that appeals to you.

5. Try the Clouds Difference filter once or twice. This filter produces stronger fractal algorithms (equations) than Clouds and inverts colors every time you use it. Fortunately, only shades of black and white are used in this 8-bit grayscale alpha channel, so the result of Difference Clouds is interesting instead of color-confused.
6. Stop applying either Clouds filter when you arrive at something interestingly splotchy-looking (see Figure 22.63).

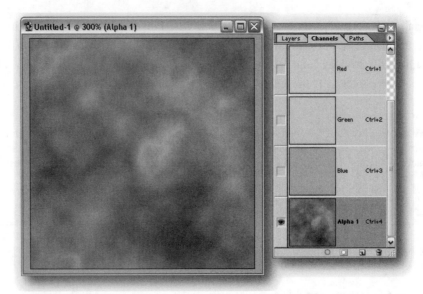

Figure 22.63   Stop brewing a fractal when you arrive at something interesting-looking.

7. Pick a very neutral shade for the foreground color (R:220, G:224, B:221). Click the Background layer on the Layers palette to make this layer active. Press Alt(Opt)+Delete (Backspace) to fill the RGB composite channel with this color.

8. Go to the Filter menu and choose Render, Lighting Effects to make bumps in the RGB composite channel by using the Texture controls. Select the Alpha 1 channel for the Texture Channel and Light type should be set at Directional. Keep the bump amount very slight, and use the directional light's point on the end of the line (in the proxy window) to make sure that the image is exposed in Lighting Effects the same as the original surface color. Check out Figure 22.64, and click OK to apply the bumps.

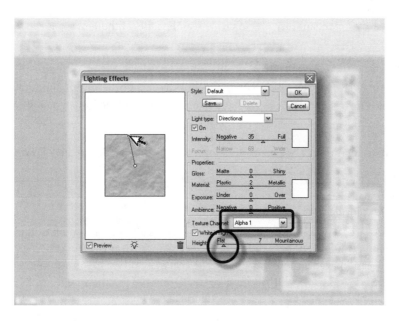

Figure 22.64   Keep the Height down to about 7% and make all the Properties 0 (zero); neither shiny nor metallic.

9. Ta-dah! You've created a seamless tiling fractal image! Use the Define Pattern command (Edit, Define Pattern) and apply this design to a large area to prove to yourself that it has no seams. You also can drag this image into ImageReady and use GIF optimization so there are only about 14 different colors in it. Doing this will preserve 90% of the visual integrity of the image, and it will result in a ti*nnnnnnny* file, which means that if you use it on a web page, download times for visitors will be courteously short (see Figure 22.65).

The fruits of your labor— in a few steps!

This image will tile seamlessly. We don't know what it is, but it looks natural and organic, huh?

Try it as a JPEG or GIF as a web page background.

Figure 22.65   The finished fractal design.

Are you ready for yet another way to create seamless tiles? I thought so…

Using the Offset Command to Shuffle a Layer

You've probably used the Offset command in other chapters, but for the uninitiated, briefly, the Offset command can turn a design inside out—the edges are repositioned at the center of the image and the center is sprawled out among the four edges of the image.

Believe it or not, this can be a handy tool for making seamless tiles, as the following steps show you:

Turning Text Inside Out

1. I prepared a little 3D file that features the letters *PS7* in celebration of this new version of Photoshop. Each letter/number is on its own layer, so copying between image windows is a cinch. The other key player in this tutorial is a file called canvas.tif. Open the canvas.tif image and the ps7.psd files from the Examples/Chap22 folder now (see Figure 22.66).

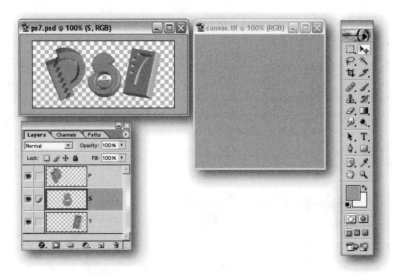

Figure 22.66   You're going to make a 3D-seamless tile!

2. With the ps7.psd document in the foreground, on the Layers palette, drag the "P" into the Canvas window. Repeat this process for the "S" and the "7", and then with the Move tool, make sure they are evenly spaced from one another. Remember, with Auto Layer Select disabled, you can Ctrl(⌘)+click over a letter/number and automatically move to that layer as the active layer.

3. With the three characters on different layers, you are hindered in your endeavors. Hide the Background layer in Canvas.tif (uncheck the eye icon next to the title), and with the top layer selected as the active layer, press Ctrl(⌘)+Shift+E (to

Merge Visible—a *very* useful shortcut to remember). See Figure 22.67 for where we are at this point.

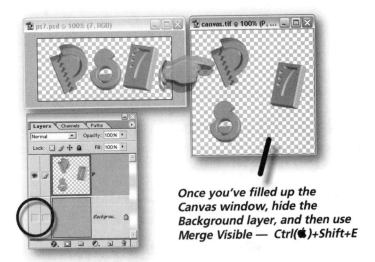

Once you've filled up the Canvas window, hide the Background layer, and then use Merge Visible — Ctrl(⌘)+Shift+E

Figure 22.67   Evenly space the characters because you will soon add characters to the canvas image once again.

4. Go to the Filter menu and choose Other, Offset. Make the Vertical and Horizontal Offset amounts about 75 pixels each, and set the Undefined Areas to Wrap Around. Make sure—and this will sound weird—that at least two if not all three of the characters are chopped in half, disappearing around one image window edge only to partially reappear on the opposite edge (see Figure 22.68).

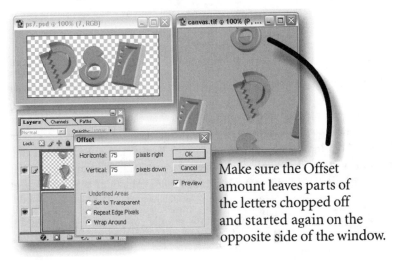

Make sure the Offset amount leaves parts of the letters chopped off and started again on the opposite side of the window.

Figure 22.68   Scatter those characters well. You'll be adding characters to fill in the gaps shortly.

5. Click OK to mess up the characters, and then repeat the process of dragging characters from the ps7.psd image to the canvas.tif image. Make sure that everything is evenly spaced.

6. On the Layers palette, the top layer should be the active layer. Click to link the remaining character layers to the top layer and press Ctrl(⌘)+E to merge the linked layers. All the characters are now on one layer and you also have the Background—which you should make visible again now.

7. With the characters layer as the current editing layer, press Ctrl(⌘)+L to display the Levels command.

8. Lighten or darken the character layer by using the Input sliders in the Levels command. This makes the characters sort of recede and almost vanish into the background color (see Figure 22.69).

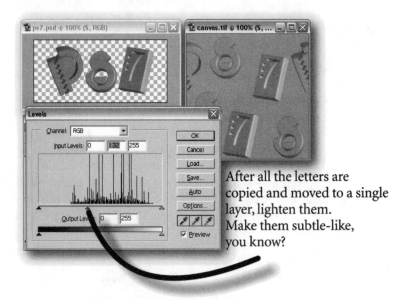

Figure 22.69   Blend the characters into the background color using the Levels command.

9. Click OK to apply the Levels command, and then flatten the image. Choose Define Pattern from the Edit menu. Then apply the pattern to a new, large document window. To bring up the pattern, you choose Edit, Fill, and then select Pattern for the Contents: Use flyout menu and select the pattern name from the Custom Pattern menu. (You can name these things when you define the pattern, and that's probably a good idea because the thumbnails are 32-by-32 pixels by default.)

As you can see in Figure 22.70, the pattern is terrific for presenting images, but text? Forget it. Textures are used often in other applications, and this has been the most visually sophisticated of the lot.

Figure 22.70   This is one visually interesting tiling pattern! What's next?

There is one more pattern-making technique I'd like to present, and this is perhaps the easiest and most effective for presentations, web pages, and lazy summer cookouts.

Cloning Away the Offset Filter's Seams

As mentioned earlier, the most valuable reason for the existence of the Offset command is to turn stuff inside out. Well, if you find a non-terminating (it will not tile seamlessly) fractal and you want to pick up the Clone Stamp tool, you can turn a non-tiling fractal into a tiling one.

Like so:

Fussing a Non-Tiling Fractal Into Shape

1. Open the Fractal eggs.tif image from the Examples/Chap22 folder on the Companion CD. Take a look at Figure 22.71—it's really gross.

This fractal pattern
does *not* repeat
seamlessly.

And God knows what
it's supposed
to be.

Figure 22.71   This is the non-tiling fractal we will mercilessly pummel into submission.

2. The only saving grace about this image is that I made the math simple. It's 200 pixels square, so you should go to the Filter menu and choose Other, Offset, and specify 100 pixels offset in both directions with the Wrap Around option checked. This makes sure that its center is composed of the four edges. Then click OK to apply the change. You will clearly see ugly edges in this ugly picture.

3. Um, pick the Clone Stamp tool, and right-click (Macintosh: hold Ctrl and click) over the image. Click the Brushes palette's flyout button and choose Reset Brushes so that you are not bound forever with the Natural Brushes! Click OK in the dialog box to replace the Natural Brushes.

4. Because the pattern is organic and not absolutely distinct in shape, you can get away with a soft brush tip (22 pixels), and then Alt(Opt)+click in a light area to set the roving sampling point. Then start stroking where you find a light area next to a visible edge in the image. Continue making new sampling points, and applying the Clone Stamp tool along the visible edges (see Figure 22.72).

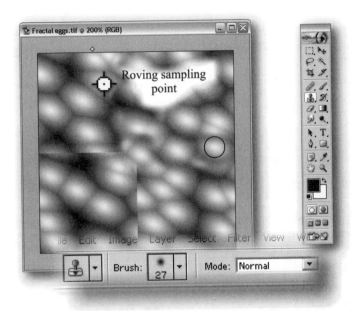

Figure 22.72   It is truly amazing how you can hide tile lines in an abstract image.

5. Press Ctrl(⌘)+F to apply the last-used filter (Offset), and the image is turned inside out again. Now, check carefully for telltale tiling lines and then remove any/all of them using the Clone Stamp tool. You can never be 100% certain of your efforts in the corner regions of the design, which are now located at 12, 3, 6, and 9 o'clock (see Figure 22.73).

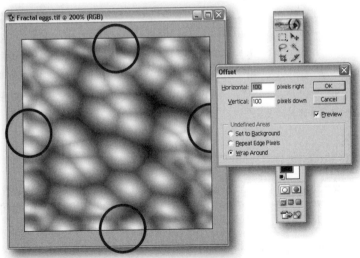

ARE THERE ANY HARD EDGES SHOWING?

Figure 22.73   Just a last-minute check before you add this design to your Pattern collection.

6. Choose Edit, Define Pattern...let's name this one. **Eggs on Rampage** is good; type this in and then press Enter (Return) to enter the pattern as a Photoshop 7 pattern.

7. As you can see in Figure 22.74, the image tiles fairly nicely. Once again, Photoshop prevails over fractals, which none of us totally understand anyway.

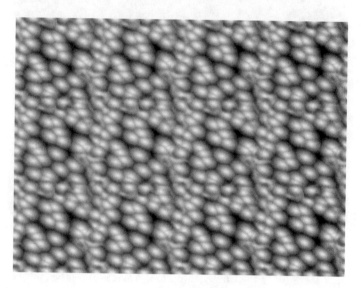

Figure 22.74   Just another way to create seamless tiling textures in Photoshop.

Trick 6 Summary

You're doing well—even the tough stuff is starting to look easier, isn't it? Creating seamless tiles, whether you use fractal math to do it or work with the Offset command and hide the seams, is now an easily repeatable process. Now that you know how to create stunning backgrounds from less-than-stunning art, are you ready for one of the most asked-for tricks in my email box?

Trick 7: Removing Red Eye

I don't use a flash anywhere near my camera's lens, so I (the all-time naive one) had to guess what "red eye" was when I first heard of it from a reader. Red eye to me was one or more of the following:

- A dye that makes clothes red.

- Something Black Bart orders at the Silver Dollar saloon during the settlement of Arkansas.

- Retinal reflection. Ding, ding, *ding*—correct answer.

Red eye happens when your flash is so close to the camera lens that the flash bounces into your pupil, hits the back of your eye which has red blood vessels, and then is captured by the camera. You can thank Kodak for manufacturing 110 film format cameras for the past 25 years that do this.

Okay, enough "whys." Here is Bouton's solution to red eye in an image.

Step-by-Step Eye Restoration

1. Open the Twins.tif picture from the Examples/Chap22 folder on the Companion CD. As you can see, I have twin brothers, (and Dave on the left has red eye). See picture Figure 25.75. And if you can count the number of times the Bouton's have used chickens in their pictures (ducks count, too), I'll send you a free Type 1 hand-crafted font in Macintosh or Windows format.

Figure 27.75   My brother Dave at left has red eye, but his twin—also called Dave—missed the flash by engrossing himself in hard disk prices.

2. Zoom in real close to the eye. Press D for the default colors. Press Q to enter Quick Mask mode. Choose a soft-edged brush that is a comfortable size for painting around and over the offending red eye areas (for this image I used a 5-pixel soft-edged brush). The Quick Mask mode tint also is red but you should still be able to see easily where it is applied. The goal is to paint around the red areas while leaving the white highlight areas and the normal color surrounding the iris intact (see Figure 22.76).

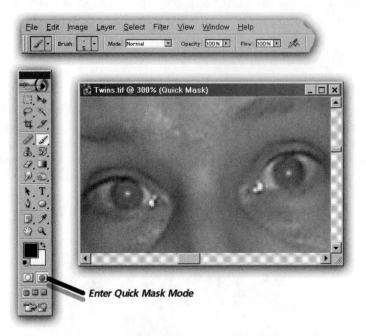

Enter Quick Mask Mode

Figure 22.76   Paint Quick Mask red tint over the red eye problem areas. In this case—the red-on-red effect can be pretty scary, so it looks like the red eye will get worse before it gets better.

3. Go to the Filter menu and choose Blur, Gaussian Blur. Add just a small amount to make your selection blend even more smoothly into the normal areas of the eye. In this case, enter a radius of .5 and click OK to apply the blur to the Quick Mask (see Figure 22.77).

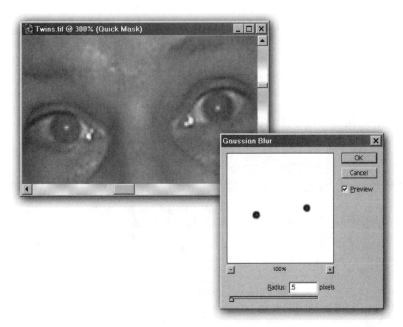

Figure 22.77   Add a Gaussian Blur to the Quick Mask red-tinted paint. This will help soften the transition of color later.

4. Press Q to exit Quick Mask. The red eye should be the only area selected (if the marching ants run up the edges of the document window, press Ctrl(⌘)+Shift+I to invert the selection). Press Ctrl(⌘)+J to put the selection on its own layer. Press Ctrl(⌘)+Shift+U to desaturate the area. You can see in Figure 22.78 that the eyes are starting to look better already.

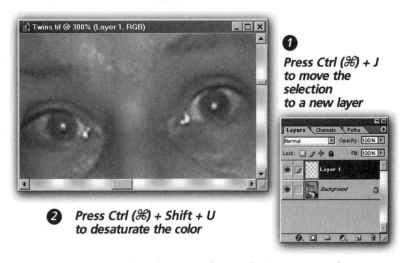

❶ *Press Ctrl (⌘) + J to move the selection to a new layer*

❷ *Press Ctrl (⌘) + Shift + U to desaturate the color*

Figure 22.78   Exit Quick Mask mode and put the eye selection on its own layer and then desaturate.

5. Layer 1 should be the active layer on the Layers palette. Click the Lock transparent pixels icon. Choose a brush big enough to encompass the entire area that used to contain the red color (I chose a 17-pixel soft-edged brush). Make sure that black is the foreground color and lower Flow to 60%. Center the brush on the offending area and click once. Then maybe move the brush toward the top edge of the area and click once more if you would like to add additional dark areas to the top of the iris area (see Figure 22.79).

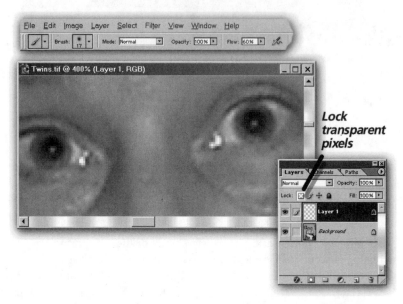

Figure 22.79   Lock transparent pixels for Layer 1 and then paint the offending area with some black. Use the Brush options shown in the figure.

6. Click the Lock transparent pixels icon to unlock Layer 1. If you would like to lower the brush size and add additional color, you should sample the colors from the original image. This is a judgment call; it's completely up to you whether you want to add any further touches to the eye. However, I decided to add to the highlight in the iris just slightly by choosing a small brush. For this image I chose a 5-pixel soft-edged brush and then pressed the left bracket ([) key to reduce it to 4 pixels. Leave the Flow at 60% and hold down the Alt(Opt) key to toggle to the Eyedropper tool. Sample the highlighted color of the eye (where light reflects). Then click once or twice in each eye to make this area a little clearer, as you see in Figure 22.80.

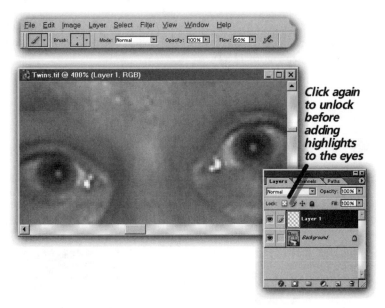

Click again
to unlock
before
adding
highlights
to the eyes

Figure 22.80   Use the Brush options shown in the figure and uncheck the Lock transparent pixels option on the Layer palette. Then enhance the existing specular highlight of the eyes.

7. For a few more final touches, go to the Filter menu and choose Noise, Add Noise. The goal is to try to match any noise you may notice in the photo. Zoom in and adjust the noise amount until it looks natural. For this image, a Gaussian noise of 1 seems to work well. Click OK to apply the filter (see Figure 22.81).

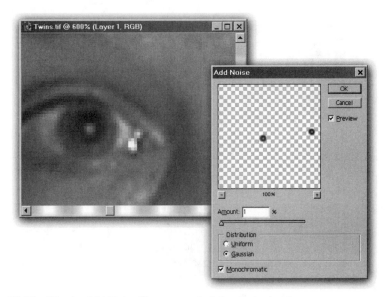

Figure 22.81   Use the Add Noise filter to match the noise in the photo.

8. Zoom out a little and watch the image as you lower the Opacity setting a little to have your changes blend in with the normal image. For this image, I lowered the Opacity to 85% (see Figure 22.82).

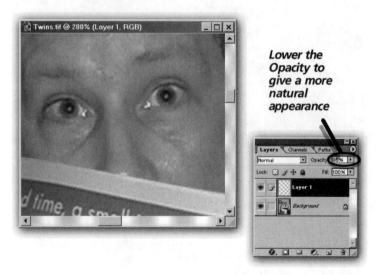

Figure 22.82   Lower the Opacity on the Layers palette to give an additional natural look.

9. When you're pleased with the results, press Ctrl(⌘)+E to merge the layer down onto the original Background layer. Save the changes. You're done. Dave looks a lot less alien-like—if you ignore the two-headed factor (see Figure 22.83).

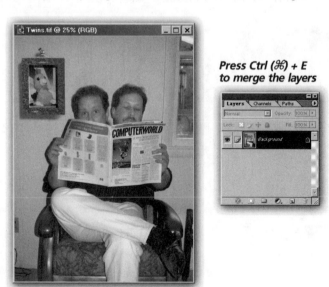

Figure 22.83   Merge the layers when you are satisfied with the results. A much more normal looking Dave (now we need a head-removal lesson for the spare head—huh?).

I think you'll have to agree now that Figure 22.84 looks a lot more natural now. And these steps were only the bare bones. Surely after you invest more time, you will come out with a more convincing banishment of red eye. Hey, it's my job to make *you* look good, and not myself!

Figure 22.84   This method helps to maintain the pre-existing specular highlights in the eye (from the photo), yet gives a realistic fix for the red eye color.

Trick 7 Summary

Nothing's more annoying than red eye in a photo you are really counting on to come out great. This section walked you through the process of fixing this easily; and, of course, you can always throw the flash out the window and try *natural* lighting...

So much for red eye. Next trick, please...

Trick 8: Creating a Bronze Guy

Don't be misled by the title. We are not going to send a pale New Yorker to Ft. Lauderdale for a weekend. Instead, I'm going to show you a behind-the-scenes piece of magic I did in a past *Inside Photoshop* book.

First of all, the assignment was to remove a person from his clothing. Um, so the clothing remained—this is a family book, you understand. It was a superbly surrealistic sight to see clothing marching down a road. But smart-aleck me had to improve upon the scene for the color plate section, and made this empty clothing into sort of a blobby bronze guy poking out of the clothing.

I received email out the Eudora asking me how I did the bronze-stylized character, mostly because the reflections in the bronze were accurate, and none of the readers thought I'd actually posed a bronze blob on the road.

Let's back up to the gracious Gary Kubicek, co-author of record with the *Inside Photoshop* series. In Figure 22.85, Gare was kind enough to flail his arms and legs while he walked, because I knew after I'd deleted him from the clothes, the clothes themselves would have to have an indicative, forced posture. Thanks, Gare!

Figure 22.85   Gary K. thinks, "How do I let Bouton talk me into this embarassing stuff?"

Using the photo and a lot of the Clone Stamp tool, I removed all fleshy parts, desaturated the collar (where fleshtones were reflecting off the white collar—think about that detail…the little stuff counts), and before long, we had a phantom Gary trucking down the street. Check out Figure 22.86 for both the top and bottom halves of the trickery.

Figure 22.86   About the only thing missing here is a nametag on the inside of the shirt collar.

In the earlier book, we left the tutorial at that. But I had an interesting idea: What if I dress a Poser model in similar clothing, and extend bronze blobs out of his clothing to reflect the scene of the photo that had been taken weeks before I got this idea?

Enter Figure 22.87. This is a screen capture of the Poser figure posing in trueSpace, without its head, arms, or wallet. (Again, trueSpace is one of those affordable modeling programs that does accurate reflection calculations.) I set up the background with a rough photo-collage of what the surroundings in the original picture looked like, and then I colored the sky a brilliant reddish-purple which is technically inaccurate but it made the blobs I added look like bronze.

Figure 22.87   Setting up a simulated scene of the original enables you to get exactly the right reflections you want in the pieces to be added later.

As you can see, the reflections are not perfect, but they are close enough to fool even the most discriminating viewer. I rendered the scene once for the reflections and then a second time to create an alpha channel that would help me separate the bronze components from the background.

In Figure 22.88, Gare is back on the road, but wow—where did he go to get that tan?

Figure 22.88   Reflections that are accurate enough to fool the casual viewer's eye can produce startling results when the whole image is presented.

And I did add the shadow, based on my modeling work and the shadows that Gare's "proxy" cast in the trueSpace scene.

Trick 8 Summary

This quirky trick takes a good eye and the willingness to experiment to get just the effect you want, but as you can see, it's worth the effort. Who knows? Maybe you have your own "Mercury Man" hiding in your wardrobe at home…

Trick 9: Becoming Gaugin in Your Spare Time

This trick is for folks who consider themselves to be non-artists and dabble in Photoshop only to color-correct stuff. I've got news for you all—although this next trick requires the purchase of Adobe Dimensions ($149 SMRP), there is not a step in this whole section that cannot be done blindfolded (okay, you can peek a little from beneath the blindfold).

I'm going to teach you simplicity of concept, of evocative colors, and you, too, might want to become a Post-Impressionist!

Doling Out the Goods from Dimensions

To me, Adobe Dimensions, which has not been updated since 1997, is sort of a wonderful utility. The program doesn't have a fraction of the modeling realism or power of say, Strata Pro, but then again, it costs about as much as a traffic fine, and what it does, it does excellently. Dimensions is particularly adept at plastic 3D-extruded text, by the way.

Okay, so step one is to make a weird squiggle in Dimensions using the same Pen tools you find in Photoshop. What does the squiggle represent? It represents half a vase shape (see Figure 22.89).

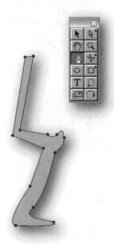

COME ON! SURELY YOU CAN DRAW THIS
SIMPLE DOODLE USING ADOBE PEN TOOLS!

Figure 22.89   This pathetic doodle is actually the makings of a vase.

In Figure 22.90, you can see that if you mirror the doodle, it indeed begins to look like
a vase. And the picture to the right in this figure shows that if a 2D path is swept by an
infinite number of points, it becomes a 3D vase.

Figure 22.90   It's easy to visualize a path swept around a central vertical line
becoming a vase, if you have the right visualization tools!

I hope it's obvious that you *will* participate in this adventure; we simply need to address how to use Dimensions first. The completed vase image, vase.tif, is on the Companion CD.

Okay, so in Dimensions, after you've used the Revolve palette to make a vase out of the path, you can color the vase any color you like. I used sand brown in this example. But wait, this gets better; you can select any facet of the vase with the Direct Selection tool, and either color the facet, or add a pattern. You can't see it in Figure 22.91, but I've made the top of the body of the vase a rusty red. The body is now selected, and I'm using the Map Artwork command, which is quite a novel feature.

Direct Selection tool chooses model faces. Each face can have a different design or color.

Figure 22.91   Dimensions sort of irons out a 3D facet into a pattern to which you can then map artwork.

In Figure 22.92, you can see how Dimensions presents a facet pattern in a workspace away from the 3D image. Areas that are invisible in your current view of the vase are grayed out. All I'm doing here is making doodles and coloring them in. When I'm done, I choose exit and the shapes have become decals on the sand-brown vase.

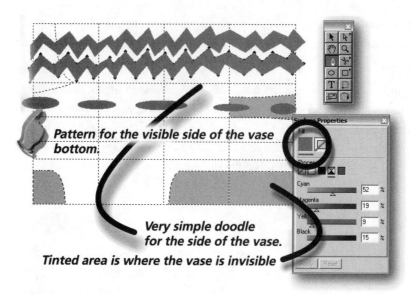

Figure 22.92   So far, has there been anything you can't draw?

After selecting the neck of the vase, I made one more trip to the Map Artwork zone. I used Symbols PS, a font I created which is on the Companion CD. Exit the zone, and I'm back to a handsomely adorned vase. See Figure 22.93 for the (undemanding) application of a symbol font character to the neck of the vase.

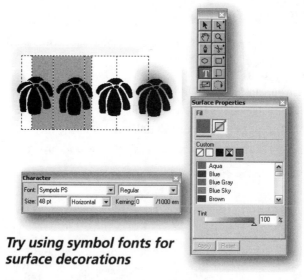

Figure 22.93   Again, I am totally confident that you can do this sort of stuff with just the little information I'm sharing here.

Back in 3D mode, I want to export a bitmap (raster) version of the vase, so I chose Dimensions and here's a secret—there's a programming error in Dimensions. Any value to which you want to export (in pixels) you must multiply by 125% because Dimensions does not export specified sizes accurately (see Figure 22.94).

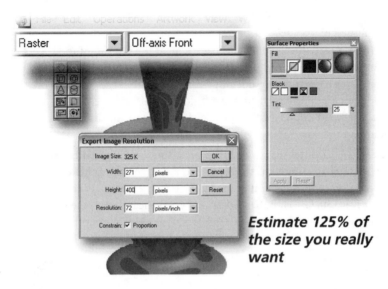

Estimate 125% of the size you really want

Figure 22.94   Export the vase to bitmap format (.bmp or .tif will do). It will render to a solid white background.

Okay, now it's your turn to put in some pixel-pushing and imitate the broad color fields and exotic tone of Gaugin's work!

Getting the Vase Out of Its Background

You are going to leave the vase right there in its little window while you remove the background and embellish the image window with modest yet tasteful creations of your own. I'm not being smart here—I'm honestly trying to take the scare out of image creation.

In the following steps, you will remove the background, pull out a couple of guides and create a ledge for the vase.

Creating a Ledge for the Vase

I. Open the vase.tif file from the Examples/Chap22 folder on the Companion CD. Press D for default colors (so white is the background color). Right-click (Macintosh: hold Ctrl and click) the title bar of the document and choose Canvas Size. In the Canvas Size dialog box, leave the middle anchor selected and type **800** (pixels) for Width and **600** (pixels) for Height. Double-click the Background layer and rename it **vase**. Press W for the Magic Wand tool and with Tolerance set at 32, click the white background color. Go to the Select menu and choose Modify, Expand and enter a value of **2**. Click OK. Press Delete (Backspace) to clear the white background. Press Ctrl(⌘)+D to deselect. Press Ctrl(⌘)+R to display the rulers in the image window. This is the only way to add guides to the image window.

2. Alt(Opt)+click the Create a new layer icon at the bottom of the Layers palette, name this new layer **Ledge,** and click OK. Drag the Ledge layer below the vase layer. Drag a horizontal guide out (from the ruler at the top) and then a vertical guide out (from the ruler on the left side) so they intersect about a screen inch to the left and middle of the vase. See Figure 22.95 for the precise location of the guides.

3. Create a horizontal shape using the Lasso tool in Polygonal Lasso mode and use the View, Snap command to keep the tool right on the guide until you make a diagonal selection segment at the left (see Figure 22.95). When you've created it, color it R:130, G:134, B:226. Then create a vertical part to the ledge (refer to Figure 22.95), and fill it with R:243, G:197, B:144. Deselect the selection.

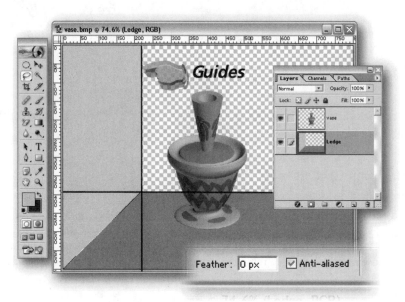

Figure 22.95   Create a primitive ledge using colors that complement the vase.

4. With the Move tool, drag the guides back into the rulers and then press Ctrl(⌘)+R to hide the rulers.

5. With the Gradient tool, set the Foreground color to R:0, G:51. B:124 and the Background color to R:255, G:211, B:123. Alt(Opt)+click on the Create a new layer icon at the bottom of the Layers palette and name the new layer **Sky**. Click OK. Drag the Sky layer below the Ledge layer. Then, in Linear mode, Foreground to Background color, drag vertically in the image window (hold the Shift key to constrain the gradient to vertical), starting about 2 screen inches from the top of the window and ending at about two screen inches from the bottom of the window (see Figure 22.96).

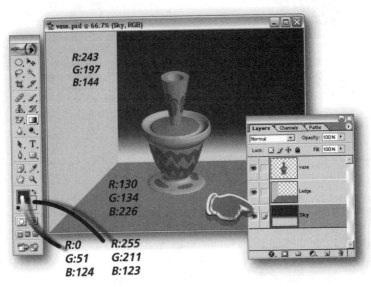

Figure 22.96   Create a sunset for the image by using the right colors and the Gradient tool in Linear mode.

6. Click the Ledge layer to make it the active layer. With the Magic Wand tool, click the vertical, peach-colored ledge area on the Ledge layer. Create an alpha channel by clicking the Create new channel icon at the bottom of the Channels palette.

7. Use the Filter, Render, Clouds filter to create a fractal pattern in the selected area in the alpha channel (see Figure 22.97). Return to the RGB view of the image. Do this on the Layers palette by clicking the Ledge layer to make it the active layer. The marquee should still be visible.

Figure 22.97   Create a texture that can then be applied to the peach side of
the ledge in the design.

8. Choose Filter, Render, and then choose Lighting Effects, as you've done several times in this chapter. Set the Texture Channel to Alpha 1, and set the Height to about 12. Make sure that the Light type is Directional and that the exposure is correct by twiddling with the point at the end of the source light—move it toward, or away from the light origin in the proxy window until the colors in the proxy window match the colors in the document window. Click OK to apply the Lighting Effects, and you now have a stucco ledge wall in the image. Press Ctrl(⌘)+D to deselect.

9. Choose the vase layer and then with the Move tool, drag the vase to the right of the image window (peek ahead at Figure 22.98 to see the vase's position).

10. Save your work to your hard disk as Vase.psd and keep the file open. We *both* need a breather!

To add some accents to the image, a moon and a shadow for the vase would be cool. Again, creating these effects is *not* hard stuff.

Adding Elements to the Composition

Let's take care of creating the moon and the shadow for the vase within one set of steps. Why? Because they are not challenging and as you will see, they don't take many steps.

Here's how to finish the Gaugin-type image:

Adding Finishing Touches to a Sunset Scene

1. Drag the vase layer title onto the Create a new layer icon at the bottom of the Layers palette. Doing this creates a copy of the vase layer.

2. Click the vase layer (below the vase copy layer) to make this the active layer. This will become the shadow layer for the vase. Press Alt(Opt)+Shift+Delete (Backspace) to fill the image on the layer with foreground color. You can see on the layers palette thumbnail that you now have a deep blue vase shape on the vase layer.

3. Press Ctrl(⌘)+T to put the blue shadow in Free Transform mode. First, hold Shift to constrain the rotation to 15-degree increments, then take hold of a corner on the Free Transform bounding box, and rotate the shadow by 90 degrees. If you cannot get a hold of the bounding box handle with a bent-arrow cursor, right-click (Macintosh: hold Ctrl and click) and choose Rotate from the context menu.

4. After the shadow has been rotated, drag the top-center handle downward, and then drag the left-center handle to the left so the shadow is thin and long.

5. Place the cursor inside the Transform box and then drag the shadow so that its base is under the vase. When you're satisfied with the effect, press Enter (Return) to accept the transformations (see Figure 22.98). As a finishing touch on the shadow, use the Lasso tool to lasso some of the areas showing past the vase base and press the Delete (Backspace) key to remove the unwanted parts of the shadow. Press Ctrl(⌘)+D to deselect.

Rotate, reposition, and then Scale.

Figure 22.98   The vase shadow is a nice touch and adds geometry to the image.

6. Now, the moon. In the sky to the right of the image, use the Elliptical Marquee tool while holding Shift to make a perfect circle. Click the Quick Mask mode icon (or press Q) and the selection becomes a red dot.

7. Choose Filter, Distort, and then choose Glass. As you can see in Figure 22.99, a moderate Glass distortion setting makes a van Gogh-like "Starry Night" moon. By the way, Gaugin and van Gogh were both Impressionists, but Gaugin was also a Post Impressionist.

Quick Mask mode.

Figure 22.99   The Glass distortion filter creates shards out of the edges of a smooth object.

8. Click OK to apply the filter, and then press Q (or click the Edit in Standard Mode icon on the toolbox) to make the Quick Mask into a selection marquee. Alt(Opt)+click the Create a new layer icon on the bottom of the Layers palette, name this layer **moon**, and click OK. Drag the new moon layer title down between the Ledge layer and the Sky layer on the palette list.

9. To be true to Impressionism, we need an odd color for the moon to create moodiness in the image. Choose R:177, G:205, B: 123 for the toolbox foreground color, and then with the Brush tool and a 65-pixel soft-edged brush, paint over the selection marquee, as shown in Figure 22.100. Press Ctrl(⌘)+D to deselect.

Figure 22.100   Add a touch of suspense in the image by using an unexpected color for the moon.

10. You're done! Press Ctrl(⌘)+S, and check out the final image in Figure 22.101.

Figure 22.101   Does your vase look like this?

That was a walk in the park, wasn't it?

Trick 9 Summary

No matter how Gaugin-ish your final result may be, you have to admit—examples like this get your hands on a lot of important Photoshop features and give you ideas for using the tools in new and adventurous ways. Simplicity can say as much as intricacy, except simplicity is easier to create!

Trick 10: Fixing a Chopped-Off Drop Shadow

I have been putting drop shadows on everything in the *Inside Photoshop* books for years. The famous Gaussian Blur drop shadow is extremely overused, starting with *PC Magazine* and ending up on both the Mac OS and the Windows XP Plus! Pack interfaces. So why do I apparently succumb to peer pressure? It's simple—the drop shadow adds dimension so you are not stuck reading a "flat" book for hours on end; if I get you to refocus every now and then, I've provided a valuable service and will be sending you my ophthalmologist's bill.

Seriously, there are hazards associated with drop-shadowing everything. One big Oops! occurs when you apply a drop shadow, make a few editing moves, and then move a drop shadowed image—only to discover that you've truncated the shadow. It travels abruptly from 10% gray to paper white.

In Figure 22.102, trouble is a-brewing. The mounty picture has just had a fresh drop shadow applied. But as you can see, the shadow doesn't fade away completely at the bottom of the image.

Figure 22.102   I might get a ticket from this mounty for imprudent use
of Alien Skin's Eye Candy filters!!!!

I want you to run through this simple trick with me, so open the Mounty.tif image from
the Examples/Chap22 folder on the Companion CD, and follow these steps.

How to Fix a Broken Drop Shadow

1. Double-click the Background layer on the Layers palette and click OK to accept
   the default name. Now you can move the mounty as you please.

2. As you can see, Bouton has already fouled up the picture with a drop shadow
   that runs off the page. With the Move tool, move the image up and to the left, as
   shown in Figure 22.103, and then choose Flatten image from the Layers palette's
   flyout menu.

Figure 22.103   The bottom edge of the shadow is cropped off. What idiot did this?

3. With the Rectangular Marquee tool, drag a selection marquee around the very bottom of the cropped shadow. Look carefully at Figure 22.104—the top of the selection should be a few pixels away from the image, and the bottom of the marquee should extend into the white area by only three or four pixels. Then press Ctrl(⌘)+Alt(Opt)+D and feather the selection by about 5 pixels. Click OK.

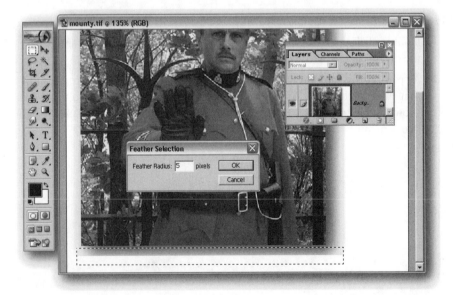

Figure 22.104   Select the "broken" part of the drop shadow and then feather the selection.

4. Apply a slight amount of Gaussian Blurring (Filter, Blur, Gaussian Blur), as shown in Figure 22.105. Four pixels should do the trick for an image and a shadow of the sizes presented to you here. See? Instant shadow restoration.

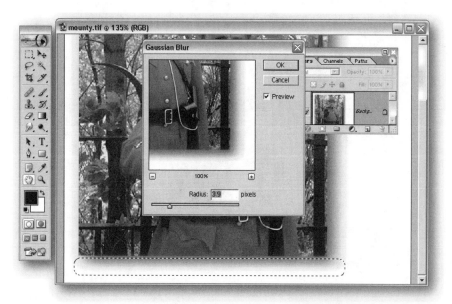

Figure 22.105 The Gaussian Blur filter restores the chopped-off drop shadow!

5. You're done! Deselect the selection marquee and save the image if you like. As you can see in Figure 22.106, the mounty is pretty happy about the repairs, too. Press Ctrl(⌘)+Shift+S if you want to save this image to your hard drive.

Figure 22.106   Drop shadows can be cropped badly, but they also can be restored in about four steps.

Trick 10 Summary

Drop shadows appear to be the staple of modern printed communications. So you might as well know how to fix them when something goes amiss. Murphy's Law is alive and well in the 21st century!

Grand Chapter Summary

Has this chapter seemed a little weird to you? But did you like it anyway? Well, welcome to the league of Photoshop pros. We do funky stuff all day, and ultimately, it's all in a day's work. You are forced to be ingenious at every turn, and this author hopes that you don't mind thinking like me at least for a little while until you get your Photoshop wings. Everything worthwhile in Photoshop is a challenge and the impossible simply takes a little longer to do.

Now, ye should be off. There's got to be a quinnch match around hayre sumplace. And wear yer bike helmets!

PostScript

Chapter 22½, right around your right elbow, doesn't talk much about Photoshop, or even computer graphics. We felt that you've been sitting here with this big book in your lap studying Photoshop long enough. Now it's time to get to the gist of the reason you picked up this book. You want to express yourself graphically, right? You want a billion-dollar-a-year job at Industrial Light and Magic, right? (So does the author—we'll both dream on, okay?)

Essentially, you want advice on where the road leads for you after you close this book. And that's what 22½ is all about: it's about you and your dreams. So bring both of them along!

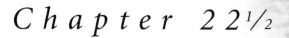

Chapter 22½

Where Do We Go from Here?

Closing Thoughts

That's right—there are definitely more pages under your left thumb than under your right. This means that *Inside Photoshop 7* must close because the publisher has run out of paper (only kidding, David!). Seriously, though, *Inside Photoshop 7* was not the beginning of your computer graphics education—you began when you developed enough of an interest in graphics to go out and look for a book— and it is not the end, either. The authors will certainly be back with a version 8 book in good time, but until then, be sure to keep this book beside your computer because there's still a lot more to learn.

Learning from Life

In the same way that you must occasionally take your face away from the monitor to catch a breath of fresh air, you also should seriously consider taking a day or two off from the computer. Go outdoors, visit a friend you respect and haven't spoken with in a while, and even stick your head into a continuing education classroom that looks interesting. The creative mind is always looking for outside stimulation—you see a beautiful scene, your mind filters it, and you eventually express what you feel about this scene, using Photoshop or even (gasp) a pencil on paper. When the creative urge strikes (and historically it has been a very strong urge), you should do two things:

- Realize firmly in your mind what the *concept* is. The concept can be as commercial as a stunning graphic to sell a car or as personal as creating a graphic to tell your spouse you love her.

  A concept is an elusive thing. Many people presume, for example, that a concept is, "Okay, we get this elephant to stand on one leg next to a clothes washer." This describes what someone wants to *see* in a composition, but it is not the *concept*. Why is the elephant there? Why is the elephant next to a clothes washer? If there's no reason, there's no concept, and as we would traditionally say, it's "back to the drawing board."

- A fair example of a concept (we don't want to give away *too* many free concepts!) would be of a clown, in color, walking down an urban street that's in black and white. The picture is saying that there is humor amidst the cold, serious world; that's the concept. Do you see the difference between the clown and the elephant?

- Gather stock photography, but also gather stock ideas, and write them down. There's a yin/yang to ideas. You give an idea life, but the idea also provokes you on an emotional level, and then more ideas are created. There's nothing sadder than sitting down in front of Photoshop without an idea. It's time wasted, time that would be better spent examining the geometric complexity of a flower or considering how clouds can create specific moods.

We, as a civilization, are so caught up in the day-to-day machinery we call a working life that we often deprive ourselves of inspiration and really good ideas. After this book is finished, this author intends to mow the lawn, inspect all the flowers his spouse has planted, look at the sky, look at an insect crawling around for food—and then open Photoshop or another application and see where these impressions of life lead. To be an artist means being able to see life with the widest vision you permit yourself, and then to filter what you're thinking about what you saw into a graphical composition. It doesn't get much easier than that; simply soak in the world around you and let the experience of life flow into your work. And don't feel intimidated about the outcome of your work, either. Simply immerse yourself in what you're creating without shame or fear of public acceptance or rejection, and gaze on what you've done as a way of expressing yourself.

Learning How to Learn

Instinctive learning isn't easy for everyone. Schools tend to make you recite instead of invent, and we tend to be conditioned, not taught, by even the best-intentioned, but often opinionated scholars. The authors feel differently about books than any other medium of communication, because you, the reader, have the option of closing the book and taking a break any time you feel like it. Additionally, try as we may, *Inside Photoshop 7* is a reference book and tutorial book above all things, so this puts us in the position of being fellow artists second, and "information vendors" first. Hopefully, we've set a conversational tone in this book, but not at the expense of our prime goal, which is teaching.

Inside Photoshop 7 is the (lucky!) 13th book we have written on Photoshop. Through the years, we've received mail from our friends and readers with questions (and a scattered complaint here and there). Like other artists, we depend on feedback to influence what we document and how we communicate with you. The most useful feedback we've received has been on how users approach this book.

Many readers never actually perform the tutorials; instead, they skip around in the book looking for a magic recipe or technique here and there. For many users, this approach works when they need to solve a specific problem quickly. But the most "successful" readers—the ones who have increased their overall relationship with art, and increased their skill level—are the ones who found time to sit with the book for an hour or two at a time and work their way through a chapter. Like most things in life, mastery of an art comes from doing. Only through action do the principles behind the steps become tangible. If you've passed over chapters on your way to this paragraph, please invest in your own talent and work completely through a favorite chapter. Follow the steps, and then do something similar with images of your own. Make the knowledge truly yours.

Also, we should tell you that we actually *read* sometimes(!), and even a tutorial-based book has some "good stuff" lodged between the pages that might not be a formal set of steps designed to help you arrive at a finished piece. What we do when we discover a nugget of wisdom is outlined in (you guessed it) a numbered list:

Indexing a Nugget of Wisdom in a Book

1. Take out a pad of fluorescent sticky notes.
2. Detach one leaf.
3. Place it on the page in the book that contains a morsel of interest.

For all the information organized into procedures found in this book, however, please *don't* treat *Inside Photoshop 7* as a workbook. We've tried to make this book an excellent *resource* guide, and a book on art, too.

Whether you are an imaging enthusiast who simply wants to retouch photos as a pastime, a designer in a large enterprise who is forced to measure output in volume, or a fine artist who is looking for that "special something" to refine your work, you might not know where you're going creatively. But we all pack toolkits for our artistic voyages, both virtual and physical. You've seen in this book that Photoshop is not only a necessary part of your computer graphics toolkit, but that it also should be located at the *top* of the toolkit, where you can reach it easily.

We have had the career privilege of never having to write about an application we do not believe in. Bringing all the examples in this book together, with the tricks, tips, techniques, and secrets, took being able to learn correctly. But it also required an imaging program as capable as Photoshop as the vehicle of our expression. You've got the right application, you've got the right book (we think), and now it's simply up to you to create your own gallery of ideas.

Part IX

The Back O'
the Book

Appendix A

The *Inside Photoshop 7* CD-ROM

So are you wondering what's on the CD-ROM and how to use it? Glad you asked! The short answer is, "Lots!" The long answer is found in the following pages. Be sure to check out these sections:

- Instructions on where to get Acrobat Reader 5 if you don't already have a copy

- Descriptions of the contents of the Companion CD

- Information concerning special offers

- What to do if you have problems with your Companion CD

Instructions for Installing Acrobat Reader 5

The *Inside Photoshop 7* Companion CD contains a number of Adobe Acrobat PDF files. Of particular importance are the PDF files in the ClipArt, Fonts, Tilers, and BeholdersEye folders inside the Boutons folder. Also check out the Online Glossary (ip7glos.pdf). Because PDF files are so important to the CD, we want to make sure that you have a copy of Acrobat Reader.

If you have already installed Photoshop, Acrobat Reader is almost certainly installed. Try opening one of the files with the PDF file extension. If your operating system complains that it doesn't know what program to use to open the file, you probably need to install a copy of Adobe Acrobat Reader. You can find a copy of Acrobat Reader on the Adobe Photoshop 7 CD, or if you want to be sure that you have the newest version of this very useful, free program, jump on the web and download it from Adobe's site at http://www.adobe.com/products/acrobat/update.html.

What's On the Companion CD?

We're really proud of the CD that accompanies this book. You won't believe all the goodies it contains!

The Online Glossary

In the Boutons folder is the ip7glos.pdf file, an Acrobat document that is the book's glossary. The glossary is more than 280 pages in color, thoroughly indexed and with scores of cross-references. You need Acrobat Reader 3 or later to access this file.

The Boutons Folder

In the Boutons folder, you'll find the following items:

- The ClipArt folder stores over 100 images, most of them 3D, which exist on a Photoshop layer. You know what that means? You can copy the layer's clip art contents to another image or use ImageReady to make a transparent GIF from the clip art (see Figure CD.1). Now, as with most BoutonWare, this stuff is CharityWare, and we'll spare you from hearing this more than once.

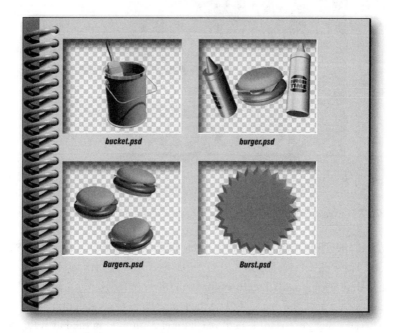

Figure CD.1   Clip art in Photoshop format galore!

CharityWare is *not* FreeWare or ShareWare. If you want to use a Bouton-generated piece of data (fonts or art) commercially, we ask that you donate a sum (dictated by your own conscience) to the charities listed in the PDF file in a particular folder. Do your heart, and someone else's life, some good as you use our work that's truly from the heart.

- In the Fonts folder, you will find Gary David Bouton-created fonts in TrueType and Type 1 for the Mac and Windows. Check out Figure CD.2. Many of these fonts are better quality than the commercial fonts you'd pay $30 or more for.

Figure CD.2   Even if you're Adobe Systems, you probably don't have all *these* fonts!

- In the Tilers folder, guess what? You get volumes 1 through 4 for free, a $29.95 value for each set (see Figure CD.3). What do you do with tilers? These are carefully designed images of textures that will tile seamlessly. And many of them have corresponding alpha channels. Use the alphas only to create bumps and organic material using Photoshop's Texture Channel command in the Filter, Render, Lighting Effects feature.

All images will tile seamlessly. To do this, you simply use Photoshop's Edit, Define Pattern command with a texture selected. You then can use the texture as a fill by using either the Edit, Fill command or the Paint Bucket tool. Additionally, if you export any of these texture files to JPEG or GIF89a format, you can use them with an HTML editor to create a seamless, tiling background texture for a web page.

The files marked with an "m" after them are mask files, also known as *bump maps*. You can use these files to create your own textures in Painter and Photoshop, or use them as the basis for a terrain map in programs such as Bryce or Terragen.

Figure CD.3   Tilers give you an effortless way to create interesting seamless tiles.

- Finally (as though there should be a "finally," right?), the Boutons are proud to present you with the Beholder's Eye collection, a digitally photographed potpourri of scenes you'll want to add to, subtract from, or simply filter and have a ball with. *Nobody* has enough digitized pictures. We have a feeling that this is only Volume 1 (see Figure CD.4)!

Figure CD.4   Stock photography you'll really want to use! The Boutons' *Beholder's Eye Collection.*

The Examples Folder

The Examples folder has subfolders, marked Chap02, Chap20, and so on. (Please note that some chapters do not require Example files, so do not freak out if there is a chapter folder "missing" from the Companion CD.) When you read the examples in the chapters, you'll be asked to open a file, such as duck.psd from the Examples/Chap22 folder. Locating the materials you need to work through this book is a snap. Double-click Examples, and then navigate to the folder listed in the text.

The Software Folder

In this folder are several subfolders that contain working demos or totally functional programs that we feel work well with Photoshop. The following sections list the programs. We're pretty proud of our legwork.

The Alien Skin Folder (Windows and Macintosh)

In this folder, you'll find collections of plug-ins by Alien Skin Software for Photoshop in both Macintosh and Windows versions. Splat! is the newest set of filters from the Aliens and we think that it is the best they've done. The seamless pattern-maker combined with the Stamp brings Painter-like nozzles to Photoshop. The fully functional demo is good for 30 days. After 30 days, we're pretty sure you will want to take Alien Skin up on their generous money-saving offer found in the back of this book. Check out Figure CD.5 for an example of what you can do with this plug-in.

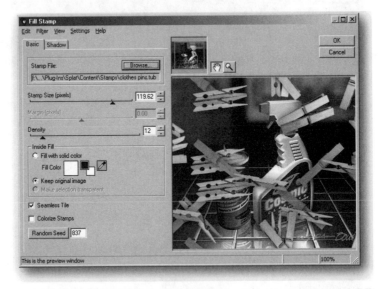

Figure CD.5   Clothspins abound, or any other seamless tiling objects you want to add to a picture. How about money? :)

Don't overlook the wild, wild Xenofex collection or Eye Candy 4000. The filters, such as Baked Earth and Constellation, are really fantastic. Check out these filters, and we're sure you'll want to purchase at least one set for yourself.

The Creoscitex Folder (Windows and Macintosh)

The demo product in this folder is Powertone. Powertone is an Adobe Photoshop plug-in for Macintosh and Windows. This incredible plug-in generates dynamic and colorful images that can be printed with only two inks. Two-color printing will never be the same!

The Art Director's Toolkit Folder (Macintosh Only)

Code Line Communications has supplied us with a 15-day demo of their Art Director's toolkit. This kit contains so many useful utilities—such as a character map, font specimen and specification tool, RGB and CMYK color tools, and a graphic arts calculator—that Apple is including the full, OS X version of Art Director's toolkit on all PowerMac G4 towers and PowerBook G4 laptops. See Figure CD.6 for a look at Art Director's Toolkit.

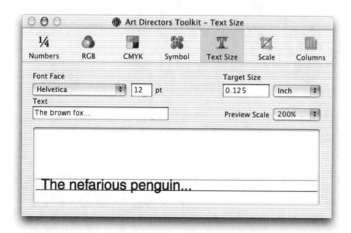

Figure CD.6   The Art Director's toolkit is so good that Apple licensed part of it for OS X!

Digital ROC and Digital SHO (Windows and Macintosh)

If you are not lucky enough to have a scanner that incorporates Applied Science Fiction, Digital ICE technology, or you are working with digital photography, you've got to give these amazing Photoshop plug-ins a try. Digital SHO uses some kind of amazing math to analyze an underexposed picture and actually bring out detail in shadow, a task you would have a hard time doing manually. Its partner plug-in, Digital ROC, uses different,

but equally complex math formulas to restore proper color balance to badly aged photos and to restore density to faded black-and-white photos. If the plug-in works for your
particular photo (and it often does take you close to where you want to be), it can save
you hours of retouching time. These are trial versions of the filters (see Figure CD.7).
The SHO filter automatically improves brightness and contrast in an image.

Figure CD.7   Applied Science Fiction does the impossible...every day!

The Auto FX Folder (Windows and Macintosh)

Take a peek into the Auto FX folder and you'll find demo versions of Auto FX Software's
seriously fun DreamSuite Series 1, DreamSuite Series 2, and DreamSuite Gel filter sets.
Make digital gummi shapes with the Gel filter, add that paste-up look to your layouts
with the masking tape filter, or just go wild exploring them all. (Just don't use every one
of the filters in a single commissioned piece, even though you might be tempted to,
okay?) And be sure to check out their ad page and save some money when it comes time
to upgrade from demo to full versions. See Figure CD.8 for a realistic duct-taped image!

Figure CD.8   DreamSuite's filters add endless fun to your projects.

The Flaming Pear Folder (Windows and Macintosh)

If you haven't acquainted yourself with the filters that Flaming Pear Software offers, you owe it to yourself to do so now. Some of these filters are ShareWare and others are FreeWare. We don't know of a better tool to use to create jewel-like buttons than Blade Pro. Super Blade Pro, Lunar Cell, Designer Sextet, Flood, Hue and Cry, Melancholytron, Flexify, Solar Cell, India Ink, Ornament, Tesselation, and additional demo versions are on the CD. Check out what Flood does in Figure CD.9.

Figure CD.9   High tide, everyone! Flaming Pear is in town!

The XARA Folder (Windows Only)

XARA is a Windows-only drawing program. Wait a minute—to say it's *only* a drawing program is like saying the Statue of Liberty won't fit in a Size 7 dress. XARA X is a fully functional, two-week time-limited program that is highly compatible with Photoshop. It slips in and out between vectors and bitmaps with ease and precision. If you know CorelDRAW, you'll feel right at home with this state-of-the-art drawing program. In fact, all the screen annotations and the color signature in this book were generated in XARA X. See Figure CD.10 for an example—Bouton's been using this program along with Photoshop for more than five years now.

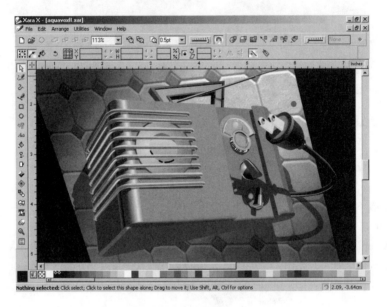

Figure CD.10   A drawing program that thinks it's a painting program.

PhotoRescue

PhotoRescue reads digital camera cards that cannot be read for one reason or another. It literally rescues digital images from chips and cards in digital cameras that refuse to download.

VisCheck

VisCheck (which is for Windows, but Macintosh users can use the site's VisCheck at http://www.vischeck.com/) isn't a "fun" plug-in, but then again, it isn't funny when your audience is colorblind and you don't know what they can see in your artwork. Be kind to the colorblind—check in with VisCheck before you post an image to the web (see Figure CD.13).

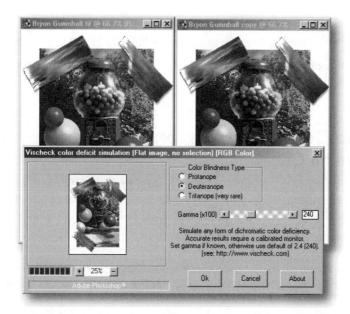

Figure CD.11   Make sure that everyone in your audience can view your artwork with VisiCheck.

Special Offers

Finally, the publisher and the authors are out to save you some bucks with firms we know and trust as being outstanding in their respective fields. In fact, many of our demo versions on the CD are accompanied with a discount ad in this book. How about that!

As mentioned earlier, check out the fantastic deal on Alien Skin filters. Take our word, graphics professionals just don't work willingly without a full set of Alien Skin filters in their tool chests.

AutoFx Software has been helping Photoshoppists turn out eye-catching work for years. And you, lucky reader, can take advantage of their offer of $50 off their award-winning DreamSuite filters. You'll want to jump on this offer fast.

Contributing author, J. Scott Hamlin also has extended a great offer to you. Be sure to check out the fine print at the bottom of the Photoshop Web Foundry ad page and get your free game, newsletter, and $5.00 off anything at Eyeland Studio (www.eyeland.com).

Daniel Will-Harris, contributing author and typography guru, invites you take him up on his offer of a free subscription to the Schmoozeletter. It is the most entertaining, thought-provoking, and information-packed email newsletter that arrives at the Bouton household. Go to Schmoozeletter.com to sign up and go to Will-Harris.com to tank-up on all font-related stuff.

Happy hunting on the CD. We think you'll discover some real gems—especially the just-for-fun pineapples!

What to Do if You Have Problems with the Companion CD

For more information about the use of this CD, please review the ReadMe.txt file in the root directory. This file includes important disclaimer information as well as information about installation, system requirements, troubleshooting, and technical support.

Note

Technical Support Issues   If you have any difficulties with this CD, you can access our tech support at http://www.newriders.com. (Hint, look under the Contact Us menu item.)

A p p e n d i x   B

Keyboard Shortcuts and Power User Tricks

Adobe has created hundreds (it seems like thousands) of special keyboard combinations to make Photoshop more productive. Just because Adobe added these features, it doesn't mean that you are required to know and use them. I want to give you some free philosophy to go with the contents of this chapter. If the tip, keyboard shortcut, or trick involves an area that you work in (such as photo restoration, web design, and so on), make the effort to learn the technique because it will save you time. If not, scan it, smile, say something like "How interesting!" and move on.

The tricks, tips, and other power user stuff in this appendix represent the distillation of things I have personally gathered over the years, by talking with close friends who also spend way too much time in front of a computer screen and by sitting (sometimes sleeping) through Photoshop workshops by the best (and worst) Photoshop instructors in the business. Good power user tricks and tips are like jokes; they circulate quickly and we never know who the original author was. Some of the contributors to the Photoshop community's collection of these shortcuts, tips, and all include (but are not limited to) Scott Kelby (Founder of National Association of Photoshop Professionals), Julieanne Kost and Daniel Brown (Adobe's Photoshop evangelists—http://www.adobeevange-lists.com/), and Photoshop authors Ben Wilmore, Jack Davis, and Dan Margulis—to name only a few.

Undoing a Potential Disaster

No matter what kind of work you are doing in Photoshop, there is nothing worse than the feeling that occurs when you realize you've unintentionally made temporary changes permanent. For example, I recently created a large composite photograph involving many layers. I wanted to show the image to my editor so I flattened it and then reduced it from 300 dpi to a 72-dpi image so that I could include it in an email. After sending the email, out of habit I saved the file, which effectively replaced my large, complex multi-layer PSD with the itty-bitty flat jpeg—wiping out many hours of work.

It made me realize two things: panic was making me rusty and more importantly, as long as the image file is still open I can still undo the inadvertent save. Although it's a fact that once a file is saved the Undo command is no longer available, the Step Backward command available with Alt(Opt)+Ctrl(⌘)+Z still works. Here is how to do it:

1. Open the History palette.
2. Apply the Step Backward command as many times as necessary to restore the image to the pre-oops stage.
3. Save the file.

Clipboards and New Images

Here are my two favorites when it comes to creating a new image—and as it turns out, they are related. To make a new image using the contents of the clipboard is a simple two stage process:

1. Create a new file (Ctrl(⌘)+N) and click OK. Photoshop automatically matches the image size of the new file to the same size, resolution, and color mode as the contents of the clipboard.
2. Apply the Paste command (Ctrl(⌘)+V). The contents of the clipboard become a layer in the new document.

So, what if you have something in the clipboard when you create a new image, but you don't want Photoshop to automatically resize to the dimensions, resolution, and color mode of the current clipboard contents? Well, you can manually change the data fields in the New dialog box when it opens or you can use Ctrl(⌘)+Alt(Opt)+N which opens the dialog box with the last values entered.

Dump Your Clipboard

If you want to keep Photoshop running as fast as possible, never leave a large amount of data on the clipboard. If you copy a huge image using the clipboard, it takes up precious RAM space and may force Photoshop to begin to use virtual RAM on your disk drive, which is at least 10× slower. After you have finished using the contents of the clipboard, choose Edit, Purge, Clipboard. This is the only case I know in which purging is a good thing.

Keep Plenty of Drive Space Available

If it seems that Photoshop is running slowly, especially if you have large images, check and see how much available free disk space you have. Both Mac OS X and every version of Windows like a lot of room to play with to get optimum performance. How much is enough? In this day and age, I think you should have at least 500MB free.

Scratch Disk No-No

Photoshop 7 will give you a friendly reminder when you start the program if you are using the startup disk as a scratch disk and there is another disk available. If there isn't much space left on the other drive, don't use it for a scratch disk. Never, *ever* use a removable drive (Zip or Jaz) as a scratch disk.

Closing All Open Images

If you have a lot of images open, you can close them all in a hurry by using Ctrl(⌘)+Shift+W.

Drawing a Straight Line in Photoshop

Many Photoshop users are unaware that the developers of this program included a feature that allows you to draw a straight line between any two points using any of the brush tools. This is really handy to use with the Airbrush to add uniform shading along the edge of an object.

1. Select a brush tool.

2. Click the starting point of the line.

3. Hold down the Shift key and click the end point, and a straight line is produced between the two points.

Note

Continuing Straight On   If you continue to hold down the Shift key, each successive click adds a straight line segment from point to point.

How to Hide Those Pesky Marching Ants

All selections that appear in Photoshop are surrounded by a marquee, which has come to be known as "marching ants." Although this is a great way to show the edge of the current selection, the effect can be somewhat distracting. If you would like to turn the selection edges off, simply press Ctrl(⌘)+H to toggle them off. Pressing Ctrl(⌘)+H again will toggle them back on again.

In addition, Ctrl(⌘)+H can come in handy on a lot of non-printing items (besides marquee selections). How many times have you highlighted text so that you could implement changes, such as changing the font, size, or color? Does the highlighted text annoy you? Press Ctrl(⌘)+H and you can see the changes to font, size, and color update without that pesky inverted highlighting problem obscuring your view. You will find that Ctrl(⌘)+H also works on the Transform bounding box.

> **Note**
>
> **Exterminating Ants on the Current Selection Only**   This action affects only the marquee of the current selection. The marching ants will reappear if you make a different selection. Also, just because you can't see the selection doesn't mean it is not there. When you hide a marquee selection, the selection remains active until you deselect it. So if you have trouble getting paint to apply to an area of an image, you might check to see whether a hidden marquee surrounds the area you're trying to paint.

Quick Frame

Did you know that Photoshop has a frame tool? Well, not really, but the way that the Canvas Size dialog box was designed, it can be used to quickly create solid color frames. Here's how it is done:

1. Change the background color to a color you want for your frame.

2. Choose Image, Canvas Size, and with the center square of the Anchor section selected in the dialog box, increase the size of the existing canvas by adding an appropriate value to Width and Height.

How many times have you wanted to increase the measurement of the canvas equally along all four sides (by a specific amount)? For example, if you want a 35-pixel border around the image, you then need to double 35 to get 70, then add 70 to the current Width and Height amount. Ugh! Wouldn't it be great if you didn't have to do the math? Then let Photoshop do the math for you. These optional steps show you how:

3. With the Canvas Size dialog box open, check the Relative option. The numbers zero out in the Width and Height fields. Now type the amount by which you want to increase the border. You will have to type the number for both Width and Height, unless you want only one dimension to increase equally.

4. Click OK. Photoshop resizes the canvas by the amount you specified equally to both sides of each dimension (using the amount you specified in Width and Height). Cool, huh?

If a solid color doesn't tickle your fancy (and for most of us, it doesn't), choose the Magic Wand tool and select the frame. Now you can apply just about anything your heart desires to the selected area.

Fade Power

The Fade command (Ctrl(⌘)+Shift+F) has become one of my very favorite commands. With Fade, you can supercharge the effects of filters. On the surface, it appears that it allows you only to reduce the amount of the last command that was applied. Although that is true, where Fade really shines is in the ability to add one of many blend modes to images. But even without making use of the blend modes, my favorite use for this command is to apply a large amount of sharpening and then use the Fade command to adjust the amount of sharpening on the image. Think of it like an "undo" on a slider. Fade enables you to scale down the effect just a little. The command works on a variety of Photoshop functions—but there's a catch—the Fade command is available only for the last function you performed.

Another Fade Trick (Windows Only)

When applying the Fade command, you can select different blend modes. A quick way to preview the affect of the different modes is to select one of them and then with the blend mode still highlighted in the dialog box, use the up- or down-arrow keys to change modes. On a Mac, the arrow keys change the percentage of Fade—sorry about that.

Stuff for Retouching

When you are retouching a photograph, you will find yourself constantly opening and closing the Brushes palette unless you learn a few important shortcuts:

- Use the B key to select the Brush tool.

- With the Brush tool selected, right-click (Macintosh: hold Ctrl and click) on the image and the Brush Preset picker opens so that you can select a brush. Press Enter (Return) to close the Brush Preset picker.

- To change brush size, use the left ([) or right bracket (]) keys. The amount of change produced by each keystroke depends on the current size of the brush. Table B.1 displays the incremental change information. Note, however, that this doesn't work while the Brushes palette is open.

- To change brush hardness, hold down the Shift key and press the bracket keys (left bracket to decrease and right bracket to increase). This changes the hardness of the brush in 25% increments.

Table B.1   Changing Brush Sizes

Brush Size	Change Increments
1—10	1 pixel
10—99	10 pixels
100—200	25 pixels
200—300	50 pixels
300—999	100 pixels

New Photoshop 7 Brushes Palette

Although the Brushes palette has changed in Photoshop 7, you can still open it by right-clicking (Macintosh: hold Ctrl and click) the image with a brush tool selected. Wait! It doesn't look like the Brush palette we have come to know and love. Never fear—just click the button in the upper-right corner and select Small Thumbnail. Isn't that better?

Making the Palettes Go Away (Temporarily)

Palettes are great but sometimes you want them to go away temporarily so that you can better view the image you are working on. That's easy: Press the Tab key and the palettes disappear. Press it again and—presto, there are back.

Think Before You Reset All Brushes

If you have created any custom brushes or changed the settings of any of the standard brushes, make sure that you save the contents of the Brush menu before restoring the default brushes. If you accidentally restore the default brushes, it cannot be undone. Consider yourself warned.

Creating Irregularly Shaped Brushes

Here is a fast way to make an irregularly shaped brush. Create the brush shape on a white background and then select the entire shape. Any part of the brush that is based on white pixels will be transparent.

Great Fill Tricks

If you have read a large majority of this book—then it's no secret that Alt(Opt)+Delete (Backspace) will fill a selection with the foreground color. But what if you want to fill with the background color? Just press Ctrl(⌘)+Delete (Backspace).

Okay—now let me ask you this one. How many times do you Ctrl(⌘)+click a layer to select the contents of that layer, then press Alt(Opt)+Delete (Backspace) to fill the selection with foreground color, then press Ctrl(⌘)+D to deselect the selection? Whew! Wouldn't it be great if there were a killer shortcut to do all of that in one swoop? There is!

Add the Shift key to the mix. In other words, click the layer in question. Then press Alt(Opt)+Shift+Delete (Backspace) to fill the objects only (that occupy that layer) with foreground color. Or press Ctrl(⌘)+Shift+Delete (Backspace) to use the Background color as a fill (for the objects on that layer). You can also think of it this way: It's as though you turned the Lock transparent pixels icon on, filled the layer, and then toggled the Lock transparent pixels icon off again.

Great Zoom Tricks

Being able to navigate quickly through many different zoom settings is essential when retouching a photograph. Adobe apparently realized this too, because they made a large number of keyboard shortcuts for zoom settings. As you may or may not know, the only way to see an accurate representation of a photographic image (without distortion introduced by the resampling of the zoom feature) is to view it at 100%, which you do by selecting Actual Pixels. I used to spend a lot of time selecting the Zoom tool and then moving between the Actual Pixels and Fit to Screen buttons on the Zoom option bar. I was thrilled when I discovered that Adobe provided a keyboard shortcut to jump between the Zoom settings I used the most. Thanks, Adobe. Here are the shortcuts:

- Fit to Screen: Ctrl(⌘)+0
- Actual Pixels: Ctrl(⌘)+Alt(Opt)+0
- Zoom In: Ctrl(⌘)+plus key
- Zoom Out: Ctrl(⌘)+minus key

The Best Zoom Setting Possible

Actually, if you are doing any significant amount of photo editing, you should seriously consider getting a second monitor. Both the Max OS and Windows OS support dual display capability. By setting one display at 100% and then zooming in on the other, you can do detailed retouching without needing to spend time with the many variations of the zoom tools.

Getting Around an Image Fast

If the current zoom level of an image is larger than the display area, scroll bars appear on the right and left sides of the image window. These bars are just for visual entertainment, don't ever use them; instead use the Hand tool. Holding down the spacebar on the keyboard toggles to the Hand tool, regardless of the tool that you have currently selected. When you release the spacebar, the currently selected tool returns. There are three situations when this doesn't work:

- The scrollbars are not present.
- The Text tool is selected, and it thinks of the spacebar as a spacebar (go figure).
- You are creating a selection with the marquee tool (in which case the spacebar allows you to move and reposition the selection you are creating—while the creation process is in progress).

Removing Blue Cast from Digital Camera Photos

Here is my favorite way to remove the blue cast that is so common in many digital photos that were taken on bright sunny days. Often if you apply Auto Levels, it only makes the blue cast worse. So, this is a quick fix for the blue cast, but many times it has improved the image dramatically enough that no other adjustment was required. Here is the technique:

1. Choose Image, Adjust, Levels (or since this chapter is about shortcuts, press Ctrl(⌘)+L).
2. Change the Channel setting in the dialog box to Blue.
3. Drag the left (shadow) slider over to the right until the image just begins to look a little green. Not seasick green, just a very light green tint.

4. Change the Channel setting to Green and drag the middle slider (midtone) slightly to the right, which will add just enough magenta to compensate for the green we got from tweaking the blue channel.

5. Check and uncheck the preview to see the before and after. When you like it, click OK and you're done.

Reapplying Filters

Adobe provided a way to reapply the last filter by using the keyboard shortcut Ctrl+F. The problem with this action is that it applies the last-used filter at the last-used settings. What if you want to reapply the filter but would like to change the settings? Adobe left a way to do that, too. If you use the keyboard shortcut Ctrl(⌘)+Alt(Opt)+F, the dialog box of the last-used filter appears and you can enter your changes.

Resetting Filters to Default Settings

So, you have fiddled with the filter setting to the point you just want to start all over again. So where is the reset button on the filter's dialog box? It's there, but it's hidden. Look at the Cancel button and press the Alt(Opt) key and it transforms into a Reset button—as long as you are holding down the key.

Adjustment Layers

Whenever possible, use Adjustment layers to make all corrections to your images. What are Adjustment layers? Well, take a trip to the Image menu and choose Adjustments. Most of the commands you find there can be applied as an Adjustment layer. They allow you the flexibility to come back to the image and tweak the adjustments made on the image at any point in time. Even further, because they are functioning as a layer, you have the added ability to mask a specific portion of the image (thus applying the command only to a particular area).

Now how much would you pay for this feature? Wait! There's more! Adjustment layers give the added bonus of allowing you to see what settings you applied at any time. Let's say that you want to come back a year later and investigate the settings used in the Levels command and apply those same settings to a different image.

Now how much would you pay for this feature? Wait! There's more. Did I mention these Adjustment layers are layers? So if you want to apply the same Adjustment to a different image—you also have the flexibility to simply drag the Adjustment layer into the new document window to apply it to a different image document.

If the image you are working on is a monster and your computer resources are under too much of a strain to have multiple Adjustment layers floating around, make a duplicate of the image layer and make changes on that layer. But hey—if it were me—I'd dump that slug of a computer and buy a more modern one that can handle Adjustment layers.

Dragging Layers Between Images

Did you know that when you press and hold the Shift key while dragging a layer from one image to another, the new layer is perfectly centered on the designation image?

If both images are the same exact document size, holding the Shift key while dragging between documents places the layer information in the exact same position (or coordinates) in the final document (relative to its position in the starting document, that is).

A Context Menu Trick

Here's the story. You have an image with a lot of layers. You would like to perform a trick on a flattened layer (or maybe a composite of several of these layers) without actually flattening the file. In other words, you want to have your cake and eat it too. You want to retain all your layers—but quickly make a layer that's a flattened version of the file.

I'm about to let you in on a trick that very few people know about…

1. First Create a new layer and position it below all the layers you want to flatten together.

2. With your new (blank) layer selected as the active layer, link it to all the layers you want to composite.

3. Hold down the Alt(Opt) key and click the arrow in the upper-right corner of the Layers palette (to access the context menu) and then choose Merge Linked. This results in your blank layer containing all the information of the linked layers, but the layers are still intact as separate layers.

Note

This works on most of the options available in the context menu. For example, to bypass linking layers, just click the new blank layer and hold down the Alt(Opt) key and choose Merge Visible. All the visible layers merge onto the blank layer, still leaving the original layers in position.

You might find that the Alt(Opt) key performs benefits on other palette context menus as well.

Auto Selecting Layers

The obvious way to select layers is to click the desired layer in the Layers palette. That's great if you have only a few layers, but if you have a lot of layers, it is difficult scroll up and down a long Layers palette. Adobe agrees with you, which explains why they added a feature way back in Photoshop 5 called Auto Select Layer.

Early on, you opened the Auto Select Layer feature by double-clicking the Move tool. In Photoshop 7, checking the Auto Select Layer feature in the Options bar when the Move tool is selected does the trick. So, what does Auto Select Layer do? When this feature is enabled, anytime you click an object in your image, the layer that contains this object is automatically selected.

Now that I explained this feature, let me give you some really great advice (and a killer tip)—forget its there. *Never* check the Auto Select Layer option on the Options bar. Instead, while the Move tool is active, hold down the Ctrl(⌘) key when you want to access this feature. This allows you the flexibility to use this feature on demand, only when you need it. There are times when this feature can become, well, a pain in the neck. It can become even more of a pain to check and uncheck the box as you toggle the feature on and off. So take my advice and try using the Ctrl(⌘) key in combination with the Move tool. It's the best of both worlds.

Layers and the Clone Tool

If you are going to be doing a lot of cloning, I have found it best to create a new layer and apply the cloning to the new layer. This makes it easy to remove the unwanted cloned area without affecting the original image, and when you get it just the way you like it, you can merge the layer. By the way, Ctrl(⌘)+E is a great shortcut for merging the active layer with the layer below (it will merge only one layer down at a time—but you'll be surprised how many times this comes in handy).

Quickly Toggling Between Measuring Tools

Pressing the I key selects the Eyedropper tool that is currently visible. A quick way to toggle between the Eyedropper, Color Sampler, and the Measure tool is to use the Shift+I keyboard shortcut. In fact, using Shift with any of the keys to access tools will toggle between the tools associated with the same letter (when applicable).

Speaking of Measuring Tool Tricks—Did Ya Know?

Have you ever scanned an image that is slightly crooked? You try to fix this by going to the Image menu and choosing Rotate Canvas, Arbitrary. The Rotate Canvas dialog box comes up and asks for the Angle. You try to guess, but maybe you guess wrong. So you undo and try again—this time guessing again how much to adjust the first guess. Wait! Stop! There's a totally simple solution. Let Photoshop do the math for you.

How is this possible, you ask? Take a look:

1. Get out the Measuring tool (if you were just reading the previous tip you already know this—press Shift+I until the Measuring tool is the active tool).

2. Click and drag the Measuring tool along the top edge (of the crooked image) as shown in Figure B.1.

Figure B.1   Just drag to stretch the Measuring tool along the crooked angle of the scanned image. Too bad this trick doesn't do something for the sun that is obviously glaring in everyone's eyes.

3. Now make a trip to the Image menu and choose Rotate Canvas, Arbitrary (check out items 1 and 2 in Figure B.2). You will see a suggested Angle amount

already displayed in the Rotate Canvas dialog box. Click OK (item 3) and accept
the amount given to you. Item 4 in the figure shows that the adjusted image is
now perfectly straight.

Figure B.2   Photoshop does the math and shows you the answer in the Rotate Canvas dialog
box. All you have to do is click OK. Oh wow! Look closely—even the sun-glare
problem was solved.

Making Better Grayscale Images from Color Ones

I have used this quick trick for years to convert color images to more vivid grayscale
images. This is most helpful when an image that looked great as a color image loses its
contrast when converted to grayscale because many of those different colors became the
same shades of gray. There are two ways to do this conversion. My favorite is as follows:

1. Open the Channel palette and look at each of the three channels.

2. When you find a channel that has the best grayscale, click that channel and
   select the entire image by pressing Ctrl(⌘)+A. Copy it to the clipboard by
   pressing Ctrl(⌘)+C. Close the original image—do not save any changes.

3. Use Ctrl(⌘)+N to open a New document and Ctrl(⌘)+V to paste the contents of the clipboard into it.

4. Choose Layers, Flatten, and you're done.

5. Figure B.3 shows a before-and-after example of a very tired runner at the finish line. Using a channel to create a grayscale image from a color photo usually results in a superior grayscale image.

Figure B.3   The original color photograph of this runner was converted to grayscale (left) and in the other (right), the red channel was selected for a grayscale conversion.

If none of the channels meets your artistic needs, there is another way to improve grayscale images. It is essentially the same technique as shown previously, except that you change the image into a Lab Color mode (go to the Image menu and choose Mode, Lab Color). Click the Channels tab to view the Channels palette. Click the Lightness channel. Then go to the Image menu again and choose Mode, Grayscale.

One of these methods will yield a better grayscale image than if you had just gone directly to the Grayscale option.

An Easy Way to Create Complex Selections Automatically

Would you like to know a way to select—quickly and perfectly—a complex, irregularly shaped subject? For example, you might be working with an image of a woman with lots of long wispy hair flying around against a multi-colored background. Hey, come to think of it, I'd like to do the same thing—let me know if you find it.

Creating a Selection Using Channels

Another issue that comes up frequently is when you try to separate a subject against a background where the division line is difficult to determine, because the colors between them are the same. This makes it difficult to differentiate between the foreground and the background. Here's a solution that might help: Using your selection tool of choice, select the parts that are obvious and when it comes to the questionable areas, open the Channels palette and look for a greater contrast between the subject and the background in one of the channels. If so, add to the existing selection by using that channel as an image source. Regardless of which channel you are viewing, all the selection additions go to the same spot.

If that doesn't work, try the following steps. They'll probably remind you of the point earlier in this appendix when we listed all the great benefits of Adjustment layers.

1. At the bottom of the Layers palette, click the Create New Fill or Adjustment layer icon (it looks like a circle with half of the circle filled) and choose Brightness/Contrast.

2. In the Brightness/Contrast dialog box, play with the sliders to see whether you can maneuver a setting that gives you a clear distinction between the object and the background. Don't worry if the image looks awful. This is an Adjustment layer—you can discard the layer after your work is done. Once you can see a clear distinction between the object and background, click OK.

3. Use the necessary tools and tricks to make your selection. Then drag the Adjustment layer to the trash. Your image looks great again, and you have a clear selection of your object.

Note

No-Go on the Adjustment Layer Fix   If working with the Brightness/Contrast Adjustment layer doesn't give you the results you want, you might try applying the same principle with another Adjustment layer, such as Curves or Levels. The idea is the same and we'll leave it up to you to try. Hopefully these basic concepts will help you think outside the box.

Index

A

F

J-K

Q-R

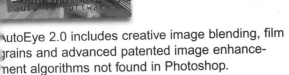

Ten great tips – all on one free CD!

Ever wanted to layer mask like the pros? Turn a digital photo into a painting? Quickly retouch old photos? The Wacom Power Tips CD has ten of our best Photoshop tips – and it's absolutely free! So go ahead – turn on Photoshop 7's power with Intuos2. Stop by and visit us today at **www.wacompowertips.com** or give us a quick call at **800-922-1490,** and we'll send you your *free* Photoshop Power Tips CD*.

Intuos2 starts at $199.⁹⁹**

Cintiq starts at $1899.⁹⁹**

HOW TO CONTACT US

VISIT OUR WEB SITE

WWW.NEWRIDERS.COM

On our web site, you'll find information about our other books, authors, tables of contents, and book errata. You will also find information about book registration and how to purchase our books, both domestically and internationally.

EMAIL US

Contact us at: **nrfeedback@newriders.com**

- If you have comments or questions about this book
- To report errors that you have found in this book
- If you have a book proposal to submit or are interested in writing for New Riders
- If you are an expert in a computer topic or technology and are interested in being a technical editor who reviews manuscripts for technical accuracy

Contact us at: **nreducation@newriders.com**

- If you are an instructor from an educational institution who wants to preview New Riders books for classroom use. Email should include your name, title, school, department, address, phone number, office days/hours, text in use, and enrollment, along with your request for desk/examination copies and/or additional information.

Contact us at: **nrmedia@newriders.com**

- If you are a member of the media who is interested in reviewing copies of New Riders books. Send your name, mailing address, and email address, along with the name of the publication or web site you work for.

BULK PURCHASES/CORPORATE SALES

The publisher offers discounts on this book when ordered in quantity for bulk purchases and special sales. For sales within the U.S., please contact: Corporate and Government Sales (800) 382-3419 or **corpsales@pearsontechgroup.com**. Outside of the U.S., please contact: International Sales (317) 581-3793 or **international@pearsontechgroup.com**.

WRITE TO US

New Riders Publishing
201 W. 103rd St.
Indianapolis, IN 46290-1097

CALL/FAX US

Toll-free (800) 571-5840
If outside U.S. (317) 581-3500
Ask for New Riders
FAX: (317) 581-4663

New Riders

WWW.NEWRIDERS.COM

Solutions from experts you know and trust.

www.informit.com

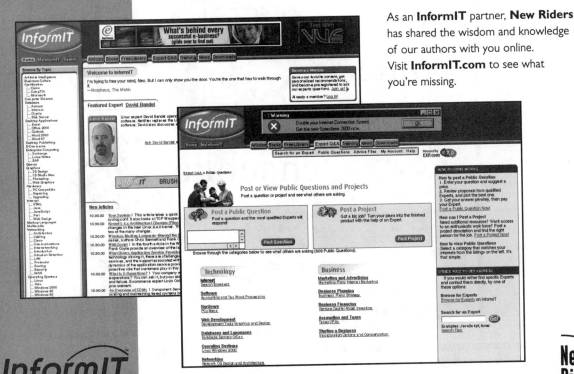

Welcome to THE BOUTONS www.boutons.com home page, where you can see our latest books, take a trip to GaryWorld gallery, get some one-of-a-kind chachke, and **FREE** education!

Adobe® Photoshop® 7

GaryWorld

Duck Chart

PDF

Photoshop Web Foundry

The Photoshop Web Foundry CD is a collection of customizable interfaces, buttons, animations, and more for the Web and Multi-media. All of the interfaces, buttons, and animations are provided in layered Photoshop format so that you can customize them to your heart's content.

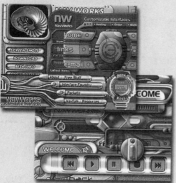

CD Contents:

- Over 120 customizable Interfaces
- Over 100 customizable buttons
- Over 25 customizable animations
- Over 40 HTML and Quicktime Video Tutorials
- Over 30 minutes of training videos

For more info visit: www.eyeland.com

Customizable Flash Resources

Flash Games

Dynamic Flash Interfaces

Flash Animations

Create your own flash games or dynamic flash interfaces with no programming experience or choose from hundrds of flash animations to spruce up your web or multi-media projects. Select from a large collection of rich backgrounds created in Photoshop.

Customizable Flash Games:

Create any number of games quickly and easily with no Flash programming experience

Flash Apps:

Create dynamic interfaces quickly and easily with no programming experience

Free Greeting Cards!

For more info visit: www.swiftlab.com

Enter the code "InsidePhotoshop" for $5 off at Eyeland Studio. Also, sign up for the Eyeland Studio newsletter and get a free Flash game.